JavaScript & DHTML Cookbook™

Other resources from O'Reilly

SECOND EDITION

JavaScript & DHTML Cookbook™

Danny Goodman

O'REILLY®

Beijing · Cambridge · Farnham · Köln · Paris · Sebastopol · Taipei · Tokyo

JavaScript and DHTML Cookbook™, Second Edition
by Danny Goodman

Published by O'Reilly Media, Inc., 1005 Gravenstein Highway North, Sebastopol, CA 95472.

O'Reilly books may be purchased for educational, business, or sales promotional use. Online editions are also available for most titles (*safari.oreilly.com*). For more information, contact our corporate/institutional sales department: (800) 998-9938 or *corporate@oreilly.com*.

Editor: Tatiana Apandi
Production Editor: Laurel R.T. Ruma
Proofreader: Audrey Doyle
Indexer: Ellen Troutman Zaig

Cover Designer: Karen Montgomery
Interior Designer: David Futato
Illustrators: Robert Romano and Jessamyn Read

Printing History:

April 2003:	First Edition.
August 2007:	Second Edition.

 This book uses RepKover™, a durable and flexible lay-flat binding.

ISBN-10: 0-596-51408-5
ISBN-13: 978-0-596-51408-2
[M]

Table of Contents

Preface

It may be difficult to imagine that a technology born as recently as 1995 would have had enough of a life cycle to experience a rise and fall in popularity, followed now by an amazing renaissance. Client-side scripting, begun initially with JavaScript embedded in Netscape Navigator 2, has experienced such a roller coaster ride. A number of early incompatibilities among major browsers caused many a content author's head to ache. But we learned to live with it, as a long period of stability in one platform—Internet Explorer 6, in particular—meant that we could use our well-worn compatibility workarounds without cause for concern. Another stabilizing factor was the W3C DOM Level 2 specification, which remained a major target for browser makers not following Microsoft's proprietary ways. Mozilla, Safari, and Opera used the W3C DOM as the model to implement, even if Microsoft didn't seem to be in a hurry to follow suit in all cases.

Two factors have contributed to the rebirth of interest in JavaScript and Dynamic HTML. The first is the wide proliferation of broadband connections. Implementing large client-side applications in JavaScript can take a bunch of code, all of which must be downloaded to the browser. At dial-up speeds, piling a 50–75 kilobyte script onto a page could seriously degrade perceived performance; at broadband speeds, nobody notices the difference.

But without a doubt, the major attraction these days is the now widespread availability in all mainstream browsers of a technology first implemented by Microsoft: the XMLHttpRequest object. It's a mouthful (leading some to refer to it as, simply, XHR), but it allows background communication between the browser and server so that a script can request incremental data from the server and update only a portion of a page. It is far more efficient than downloading a bunch of data with the page and less visually disruptive than the old submit-and-wait-for-a-new-page process. To help put a label on the type of applications one can build with this technology, the term *Asynchronous JavaScript and XML (Ajax)* was coined. In truth, Ajax is simply a catchy handle for an existing technology.

Ajax has opened the floodgates for web developers. Perhaps the most popular first implementation was Google Maps, whereby you could drag your way around a map, while scripts and the XMLHttpRequest object in the background downloaded adjacent blocks of the map in anticipation of your dragging your way over there. It was smooth, fast, and a real joy to use. And now, more powerful applications—word processors, spreadsheets, email clients—are being built with JavaScript and DHTML.

JavaScript in the browser was originally designed for small scripts to work on small client-side tasks. It is still used that way quite a bit around the Web. Not every application is a mega DHTML app. Therefore, this collection of recipes still has plenty of small tasks in mind. At the same time, however, many recipes from the first edition have been revised with scripting practices that will serve both the beginner and the more advanced scripter well. Examples prepare you for the eventuality that your scripting skills will grow, perhaps leading to a mega DHTML app in the future. Even so, there are plenty of times when you need an answer to that age-old programming question: "How do I…?"

About You

Client-side scripting and DHTML are such broad and deep subjects that virtually every reader coming to this book will have different experience levels, expectations, and perhaps, fears. No book could hope to anticipate every possible question from someone wishing to use these technologies in his web pages. Therefore, this book makes some assumptions about readers at various stages of their experience:

- You have at least rudimentary knowledge of client-side JavaScript concepts. You know how to put scripts into a web page—where <script> tags go, as well as how to link an external .js file into the current page. You also know what variables, strings, numbers, Booleans, arrays, and objects are—even if you don't necessarily remember the precise way they're used with the JavaScript language. This book is not a tutorial, but you can learn a lot from reading the introductions to each chapter and the discussions following each solution.

- You may be a casual scripter, who wants to put a bit of intelligence into a web page for some project or other. You don't use the language or object model every day, so you need a refresher about even some simple things, such as the correct syntax for creating an array or preloading images for fast image rollover effects.

- While surfing the Web, you may have encountered some scripted DHTML effect that you'd like to implement or adapt for your own pages, but either you can't decipher the code you see or you want to "roll your own" version to avoid copyright problems with the code's original owner. If the effect or technique you've seen is fairly popular, this cookbook probably has a recipe for it. You can use these recipes as they are or modify them to fit your designs. There are no royalties or copyrights to worry about, as long as you don't offer these recipes to others as part of a collection of scripts. Of course, if you wish to acknowledge this book in your source code comments, that would be great!

- You may be an experienced web developer who has probed gingerly, if at all, into client-side scripting. The horror stories of yore about browser incompatibilities have kept your focus entirely on server-side programming. But now that so many mainstream sites are using client-side scripting to improve the user experience, you are ready to take another look at what is out there.

- At the far end of the spectrum, you may be an experienced client-side DHTML developer in search of new ideas and techniques. For instance, you may have developed exclusively for the Internet Explorer browser on the Windows platform, but you wish to gravitate toward standards-compatible syntax for future coding.

Virtually every reader will find that some recipes in this book are too simple and others are too complex for their experience level. I hope the more difficult ones challenge you to learn more and improve your skills. Even if you think you know it all, be sure to check the discussions of the easier recipes for tips and insights that may be new to you.

About the Recipes

It's helpful for a reader to know upfront what biases an author has on the book's subject. To carry the cookbook metaphor too far, just as a culinary chef has identifiable procedures and seasonings, so do I format my code in a particular way and employ programming styles that I have adopted and updated over the years.

More important than scripting style, however, are the implementation threads that weave their way throughout the code examples. Because these examples may serve as models for your own development, they are written for maximum clarity to make it easy (I hope) for you to follow the execution logic. Names assigned to variables, functions, objects, and the like are meant to convey their purpose within the context of the example. One of the goals of coding is that the operation of a program should be self-evident to someone else reading the code, even if that "someone else" is the programmer who revisits the code six months later to fix a bug or add a feature. There's no sense in being cryptically clever if no one can understand what you mean by assigning some value to a variable named x.

This book unabashedly favors the W3C DOM way of addressing document objects. You can use this format to reference element objects in browsers starting with Microsoft Internet Explorer 5 and the other mainstream browsers addressed in this edition (Mozilla-based browsers, Safari, and Opera 7 or later), which means that the vast majority of browsers in use today support this standard. Where IE (including

IE 7) does not support the standard (as in handling events), all recipes here include efficient cross-browser implementations. You won't find too much in the way of IE-only solutions, especially if they would cover only the Windows version of IE.

The long period of browser stability we have enjoyed since the first edition means that visitors to public sites almost never use what are now antique browsers—IE prior to 5.5 and Netscape Navigator 4 or earlier. All recipes are optimized for the current browsers, but they also try to prevent hassles for anyone driving by in her steam-powered browser.

One credo dominates the recipes throughout this book: scripting must add value to static content on the page. Don't look to this book for scripts that cycle background colors to nauseate visitors or make elements bounce around the page while singing "Happy Birthday." You may be able to figure out how to do those horrible things from what you learn in this book, but that's your business. The examples here, while perhaps conservative, are intended to solve real-world problems that scripters and developers face in professional-quality applications.

The scripting techniques and syntax you see throughout this book are designed for maximum forward compatibility. It's difficult to predict the future of any technology, but the W3C DOM and ECMAScript standards, as implemented in today's latest browsers, are the most stable platforms on which to build client-side applications since client-side scripting began. With a bit of code added here and there to degrade gracefully in older browsers, your applications should be running fine well into the future.

What's in This Book

The first four chapters focus on fundamental JavaScript topics. In Chapter 1, *Strings*, you will see the difference between a string value and a string object. Regular expressions play a big role in string parsing for these recipes. You will also see a reusable library for reading and writing string data to cookies. Chapter 2, *Numbers and Dates*, includes recipes for handling number formatting and conversions, as well as date calculations that get used in later recipes. Perhaps the most important core JavaScript language chapter is Chapter 3, *Arrays and Objects*. Recipes in this chapter provide the keys to one- and multidimensional array creation, array sorting, object creation, hash table simulation, and exploration of the prototype inheritance powers of objects. You also see how creating custom objects for your libraries can reduce potential naming conflicts as projects grow. Chapter 4, *Variables, Functions, and Flow Control*, includes a recipe for improving overall script performance.

Chapter 5 through Chapter 8 provide solutions for problems that apply to almost all scriptable browsers. In Chapter 5, *Browser Feature Detection*, you will learn how to free yourself of the dreaded "browser sniffing" habit and use forward-compatible techniques for determining whether the browser is capable of running a block of script statements. If multiple windows are your nemesis, then Chapter 6, *Managing Browser Windows*, provides plenty of ideas to handle communication between windows. A few recipes present suggestions for modal windows (or facsimiles thereof). Not everyone is a frame lover, but Chapter 7, *Managing Multiple Frames*, may be of interest to all, especially if you don't want your site being "framed" by another site. Intelligent forms—one of the driving forces behind the creation of client-side scripting—are the subject of Chapter 8, *Dynamic Forms*. Updated to modern techniques, recipes include form validation (with or without regular expressions) and some cool but subtle techniques found on some of the most popular web sites on the Internet.

Interactivity with the user is driven by event processing, and Chapter 9, *Managing Events*, covers the most common event processing tasks you'll encounter with DHTML scripting. Events (and one of the libraries shown in Chapter 9) ripple through most of the remaining chapters' recipes. That includes many recipes in Chapter 10, *Page Navigation Techniques*, where you'll see how to implement a variety of menuing designs and pass data from one page to the next. Chapter 11, *Managing Style Sheets*, provides recipes for both basic and advanced style sheet techniques as they apply to dynamic content, including how to load a browser- or operating system-specific stylesheet into the page. Style sheets play a big role in Chapter 12, *Visual Effects for Stationary Content*, where recipes abound for image rollovers and user-controlled font sizes, to name a couple.

Chapter 13, *Positioning HTML Elements*, addresses numerous challenges in keeping positioned elements under tight rein. A positioning library recipe is used extensively throughout the rest of the book, including more recipes in this chapter for animating elements, scrolling content, and creating a draggable element. In Chapter 14, *Creating Dynamic Content*, the W3C DOM and XMLHttpRequest object get good workouts with recipes for tasks such as embedding JavaScript and XML data within a document, transforming data into renderable HTML content, and sorting HTML tables instantly on the client. Additional dynamic content recipes come in Chapter 15, *Dynamic Content Applications*, where more complex recipes show you how to use DHTML for a slide show, a user-editable document, and a pop-up calendar date picker, among others.

Browser Platforms

Freed from having to worry much about compatibility with very old browsers, the goal of each recipe's design in this edition is to work in the following browsers:

- Microsoft Internet Explorer 6 or later
- Mozilla 1.7.5 (Firefox 1.0, Netscape 8.0, Camino 1.0) or later
- Apple Safari 1.2 or later (including the Windows version)
- Opera 7 or later

Many of the simpler scripts in early chapters work in browsers all the way back to Netscape Navigator 2, but that is hardly the focus here. Occasionally, a recipe may require a later version of Mozilla, Safari, or Opera, as noted clearly in the recipe. In those cases, the recipe is designed to prevent script errors from appearing in slightly older versions of these modern browsers.

You will also see many references in this book to designing pages to convey mission-critical information for browsers that either aren't equipped with JavaScript or have scripting turned off. Beyond the browsers mentioned in the previous list, there are a lot of users of browsers in portable wireless devices and browsers for users with vision or motor skill impairments. Always keep accessibility in mind with your designs.

Conventions Used in This Book

The following typographical conventions are used throughout this book:

Italic

> Indicates pathnames, filenames, program names, sample email addresses, and sample web sites; and new terms where they are defined

`Constant width`

> Indicates any HTML, CSS, or scripting term, including HTML tags, attribute names, object names, properties, methods, and event handlers; and all HTML and script code listings

`Constant width italic`

> Indicates method and function parameters or assigned value placeholders that represent an item to be replaced by a real value in actual use

`Constant width bold`

> Used to draw attention to specific parts of code

 This icon signifies a tip, suggestion, or general note.

 This icon indicates a warning or caution.

Using Code Examples

This book is here to help you get your job done. In general, you may use the code in this book in your programs and documentation. You do not need to contact us for permission unless you're reproducing a significant portion of the code. For example, writing a program that uses several chunks of code from this book does not require permission. Selling or distributing a CD-ROM of examples from O'Reilly books *does* require permission. Answering a question by citing this book and quoting example code does not require permission. Incorporating a significant amount of example code from this book into your product's documentation *does* require permission.

We appreciate, but do not require, attribution. An attribution usually includes the title, author, publisher, and ISBN. For example: "*JavaScript & DHTML Cookbook*, Second Edition, by Danny Goodman. Copyright 2007 Danny Goodman, 978-0-596-51408-2."

If you feel your use of code examples falls outside fair use or the permission given here, feel free to contact us at *permissions@oreilly.com*.

Request for Comments

We have tested and verified the information in this book to the best of our ability, but you may find that features have changed (or even that we have made mistakes!). Please let us know about any errors you find, as well as your suggestions for future editions, by writing to:

> O'Reilly Media, Inc.
> 1005 Gravenstein Highway North
> Sebastopol, CA 95472
> 800-928-9938 (in the United States or Canada)
> 707-829-0515 (international or local)
> 707-829-0104 (fax)

There is a web page for this book, which lists errata, downloadable examples, and any additional information. You can access this page at:

> *http://www.oreilly.com/catalog/9780596514082*

To ask technical questions or comment on the book, send email to:

> *bookquestions@oreilly.com*

For more information about books, conferences, resource centers, and the O'Reilly Network, see the O'Reilly web site at:

> *http://www.oreilly.com*

Safari® Enabled

 When you see a Safari® Enabled icon on the cover of your favorite technology book, that means the book is available online through the O'Reilly Network Safari Bookshelf.

Safari offers a solution that's better than e-books. It's a virtual library that lets you easily search thousands of top tech books, cut and paste code samples, download chapters, and find quick answers when you need the most accurate, current information. Try it for free at *http://safari.oreilly.com*.

Acknowledgments

The physical act of writing a book—converting thoughts to keystrokes and characters on the screen—is a solitary one. But once the first draft is submitted, an army of dedicated professionals join the author in shaping the work into a finished product. When the army marches under the O'Reilly banner, the author can be assured of a commitment to quality, even from many individuals whom the author never meets.

I extend my sincere appreciation to my editor, Tatiana Apandi, who magically kept me on schedule. I also thank Rob Hoexter and Sergio Pereira, who provided invaluable contributions to improving the writing and scripting.

Much of the impetus for selecting the recipes for this book has come from the scripting public. Having read thousands of online forum threads since 1996, having listened to readers of my JavaScript and Dynamic HTML books for years, and having observed search queries that lead visitors to my web site (*http://www.dannyg.com*), I believe I have distilled the essence of the needs of most client-side scripters. Your pain, confusion, and frustration with the technologies have not gone unnoticed. I hope this book provides the relief and understanding you deserve.

CHAPTER 1

Strings

1.0   Introduction

A string is one of the fundamental building blocks of data that JavaScript works with. Any script that touches URLs or user entries in form text boxes works with strings. Most document object model properties are string values. Data that you read or write to a browser cookie is a string. Strings are everywhere!

The core JavaScript language has a repertoire of the common string manipulation properties and methods that you find in most programming languages. You can tear apart a string character by character if you like, change the case of all letters in the string, or work with subsections of a string. Most scriptable browsers now in circulation also benefit from the power of regular expressions, which greatly simplify numerous string manipulation tasks—once you surmount a fairly steep learning curve of regular expression syntax.

Your scripts will commonly be handed values that are already string data types. For instance, if you need to inspect the text that a user has entered into a form's text box, the value property of that text box object returns a value already typed as a string. All properties and methods of any string object are immediately available for your scripts to operate on that text box value.

Creating a String

If you need to create a string, you have a couple of ways to accomplish it. The simplest way is to simply assign a quoted string of characters (known as a *string literal*) to a variable (or object property):

```
var myString = "Fluffy is a pretty cat.";
```

Quotes around a JavaScript string can be either single or double quotes, but each pair must be of the same type. Therefore, both of the following statements are acceptable:

```
var myString = "Fluffy is a pretty cat.";
var myString = 'Fluffy is a pretty cat.';
```

But the following mismatched pair is illegal and throws a script error:

```
var myString = "Fluffy is a pretty cat.';
```

Having the two sets of quote symbols is handy when you need to embed one string within another. The following document.write( ) statement that would execute while a page loads into the browser has one outer string (the entire string being written by the method) and nested sets of quotes that surround a string value for an HTML element attribute:

```
document.write("<img src='img/logo.jpg' height='30' width='100' alt='Logo' />");
```

You are also free to reverse the order of double and single quotes as your style demands. Thus, the above statement would be interpreted the same way if it were written as follows:

```
document.write('<img src="img/logo.jpg" height="30" width="100" alt="Logo" />');
```

Two more levels of nesting are also possible if you use escape characters with the quote symbols. See Recipe 1.9 for examples of escaped character usage in JavaScript strings.

If you need to include only one instance of a single or double quote within a string (e.g., "Welcome to Joe's Diner."), you can do so without special characters. This is because upon encountering the start of a string, JavaScript treats ensuing characters— up to the next occurrence of the same quote symbol that starts the string—as part of the string. Trouble arises, however, when two or more alternate quote symbols are nested within the string (e.g., "Welcome to Joanne's and Joe's Diner."). In such cases, you would have to use escaped apostrophes to keep the string together ("Welcome to Joanne\'s and Joe\'s Diner."). Or, you can always use escaped quotes (even just one) inside a string, and then you won't have to worry about the balancing act.

Technically speaking, the strings described so far aren't precisely string *objects* in the purest sense of JavaScript. They are string *values*, which, as it turns out, lets the strings use all of the properties and methods of the global String object which inhabits every scriptable browser window. Use string values for all of your JavaScript text manipulation. In a few rare instances, however, a JavaScript string value isn't quite good enough. You may encounter this situation if you are using JavaScript to communicate with a Java applet, and one of the applet's public methods requires an argument as a string data type. In this case, you might need to create a full-fledged instance of a String object and pass that object as the method argument. To create such an object, use the constructor function of the String object:

```
var myString = new String("Fluffy is a pretty cat.");
```

The data type of the myString variable after this statement executes is object rather than string. But this object inherits all of the same String object properties and methods that a string value has, and works fine with a Java applet.

Regular Expressions

For the uninitiated, regular expressions can be cryptic and confusing. This isn't the forum to teach you regular expressions from scratch, but perhaps the recipes in this chapter that demonstrate them will pique your interest enough to pursue their study.

The purpose of a regular expression is to define a pattern of characters that you can then use to compare against an existing string. If the string contains characters that match the pattern, the regular expression tells you what the text is that matches the pattern and where the match occurs within the string, facilitating further manipulation (perhaps a search-and-replace operation). Regular expression patterns are powerful entities because they let you go much further than simply defining a pattern of fixed characters. For example, you can define a pattern to be a sequence of five numerals bounded on each side by whitespace. Another pattern can define the format for a typical email address, regardless of the length of the username or domain, but the full domain must include at least one period.

The cryptic part of regular expressions is the notation they use to specify the various conditions within the pattern. JavaScript regular expressions notation is nearly identical to regular expressions found in languages such as Perl. The syntax is the same for all except for some of the more esoteric uses. One definite difference is the way you create a regular expression object from a pattern. You can use either the formal constructor function or the more compact literal syntax. The following two syntax examples create the same regular expression object:

```
var re = /pattern/ [g | i | m];                    // Literal syntax
var re = new RegExp(["pattern", ["g"| "i" | "m"]]); // Formal constructor
```

The optional trailing characters (g, i, and m) indicate whether:

g   The pattern should be applied globally (i.e., to every instance of the pattern in a string)

i   The pattern is case-insensitive

m   Each physical line of the target string is treated as the start of a string

If you have been exposed to regular expressions in the past, Table 1-1 lists the regular expression pattern notation available in today's browsers.

Table 1-1. Regular expression notation

Character	Matches	Example
\b	Word boundary	/\bto/ matches "tomorrow"
		/to\b/ matches "Soweto"
		/\bto\b/ matches "to"
\B	Word nonboundary	/\Bto/ matches "stool" and "Soweto"
		/to\B/ matches "stool" and "tomorrow"
		/\Bto\B/ matches "stool"
\d	Numeral 0 through 9	/\d\d/ matches "42"

Table 1-1. Regular expression notation (continued)

Character	Matches	Example
\D	Nonnumeral	/\D\D/ matches "to"
\s	Single whitespace	/under\sdog/ matches "under dog"
\S	Single nonwhitespace	/under\Sdog/ matches "under-dog"
\w	Letter, numeral, or underscore	/1\w/ matches "1A"
\W	Not a letter, numeral, or underscore	/1\W/ matches "1%"
.	Any character except a newline	/../ matches "Z3"
[...]	Any one of the character set in brackets	/J[aeiou]y/ matches "Joy"
[^...]	Negated character set	/J[^eiou]y/ matches "Jay"
*	Zero or more times	/\d*/ matches "", "5", or "444"
?	Zero or one time	/\d?/ matches "" or "5"
+	One or more times	/\d+/ matches "5" or "444"
{n}	Exactly n times	/\d{2}/ matches "55"
{n,}	n or more times	/\d{2,}/ matches "555"
{n,m}	At least n, at most m times	/\d{2,4}/ matches "5555"
^	At beginning of a string or line	/^Sally/ matches "Sally says..."
$	At end of a string or line	/Sally.$/ matches "Hi, Sally."

See Recipes 1.6 through 1.8, as well as Recipe 8.2, to see how regular expressions can empower a variety of string examination operations with less overhead than more traditional string manipulations. For in-depth coverage of regular expressions, see *Mastering Regular Expressions* by Jeffrey E. F. Friedl (O'Reilly).

1.1   Concatenating (Joining) Strings

Problem

You want to join together two strings or accumulate one long string from numerous sequential pieces.

Solution

Within a single statement, use the plus (+) operator to concatenate multiple string values:

```
var longString = "One piece " + "plus one more piece.";
```

To accumulate a string value across multiple statements, use the add-by-value (+=) operator:

```
var result = "";
result += "My name is " + document.myForm.myName.value;
result += " and my age is " + document.myForm.myAge.value;
```

The add-by-value operator is fully backward-compatible and is more compact than the less elegant approach:

```
result = result + "My name is " + document.myForm.myName.value;
```

Discussion

You can use multiple concatenation operators within a single statement as needed to assemble your larger string, but you must be cautious about word wrapping of your source code. Because JavaScript interpreters have a built-in feature that automatically inserts semicolons at the logical ends of source code lines, you cannot simply break a string with a carriage return character in the source code without putting the syntactically correct breaks in the code to indicate the continuation of a string value. For example, the following statement and format triggers a syntax error as the page loads:

```
var longString = "One piece " + "plus one
more piece.";
```

The interpreter treats the first line as if it were:

```
var longString = "One piece " + "plus one;
```

To the interpreter, this statement contains an unterminated string and invalidates both this statement and anything coming after it. To break the line correctly, you must terminate the trailing string, and place a plus operator as the final character of the physical source code line (do not put a semicolon there because the statement isn't finished yet). Also, be sure to start the next line with a quote symbol:

```
var longString = "One piece " + "plus one " +
"more piece.";
```

Additionally, whitespace outside of the quoted string is ignored. Thus, if you wish to format the source code for improved readability, you can even indent the second line without affecting the content of the string value:

```
var longString = "One piece " + "plus one " +
    "more piece.";
```

Source code carriage returns do not influence string text. If you want to include a carriage return in a string, you need to include one of the special escaped characters (e.g., \n) in the string. For example, to format a string for a confirm dialog box so that it creates the illusion of two paragraphs, include a pair of the special newline characters in the string:

```
var confirmString = "You did not enter a response to the last " +
    "question.\n\nSubmit form anyway?";
```

Note that this kind of newline character is for string text that appears in dialog boxes or other string-only containers. It is not a newline character for text that is to be rendered as HTML content. For that kind of newline, you must explicitly include a <br> tag in the string:

```
var htmlString = "First line of string.<br />Second line of string.";
```

See Also

Recipe 1.2 for a technique to improve performance; Recipe 1.9 to see how to include special control characters (such as a carriage return) in a string value.

1.2 Improving String Handling Performance

Problem

You wish to improve the execution speed of routines manipulating large amounts of text.

Solution

Use a JavaScript array as a temporary storage device when accumulating large chunks of text. The push( ) method of an array object allows you to assemble individual text blocks in the desired order—the method appends to the end of the array. When it comes time to use the full text (e.g., to assign a large string of HTML code to the innerHTML property of an element object), use the join( ) method of the array object, specifying an empty string as the delimiter character.

Although the technique is intended for large text blocks, the following example uses small strings to demonstrate the sequence:

```
var txtArray = new Array( );
txtArray.push("<tr>");
txtArray.push("<td>Boston</td><td>24</td><td>10</td><td>Partly Cloudy</td>");
txtArray.push("</tr>");
txtArray.push("<tr>");
txtArray.push("<td>New York</td><td>21</td><td>14</td><td>Snow</td>");
txtArray.push("</tr>");
document.getElementById("weatherTBody").innerHTML = txtArray.join("");
txtArray = null;
```

The sequence ends by emptying the array so that the browser will free up memory occupied by the array.

Discussion

String concatenation, especially when it involves either large amounts of text or an inordinate amount of pieces being stitched together via the add-by-value (+=) operator, can be a performance hog in browsers. You may never notice the problem if your strings are not very large, but the signs start to appear when you use standard string concatenation in repeat loops that assemble huge strings. These situations are excellent candidates for using an array as the temporary string data holder. Scripts typically execute array manipulation with much better performance than string manipulation.

Note that, just as with strings, your code is responsible for handling details, such as spaces between words in joined text. If spaces are needed, they should go in the text being pushed onto the end of the array. Alternatively, if a space is needed between absolutely every string stored in the array, you can specify a space character as the parameter to the join( ) method:

```
var finalString = txtArray.join(" ");
```

The character you specify as the parameter (if any) is inserted *between* array items as they are output as a single string.

Invoking the join( ) method does not alter the contents of the array. To minimize the impact on browser memory once the array's contents are no longer needed, you should assign null to the array, thus allowing the browser's garbage collector to do its job.

1.3 Accessing Substrings

Problem

You want to obtain a copy of a portion of a string.

Solution

Use the substring( ) method (in all scriptable browsers) to copy a segment starting at a particular location and ending either at the end of the string (omitting the second parameter does that) or at a fixed position within the string, counting from the start of the string:

```
var myString = "Every good boy does fine.";
var section = myString.substring(0, 10);    // section is now "Every good"
```

Use the slice( ) method (in IE 4 or later and all modern scriptable browsers) to set the end position at a point measured from the end of the string, using a negative value as the second parameter:

```
var myString = "Every good boy does fine.";
var section = myString.slice(11, -6);      // section is now "boy does"
```

Use the nonstandard, but widely supported, variant called substr( ) to copy a segment starting at a particular location for a string length (the second parameter is an integer representing the length of the substring):

```
var myString = "Every good boy does fine.";
var section = myString.substr(6, 4);       // section is now "good"
```

If the sum of the two arguments exceeds the length of the string, the method returns a string from the start point to the end of the string.

Discussion

Parameters for the ECMA-compatible slice( ) and substring( ) methods are numbers that indicate the zero-based start and end positions within the string from which the extract comes. The first parameter, indicating the start position, is required. When you use two positive integer values for the slice( ) method arguments (and the first argument is smaller than the second), you receive the same string value as the substring( ) method with the same arguments.

Note that the integer values for substring( ) and slice( ) act as though they point to spaces between characters. Therefore, when a substring( ) method's arguments are set to 0 and 4, it means that the substring starts to the right of the "zeroeth" position and ends to the left of the fourth position; the length of the string value returned is four characters, as shown in Figure 1-1.

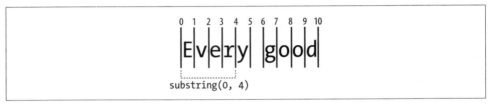

Figure 1-1. How substring end points are calculated

If you should supply argument values for the substring( ) or substr( ) methods in an order that causes the first argument to be larger than the second, the JavaScript interpreter automatically reverses the order of arguments so that the end pointer value is always larger than the start pointer. The slice( ) method isn't as forgiving and returns an empty string.

None of the substring methods modifies the original string object or value in any way. This is why you must capture the returned value in a variable, or apply the returned value as an argument to some other function or method.

See Also

Recipe 1.7 for testing whether a string contains a substring.

1.4   Changing String Case

Problem

You want to convert a string to all upper- or lowercase letters.

Solution

Use the two dedicated String object methods, toLowerCase( ) and toUpperCase( ), for case changes:

```
var myString = "New York";
var lcString = myString.toLowerCase( );
var ucString = myString.toUpperCase( );
```

Both methods return modified copies of the original string, leaving the original intact. If you want to replace the value of a variable with a case-converted version of the original string (and thus eliminate the original string), reassign the results of the method to the same variable:

```
myString = myString.toLowerCase( );
```

Do not, however, redeclare the variable with a var keyword.

Discussion

Because JavaScript strings (like just about everything else in the language) are case-sensitive, it is common to use case conversion for tasks such as testing the equivalency of a string entered into a text box by a user against a known string in your code. Because the user might include a variety of case variations in the entry, you need to guard against unorthodox entries by converting the input text to all uppercase or all lowercase letters for comparison (see Recipe 1.5).

Another common need for case conversion is preparing user entries for submission to a database that prefers or requires all uppercase (or all lowercase) letters. You can accomplish this for a user either at the time of entry or during batch validation prior to submission. For example, an onchange event handler in a text box can convert the text to all uppercase letters as follows:

```
<input type="text" name="firstName" id="firstName" size="20" maxlength="25"
    onchange="this.value=this.value.toUpperCase( )" />
```

Simply reassign a converted version of the element's value to itself.

See Also

Recipe 1.5 for a practical example of case conversion simplifying an important string task.

1.5   Testing Equality of Two Strings

Problem

You want to compare a user's text entry against a known string value.

Solution

Convert the user input to either all uppercase or all lowercase characters, and then use the JavaScript equality operator to make the comparison:

```
if (document.myForm.myTextBox.value.toLowerCase( ) == "new york") {
    // process correct entry }
```

By using the results of the case conversion method as one of the operands of the equality expression, you do not modify the original contents of the text box. (See Recipe 1.4 if you want to convert the text in the text box to all of one case.)

Discussion

JavaScript has two types of equality operators. The fully backward-compatible, standard equality operator (==) employs data type conversion in some cases when the operands on either side are not of the same data type. Consider the following variable assignments:

```
var stringA = "My dog has fleas.";
var stringB = new String("My dog has fleas.");
```

These two variables might contain the same series of characters but are different data types. The first is a string value, while the second is an instance of a String object. If you place these two values on either side of an equality (==) operator, JavaScript tries various evaluations of the values to see if there is a coincidence somewhere. In this case, the two variable values would show to be equal, and the following expression:

```
stringA == stringB
```

returns true.

But the other type of equality operator, the strict equality operator (===), performs no data type conversions. Given the variable definitions above, the following expression evaluates to false because the two object types differ, even though their payloads are the same:

```
stringA === stringB
```

If the logic of your code requires you to test for the inequality of two strings, you can use the inequality (!=) and strict inequality (!==) operators. For example, if you want to process an incorrect entry, the branching flow of your function would be like the following:

```
if (document.getElementById("myTextBox").value.toLowerCase( ) != "new york") {
    // process incorrect entry
}
```

The same data type conversion issues apply to the inequality and strict inequality operators as to their opposite partners.

Although the equality and inequality operators go to great lengths to find value matches, you may prefer to assist the process by performing obvious data type conversions in advance of the operators. For instance, if you want to see if an entry to a numeric text box (a string value) is a particular number, you could let the equality operator perform the conversion for you, as in:

```
if (document.getElementById("myTextBox").value == someNumericVar) { ... }
```

Or you could act in advance by converting one of the operands so that both are the same data type:

```
if (parseInt(document.getElementById("myTextBox").value) == someNumericVar) { ... }
```

If you are accustomed to more strongly typed programming languages, you can continue the practice in JavaScript without penalty, while perhaps boosting your script's readability.

See Also

Recipe 2.1 for converting between string and number values; Recipe 3.3 for converting between strings and arrays; Recipe 3.13 for converting a custom object to a string value.

1.6 Testing String Containment Without Regular Expressions

Problem

You want to know if one string contains another, without using regular expressions.

Solution

Use the JavaScript indexOf( ) string method on the longer string section, passing the shorter string as an argument. If the shorter string is inside the larger string, the method returns a zero-based index integer of the start position of the smaller string within the larger string. If the shorter string is not in the larger string, the method returns –1.

For logic that needs to branch if the smaller string is not contained by the larger string, use the following construction:

```
if (largeString.indexOf(shortString) == -1) {
    // process due to missing shortString
}
```

For logic that needs to branch if the smaller string is contained somewhere within the larger string, use the following construction:

```
if (largeString.indexOf(shortString) != -1) {
    // process due to found shortString
}
```

In either case, you are not interested in the precise position of the short string but simply whether it is anywhere within the large string.

Discussion

You may also find the integer returned by the indexOf( ) method to be useful in a variety of situations. For example, an event handler function that gets invoked by all kinds of elements in the event-propagation (bubbling) chain wants to process events that come only from elements whose IDs begin with a particular sequence of characters. This is an excellent spot to look for the returned value of zero, pointing to the start of the larger string:

```
function handleClick(evt) {
    var evt = (evt) ? evt : ((window.event) ? window.event : null);
    if (evt) {
        var elem = (evt.target) ? evt.target : ((evt.srcElement) ?
            evt.srcElement : null);
        if (elem && elem.id.indexOf("menuImg") == 0) {
            // process events from elements whose IDs begin with "menuImg"
        }
    }
}
```

Be aware that if the larger string contains multiple instances of the shorter string, the indexOf( ) method returns a pointer only to the first instance. If you're looking to count the number of instances, you can take advantage of the indexOf( ) method's optional second parameter, which specifies the starting position for the search. A compact repeat loop can count up the instances quickly:

```
function countInstances(mainStr, srchStr) {
    var count = 0;
    var offset = 0;
    do {
        offset = mainStr.indexOf(srchStr, offset);
        count += (offset != -1) ? 1 : 0;
    } while (offset++ != -1)
    return count
}
```

Counting instances is much easier, however, using regular expressions (see Recipe 1.7). Although many factors can influence performance, for the task of testing only for string containment, the indexOf( ) approach is typically faster than using a regular expression.

See Also

Recipe 1.7 for using regular expressions to test string containment.

1.7   Testing String Containment with Regular Expressions

Problem

You want to use regular expressions to know whether one string contains another.

Solution

Create a regular expression with the short string (or pattern) and the global (g) modifier. Then pass that regular expression as a parameter to the match( ) method of a string value or object:

```
var re = /a string literal/g;
var result = longString.match(re);
```

When a global modifier is attached to the regular expression pattern, the match( ) method returns an array if one or more matches are found in the longer string. If there are no matches, the method returns null.

Discussion

To work this regular expression mechanism into a practical function, you need some helpful surrounding code. If the string you are looking for is in the form of a string variable, you can't use the literal syntax for creating a regular expression as just shown. Instead, use the constructor function:

```
var shortStr = "Framistan 2000";
var re = new RegExp(shortStr, "g");
var result = longString.match(re);
```

After you have called the match( ) method, you can inspect the contents of the array value returned by the method:

```
if (result) {
    alert("Found " + result.length + " instances of the text: " + result[0]);
} else {
    alert("Sorry, no matches.");
}
```

When matches exist, the array returned by match( ) contains the found strings. When you use a fixed string as the regular expression pattern, these returned values are redundant. That's why it's safe in the previous example to pull the first returned value from the array for display in the alert dialog box. But if you use a regular expression pattern involving the symbols of the regular expression language, each of the returned strings could be quite different, but equally valid because they adhere to the pattern.

As long as you specify the g modifier for the regular expression, you may get multiple matches (instead of just the first). The length of the array indicates the number of matches found in the longer string. For a simple containment test, you can omit the g modifier; as long as there is a match, the returned value will be an array of length 1.

See Also

"Regular Expressions" in the introduction to this chapter; Recipe 8.2 for using regular expressions in form field validations.

1.8   Searching and Replacing Substrings

Problem

You want to perform a global search-and-replace operation on a text string.

Solution

The most efficient way is to use a regular expression with the replace( ) method of the String object:

```
var re = /a string literal/g;
var result = mainString.replace(re, replacementString);
```

Invoking the replace( ) method on a string does not change the source (original) string. Capture the changed string returned by the method, and apply the result where needed in your scripts or page. If no replacements are made, the original string is returned by the method. Be sure to specify the g modifier for the regular expression to force the replace( ) method to operate globally on the original string; otherwise, only the first instance is replaced.

Discussion

To work this regular expression mechanism into a practical function, you need some helpful surrounding code. If the string you are looking for is in the form of a string variable, you can't use the literal syntax for creating a regular expression as just shown. Instead, use the constructor function:

```
var searchStr = "F2K";
var replaceStr = "Framistan 2000";
var re = new RegExp(searchStr , "g");
var result = longString.replace(re, replaceStr);
```

In working with a text-based form control or an element's text node, you can perform the replace( ) operation on the value of the existing text, and immediately assign the results back to the original container. For example, if a div element contains one text node with scattered place holders in the form of (ph), and the job of the replace( ) method is to insert a user's entry from a text box (called myName), the sequence is as follows:

```
var searchStr = "\\(ph\\)";
var re = new RegExp(searchStr, "g");
var replaceStr = document.getElementById("myName").value;
var div = document.getElementById("boilerplate");
div.firstChild.nodeValue = div.firstChild.nodeValue.replace(re, replaceStr);
```

The double backslashes are needed to escape the escape character before the parentheses characters, which are otherwise meaningful symbols in the regular expression pattern language.

It is also possible to implement a search-and-replace feature without regular expressions, but it's a cumbersome exercise. The technique involves substantial text parsing using the indexOf( ) method to find the starting location of text to be replaced. You need to copy preceding text into a variable and strip away that text from the original string; keep repeating this find-strip-accumulate tactic until the entire string is accounted for, and you have inserted the replacement string in place of each found search string. This was necessary in the early browsers, but the far more convenient and efficient regular expressions are implemented in almost all scriptable browsers that are now in use.

See Also

"Regular Expressions" in the introduction to this chapter; Recipe 14.15 for additional body text replacement techniques in modern browsers.

1.9 Using Special and Escaped Characters

Problem

You want to add low-order ASCII characters (tab, carriage return, etc.) to a string.

Solution

Use the escape sequences shown in Table 1-2 to represent the desired character. For example, to include a quotation mark inside a literal string, use \", as in:

```
var msg = "Today's secret word is \"thesaurus.\"";
```

Discussion

The core JavaScript language includes a feature common to most programming languages that lets you designate special characters. A *special character* is not one of the plain alphanumeric characters or punctuation symbols, but has a particular meaning with respect to whitespace in text. Common characters used these days include the tab, newline, and carriage return.

A special character begins with a backslash, followed by the character representing the code, such as \t for tab and \n for newline. The backslash is called an *escape character*, instructing the interpreter to treat the next character as a special character. To include these characters in a string, include the backslash and special character inside the quoted string:

```
var confirmString = "You did not enter a response to the last " +
    "question.\n\nSubmit form anyway?";
```

If you want to use one of these symbols between variables that contain string values, be sure the special character is quoted in the concatenation statement:

```
var myStr = lineText1 + "\n" + lineText2;
```

Special characters can be used to influence formatting of text in basic dialog boxes (from the alert( ), confirm( ), and prompt( ) methods of the window object) and textarea form controls. Table 1-2 shows the recognized escaped characters and their meanings.

Table 1-2. String escape sequences

Escape sequence	Description
\b	Backspace
\t	Horizontal tab (ASCII 9)
\n	Line feed (newline, ASCII 10)
\v	Vertical tab
\f	Form feed
\r	Carriage return (ASCII 13)
\"	Double quote
\'	Single quote
\\	Backslash

Note that to include a visible backslash character in a string, you must use a double backslash because a single one is treated as the invisible escape character. Use the escaped quote symbols to include single or double quotes inside a string.

While you can use an escaped character in tests for the existence of, say, line feed characters in a string, you have to exercise some care when doing so with the content of a textarea element. The problem accrues from a variety of implementations of how user-entered carriage returns are coded in the textarea's content. IE for Windows and Opera (all platforms) inserts two escaped characters (\r\n in that sequence) whenever a user presses the Enter key to make a newline in a textarea. Other browsers, including Mozilla and Safari, have settled on a single \n character. This variety in character combinations makes searches for user-typed line breaks difficult to perform accurately across browsers and operating systems.

Going the other way—creating a string for script insertion into a textarea value—is easier because modern browsers accommodate all symbols. Therefore, if you assign just \n or the combination \r\n, all browsers interpret any one of them as a carriage return, and convert the escape character(s) to match their internal handling.

See Also

Recipe 1.1 for tips on concatenating strings—tips that apply equally to escaped string characters.

1.10   Reading and Writing Strings for Cookies

Problem

You want to use cookies to preserve string data from one page visit to the next.

Solution

Use the *cookies.js* library shown in the Discussion as a utility for saving and retrieving cookies in modern browsers. To set a cookie via the library, invoke the setCookie( ) function, passing, at a minimum, the cookie's name and string value as arguments:

```
setCookie("userID", document.entryForm.username.value);
```

To retrieve a cookie's value, invoke the library's getCookie( ) function, as in:

```
var user = getCookie("userID");
```

Discussion

Example 1-1 shows the code for the entire *cookies.js* library.

Example 1-1. cookies.js library

```
// utility function to retrieve an expiration date in proper
// format; pass three integer parameters for the number of days, hours,
// and minutes from now you want the cookie to expire (or negative
// values for a past date); all three parameters are required,
// so use zeros where appropriate
function getExpDate(days, hours, minutes) {
    var expDate = new Date( );
    if (typeof days == "number" && typeof hours == "number" &&
        typeof minutes == "number") {
        expDate.setDate(expDate.getDate( ) + parseInt(days));
        expDate.setHours(expDate.getHours( ) + parseInt(hours));
        expDate.setMinutes(expDate.getMinutes( ) + parseInt(minutes));
        return expDate.toUTCString( );
    }
}

// utility function called by getCookie( )
function getCookieVal(offset) {
    var endstr = document.cookie.indexOf (";", offset);
    if (endstr == -1) {
        endstr = document.cookie.length;
    }
```

Example 1-1. cookies.js library (continued)

```
        return decodeURI(document.cookie.substring(offset, endstr));
}

// primary function to retrieve cookie by name
function getCookie(name) {
    var arg = name + "=";
    var alen = arg.length;
    var clen = document.cookie.length;
    var i = 0;
    while (i < clen) {
        var j = i + alen;
        if (document.cookie.substring(i, j) == arg) {
            return getCookieVal(j);
        }
        i = document.cookie.indexOf(" ", i) + 1;
        if (i == 0) break;
    }
    return "";
}

// store cookie value with optional details as needed
function setCookie(name, value, expires, path, domain, secure) {
    document.cookie = name + "=" + encodeURI(value) +
        ((expires) ? "; expires=" + expires : "") +
        ((path) ? "; path=" + path : "") +
        ((domain) ? "; domain=" + domain : "") +
        ((secure) ? "; secure" : "");
}

// remove the cookie by setting ancient expiration date
function deleteCookie(name,path,domain) {
    if (getCookie(name)) {
        document.cookie = name + "=" +
            ((path) ? "; path=" + path : "") +
            ((domain) ? "; domain=" + domain : "") +
            "; expires=Thu, 01-Jan-70 00:00:01 GMT";
    }
}
```

The library begins with a utility function (getExpDate( )) that your scripts use to assist in setting an expiration date for the cookie. A second utility function (getCookieVal( )) is invoked internally during the reading of a cookie.

Use the getCookie( ) function in your scripts to read the value of a named cookie previously saved. The name you pass to the function is a string. If no cookie by that name exists in the browser's cookie filing system, the function returns an empty string.

To save a cookie, invoke the setCookie( ) function. The first two parameters (the cookie's name and the value to be preserved on the client) are required. If you intend the cookie to last beyond the user quitting the browser, be sure to set an expiration date as the third parameter. Filter the expiration time period through the getExpDate( ) function shown earlier so that the third parameter of setCookie( ) is in the correct format.

One last function, deleteCookie( ), lets you delete an existing cookie before its expiration date. The function is hardwired to set the expiration date to the start of the JavaScript date epoch.

Load the library into your page in the head portion of the document:

```
<script src="cookies.js"></script>
```

All cookie values you save must be string values; all cookie values you retrieve are string values. Strings, however, can contain characters that upset their storage and proper retrieval later on. To compensate for this issue, the *cookies.js* library uses the global encodeURI( ) and decodeURI( ) methods to handle conversions. These methods improve on (and supercede) the old escape( ) and unescape( ) methods.

A browser cookie is the only way to preserve a string value on the client between visits to your web site. Scripts on your page may read only cookies that were saved from your domain and server. If you have multiple servers in your domain, you can set the fifth parameter of setCookie( ) to share cookies between servers at the same domain.

Browsers typically limit capacity to 20 name/value pairs of cookies per server; a cookie should be no more than 4,000 characters, but more practically, the value of an individual named cookie should be less than 2,000 characters. In other words, cookies are not meant to act as high-volume data storage facilities on the client. Also, browsers automatically send domain-specific cookie data to the server as part of each page request. Keep the amount of data small to limit the impact on dial-up users.

When you save a cookie, the name/value pair resides in the browser's memory. The data, if set to expire sometime in the future, is written to the cookie filesystem only when the browser quits. Therefore, don't be alarmed if you don't see your latest entry in the cookie file while the browser is still running. Different browsers save their cookies differently (and in different places in each operating system). IE stores each domain's cookies in its own text file, whereas Mozilla gangs all cookies together in a single text file.

All of this cookie action is made possible through the document.cookie property. The purpose of the *cookies.js* library is to act as a friendlier interface between your scripts and the document.cookie property, which isn't as helpful as it could be in extracting cookie information. Although you can save a cookie with several parameters, only the value of a cookie is available for reading—not the expiration date, path, or domain details.

Cookies are commonly used to preserve user preference settings between visits. A script near the top of the page reads the cookie to see if it exists, and, if so, applies settings to various content or layout attributes while the rest of the page loads. Recipe 12.7 shows how this can work to let users select a relative font size and preserve the settings between visits. For example, the function that preserves the user's font size choice saves the value to a cookie named fontSize, which is set to expire in 180 days if not updated before then:

```
setCookie("fontSize", styleID, getExpDate(180, 0, 0));
```

The next time the user visits, the cookie is read while the page loads:

```
var styleCookie = getCookie("fontSize");
```

With the information from the cookie, the script applies the previously selected style sheet to the page. If the cookie was not previously set, the script assigns a default style sheet to use in the interim.

Just because cookies can store only strings, don't let that get in the way of preserving information normally stored in arrays or custom objects. See Recipe 3.12 and Recipe 8.14 for ways to convert more complex data types to strings for preservation, and then restore their original form after retrieval from the cookie on the next visit.

See Also

Recipe 10.4 for passing data between pages via cookies; Recipe 12.7 for an example of using cookies to preserve a user's style preference; Recipe 3.12 and Recipe 8.14 for ways of converting arrays and objects to cookie string values; Recipe 3.14 for a way to reduce the global "footprint" of this library.

1.11 Converting Between Unicode Values and String Characters

Problem

You want to obtain the Unicode code number for an alphanumeric character or vice versa.

Solution

To obtain the Unicode value of a character of a string, use the charCodeAt( ) method of the string value. A single parameter is an integer pointing to the zero-based position of the character within the string:

```
var code = myString.charCodeAt(3);
```

If the string consists of only one character, use the 0 argument to get the code for that one character:

```
var oneChar = myString.substring(12, 13);
var code = oneChar.charCodeAt(0);
```

The returned value is an integer.

To convert a Unicode code number to a character, use the fromCharCode( ) method of the static String object:

```
var char = String.fromCharCode(66);
```

Unlike most string methods, this one must be invoked only from the String object and not from a string value.

Discussion

ASCII values and Unicode values are the same for the basic Latin alphanumeric (low-ASCII) values. But even though Unicode encompasses characters from many written languages around the world, do not expect to see characters from other writing systems displayed in alert boxes, text boxes, or rendered pages simply because you know the Unicode values for those characters; the browser and operating system must be equipped for the language encompassed by the characters. If the character sets are not available, the characters generated by such codes will be question marks or other symbols. A typical North American computer won't know how to produce a Chinese character on the screen unless the target writing system and font sets are installed for the OS and browser.

See Also

Recipe 1.3 for other ways to extract single-character substrings.

1.12   Encoding and Decoding URL Strings

Problem

You want to convert a string of plain text to a format suitable for use as a URL or URL search string, or vice versa.

Solution

To convert a string consisting of an entire URL to a URL-encoded form, use the encodeURI( ) global method, passing the string needing conversion as an argument. For example:

```
document.myForm.action = encodeURI(myString);
```

If you are assembling content for values of search string name/value pairs, apply the encodeURIComponent( ) global method:

```
var srchString = "?name=" + encodeURIComponent(myString);
```

Both methods have complementary partners that perform conversions in the opposite direction:

```
decodeURI(encodedURIString)
decodeURIComponent(encodedURIComponentString)
```

In all cases, the original string is not altered when passed as an argument to these methods. Capture the results from the value returned by the methods.

Discussion

Although the escape( ) and unescape( ) methods have been available since the first scriptable browsers, they have been deprecated in the formal language specification (ECMA-262) in favor of a set of new methods. The new methods are available in IE 5.5 or later and other modern browsers.

These new encoding methods work by slightly different rules than the old escape( ) and unescape( ) methods. As a result, you must encode and decode using the same pairs of methods at all times. In other words, if a URL is encoded with encodeURI( ), the resulting string can be decoded only with decodeURI( ).

The method names use "URI" (Universal Resource Identifier). A URI is an all-encompassing reference to obtain any network-accessible item (document, object, etc.). A URL (Universal Resource Locator) is a type of URI that includes both a network location for the item, as well as an indication of the access mechanism (e.g., http:). That the method names adopt the more general URI nomenclature is not unusual. For most client-side web authoring in HTML, CSS, and JavaScript, the terms *URI* and *URL* are interchangeable.

The differences between encodeURI( ) and encodeURIComponent( ) are defined by the range of characters that the methods convert to the URI-friendly form of a percent sign (%) followed by the hexadecimal Unicode value of the symbol (e.g., a space becomes %20). Regular alphanumeric characters are not converted, but when it comes to punctuation and special characters, the two methods diverge in their coverage. The encodeURI( ) method converts the following symbols from the characters in the ASCII range of 32 through 126:

> *space* " % < > [\ ] ^ ` { | }

For example, if you are assembling a URL with a simple search string on the end, pass the URL through encodeURI( ) before navigating to the URL to make sure the URL is well formed:

```
var newURL = "http://www.megacorp.com?prod=Gizmo Deluxe";
location.href = encodeURI(newURL);
// encoded URL is: http://www.megacorp.com?prod=Gizmo%20Deluxe
```

In contrast, the encodeURIComponent( ) method encodes far more characters that might find their way into value strings of forms or script-generated search strings. Encodable characters unique to encodeURIComponent( ) are shown in bold:

> *space* " **# $** % **& + , / : ;** < **=** > **? @** [\ ] ^ ` { | }

You may recognize some of the encodeURIComponent( ) values as those frequently appearing within complex URLs, especially the ?, &, and = symbols. For this reason, you want to apply the encodeURIComponent( ) only to values of name/value pairs before those values are inserted or appended to a URL. But then it gets dangerous to pass the composite URL through encodeURI( ) again because the % symbols of the encoded characters will, themselves, be encoded, probably causing problems on the server end when parsing the input from the client.

If, for backward-compatibility reasons, you need to use the escape( ) method, be aware that this method uses a heavy hand in choosing characters to encode. Encodable characters for the escape( ) method are as follows:

    space ! \ " # $ % & ' ( ) , : ; < = > ? @ [\ ] ^ ` { | } ~

The @ symbol, however, is not converted in Internet Explorer browsers via the escape( ) method.

You can see now why it is important to use the matching decoding method if you need to return one of your encoded strings back into plain language. If the encoded string you are trying to decode comes from an external source (e.g., part of a URL search string returned by the server), try to use the decodeURIComponent( ) method on only those parts of the search string that are the value portion of a name/value pair. That's typically where the heart of your passed information is, as well as where you want to obtain the most correct conversion.

See Also

Recipe 10.6 for passing data to another page via URLs, during which value encoding is used.

1.13 Encoding and Decoding Base64 Strings

Problem

You want to convert a string to or from Base64 encoding.

Solution

Use the functions of the *base64.js* library shown in the Discussion. Syntax for invoking the two functions is straightforward. To encode a string, invoke:

```
var encodedString = base64Encode("stringToEncode");
```

To decode a string, invoke:

```
var plainString = base64Decode("encodedString");
```

Discussion

Example 1-2 shows the entire *base64.js* library.

Example 1-2. base64.js library

```
// Global lookup arrays for base64 conversions
var enc64List, dec64List;

// Load the lookup arrays once
function initBase64() {
    enc64List = new Array();
    dec64List = new Array();
    var i;
    for (i = 0; i < 26; i++) {
        enc64List[enc64List.length] = String.fromCharCode(65 + i);
    }
    for (i = 0; i < 26; i++) {
        enc64List[enc64List.length] = String.fromCharCode(97 + i);
    }
    for (i = 0; i < 10; i++) {
        enc64List[enc64List.length] = String.fromCharCode(48 + i);
    }
    enc64List[enc64List.length] = "+";
    enc64List[enc64List.length] = "/";
    for (i = 0; i < 128; i++) {
        dec64List[dec64List.length] = -1;
    }
    for (i = 0; i < 64; i++) {
        dec64List[enc64List[i].charCodeAt(0)] = i;
    }
}

// Encode a string
function base64Encode(str) {
    var c, d, e, end = 0;
    var u, v, w, x;
    var ptr = -1;
    var input = str.split("");
    var output = "";
    while(end == 0) {
        c = (typeof input[++ptr] != "undefined") ? input[ptr].charCodeAt(0) :
            ((end = 1) ? 0 : 0);
        d = (typeof input[++ptr] != "undefined") ? input[ptr].charCodeAt(0) :
            ((end += 1) ? 0 : 0);
        e = (typeof input[++ptr] != "undefined") ? input[ptr].charCodeAt(0) :
            ((end += 1) ? 0 : 0);
        u = enc64List[c >> 2];
        v = enc64List[(0x00000003 & c) << 4 | d >> 4];
        w = enc64List[(0x0000000F & d) << 2 | e >> 6];
        x = enc64List[e & 0x0000003F];

        // handle padding to even out unevenly divisible string lengths
        if (end >= 1) {x = "=";}
        if (end == 2) {w = "=";}
        if (end < 3) {output += u + v + w + x;}
    }
    // format for 76-character line lengths per RFC
```

Example 1-2. base64.js library (continued)

```
    var formattedOutput = "";
    var lineLength = 76;
    while (output.length > lineLength) {
        formattedOutput += output.substring(0, lineLength) + "\n";
        output = output.substring(lineLength);
    }
    formattedOutput += output;
    return formattedOutput;
}

// Decode a string
function base64Decode(str) {
    var c=0, d=0, e=0, f=0, i=0, n=0;
    var input = str.split("");
    var output = "";
    var ptr = 0;
    do {
        f = input[ptr++].charCodeAt(0);
        i = dec64List[f];
        if ( f >= 0 && f < 128 && i != -1 ) {
            if ( n % 4 == 0 ) {
                c = i << 2;
            } else if ( n % 4 == 1 ) {
                c = c | ( i >> 4 );
                d = ( i & 0x0000000F ) << 4;
            } else if ( n % 4 == 2 ) {
                d = d | ( i >> 2 );
                e = ( i & 0x00000003 ) << 6;
            } else {
                e = e | i;
            }
            n++;
            if ( n % 4 == 0 ) {
                output += String.fromCharCode(c) +
                          String.fromCharCode(d) +
                          String.fromCharCode(e);
            }
        }
    } while (typeof input[ptr] != "undefined");
    output += (n % 4 == 3) ? String.fromCharCode(c) + String.fromCharCode(d) :
              ((n % 4 == 2) ? String.fromCharCode(c) : "");
    return output;
}

// Self-initialize the global variables
initBase64();
```

The library begins with two global declarations and an initialization function that creates lookup tables for the character conversions. At the end of the library is a statement that invokes the initialization function.

Scripts may call the base64Encode( ) function directly to convert a standard string to a Base64-encoded string. The value of the original string is not changed, but the function returns an encoded copy. To convert an encoded string to a standard string, use the base64Decode( ) function, passing the encoded string as an argument.

All Mozilla-based browsers include global methods that perform the same conversions shown at length in the solution. The atob( ) method converts a Base64-encoded string to a plain string; the btoa( ) method converts a plain string to a Base64-encoded string. These methods are not part of the ECMAScript standard used as the foundation for these browser versions, so it's unclear when or if they will find their way into other browsers.

Frankly, there hasn't been a big need for Base64 encoding in most scripted web pages, but that's perhaps because the facilities weren't readily available. A Base64-encoded string contains a very small character set: a–z, A–Z, 0–9, +, /, and =. This low common denominator scheme allows data of any type to be conveyed by virtually any Internet protocol. Binary attachments to your email are encoded as Base64 strings for their journey en route. Your email client decodes the simple string and generates the image, document, or executable file that arrives with the message. You may find additional ways to apply Base64-encoded data in your pages and scripts. To learn more about Base64 encoding, visit *http://www.ietf.org/rfc/rfc2045.txt*.

See Also

Recipe 1.12 for URL-encoding techniques.

CHAPTER 2

Numbers and Dates

2.0 Introduction

Designers of friendly scripting languages might have nonprogrammers in mind when they first define the scope of their languages, but it's difficult for any such language to be taken seriously by professional programmers unless some of the nerdy basics are there. Math may be anathema to scripters not schooled in computer science, but even an accessible language such as JavaScript has a solid complement of features to accommodate the kinds of arithmetic, trigonometric, and other operations typically supported by a programming language. Date manipulation—also numerically intensive, as it turns out—is well supported in JavaScript as well. This chapter includes recipes for both of these areas.

JavaScript Numbers

For most scripters, the interior details about how JavaScript treats numbers is of little importance. In fact, the more you know about programming languages and different types of numbers, the more you need to forget in order to use JavaScript numbers. Unlike other languages, JavaScript has only one kind of number data type. All integers and floating-point values are represented by the same data type in Java-Script: `number`.

Internally, a JavaScript number is an IEEE double-precision 64-bit value. JavaScript provides a usable range of number values from 2.2E-208 to 1.79E+308 (boundary values obtainable by the static `Number` object properties `Number.MIN_VALUE` and `Number.MAX_VALUE`, respectively). JavaScript treats numbers beyond these limits as infinity, represented by `Number.NEGATIVE_INFINITY` and `Number.POSITIVE_INFINITY`. It is unlikely that you will ever refer to these four properties in your scripts, but the language has them for the sake of completeness.

Number values do not carry any formatting with them. If a value needs places to the right of the decimal to signify a fractional part of an integer, those places are there. But if a variable that once held a number with 10 digits to the right of the decimal is modified through an arithmetic operation to become an integer, the decimal and zeros to the right of the decimal disappear.

As with JavaScript strings (see Chapter 1), numbers are most commonly values (of data type number), but may also be created as more formal objects through the Number object constructor. Therefore, both of the following statements produce a piece of data that evaluates to the same number:

```
var myNum = 55;
var myNum = new Number(55);
```

But if you examine the data types of the two objects (via the typeof operator), the first is number and the second is object. A number value inherits the properties and methods of the Number object, many of which are discussed in this chapter.

The Math Object

Available in every JavaScript context is a static Math object that provides a standard set of math constants and methods for working with numbers and trigonometry. At no time do your scripts create an instance of the Math object. It is simply "there" as a resource for your scripts to use as needed.

Table 2-1 shows the properties of the Math object. All of them are well-known constants in math circles. You can use these constants within JavaScript expressions. For example, to calculate the circumference of a circle (π times the diameter) whose diameter measure is in a variable d, the statement is:

```
var circumference = d * Math.PI;
```

Table 2-1. Math object properties (constants)

Property	Description
E	Euler's constant (2.718281828459045)
LN2	Natural logarithm of 2 (0.6931471805599453)
LN10	Natural logarithm of 10 (2.302585092994046)
LOG2E	Log base-2 of Euler's constant (1.4426950408889634)
LOG10E	Log base-10 of Euler's constant (0.4342944819032518)
PI	π (3.141592653589793)
SQRT1_2	Square root of 1/2 (0.7071067811865476)
SQRT2	Square root of 2 (1.4142135623730951)

The long list of Math object methods is located in Table 2-2. Many of them support trigonometric operations, some of which can come into play for path animation with positioned elements. Others provide math services that are useful from time to time, such as taking a number to a power, rounding, and getting the minimum or maximum of a pair of number values. As with most JavaScript methods, the values passed as arguments to the methods are not altered in any way. Capture the results in a variable.

Table 2-2. Math object methods

Method	Description
abs(*number*)	Returns the absolute value of *number*
acos(*number*)	Returns the arc cosine (in radians from +0 to π) of *number* (from -1 to +1)
asin(*number*)	Returns the arc sine (in radians from -π/2 to +π/2) of *number* (from -1 to +1)
atan(*number*)	Returns the arc tangent (in radians from -π/2 to +π/2) of *number* (between NEGATIVE_INFINITY and POSITIVE_INFINITY)
atan2(*y*, *x*)	Returns the arc tangent (in radians from -π to +π) of the quotient *y*/*x*
ceil(*number*)	Returns the next higher integer that is greater than or equal to *number*
cos(*number*)	Returns the cosine (in radians) of *number* (also in radians between NEGATIVE_INFINITY and POSITIVE_INFINITY)
exp(*number*)	Returns Euler's constant raised to the *number* power
floor(*number*)	Returns the next lower integer that is less than or equal to *number*
log(*number*)	Returns the natural logarithm (base e) of *number*
max(*number1*, *number2*)	Returns the greater value of *number1* or *number2*
min(*number1*, *number2*)	Returns the lesser value of *number1* or *number2*
pow(*number1*, *number2*)	Returns the value of *number1* raised to the *number2* power
random( )	Returns a pseudorandom number between 0 and 1
round(*number*)	Returns an integer of *number*+1 if *number* is greater than or equal to *number* + 0.5; otherwise, returns integer of *number*
sin(*number*)	Returns the sine (in radians) of *number* (also in radians)
sqrt(*number*)	Returns the square root of *number*
tan(*number*)	Returns the tangent (in radians) of *number* (also in radians)

Dates and Times

Since the very beginning of the JavaScript language, one of its most powerful objects has been the Date object. It is a global object in that every window (or frame) has a static Date object sitting in the background, ready to be invoked at any time. With only a couple of exceptions, the way you work with dates is to create an instance of the Date object via the constructor function for this object:

```
var myDate = new Date();
```

Creating an instance of the Date object (which I call a date object—with a lowercase *d*) is like taking a snapshot of an instant in time. A date object contains information about the date and time, down to the millisecond, but it is not a ticking clock. Even so, you can use the myriad functions associated with every date object to read individual components of the date and time (year, month, day, hour, and so on). A parallel set of methods let you set the date and/or time of that date object instance. That's one way you can perform some date or time arithmetic, as shown in Recipes 2.10 and 2.11.

Be aware that the date object operates solely on the client computer in which the page is loaded. There is no connection with the server clock or its timekeeping abilities. This means that your date and time calculations are entirely at the mercy of the accuracy (and proper setting) of the client computer's internal clock. Not only must the date and time be reasonably accurate, but the time zone setting is critical. If the user is located in California, but the computer's time zone settings are for New York, the computer will be thinking strictly in New York time. This could disturb some date and time calculations, as shown in Recipe 15.9.

If a script is concerned with the "ticking clock," the script must periodically create a new date object instance to get the latest snapshot of the clock—and then perhaps compare it against some known deadline. Again, the discussion in Recipe 15.9 shows how to do this.

Working with dates in JavaScript can be rather puzzling at times. Perhaps the most difficult concept to comprehend is when you create a date object (either for the present or for some other date and time), the object instance stores its value as an integer representing the number of milliseconds from the start of January 1, 1970. More importantly, the point of reference for all date values is Coordinated Universal Time (UTC), which is essentially the same as Greenwich Mean Time (GMT). What makes this hard to understand is that when you create a date object instance and ask to view its value, the JavaScript interpreter automatically returns the computer's local date and time for that object, even though the GMT value is stored. For example, if you create a date object on a computer running in New York City at 10:00 P.M. on Friday night, the date object preserves that date and time in GMT, or (during standard time months) five hours later than the time in New York (3:00 A.M. on Saturday). But if you ask to view the value of the date object (say, in an alert dialog box), the value reports itself to be 10:00 P.M. on Friday.

For the most part, this discrepancy between a date object's internal calculation and external display is of no consequence. Since all of your date objects behave the same way, calculations such as the amount of time separating two date objects yield the same results. You need to worry about this GMT offset business only when your calculations involve times in two different time zones. See Recipe 15.9 for an example of how to account for time zone offsets.

Look to recipes in this chapter for examples of how to perform date calculations; see Chapter 15's recipes for additional practical applications in dynamic pages. The Date object is a powerful beast that, once tamed, can enliven the personalization features and dynamic aspects of your pages.

2.1 Converting Between Numbers and Strings

Problem

You want to change a number data type to a string data type, or vice versa.

Solution

To convert a number value to a string value, use the `toString()` method of a number value:

```
var numAsStringValue = numValue.toString();
```

You can also create an instance of a `String` object by passing the number as an argument to the `String` object constructor:

```
var numAsStringObject = new String(numValue);
```

To convert a string to a number, use the `parseInt()` global method if the desired result is an integer only, or the `parseFloat()` global method if the number could be or is definitely a floating-point number:

```
var intValue = parseInt(numAsString, 10);
var floatValue = parseFloat(numAsString);
```

If you use `parseFloat()` and the number passed as an argument is an integer, the result will also be formatted as an integer, without a decimal and trailing zero. Both the `parseInt()` and `parseFloat()` functions work with all scriptable browser versions.

Discussion

In many cases, the JavaScript interpreter tries to cast values between number and string data types automatically. For example, if you multiply a number times a string version of the number, the string is automatically converted to a number value, and the operation succeeds. This kind of casting doesn't always work, however. For instance, the addition (+) operator plays two roles in JavaScript: adding numbers and concatenating strings. When you place this operator between a number and a number that is actually a string value, the string wins the battle, and the two numbers get concatenated together as a string. Thus, the expression 2 + "2" equals "22" in JavaScript.

Most commonly, you need to convert a string to a numeric value when you perform math operations on values entered by the user in form text boxes. The `value` property of any text field supplies the data as a string value. To add values from two text boxes to fill a third requires converting each operand to a number before doing the math. Then you can assign the resulting number value to the `value` property of the third text box, where the number automatically converts to a string value because that's the only data type acceptable in a text box. For example:

```
var val1 = parseFloat(document.getElementById("firstNum").value);
var val2 = parseFloat(document.getElementById("secondNum").value);
var result = val1 + val2;
document.getElementById("sum").value = result;
```

Unlike most other programming languages, JavaScript does not differentiate numeric data types by the kind of number. A number is a number, whether it happens to be an integer or a floating-point number. The distinction made by the two number parsing methods is that even if the source string contains a number with a decimal point and digits to the right of the decimal, only the integer portion is returned from parseInt( ). This behavior comes in handy when the source string starts with a number but has additional string characters following it. For example, the navigator. appVersion property returns a string similar to the following:

```
4.0 (compatible; MSIE 6.0; Windows 98; Q312461)
```

If you want to get the integer that starts this string, you can apply the parseInt( ) method:

```
var mainVer = parseInt(navigator.appVersion, 10);
```

Similarly, if the string starts with a floating-point number (say, 4.2), you could use parseFloat( ) to get a numeric copy of just the leading number. In other words, both methods try to grab as much of their kinds of numbers as they can from the front of the string. When they encounter a nonnumeric value, the copying stops, and they return whatever number has been collected up to that point.

It's a good idea to specify the optional second parameter to parseInt( ) as a 10, signifying that you want the value treated as a base-10 value. If you don't, and the string begins with a zero and either an 8 or a 9, the string number is treated as an octal value (whose allowable digits are 0 through 7), and the 8 and 9 digits are treated as nonnumeric. The parseFloat( ) method always returns a base-10 value (see Recipe 2.6).

As for converting a number to a string, an old trick from the earliest days of JavaScript still works. It's simply an extrapolation of the behavior just explained that forces the addition operator to give priority to string concatenation over numeric addition. If you "add" an empty string to a number value, the result of the operation is a string version of that number:

```
var numAsString = numVal + "";
```

The syntax isn't particularly elegant, but it is compact and fully backward-compatible. If you see this construction in some old code, now you know where it comes from.

See Also

Recipe 2.6 for converting between different number bases.

2.2 Testing a Number's Validity

Problem

You want to be sure a value is a number before performing a math operation on it.

Solution

If the value you're testing can come from any kind of source, the safest bet is to use the typeof operator on the value. Applying this operator to any numeric value evaluates to the string number. Therefore, using it in a conditional expression looks like this:

```
if (typeof someVal == "number") {
    // OK, operate on the value numerically
}
```

But some JavaScript methods, such as parseInt( ) and parseFloat( ), return a special value, NaN ("Not a Number"), signifying that they were unable to derive the number you desired. Operations expecting numeric operands or arguments that encounter values evaluating to NaN also generally return NaN. To test for this condition, use the isNaN( ) method, which returns true if the value is not a number. For example:

```
var myVal = parseInt(document.getElementById("myAge").value);
if (isNaN(myVal)) {
    alert("Please check the Age text box entry.");
} else {
    // OK, operate on the value numerically
}
```

Discussion

Don't get the wrong impression about the isNaN( ) method from the second example just shown. It is not a suitable approach to validating numeric input to a text box. That's because the parseInt( ) and parseFloat( ) methods return the first numbers (if any) they encounter in the string value passed as an argument. If someone enters 32G into a text box intended for an age, the parseInt( ) method pulls off the 32 portion, but the full value of the text box is not valid for your database that expects a strictly numeric value for that field. See Recipe 8.2 for more robust ways of validating numeric text entries.

You don't have to perform validity testing on absolutely every value about to undergo a math operation. Most values in your scripts tend to be under strict control of the programmer, allowing data-typing kinks to be worked out before the script is put into production. You need to exercise care, however, whenever user input enters the equation.

Look to the NaN value as a debugging aid. If some calculation is failing, use alert dialog boxes or debuggers to show the values of the operands and components. Any value that reports itself to be NaN means that it has problems at its source that need fixing before your calculation can even get started.

As a point of trivia, the NaN value is, believe it or not, a number data type, and is also a property of the static Number object.

See Also

Recipe 8.2 for numeric data entry validation in a form.

2.3   Testing Numeric Equality

Problem

You want to know whether two numeric values are equal (or not equal) before continuing processing.

Solution

Use the standard equality operator (==) in a conditional statement:

```
if (firstNum == secondNum) {
    // OK, the number values are equal
}
```

Values on either side of the equality operator may be variables or numeric literals. Typical practice places the suspect value to the left of the operator, and the fixed comparison on the right.

Discussion

JavaScript has two types of equality operators. The fully backward-compatible, standard equality operator (==) employs automatic data type conversion in some cases when the operands on either side are not of the same data type. Consider the following variable assignments:

```
var numA = 45;
var numB = new Number(45);
```

These two variables might contain the same numeric value, but they are different data types. The first is a number value, while the second is an instance of a Number object. If you place these two values on either side of an equality (==) operator, Java-Script tries various evaluations of the values to see if there is a coincidence somewhere. In this case, the two variable values would show to be equal, and the following expression:

```
numA == numB
```

returns true.

But the other type of equality operator, the strict equality operator (===), performs no data type conversions. Given the variable definitions above, the following expression evaluates to false because the two object types differ, even though their payloads are the same:

```
numA === numB
```

If one equality operand is an integer and the other is the same integer expressed as a floating-point number (such as 4 and 4.00), both kinds of equality operators find their values and data types to be equal. A number is a number in JavaScript.

If the logic of your code requires you to test for the inequality of two numbers, you can use the inequality (!=) and strict inequality (!==) operators. For example, if you want to process an entry for a special value, the branching flow of your function would be like the following:

```
if (parseInt(document.getElementById("myTextBox").value) != 0) {
    // process entry for non-zero values
}
```

The same issues about data type conversion apply to the inequality and strict inequality operators as to their opposite partners.

See Also

Recipe 2.1 for converting between number and string value types.

2.4   Rounding Floating-Point Numbers

Problem

You want to round a floating-point value to the nearest whole number.

Solution

Use the Math.round( ) method on the value:

```
var roundedVal = Math.round(floatingPointValue);
```

The operation does not disturb the original value. Capture the rounded result in a variable.

Discussion

The Math.round( ) method uses the following algorithm: any floating-point value that is greater than or equal to x.5 is rounded up to x+1; otherwise, the returned value is x.

JavaScript's Math object contains some other useful methods for trimming floating-point numbers of their fractional parts. Math.floor( ) and Math.ceil( ) return the next lowest and next highest integer values, respectively. For example, Math.floor(3.25) returns 3, while `Math.ceil(3.25)` returns 4. With negative values, the rules still apply, but the results seem backward at first glance: `Math.floor(-3.25)` returns the next lowest integer, -4; `Math.ceil(-3.25)` returns -3. For positive values, you can use the `Math.floor()` method as a substitute for what some other languages treat as obtaining the integer part of a number.

Anytime a floating-point number evaluates to a number equal to an integer value, the decimal and digits to the right of the decimal go away. A variable can hold a floating-point number in one statement and be modified to an integer in the next. This drives some programmers crazy because they were indoctrinated by other languages to treat each type of number as a different data type.

See Also

"The Math Object" in the introduction to this chapter.

2.5   Formatting Numbers for Text Display

Problem

You want to display the results of numeric calculations with a fixed number of digits to the right of the decimal.

Solution

Two global methods of the JavaScript language (and ECMA standard) simplify the display of numbers with a specific number of digits. These methods are implemented in IE 5.5 or later for Windows and other modern browsers (Mozilla, Safari, and Opera). To obtain a string containing a number with digits to the right of the decimal, use the `toFixed()` method, as in the following:

```
document.getElementById("total").value = someNumber.toFixed(2);
```

The argument to the `toFixed()` method is the number of digits to the right of the decimal. Even if the number is an integer, the resulting string has a decimal and two zeros to the right of the decimal.

To obtain a string containing a number with a total fixed number of digits, use the `toPrecision()` method, as in the following:

```
document.getElementById("rate").value = someNumber.toPrecision(5);
```

The argument to the `toPrecision()` method is the total number of digits in the returned string value, including digits to the left and right of the decimal (the decimal is not counted). If the original value has fewer digits than the method argument calls for, the result is padded with zeros to the right of the decimal; an argument smaller than the number of integer digits yields a value in scientific notation. Here are some examples:

```
var num = 123.45;
preciseNum = num.toPrecision(7);        // preciseNum is now 123.4500
preciseNum = num.toPrecision(4);        // preciseNum is now 123.5
preciseNum = num.toPrecision(3);        // preciseNum is now 123
preciseNum = num.toPrecision(2);        // preciseNum is now 1.2e+2
```

For older browsers, number formatting is a more cumbersome process, but one that can be encapsulated in the formatNumber( ) utility function shown in the Discussion. Invoke the function by passing either a number or string that can be cast to a number and an integer signifying the number of places to the right of the decimal for the returned string:

```
document.myForm.total.value = formatNumber(someNumber, 2);
```

The result from this function is a string intended for display on the page, not further calculation. The string can conceivably contain an error message, but you can modify the function to change how errors are reported.

Discussion

In the now rare case that you need number formatting for browsers such as IE 5 or Netscape 4, you can use the formatNumber( ) reusable utility function shown in Example 2-1. It also works in the newest browsers.

Example 2-1. formatNumber( ) function for text display of numbers

```
function formatNumber (num, decplaces) {
    // convert in case it arrives as a string value
    num = parseFloat(num);
    // make sure it passes conversion
    if (!isNaN(num)) {
        // multiply value by 10 to the decplaces power;
        // round the result to the nearest integer;
        // convert the result to a string
        var str = "" + Math.round (eval(num) * Math.pow(10,decplaces));
        // exponent means value is too big or small for this routine
        if (str.indexOf("e") != -1) {
            return "Out of Range";
        }
        // if needed for small values, pad zeros
        // to the left of the number
        while (str.length <= decplaces) {
            str = "0" + str;
        }
        // calculate decimal point position
        var decpoint = str.length - decplaces;
        // assemble final result from: (a) the string up to the position of
        // the decimal point; (b) the decimal point; and (c) the balance
        // of the string. Return finished product.
        return str.substring(0,decpoint) + "." + str.substring(decpoint,str.length);
    } else {
        return "NaN";
    }
}
```

When you use the newer built-in methods (toFixed( ) and toPrecision( )) to set the number format, you should be aware of the way truncated numbers are rounded. All rounding is based on the value of the next digit to the right of the last visible digit in the returned string. For example, if you format the number 1.2349 to two digits to the right of the decimal, the returned value is 1.23 because the next digit to the right of the 3 is a 4.

It should be clear that none of the methods or functions shown in this recipe operate in the same way that more sophisticated number formatting in other programs work. There is nothing about adding commas for large numbers or a leading currency symbol. Such extras need to be handled through your own scripts.

Inserting commas for displaying large numbers can be accomplished easily on the integer portion of a number through regular expressions. Here is a simple function that inserts commas in the appropriate places, regardless of the size of the number (in plain, nonscientific notation, that is):

```
function formatCommas(numString) {
    // extract decimal and digits to right (if any)
    var re = /\.\d{1,}/;
    var frac = (re.test(numString)) ? re.exec(numString) : "";
    // divide integer portion into three-digit groups
    var int = parseInt(numString,10).toString();
    re = /(-?\d+)(\d{3})/;
    while (re.test(int)) {
        int = int.replace(re, "$1,$2");
    }
    return int + frac;
}
```

This function accepts as a parameter a string version of any integer or floating-point value.

While on the subject of commas, it's not unusual for users to enter large numbers with commas, but the database or other backend processing does not allow commas in numbers. If that's the case, you can use a form's submit event handler to modify the value of a text box that contains commas and strip those commas before submitting the form. It can all take place during the client-side batch validation of the form. The function to remove commas also uses regular expressions, and looks like the following:

```
function stripCommas(numString) {
    var re = /,/g;
    return numString.replace(re,"");
}
```

One final point about number formatting involves a comparatively new JavaScript method of the Number object called toLocaleString( ), invoked as:

```
var formattedString = myNumber.toLocaleString( );
```

The formal ECMAScript specification does not recommend any particular formatting for this method because it is largely dependent on how the browser maker wishes to align formatting with localized customs. For now, only Internet Explorer (at least for the U.S. version) does anything special when invoking this method on a number value. All numbers are formatted to two places to the right of the decimal (dollars and cents without any currency symbol). IE for Windows also inserts commas for large numbers. While Mozilla, Safari, and Opera support this method, they perform no additional formatting for numbers.

Bear in mind that other parts of the world use different symbols where North Americans use commas and decimals. For example, in Europe, it's not uncommon to find commas and periods used in the opposite manner, so that the number 20,000.50 would be displayed as 20.000,50. If your audience uses that system, you could modify the functions above to work within that system. The most deeply nested statement of the formatCommas( ) function would be:

```
numString = numString.replace(re, "$1.$2");
```

and the first statement of the stripCommas( ) function would be:

```
var re = /\./g;
```

You'd also probably want to change the names of both functions to formatPeriods( ) and stripPeriods( ), respectively. This is just the kind of cultural variation that the toLocaleString( ) method was intended to solve. Now it is up to the browser makers to agree on an implementation that works across the board.

See Also

Recipe 8.3 for using the submit event handler to trigger batch validation and other last-instant tasks on a form prior to submission.

2.6 Converting Between Decimal and Hexadecimal Numbers

Problem

You want to change a decimal number to its hexadecimal equivalent, and vice versa.

Solution

The core JavaScript language provides facilities for going from hexadecimal to decimal and back again, but through two separate mechanisms.

To get a hexadecimal number as a string into its decimal equivalent, use the parseInt( ) method and specify the second parameter as 16:

```
var decimalVal = parseInt(myHexNumberValue, 16);
```

For *myHexNumberValue*, you can use either the hexadecimal characters for the number, or the format required for hexadecimal arithmetic in JavaScript: the hexadecimal characters preceded by 0x or 0X (a zero followed by an X). Here are some examples with string literals in the two formats:

```
var decimalVal = parseInt("1f", 16);
var decimalVal = parseInt("0x1f", 16);
```

To convert a decimal number to a hexadecimal string equivalent, use the toString( ) method of the Number object, specifying base 16 as the argument:

```
var hexVal = (255).toString(16)      // result = "ff"
```

Because JavaScript automatically converts hexadecimal numbers to their decimal equivalents for arithmetic operations, the hexadecimal conversion is needed only for display of a hexadecimal result.

Discussion

Hexadecimal arithmetic isn't used much in JavaScript, but the language provides rudimentary support for base 16 numbers. As long as you signify a hexadecimal number value with the leading 0x, you can perform regular arithmetic on that value to your heart's content. But be aware that the results of those operations are returned in base 10, which allows the odd possibility of using hexadecimal and decimal values in the same expression:

```
var result = 0xff - 200;
```

Hexadecimal digits a through f may be expressed in your choice of upper- or lower-case letters.

The parseInt( ) method is frequently a handy tool for getting values in other bases into decimal. For example, you obtain a decimal equivalent of a binary number string by specifying base 2 as the second argument of the method:

```
var decimalVal = parseInt("11010011", 2);
```

Converting in the other direction (from decimal to other bases) is aided by the toString( ) method that you can apply to any number value (not string values). This works not only for hexadecimal values, as shown earlier, but for octal (base 8) and binary (base 2) values as well:

```
var decimalVal = parseFloat(document.getElementById("textBox").value);
var binaryVal = decimalVal.toString(2);
```

See Also

Recipe 2.1 for converting between number and string value types.

2.7   Generating Pseudorandom Numbers

Problem

You want to generate a random number.

Solution

The Math.random( ) method returns a pseudorandom number between 0 and 1. To calculate a pseudorandom integer value within a range starting with zero, use the formula:

```
var result = Math.floor(Math.random( ) * (n + 1));
```

where n is the highest acceptable integer of the range. To calculate a pseudorandom integer number within a range starting at a number other than zero, use the formula:

```
var result = Math.floor(Math.random( ) * (n - m + 1)) + m;
```

where m is the lowest acceptable integer of the range, and n is the highest acceptable integer of the range.

Discussion

The previous examples focus on random integers, such as the kind you might use for values of a game cube (a die with numbers from 1 through 6). But you can remove the Math.floor( ) call to let the rest of the expression create random numbers with decimal fractions if you need them.

JavaScript's random number generator does not provide a mechanism for adjusting the seed to ensure more genuine randomness. Thus, at best you can treat it as a pseudorandom number generator.

See Also

"The Math Object" in the introduction to this chapter.

2.8   Calculating Trigonometric Functions

Problem

You want to invoke a variety of trigonometric functions, perhaps for calculating animation paths of a positioned element.

Solution

JavaScript's Math object comes with a typical complement of functions for trigonometric calculations. Each one requires one or two arguments and returns a result in radians. Arguments representing angles must also be expressed in radians. The following statement assigns the sine of a value to a variable:

```
var sineValue = Math.sin(radiansInput);
```

All Math object methods must be invoked as methods of the static Math object, as shown above.

Discussion

See the introduction to this chapter for a summary of all Math object methods and constants. You can see an application of trigonometric functions in Recipe 13.10, which calculates the circular path for a positioned element to follow on the page.

See Also

"The Math Object" in the introduction to this chapter; Recipe 13.10 where some trigonometric operations help calculate points around a circular path.

2.9   Creating a Date Object

Problem

You want to create an instance of a Date object to use for date calculations or display.

Solution

Use the Date object constructor method with any of the acceptable arguments signifying a date (and, optionally, a time for that date):

```
var myDate = new Date(yyyy, mm, dd, hh, mm, ss);
var myDate = new Date(yyyy, mm, dd);
var myDate = new Date("monthName dd, yyyy hh:mm:ss");
var myDate = new Date("monthName dd, yyyy");
var myDate = new Date(epochMilliseconds);
```

With all of these constructions, you can generate a date object for any point in history (reliably back to approximately 100 A.D.) or the future (thousands of millennia hence). When you create a date object without specifying the time, all time values are automatically set to zero—the very start of that day.

To create a date object with the current date and time, omit all arguments:

```
var now = new Date();
```

The accuracy of the value assigned by the Date object constructor is entirely dependent upon the accuracy of the client computer's internal clock and control panel settings. Correct setting of the computer's local time zone and daylight saving time option is essential to accurate date and time calculations based on the current date.

Discussion

Notice that the arguments for the Date object constructor—as specified in the ECMAScript standard—have no variation that readily accepts shortcut ways of entering dates (such as *mm/dd/yyyy*, or the numerous variations used around the world). Instead, numerical entries need to be broken into the component parts to be passed as discrete arguments for the constructor. If you need to generate a date object from user entries in a text box (or, better still, a series of three text boxes), you can pass the value properties of those text boxes directly as arguments of the constructor:

```
var dateEntry = new Date(document.getElementById("year").value,
                         document.getElementById("month").value,
                         document.getElementById("date").value);
```

This is one of those many places where the JavaScript engine automatically attempts to cast a string value to the required number value.

Despite the lack of ECMA standard support for entry in formats such as *mm/dd/yyyy* or *mm-dd-yyyy*, browsers support them. Therefore, you can get away with supplying one of those formats to a constructor method, but remember that the sequence is assured to work only in browsers and operating systems whose date formats support that sequence. A North American browser, for instance, will misinterpret dates formatted as *dd/mm/yyyy*, which is a very common format outside North America.

It's important to remember that all of this date object creation and manipulation occurs strictly on the client. A client-side date object has no connection with the server's clock or time zone. At best, a server can timestamp a page as it leaves the server, but that has nothing to do with a date object on the client. Any attempt at synchronizing a client-side date object with the server clock is doomed due to latency between the serving of the page and the rendering in the client.

See Also

Recipes 2.10 and 2.11 for date calculations; Recipe 2.12 for using regular expressions to validate date entries in a form; Recipes 15.8 and 15.9 for applications of a date object in showing how much time is left before a future event.

2.10 Calculating a Previous or Future Date

Problem

You want to obtain a date based on a specific number of days before or after a known date.

Solution

The basic technique is to create a date object with a known date, and then add or subtract any number of units from that known date. After that, you can read the components of the modified date object to obtain the string or numerical representation of the date.

For example, we'll calculate the date that is 10 days from the current date. After creating a date object for now, a statement reads the date component (a calendar date within the month) and then sets the date value ahead by 10 days:

```
var myDate = new Date( );
myDate.setDate(myDate.getDate( ) + 10);
```

At this point, the myDate object contains the future date in milliseconds, irrespective of months, dates, and years. But if you then read myDate's string version (or locale string), you see the future date correctly calculated:

```
document.myForm.deadline.value = myDate.toLocaleDateString( );
```

Discussion

You can move the date forward or back by any increment you like, even when it doesn't seem logical. For example, if a date object is currently pointing to the 25th of a month, you can get the date 10 days in the future by adding 10 to the date:

```
myDate.setDate(myDate.getDate( ) + 10);
```

Even though 25 plus 10 is 35, the date object corrects for the number of days in the object's month, and calculates the correct date in the following month, 10 days after the 25th.

By keeping its internal workings strictly at the millisecond level, a date object can easily adapt itself to month and year boundaries. Details about the month, date, and year are calculated internally and returned only upon request. For example, you add 10 days to the 25th of June (which has 30 days), you arrive at the 5th of July; but add 10 days to the 25th of July (which has 31 days), and you reach the 4th of August. The JavaScript interpreter takes care of all such irregularities for you.

A date object has numerous functions for getting and setting components of the date, ranging from the millisecond to the year. Table 2-3 shows the most common methods and their value ranges.

Table 2-3. Date methods

Read	Write	Values	Description
getTime( )	setTime(*val*)	0–...	Number of milliseconds since 1Jan1970 at 00:00:00 UTC
getSeconds( )	setSeconds(*val*)	0–59	Number of seconds after the minute stored in the object

Table 2-3. Date methods (continued)

Read	Write	Values	Description
getMinutes( )	setMinutes(*val*)	0–59	Number of minutes after the hour stored in the object
getHours( )	setHours(*val*)	0–23	Number of hours in the date stored in the object
getDay( )	setDay(*val*)	0–6	Day of the week (Sunday = 0, Monday = 1, etc.)
getDate( )	setDate(*val*)	1–31	Date number
getMonth( )	setMonth(*val*)	0–11	Month in the object's year (January = 0)
getFullYear( )	setFullYear(*val*)	1970–...	Four-digit year

All of these methods deal with time in the client computer's local time zone. If you need to work on a more global scale, see Recipe 15.9.

See Also

Recipe 2.9 for creating a date object; Recipe 2.11 for calculating the number of days between two dates; Recipes 15.7, 15.8, and 15.9 for more date applications.

2.11 Calculating the Number of Days Between Two Dates

Problem

You want to find out how many days come between two known dates.

Solution

Use the daysBetween( ) function shown in the Discussion to obtain an integer signifying the number of whole days between two dates that are passed as parameters to the function. For example:

```
var projectLength = 0;
// validate form entries with checkDate() function from Recipe 2.12
var startField = document.getElementById("startDate");
var endField = document.getElementById("endDate");
if (checkDate(startField) && checkDate(endField)) {
    var startDate = new Date(startField.value);
    var endDate = new Date(endField.value);
    projectLength = daysBetween(startDate, endDate);
}
if (projectLength > 0) {
    alert("You\'ve specified " + projectLength + " days for this project.");
}
```

Discussion

Example 2-2 shows the daysBetween( ) utility function. The function's two arguments are date objects.

Example 2-2. daysBetween() function for calculating days between dates

```
function daysBetween(date1, date2) {
    var DSTAdjust = 0;
    // constants used for our calculations below
    oneMinute = 1000 * 60;
    var oneDay = oneMinute * 60 * 24;
    // equalize times in case date objects have them
    date1.setHours(0);
    date1.setMinutes(0);
    date1.setSeconds(0);
    date2.setHours(0);
    date2.setMinutes(0);
    date2.setSeconds(0);
    // take care of spans across Daylight Saving Time changes
    if (date2 > date1) {
        DSTAdjust =
            (date2.getTimezoneOffset() - date1.getTimezoneOffset()) * oneMinute;
    } else {
        DSTAdjust =
            (date1.getTimezoneOffset() - date2.getTimezoneOffset()) * oneMinute;
    }
    var diff = Math.abs(date2.getTime() - date1.getTime()) - DSTAdjust;
    return Math.ceil(diff/oneDay);
}
```

The calculation is based on the number of milliseconds between the two dates. Because it is possible that one or both of the arguments' date objects could have been created with times (as happens when invoking the Date( ) constructor method without parameters), the function sets the times of both objects to zero.

You probably noticed the code in the daysBetween( ) function that revolves around the DSTAdjust variable. This adjustment is needed when the span of time between the two dates includes a local time change—known as Daylight Saving Time in North America, and Summer Time in many other parts of the world.

While every day has a fixed number of milliseconds (as far as JavaScript is concerned), the days in which the time changes occur can have an artificial measure of 23 or 25 hours. When the function sets the hours, minutes, and seconds of the date objects to zero, the values are assigned to the local time of the client computer. Consider what happens during the change back to standard time, when the day with the change lasts for 25 hours. If that day is a Sunday, and you want to count the number of days between Friday and Monday, the total number of milliseconds between those two days will have one hour's worth of extra milliseconds in the total difference between the two dates. Without adjusting for this extra hour, the daysBetween( )

function returns an integer showing one more day than is actually there (by taking the ceiling of the result of dividing the total number of elapsed milliseconds by the number of milliseconds in one day).

It's almost magic that the date management mechanism of the JavaScript interpreter (working in concert with the operating system) knows that for a given locale (as determined by the operating system), the offset from GMT is one measure during Daylight Saving Time and another measure during standard time. It is that intelligent offset measure that the daysBetween( ) function uses to determine the amount of adjustment to make to the calculation (and is not affected by legislated changes to Daylight Saving Time start and end dates). For a date span that does not cross one of these boundary cases, the value of DSTAdjust is zero; but during those breaks, the variable holds the number of minutes difference between the two dates (the getTimezoneOffset( ) method returns a value in minutes).

See Also

Recipe 15.8 for a dynamic display of the number of shopping days until Christmas; Recipe 15.9 for a dynamic countdown timer.

2.12   Validating a Date

Problem

You want to validate a date entered by the user in a form.

Solution

Use the checkDate( ) function shown in the Discussion. This function takes a text input element as its sole argument and expects the user to enter a date value in either *mm*/*dd*/*yyyy* or *mm-dd-yyyy* format. For example, the following validation function could be triggered from a change event handler of a date entry form field:

```
function validateDate(fld) {
    if (!checkDate(fld)) {
        // focus if validation fails
        fld.focus( );
        fld.select( );
    }
}
```

Discussion

Before you undertake validating a date entry, you must clearly understand your assumptions about the users, the purpose of the entry, and what you want to report back to the users for invalid entries. It's comparatively easy to test whether a field expecting a date in the *mm*/*dd*/*yyyy* format has numbers in the right places, but that typically is not good enough. After all, you don't want someone to get away with entering the 45th of June into a date field.

The checkDate( ) validation function in Example 2-3 assumes that users will enter dates in either *mm/dd/yyyy* or *mm-dd-yyyy* formats (in that order only), and that the validation must test for the entry of a true date. There is no boundary checking here, so practically any year is accepted. As a form-validation function, this one takes a reference to the text input element as the sole argument. Upon successful validation, the function returns true; otherwise, the user receives an alert message with some level of detail about the error, and the function returns false.

Example 2-3. Basic date validation function

```
function checkDate(fld) {
    var mo, day, yr;
    var entry = fld.value;
    var re = /\b\d{1,2}[\/-]\d{1,2}[\/-]\d{4}\b/;
    if (re.test(entry)) {
        var delimChar = (entry.indexOf("/") != -1) ? "/" : "-";
        var delim1 = entry.indexOf(delimChar);
        var delim2 = entry.lastIndexOf(delimChar);
        mo = parseInt(entry.substring(0, delim1), 10);
        day = parseInt(entry.substring(delim1+1, delim2), 10);
        yr = parseInt(entry.substring(delim2+1), 10);
        var testDate = new Date(yr, mo-1, day);
        if (testDate.getDate( ) == day) {
            if (testDate.getMonth( ) + 1 == mo) {
                if (testDate.getFullYear( ) == yr) {
                    return true;
                } else {
                    alert("There is a problem with the year entry.");
                }
            } else {
                alert("There is a problem with the month entry.");
            }
        } else {
            alert("There is a problem with the date entry.");
        }
    } else {
        alert("Incorrect date format. Enter as mm/dd/yyyy.");
    }
    return false;
}
```

The basic operation of the checkDate( ) function is to first validate the format of the entry against a regular expression pattern. If the format is good, the function creates a date object from the entered numbers. Then the components of the resulting date object are compared against the initial entries. If there is any discrepancy between the two sets of numbers, a problem with the entry exists. It helps that the JavaScript Date object constructor accepts out-of-range dates and calculates the effective date from those wacky values. When the user enters 2/30/2007, the resulting date object is for 3/2/2007. Since the month and date no longer coincide with the entries, it's clear that the user entered an invalid date.

Although this function uses a regular expression only to verify the basic format of the date entry, it uses more rudimentary string parsing for the detailed analysis of the entry. This tactic is needed for backward-compatibility to overcome incomplete implementations of advanced regular expression handling in browsers prior to IE 5.5 for Windows. The checkDate( ) function works in all mainstream browsers from Version 4 onward.

In a high-volume data-entry environment, where productivity is measured in operators' keystrokes and time spent per form, you want to build more intelligence in a form. For example, you want to allow two-digit year entries, but code the validation routine so that it fills the field with the expanded version of the date because the backend database requires it. Moreover, the two-digit entry needs to be done in a maintenance-free way so that the range of allowable years for two-digit dates continues to modify itself as the years progress. Example 2-4 is an enhanced version of the checkDate( ) function with these upgrades shown in bold.

Example 2-4. Enhanced date validation function

```
function checkDate(fld) {
    var mo, day, yr;
    var entry = fld.value;
    var reLong = /\b\d{1,2}[\/-]\d{1,2}[\/-]\d{4}\b/;
    var reShort = /\b\d{1,2}[\/-]\d{1,2}[\/-]\d{2}\b/;
    var valid = (reLong.test(entry)) || (reShort.test(entry));
    if (valid) {
        var delimChar = (entry.indexOf("/") != -1) ? "/" : "-";
        var delim1 = entry.indexOf(delimChar);
        var delim2 = entry.lastIndexOf(delimChar);
        mo = parseInt(entry.substring(0, delim1), 10);
        day = parseInt(entry.substring(delim1+1, delim2), 10);
        yr = parseInt(entry.substring(delim2+1), 10);
        // handle two-digit year
        if (yr < 100) {
            var today = new Date( );
            // get current century floor (e.g., 2000)
            var currCent = parseInt(today.getFullYear( ) / 100) * 100;
            // two digits up to this year + 15 expands to current century
            var threshold = (today.getFullYear( ) + 15) - currCent;
            if (yr > threshold) {
                yr += currCent - 100;
            } else {
                yr += currCent;                }
        }
        var testDate = new Date(yr, mo-1, day);
        if (testDate.getDate( ) == day) {
            if (testDate.getMonth( ) + 1 == mo) {
                if (testDate.getFullYear( ) == yr) {
```

Example 2-4. Enhanced date validation function (continued)

```
                    // fill field with database-friendly format
                    fld.value = mo + "/" + day + "/" + yr;
                    return true;
                } else {
                    alert("There is a problem with the year entry.");
                }
            } else {
                alert("There is a problem with the month entry.");
            }
        } else {
            alert("There is a problem with the date entry.");
        }
    } else {
        alert("Incorrect date format. Enter as mm/dd/yyyy.");
    }
    return false;
}
```

You can short-circuit a lot of the potential problems for date validation—including the one involving cultural differences in date formats—by providing either three text boxes (for month, day, and year in any order), or three select lists. Even the select list solution isn't free from validation, however, because you have to make sure that the user has chosen a valid combination (e.g., not something like June 31). You can get creative in this regard by using dynamic forms to repopulate the date list each time the user changes the month (see Recipe 8.14).

Date fields are generally important to the form in which they exist. Don't skimp on the thoroughness of validation for dates either on the client or on the server.

See Also

Recipe 8.2 for additional form field validation functions.

CHAPTER 3

Arrays and Objects

3.0 Introduction

Most programming tasks involve moving data around in memory. A lot of the data involved in browser-based JavaScript activity consists of objects that are part of the rendered document. But very often your scripts arrive at the client accompanied by data provided by a server or hardwired in the script (as arrays or custom objects). Or you may find it convenient to create more flexible data structures that mirror the rendered content on the page. For example, it may be easier and faster to sort a table's data inside a JavaScript array and re-render the table rather than playing Tower of Hanoi games with cells and rows of a table one by one.

One of the most important jobs you have as a programmer is designing the data structures that your scripts will be working with. It's not unusual to start the planning of a major scripting job by scoping out the data structures that will facilitate DHTML-enhanced user interface features. When you do so, you will find JavaScript arrays and custom objects to be the containers and organizers of your data. These containers give your scripts a regular way to access the data points and a clean way to structure the data to make it easy to visualize the abstract comings and goings during script execution.

JavaScript Arrays

The loose data typing that pervades JavaScript carries over to arrays, but even more so. Unlike similar structures in many other programming languages, a JavaScript array is not limited to a specific size chiseled in stone at the time of its creation. You can add or delete items from an array at will. It is an extraordinarily flexible data store.

Another feature of the JavaScript array is that each entry in the array can hold data of any type. It's no problem mixing strings, numbers, Booleans, and objects within the same array. You can even change the data and data type for a single array entry at any time. Neither of these practices may be advisable from a programming-style point of view, but they're possible nevertheless.

Arrays are indexed by zero-based integers. In other words, to reference the first entry in an array named myArray, use myArray[0]. A reference to the array entry returns the entry's value. To assign a value to an entry, use the simple assignment (=) operator. You may also use the add-by-value (+=) operator to add a number or append a string to an array entry, as appropriate.

The basic JavaScript array is a one-dimensional kind of array. But as you will see in Recipes 3.2 and 3.9, you can create more complex array structures, including multi-dimensional arrays (arrays of arrays), and arrays whose entries are complex custom objects.

JavaScript Custom Objects

The "looseness" of the JavaScript language, as exhibited in the way it handles data typing, arrays, and variable values, extends to its concept of objects. Forget what you know about object-oriented programming techniques and relationships between objects. The notions of traditional classes, subclasses, and message passing have little application in JavaScript (although some of these ideas may come to the language in the future). Instead, think of a custom object as simply a convenient container for data in which the data values have labels that make it easier to remember what's what. Custom object syntax is just like the syntax you use for other JavaScript and DOM objects: it follows the "dots" rule (e.g., *myObject.myProperty* and *myObject. myMethod( )*).

One of the hazards of bringing too much object-oriented programming experience to scripting is that you might tend to turn every piece of data into an object, even when the overhead (in terms of source code space) to generate the object outweighs any functional or readability benefit you might get from using objects. It's not uncommon for an object-oriented approach to a simple problem to obfuscate the relationships among data points. But if your scripts frequently need to refer to some data associated with an entity that hangs around in the global variable space, it probably makes good sense to use an object there. In later chapters of this book, you will see many objects used as repositories for bits of information related to a particular item, such as the details of a drop-down menu.

Despite the cautions expressed here about the difference between objects in JavaScript (which are based on a concept called *prototype inheritance*) and true object-oriented environments, you can simulate a goodly amount of genuine OOP ideas with custom objects. Recipe 3.12 demonstrates a few of these simulations.

Choosing Between Arrays and Objects

So, when do you use an array, and when do you use an object? Think of an array as an ordered list of similar kinds of data. The list, itself, signifies the purpose or kind of data it contains, such as a series of coworker names or the titles of all books on a shelf. The position of one item among the others is not important, although you might like to sort the list to, perhaps, show the contents in alphabetical order. Having the items in this kind of "blind" list means that at some point you will be looking through all items in the list, perhaps to pull out their values for insertion into an HTML element for display.

An object, on the other hand, is best used to encapsulate information about a single entity. A coworker object might contain properties for the person's name and age; a book object could have dozens of properties for information points such as title, author, publisher, category, and so on. The properties are explicitly named so that you can readily access the value of a single property directly (e.g., book3.publisher). You can also equip an object with methods whose actions operate on the object and its properties (see Recipe 3.8).

As you will see in Recipe 3.7 and elsewhere, there is an advantage in creating an array of objects. The "array-ness" gives your scripts the ability to iterate through the entire list of objects; the "object-ness" lets the same script inspect a specific property of each object in the array to perform tasks like lookups. An array of book objects, for instance, lets a looping construct look through the entire list of books and inspect the author property of each item to accumulate the title property values of those objects whose author property meets a particular criterion.

Be prepared to use arrays and objects by themselves, as well as in combination. Not only are you likely to use an array of objects, but a property of an object may be an array. For example, an object that represents a book might define the author property as an array to accommodate multiple authors. A book with a single author has a one-entry array for that property, but the scripts that go diving for authors know to expect an array data type there, as well as use appropriate comparison tools against the entries in the array.

As dry as this chapter's subject may seem at first glance, it may be the most important one in the entire book. Most of the recipes from this chapter are used in later chapters repeatedly because they are fundamental building blocks for a lot of Dynamic HTML and other scripting.

Getting Data into the Page

Most of the recipes in this chapter show data arrays and objects embedded directly within the page of the examples. This approach works for a fixed set of data or, after the page has loaded, data dynamically read from the page or user entry forms. But you can also embed data from live sources—server databases—with the help of server programming.

If you use a server environment (such as ASP, JSP, ColdFusion, PHP, and many more) that assembles each page's content by way of server-side templates and programs, you can use the same environment to retrieve data from your databases and convert the returned data sets into JavaScript arrays and objects to be delivered with the rest of the page. Another approach is to let the external script-loading capability of browsers (via the src attribute of the <script> tag) point to a server process URL. The URL contains query data that the server program uses to fetch the database data, then the server converts the returned data into JavaScript arrays and objects for output to the client, delivered in the format and MIME type of a *.js* file. The data becomes part of the page's scripts, just as if it were directly embedded in the page.

Perhaps the most intriguing possibilities, however, arise from a technology that is now common to every scriptable browser. An object called XMLHttpRequest makes it possible for a rendered page to make requests to a server process without disturbing the current page. Typically, the process returns data in the form of an XML document, from which a browser script may readily extract data to update portions of the rendered page. The technology has been given a more convenient name: Asynchronous JavaScript and XML, or Ajax for short.

Such data retrieval is not limited to XML. Instead, a server process can return to the XMLHttpRequest object a string consisting of a JavaScript array and custom object code. Once received at the browser, a single statement (eval( )) converts the string into full-fledged JavaScript arrays and objects, ready for further manipulation. This so-called JavaScript Object Notation (JSON) is yet another way to feed server data to an already rendered page.

3.1   Creating a Simple Array

Problem

You want to create a simple array of data.

Solution

JavaScript provides both a long way and a shortcut to generate and populate an array. The long way is to use the Array object constructor. If you specify no parameters for the constructor, you create an empty array, which you may then populate with data entry by entry:

```
var myArray = new Array( );
myArray[0] = "Alice";
myArray[1] = "Fred";
...
```

You do not have to declare a fixed size for an array when you create it, but you may do so if you wish, by passing a single integer value as a parameter to the constructor method:

```
var myArray = new Array(12);
```

This creates an array of 12 entries whose values are null.

If you supply more than one comma-delimited parameter to the constructor method, the arguments are treated as data for the array entries. Thus, the following statement:

```
var myArray = new Array("Alice", "Fred", "Jean");
```

creates a three-item array, each item containing a string value.

A shortcut approach to the same action lets you use square brackets to symbolize the array constructor:

```
var myArray = ["Alice", "Fred", "Jean"];
```

Discussion

After you create an array (through any of the syntaxes just shown), you can add to it by assigning a value to the array with the next numeric index in sequence. If your script doesn't know how large an array is when it needs to add to it, you can use the length property of the array to help out. Because the length integer is always one larger than the highest zero-based index value of the array, the length value can act as the index for the next item:

```
myArray[myArray.length] = "Steve";
```

In fact, you can use this construction to populate any existing array object, including an empty one. This is particularly helpful if you are populating a large array and need to change values in the source code from time to time. Rather than trying to juggle fixed index numbers in a long series of assignment statements, use the length property, and order the assignment statements so that all items are in the desired array order. The indexes will take care of themselves when the statements run, even if you change the order in the source code tomorrow.

If your pages limit IE browsers to version 5.5 or later, you should use the ECMA-standard push( ) method of arrays to append items to an existing array. Thus, in place of the first example shown in the Solution, you would use the following syntax:

```
var myArray = new Array( );
myArray.push("Alice");
myArray.push("Fred");
...
```

Your code can use the same method to add new items to the array at any time. If the order of items in an array requires that a new item be inserted as the first array entry (occupying the zeroth position), use the unshift( ) method of an array. Index values for all subsequent items increment by one as a result of the insertion.

See Also

Recipe 3.2 for creating a more complex array; Recipe 3.8 for a discussion about creating an array of objects; Recipe 3.3 for converting an array's entries to a string value.

3.2   Creating a Multidimensional Array

Problem

You want to consolidate data in an array construction of two dimensions—such as a table—or even more dimensions.

Solution

Create an array of arrays. As an example, consider the following small table of regional sales data:

Description	Q1	Q2	Q3	Q4
East	2300	3105	2909	4800
Central	1800	1940	2470	4350
West	900	1200	1923	3810

To place the data portions of this table into an array that has three items (one for each region row), in which each item contains an array of four nested items (sales figures for each quarter column for that region), you can use a variety of array-creation syntaxes. A comparatively long version creates each of the nested arrays first, and then assigns those nested arrays to the outer array:

```
var eastArray = new Array(2300, 3105, 2909, 4800);
var centralArray = new Array(1800, 1940, 2470, 4350);
var westArray = new Array(900, 1200, 1923, 3810);
var salesArray = new Array(eastArray, centralArray, westArray);
```

The most compact array creation approach is to use the bracket shortcuts exclusively:

```
var salesArray = [[2300, 3105, 2909, 4800],
                  [1800, 1940, 2470, 4350],
                  [900, 1200, 1923, 3810]];
```

To access any nested item within salesArray, use a double index. For example, to reach the first item (East Q1), the reference is:

```
salesArray[0][0]      // 2300
```

There are no commas or other symbols allowed between the bracketed index values in this kind of reference. The first index applies to the first-level array, while the second applies to the nested arrays. Therefore, to reach the Central region's Q3 sales, the reference is:

```
salesArray[1][2]      // 2470
```

You may read and write to these multidimensional array items just like any other array items.

Discussion

There is no practical limit to the number of nesting levels you can create for a multidimensional array. For each dimension, lengthen the reference to the most deeply nested items with another bracketed index value. See Recipe 3.4 for using loops to inspect every item in a deeply nested array.

One potential problem with using a multidimensional array is that you may lose track of what a particular entry represents. When you look at the array creation examples just shown, the numbers lose their contextual meaning with respect to region or quarter. Their position in the two-dimensional array is all that the numbers know about. It is up to the rest of your scripts to keep the relationships between the data points and their meanings straight. In many cases, you may be better served by creating an array of custom objects. The objects can contain properties that provide labels and context for the raw data. See Recipes 3.8 and 3.9 for additional thoughts on the issue.

See Also

Recipe 3.4 to see how to iterate through simple and multidimensional arrays; Recipe 3.8 for using an array of objects in place of a multidimensional array; Recipe 3.9 for a custom object implementation of the sales example and how to create a simulated hash table to speed access to a particular entry.

3.3   Converting Between Arrays and Strings

Problem

You want to obtain a string representation of an array's data or change a string to an array.

Solution

Array objects and string values have methods that facilitate conversion between these data types, thus allowing arrays to be conveyed to other pages via URL search strings or cookies.

To convert a simple (one-dimensional) array to a string, first select a character that can act as a unique delimiter character between the array values when they become embedded in a string. The character cannot appear in any of the data entries. Specify that character as the sole parameter to the join( ) method of the array. The following statement uses a comma as a delimiter between entries after the conversion to string form:

```
var arrayAsString = myArray.join(",");
```

The original array is not disturbed in the course of this transformation.

If you have a string with a delimiter character separating individual points of data that you want to convert to an array, specify that character as the parameter of the `split()` method of your string value or object:

```
var restoredArray = myRegularString.split(",");
```

The `split()` method performs the task of an array constructor, automatically passing the values between delimiters as items of the new array. The delimiter characters do not become part of the array's value.

Discussion

Although the preceding examples show only single characters used as the so-called separators for the string versions, you can use any string. For example, if you intended to display the array entries as a vertical list in a `textarea` element, you could use the `\n` special character to force carriage returns between the items. Similarly, if the data was to be formatted as an XHTML list, you could use the string `<br />` as the separator of the `join()` method; or if the array items have all the necessary XHTML code in them, specify an empty string as the `join()` method parameter. Then use the resulting string as a value to assign to an element's `innerHTML` property for display in the body text of a page.

Use the `join()` method only on simple arrays. For a multidimensional array, the method is safe to use on any of the most deeply nested arrays, which are, themselves, simple arrays.

Even more powerful is the `split()` method of a string value or object. You can use regular expressions as the separator parameter. For example, consider the string of comma-delimited dollar values:

```
var amounts = "30.25,120.00,45.09,200.10";
```

If you want to create an array of just the integer portions of those values, you could create a regular expression whose pattern looks for a period, followed by two numerals and an optional comma (to accommodate the final entry):

```
var amtArray = amounts.split(/\.\d{2},?/);   // result = [30, 120, 45, 200,]
```

One by-product of the use of the `split()` method on a string when the separator is at the end of the string is that the method creates an array entry for the nonexistent item following the end separator. Most typically, the separator does not come at the end of the string, but if it does, watch out for this extra empty array entry.

An optional second parameter of the `split()` method lets you supply an integer representing the number of items from the string to send to the new array. Thus, if the string value always ends in the separator character or sequence, you can limit the `split()` method to the actual number of items in the string (assuming your scripts know or derive that information from string parsing or other activities). This parameter is not part of the formal ECMAScript standard, but is implemented in mainstream browsers.

In practice, converting arrays to a string is limited to array data that is easily represented in strings, such as numbers, Booleans, and other strings. If an array's items consist of references to objects (either custom or DOM), such objects don't have a suitable or meaningful string representation. For an array of DOM objects, you might consider grabbing the id properties of the objects and preserving them in the string. Although the characteristics of the objects won't be conveyed, if the same objects exist in another page, the IDs can be used (via the document. getElementById( ) method) to resurrect a proper reference to the object. See Recipes 3.13 and 8.14 for ideas about converting objects to strings.

See Also

Recipe 3.13 for a way to convert data consisting of custom objects and arrays to a string that can later rebuild the objects and arrays; Recipe 8.14 to convert form data to strings for transfer to another page.

3.4   Doing Something with the Items in an Array

Problem

You want to loop through all entries of an array and read their values.

Solution

Use a for loop to build an incrementing index counter, limited by the length of the array. Although not particularly practical, the following sequence demonstrates how to iterate through an array and reference individual entries of the array from inside the loop:

```
var myArray = ["Alice", "Fred", "Jean", "Steve"];
for (var i = 0; i < myArray.length; i++) {
    alert("Item " + i + " is:" + myArray[i] + ".");
}
```

The limit expression portion of the for loop uses the less-than (<) operator on the length property of the array. Because index values are zero-based, but the length property contains the actual count of items, you want to keep the maximum index value at one less than the count of items. Therefore, do not use the less-than or equal to (<=) operator. If you want the loop to operate in reverse order, initialize the loop counter variable (i) to be the length minus 1:

```
for (var i = myArray.length - 1; i >= 0; i--) {
    alert("Item " + i + " is:" + myArray[i] + ".");
}
```

You don't have to redeclare the counter variable with the var statement if you have initialized it in a separate var statement or in a previous loop earlier within the same function.

Discussion

It's not uncommon to loop through an array (or collection of DOM objects) to find a match for some value within the array, and then use the index of the found item to assist with other lookup tasks. For example, the following parallel (but distinctly separate) arrays contain data with individuals' names and their corresponding ages:

```
var nameList = ["Alice", "Fred", "Jean", "Steve"];
var ageList = [23, 32, 28, 24];
```

You can use these parallel arrays as a lookup table. The following function receives a name string as a parameter, and looks for the matching age in the second array:

```
function ageLookup(name) {
    for (var i = 0; i < nameList.length; i++) {
        if (nameList[i] = = name) {
            return ageList[i];
        }
        return "Could not find " + name + ".";
    }
}
```

Similarly, you can examine a property of objects within a collection, and use the "found" index to read or write properties of the target items. The following function empties all of the text boxes on a page, even if the page contains multiple forms:

```
function clearTextBoxes( ) {
    var allInputs = document.getElementsByTagName("input");
    for (var i = 0; i < allInputs.length; i++) {
        if (allInputs[i].type = = "text") {
            allInputs[i].value = "";
        }
    }
}
```

For a multidimensional array, you need a multidimensional (i.e., nested) for loop construction to access each item. For example, given the two-dimensional array demonstrated in Recipe 3.2, the following nested for loops are able to reference each item and accumulate the numeric values from all entries of the two-dimensional array:

```
var total = 0;
var i, j;
for (i = 0; i < salesArray.length; i++) {
    for (j = 0; j < salesArray[i].length; j++) {
        total += salesArray[i][j];
    }
}
```

The nested array uses a separate loop counting variable (j). If you visualize the multidimensional array as the table shown in Recipe 3.2, the outer-counting variable (i) works along the rows, and the nested counting variable (j) works down the columns.

Thus, the sequence of operations in this construction goes across the rows of the corresponding table as follows:

```
row 0, cell 0
row 0, cell 1
row 0, cell 2
row 0, cell 3
row 1, cell 0
row 1, cell 1
...
```

See Also

Recipe 3.9 for a speedy alternative to parallel array lookups using a simulated hash table; Recipe 3.2 for creating a multidimensional array.

3.5   Sorting a Simple Array

Problem

You want to sort an array of numbers or strings.

Solution

To sort an array of numbers from lowest to highest, use the plain sort( ) method of the array object:

```
myArray.sort( );
```

This action modifies the order of the items within the array, and its original order cannot be restored unless your scripts have preserved that information elsewhere. Sorting a multidimensional array sorts only the outermost level.

Discussion

You can use the same parameter-less method on an array of string items, but the sorting is performed according to the ASCII values of the string characters. Therefore, if the strings in the array are not homogenous with respect to case, you may receive the array sorted such that all strings starting with uppercase letters sort ahead of those starting with lowercase letters (because ASCII values for uppercase letters are smaller than those for lowercase letters, as shown in Appendix A). For more complex and numeric sorting, however, you need to define a comparison function and invoke it from the sort( ) method.

A comparison function used with array sorts is a very powerful component of the JavaScript language and data manipulation. To invoke the comparison function, pass a reference to the function as the sole parameter of the sort( ) method.

Sorting through a comparison function causes the interpreter to repeatedly send pairs of values from the array to the function. The function should have two parameter variables assigned to it. The job of the function is to compare each pair of values, and return a value of less than zero, zero, or greater than zero, depending on the relationships between the two values:

<0   The second passed value should sort later than the first value.

0   The sort order of the two values should not change.

>0   The first passed value should sort later than the second.

As an example, consider an array consisting of numeric values. If you invoke the `sort( )` method without any parameters, the default sorting routine treats the values like strings and sorts them according to their ASCII values, which puts the number 10 sorting earlier than 4 because the first character of 10 is a lower ASCII value than that for 4.

To sort the values in genuine numerical order, you need to create a sorting function that explicitly compares the values as numbers:

```
function compareNumbers(a, b) {
    return a - b;
}
```

Invoke the sort through the statement:

```
myArray.sort(compareNumbers);
```

Behind the scenes, the JavaScript interpreter repeatedly sends pairs of values from the array to the function. If, during one of the trips to the comparison function the returned value is less than zero, it means that the second value is larger than the first and should be pushed down the sorting order. After rippling through all the values, the array is in the desired sorting order. To change the order of the sorting so that numbers are sorted in descending order, rework the comparison function as follows:

```
function compareNumbers(a, b) {
    return b - a;
}
```

For more complex sorting, including how you could sort by the number of characters in array item strings, see Recipe 3.11.

See Also

Recipe 3.11 for sorting arrays of objects based on values of a property in the objects.

3.6 Combining Arrays

Problem

You want to blend two or more separate arrays into one larger array.

Solution

To join arrays together, use the `concat()` method of the array object, passing a reference to the other array as a parameter:

```
var comboArray = myArray.concat(anotherArray);
```

Arrays joined through the `concat()` method are not altered. Instead, the `concat()` method returns the combined array as a new value, which you can preserve in a separate variable. The base array (the one used to invoke the `concat()` method) comes first in the combined array.

For combining multiple arrays, pass the additional arrays as comma-delimited parameters to the `concat()` method:

```
var comboArray = myArray.concat(otherArray1, otherArray2, otherArray3);
```

The combined array has items in the same order as they appear in the comma-delimited arguments.

Discussion

The `concat()` method is not limited to tacking one array onto another. Comma-delimited parameters to the method can be any data type. A value of any data type other than an array becomes another entry in the main array—in the same sequence as the parameters. You can even combine arrays and other data types in the group of parameters passed to the method.

In addition to the `concat()` method, a quartet of array methods let you treat an array like a stack for tacking on and removing items from the frontend or backend of the array. The `push()` method lets you append one or more items to the end of an array; the corresponding `pop()` method removes the last item from the array and returns its value. You can perform the same operations at the beginning of the array with the `unshift()` (append) and `shift()` (remove) methods. All four of these methods are implemented in IE 5.5 or later and all modern scriptable browsers.

See Also

Recipe 3.5 for sorting an array—something you may wish to do once you add to an array; Recipe 3.7 for dividing an array.

3.7   Dividing Arrays

Problem

You want to divide one array into two or more array segments.

Solution

To divide an array into two pieces, use the splice( ) method on the original array (the method is available in IE 5.5 or later and all modern scriptable browsers). The splice( ) method requires two parameters that signify the zero-based index of the first item, and the number of items from there to be removed from the original array. For example, consider the following starting array:

```
var myArray = [10, 20, 30, 40, 50, 60, 70];
```

To create two arrays that have three and four items, respectively, first decide which items are to remain in the original array. For this example, we'll remove the first three items to their own array:

```
var subArray = myArray.splice(0, 3);
```

After the splice( ) method executes, there are now two arrays as follows:

```
myArray: [40, 50, 60, 70]
subArray: [10, 20, 30]
```

You can extract any sequence of contiguous items from the original array. After the extraction, the original array collapses to its most compact size, reducing its length to the number of items remaining. The two arrays do not maintain any connection with each other after the splice( ) method executes.

Discussion

The splice( ) method does more than merely cut out a group of entries from an array. Optional parameters to the method let you both remove and insert items in their place all in one step. Moreover, you don't have to replace removed items with the same quantity of new items. To demonstrate, we'll start with a simple array:

```
var myArray = [10, 20, 30, 40, 50, 60, 70];
```

Our goal is to extract the middle three items (preserved as their own array for use elsewhere), and replace these items with two new items:

```
var subArray = myArray.splice(2, 3, "Jane", "Joe");
```

After the splice( ) statement executes, the two arrays have the following content:

```
myArray: [10, 20, "Jane", "Joe", 60, 70]
subArray: [30, 40, 50]
```

Using the splice( ) method is the best way to delete entries from within an array. If you simply invoke the method without capturing the returned result, the items specified by attributes are gone, and the length of the array closes up to the remaining items.

To insert an item into an array at a specific location, specify the zero-based index location as the first parameter, zero for the second parameter (deleting zero items), and the inserted value (or comma-separated values) as the last parameter. For example:

```
var myArray = [10, 20, 30, 40];
myArray.splice(2, 0, 25);
// myArray is now [10, 20, 25, 30, 40]
```

One other array method, slice( ), allows you to copy a contiguous section of an array and create a separate, new array with those entries. The difference between slice( ) and splice( ) is that slice( ) does not alter the original array. Parameters to slice( ) are integers of the starting index of the group to extract and the ending index. (Or else, omit the ending index to take every entry to the end of the array.)

See Also

Recipe 3.6 for combining two or more arrays into a single array.

3.8   Creating a Custom Object

Problem

You want to create a custom object for your data structure.

Solution

As with creating arrays, object creation has both a long form and a compact form. The long form requires that you define a constructor function, while the compact form uses special inline symbols to denote the structure of the object.

A *constructor function* looks like any other JavaScript function, but its purpose is to define the initial structure of an object—its property and method names—and perhaps to populate some or all of the properties with initial values. Values to be assigned to properties of the object are typically passed as parameters to the function, and statements in the function assign those values to properties. The following constructor function defines an object with two properties:

```
function coworker(name, age) {
    this.name = name;
    this.age = age;
}
```

To create objects with this constructor, invoke the function with the new keyword:

```
var emp1 = new coworker("Alice", 23);
var emp2 = new coworker("Fred", 32);
```

The this keyword in the constructor function localizes the context of the function to the object being created. As the function is reused for each object it creates, the context limits itself just to the one object under construction.

If you prefer not to use a constructor function, you can create objects with a shortcut syntax that defines an object inside curly braces. Property names and values are defined inside the curly braces as name/value pairs with a colon between the name and value, and each pair is comma-delimited. Property names cannot begin with a numeral. For example, the two objects just shown can be created using the shortcut syntax as follows:

```
var emp1 = {name:"Alice", age:23};
var emp2 = {name:"Fred", age:32};
```

After the objects are created, you access a property value just like you do with other JavaScript objects. For example, to display data from the emp2 object in an alert dialog box, the statement looks like the following:

```
alert("Employee " + emp2.name + " is " + emp2.age + " years old.");
```

After an object exists, you can add a new property to that instance by simply assigning a value to the property name of your choice. For example, to add a property about the cubicle number for Fred, the statement is:

```
emp2.cubeNum = 320;
```

After that assignment, only emp2 has that property (see Recipe 3.12 for more powerful assignments). There is no requirement that a property be predeclared in its constructor or shortcut creation code. This also means that you can be quite cavalier in your object creation to the point of generating a blank object and then populating it explicitly property by property:

```
var emp1 = new Object( );
emp1.name = "Alice";
emp1.age = 23;
```

This kind of object creation is usually more difficult to maintain in the source code and also takes up much more space if you need to create many similar objects.

Discussion

We've covered how to create properties for a custom object. Doing the same with methods is no more difficult. All it requires is that the method initially be defined in your source code as a JavaScript function; then assign a reference to that function as a value for a method name in either the constructor function or name/value pair inside curly braces. Continuing with the simple employee objects just shown, let's add a method to the object that displays an alert dialog box with the employee's name and age. Begin by defining the function that will do the work when invoked through one of the objects:

```
function showAll( ) {
    alert("Employee " + this.name + " is " + this.age + " years old.");
}
```

Then assign the function to a method name in the constructor function:

```
function coworker(name, age) {
    this.name = name;
    this.age = age;
    this.show = showAll;
}
```

Or add the assignment to the shortcut constructors:

```
var emp1 = {name:"Alice", age:23, show:showAll};
var emp2 = {name:"Fred", age:32, show:showAll};
```

To invoke the method, do so via one of the objects:

```
emp1.show( );
```

Note how the context of the object passes through to the function when it is invoked as a method of the object. The this keyword in the function definition points back to the context of the object that invoked the method, and thus has immediate access to its companion properties.

JavaScript provides an extra shortcut operator in constructor functions that lets you automatically assign a default value to any property that has a null value passed to it in the function's parameter variables. For example, in the coworker object constructor function, if the statement that invokes the function leaves the second parameter blank, the age parameter variable is initialized as a null value. To provide a valid but harmless default value (of zero) to that property, the syntax is as follows:

```
function coworker(name, age) {
    this.name = name;
    this.age = age || 0;
    this.show = showAll;
}
```

The operator is the regular JavaScript OR operator. If the first value evaluates to a boolean false (e.g., null, undefined, zero, an empty string, and so on), the second value is assigned to the property. You can use this construction in any variable assignment in JavaScript.

One advantage to the longer constructor function approach is that you can include calls to other functions from inside the constructor. For example, you might wish to invoke some initialization routines with the object immediately as it is being created. Simply add the call to the function as another statement inside the constructor function. You can even pass a reference to the object under construction by passing this as a parameter. The following example builds on the coworker( ) constructor function previously shown.

A separate function displays an alert dialog box each time an object is created:

```
function verify(obj) {
    alert("Just added " + obj.name + ".");
}
function coworker(name, age) {
    this.name = name;
    this.age = age;
    this.show = showAll;
    verify(this);
}
```

If the external function returns a value, the constructor function can assign that value to a property of the object.

If you are going to the trouble of creating a constructor function for a complex data structure, more than likely you are doing it for multiple instances of that object. But instead of having these objects floating around the window's scripting space as independent global variables, it will probably be more convenient to store these objects in an array of objects. As shown in Recipe 3.4, the array data structure facilitates iterating through a collection of similar items. For example, you could use an array of coworker objects to look through all records in search of those coworkers within a specific age range, and accumulate the names of those who meet your criteria.

Very little extra is needed to generate an array of objects while you are in the process of generating the objects themselves. The following demonstrates how a series of calls to a constructor function can be blended into an array constructor:

```
var employeeDB = new Array( );
employeeDB[employeeDB.length] = new coworker("Alice", 23);
employeeDB[employeeDB.length] = new coworker("Fred", 32);
employeeDB[employeeDB.length] = new coworker("Jean", 28);
employeeDB[employeeDB.length] = new coworker("Steve", 24);
```

You can do the same with shortcut syntax:

```
var employeeDB = new Array( );
employeeDB[employeeDB.length] = {name:"Alice", age:23, show:showAll};
employeeDB[employeeDB.length] = {name:"Fred", age:32, show:showAll};
employeeDB[employeeDB.length] = {name:"Jean", age:28, show:showAll};
employeeDB[employeeDB.length] = {name:"Steve", age:24, show:showAll};
```

Or you can go the whole route with shortcut syntax (albeit with one long statement):

```
var employeeDB = [{name:"Alice", age:23, show:showAll},
                  {name:"Fred", age:32, show:showAll},
                  {name:"Jean", age:28, show:showAll},
                  {name:"Steve", age:24, show:showAll}];
```

Finally, here's the function that looks for all coworkers in a certain age group:

```
function findInAgeGroup(low, high) {
    var result = new Array( );
    for (var i = 0; i < employeeDB.length; i++) {
```

```
            if (employeeDB[i].age >= low && employeeDB[i].age <= high) {
                result = result.concat(employeeDB[i].name);
            }
        }
        return result;
    }
```

This function returns an array of the names of those whose ages fall between the low and high values passed as parameters.

As discussed in Recipes 3.9 and 3.11, an array of objects is one of the most flexible complex data structures available to JavaScript coders. During the design phase of your applications, look for opportunities to group together similar objects in arrays.

See Also

Recipe 3.9 for generating a fast hash table from an array of objects; Recipe 3.11 for sorting an array of objects based on object property values; Recipe 3.14 for minimizing object naming conflicts; Recipe 4.4 for using anonymous functions in object creation.

3.9   Simulating a Hash Table for Fast Array Lookup

Problem

You want to be able to go directly to an entry in an array (especially an array of objects or a multidimensional array) without having to loop through the entire array in search of that item.

Solution

By taking advantage of the fact that a JavaScript array is a JavaScript object, you can define properties for an array without interfering with the true array portion of the object. Properties can be referenced by name either by string (in parentheses, like array index value) or following a period like a typical object property.

The key to implementing this construction for an existing array is that you must generate a property for each entry with a unique value. If you are implementing this for an array of objects, use a property value that is unique for each entry as the hash table lookup index.

As a simple example with the coworker objects created in other recipes of this chapter, we'll assume no two coworkers have the same name. Thus, we'll use the name property of the coworker objects as property names for the hash table. Immediately after the array of coworker objects is populated, we execute the following statements:

```
for (var i = 0; i < employeeDB.length; i++) {
    employeeDB[employeeDB[i].name] = employeeDB[i];
}
```

Without the hash table, to find the age of a coworker, you have to loop through the employeeDB array in search of a match against the name property of each entry. With the simulated hash table, however, simply reference the unique object bearing the name of the person you're looking for, and retrieve the age property of that object:

```
var JeansAge = employeeDB["Jean"].age;
```

You typically use the string way of referring to the object because variable lookup information will likely be coming from a text source: a text input box or a string value of a select element.

Discussion

I cannot overemphasize the importance of the uniqueness of the property name. If you unknowingly have two assignments to the same property value, the last one to execute is the one that sticks.

If one property of an object is not enough to make it unique, you may need to combine values to obtain that uniqueness. For example, the following table's data could be made into a convenient array of objects:

Description	Q1	Q2	Q3	Q4
East	2300	3105	2909	4800
Central	1800	1940	2470	4350
West	900	1200	1923	3810

Each cell of numeric data should be its own object, with other properties assisting in identifying the context of the number. For example:

```
var sales = new Array();
sales[sales.length] = {period:"q1", region:"east", total:2300};
sales[sales.length] = {period:"q2", region:"east", total:3105};
...
sales[sales.length] = {period:"q4", region:"west", total:3810};
```

None of the label properties—the properties you'd likely be using to look up sales information—is totally unique. The East region is shared by four objects, and the Q1 period is shared by three objects. But a combination of the region and period names generates a unique identifier for a given object. Thus, if we use a name of the form *region_period* (e.g., east_q1), other scripts can perform lookups to reach individual records. Therefore, the hash table maker comes after the object creation statements above:

```
for (var i = 0; i < sales.length; i++) {
    sales[sales[i].region + "_" + sales[i].period] = sales[i];
}
```

To access the third quarter sales for the central region, use the following reference:

```
sales["central_q3"].total
```

Another important point about the names of hash table indices is that they cannot be numbers or start with a numeral. Remember that these indices are property names, and therefore must follow the same rules of all properties of JavaScript objects, including the avoidance of reserved keywords (see Appendix C) and native property and methods names of JavaScript objects (e.g., `constructor`, `length`, `join`, `push`, `pop`, `sort`).

When a hash table entry is assigned a reference to an object (as happens in the preceding examples), each hash table entry simply points to the original object without duplicating the data. Any change you assign to an object's property in the array of objects is reflected in the hash table reference to that object's property.

Anytime you have a large multidimensional array or collection of objects through which your scripts will be looking for matching records, try to add the simulated hash table to your array. It gives you the best of both worlds: the ability to iterate through the collection when you need to use every entry, and the ability to dive into a specific record without any looping.

See Also

Recipes 8.13, 10.8, and 14.5 for real-world examples of the simulated hash table in action.

3.10 Doing Something with a Property of an Object

Problem

You want to examine (or modify) the values of properties belonging to an object, but the object and its properties may change from one examination to another.

Solution

Use a for/in loop to access every property of an object, regardless of the property's name. The following function assembles a list of properties and their values for any object passed as an argument to the function:

```
function listProperties(obj, objName) {
    var result = "";
    for (var i in obj) {
        result += objName + "." + i + "=" + obj[i] + "\n";
    }
    alert(result);
}
```

In this special type of loop, the variable (i in this example) is automatically assigned the name of each property (in string form) as the loop progresses through the list of available properties for the object. By using the string name as an index to the object (obj[i] in this example), the value of that property is returned.

Discussion

Figure 3-1 shows what the alert dialog box generated by the function would display for one of the `sales` objects defined in Recipe 3.9 if you invoke the following:

```
listProperties(sales[0], "sales[0]");
```

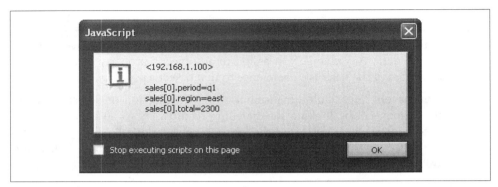

Figure 3-1. Object property enumeration example

The type of property enumeration shown in the `listProperties( )` function in the Solution is useful not only for custom objects but also for DOM objects. When using it with DOM objects, some browser-specific behaviors reveal themselves. For example, IE for Windows enumerates all of the event handler properties of the object. Mozilla, Safari, and Opera enumerate properties and methods. The order of enumerated items is determined by the inner workings of the browser (rarely alphabetical), but your scripts can accumulate results in an array and sort the array before displaying the data.

See Also

Recipe 3.4 for looping through all entries of an array; Recipe 3.11 for sorting arrays.

3.11   Sorting an Array of Objects

Problem

You want to sort an array of objects based on the value of one of the properties of the objects.

Solution

Sorting an array of objects relies on a logical extension of the comparison function described for simple arrays in Recipe 3.5. Define a comparison function as usual, but let the actual comparisons work on the properties of the objects being passed to the function two at a time.

To demonstrate the concept, we'll start with the array of sales objects:

```
var sales = new Array( );
sales[sales.length] = {period:"q1", region:"east", total:2300};
sales[sales.length] = {period:"q2", region:"east", total:3105};
...
sales[sales.length] = {period:"q4", region"west", total:3810};
```

If you want to sort the sales array in descending order of the values of the total properties of each object, define a comparison function that returns the appropriate values based on the arithmetic:

```
function compareTotals(a, b) {
    return b.total - a.total;
}
```

Because each array entry passed as parameters a and b is an object, you can use those parameter variables to reference the properties of the objects as they pass through in waves during the full sort operation. To sort the array by way of the comparison function, pass the function's reference to the sort( ) method of the array:

```
sales.sort(compareTotals);
```

Recall that the sort( ) method modifies the order of the original array. But you can invoke other sort( ) methods (that call other comparison functions) to re-sort the array by other criteria.

Discussion

Comparison functions can get rather elaborate if necessary. It all depends on the kind of data in your object properties and what kind of sorting you need to perform. For example, if an object is defined with separate properties for month, day, and year, and if you want to sort the objects by the dates that those numbers represent, the comparison function can create date objects from those values and then compare the resulting date objects:

```
function compareDates(a, b) {
    var dateA = new Date(a.year, a.month, a.date);
    var dateB = new Date(b.year, b.month, b.date);
    return dateA - dateB;
}
```

If sorting is required of string values in properties, you have to be more explicit in the comparisons you perform and the values you return. You may also want to eliminate case as a factor by comparing values converted to all upper- or all lowercase characters. The following function sorts string values of the lastName property of an array of objects:

```
function compareNames(a, b) {
    var nameA = a.lastName.toLowerCase( );
    var nameB = b.lastName.toLowerCase( );
    if (nameA < nameB) {return -1}
```

```
        if (nameA > nameB) {return 1}
        return 0;
    }
```

The return values from the function fall into the three categories described for all array sorting in Recipe 3.5. And because the `toLowerCase( )` method of a string doesn't disturb the case of the original string, the object values are ready to be displayed as entered into the data structure.

Avoid excessive string manipulation in comparison functions. They can negatively impact performance on large (hundreds of items) arrays.

See Also

Recipe 3.5 for basic array sorting concepts; Recipe 14.19 for using object sorting to sort data for rendering in a Dynamic HTML table.

3.12   Customizing an Object's Prototype

Problem

You want to add a property or method to objects that have already been created or are about to be created.

Solution

To add a property or method to a group of objects built from the same constructor, assign the property or method name and its default value to the `prototype` property of the object. To demonstrate this concept, we'll start with the `coworker` object constructor from Recipe 3.8 and create four instances of this object, all stored in an array:

```
function coworker(name, age) {
    this.name = name;
    this.age = age || 0;
    this.show = showAll;
}
var employeeDB = new Array( );
employeeDB[employeeDB.length] = new coworker("Alice", 23);
employeeDB[employeeDB.length] = new coworker("Fred", 32);
employeeDB[employeeDB.length] = new coworker("Jean", 28);
employeeDB[employeeDB.length] = new coworker("Steve", 24);
```

Each object has two properties and one method assigned to it. Each object's property values are private to that particular object instance. And although each object shares a method name (and the same function code for that method), when the method executes, it does so within the private context of the single object's instance (e.g., the `this` keyword in the method code refers to the object instance only).

Before or after the object instances exist, you can add a property that belongs to the prototype—an abstract object that represents the "mold" from which the object instances are made. When you assign a property and value to the prototype of the constructor, all object instances—including those that have already been created—gain this new property and value. For example, we can add a property to the coworker constructor that provides employment status information. The default value at the time the prototype property is assigned is the string "on duty":

```
coworker.prototype.status = "on duty";
```

Each object in the employeeDB array immediately inherits the status property, which is read via the following reference (for any item in the array indexed with integer *i*):

```
employeeDB[i].status
```

Here is where things get interesting. If you modify the value of the status property of an instance of the object, the value is private to that instance only (akin to overriding a property in a subclass in other languages). All other objects continue to share the default prototype property value. Therefore, if you execute the following statement:

```
employeeDB[2].status = "on sick leave";
```

the value of all of the other object instances (and any new objects you create via the coworker constructor) show their status to be "on duty."

Overridden property values are durable. If, after the above modifications, you change the value of the prototype property, the private property values assigned individually do not reflect the prototype change. For example, changing the prototype status property to reflect the company-wide vacation period is accomplished as follows:

```
coworker.prototype.status = "on vacation";
```

But the value of employeeDB[2].status continues to be "on sick leave" because the local value was explicitly overridden.

From any object reference that inherits a prototype property, you can reach the prototype's value, even if that value has been overridden by the object instance. The object's constructor property points to the constructor function that maintains information about the prototype. For example, the following statement tests the equality of the local status property against the prototype status property:

```
if (employeeDB[2].status != employeeDB[2].constructor.prototype.status) {
    // the two values aren't the same, so the local value has been overridden
}
```

Referencing the constructor's prototype is the JavaScript equivalent of calling super in some truly object-oriented languages.

Discussion

The following discussion assumes you have experience with, or working knowledge of, object-oriented programming concepts in languages such as Java. Even if you don't, feel free to read along to witness some of the advanced intricacies and possibilities with the JavaScript language.

All objects accessible by JavaScript—custom objects, global language objects, and DOM objects (in Mozilla and Opera 9)—are subject to prototype inheritance. Whenever a statement includes a reference to an object's property (or method), the JavaScript interpreter follows a prototype inheritance chain to find the value (if it exists along the chain) that currently applies. The rules that the interpreter follows are relatively simple:

- If the object has a private value assigned to that property (as is the case more than 99 percent of the time), that is the value returned by the reference.
- If no local value exists, the interpreter looks for that property and value in the constructor prototype for that object.
- If no property or value exists in the constructor prototype, the interpreter follows the prototype chain all the way to the basic Object object if necessary.
- When no property by that name exists in the prototype inheritance chain, the interpreter indicates an "undefined" value for that property.

When a prototype inheritance chain consists of two or more objects, you can also use scripts to access points higher up the chain. For example, an Array constructor inherits from the basic Object constructor. In other words, it is conceivable that a prototype property influencing an instance of an array could be defined for the Object or Array constructor prototype. As shown in the Solution, a reference to the Array's prototype property is:

```
myArray.constructor.prototype.propertyName
```

To reach one level higher, access the (Object) constructor of the (Array) constructor:

```
myArray.constructor.constructor.prototype.propertyName
```

Mozilla-based browsers implement a proprietary shortcut syntax for these kinds of upward prototype traversals: the __proto__ property (with a double underscore before and after the word). I mention it here in case you encounter this syntax in further research about simulating object-oriented techniques in JavaScript. The shortcut equivalents to these references are:

```
myArray.__proto__.propertyName
myArray.__proto__.__proto__.propertyName
```

There is no shortcut equivalent in other browsers.

It is possible in JavaScript to simulate what some programming languages describe as an interface or implements construction—a way of empowering one object with the properties and methods of another object without creating a subclass of the shared object. The approach to this implementation is not particularly intuitive, but it works nicely once you have it set up.

To demonstrate, we'll start with the now familiar coworker object, which contains basic information about a person. In creating another object for project team members, we find that the coworker object already contains some properties that we'd like to reuse in the project team members object. We'll use two object constructors: one for coworker objects and one for project team members:

```
// coworker object constructor
function coworker(name, age) {
    this.name = name;
    this.age = age;
    this.show = showAll;
}
// teamMember object constructor
function teamMember(name, age, projects, hours) {
    this.projects = projects;
    this.hours = hours;
    this.member = coworker;
    this.member(name, age);
}
```

Notice in the teamMember constructor function that the coworker constructor function is assigned to this.member. In other words, invoking the member( ) method of a teamMember object creates a new coworker object. And in fact, the next statement of the teamMember constructor function invokes the member( ) method, passing two of the incoming parameters to the coworker( ) function. Creating a series of teamMember objects takes the following form:

```
var projectTeams = new Array( );
projectTeams[projectTeams.length] = new teamMember("Alice", 23, ["Gizmo"], 240);
projectTeams[projectTeams.length] = new teamMember("Fred", 32, ["Gizmo","Widget"],
    325);
projectTeams[projectTeams.length] = new teamMember("Jean", 28, ["Gizmo"], 200);
projectTeams[projectTeams.length] = new teamMember("Steve", 23, ["Widget"], 190);
```

The result of blending these two constructor functions is that when you create a teamMember object, it has four properties (projects, hours, name, and age) and two methods (showAll( ) and member( )). Your scripts wouldn't have much reason to invoke the member( ) method because it's used internally by the teamMember( ) function. But all other pieces of the teamMember object are readily accessible and meaningful to your scripts.

An unusual side effect to the connection between these nested objects is that the teamMember objects do not have the coworker constructor in their prototype chain. Therefore, if you assign a property and value to the prototype of the coworker constructor, none of the teamMember objects gains that property.

There is, however, a way to place the coworker constructor in the prototype chain of the teamMember object: assign a blank coworker object to the prototype of the teamMember constructor:

```
teamMember.prototype = new coworker( );
```

You must do this before creating instances of the teamMember object, but you can hold off on assigning specific coworker object prototype properties or methods until later. Then you can do something like the following:

```
coworker.prototype.status = "on duty";
```

After this statement runs, all instances of teamMember have the additional status property with the default setting. And, just like any prototype property or method, you can override the private value for a single instance without disturbing the default values of the other objects.

In Mozilla and Opera 9, many of these language capabilities add potentially enormous power to the DOM you use every day. These browsers give scripters access to the constructors of every type of DOM object, thus allowing you to add prototype properties and methods to any class of DOM object. For example, if you wish to empower all table elements with a method that removes all rows of nested tbody elements, first define the function that acts as the method, and then assign the function to a prototype method name:

```
function clearTbody( ) {
    var tbodies = this.getElementsByTagName("tbody");
    for (var i = 0; i < tbodies.length; i++) {
        while (tbodies[i].rows.length > 0) {
            tbodies[i].deleteRow(0);
        }
    }
}
HTMLTableElement.prototype.clear = clearTbody;
```

Thereafter, you can invoke the clear( ) method of any table element object to let it remove all of its rows:

```
document.getElementById("myTable").clear( );
```

Given the fact that Mozilla-based browsers and Opera 9 expose every W3C DOM object type to scripts, just like the HTMLTableElement, you may get all kinds of wild ideas about extending the properties or methods of all HTML elements or text nodes. Go crazy!

3.13   Converting Arrays and Custom Objects to Strings

Problem

You want to convert the details of an array or a custom object into string form for conveyance as a URL search string or preservation in a cookie, and then be able to reconstruct the array or object data types from the string when needed later.

Solution

Use the *objectsArraysStrings.js* script library shown in the Discussion. To convert a custom object to string form, invoke the `object2String()` function, passing a reference to the object as a parameter:

```
var objAsString = object2String(myObj);
```

To convert an array (including an array of custom objects) to string form, invoke the `array2String()` function, passing a reference to the array as a parameter:

```
var arrAsString = array2String(myArray);
```

To reconvert the strings to native data types, use the corresponding library function:

```
var myArray = string2Array(arrayString);
var myObj = string2Object(objString);
```

Discussion

Example 3-1 shows the code for the *objectsArraysString.js* library.

Example 3-1. objectsArraysString.js conversion library

```
function object2String(obj) {
    var val, output = "";
    if (obj) {
        output += "{";
        for (var i in obj) {
            val = obj[i];
            switch (typeof val) {
                case ("object"):
                    if (val[0]) {
                        output += i + ":" + array2String(val) + ",";
                    } else {
                        output += i + ":" + object2String(val) + ",";
                    }
                    break;
                case ("string"):
                    output += i + ":'" + encodeURI(val) + "',";
                    break;
                default:
                    output += i + ":" + val + ",";
```

Example 3-1. objectsArraysString.js conversion library (continued)

```
                }
            }
        output = output.substring(0, output.length-1) + "}";
    }
    return output;
}

function array2String(array) {
    var output = "";
    if (array) {
        output += "[";
        for (var i in array) {
            val = array[i];
            switch (typeof val) {
                case ("object"):
                    if (val[0]) {
                        output += array2String(val) + ",";
                    } else {
                        output += object2String(val) + ",";
                    }
                    break;
                case ("string"):
                    output += "'" + encodeURI(val) + "',";
                    break;
                default:
                    output += val + ",";
            }
        }
        output = output.substring(0, output.length-1) + "]";
    }
    return output;
}

function string2Object(string) {
    eval("var result = " + decodeURI(string));
    return result;
}

function string2Array(string) {
    eval("var result = " + decodeURI(string));
    return result;
}
```

The first two functions of the library perform the conversion to strings. The first, object2String( ), works through the properties of a custom object, and assembles a string in the same format used to generate the object in the curly-braced shortcut syntax. The sole parameter to the function is a reference to the custom object you wish to convert. The returned value is a string, including the curly braces surrounding the text.

To demonstrate the effect of object2String( ), start with a simple object constructor:

```
function coworker(name, age, dept) {
    this.name = name;
    this.age = age;
    this.department = dept;
}
```

Create an instance of the object:

```
var kevin = new coworker("Kevin", 28, "Accounts Payable");
```

Convert the object to a string via the object2String( ) library function:

```
var objStr = object2String(kevin);
```

The value of objStr becomes the following string:

```
{name:'Kevin',age:28,department:'Accounts%20Payable'}
```

In the second library function, array2String( ), an array passed as the parameter is converted to its square bracket-encased shortcut string equivalent. Each function relies on the other at times. For example, if you are converting an object to a string, and one of its properties is an array, the array portion is passed through array2String( ) to get the desired format for that segment of the full string. Conversely, converting an array of objects requires calls to object2String( ) to format the object portions.

To reconstruct the object or array data type from the string, use one of the final two functions that applies to the outermost construction of the string. The two functions perform the same operation, but the names are provided for each conversion type to improve readability of the code that invokes them. Despite warnings elsewhere in this book about performance degradation of the eval( ) function, its use is necessary here.

Let the type of the outermost data structure govern which of the two convert-to-string functions you use. Even though your custom objects may be the most important part of your script data structure conceptually, they may be found within an array of those objects, as shown in Recipe 3.8. In this case, convert the entire array of objects to a single string by invoking array2String( ), and let it handle the object conversion along the way.

Conversions between objects and strings are the foundation of JSON (JavaScript Object Notation), one of the ways you can use Ajax technology to access server data from the current page. See Recipe 14.5 for more details.

See Also

Recipes 3.1 and 3.8 to see the shortcut array and object creation syntax emulated here in string form; Recipe 4.8 for a discussion about the eval( ) function; Recipe 10.6 for an example of this library being used to pass objects between pages via URLs; Recipes 14.5 and 14.7 for using strings to transfer objects from server to page via Ajax.

3.14   Using Objects to Reduce Naming Conflicts

Problem

You want to minimize the possibility of script object naming conflicts, especially in larger projects involving multiple script sources.

Solution

Make use of what is known as *encapsulation*, an automatic feature of JavaScript objects. Each property or method name you define for an object is private to that object. For example, if you define an object that contains three properties and two methods, the only name that is accessible to other script statements outside of the object is the identifier you use for the entire object. The five names you use for the properties and methods can be used anywhere else without fear of naming conflicts. Access to the internal properties and methods is via the standard objectName. *propertyName* and objectName.*methodName*( ) syntax.

Discussion

At issue here is the global (i.e., window-wide) scope for scriptable objects. Every global variable and, importantly, every non-nested named function has global scope. For example, if you import two external *.js* libraries into a page, and both define a function using the same function name, only the one that is defined later in source code order prevails. So, too, with global variables that may be defined in multiple *.js* files. When multiple authors work on a project, or if you use third-party script files, you may be unaware of the conflicts looming when all files are loaded into a single page.

Contributing even more to the problem is that some browsers—notably IE and Safari—expose IDs of all named HTML elements to the global scope. Thus, if you have a form containing a text input element whose ID is total, you cannot have any JavaScript global variable or function by that name.

To demonstrate the "savings" in global names, we will transform the *cookies.js* library from Recipe 1.10. The original library contains five functions, each of which occupies a global name spot: getExpDate, getCookieVal, getCookie, setCookie, and deleteCookie. The replacement library contains a single object, cookieMgr, which becomes the gateway to invoking the functions.

Example 3-2 shows the code for the revised cookie manager library, with changes shown in bold.

Example 3-2. cookieManager.js library

```javascript
var cookieMgr = {
    // utility function to retrieve an expiration date in proper
    // format; pass three integer parameters for the number of days, hours,
    // and minutes from now you want the cookie to expire (or negative
    // values for a past date); all three parameters are required,
    // so use zeros where appropriate
    getExpDate : function(days, hours, minutes) {
        var expDate = new Date();
        if (typeof days == "number" && typeof hours == "number" &&
            typeof minutes == "number") {
            expDate.setDate(expDate.getDate() + parseInt(days));
            expDate.setHours(expDate.getHours() + parseInt(hours));
            expDate.setMinutes(expDate.getMinutes() + parseInt(minutes));
            return expDate.toGMTString();
        }
    },
    // utility function called by getCookie()
    getCookieVal : function(offset) {
        var endstr = document.cookie.indexOf (";", offset);
        if (endstr == -1) {
            endstr = document.cookie.length;
        }
        return decodeURI(document.cookie.substring(offset, endstr));
    },
    // primary function to retrieve cookie by name
    getCookie : function(name) {
        var arg = name + "=";
        var alen = arg.length;
        var clen = document.cookie.length;
        var i = 0;
        while (i < clen) {
            var j = i + alen;
            if (document.cookie.substring(i, j) == arg) {
                return this.getCookieVal(j);
            }
            i = document.cookie.indexOf(" ", i) + 1;
            if (i == 0) break;
        }
        return "";
    },
    // store cookie value with optional details as needed
    setCookie : function(name, value, expires, path, domain, secure) {
        document.cookie = name + "=" + encodeURI(value) +
            ((expires) ? "; expires=" + expires : "") +
            ((path) ? "; path=" + path : "") +
            ((domain) ? "; domain=" + domain : "") +
            ((secure) ? "; secure" : "");
    },
    // remove the cookie by setting ancient expiration date
    deleteCookie : function(name,path,domain) {
```

Example 3-2. cookieManager.js library (continued)

```
        if (this.getCookie(name)) {
            document.cookie = name + "=" +
                ((path) ? "; path=" + path : "") +
                ((domain) ? "; domain=" + domain : "") +
                "; expires=Thu, 01-Jan-70 00:00:01 GMT";
        }
    }
};
```

The new library consists of one global object and five internal functions. Each function is coded as an anonymous function (see Recipe 4.4). When a JavaScript custom object property name (to the left of the colon) is defined as an anonymous function (to the right of the colon), the property becomes a method of the object. Therefore, following the example from the Discussion section of Recipe 1.10, invoking the methods to set and get cookie values from other script statements would look like the following:

```
cookieMgr.setCookie("fontSize", styleID, cookieMgr.getExpDate(180, 0, 0));
var styleCookie = cookieMgr.getCookie("fontSize");
```

Notice in Example 3-2 that when a script statement within the object needs to invoke another method of the same object, it must provide the context within which the method operates. While you could refer to the object by name (cookieMgr), that tactic limits you to always using that specific name for the object. Instead, use the this operator to point to the current object, as shown in the getCookie( ) and deleteCookie( ) methods.

See Also

Recipe 3.8 for creating JavaScript objects; Recipe 4.4 for more on anonymous functions.

CHAPTER 4

Variables, Functions, and Flow Control

4.0 Introduction

This chapter covers a miscellany of core JavaScript topics. A couple of these recipes (or your own variations on them) may be part of your daily menu. If you don't use these constructions frequently, let this chapter serve to refresh your memory, and give you models to get you back on track when you need them.

Even simple subjects, such as JavaScript variables and functions, have numerous nuances that are easy to forget over time. On another front, scripters without formal programming training tend to be rather loose in their attention to detail in the error department—something that can come back to bite you. On the other hand, the browser implementations of some of the details of exception handling are far from compatible. If you aren't yet using exception-handling techniques in your scripts, you should get to know the concepts. As time goes on and the full W3C DOM becomes implemented in browsers, the notion of "safe scripting" will include regular application of exception-handling practices.

This chapter ends with some suggestions about improving script performance. Most scripts can scrape by with inefficiencies, but larger projects that deal with complex document trees and substantial amounts of hidden data delivered to the client must pay particular attention to performance. You'll learn some practices here that you should apply even to short scripts.

4.1 Creating a JavaScript Variable

Problem

You want to create a JavaScript variable value either in the global space or privately within a function.

Solution

Use the var keyword to define the first instance of every variable, whether you assign a value to the variable immediately or delay the assignment until later. Any variable defined outside of a function is part of the global variable scope:

```
var myVar = someValue;
```

All script statements on the page, including those inside functions, have read/write access to a global variable.

When you define a variable with var inside a function, only statements inside the function can access that variable:

```
function myFunction( ) {
    var myFuncVar = someValue;
    ...
}
```

Statements outside of the function cannot reach the value of a variable whose scope is limited to its containing function.

Discussion

A JavaScript variable has no inherent limit to the amount of data it can hold. Maximum capacity is determined strictly by memory available to the browser application—information not accessible to your scripts.

Variable scope is an important concept to understand in JavaScript. Not only is a global variable accessible by all script statements in the current window or frame, but statements in other frames or windows (served from the same domain and server) can access those global variables by way of the window or frame reference. For example, a statement in a menu frame can reference a global variable named myVar in a frame named content as follows:

```
parent.content.myVar
```

You don't have to worry about the same global variable names colliding when they exist in other windows or frames, because the references to those variables will always be different.

Where you must exercise care is in defining a new variable inside a function with the var keyword. If you fail to use the keyword inside the function, the variable is treated as a global variable. If you have defined a global variable with the same name, the function's assignment statement overwrites the value originally assigned to the global variable. The safest way to avoid these kinds of problems is to always use the var keyword with the first instance of any variable, regardless of where it's located in your scripts. Even though the keyword is optional for global variable declarations, it is good coding style to use var for globals as well. That way you can readily see where a variable is first used in a script.

Although some programming languages distinguish between the tasks of declaring a variable (essentially reserving memory space for its value) and initializing a variable (stuffing a value into it), JavaScript's dynamic memory allocation for variable values unburdens the scripter of memory concerns. A variable is truly variable in JavaScript in that not only can the value stored in the variable change with later reassignments of values, but even the data type of the variable's value can change (not that this is necessarily good programming practice, but that's simply a by-product of Java-Script's loose data typing).

Speaking of good programming practice, it is generally advisable to define global variables near the top of the script, just as it's also advisable to define heavily used variables inside a function at the top of the function. Even if you don't have a value ready to assign to the variable, you can simply declare the variable as undefined with a statement like the following:

```
var myVar;
```

If you have multiple variables that you'd like to declare, you may do so compactly by separating the variable names with commas:

```
var myVar, counter, fred, i, j;
```

You may even combine declarations and initializations in a comma-delimited statement:

```
var myVar, counter = 0, fred, i, j;
```

In examples throughout this book, you typically find variables being declared or initialized at the top of their scope regions, but not always. It's not unusual to find variables that are about to be used inside a for loop defined (with their var keywords) just before the loop statements. For example, if a nested pair of loops is in the offing, I may define the loop counter variables prior to the outer loop's start:

```
var i, j;
for (i = 0; i < array1.length; i++) {
    for (j = 0; j < array1[i].array2.length; j++) {
        ...
    }
}
```

This is merely my style preference. But in any case, this situation definitely calls for declaring the variables outside of the loops for another reason. If you were to use the var keywords in the loop counter initialization statements (e.g., var j = 0;), the nested loop would repeatedly invoke the var declaration keyword each time the outer loop executes. Internally, the JavaScript interpreter creates a new variable space for each var keyword. Fortunately, the interpreter is also able to keep track of which variable repeatedly declared is the current one, but it places an unnecessary burden on resources. Declare once, then initialize and reassign values as often as needed. Thus, in complex functions that have two or more outer for loops, you should declare the counter variable at the top of the function, and simply initialize the value at the start of each loop.

As for selecting the names for your variables, there are some explicit rules and implicit customs to follow. The explicit rules are more important. A variable name cannot:

- Begin with a numeral
- Contain any spaces or other whitespace characters
- Contain punctuation or symbols except the underscore character
- Be surrounded by quote marks
- Be a reserved ECMAScript keyword (see Appendix C)

Conventions among programmers with respect to devising names for variables are not rigid, nor do they affect the operation of your scripts. They do, however, help in readability and maintenance when it comes time to remember what your script does six months from now.

The main idea behind a variable name is to help you identify what kind of value the variable contains (in fact, names are commonly called identifiers). Littering your scripts with a bunch of one- or two-letter variables won't help you track values or logic when reading the script. On the other hand, there are performance reasons (see Recipe 4.8) to keep names from getting outrageously long. The shorter the better, but not to the point of cryptic ciphers. If you need two or more words to describe the value, join the words together via underscore characters, or capitalize the first character of any words after the first word (a convention used throughout this book). Thus, either of the variable names in the following initializations is fine:

```
var teamMember = "George";
var team_member = "George";
```

Apply these rules and concepts to the identifiers you assign to HTML element name and id attributes, as well. Your scripts will then have no trouble using these identifiers in DOM object references.

Variable names are case-sensitive. Therefore, it is permissible (although not necessarily advisable) to reuse an identifier with different case letters to carry different values. One convention that you might employ is to determine which variables won't be changing their values during the execution of your scripts (i.e., you will treat them as constants) and make their names all uppercase. Mozilla-based browsers implement a forthcoming ECMAScript keyword called const, which you use in place of var to define a true constant value. No other browser supports this keyword yet, so you can use variables as constants and keep modification statements away from them.

JavaScript assigns data to a variable both "by reference" and "by value," depending on the type of data. If the data is a true object of any kind (e.g., DOM object, array, custom object), the variable contains a "live" reference to the object. You may then use that variable as a substitute reference to the object:

```
var elem = document.getElementById("myTable");
var padWidth = elem.cellPadding;
```

But if the data is a simple value (string, number, Boolean, object property other than an object), the variable holds only a copy of the value, with no connection to the object from which the value came. Therefore, the `padWidth` variable shown above simply holds a string value; if you were to assign a new value to the variable, it would have no impact on the `table` element. To set the object's property, go back to the object reference and assign a value to the property:

```
elem.cellPadding = "10";
```

If an object's property value is itself another object, the variable receives that data as an object reference, still connected to its object:

```
var elem = document.getElementById("myTable");
var elemStyle = elem.style;
elemStyle.fontSize = "18px";
```

Exercise care with DOM objects assigned to variables. It may seem as though the variable is a mere copy of the object reference, but changes you make to the variable value affect the document node tree.

Global variables share the same scope with all non-nested named functions. In IE and Safari, this same scope is shared with IDs of HTML element objects. In large projects, you may wish to move the declaration of related groups of variables into a custom object as properties. See Recipe 3.14 for more on this subject.

See Also

Chapters 1, 2, and 3 for a discussion on assigning values of different types—strings, numbers, arrays, and objects—to variables; Recipe 4.8 for the impact of variable name length on performance; Recipe 3.14 for ways to minimize global variable space naming collisions.

4.2   Creating a Named Function

Problem

You want to define a function that can be invoked from any statement in the page.

Solution

For a function that receives no parameters, use the simple function declaration format:

```
function myFunctionName( ) {
    // statements go here
}
```

If the function is designed to receive parameters from the statement that invokes the function, define parameter variable names in the parentheses following the function name:

```
function myFunctionName(paramVar1, paramVar2[, ..., paramVarN]) {
    // statements go here
}
```

You can define as many unique parameter variable identifiers as you need. These variables become local variables inside the function (var declarations are implied). Following JavaScript's loosely typed conventions, parameter variables may hold any valid data type, as determined by the statement that invokes the function and passes the parameters.

Curly braces that contain the statements belonging to the function are required only when two or more statements are inside the function. It is good practice to use curly braces anyway, even for one-line statements, to assist in source code readability (a convention followed throughout this book).

The majority of long scripts throughout this book employ named functions, some with parameters, others without. Real-world examples abound, especially in recipes containing external JavaScript libraries, such as the DHTML API library in Recipe 13.3.

Discussion

A function is an object type in JavaScript, and the name you assign to the function becomes a case-sensitive identifier for that object. As a result, you cannot use a JavaScript-reserved keyword as a function name, nor should you use a function name that is also an identifier for one of your other global entities, such as variables or (in IE and Safari) element IDs. If you have two functions with the same name in a page, the one that comes last in source code order is the only available version. JavaScript does not implement the notion of function or method overloading found in languages such as Java (where an identically named method with a different number of parameter variables is treated as a separate method).

Invoke a function using parentheses:

```
myFunc();
myFunc2("hello",42);
```

At times, you will need to assign a function's reference to a property. For example, when you assign event handlers to element object properties (see Chapter 9), the assignment consists of a function reference. Such a reference is the name of the function but without parentheses, parameters, or quotes:

```
document.onclick = myFunc;
```

This kind of property assignment is merely setting the stage for a future invocation of the function, where parameters may be passed, if necessary.

Some programming languages distinguish between executable blocks of code that operate on their own and those that return values. In JavaScript, there is only one kind of function. If the function includes a return statement, the function returns a value; otherwise, there is no returned value. Functions used as what other environments might call subroutines commonly return values simply because you define them to perform some kind of information retrieval or calculation, and then return the result to the statement that invoked the routine. When a function returns a value, the call to the function evaluates to a value that can be assigned immediately to a variable or be used as a parameter value to some other function or method. Recipe 15.7 demonstrates this feature. Its job is to display the part of the day (morning, afternoon, or evening) in a welcome greeting that is written to the page as it loads. A function called getDayPart( ) (defined in the head portion of the page) calculates the current time and returns a string with the appropriate day part:

```
function dayPart( ) {
    var oneDate = new Date( );
    var theHour = oneDate.getHours( );
    if (theHour < 12) {
        return "morning";
    } else if (theHour < 18) {
        return "afternoon";
    } else {
        return "evening";
    }
}
```

That function is invoked as a parameter to the document.write( ) method that places the text in the rendered page:

```
<script type="text/javascript">
document.write("Good " + dayPart( ) + " and welcome")
</script>
<noscript>Welcome</noscript>
 to GiantCo.
```

It is not essential to pass the same number of arguments to a function, as you have defined parameter variables for that function. For example, if the function is called from two different places in your script, and each place provides a different number of parameters, you can access the parameter values in the function by way of the arguments property of the function rather than by parameter variables:

```
function myFunc( ) {
    for (var i = 0; i < myFunc.arguments.length; i++) {
        // each entry in the arguments array is one parameter value
        // in the order in which they were passed
    }
}
```

A typical function (except a nested function, as described in Recipe 4.3) exists in the global context of the window housing the current page. Just as with global variables, these global functions can be referenced by script statements in other windows and frames. See "Frames As Window Objects" in Chapter 7 for examples of referencing content in other frames.

How large a function should be is a matter of style. For ease of debugging and maintenance, it may be appropriate to divide a long function into sections that either branch out to subroutines that return values or operate in sequence from one function to the next. When you see that you use a series of statements two or more times within a large function, these statements are excellent candidates for removal to their own function that gets called repeatedly from the large function.

The other stylistic decision in your hands is where you place the curly braces. This book adopts the convention of starting a curly brace pair on the same line as the function name, and closing the pair at the same tab location as the function declaration. But you can place the opening curly brace on the line below the function name, and left-align it if you like:

```
function myFunc( )
{
    // statements go here
}
```

Some coders feel this format makes it easier to keep brace pairs in sync. For a one-line function, the single statement can go on the same line as the function name:

```
function myFunc( ) {//statement goes here}
```

Adopt the style that makes the most logical sense to you and your code-reading eye.

See Also

Recipe 4.1 for a discussion about variables "by reference" and "by value"—a discussion that applies equally to function parameter variables; Recipe 4.3 for nesting functions.

4.3   Nesting Named Functions

Problem

You want to create a function that belongs to only one other function.

Solution

You can nest a function inside another function according to the following syntax model:

```
function myFuncA( ) {
    // statements go here
    function.myFuncB( ) {
        // more statements go here
    }
}
```

In this construction, the nested function may be accessed only by statements in the outer function. Statements in the nested function have access to variables declared in the outer function, as well as to global variables. Statements in the outer function, however, do not have access to the inner function's variables.

Discussion

The basic idea behind nested functions is that you can encapsulate all activity related to the outer function by keeping subroutine functions private to the outer function. Because the nested function is not directly exposed to the global space, you can reuse the function name in the global space or for a nested function inside some other outer function.

See Also

Recipe 4.1 for a discussion of variable scope.

4.4   Creating an Anonymous Function

Problem

You want to define a function in the form of an expression that you can, for example, pass as a parameter to an object constructor or assign to an object's method.

Solution

You can use an alternative syntax for defining functions without creating an explicitly named function (as shown in Recipe 4.2). Called an *anonymous function*, this syntax has all the components of a function definition except its identifier. The syntax model is as follows:

```
var someReference = function( ) {statements go here};
```

Statements inside the curly braces are semicolon-delimited JavaScript statements. You can define parameter variables if they're needed:

```
var someReference = function(paramVar1[,..., paramVarN]) {statements go here};
```

Invoke the function via the reference to the function:

```
someReference( );
```

Discussion

Anonymous function creation returns an object of type function. Therefore, you can assign the right side of the statement to any assignment statement where a function reference (the function name without parentheses) is expected. To demonstrate, we'll make a version of a shortcut object constructor from Recipe 3.8. It starts with an ordinary function definition that gets invoked as a method of four objects defined with shortcut syntax:

```
function showAll() {
    alert("Employee " + this.name + " is " + this.age + " years old.");
}
var employeeDB = [{name:"Alice", age:23, show:showAll},
                  {name:"Fred", age:32, show:showAll},
                  {name:"Jean", age:28, show:showAll},
                  {name:"Steve", age:24, show:showAll}];
```

Notice how in the object constructors, a reference to the showAll( ) function is assigned to the show method name. Invoking this method from one of the objects is done in the following manner:

```
employeeDB[2].show( );
```

For the sake of example, we assign an anonymous function to the first object. The anonymous function is custom-tailored for the first object and replaces the reference to showAll( ):

```
var employeeDB = [{name:"Alice", age:23,
                   show:function( )
                   {alert("Alice\'s age is not open to the public.")}},
                  {name:"Fred", age:32, show:showAll},
                  {name:"Jean", age:28, show:showAll},
                  {name:"Steve", age:24, show:showAll}];
```

Now, if you invoke employeeDB[0].show( ), the special alert displays itself because the anonymous function is running instead of the showAll( ) function. We have saved the need to create an external function with its own identifier just to act as an intermediary between the show method name and the statements to execute when the method is invoked.

Assigning anonymous function definitions to object properties—thus creating object methods—is a good way to remove groups of related functions from the global scope. In large projects containing multiple libraries or frameworks (often from multiple authoring sources), unintentionally redundant function names can cause havoc. See Recipe 3.14 for suggestions on minimizing such conflicts.

See Also

Recipe 4.3 for creating traditional named functions; Recipe 3.14 for using anonymous functions to reduce global naming conflicts.

4.5   Delaying a Function Call

Problem

You want a function to run at a specified time in the near future.

Solution

Use the `window.setTimeout()` method to invoke a function one time after a delay of a number of milliseconds. You essentially set a timer to trigger a function of your choice. In its most common form, the function is referenced as a string, complete with parentheses, as in the following example:

```
var timeoutID = setTimeout("myFunc()", 5000);
```

The method returns an ID for the time-out operation and should be preserved in a global variable or property of a global object. If, at any time before the delayed function fires, you wish to abort the timer, invoke the `clearTimeout()` method with the time-out ID as the parameter:

```
clearTimeout(timeoutID);
```

Once the timer is set, other script processing may proceed as usual, so it is often a good idea to place the `setTimeout()` call as the final statement of a function.

Discussion

It's important to understand what the `setTimeout()` method doesn't do: it does not halt all processing in the manner of a delay that suspends activity until a certain time. Instead, it simply sets an internal countdown timer that executes the named function when the timer reaches zero. For example, if you are creating a slide show that should advance to another page after 15 seconds of inactivity from the user, you would initially set the timer via the `load` event handler for the page and the `resetTimer()` function:

```
var timeoutID;
function goNextPage() {
    location.href = "slide3.html";
}
function resetTimer() {
    clearTimeout(timeoutID);
    timeoutID = setTimeout("goNextPage()", 15000);
}
```

You would also set an event handler for, say, the `mousemove` event so that each time the user activates the mouse, the autotimer resets to 15 seconds:

```
window.onmousemove = resetTimer;
```

The `resetTimer()` function automatically cancels the previously set time-out before it triggers the `goNextPage()` function, and then it starts a new 15-second timer.

If the function you are invoking via the delay requires parameters, you can assemble a string with the values, even if those values are in the form of variables within the function. But—and this is important—the variable values cannot be object references. Parameters must be in a form that will survive the conversion to the string needed for the first argument of the `setTimeout()` method. Recipe 8.4 demonstrates how you can convey names of DOM form-related objects as ways of passing an object reference. The tricky part is in keeping the quotes in order:

```
function isEMailAddr(elem) {
    var str = elem.value;
    var re = /^[\w-]+(\.[\w-]+)*@([\w-]+\.)+[a-zA-Z]{2,7}$/;
    if (!str.match(re)) {
        alert("Verify the e-mail address format.");
        setTimeout("focusElement('" + elem.form.name + "', '" + elem.name + "')", 0);
        return false;
    } else {
        return true;
    }
}
```

In this example, the focusElement( ) function requires two parameters that are used to devise a valid reference to both a form object and a text input object. Both parameters of the focusElement( ) function are strings. Because the first argument of setTimeout( ) is, itself, a string, you have to force the "stringness" of the parameters to focusElement( ) by way of single quotes placed within the extended string concatenation sequence. (The zero milliseconds shown in the example is not a mistake for this application. Learn why in the Discussion for Recipe 8.4.)

Conveniently, setTimeout( ) also accepts a function reference as its first parameter, thus opening up the possibility of using an anonymous function in that spot. Staying with the previous example, we can invoke multiple method calls within a single anonymous function, as in the following:

```
setTimeout(function() {elem.focus(); elem.select();}, 0);
```

This approach circumvents all the string machinations of the other format.

If you are looking for a true delay between the execution of statements within a function or sections of a function, JavaScript has nothing comparable to commands available in some other programming languages. But you can accomplish the same result by dividing the original function into multiple functions—one function for each section that is to run after a delay. Link the end of one function to the next by ending each function with setTimeout( ), which invokes the next function in sequence after the desired amount of time:

```
function mainFunc( ) {
    // initial statements here
    setTimeout("funcPart2( )", 10000);
}
function funcPart2( ) {
    // initial statements here
    setTimeout("finishFunc( )", 5000);
}
function finishFunc( ) {
    // final batch of statements here
}
```

The related functions don't have to be located adjacent to each other in the source code. If all related functions need to operate on the same set of values, you can cascade the value as parameters (provided the parameters can be represented as nonobject values), or you can preserve them as global variables. If the values are related, it may be a good reason to define a custom object with values assigned to labeled properties of that object to make it easier to see at a glance what each function segment is doing with or to the values.

Another JavaScript method, setInterval( ), operates much like setTimeout( ), but repeatedly invokes the target function until told to stop (via the clearInterval( ) method). The second parameter (an integer in milliseconds) controls the amount of time between calls to the target function.

See Also

Recipe 8.4 for using setTimeout( ) to keep script execution synchronized; Recipe 12.6 for an example of using a self-contained counter variable in a repeatedly invoked function to execute itself a fixed number of times; Recipes 13.9 and 13.10 for applications of setInterval( ) in animation.

4.6   Branching Execution Based on Conditions

Problem

You want your scripts to execute sections of code based on external values, such as Booleans, user entries in text boxes, or user choices from select elements.

Solution

Use the if, if/else, or switch flow control construction to establish an execution path through a section of your scripts. When you need to perform a special section of script if only one condition is met, use the simple if construction with a conditional expression that tests for the condition:

```
if (condition) {
    // statements to execute if condition is true
}
```

To perform one branch under one condition and another branch for all other situations, use the if/else construction:

```
if (condition) {
    // statements to execute if condition is true
} else {
    // statements to execute if condition is false
}
```

You can be more explicit in the else clause by performing additional condition tests:

```
if (conditionA) {
    // statements to execute if conditionA is true
} else if (conditionB) {
    // statements to execute if conditionA is false and conditionB is true
} else {
    // statements to execute if both conditionA and conditionB are false
}
```

For multiple conditions, you should consider using the switch statement if the conditions are based on string or numeric value equivalency:

```
switch (expression) {
    case valueA:
        // statements to execute if expression evaluates to valueA
        break; // skip over default
    case valueB:
        // statements to execute if expression evaluates to valueB
        break; // skip over default
    ...
    default:
        // statements to execute if expression evaluates to no case value
}
```

The break statements in each of the case branches ensure that the default branch (which is optional) does not also execute.

Discussion

A condition expression in the if and if/else constructions is an expression that evaluates to a Boolean true or false. Typically, such expressions use comparison operators (==, ===, !=, !==, <, <=, >, >=) to compare the relationship between two values. Most of the time, you are comparing a variable value against some constant or known value:

```
var theMonth = myDateObj.getMonth();
if (theMonth == 1) {
    // zero-based value means the date is in February
    monLength = getLeapMonthLength(myDateObj);
} else {
    monLength = getMonthLength(theMonth);
}
```

JavaScript offers some additional shortcut evaluations for condition expressions. These shortcuts come in handy when you need to branch based on the existence of an object or property. Table 4-1 lists the conditions that automatically evaluate to true or false when placed inside the parentheses of a condition expression. For example, the existence of an object evaluates to true, which allows a construction such as the following to work:

```
if (myObj) {
    // myObj exists, so use it
}
```

Table 4-1. Condition expression equivalents

True	False
String has one or more characters	Empty string
Number other than zero	0
Nonnull value	`null`
Referenced object exists	Referenced object does not exist
Object property is defined and evaluates to a string of one or more characters or a nonzero number	Object property is undefined, or its value is an empty string or zero

When testing for the existence of an object property (including a property of the global `window` object), be sure to start the reference with the object, as in the following:

```
if (window.innerHeight) { ... }
```

But you also need to be careful when testing for the existence of a property if there is a chance that its value could be an empty string or zero. Such values force the conditional expression to evaluate to `false`, even though the property exists. Therefore, it is better to test for the data type of the property with the `typeof` operator. If you're not sure about the data type, test the data type against the `undefined` constant:

```
if (typeof myObj.myProperty != "undefined" ) {
    // myProperty exists and has a value of some kind assigned to it
}
```

If there is a chance that neither the object nor its property exists, you need to group together conditional expressions that test for the existence of both. Do this by testing for the object first, then the property. If the object does not exist, the expression short-circuits the test of the property:

```
if (myObj && typeof myObj.myProperty != "undefined") {
    // myObj exists, and so does myProperty
}
```

If, instead, you test for the property first, the test fails with a script error because the expression with the object fails unceremoniously.

JavaScript also provides a shortcut syntax that lets you avoid the curly braces for simple assignment statements that execute differently based on a condition. The syntax is as follows:

```
var myValue = (condition) ? value1 : value2;
```

If the condition evaluates to `true`, the righthand expression evaluates to the first value; otherwise, it evaluates to the second value. For example:

```
var backColor = (temperature > 100) ? "red" : "blue";
```

Several recipes in later chapters use this shortcut construction frequently, even to two levels deep. For example:

```
var backColor = (temperature > 100) ? "red" : ((temperature < 80) ?
    "blue" : "yellow"));
```

This shortcut expression is the same as the longer, more readable, but less elegant version:

```
var backColor ;
if (temperature > 100) {
    backColor = "red";
} else if (temperature < 80) {
    backColor = "blue";
} else {
    backColor = "yellow";
}
```

When you have lots of potential execution branches, and the triggers for the various branches are not conditional expressions per se, but rather the value of an expression, then the switch construction is the way to go. In the following example, a form contains a select element that lets a user choose a size for a product. Upon making that choice, a change event handler in the select element triggers a function that inserts the corresponding price for the size in a text box:

```
function setPrice(form) {
    var sizeList = form.sizePicker;
    var chosenItem = sizeList.options[sizeList.selectedIndex].value;
    switch (chosenItem) {
        case "small" :
            form.price.value = "44.95";
            break;
        case "medium" :
            form.price.value = "54.95";
            break;
        case "large" :
            form.price.value = "64.95";
            break;
        default:
            form.price.value = "Select size";
    }
}
```

If the switch expression always evaluates to one of the cases, you can omit the default branch, but while you are in development of the page, you might leave it there as a safety valve to alert you of possible errors if the expression should evaluate to an unexpected value.

See Also

Most of the recipes in Chapter 15 use the shortcut conditional statement to equalize disparate event models.

4.7 Handling Script Errors Gracefully

Problem

You want to process all script errors out of view of users, and thus prevent the browser from reporting errors to the user.

Solution

The quick-and-dirty, backward-compatible way to prevent runtime script errors from showing themselves to users is to include the following statements in a script within the head portion of a page:

```
function doNothing( ) {return true;}
window.onerror = doNothing;
```

This won't stop compile-time script errors (e.g., syntax errors that the interpreter discovers as the page loads). It also won't reveal to you, the programmer, where errors lurk in your code. Add this only if you need to deploy a page before you have fully debugged the code (essentially sweeping bugs under the rug); remove it to test your code.

In IE 5 or later, Mozilla, Safari, and Opera 7 or later, you can use more formal error (exception) handling. If you are allowing your pages to load in older browsers, you may need to prevent those browsers from coming into contact with the error-handling code. To prevent earlier browsers from tripping up on the specialized syntax used for this type of processing, embed these statements in <script> tags that specify Java-Script 1.5 as the language attribute (language="JavaScript1.5").

Wrap statements that might cause (throw) an exception in a try/catch construction. The statement to execute goes into the try section, while the catch section processes any exception that occurs:

```
<script type="text/javascript" language="JavaScript1.5">
function myFunc( ) {
    try {
        // statement(s) that could throw an error if various conditions aren't right
    }
    catch(e) {
        // statements that handle the exception (error object passed to e variable)
    }
}
</script>
```

Even if you do nothing in the required catch section, the exception in the try section is not fatal. Subsequent processing in the function, if any, goes on, provided it is not dependent upon values created in the try section. Or, you can bypass further processing in the function and gracefully exit by executing a return statement inside the catch section.

Discussion

Each thrown exception generates an instance of the JavaScript Error object. A reference to this object reaches the catch portion of a try/catch construction as a parameter to the catch clause. Script statements inside the catch clause may examine properties of the object to learn more about the nature of the error. Only a couple of properties are officially sanctioned in the ECMAScript standard so far, but some browsers implement additional properties that contain the same kind of information you see in script error messages. Table 4-2 lists informative Error object properties and their browser support.

Table 4-2. Error object properties

Property	IE/Windows	Mozilla	Safari	Opera	Description
description	5	n/a	n/a	n/a	Plain-language description of error
fileName	n/a	all	n/a	n/a	URI of the file containing the script throwing the error
lineNumber	n/a	all	n/a	n/a	Source code line number of error
message	5.5	all	all	7	Plain-language description of error (ECMA)
name	5.5	all	all	7	Error type (ECMA)
number	5	n/a	n/a	n/a	Microsoft proprietary error number
stack	n/a	1.0.1	n/a	n/a	Multi-line string of function references leading to error

Error messages are never intended to be seen by users. Use the description or message property of an Error object in your own exception handling to decide how to process the exception. Unfortunately, the precise message from the various browsers is not always identical for a given error. For example, if you try to reference an undefined object, IE reports the description string as:

```
'myObject' is undefined
```

Mozilla, on the other hand, reports:

```
myObject is not defined
```

This makes cross-browser exception handling a bit difficult. In this case, you could try to fudge it by performing string lookups (regular expression matches) for the object reference and the fragment "defined" as in the following:

```
try {
    window.onmouseover = trackPosition;
}
catch(e) {
    var msg = (e.message) ? e.message : e.description;
    if (/trackPosition/.exec(msg) && /defined/.exec(msg)) {
        // trackPosition function does not exist within page scope
    }
}
```

You can also intentionally throw an exception as a way to build exception handling into your own processing. The following function is a variation of a form validation function that tests for the entry of only a number in a text box. The try clause tests for an incorrect value. If found, the clause creates its own instance of an Error object and uses the throw method to trigger an exception. Of course, the thrown exception is immediately caught by the following catch clause, which displays the alert message and refocuses the text box in question:

```
function processNumber(inputField) {
    try {
        var inpVal = parseInt(inputField.value, 10);
        if (isNaN(inpVal)) {
            var msg = "Please enter a number only.";
            var err = new Error(msg);
            if (!err.message) {
                err.message = msg;
            }
            throw err;
        }
        // it's safe to process number here
    }
    catch (e) {
        alert(e.message);
        inputField.focus();
        inputField.select();
    }
}
```

This kind of function is invoked by both a change event handler for the text field and a batch validation routine, as described in Chapter 8.

4.8   Improving Script Performance

Problem

You want to speed up a sluggish script.

Solution

When swallowing small doses of code, JavaScript interpreters tend to process data speedily. But if you throw a ton of complex and deeply nested code at a browser, you may notice some latency, even after all the data has been downloaded in the browser.

Here are a handful of useful tips to help you unclog potential processing bottlenecks in your code:

- Avoid using the eval( ) function.
- Avoid the with construction.
- Minimize repetitive expression evaluation.

- Use simulated hash tables for lookups in large arrays of objects.
- Avoid excessive string concatenation.
- Investigate download performance.
- Avoid multiple document.write( ) method calls.

Look for these culprits especially inside loops, where delays become magnified.

Discussion

One of the most inefficient functions in the JavaScript language is eval( ). This function converts a string representation of an object to a genuine object reference. It becomes a common crutch when you find yourself with a string of an object's name or ID, and you need to build a reference to the actual object. For example, if you have a sequence of mouse rollover images comprising a menu, and their names are menuImg1, menuImg2, and so on, you might be tempted to create a function that restores all images to their normal image with the following construction:

```
for (var i = 0; i < 6; i++) {
    var imgObj = eval("document.menuImg" + i);
    imgObj.src = "images/menuImg" + i + "_normal.jpg";
}
```

The temptation is there because you are also using string concatenation to assemble the URL of the associated image file. Unfortunately, the eval( ) function in this loop is very wasteful.

When it comes to referencing element objects, there is almost always a way to get from a string reference to the actual object reference without using the eval( ) function. In the case of images, the document.images collection (array) provides the avenue. Here is the revised, more streamlined loop:

```
for (var i = 0; i < 6; i++) {
    var imgObj = document.images["menuImg" + i];
    imgObj.src = "images/menuImg" + i + "_normal.jpg";
}
```

If an element object has a name or ID, you can reach it through some collection that contains that element. The W3C DOM syntax for document.getElementById( ) is a natural choice when working in browsers that support the syntax and you have the element's ID as a string. But even for older code that supports names of things like images and form controls, there are collections to use, such as document.images and the elements collection of a form object (document.myForm.elements["elementName"]). For custom objects, see the later discussion about simulated hash tables. Hunt down every eval( ) function in your code and find a suitable, speedier replacement.

Another performance grabber is the with construction. The purpose of this control statement is to help narrow the scope of statements within a block. For example, if you have a series of statements that work primarily with a single object's properties and/or methods, you can limit the scope of the block so that the statements assume properties and methods belong to that object. In the following script fragment, the statements inside the block invoke the sort( ) method of an array and read the array's length property:

```
with myArray {
    sort( );
    var howMany = length;
}
```

Yes, it may look efficient, but the interpreter goes to extra lengths to fill in the object references before evaluating the nested expressions. Don't use this construction.

It takes processing cycles to evaluate any expression or reference. The more "dots" in a reference, the longer it takes to evaluate the reference. Therefore, you want to avoid repeating a lengthy object reference or expression if it isn't necessary, especially inside a loop. Here is a fragment that may look familiar to you from your own coding experience:

```
function myFunction(elemID) {
    for (i = 0; i < document.getElementById(elemID).childNodes.length; i++) {
        if (document.getElementById(elemID).childNodes[i].nodeType = = 1) {
            // process element nodes here
        }
    }
}
```

In the course of this function's execution, the expression document.getElementById( ) evaluates twice as many times as there are child nodes in the element whose ID is passed to the function. At each start of the for loop's execution, the limit expression evaluates the method; then the nested if condition evaluates the same expression each time through the loop. More than likely, additional statements in the loop evaluate that expression to access a child node of the outer element object. This is very wasteful of processing time.

Instead, at the cost of one local variable, you can eliminate all of this repetitive expression evaluation. Evaluate the unchanging part just once, and then use the variable reference as a substitute thereafter:

```
function myFunction(elemID) {
    var elem = document.getElementById(elemID);
    for (i = 0; i < elem .childNodes.length; i++) {
        if (elem .childNodes[i].nodeType = = 1) {
            // process element nodes here
        }
    }
}
```

If all of the processing inside the loop is with only child nodes of the outer loop, you can further compact the expression evaluations:

```
function myFunction(elemID) {
    var elemNodes = document.getElementById(elemID).childNodes;
    for (i = 0; i < elemNodes.length; i++) {
```

```
            if (elemNodes[i].nodeType = = 1) {
                // process element nodes here
            }
        }
    }
```

As an added bonus, you have also reduced the source code size. If you find instances of repetitive expressions whose values don't change during the course of the affected script segment, consider them candidates for pre-assignment to a local variable.

Next, eliminate time-consuming iterations through arrays, especially multidimensional arrays or arrays of objects. If you have a large array (say, more than about 100 entries), even the average lookup time may be noticeable. Instead, use the techniques shown in Recipe 3.9 to perform a one-time generation of a simulated hash table of the array. Assemble the hash table while the page loads so that any delay caused by creating the table is blended into the overall page-loading time. Thereafter, lookups into the array will be nearly instantaneous, even if the item found is the last item in the many-hundred member array.

As discussed in depth in Recipe 1.2, string concatenation can be a resource drain. Using arrays as temporary storage of string blocks can streamline execution.

Getting a ton of JavaScript code from server to browser can be a bottleneck on its own. Bear in mind that each external *.js* file loaded into a page incurs the overhead of an HTTP request (with at most two simultaneous connections possible). Various techniques for condensing *.js* source files are available, such as utilities that remove whitespace and shorten identifiers (often at the cost of ease of source code management and debugging). Most modern browsers can also accept external JavaScript files compressed with gzip (although IE 6 exhibits problems). As you can see, no single solution is guaranteed to work in every situation.

One other impact on loading time is where in the page you place `<script>` tags that load external *.js* files. The user may perceive that the entire page is loading faster if your `<script src="">` tags are just above the closing `</body>` tag because images and text start to appear faster. Interaction on the elements that relies on the scripts will still be delayed until the scripts fully load.

The final tip addresses use of the `document.write( )` method to generate content while the page loads. Treat this method as if it were an inherently slow input/output type of operation. Invoke the method as infrequently as possible. If you are writing a lot of content to the page, accumulate the HTML into one string variable, and blast it to the page with one call to `document.write( )`.

See Also

Recipe 3.9 for details on creating a simulated hash table from an array; Recipe 3.13 for a rare case where the `eval( )` function can't be avoided; Recipe 1.2 for details on using an array to speed large string assembly.

CHAPTER 5

Browser Feature Detection

5.0   Introduction

Perhaps the greatest challenge that faces any web author who needs scripting or Dynamic HTML features embedded within content is how to select features that work with the widest set of browsers for the target audience. Despite claims of compatibility with industry standards, every browser is guilty of one or more of the following charges:

- It implements some features in a peculiar way.
- It offers its preliminary vision of proposed standards.
- It includes proprietary features never intended for the standards track.

From an authoring standpoint, the most dramatic changes to browser functionality from version to version tend to be in two areas: the core JavaScript language (covered in Chapter 1 through Chapter 4) and the document object model (the "things" you manipulate on the page using the JavaScript vocabulary). After several years of rapid escalation of the browser feature wars among major brands, the dominant browser—Internet Explorer for Windows—remained stagnant after IE 6's final release in October 2001. Given that almost nothing in the way of scriptable improvements arrived with IE 7 in late 2006, this period of IE stability continues. Unfortunately for developers, however, the IE 6 implementation failed to support several key W3C DOM standards, most annoyingly, the event model. In the meantime, other browsers, including Mozilla-based browsers (Firefox is the most popular), Apple's Safari, and the cross-platform Opera browser, continued to implement more or newer W3C and other standards (such as the WHATWG effort). The browser wars are still being fought.

Complicating the issue is the fact that just because a new generation of web browser is available to the world doesn't mean that the world's user base rushes to adopt it. Even if IE 8 magically appears with superb standards support, universal adoption won't be immediate. The cost of upgrading an organization-wide deployment of web browser software may be too high to let employees keep pace with the available software. At the same end of the scale, oddly enough, is the consumer who would rather use a stable, reliable browser for years as if it were an appliance—not something that is upgraded every 12 to 18 months. It's all too easy for the web-literate to get caught up in the latest pre-release browser version frenzy, failing to realize that web server logs won't show the audience reaching a critical mass of that new browser version for as much as one year after its release.

These and other factors conspire to fragment the installed base of browsers in the real world. As a web application author, your task is to balance the desire to spiff up your content with DHTML features against the trouble of making sure the content degrades well on less-capable browsers. Part of achieving this balance is determining how maintainable your content should be. Sure, in an ideal world, you might have many versions of a given page, each optimized for a combination of browser brand, browser version, and operating system. But unless you have very sophisticated content management tools, a single text change to a page may become an unthinkable nightmare to deploy. In truth, the more palatable ideal world lets one HTML file (or server routine under PHP, ASP, JSP, and others) handle browser- and operating system-specific idiosyncrasies. That's what browser feature detection and scripting are all about.

Unfortunately, there are no hard and fast rules to follow when it comes to handling browser detection. Each combination of content and target audience has its own compatibility requirements. It's helpful to know this ahead of time, because you can start thinking about the level of browser detection you need to deploy for your content. In fact, it's one of the first things I address when embarking on a new project.

Developing a Browser Strategy

An approach I frequently recommend is to start with a mock-up of the art and content for related pages. Next, visualize the ideal user interaction that adds value to the content. For example: would site navigation be faster with pop-up submenus associated with main menu icons? Do you want to offer customized visual settings that are invoked automatically when a user accesses the site next time? Would it be more fun and convenient for users to build components of their online order by dragging icons representing features or modules?

With your wish list in hand, it's time to figure out what browser versions can support those features, and then map that support to the profiles of users you expect for the site. You may want to have all the fancy user interface features available for users of only the most recently released browsers and shuttle all others to a simpler presentation. A lot of scriptable and DHTML features can be added to a page such that the same HTML file serves both older and newer browsers, with users of new browsers getting the benefit of the added features—thanks to scripts that modify the document in the browser.

To make any these grand ideas work, you must include browser or feature detection scripts in your document. Such detection can be as simple as creating separate script-processing paths in the same document for different levels of scriptable feature support. Your designs may call for two or more HTML document paths through your web site, depending not only on various levels of scriptability but also on whether the browser is scriptable at all. You might even have your default page act as a filter for the browser flavors you are prepared to handle.

When There Is No JavaScript

It's not unusual for newcomers to client-side scripting to wonder how a script might detect the absence of JavaScript. Only after a bit of thought do they realize the ridiculous proposition of using JavaScript for decision-making when the browser completely ignores all scripts.

A user won't have JavaScript available for one of two reasons—one by force, one by choice. The most common reason is that the browser knows nothing about JavaScript. This isn't limited only to nongraphical browsers such as Lynx or special-purpose browsers for disabled users. Some portable wireless devices use browsers endowed with little or none of the scripting support found in full-fledged browsers (Apple's iPhone Safari browser being a notable exception).

Regardless of the latest browser bells and whistles, or the "preferred" way to apply certain content constructs, many thousands of web pages on the Net use techniques long ago deprecated in the standards documents. Web browser makers, however, bear the burden of this "ancient" baggage, as their browsers (with rare exception) continue to be backward-compatible with earlier technologies. Unfortunately, this continued support can lead casual page authors to believe that the old ways are just fine, so they believe they have little incentive to use the latest techniques. Conversely, a tuned-in content author who blindly follows standards—essentially treating the standards as platforms—may be even more foolhardy because browser makers haven't caught up with the standards or have implemented them oddly in the early development stages.

The second reason JavaScript may be unavailable is that for personal or MIS policy reasons, JavaScript is turned off in a browser that is otherwise capable of JavaScript. When scripting is turned off in a scriptable browser, any HTML content contained by the <noscript> tag pair is rendered by the browser. This is where you might include a message that alerts users about what they're missing:

```
<noscript>
<p>
If you are able to turn on JavaScript in your browsers, you will enjoy
convenient shortcuts to speed your site navigation. To learn how to enable
JavaScript for your browser, click the link for your browser:
<a href="jsiewin.html">Internet Explorer for Windows</a>,
<a href="jsmoz.html">Firefox</a>,
<a href="jssaf.html">Safari</a>.
<a href="jsop.html">Opera</a>.
```

```
    </p>
  </noscript>
```

With a little server programming, you can help the visitor even more. By analyzing the HTTP USERAGENT string arriving with the page request, the server can examine the browser and operating system type, and thus provide a single link in the `<noscript>` tag to the script-enabling instructions tailored for that browser class. Not all visitors know (or care) which browser brand or version they're using. A little extra server programming (if you have access to it for your web hosting) can simplify life for nontechnical visitors.

Masking Scripts from Nonscriptable Browsers

Scripting has been a part of web page development for so many years now, it's extremely rare to be visited by a browser that doesn't know what to do with a `<script>` tag, even if just to ignore the tag and its content. Such wasn't always the case. For scripting's first few years, it was necessary to guard against old browsers that ignored the `<script>` tag, but rendered the script contents as if it were body content. To prevent the display of scripts, you had to wrap script statements with HTML comment tags:

```
<script language="JavaScript">
<!--
script statements go here
//-->
</script>
```

This practice is no longer necessary, although you will see it deployed widely in pages that have been on the Web for a long time.

Incidentally, this masking technique is not a way to prevent inquisitive visitors from viewing the source code of your HTML or scripts. And before you ask, there is no sure-fire way to prevent someone from seeing your client-side scripts. While numerous ways exist to obfuscate your code, a determined visitor will be able to view your scripts one way or another.

Detecting the JavaScript Version

A somewhat imprecise way of providing multiple levels of functionality in a single page is possible by letting scripts branch based on the version of JavaScript built into the browser. This strategy is called *browser detection*; it was practical in the early days of scripting when increments in the scripting language version were more closely tied to specific browser versions from the only two scriptable browsers: Internet Explorer and Netscape Navigator. For example, JavaScript 1.2 was the language deployed in Navigator 4 and Internet Explorer 4.

Since then, the correlation between JavaScript version number and scriptable features of browsers—the latter determined by the separate document object models— is too loose to be useful. I no longer recommend language version branching. But, because a lot of legacy code deployed on the Web demonstrates this technique, I present a brief discussion of how it works.

Just like HTML, scripts load into the browser in source code order (i.e., from top to bottom). If the browser encounters more than one function of the same name, the last one to be read overrides all others that appear earlier in the document. But the browser recognizes `<script>` tags only for the JavaScript language versions it knows about. For example, consider the following parallel sets of tags:

```
<script language="JavaScript" type="text/javascript">
function myFunction( ) {
    function statements
}
</script>
<script language="JavaScript1.2" type="text/javascript">
function myFunction( ) {
    function statements
}
</script>
```

A browser that knows only JavaScript 1.0 or 1.1 keeps the first definition of `myFunction( )` in memory ready to be invoked by any event handler or script statement. A browser that knows JavaScript 1.2 (or later) loads the first definition into memory as the page loads, but the function is immediately overwritten in memory by the second definition. Only the second function runs when invoked by an event handler elsewhere in the document.

Object Detection: The Way to Go

Using browser brand, version, or operating system detection assumes that you know for certain which browser versions support a particular document object, property, or method. With so many scriptable browsers prowling the Web these days, it is impossible to know which current or future subversion of each browser supports the object model features you need. This is where a technique known as *object detection* picks up the slack. As demonstrated in Recipes 5.8 and 5.9, your scripts can make sure the browser supports a new or limited object model feature before using that feature.

Use object detection wisely. Do not assume that because a browser supports one feature of some other browser that all other features of that other browser are supported. For example, it is an unfortunately common practice to assume that just because a browser supports the `document.all` collection, the browser is Internet Explorer 4 or later. If you are familiar with that browser class in the Windows environment, you're probably aware of a wide range of IE DOM features. But some of those features are not available in IE 4 or later for other operating systems, nor in the Opera browser set to behave like IE—all of which support the `document.all` collection. On the other hand, you don't need to be a JavaScript guru to know that support for `document.all` universally equates with support for the `document.all.length` property—all object collections have a `length` property.

Deploying object detection intelligently requires a good source of language- and object-compatibility ratings. The latest edition of my book *Dynamic HTML: The Definitive Reference* (O'Reilly) is tailored for this task.

Setting Global Variables

How often your scripts need to perform the actual browser or object detection depends a lot on how large your scripts are and how often those scripts need to differentiate among support profiles for browsers. Most browser detection occurs via the `navigator` object, sometimes involving compound detection statements (e.g., you're looking for a particular browser brand and version). Because browser detection is most often used to branch script execution within an `if` construction, it is generally more convenient to establish one or more global variables at the start of your script to be used as flags later on. Let the assignment statements perform the examination and assign `true` or `false` Boolean values to the global(s). Then use the global variable(s) as expressions within your branching `if` conditions:

```
var isMacOS = (navigator.userAgent.indexOf("Mac") != -1);
...
if (isMacOS) {
    Macintosh-specific scripts here
} else {
    Other scripts here
}
```

You can do the same for object detection (and reduce excessive expression evaluation throughout your scripts):

```
var isW3C = (document.getElementById) ? true : false;
```

After some experience, you'll get to know the kinds of branching a particular job requires. Assigning the browser global variables at the start of your scripts will become second nature to you.

DHTML and Accessibility

Many countries have enacted laws that require employers and organizations open to the public to provide site access to employees, customers, and visitors who have a variety of disabilities. It's not uncommon for such users to visit web pages with browsers that permit navigation exclusively via keyboard or render content through speech synthesis. Implementing an application that relies solely on DHTML techniques to convey its content may place such content in violation of these laws. For information about the U.S. law covering this topic, visit *http://www.section508.gov*.

A related issue is how accessible the content is to search engine spiders and bots that troll the Web to build their databases. These services tend to follow HTML links found on a page, but do not execute scripts. Thus, they see only explicit HTML content as delivered by the web server. If all links from the home page activate only through script control, the search engines won't get past your site's lobby.

5.1   Detecting the Browser Brand

Problem

You want script execution to branch one way for IE users and another way for all other browser users.

Solution

Use the navigator.appName property to find out which brand the browser purports to be. The following statement sets a global Boolean variable for browser brands:

```
var isIE = (navigator.appName == "Microsoft Internet Explorer");
```

Discussion

The navigator.appName property returns a string that the browser maker determines. Firefox and Safari always return the string "Netscape", while Internet Explorer returns "Microsoft Internet Explorer". These strings and the equivalency operator are case-sensitive.

You will also encounter some interesting aberrations to this scheme with Opera, which reports that its appName is "Microsoft Internet Explorer", "Netscape", or "Opera", depending on how the user sets the preferences. Settings for IE and NN force the browser to react to script syntax and objects along the lines of the selected browser (at least for simple tasks). If you want to find out for sure whether the browser is Opera, you must dig into the navigator.userAgent property, which contains more information about the browser. See Recipe 5.6 for more details.

With respect to Internet Explorer, you should be aware that substantial differences exist between the Windows and now-defunct Macintosh versions. Thus, you may need operating-system detection as well (covered in Recipe 5.7).

See Also

Recipes 5.2 through 5.6 for more granular browser version sniffing; Recipe 5.7 for operating-system detection.

5.2   Detecting an Early Browser Version

Problem

You want script execution to branch based on Internet Explorer or pre-Mozilla Netscape Navigator.

Solution

For IE and Netscape browsers through version 4, the `navigator.appVersion` property returns the complete version of the browser along with further information about the operating system platform. To determine the major generation of the browser, use the `parseInt( )` function to extract the integer value of the version:

```
var isVer4 = (parseInt(navigator.appVersion) == 4);
```

To get the version number that includes incremental upgrades of the browser (represented as numbers to the right of the decimal, such as 4.74), use the `parseFloat( )` function:

```
var isVer4_74 = (parseFloat(navigator.appVersion) == 4.74);
```

If you want your variable to indicate that a certain minimum version is available, use the `>=` operator instead of the equality (`==`) operator:

```
var isVer4Min  = (parseInt(navigator.appVersion) >= 4);
var isVer4_5Min = (parseFloat(navigator.appVersion) >= 4.5);
```

Discussion

For any browser version up to Microsoft Internet Explorer 4.0 and the last released version of the Netscape Navigator 4 family (4.8), the `navigator.appVersion` string begins with accurate information about the browser's version. For example:

```
Microsoft Internet Explorer 4.01 running on Windows 98:
    4.0 (compatible; MSIE 4.01; Windows 98)
Netscape Navigator 4.79 for the Macintosh PowerPC:
    4.79 (Macintosh; U; PPC)
```

For all subsequent browser versions, the leading characters of the `navigator.appVersion` string no longer correspond to the browser's actual version number. Instead, the leading number represents the generation of core browser code. Thus, the lead part of the `navigator.appVersion` string, even for Internet Explorer 7 for Windows, continues to read 4.0.

Newer browsers that succeeded Netscape 4.x are built with an entirely new core engine (the Gecko engine developed by Mozilla). For a variety of historical reasons, this generation of code is counted as the fifth generation. Therefore, because the fifth-generation core engine is used in Mozilla-based browsers, the `navigator.appVersion` string for those browsers begins with 5.0, rather than a number corresponding to the actual browser version.

To determine the precise browser version number for newer browsers, you must use other techniques that are, unfortunately, not cross-browser compatible. These are described in Recipes 5.3 through 5.6.

See Also

Recipe 5.1, and Recipes 5.3 through 5.6 for additional browser detection tips.

5.3 Detecting the Internet Explorer Version

Problem

You want script execution to branch based on a specific or minimum version of Internet Explorer.

Solution

Access the complete version number by parsing the string of the `navigator.userAgent` property. Internet Explorer identifies itself with the string `MSIE`, followed by a space, the version number (with one or more digits to the right of the decimal), and a semicolon. Here's a function that returns the numeric portion of the pertinent information:

```
function getIEVersionNumber() {
    var ua = navigator.userAgent;
    var MSIEOffset = ua.indexOf("MSIE ");
    if (MSIEOffset == -1) {
        return 0;
    } else {
        return parseFloat(ua.substring(MSIEOffset + 5, ua.indexOf(";", MSIEOffset)));
    }
}
```

You can use the returned value to establish a global variable that gets used elsewhere in code execution branch condition statements. For example, here's how to execute code only if the browser identifies itself as being compatible with IE 5 or later:

```
var isIE5Min = getIEVersionNumber() >= 5;
...
if (isIE5Min) {
    // perform statements for IE 5 or later
}
```

Discussion

Because the function in the Solution returns a number data type, it does not reveal whether the version number is followed by any letters, such as B for beta versions. If you omit the `parseFloat()` function, the returned result will be a string value. But by and large, you will be looking for a numeric value to use for a comparison, as shown previously.

The userAgent string for IE 7 continues the same format as in earlier versions. In Windows Vista, IE 7 also reports itself as `MSIE 7.0`, but the operating system reports in as `Windows NT 6.0`.

Using a numerical comparison of the version number is a two-edged sword. On one side is a warning against using a simple equality operator (==) instead of a greater-than or equals operator (>=). Using the equality operator is a frequent mistake of a routine that is designed to run on only the latest version. The problem with this is that when the next version appears, the comparison operation fails. On the other side is that the >= operator assumes that future versions of the browser will continue to support the branched feature. While browsers tend to be backward-compatible, scripters familiar with the removal of the layer object between Netscape Navigator 4 and 6 know how this assumption can get you into trouble. This is one more reason to look toward object detection rather than version detection in most cases. Version detection is valuable, however, when you are aware of a bug in a particular version and you want your script to bypass that bug when running on the rogue browser.

See Also

Recipes 5.2 and 5.4 through 5.6 for additional browser detection tips; Recipe 2.1 for uses of the parseFloat( ) function; Recipe 1.6 for uses of the indexOf( ) method.

5.4 Detecting the Mozilla Version

Problem

You want script execution to branch based on a specific or minimum version of a Mozilla-based browser.

Solution

Script execution tends to rely on core JavaScript, DOM, and CSS features that are built into the Gecko rendering engine that Mozilla-based browsers have in common. The navigator.userAgent string for all of these browsers contains the string Gecko, followed by a slash and the date (in YYYYMMDD form) of the engine build used in the browser. The date varies with virtually every build, including those that don't necessarily result in new application versions, but just minor bug fixes. Mozilla does not explicitly publish the Gecko engine dates corresponding to each build release, but you can install archived versions of several browsers to discover the Gecko reporting date for a specific browser version.

In recent implementations, the navigator.userAgent string also contains a reference to the Mozilla build version from which the current browser was taken. A table of various browser versions and their corresponding Mozilla build numbers appears in the Discussion section. Some sample navigator.userAgent strings are as follows:

```
Mozilla/5.0 (Macintosh; U; PPC Mac OS X Mach-O; en-US; rv:1.8.1.2) Gecko/20070219
Firefox/2.0.0.2
Mozilla/5.0 (Windows; U; Windows NT 5.1; en-US; rv:1.8.0.10) Gecko/20070216 Firefox/
1.5.0.10
Mozilla/5.0 (Windows; U; Windows NT 5.1; en-US; rv:1.7.5) Gecko/20060912 Netscape/
8.1.2
```

Given these patterns, your scripts can first test for the presence of Gecko/ in the navigator.userAgent string to determine if you are using a Mozilla-based browser (an early version of Safari contained the phrase like Gecko, without the slash). From there, you can extract the revision number using the following script fragment:

```
var re = /(rv:)(\d+\.\d+\.?\d*\.?\d*)/;
var mozVer = a.exec(navigator.userAgent)[2];
```

The returned value is a string of only the revision number (e.g., 1.8.1.2). This value cannot easily be converted to a number that can be used for numeric comparisons. You can, of course, divide the string into array items (via the split( ) method) and compare desired items against your baseline requirements.

Discussion

Use Table 5-1 as a guide to the Mozilla build version, Gecko version, and three of the most popular Mozilla-based browsers. The m18 designation stands for milestone build number 18, a convention later dropped in favor of traditional numbering. Gecko dates are the earliest dates obtained from a released browser using the Mozilla build version in the same row. As you can see, there is little tracking between the Mozilla version and the version of a particular branded browser.

Table 5-1. Mozilla build versions versus branded browser versions

Mozilla	Gecko	Netscape	Firefox	Camino
m18	20001108	6.0		
0.9.4	20011022	6.2		
1.0.1	20020823	7.0		
1.4	20030624	7.1		
1.7.2	20040804	7.2		
1.7.5	20041217	8.0–8.2	1.0	
1.8	20051111		1.5	1.0
1.8.1	20061010		2.0	

If you are interested in knowing if the Mozilla-based browser is of a particular brand, check the navigator.userAgent property value for the desired browser to see how it reports itself. Although the examples above demonstrate that Firefox and Netscape use a similar format (the brand name followed by a slash and version number), other brands may not necessarily follow this format. In fact, Mozilla's own documentation recommends avoiding using the navigator.userAgent string for browser identification, but offers no alternative suggestion.

See Also

Recipe 5.1 for primary browser brand detection; Recipes 5.3, 5.5, and 5.6 for detecting other browser brands; Recipe 3.3 for converting between arrays and strings.

5.5 Detecting the Safari Version

Problem

You want script execution to branch based on a specific or minimum version of Apple's Safari browser.

Solution

Apple recommends performing version detection not on the Safari indicator of the navigator.userAgent string, but rather on the AppleWebKit version. This version indicates the fundamental rendering engine that influences your scripting decisions.

The following script fragment sets a global flag for whether the current Safari version is one that implements a rich set of scriptable CSS and DOM support beginning with Safari 1.3 (Mac OS X 10.3) and Safari 2.0 (Mac OS X 10.4):

```
var isModernSafari = false;
if (navigator.userAgent.indexOf("AppleWebKit") != -1) {
    var re = /\(.*\) AppleWebKit/(.*) \((.*)/;
    var webkitVersion = re.exec(ua)[1].split(".")[0];
    if (webkitVersion > 312) {
        isModernSafari = true;
    }
}
```

Apple provides a complete list of AppleWebKit versions for each release and update since the first release at *http://developer.apple.com/internet/safari/uamatrix.html*.

Discussion

The best reason to use the AppleWebKit version is that the engine may be built into other applications capable of rendering HTML and running scripts. You therefore do not want to be tied down only to Safari, when your scripts could run elsewhere.

The relative complexity of the regular expression shown in the Solution is due to the fact that AppleWebKit versions can contain multiple sub-versions, each separated by periods, such as 418.9.1. By and large, your branching will consider only whole version numbers. During the transition between Mac OS X 10.3 (Panther) and Mac OS X 10.4 (Tiger), Safari was released with similar functionality, but with different version numbers and AppleWebKit series. Safari 1.3 for Panther was released at approximately the same time as Safari 2.0 for the newly released Tiger. Therefore, although the AppleWebKit version for Tiger begins at 412, the corresponding Panther release was 312. Thus, the example above uses the 312 version as a baseline for what the script considers "modern" Safari at the time.

See Also

Recipe 5.1 for primary browser brand detection; Recipes 5.3, 5.4, and 5.6 for detecting other browser brands; Recipe 3.3 for converting between arrays and strings.

5.6 Detecting the Opera Version

Problem

You want script execution to branch based on a specific or minimum version of the Opera browser.

Solution

Although Opera can identify itself in its `navigator.userAgent` string as being Opera, Firefox, or Internet Explorer (depending on user preference settings), the string always contains some representation of the Opera name and version. Here are the possibilities from a recent version of the browser:

```
Opera/9.10 (Windows NT 5.1; U; en)
Mozilla/5.0 (Windows NT 5.1; U; en; rv:1.8.0) Gecko/20060728 Firefox/1.5.0 Opera 9.10
Mozilla/4.0 (compatible; MSIE 6.0; Windows NT 5.1; en) Opera 9.10
```

Because some of these strings contain text that you might use to inspect for a Mozilla-based browser or IE, it is important to look for Opera prior to the other browser types. The following script fragment extracts the version number from any of the above `navigator.userAgent` strings:

```
var ua = navigator.userAgent;
var operaVersion = null;
if (ua.indexOf("Opera") != -1) {
    var re = /(Opera\W)(\d*\.\d*)/;
    var operaVersion = re.exec(ua)[2];
}
```

If you are interested only in the major version, you can apply the `parseInt( )` global function to the extracted version, and perform numeric comparisons for branching.

Discussion

Be sure not to rely on the `navigator.appName` or `navigator.appVersion` properties when inspecting Opera. The `appName` property value reflects the user preference choice, offering values of `Opera`, `Netscape`, and `Microsoft Internet Explorer` based on user settings.

Also, exercise caution with the version string. Applying `parseFloat( )` to version 9.10 returns 9.1, not the actual sub-version. To numerically compare the sub-version, use string extraction routines to obtain the characters to the right of the decimal; then use `parseInt( )` to obtain an arithmetically friendly value.

See Also

Recipe 5.1 for primary browser brand detection; Recipes 5.3, 5.4, and 5.5 for detecting other browser brands; Recipe 3.3 for converting between arrays and strings.

5.7   Detecting the Client Operating System

Problem

You want to apply styles or other content features tailored to a particular operating system.

Solution

The string returned by the `navigator.userAgent` property usually contains information about the basic operating system platform on which the browser is running. Unfortunately, there is no standard nomenclature that you can search the `userAgent` string for a particular operating system. The values are not only different with each browser brand, but have evolved over time and may be different for OEM versions of the browser.

The widest difference is in the depiction of the Windows platforms in various browsers, in which Windows 98, for example, might be displayed as "Win98" or "Windows 98." A better solution is to test for the presence of strings that identify other operating systems more uniformly. For instance, all Macintosh versions have the string "Mac" somewhere in the `navigator.userAgent` property. By the same token, all Windows versions have the string "Win" in them, but that could represent anything from Windows 3.1 to Windows Vista. Furthermore, all Unix versions of Navigator have the string "X11". If you're just looking for a rough cut, the following global variable assignment statements will do the job of setting Boolean flags:

```
var isWin = (navigator.userAgent.indexOf("Win") != -1);
var isMac = (navigator.userAgent.indexOf("Mac") != -1);
var isUnix = (navigator.userAgent.indexOf("X11") != -1);
```

Browsers running under Linux include both "X11" and "Linux" in the `navigator.userAgent` property.

Discussion

As you can see, operating-system detection is a tricky business and should be used with care. While some OEM versions of a browser might have more specific information about the operating system in the `navigator.userAgent` property (such as the specific release number of the operating system), you are not assured of this information being there for all browsers on a given operating system. For example, Windows XP and Vista identify themselves as versions of Windows NT.

Mozilla includes a new `navigator` object property, `oscpu`, that returns that portion of the `userAgent` value containing as much operating system and CPU information as is revealed by the browser. When running under Windows, the property conveys only the operating system information, such as "Win98" or "Windows NT 5.1." For the Mac, the property always returns the CPU class ("Intel") and the operating system for Mac OS X (as "Mac OS X").

Once you are satisfied that the global variables you set for operating system versions are doing what you need, you can use them efficiently in making operating system-dependent settings for page characteristics such as font size. For example, it is well-known by designers that a given font point size looks smaller on a Macintosh screen than on a Windows display. If you are intent on specifying font sizes in point units, you can make the content look more similar across operating systems by dynamically writing the style sheet, using the operating system global variables to set the desired font size:

```
<script language="JavaScript" type="text/javascript">
document.write("<style type='text/css'>");
document.write("body {font-size:" + ((isMac) ? "12" : "10") + "pt}");
document.write("</style>");
</script>
```

Similar decision constructions can be used to apply operating system-specific element position coordinates if your design requires it. In fact, you can nest inline if constructions to get three-way switching. For example, if you need to establish a variable for a pixel offset between elements, you can set an offset for each of the three major OS categories as follows:

```
var elemOffset = (isMac) ? 15 : ((isWin) ? 12 : 10);
```

After execution, the elemOffset variable is 15 for the Mac, 12 for all Windows flavors, and 10 for all others (presumably Unix).

See Also

Recipe 5.1, particularly if one operating system version of a particular browser brand is giving you design headaches; Recipe 11.5 for importing operating system-specific style sheet definitions; Recipe 4.6 for conditional branching.

5.8   Detecting Object Support

Problem

You want scripts to run on all browsers that support the objects that your scripts address, and to degrade gracefully in other browsers.

Solution

Surround the script statements that reference potentially incompatible objects with if statements that test for the existence of the objects. The objects you test for can be core JavaScript language objects, as well as DOM objects. Facilitating this kind of condition testing is the fact that a reference to a nonexistent object inside an if condition evaluates to the equivalent of false. A very common usage of object detection from earlier scriptable browsers is in scripts that work with img elements as objects for rollover image swaps (covered in depth in Chapter 12). Support for the img element object was very uneven until the version 4 browsers. Creating browser version filters for all the possibilities would have been tedious at best. Instead, all script statements that referenced img element objects were wrapped inside an if construction that looks for the presence of the document.images array:

```
function rollover(imgName, imgSrc) {
    if (document.images) {
        document.images[imgName].src = imgSrc;
    }
}
```

This function is invoked by a mouseover event handler associated with a link surrounding an image:

```
<a href="product.html"
    onmouseover="rollover('products', 'images/products_on.gif'); return false"
    onmouseout="rollover('products', 'images/products_off.gif'); return false">
<img src="images/products_off.gif" name="products" border="0" alt="Products Page">
</a>
```

The check for document.images works conveniently because if a browser recognizes an img element as a scriptable object, the document object always has an images[ ] array associated with it. If there are no images on the page, the array is empty—but it still exists with length zero. If the browser has no document.images array, however, the if condition fails, and no internal statements of the function execute. Browsers that would otherwise choke on the invalid reference to the img element object glide past the offensive statements.

Discussion

Object detection frees you from the tyranny and tedium of browser-version sniffing, but you must also deploy this technique in such a way that browsers not supporting your desired objects degrade gracefully. This means that you must anticipate what will happen to a script that runs in a browser that supports only some, but not all, desired objects. For example, consider the scenario in which you have a complex operation running under script control, and execution branches periodically to other functions to retrieve a calculated value. If one of those remote functions performs object detection, how well does your main execution thread respond to the inability of one remote function to return a suitable value?

The following two functions are written without the benefit of object detection. After the main function invokes a subroutine function to calculate the area of all images on the page, the main function enters the values into a form field:

```
function getImgAreas( ) {
    // initialize return value so we can add to it
    var result = 0;
    // loop through all img objects on the page
    for (var i = 0; i < document.images.length; i++) {
```

```
        // accumulate image areas
        result += (document.images[i].width * document.images[i].height);
    }
    return result;
}

function reportImageArea( ) {
    document.reportForm.imgData.value = getImgAreas( );
}
```

A browser that does not know about the img element object would report a script error when executing the getImgAreas( ) function. Even if the errors were hidden from view (see Recipe 4.8), the user might expect some information to appear in the text box, but none would come.

A smarter scripter would recognize that the preceding scripts might fail in very old browsers, where script errors tend to be rather invasive. To prevent such errors, the author makes two modifications. First, the potentially offending script statements in the getImgAreas( ) function wrap themselves in an object detection block. Second, the main function intelligently accommodates the possibility that the getImgAreas( ) function won't be doing any calculations at all:

```
function getImgAreas( ) {
    var result;
    // make sure browser supports img element objects
    if (document.images) {
        // initialize return value so we can add to it
        result = 0;
        // loop through all img objects on the page
        for (var i = 0; i < document.images.length; i++) {
            // accumulate image areas
            result += (document.images[i].width * document.images[i].height);
        }
    }
    // returned value is either a number or null
    return result;
}
function reportImageArea( ) {
    // grab result so we can verify it
    var imgArea = getImgAreas( );
    var output;
    if (imgArea == null) {
        // message for browsers not supporting img object
        output = "Unknown";
    } else {
        output = imgArea;
    }
    document.reportForm.imgData.value = output;
}
```

Notice that the main function does not perform any object detection for the form-related statement at the end. A knowledgeable scripter (or one with a good DOM reference resource) knows that the syntax used to reference the form's text field is completely backward-compatible to the very earliest browsers.

Object detection alone is not always a savior, however. Sometimes you must also employ property and method detection. For example, in the preceding subroutine function, there was no compatibility problem with accessing the height and width properties of the img element object, since these properties have been available for this object since the first implementation of that object in the various DOMs. But some other properties, such as the alt property, are not supported in all browsers that support the img object. If the subroutine function needed the alt property, further object property detection, as shown in Recipe 5.9, would be in order.

See Also

Recipe 5.9 to test for the presence of an object property or method; Recipe 4.6 for special values you can use in condition statements that evaluate to true and false.

5.9   Detecting Object Property and Method Support

Problem

You want scripts to run on all browsers that support the object properties and/or methods that your scripts address, and to degrade gracefully in other browsers.

Solution

Surround the script statements that reference potentially incompatible object properties or methods with if statements that test for the existence of the objects and their properties or methods. The items you test for can belong to core JavaScript language objects, as well as to DOM objects. Testing for the existence of a property or method is a little more complicated than testing for the object alone. If your condition expression references a property of a nonexistent object, a script error results. Therefore, you must precede your property/method test with a test for the object (assuming the object is not one that is fully backward-compatible):

```
if (objectTest && objectPropertyTest) {
    // OK to work with property
}
```

This combination works smoothly because if the first condition test fails, JavaScript short-circuits the rest of the expression, bypassing the second condition.

It is not advisable, however, to use the simple existence test for an object's property in an if condition. The main reason is that some legitimate property values are zero or empty strings. A conditional test with these values evaluates the same as false, which gives an incorrect reading about support for the property (see Recipe 4.6). The best way around this problem is to test for the data type of the property being something other than undefined:

```
if (objectReference && typeof objectReference.propertyName != "undefined") {
    // OK to work with property
}
```

References to object methods take the same form as references to functions: the
name of the method without the parentheses. If the method exists, the reference
evaluates to a valid object type and the conditional test succeeds:

```
if (objectReference && objectReference.methodName) {
    // OK to work with method
}
```

For example, to protect scripts written with W3C DOM element referencing from
tripping up older browsers, you can wrap function execution inside conditions that
test for the existence of the document.getElementById( ) method:

```
function myFunction( ) {
    if (document.getElementById) {
        // OK to use document.getElementById( ) here
    }
}
```

To save some bytes on the page and extraneous expression evaluation, you can also
set a Boolean global variable as the page loads to use in later condition statements:

```
var isW3 = (document.getElementById) ? true : false;
...
if (isW3) {
    // OK to use document.getElementById( ) here
}
```

Discussion

Be careful about the assumptions you make when you qualify a browser for an object
and one of its properties or methods. For instance, it would be a mistake to assume
that because the browser indicates support for the document.getElementById( )
method that it supports the rest of the W3C DOM Core module objects, properties,
and methods. With experience, however, you will gain the knowledge that all browsers that recognize the all-important method also know about the basic element node
properties, such as nodeType, nodeName, and nodeValue. Again, a good DOM reference
will help you with those kinds of decisions.

Don't be afraid to nest multiple levels of object and property/method detection in a
function. You can see examples of this when processing events for the incompatible
IE and W3C event models (Recipe 9.1). But always make sure that your functions are
structured in such a way that any one condition failure is handled gracefully so that
no script errors accrue in the absence of support for your desired object, property, or
method.

If your scripts or pages are pre-screened to work only in IE 6 or later and other modern browsers, you can consider using the document.implementation.hasFeature( )
method (see Recipe 5.10) to query about support for numerous related DOM

objects, properties, and methods. You should still test this approach extensively, especially on early versions of browsers that support the method to make sure the browsers are telling the whole truth about support for a particular W3C DOM module.

See Also

Recipe 5.8 for detecting object support; Recipe 4.6 for special condition expressions that evaluate to true and false; Recipe 9.1 for nested object detection in event processing; Recipe 5.10 for using the hasFeature( ) method.

5.10   Detecting W3C DOM Standard Support

Problem

You want to know if the current browser supports a particular W3C DOM module.

Solution

The W3C DOM provides the hasFeature( ) method of the implementation object. The method lets scripts query the browser about its support for any of several modules in the W3C specification. For example, if you wish to load a more complex style sheet for any browser that claims to support scripting of CSS Level 2, you could add the following code to the document's head portion:

```
var cssFile;
if (document.implementation.hasFeature("CSS2", "2.0")) {
    cssFile = "styles/corpStyle2.css";
} else {
    cssFile = "styles/corpStyle1.css";
}
document.write("<link rel='stylesheet' type='text/css' href='" + cssFile + "'>");
```

This feature is implemented in IE 6 or later, as well as Mozilla, Safari, and Opera 7 or later.

Discussion

Beginning with Level 2, the W3C DOM was compartmentalized into modules of related functionality so that browser makers could elect to implement only selected segments of the W3C DOM and still claim standard support. You can view a list of all Level 2 modules at *http://www.w3.org/TR/DOM-Level-2-Core/introduction. html#ID-Conformance.*

You can therefore query the browser for any of the following case-sensitive Level 2 module names: Core, XML, HTML, Views, StyleSheets, CSS, CSS2, Events, UIEvents, MouseEvents, MutationEvents, HTMLEvents, Range, Traversal, and Views. DOM Level 3 offers the following additional modules: `BasicEvents`, `TextEvents`, `KeyboardEvents`, and `LS` (Load and Save module).

The second parameter of the `hasFeature( )` method is a string of the DOM level whose module is under test. For example, if you wanted to see if the browser supports the full Core module of Level 3, the method would be invoked as follows:

```
document.implementation.hasFeature("Core", "3.0")
```

Note that when the module refers to a standard that the DOM addresses, the version referenced in the method's second parameter is of the DOM module, not the external standard. Therefore, although the HTML module of DOM Level 2 is in support of HTML 4.01, your test is whether the current browser supports all the DOM-accessible features of HTML as defined in the Level 2 specification.

5.11   Detecting the Browser Written Language

Problem

You wish to direct users automatically to a path in your web site tailored for a specific written language.

Solution

Current browsers provide properties of the `navigator` object that let you read the code for the native language for which the user's browser was developed. Unfortunately, the property names are different for each browser, so you must perform some object property detection in the process. The solution below assumes that all users will be shunted to the English page unless their browsers indicate that the native language is German:

```
// verify browser language
function getLang(type) {
    var lang;
    if (typeof navigator.userLanguage != "undefined") {
        lang = navigator.userLanguage.toUpperCase( );
    } else if (typeof navigator.language != "undefined") {
        lang = navigator.language.toUpperCase( );
    }
    return (lang && lang.indexOf(type.toUpperCase( )) == 0)
}
...
location.href = (getLang("de")) ? "de/home.html" : "en/home.html";
```

The case conversions eliminate potential differences in the case of the letters returned by the language-related properties of browsers. In the end, the return statement performs string equality testing on all uppercase letters (see Recipes 1.4 and 1.5).

Discussion

Language codes consists of a primary two-letter code indicating the basic language. An optional two-letter subcode may also be used to identify a country or region for which the primary language is tailored (e.g., "en-us" for United States English). Therefore, you cannot always rely on the navigator object's language-related property returning only a two-letter code. But since the primary code always comes first, you can look for the code being at the beginning of whatever string is returned by the property. Also, be sure to force the case of the values so that your eventual comparison operation works on a level playing field, regardless of the case of the returned data. Nonscriptable browsers will still need links on the page to provide manual selection of the desired language path through the site. Common two-letter primary codes are cataloged in ISO-639 (an excerpted list of codes is available at *http://www. ietf.org/rfc/rfc1766.txt*).

See Also

Recipes 5.1 and 5.2 for browser brand and version detection; Chapter 1 for string parsing.

5.12 Detecting Cookie Availability

Problem

You want your scripts to know whether the user's browser has cookies enabled.

Solution

Current browsers feature the navigator.cookieEnabled property, which you can test at anyplace within a script:

```
if (navigator.cookieEnabled) {
    // invoke cookie statements here
}
```

For early versions of mainstream browsers (pre-Mozilla Netscape Navigator and before IE 4), you can test whether cookies are enabled by first checking for the presence of a value stored in the cookie. If no data is there, you can test write a cookie to see if it "sticks":

```
var cookieEnabled = false;
if (typeof document.cookie == "string") {
    if (document.cookie.length == 0) {
        document.cookie = "test";
        cookieEnabled = (document.cookie == "test");
        document.cookie = "";
    } else {
        cookieEnabled = true;
    }
}
```

Discussion

The longer solution also works with browsers that have the `navigator.cookieEnabled` property, so you can use one solution for all scriptable browsers. The first `if` construction verifies that the `document.cookie` property returns a string value, which it does even when cookies are disabled by the user. If the string has any content, you know that cookies are enabled and that the cookie is in use for the domain that served up the current page. But if the string is empty, you can assign a simple value to it and see if it "sticks." If the value can be read back, cookies are enabled, and you empty the cookie so as not to disturb it for regular usage.

See Also

Recipe 1.10 for using client-side cookies; Recipe 10.4 for using cookies to pass data from document to document.

5.13 Defining Browser- or Feature-Specific Links

Problem

You want a link to navigate to different destinations based on browser or object model feature support.

Solution

A link can have multiple destinations, usually with one URL hardwired to the `href` attribute of the `<a>` tag, and scripted URLs invoked from the `<a>` element's `click` event handler. The latter must cancel the default behavior of the `href` attribute.

In the following example, the scripted navigation goes to one of two destinations: one for Windows Internet Explorer users and one for all other users who are using browsers capable of referencing elements via the W3C DOM `document.getElementById()` syntax. For all other browsers, the hardwired URL is the destination:

```
function linkTo(ieWinUrl, w3Url) {
    var isWin = (navigator.userAgent.indexOf("Win") != -1);
    // invoke function from Recipe 5.3
    var isIE5Min = getIEVersionNumber() >= 5;
    var isW3 = (document.getElementById) ? true : false;
    if (isWin && isIE5Min) {
        location.href = ieWinUrl;
        return false;
    } else if (isW3) {
        location.href = w3Url;
        return false;
    }
    return true
}
```

```
...
<a href="std/newProds.html" title="To New Products"
onclick="return linkTo('ieWin/newProds.html', 'w3/newProds.html')">New Products</a>
```

When the scripted navigation succeeds, the function returns a value of `false`, which forces the `onclick` event handler to evaluate to `return false`. This automatically cancels the default behavior of the `<a>` tag. But if the browser is scriptable and not in either of the desired categories, the `onclick` event handler evaluates to `return true`, allowing the default navigation action of the `<a>` tag to prevail.

Discussion

For a public web site that you hope will be indexed by search engine spiders and "bots," make sure that every `<a>` tag has a default destination assigned to its `href` attribute, even if you expect most of your visitors' browsers to follow the scripted path. Most automated services don't interpret JavaScript, but avidly follow `href` links.

Another technique favored by some developers is to let a script triggered by the page's `load` event handler change the destination of a link based on whatever scripted criteria you have. One big advantage to this approach is that you don't need to assign an event handler to the link. The following example uses the `load` event routine from Recipe 9.3 to cause a script to modify a product catalog link to a special section for Macintosh users:

```
function setCatalogLink( ) {
    if (navigator.userAgent.indexOf("Mac") != -1) {
        document.getElementById("catalogLink").href = "products/mac/index.html";
    }
}
addOnLoadEvent(setCatalogLink);
```

You can go even further along these lines to use scripting to insert new link elements only for scriptable browser users. Use DOM tree modification (see Chapter 14) to tailor the page just for scriptable browsers.

See Also

Recipe 10.6 for using URLs to pass data from document to document; Recipe 14.2 for inserting script-generated content into the current page.

5.14   Testing on Multiple Browser Versions

Problem

You want to test a page on as many browser brands, versions, and operating systems as you can to verify compatibility, but some browsers don't allow multiple versions to be installed or run on one computer at the same time.

Solution

The commercial software program called Virtual PC by Microsoft allows you to create multiple instances of a Windows computer on a single computer. Each instance runs inside its own window and does not conflict with other instances. If you are a Windows-only user, this means that you can create and run virtual computers for different Windows and Internet Explorer versions (although Windows Vista is limited to the Enterprise, Business, or Ultimate versions). Microsoft offers the Windows version as a free download. On a PowerPC-based Macintosh, you can have the same multiple-PC setup, as well as your regular Mac OS running at the same time. Since both the virtual Windows machines and Mac can share common folders, you can edit an HTML file where you like, and load the same file into many browsers and versions at once.

Virtual PC 7 for the Macintosh does not run on the newer, Intel-based Macs, nor does it appear that Microsoft is continuing the product's development into the future. A new third-party product, called Parallels, does the job very well. The downside is that while Virtual PC for the Mac comes with a licensed copy of Windows, for Parallels you must buy a separate copy of Windows.

Discussion

As yet there is no Macintosh emulator that runs on Wintel hardware, so virtualizing Windows on a Mac is a more versatile environment than on the PC. Both are capable of creating Wintel-based instances of Linux, and both have had the x86 version of Solaris 8 install successfully (although it is officially supported only on Virtual PC for Windows).

In 2007, Apple announced a Windows version of Safari. That should help Windows-only developers test basic compatibility on that browser without owning a Mac OS X computer.

If you are in search of older browser versions to install on your virtual machines, you have a few online resources to help. The biggest repository of past browsers of many, many brands can be found at evolt's Browser Archive (*http://browsers.evolt.org*). For more recent versions of Firefox and Mozilla, visit the Mozilla.org FTP server (*ftp:// ftp.mozilla.org/pub/mozilla.org*). Recent Netscape versions can be found at Netscape's FTP server (*ftp://ftp.netscape.com/pub*). Opera 8 and later versions are available at Opera's FTP server (*ftp://ftp.opera.com/pub/opera*). With the exception of Internet Explorer, you can install multiple versions (even incremental bug fix versions) on the same computer (virtual or otherwise), provided you create a separate directory for each version in the Program Files folder. You may, however, find some browsers not wanting to run simultaneously with other versions of itself on the same computer.

CHAPTER 6

Managing Browser Windows

6.0 Introduction

Perhaps the most controversial aspect of applying DHTML techniques to web sites is messing with the browser window or windowing system. On the one hand, windows are pretty much outside the scope of Dynamic HTML, inasmuch as windows are merely containers for documents that adhere to one object model or another. But since the earliest days, windows have been part of the scripter's bag of tricks, standing ready to enhance a user's experience or torment the user with a variety of unexpected nonsense.

Most activity surrounding windows involves the `window` object. Although the `window` object has gained a large number of properties and methods over the years, the implementation across browsers is far from uniform. Part of the reason behind the disparity of `window` object features in browsers is that the `window` object is the most global context for scripting tasks. Browsers such as Internet Explorer for Windows take advantage of this context to embed numerous properties and methods that are tied to the browser application and the Windows operating system. In contrast, Mozilla empowers the `window` object with properties that are so potentially threatening to user privacy that they are accessible only through scripts that are electronically tagged on the server as being from a source to whom the user has explicitly given permission to operate (called *signed scripts*).

Window Abuse

It's unfortunate that unscrupulous web sites have abused the privilege of opening one or more additional windows automatically with JavaScript. The result has been the dreaded "pop-up" or "pop-under" advertisement that so many users find annoying. Most of us at one time or another have accidentally arrived at a web site that drops us into "pop-up hell," where each window you close opens one or more additional windows of equally unwanted content. The problem has gotten so out of hand that some Internet service providers filter web pages to strip out the offending

JavaScript code that opens subsidiary windows. Additionally, most of today's browsers build in user-selectable pop-up blocking, which intercepts some scripted attempts to open subwindows. Also, some users go so far as to turn off scripting in their browsers, thus preventing them from gaining any advantages added to sites employing Dynamic HTML. As often happens with anti-abuse software, however, these kinds of "pop-up blockers" can also block well-intentioned and otherwise harmless secondary windows.

Pop-up blocking is becoming so prevalent these days, it may be sending you a message with regard to your own development: do your best to keep everything in a single window. If a user wishes to open one of your links in a new window, a choice from the browser's context menu allows this without any difficulty. Or, you can simulate a window in modern browsers with positioned elements (see Recipe 6.11).

Window No-Nos

The more you might like to control the user's window line up to control the viewing experience of your web site, the less that browsers allow such activity. Numerous security holes would exist if browsers and scripting engines didn't have substantial safeguards built into them (some holes did exist in earlier browsers, but they are patched in the predominant versions surfing the Web today). Therefore, before you get any big ideas about window trickery, here is a compendium of the things you cannot do with scripted windows, even if your intentions are good ones:

Modifying main window chrome
> While you can resize and reposition the main browser window (Recipes 6.2, 6.3, and 6.4), you cannot add or remove window chrome—the menu bar, status bar, scrollbars, resizing widgets, toolbars, and titlebar. Mozilla lets you do this with signed scripts, but the user is queried for permission first, so you won't be able to do this without the user's knowledge. The only way to customize a window with regard to window chrome is by opening a brand new window. As you can see in Recipe 6.5, you can choose the chrome features that you want on or off in the new window.

Closing the main window from a script in a subwindow
> If you attempt to close the main window via the close( ) method (specifically, the opener.close( ) method), the user sees an alert dialog that requests permission to let the main window be closed. This warning prevents a script in a subwindow from automatically closing the main window that contains recent browser history. If the subwindow has no menu bar or titlebar, automatically closing the main window could leave the casual browser user in a pickle.

Closing other windows not created by the main window document's script

As yet, none of the browser object models provides a property that returns an array of available window references. If your page arrives in someone's browser, but is in one of several open windows, scripts in your document cannot reference the other windows, or even know how many windows are open.

Accessing document properties from other windows served by other domains

It could be potentially nasty business if a script in one window could look into another window and retrieve its URL or any of its HTML content. Browsers implement what is known as a *same-origin security policy*, which means that a script in one window (or frame) cannot access critical details (URL, DOM structure, form control settings, text content) from another window (or frame) unless both pages are delivered by the same domain and server and arrived via the same protocol (such as HTTP or HTTPS, but not both).

Intercepting or activating most browser application window buttons

Many scripters would like to intercept the Back and Forward buttons to control navigation, but these user actions do not expose themselves to the `window` object. At most, JavaScript can re-create the equivalent of clicking the Print button, but the Print dialog window always appears, and the user must click the appropriate button in that dialog box to begin actual printing.

Changing the content of the Address/Location text field

Scripts cannot override the browser's display of the current page's URL as requested from the server. The only change scripts can make in this regard is to load another page into the window (via the `location.href` property), but then the window's rendered content changes to the new destination URL.

Adding or removing entries in the Favorites/Bookmarks list

The closest one can come to automatically adding the current page to the Favorites list is in IE for Windows (via the `window.external.AddFavorite("URL", "title")` method). But even then, the browser asks for the user's permission before adding the item to the Favorites list. This list is private to the user, and is not exposed to scripts.

Modifying browser preferences

Mozilla lets signed scripts (again, with the user's permission) modify application preferences. This was built in as a networked administrative function, and is not intended for web site scripts.

The list of things you cannot do with the `window` object is long, but if you study the items carefully, you'll realize that although these taboo tasks may be common in standalone applications, they can be downright dangerous in an Internet environment. Respect every visitor's right to privacy and window layout.

6.1 Living with Browser Window Control Limitations

Problem

You or your site visitors encounter various difficulties when scripting multiple windows.

Solution

It's a sign of the times: thanks to so much abuse by pesky web sites and adware, browser makers now give substantial control over window behavior to the user. Although the scripting powers are still in the browsers, your scripts cannot determine at a glance whether the user allows pop-up windows to open or the main window to be move or resized. Designing a site that relies on these capabilities is an extremely risky proposition these days. You must assume that a visitor has every malleable feature disabled.

An all-too-common situation is that the page author creates scripts with pop-up blocking turned off in the test browser. But when the page loads into a browser with pop-up blocking turned on, the scripting fails to work, and the scripter is flummoxed. It's best to design in a restricted environment because increasingly, your visitors will be arriving the same way. Several recipes in this chapter provide scripts that may not work in a restricted environment.

Discussion

A large percentage of attempts to open subwindows occur in response to the main window's load or unload events. It is these events' trigger of the window.open( ) method that has caused the most pop-up window grief among browser users (see Recipe 6.5). It is precisely this activity that browser pop-up blockers prevent from executing. You may find that invoking window.open( ) in other event contexts (such as clicking a button) still works, but you need to test on a wide variety of browsers, each set to all possible pop-up blocker settings in their preferences.

Even if you are successful at opening a subwindow or convincing your visitors to allow scripted window movement and resizing for your site (if the browser allows domain-specific settings), other restrictions may apply. For example, Mozilla and Safari do not allow moving a browser window off the screen by way of scripts.

See Also

Recipes 6.2 through 6.5 for various window control solutions whose success may be influenced by user preference settings.

6.2   Setting the Main Window's Size

Problem

You want to resize the browser window that contains the current page.

Solution

Ever since version 4 of Internet Explorer and Netscape, scripters have been able to adjust the pixel size of the browser window with two `window` object methods: `resizeTo()` and `resizeBy()`. To resize the window to a specific pixel size, use the `resizeTo()` method:

```
window.resizeTo(800, 600);
```

To increase or decrease the size of the window by a fixed pixel amount, use the `resizeBy()` method:

```
window.resizeBy(50, -10);
```

Adjustments affect the outside measure of the browser window.

Discussion

Both parameters are in pixel measures and are required for both methods. The first value affects the width of the window, and the second value affects the height. In the case of the `resizeBy()` method, if you want to modify only one axis value, pass a value of 0 as the other parameter.

When you resize a window, the position of the top-left corner of the window does not change. Instead, the right and bottom edges of the window move to meet the requirements of the method parameters. See Recipes 6.3 and 6.4 for ways to move and maximize the window.

These two `window` object methods may also be applied to subwindows that your scripts open (see Recipe 6.5). As long as the script that creates the new window maintains a reference to the subwindow in a global variable, you can reference that window's `resizeTo()` and `resizeBy()` methods.

Resizing the window to accommodate content of a known size isn't as easy to do across browsers as it might seem. Only Mozilla, Safari, and Opera provide a pair of read/write properties—`innerHeight` and `innerWidth`—that let you specifically control the content region of the browser window. Internet Explorer provides no comparable scriptable feature (the dimensions are read-only via `document.body.parentNode.clientHeight` and `document.body.parentNode.clientWidth`). Trying to use the outer window dimensions as a guide to the content region size is not reliable. Users can select different sets of toolbars and toolbar settings that can throw off careful calculations you make on test browsers.

Whether you should script the size of a window that is already open is hotly debated among user interface designers. By and large, users are not fond of web pages hijacking their browser windows. It's not uncommon, especially for experienced users, to have a carefully customized layout of application windows on the desktop. Along comes a maverick web page that makes the browser window take over nearly the entire screen. Upon leaving the site, the web browser window remains in its giant size, and the user must reconstruct the desktop arrangement. Take these considerations into account before you deploy window resizing.

See Also

Recipe 6.1 for potential problems adjusting a window's size; Recipe 6.3 for setting the position of the window on the screen; Recipe 6.4 for a way to approximate a maximized window; Recipe 6.5 for how to open a new window.

6.3   Positioning the Main Window

Problem

You want to move the top-left corner of the browser window to a specific point on the screen.

Solution

Modern browsers provide two `window` object methods that adjust the position of the browser window: `moveTo( )` and `moveBy( )`. To move the window to a screen coordinate point, use the `moveTo( )` method:

```
window.moveTo(10, 20);
```

To shift the position of the window by a known pixel amount, use the `moveBy( )` method:

```
window.moveBy(0, 10);
```

The window remains the same size when you move it.

Discussion

The coordinate space of the screen is laid out such that the top-left corner of the video display area is point 0,0. The viewable area of your screen has positive coordinate values for both numbers. Negative values are "off the screen," as are values that are larger than the number of pixels displayed on the screen.

While Internet Explorer used to allow scripts to move the window completely off screen if the parameters dictate it, Mozilla and Safari resist doing so, and IE's recent security upgrades turn off that option by default. In fact, the browsers resist moving any portion of the window out of view if at all possible. Moving the browser window completely out of view is an unfriendly thing to do, especially in Windows, where the window will reveal its existence in the Taskbar, but the user won't be able to see its contents. The user must then use the Taskbar's context menu to close the window and application. Hidden windows such as this have, in the past, been used to exploit security flaws in Internet Explorer to carry out such nefarious tasks as monitoring activity in another window.

While you can set the position of a window created by a script (see Recipe 6.5), you can also modify the position after the window has appeared. As long as the script that creates the new window maintains a reference to the subwindow in a global variable, you can reference that window's moveTo( ) and moveBy( ) methods.

See Also

Recipe 6.5 for resizing a script-generated window.

6.4   Maximizing the Main Window

Problem

You want to expand the browser window so that it occupies the same screen real estate as a maximized (Windows) application window.

Solution

Use the following function, which operates best in Internet Explorer 5 or later, Mozilla, and Safari:

```
function maximizeWindow( ) {
    window.moveTo(0, 0);
    window.resizeTo(screen.availWidth, screen.availHeight);
}
```

Although the window may occupy the entire screen and appear to be maximized (in the Windows OS sense), the browser is not officially maximized.

Discussion

The notion of maximizing (and minimizing) a window is primarily a Windows phenomenon. Macintosh windows, for example, have an icon that performs an optimization for window size, but it tends to leave a space along the right edge of the screen so that a portion of the underlying Desktop is still visible. A maximized window under Windows, however, occupies the entire screen except for the Taskbar (if the Taskbar is visible in your preferences settings).

Scripts can, at best, simulate a maximized window, but even then, there are some limitations for one browser or another. First of all, a truly maximized window in Windows XP is not positioned at point 0,0 of the screen. Instead, the top-left corner of the window is located at point -4,-4, which is just slightly off-screen. This hides the four-pixel border around the window, and lets the active part of the window (including titlebar, toolbars, and scrollbars) "bleed" right to the edge of the video screen. The Macintosh doesn't behave this way, choosing instead to allow the thin window border to be visible at all times.

Due to security restrictions (or preferences) in current browsers, it is not good to rely on moving the pseudo-maximized window outside the bounds of the display by script. Old techniques of faking the "bleed" beyond the screen in IE no longer work everywhere.

To determine the space available for a simulated maximized window, the screen object's availWidth and availHeight properties provide sufficient detail for most operating systems and browsers. In the case of Windows, these properties return dimensions of the space other than that occupied by the Taskbar. The only detail you cannot deduce is whether the Taskbar is in its default location at the bottom of the screen or the user has moved it to the top. On the Macintosh side, the screen. availHeight property begins its measure immediately below the universal menu bar. In fact, browsers treat the screen space so that coordinate 0,0 is at the top-left corner of the available space. Thus, positioning the window at 0,0 to simulate a maximized window does not slip the window underneath and make it partially obscured by the menu bar. To make a pseudomaximized window appear more Mac-friendly, consider altering the width component of the resizeTo( ) method to leave about 100 horizontal pixels uncovered on the right side.

Just as there is no scripted way to officially maximize a window, there is no equivalent to minimizing the window either. IE for Windows no longer allows scripts to move a window off-screen.

See Also

Recipe 6.2 for other window resizing advice.

6.5   Creating a New Window

Problem

You want to open a separate subwindow based on scripted action in the main window.

Solution

To generate a new window, use the window.open( ) method, passing parameters for the (absolute or relative) URL of the page to occupy the new window, a text name for the window, and a comma-delimited string of parameters that specify the window's physical characteristics. For example:

```
var newWind = window.open("subDoc.html", "subWindow",
                "status,menubar,height=400,width=300");
```

Preserve the value returned by the method (a reference to the subwindow object) in a global variable if you intend to reference the subwindow from the main window's scripts in other functions later on.

Discussion

If you are not loading an existing document (or one returned by a server process) into the new window, pass an empty string as the first parameter to open the window with a blank content region (so that you can later write dynamic content to it). The window name in the second parameter is the same kind of name that a hyperlink or form's target attribute points to. You should always provide a unique name, to keep multiple subwindows from accidentally colliding with each other in the global naming scope.

Probably the trickiest part of creating a new window is defining the third parameter, a comma-delimited string of window properties. If you omit the third parameter altogether, the browser creates a window of the same dimensions and characteristics as the one that it would create if the user were to select New Window from the File menu (which is not necessarily the same size as the current window). But more typically, you want to control attributes such as size, location, and the amount of window "chrome" displayed in the window. Table 6-1 lists all of the window attributes that you can specify as part of the third parameter to window.open( ), and the browser versions that support them.

Table 6-1. Window attributes for window.open() method

Attribute	IE	Mozilla	Safari	Opera	Description
alwaysLowered	n/a	<1.7	n/a	n/a	Always behind all other browser windows. Signed script required.
alwaysRaised	n/a	<1.7	n/a	n/a	Always in front of all other browser windows. Signed script required.
channelMode	4	n/a	n/a	n/a	Show in theater mode with channel band.
chrome	n/a	1.7	n/a	n/a	Displays content with no chrome, user interface features, or keyboard commands. Signed script required.
close	n/a	all	n/a	n/a	For dialog type, set to no to remove close box. Signed script required.
copyhistory	3	all	n/a	n/a	Copy history listing from opening window to new window.
dependent	n/a	all	n/a	n/a	Subwindow closes if the window that opened it closes.
dialog	n/a	1.2	n/a	n/a	Window controls for minimize and maximize hidden.

Table 6-1. Window attributes for window.open( ) method (continued)

Attribute	IE	Mozilla	Safari	Opera	Description
directories	3	all	n/a	n/a	Display directory buttons.
fullscreen	4	n/a	n/a	n/a	Display no titlebar or menus.
height	3	all	all	7	Window height in pixels.
hotkeys	n/a	all	n/a	n/a	Disables menu keyboard shortcuts (except Quit and Security Info).
innerHeight	n/a	all	n/a	n/a	Content region height. Signed script required for very small measures.
innerWidth	n/a	all	n/a	n/a	Content region width. Signed script required for very small measures.
left	4	all	all	n/a	Offset of window's left edge from left edge of screen.
location	3	all	all	n/a	Display Location (or Address) text field.
menubar	3	all	n/a	n/a	Display menubar (a menubar is always visible on Mac).
minimizable	n/a	1.2	n/a	n/a	For dialog type, includes minimize control.
modal	n/a	1.2	n/a	n/a	Open window as a modal. Signed script required.
outerHeight	n/a	all	n/a	n/a	Total window height. Signed script required for very small measures.
outerWidth	n/a	all	n/a	n/a	Total window width. Signed script required for very small measures.
personalbar	n/a	all	n/a	n/a	Mozilla-specific alternative to the directories attribute.
resizable	3	all	all	n/a	Allow window resizing (always allowed on Mac).
screenX	n/a	all	n/a	n/a	Offset of window's left edge from left edge of screen. Signed script required to move window off-screen.
screenY	n/a	all	n/a	n/a	Offset of window's top edge from top edge of screen. Signed script required to move window off-screen.
scrollbars	3	all	all	n/a	Display scrollbars if document is too large for window.
status	3	all	n/a	n/a	Display status bar.
titlebar	n/a	all	n/a	n/a	Displays titlebar. Set this value to no to hide the titlebar. Signed script required.
toolbar	3	all	n/a	n/a	Display toolbar (with Back, Forward, and other buttons).
top	4	all	all	7	Offset of window's top edge from top edge of screen.
width	3	all	all	n/a	Window width in pixels.
z-lock	n/a	all	n/a	n/a	New window is fixed below browser windows. Signed script required.

You can include attributes supported by some browsers but not others in the attribute string. Browsers that don't know about a particular attribute simply ignore the attribute. Most of the attributes are Boolean types, indicating whether the feature should be turned on in the new window. For these attributes, you can either assign them values (yes or 1 to switch them on; no or 0 to switch them off), or simply include the attribute name by itself to signify that the feature should be turned on. The following two examples display the menu bar and status bar and allow the window to be resized:

```
window.open("someDoc.html", "newWind", "menubar,status,resizable");
window.open("someDoc.html", "newWind", "menubar=1,status=1,resizable=1");
```

For Boolean attributes that control window chrome (such as location, resizable, and status), the features are turned on by default; other Booleans (such as alwaysRaised and fullscreen) are turned off by default. An important point to remember is that if you specify even just one attribute, all Boolean values are automatically switched off. Therefore, if you assign a height and width for the window, also turn on the window chrome features you wish to appear in the window. Also, for optimum backward-compatibility, assemble the string of attributes and their values without any spaces after the commas.

In addition to controlling the window chrome that appears in the window, you can set the location of the window on the screen. For example, you can come close to centering the window with a little bit of calculation prior to assigning a value to the left and top attributes (in browsers that support them). The hedge is that the dimensions you can specify for the window across browsers control only the content region of the window, and not any chrome. Thick toolbars of unknown height can throw off the calculations just a bit. Here is a function that opens a new window to a fixed interior size and centers that space on the screen:

```
var myWindow;
function openCenteredWindow(url) {
    var width = 400;
    var height = 300;
    var left = parseInt((screen.availWidth/2) - (width/2));
    var top = parseInt((screen.availHeight/2) - (height/2));
    var windowFeatures = "width=" + width + ",height=" + height +
        ",status,resizable,left=" + left + ",top=" + top +
        ",screenX=" + left + ",screenY=" + top;
    myWindow = window.open(url, "subWind", windowFeatures);
}
```

If it's possible for the user to open the window more than once, there are other factors to consider when creating the window. See Recipe 6.6 for the case in which the user has hidden the subwindow, and all your script needs to do is bring it in front of the main window.

The issue of whether you should open a subwindow automatically for a visitor is another one of those hotly contested user interface design topics. Unfortunately for scripters who may have valid reasons for opening a secondary window, the world of the "pop-up" advertisement has turned many users against any web site that starts opening multiple windows. A case that used to be made for using secondary windows as the targets for hyperlinks and form submissions was that the site developer didn't want to lose the visitor to another site in the course of web surfing, for fear that the visitor would not come back quickly. The result, however, was that users could find themselves with many windows open on their desktop, cluttering up their workspace.

Cases against opening secondary windows abound. For one, users who know about their browser's context menu (right-click in Windows and Unix, Ctrl-click in Mac OS X) can choose to open a new window on any link they see. That puts the visitor in control of the window madness. Another case from the document markup purist point of view is that secondary windows (and even frames) have no place in electronic documents. It is no accident, for instance, that the target attribute is removed from the strict XHTML specification for hyperlinks and forms. And one final case, which may have the most impact on the development world, is a result of the backlash against pop-up ads. Many service providers use a variety of techniques to filter the window.open( ) method from pages they serve or pass through to their users.

If you decide to use secondary windows, apply them judiciously and only when they add value to the visitor's experience or solve some other technical requirement of your application. The more you try to trap your visitors with tricks, the less likely it is that they'll come back or recommend the site to others.

See Also

Recipe 6.6 for controlling window layering; Recipes 6.7 and 6.8 for script communication between a main window and script-generated window; Recipe 6.10 to use a subwindow as a simulated cross-browser modal window.

6.6   Bringing a Window to the Front

Problem

You want to bring a window that is buried beneath other windows back to the top of the pile.

Solution

For any window to which you have a valid reference, invoke the focus( ) method. The following function expands on topics addressed in Recipe 6.5. This expanded function not only opens a subwindow, but brings it forward if it was previously opened, and is currently hidden behind the main window:

```
var newWindow;
function makeNewWindow(url) {
```

```
    if (!newWindow || newWindow.closed) {
        newWindow = window.open(url,"subwind","status,height=200,width=300");
    } else {
        // window is already open, so bring it to the front
        newWindow.focus();
    }
}
```

Thus, if you have a link, button, or other script action that invokes makeNewWindow( ) after the window has been created and (accidentally or intentionally) hidden, the next activation of the function brings the new window into view.

Discussion

A global variable, newWindow in the preceding example, is initialized as null when the main page loads. The first time the makeNewWindow( ) method is called, the first conditional expression evaluates to true because the variable is still null. The new window is created, and the variable now holds a reference to the subwindow. Let's say that rather than closing the subwindow, the user clicks somewhere on the main window, causing the subwindow to submarine underneath the main window. If the user clicks on the button that invokes makeNewWindow( ) again, the first if condition fails (because newWindow contains an object reference), but a test of the closed property of the subwindow returns false. Execution branches to the alternate section, invoking the focus( ) method on the new window.

You can begin to see in this example how valuable it is to maintain a reference to the subwindow when you create it with window.open( ). But you also have to be careful to check with the closed property before referencing the object to do things like giving it focus or closing it via the close( ) method. Once you assign the subwindow's reference to the variable, the reference doesn't go away when the window closes. The variable still contains what it thinks is a valid window object reference. But when you attempt to use that reference in a statement to access one of its methods or properties, the reference fails, leading to a script error. And, since you cannot control whether a user closes a subwindow or leaves it open, it's up to your scripts to do the checking behind the scenes.

See Also

Recipe 6.5 for opening multiple windows by script; Recipe 6.10 for a simulated cross-browser modal window that always stays on top.

6.7   Communicating with a New Window

Problem

You want to access the subwindow and its document from scripts in the main window.

Solution

Provided you preserve the reference to the subwindow returned by the window.open( ) method, and if the content of the subwindow is served by the same domain and server as the main window document, you can access any property or method that you are able to from scripts within the subwindow.

The following complete HTML page contains two functions that create a new window and populate its content with dynamically written content:

```html
<html>
<head>
<title>A New Window</title>
<script type="text/javascript">
// global variable for subwindow reference
var newWindow;
// generate and fill the new window
function makeNewWindow( ) {
    // make sure it isn't already opened
    if (!newWindow || newWindow.closed) {
        newWindow = window.open("","sub","status,height=200,width=300");
        // delay writing until window exists in IE/Windows
        setTimeout("writeToWindow( )", 50);
    } else if (newWindow.focus) {
        // window is already open and focusable, so bring it to the front
        newWindow.focus( );
    }
}
function writeToWindow( ) {
    // assemble content for new window
    var newContent = "<html><head><title>Secondary  Window</title></head>";
    newContent += "<body><h1>This is a script-created window.</h1>";
    newContent += "</body></html>";
    // write HTML to new window document
    newWindow.document.write(newContent);
    newWindow.document.close( ); // close layout stream
}
</script>
</head>
<body>
<form>
<input type="button" value="Create New Window" onclick="makeNewWindow( );" />
</form>
</body>
</html>
```

Discussion

The example in the Solution points out an important aspect of referencing a newly created window. Internet Explorer for Windows tends to race ahead of script execution (presumably to improve performance). The downside of this feature is that in the case of a newly created external object, a reference to the new object may not be valid when the subsequent statements execute in the shadows. To prevent this race-ahead execution from causing script errors, you need to place statements referencing the object in a separate function that begins executing after the current function thread completes. The setTimeout( ) method is the mechanism that assists in this task.

How much time you build into the setTimeout( ) delay is not important. The 50 milliseconds shown in the example is an exceptionally small amount of time (from the user's perspective), but it's enough to keep processing in order, and allow global variable references to the new window to be valid when needed. You can use this same technique for any kind of immediate access to a newly created window. But if, for example, you have two distinct user actions (e.g., two buttons)—one to create the window and one to populate it—you don't need the setTimeout( ) because the second button's event handler function will be executing in a separate thread anyway.

Some versions of IE for Windows are particularly sensitive to potential cross-domain security breeches. Moreover, the results can be different when the main page is hosted on a local hard disk (for testing) and a web server (for deployment). You'll know if you're having the problem when a reference to the subwindow or one of its properties results in an "Access is denied" script error.

Because a subwindow reference returned from the window.open( ) method is an object reference (with no string equivalent), you cannot pass this reference between pages that occupy the main window. In other words, do not expect to open a subwindow from one page and have a script in a subsequent main window page be able to reference it. The only possible workaround is to display your main window document in a frame of a frameset (with the other frame hidden if you don't want the user to see the frames). When you create the new window, copy the returned reference to a global variable either in the frameset (parent window) or the other child frame. A new visible document in the main window can then read that global variable to obtain a reference to the subwindow.

Regard a reference to a subwindow just like any window or frame reference. Any global variables defined in the subwindow's document scripts are accessible from the main window in the subwindow's global variable space:

```
var remoteValue = newWind.someVar;
```

Access to the document's contents goes through the document object of the subwindow, as in the following examples:

```
var remoteBody = newWind.document.body;
newWind.document.getElementById("myTextBox").value = "fred";
```

Adjusting the URL of the subwindow is just like doing the same for the main window, but with the leading subwindow reference:

```
newWind.location.href = "yetAnotherPage.html";
```

Be careful when you start loading new documents into either the main or secondary window, however. The only error-free way to close a subwindow from a script in the main window is if the document invoking `close()` is also the document that opened the window. Plus, if your script or the user loads a document into the subwindow from a different server and domain, your main window scripts lose the ability to read the `location` object or any document content objects in the subwindow—all in the name of securing the browser from nefarious scripts capable of tracking surfing habits.

See Also

Recipe 6.8 to see how scripts in a subwindow talk to the main window; Recipe 10.5 for passing data between pages via frames.

6.8   Communicating Back to the Main Window

Problem

You want a script in a subwindow to access variables or document content in the main window.

Solution

With one very early exception (Netscape 2), all scriptable browsers automatically assign an `opener` property to a window created via the `window.open()` method. Scripts in the subwindow can reach the main window or frame via this `opener` property. Here is an example of a subwindow script that copies a text box value from the subwindow to a hidden input field in the main window:

```
opener.document.forms["userData"].age.value = document.forms["entry"].userAge.value;
```

The `opener` property references the window or frame whose script executed the `window.open()` method.

Discussion

Any window opened by the user reports that the `opener` property is `null`. Therefore, your scripts can test whether the current window was opened by script or manually by comparing the value or type of opener:

```
if (typeof window.opener == "object") {
    // current subwindow opened by script
}
```

If the subwindow is opened by a script running inside a frame, the `opener` property of the subwindow points to the frame holding the document whose `window.open()` method created the window. This means that you can still script your way through the main frameset, if needed. For example, a subwindow can access a form value in another frame of the main window frameset with syntax like the following:

```
opener.parent.frames["prefs"].document.dataForm.colorChoice.value = "#66eeff";
```

The same-origin security policy observed in access to a subwindow (Recipe 6.7) also applies going in the other direction. If the document in the main window or frame changes to one from a different server and domain, attempted access to details of that document via the opener property fails with security errors.

See Also

Recipe 6.7 to see how scripts in the main window communicate with content in a script-generated window.

6.9   Using Internet Explorer Modal/Modeless Windows

Problem

You want to stop script processing while a modal dialog window appears, and then capture user-entered values from the dialog window to continue processing.

Solution

Internet Explorer 4 or later (both Windows and Macintosh versions) and Safari 2.01 or later provide a window object method that displays a true modal dialog window (preventing user access to the main window until the dialog window closes). IE 5 or later for Windows provides an additional choice that creates a modeless window, which always stays in front of the main window, but allows access to the main window's user interface elements. The methods are called window.showModalDialog( ) and window.showModelessDialog( ), respectively.

To use either method, begin by assembling the data or object references you wish to pass to the dialog window (if any) as a JavaScript object (of any data type) in a variable. We use dialogArgs here. Find the place in your script where you need to query the user for input, and then invoke the method:

```
var dialogAnswer = window.showModalDialog("dialog.html", dialogArgs,
    "dialogWidth:300px; dialogHeight:201px; center:yes");
```

Scripts in the document loaded into the dialog window can access the passed arguments by reading the window.dialogArguments property. To get values back to the main window's script from a modal dialog, assign those values (again, of any JavaScript data type) to the window.returnValue property of the dialog window's document. When the user closes the dialog window, the returned value is assigned to the variable at the left side of the expression (dialogAnswer in the preceding example).

Discussion

IE modal dialog windows do not maintain the same kind of live connection between main and dialog windows as you use with full windows created via `window.open( )`. But the chord between main and dialog windows isn't entirely broken, either.

For example, a script in the main window can pass a reference to one of the main document's element objects to the `showModalDialog( )` method; a script in the dialog window can then use the passed reference as a way to inspect a property of that object. Here is a simple example, starting with the main window that passes a reference to a `form` element to the modal dialog window:

```html
<html>
<head>
<title>Launch a Modal Dialog</title>
<script type="text/javascript">
function openDialog(form) {
    var result = window.showModalDialog("dialogDoc.html", form,
        "dialogWidth:300px; dialogHeight:201px; center:yes");
}
</script>
</head>
<body>
<form name="sample" action="#" onsubmit="return false">
Enter your name for the dialog box:<input name="yourName" type="text" />
<input type="button" value="Send to Dialog" onclick="openDialog(this.form)" />
</form>
</body>
</html>
```

The document in the dialog window can read the value of the main window's text box as needed:

```html
<html>
<head>
<title>Modal Dialog</title>
</head>
<body>
<script type="text/javascript">
document.write("Greetings from " + window.dialogArguments.yourName.value + "!");
</script>
</body>
</html>
```

A modeless dialog window behaves slightly differently from a scripting point of view. Most important, main document script processing does not stop when the modeless window appears. This is logical because a modeless window is intended to allow user interaction in both windows, while the modal dialog window simply stays in front of the main window. Second, the value returned by the `showModelessDialog( )` method is a reference to the modeless dialog window. This allows scripts in the main window to communicate with the modeless dialog after it is created.

It's not uncommon for a call that invokes showModelessDialog() to pass either a reference to the main window or a reference to a main window function that needs to be invoked from the dialog window while it is still open (similar to the notion of an Apply button in many Windows system dialog boxes). Passing the main window reference looks like the following:

```
var dialogWind = window.showModelessDialog("myModeless.html", window,
    "dialogWidth:300px; dialogHeight:201px; center:yes");
```

A script in the dialog window's document can then use the value of window. dialogArguments as a starting point to any global variable, function, or element object in the main window's context:

```
var mainWind = window.dialogArguments;
mainWind.document.body.style.backgroundColor = "lightyellow";
```

The window.returnValue property is not used in the modeless dialog. Communicate back to the main window directly. In fact, you can invoke main document functions from the modeless window. One way is to use the window reference passed to the dialogArguments property:

```
// in main window script
window.showModelessDialog("myModeless.html", window, "...");

// in dialog window script
var mainWind = window.dialogArguments;
mainWind.myFunction();
```

Or pass a reference to the main document function:

```
// in main window script
window.showModelessDialog("myModeless.html", myFunction, "...");

// in dialog window script
var mainFunc = window.dialogArguments;
mainFunc();
```

When you open either type of dialog window, the optional third parameter is a comma-delimited string of properties for the window. The syntax for this string is reminiscent of CSS name:property formatting, as shown in the previous examples. Table 6-2 lists the properties you can use and a description of their values.

Table 6-2. Properties for showModalDialog() and showModelessDialog()

Property	Value	Default	Description
center	yes | no | 1 | 0 | on | off	yes	Center the dialog
dialogHeight	Length/units	n/a	Outer height of dialog (must be >200 for IE/Mac)
dialogLeft	Integer	n/a	Left pixel offset (overrides center)
dialogTop	Integer	n/a	Top pixel offset (overrides center)
dialogWidth	Length/units	n/a	Outer width of dialog (must be >200 for IE/Mac)
edge	raised | sunken	raised	Transition style between border and content area

Property	Value	Default	Description
help	yes | no | 1 | 0 | on | off	Yes	Display help icon in titlebar
resizable	yes | no | 1 | 0 | on | off	No	Dialog is resizable
status	yes | no | 1 | 0 | on | off	Yes	Display status bar

As with any potentially intrusive user interface element, don't overuse the modal or modeless window.

If you intend to use the showModalDialog( ) window to display a form that is to be submitted to a server, the default behavior of IE is to open yet another window to display the page returned by the server. Another problem is that cookies to not carry over from the main window to the modal window, even when the content of both windows originate from the same domain and server. Steinar Overbeck Cook has solved these issues in a library you can download from *http://dannyg.com/support/ SOCmodalWindow.js*.

See Also

Recipe 6.10 for a way to produce a modal window for IE and NN browsers with a subwindow; Recipe 6.11 for a layer-based modal window simulator.

6.10 Simulating a Cross-Browser Modal Dialog Window

Problem

You want to present a consistent modal dialog on multiple browsers.

Solution

Although IE provides the showModalDialog( ) method, no other browser supports it, except Safari. This recipe uses a browser subwindow to simulate the behavior of a modal dialog box. It operates in IE 4 or later, Mozilla, Safari, and Opera 7 or later. Note that this is a simulation of true modality. Due to some odd behavior in IE for Windows with respect to disabling hyperlinks in the main window, a determined user can bypass the modality of this solution. For casual users, however, the window behaves much like a modal dialog box.

Assemble your main HTML page around the *simModal.js* script library described in the Discussion. This library works by disabling form controls and links in the main page after the modal dialog is displayed and making sure the dialog keeps the focus, so that the user is forced to deal with the dialog. After the dialog is dismissed, the form controls and links are enabled again. All of this work occurs through a single dialogWin object defined in the library.

The following skeletal HTML main page shows the event handler additions that the *simModal.js* library relies upon, and a demonstration of how to invoke the function that displays a simulated modal window (in this example, a Preferences window):

```html
<html>
<head>
<title>Main Application Page</title>
<script type="text/javascript" src="eventsManager.js"></script>
<script type="text/javascript" src="simModal.js"></script>
<script type="text/javascript">
// function to run upon closing the dialog with "OK".
function setPrefs( ) {
    // Statements here to apply choices from the dialog window
}
</script>
</head>
<body>
<!-- Page Content Here -->
<button onclick="dialogWin.openSimDialog('dialog_main.html', 400, 300, setPrefs)">
Preferences
</button>
<!-- More Page Content Here -->
</body>
</html>
```

Note that the *simModal.js* library relies on the *eventsManager.js* library from Recipe 9.1. No other modifications are needed in the host page.

Call the openSimDialog( ) function to display the window, passing the URL of the page to load into the dialog window, the window's width and height (in pixels), and a reference to a function in the main page that the modal window invokes when the window closes (setPrefs( ) in this case).

In the document that loads into the dialog window, add the closeme( ), handleOK( ), and handleCancel( ) functions shown in the following extract to take care of the actions from the dialog window's Cancel and OK buttons. The load and unload event handlers of the <body> tag trigger essential event-blocking services controlled by the blockEvents( ) and unblockEvents( ) event handlers in the *simModal.js* library.

```html
<html>
<head>
<title>Preferences</title>
<script language="JavaScript" type="text/javascript">
// close the dialog
function closeme( ) {
    window.close( );
}

// handle click of OK button
function handleOK( ) {
```

```
            if (opener && !opener.closed && opener.dialogWin) {
                opener.dialogWin.returnFunc();
            } else {
                alert("You have closed the main window.\n\nNo action will be taken on the " +
                    "choices in this dialog box.");
            }
            closeme();
            return false;
        }

        // handle click of Cancel button
        function handleCancel() {
            closeme();
            return false;
        }
    </script>
    </head>
    <body onload="if (opener && opener.dialogWin.blockEvents) opener.dialogWin.
    blockEvents()" onunload="if
    (opener && opener.dialogWin.unblockEvents) opener.dialogWin.unblockEvents()">
    <!--- Dialog Window Page Content Here -->
    <form>
    <input type="button" value="Cancel" onclick="handleCancel()">
    <input type="button" value="  OK  " onclick="handleOK()">
    </form>

    </body>
    </html>
```

If the dialog window contains a frameset (where the Cancel and OK buttons are in one of the frames), locate the load and unload event handlers in the `<frameset>` tag. Keep the three functions in the framesetting document, and have the onclick event handlers of the buttons reference parent.handleCancel() and parent.handleOK().

Discussion

Example 6-1 shows the entire *simModal.js* library, which you link into the main HTML page, as shown in the Solution.

Example 6-1. The simulated modal dialog window script library (simModal.js)

```
// One object tracks the current modal dialog opened from this window.
var dialogWin = {
    // Since links in some browsers cannot be truly disabled, preserve
    // link click & mouseout event handlers while they're "disabled."
    // Restore when re-enabling the main window.
    linkClicks : null,
    // Event handler to inhibit Navigator 4 form element
    // and IE link activity when dialog window is active.
    deadend : function(evt) {
        if (this.win && !this.win.closed) {
            if (evt) {
                evt.preventDefault();
                evt.stopPropagation();
```

Example 6-1. The simulated modal dialog window script library (simModal.js) (continued)

```
            }
            this.win.focus( );
            return false;
        }
    },
    // Disable form elements and links in all frames.
    disableForms : function( ) {
        this.linkClicks = new Array( );
        for (var i = 0; i < document.forms.length; i++) {
            for (var j = 0; j < document.forms[i].elements.length; j++) {
                document.forms[i].elements[j].disabled = true;
            }
        }
        for (i = 0; i < document.links.length; i++) {
            this.linkClicks[i] = {click:document.links[i].onclick, up:null};
            this.linkClicks[i].up = document.links[i].onmouseup;
            document.links[i].onclick = dialogWin.deadend;
            document.links[i].onmouseup = dialogWin.deadend;
            document.links[i].disabled = true;
        }
    },
    // Restore form elements and links to normal behavior.
    enableForms : function( ) {
        for (var i = 0; i < document.forms.length; i++) {
            for (var j = 0; j < document.forms[i].elements.length; j++) {
                document.forms[i].elements[j].disabled = false;
            }
        }
        for (i = 0; i < document.links.length; i++) {
            document.links[i].onclick = this.linkClicks[i].click;
            document.links[i].onmouseup = this.linkClicks[i].up;
            document.links[i].disabled = false;
        }
    },
    // Disable form elements.
    blockEvents : function( ) {
        this.disableForms( );
        window.onfocus = dialogWin.checkModal;
        document.body.onclick = dialogWin.checkModal;
        addEvent(document, "click", dialogWin.checkModal, true);
        addEvent(document, "mousemove", dialogWin.checkModal, true);
    },
    // As dialog closes, restore the main window's original
    // event mechanisms.
    unblockEvents : function( ) {
        this.enableForms( );.
        window.onfocus = null;
        removeEvent(document, "click", dialogWin.checkModal, true);
        removeEvent(document, "mousemove", dialogWin.checkModal, true);
    },
    // Generate a modal dialog.
```

```
// Parameters:
//    url -- URL of the page/frameset to be loaded into dialog
//    width -- pixel width of the dialog window
//    height -- pixel height of the dialog window
//    returnFunc -- reference to the function (on this page)
//                  that is to act on the data returned from the dialog
//    args -- [optional] any data you need to pass to the dialog
openSimDialog : function(url, width, height, returnFunc, args) {
    if (!this.win || (this.win && this.win.closed)) {
        // Initialize properties of the modal dialog object.
        this.url = url;
        this.width = width;
        this.height = height;
        this.returnFunc = returnFunc;
        this.args = args;
        this.returnedValue = "";
        // Keep name unique.
        this.name = (new Date()).getSeconds().toString();
        // Assemble window attributes and try to center the dialog.
        if (window.screenX) {               // Moz, Saf, Op
            // Center on the main window.
            this.left = window.screenX +
                ((window.outerWidth - this.width) / 2);
            this.top = window.screenY +
                ((window.outerHeight - this.height) / 2);
            var attr = "screenX=" + this.left +
                ",screenY=" + this.top + ",resizable=no,width=" +
                this.width + ",height=" + this.height;
        } else if (window.screenLeft) {     // IE 5+/Windows
            // Center (more or less) on the IE main window.
            // Start by estimating window size,
            // taking IE6+ CSS compatibility mode into account
            var CSSCompat = (document.compatMode &&
                document.compatMode != "BackCompat");
            window.outerWidth = (CSSCompat) ?
                document.body.parentElement.clientWidth :
                document.body.clientWidth;
            window.outerHeight = (CSSCompat) ?
                document.body.parentElement.clientHeight :
                document.body.clientHeight;
            window.outerHeight -= 80;
            this.left = parseInt(window.screenLeft+
                ((window.outerWidth - this.width) / 2));
            this.top = parseInt(window.screenTop +
                ((window.outerHeight - this.height) / 2));
            var attr = "left=" + this.left +
                ",top=" + this.top + ",resizable=no,width=" +
                this.width + ",height=" + this.height;
        } else {                            // all the rest
            // The best we can do is center in screen.
            this.left = (screen.width - this.width) / 2;
            this.top = (screen.height - this.height) / 2;
```

```
                var attr = "left=" + this.left + ",top=" +
                    this.top + ",resizable=no,width=" + this.width +
                    ",height=" + this.height;
            }
            // Generate the dialog and make sure it has focus.
            this.win=window.open(this.url, this.name, attr);
            this.win.focus( );
        } else {
            this.win.focus( );
        }
    },
    // Invoked by focus event handler of EVERY frame,
    // return focus to dialog window if it's open.
    checkModal : function( ) {
        setTimeout("dialogWin.finishChecking( )", 50);
        return true;
    },
    finishChecking : function( ) {
        if (this.win && !this.win.closed) {
            this.win.focus( );
        }
    }
}
};
```

The library creates one global variable, named `dialogWin`, which becomes the object through which all dialog-related operations flow.

The `deadend( )` function is an event handler function that the *simModal.js* library assigns to all main page hyperlinks whenever the dialog box is visible. The function does its best to block the default action of clicking on a hyperlink.

Next are a pair of functions that disable or enable form controls and links. The `disableForms( )` method is ultimately invoked when the modal window appears (the dialog window's onload event handler invokes `blockEvents( )`, which, in turn, calls `disableForms( )`). Default event handler assignments for hyperlinks are preserved in a global variable called `linkClicks` before the links are temporarily assigned the `deadend( )` function. When the modal window closes, `enableForms( )` restores default states.

The heart of the `dialogWin` object is `openSimDialog( )`. This function takes several parameters that let you specify the URL of the document to occupy the dialog box, the size of the window, the name of the function from the main document that can be invoked easily from the dialog, and optional values to be passed directly to the dialog window (although the traditional subwindow relationships are in force if you want to communicate between windows that way, as described in Recipe 6.7 and Recipe 6.8). Most of the code here is devoted to calculating the (sometimes approximate) center of the browser window to place the dialog window, but the function also populates numerous properties of the global `dialogWin` object to maintain important values that the dialog window's scripts access (described shortly).

After all this setup code, the final two functions, checkModal() and the chained finishChecking(), force the subwindow to act like a modal window by giving the subwindow focus whenever the main window tries to come forward. A time-out takes care of the usual window synchronizing stuff that particularly affects IE for Windows.

The simulated modal dialog window library is a fairly complex application of Java-Script. It came into being not so much to get modality for non-IE browsers, but to work around a problem in earlier IE versions for Windows that prevented scripts in showModalDialog() windows from working with framesets in the modal window. By employing regular browser windows, the problem was solved.

One significant way that this simulated modal dialog differs from the IE showModalDialog() approach is that script execution in the main window does not halt while the simulated window is open. Instead, the simulated version operates more like IE's showModelessDialog(). Notice in the large openSimDialog() function that several arguments to the function are assigned to properties of the dialogWin global object. This object acts as a warehouse for key data about the window, including a reference to the dialog window itself (the dialogWin.win property). One property, returnFunc, is a reference to a main window function that the subwindow can invoke easily. Although the syntax, modeled after showModelessDialog(), is intended to be invoked when the dialog window closes (perhaps the result of a click of an OK button), a script in the dialog window can reach out to the main window function at any time. It's just that handling it in batch mode as the dialog closes reinforces the modality you're trying to convey to the user. Invoking the function from the subwindow is as easy as:

```
opener.dialogWin.returnFunc();
```

If the function takes parameters, you can include them in the call as well:

```
opener.dialogWin.returnFunc(document.myForm.myTextBox.value);
```

Going in the direction of passing data to the dialog window, the optional fifth parameter to openSimDialog() is a value of any JavaScript data type that you want scripts in the dialog to access easily. You can pack a bunch of values together as an array or custom object. Access the value via the dialogWin.args property. Thus, a script in the dialog window can read the value as follows:

```
var passedValue = opener.dialogWin.args;
```

A typical modal dialog window asks the user to make some settings or entries that affect the main window and its document or data. Good user interface design suggests that you always include a way for the user to back out of the dialog box without making any changes to the main document. As shown in the Solution, a pair of buttons (or button equivalents) that connote Cancel and OK should let users choose between aborting the dialog or committing the data to the application. Notice that the code watches out for the possibility that the user has closed the main window (because scripts cannot block access to the main browser window's Close button).

See Also

Recipe 6.9 for the IE proprietary (and more robust) modal and modeless window methods; Recipe 6.11 for using layers to simulate an overlaid window; Recipe 3.1 and Recipe 3.7 for creating an array or custom object as a chunk of data to be passed as arguments to the modal window; Recipe 9.1 for the *eventsManager.js* library.

6.11   Simulating a Window with Layers

Problem

You want to create the impression of a separate draggable window but without actually creating a new window.

Solution

This solution consists of many individual files, including four *.js* JavaScript library files and several *.css* style sheet files. Two the library files, *eventsManager.js* and *DHTML3API.js*, are applied directly from Recipes 9.1 and 13.3, respectively; the other libraries, *layerDialog.js* and *layerDialogDrag.js*, which take care of creating the window and making it draggable are shown in the Discussion. The *.css* files provide different looks for the window on different operating systems; they are also shown in the Discussion.

The following skeletal HTML main page shows the JavaScript libraries as they are linked into the page, the makeup of the required elements (some div, span, and iframe elements) that comprise the pseudowindow, and a sample button element that invokes the openLayerDialog( ) function to display the modeless, draggable pseudowindow (in this example, a Preferences window):

```
<html>
<head>
<title>Main Application Page</title>
<script src="eventsManager.js"></script>
<script src="DHTML3API.js"></script>
<script src="layerDialog.js"></script>
<script src="layerDialogDrag.js"></script>
<script language="JavaScript" type="text/javascript">
// function to run upon closing the dialog with "OK".
function setPrefs( ) {
    // Statements here to apply choices from the dialog window
}
</script>
</head>
<body>
```

```
<!-- PAGE CONTENT HERE -->
<button onclick="dialogLayer.openLayerDialog('dialog_main.html', 'User Preferences',
    setPrefs, null);return false">
Preferences
</button>
<!-- More Page Content Here -->
<div id="pseudoWindow">

<div id="titlebar" class="draggable"><img id="closebox"
src="closeBox_win9x.jpg" onclick="closeLayerDialog()" />
<span id="barTitle">Titlebar</span></div>

<iframe id="contentFrame" src="" frameborder="0" vspace="0" hspace="0"
marginwidth="14" marginHeight="14" width="100%" height="480" scrolling="auto">
</iframe>

</div>
</body>
</html>
```

All library initialization routines are self-invoked by way of the `addOnLoadEvent()`
function in *eventsManager.js* (described in Recipe 9.3).

Discussion

Specifying the functional characteristics of a positioned element acting as a simulated window gets a bit complicated if you wish to take into account the wide variety of looks and feels of popular operating systems. A window design tailored for
Windows 98 won't look anything like a Windows XP window. Even in the Mac
world, the looks of titlebars have evolved with subsequent releases of Mac OS X.
This recipe makes the following assumptions about the pseudowindow constructed
from positioned elements:

- The window is a fixed size, governed by style sheets (the example shows approximately 600 × 500).

- Titlebars and close boxes are customized for Windows 9*x*, Windows XP, and
  one version of Mac OS X.

- Other operating systems default to the Windows 9*x* look.

- The content of the window can be loaded from any URL.

- The window is draggable, behaving like a modeless dialog window.

The element-based pseudowindow is a draggable composite object. An outer wrapper div (`pseudoWindow`) is the overall container for the pseudowindow. Nested inside
are two child elements. The first represents the pseudowindow's titlebar. Two child
nodes of the titlebar div element are an image for the window's close box and a span
for the window's text title. The second is an `iframe` element, which holds the content in two nested subframes.

At the core of the interactivity built into the pseudowindow are four JavaScript libraries: *eventsManager.js*, *DHTML3API.js*, *layerDialog.js*, and *layerDialogDrag.js*. Because the *eventsManager.js* and *DHTML3API.js* libraries (Recipes 9.3 and 13.3) contain numerous cross-browser functions for element positioning, the current recipe loads these libraries to support the positioning tasks required of the pseudowindow.

Example 6-2 shows the code for the *layerDialog.js* library, which has two important jobs: linking in the OS-specific style sheets for the pseudowindow, and controlling the creation, initial position, and display of the pseudowindow.

Example 6-2. layerDialog.js library

```
// Help choose from four UI pseudowindow flavors
function getCurrOSUI( ) {
    var ua = navigator.userAgent;
    if (ua.indexOf("Mac") != -1) {
        if (ua.indexOf("OS X") != -1 || ua.indexOf("MSIE 5.2") != -1) {
            return "macosX";
        } else {
            return "win9x";
        }
    } else if (ua.indexOf("Windows XP") != -1 || ua.indexOf("NT 5.1") != -1) {
        return "winxp";
    } else if ((document.compatMode && document.compatMode != "BackComp") ||
        (navigator.product && navigator.product == "Gecko")) {
        // Win9x and CSS-compatible
        return "win9x";
    } else {
        // default for Windows 9x in quirks mode, Unix/Linux, & unknowns
        return "win9xQ";
    }
}
var currOS = getCurrOSUI( );
// Load OS-specific style sheet for pseudo dialog layer
document.write("<link rel='stylesheet' type='text/css' href='dialogLayer_" + currOS + ".
css'>");

//*****************************
//  BEGIN LAYER DIALOG CODE
//*****************************/
// Requires DHTML3API.js library pre-loaded
// One object tracks the current pseudowindow layer.
var dialogLayer = {
    layer : null,
    visible : false,
    // Center a positionable element whose name is passed as
    // a parameter in the current window/frame, and show it
    centerOnWindow : function(elemID) {
        // 'obj' is the positionable object
        var obj = DHTMLAPI.getRawObject(elemID);
        // window scroll factors
        var scrollX = 0, scrollY = 0;
```

Example 6-2. layerDialog.js library (continued)

```
        if (document.body && typeof document.body.scrollTop != "undefined") {
            scrollX += document.body.scrollLeft;
            scrollY += document.body.scrollTop;
            if (document.body.parentNode &&
                typeof document.body.parentNode.scrollTop != "undefined") {
                scrollX += document.body.parentNode.scrollLeft;
                scrollY += document.body.parentNode.scrollTop
            }
        } else if (typeof window.pageXOffset != "undefined") {
            scrollX += window.pageXOffset;
            scrollY += window.pageYOffset;
        }
        var x = Math.round((DHTMLAPI.getInsideWindowWidth( )/2) -
            (DHTMLAPI.getElementWidth(obj)/2)) + scrollX;
        var y = Math.round((DHTMLAPI.getInsideWindowHeight( )/2) -
            (DHTMLAPI.getElementHeight(obj)/2)) + scrollY;
        DHTMLAPI.moveTo(obj, x, y);
    },
    initLayerDialog : function( ) {
        document.getElementById("closebox").src = "closeBox_" + currOS + ".jpg";
        dialogLayer.layer = document.getElementById("pseudoWindow");
    },
    // Set up and display pseudowindow.
    // Parameters:
    //    url -- URL of the page/frameset to be loaded into iframe
    //    returnFunc -- reference to the function (on this page)
    //                  that is to act on the data returned from the dialog
    //    args -- [optional] any data you need to pass to the dialog
    openLayerDialog : function(url, title, returnFunc, args) {
        if (!this.visible) {
            // Initialize properties of the modal dialog object.
            this.url = url;
            this.title = title;
            this.returnFunc = returnFunc;
            this.args = args;
            this.returnedValue = "";

            // Load URL
            document.getElementById("contentFrame").src = url;

            // Set title of "window"
            document.getElementById("barTitle").firstChild.nodeValue = title;

            // Center "window" in browser window or frame
            this.layer.style.visibility = "hidden";
            this.layer.style.display = "block"
            this.centerOnWindow("pseudoWindow");

            // Show it and set visibility flag
            this.layer.style.visibility = "visible"
            this.visible = true;
        }
    },
```

Example 6-2. layerDialog.js library (continued)

```
    closeLayerDialog : function( ) {
        this.layer.style.display = "none"
        this.visible = false;
    }
};

addOnLoadEvent(dialogLayer.initLayerDialog);

//***************************
//  END LAYER DIALOG CODE
//***************************/
```

Because this solution links in several libraries with a fair amount of code in them, they feature heavy use of custom objects that encapsulate functions and properties (Recipe 3.10). Only a tiny handful of objects are exposed to the global naming space.

The *layerDialog.js* library begins by loading the external style sheet file matching the user's operating system. The getCurrOSUI( ) function uses browser operating system detection to determine which of the four supported styles applies to the current browser. Then the function dynamically writes the <link> tag with the desired URL. The code for the four *.css* files can be found in Examples 6-4 through 6-7 later in this recipe.

The library continues by defining a global variable—dialogLayer—that acts as an abstract object holding various pieces of information about the actual pseudowindow. A utility function adapted from Recipe 13.7 (centerOnWindow( )) centers the layer in the current browser window when asked to by the function that prepares the window for display. This application of the recipe, however, removes the final show( ) function call (to the DHTML API) because another function of the library controls the pseudowindow's visibility.

A brief initialization routine in initLayerDialog( ) runs just after the page loads so that the correct close box art is downloaded at the outset. The dialogLayer global object also is assigned a reference to the layer for a shortcut reference in functions that operate on the layer.

The main method of the dialogLayer object, openLayerDialog( ), is invoked by your scripts when they need to display the pseudowindow. This function shares many arguments with the functions in Recipe 6.10 that are used for simulating a modal dialog. However, the dimensions of the window are not needed here, since the pseudowindow is a fixed size. One final method, closeLayerDialog( ), is invoked when the user clicks on the pseudowindow's close box.

If you're wondering why the openLayerDialog( ) function includes code that modifies both the style.display and style.visibility properties to show the layer, it is a result of a rendering bug in IE 6 for Windows. Using only the style.visibility property to hide the pseudowindow can leave the rectangular area of the iframe completely blank (white) after the layer hides itself. Using the `style.display` settings takes care of the bug. But this introduces a different problem with positioning the layer prior to showing it. The odd combination of turning the layer's visibility to `hidden` and the display to `block` before centering the window does the trick. Then it's safe to use the `visibility` property to present the layer to the user.

Because this pseudowindow does not pick up the title from the document loaded into the `iframe` (security restrictions prevent such actions if the pseudowindow content is served from a different domain and server), you must pass the desired window titlebar text as the parameter to the `openLayerDialog()` function. The third parameter is a reference to a function that you want to invoke when the user clicks on an OK or Apply button in the window—very much like the function passed to the simulated dialog window in Recipe 6.10. This reference is also available as a property of the global `dialogLayer` object. The same is true for the fourth parameter of `openLayerDialog()`, which you can use to pass data to the pseudowindow. Be aware, however, that the document in the pseudowindow's `iframe` won't be able to access the `dialogLayer` object if the content arrives from another domain and server. To display a new document in the pseudowindow without passing any function reference or arguments, supply a `null` parameter, as in:

```
openLayerDialog("prefs.html", "User Preferences", null, null);
```

Example 6-3 shows the *layerDialogDrag.js* library, which provides support for dragging the pseudowindow around by the element standing in for the titlebar.

Example 6-3. layerDialogDrag.js library

```
// dragObject contains data for currently dragged element
var dragObject = {
    selectedObject : null,
    offsetX : 0,
    offsetY : 0,
    // invoked onmousedown
    engageDrag : function(evt) {
        evt = (evt) ? evt : window.event;
        dragObject.selectedObject = (evt.target) ? evt.target : evt.srcElement;
        var target = (evt.target) ? evt.target : evt.srcElement;
        var dragContainer = target;
        // in case event target is nested in draggable container
        while (target.className != "draggable" && target.parentNode) {
            target = dragContainer = target.parentNode;
        }
        // modification for pseudowindow use
        if (target.id == "titlebar") {
            target = dragContainer = target.parentNode;
        }
        if (dragContainer) {
            dragObject.selectedObject = dragContainer;
            DHTMLAPI.setZIndex(dragContainer, 100);
            dragObject.setOffsets(evt, dragContainer);
```

Example 6-3. layerDialogDrag.js library (continued)

```
            dragObject.setDragEvents( );
            evt.cancelBubble = true;
            evt.returnValue = false;
            if (evt.stopPropagation) {
                evt.stopPropagation( );
                evt.preventDefault( );
            }
        }
        return false;
    },
    // calculate offset of mousedown within draggable element
    setOffsets : function (evt, dragContainer) {
        if (evt.pageX) {
            dragObject.offsetX = evt.pageX - ((typeof dragContainer.offsetLeft =="number") ?
                dragContainer.offsetLeft : dragContainer.left);
            dragObject.offsetY = evt.pageY - ((typeof dragContainer.offsetTop == "number") ?
                dragContainer.offsetTop : dragContainer.top);
        } else if (evt.offsetX || evt.offsetY) {
            dragObject.offsetX = evt.offsetX - ((evt.offsetX < -2) ?
                0 : document.body.scrollLeft);
            dragObject.offsetY = evt.offsetY - ((evt.offsetY < -2) ?
                0 : document.body.scrollTop);
        }
    },
    // invoked onmousemove
    dragIt : function (evt) {
        evt = (evt) ? evt : window.event;
        var obj = dragObject;
        if (evt.pageX) {
            DHTMLAPI.moveTo(obj.selectedObject, (evt.pageX - obj.offsetX),
                (evt.pageY - obj.offsetY));
        } else if (evt.clientX || evt.clientY) {
            DHTMLAPI.moveTo(obj.selectedObject, (evt.clientX - obj.offsetX),
                (evt.clientY - obj.offsetY));
        }
        evt.cancelBubble = true;
        evt.returnValue = false;
    },
    // invoked onmouseup
    releaseDrag : function (evt) {
        DHTMLAPI.setZIndex(dragObject.selectedObject, 0);
        dragObject.clearDragEvents( );
        dragObject.selectedObject = null;
    },
    // set temporary events
    setDragEvents : function ( ) {
        addEvent(document, "mousemove", dragObject.dragIt, false);
        addEvent(document, "mouseup", dragObject.releaseDrag, false);
        // make sure nested frames react to events for Mozilla
        if (window.frames.length > 0) {
            var i, j;
            for (i = 0; i < window.frames.length; i++) {
```

Example 6-3. layerDialogDrag.js library (continued)

```
                if (window.frames[i].frames.length == 0) {
                    addEvent(window.frames[i], "mousemove", top.dragObject.dragIt, false);
                    addEvent(window.frames[i], "mouseup", top.dragObject.releaseDrag,
                        false);
                } else {
                    for (j = 0; j < window.frames[i].frames.length; j++) {
                        addEvent(window.frames[i].frames[j], "mousemove",
                            top.dragObject.dragIt, false);
                        addEvent(window.frames[i].frames[j], "mouseup",
                            top.dragObject.releaseDrag, false);
                    }
                }
            }
        }
    },
    // remove temporary events
    clearDragEvents : function () {
        removeEvent(document, "mousemove", dragObject.dragIt, false);
        removeEvent(document, "mouseup", dragObject.releaseDrag, false);
        if (window.frames.length > 0) {
            var i, j;
            for (i = 0; i < window.frames.length; i++) {
                if (window.frames[i].frames.length == 0) {
                    removeEvent(window.frames[i], "mousemove", top.dragObject.dragIt,
                        false);
                    removeEvent(window.frames[i], "mouseup", top.dragObject.releaseDrag,
                        false);
                } else {
                    for (j = 0; j < window.frames[i].frames.length; j++) {
                        removeEvent(window.frames[i].frames[j], "mousemove",
                            top.dragObject.dragIt, false);
                        removeEvent(window.frames[i].frames[j], "mouseup",
                            top.dragObject.releaseDrag, false);
                    }
                }
            }
        }
    },
    // initialize, assigning mousedown events to all
    // elements with class="draggable" attributes
    init : function (tagName) {
        var elems = [];
        if (document.all) {
            // IE 5 & 5.5 don't know wildcard for getElementsByTagName
            // so use document.body.all, which lets IE 4 work OK
            elems = document.body.all;
        } else if (document.body && document.body.getElementsByTagName) {
            elems = document.body.getElementsByTagName("*");
        }
```

Example 6-3. layerDialogDrag.js library (continued)

```
        for (var i = 0; i < elems.length; i++) {
            if (elems[i].className.match(/draggable/)) {
                addEvent(elems[i], "mousedown", dragObject.engageDrag, false);
            }
        }
    }
};
addOnLoadEvent(function( ) {dragObject.init("div");});
```

The *layerDialogDrag.js* library is identical to the element-dragging library from Recipe 13.11, with two small modifications. The setSelectedElement( ) function needs to acknowledge events only from the titlebar layer, but it must set the draggable layer to be the outer pseudoWindow layer. Thus, when the user drags the titlebar, the entire pseudowindow div element moves.

The other modification occurs in the setDragEvents( ) and clearDragEvents( ) method definitions. Because the primary content of this pseudowindow loads into frames, and because Mozilla and IE don't let mousemove or mouseup events bubble to the main window, we must define event handlers to these nested frame elements. Thus, when a user drags the titlebar in a downward motion quickly—causing the cursor to momentarily slide into the frame region—the frame events will cause the pseudowindow to move downward with the cursor.

You may experience a cosmetic annoyance in some circumstances, however. If the content of the pseudowindow has form controls, browsers running on slow computers don't refresh the screen promptly, leading to temporary ghosts while the pseudowindow is dragged. You'll have to evaluate how troubling this might be to your users based on the types of pages you load into the iframe.

Let's now come back to the issue of style sheets and their influence on the pseudowindow elements. When style sheets are applied to the basic HTML of the pseudoWindow div element, you get a range of looks, as shown in Figure 6-1.

One of the stated goals of this application was to have the pseudowindow blend into the operating system look and feel as much as possible. The example shown in Figure 6-1 tries to match the look and feel of three different operating system versions. To that end, a set of four separate external style sheets are created to handle the specific art files and sizes to come close to simulating the native look and feel of the host operating system. This assumes, of course, that you have available to you the art files for titlebar backgrounds (just small vertical slices are needed because the backgrounds repeat to fit the space) as well as close boxes. So that you can compare the subtle differences needed between the versions, we'll begin with *dialogLayer_win9xQ.css* (shown in Example 6-4), which is the style sheet used for backward-compatible IE versions (IE 5, 5.5, and 6 running in quirks mode).

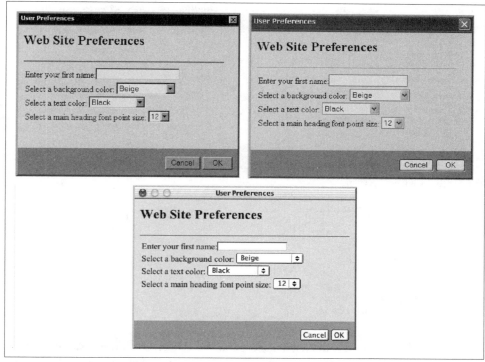

Figure 6-1. Pseudowindows of Window9x, XP, and Mac OS X designs

Example 6-4. dialogLayer_win9xQ.css for backward-compatible IE/Windows versions

```
#pseudoWindow {position:absolute;
               top:0px;
               left:0px;
               width:600px;
               height:502px;
               border:2px solid black;
               background-color:#ffffff;
               border-top:3px solid #cccccc;
               border-left:3px solid #cccccc;
               border-right:3px solid #666666;
               border-bottom:3px solid #666666;
               display:none
               }

#titlebar {position:absolute;
           top:0px;
           left:0px;
           height:16px;
           width:596px;
           background-image:url(titlebar_win9x.jpg);
           color:#ffffff;
           border-bottom:2px solid #666666;
```

Example 6-4. dialogLayer_win9xQ.css for backward-compatible IE/Windows versions (continued)

```
            font-family:Tahoma;
            font-size:8pt;
            font-weight:bold;
            padding:2px;
            text-align:left
            }

#closebox {position:absolute;
        right:0px;
        top:1px
        }

#barTitle {padding-left:3px}

#contentFrame{position:absolute;
            top:19px;
            left:0px;
            height:477px;
            width:594px;
            background-color:#ffffff;
            margin-left:0px;
            margin-top:0px;
            overflow:visible
            }
```

Only minor differences in dimensions accrue to the CSS and Windows 9x-compatible versions of the style sheet: *dialogLayer_win9x.css* (shown in Example 6-5). This variation is needed to account for the different ways that CSS-compatible browsers measure element widths when borders, margins, and padding are involved. The titlebar background art file is the same for both Windows 9x versions, as is the entire look of the pseudowindow.

Example 6-5. dialogLayer_win9x.css CSS-compatible stylesheet for Windows 9x

```
#pseudoWindow {position:absolute;
            top:0px;
            left:0px;
            width:600px;
            height:502px;
            border:2px solid black;
            background-color:#ffffff;
            border-top:3px solid #cccccc;
            border-left:3px solid #cccccc;
            border-right:3px solid #666666;
            border-bottom:3px solid #666666;
            display:none
            }

#titlebar {position:absolute;
        top:0px;
        left:0px;
```

```
            height:16px;
            width:596px;
            background-image:url(titlebar_win9x.jpg);
            color:#ffffff;
            border-bottom:2px solid #666666;
            font-family:Tahoma;
            font-size:8pt;
            font-weight:bold;
            padding:2px;
            text-align:left
            }

#closebox {position:absolute;
            right:0px;
            top:1px
            }

#barTitle {padding-left:3px}

#contentFrame{position:absolute;
                top:22px;
                left:0px;
                height:480px;
                width:600px;
                background-color:#ffffff;
                margin-left:0px;
                margin-top:0px;
                overflow:visible
                }
```

The Windows XP version, *dialogLayer_winxp.css* (shown in Example 6-6), adjusts its dimensions to accommodate a thicker titlebar.

Example 6-6. dialogLayer_winxp.css for browsers running in Windows XP

```
#pseudoWindow {position:absolute;
                top:0px;
                left:0px;
                width:600px;
                height:502px;
                border:2px solid black;
                background-color:#ffffff;
                border-top:3px solid #cccccc;
                border-left:3px solid #cccccc;
                border-right:3px solid #666666;
                border-bottom:3px solid #666666;
                display:none
                }

#titlebar {position:absolute;
            top:0px;
            left:0px;
```

```
            height:26px;
            width:596px;
            background-image:url(titlebar_winxp.jpg);
            color:#ffffff;
            border-bottom:2px solid #666666;
            font-family:Tahoma;
            font-size:10pt;
            font-weight:bold;
            padding:2px;
            text-align:left
            }

#closebox {position:absolute;
            right:1px;
            top:1px
            }

#barTitle {padding-left:3px}

#contentFrame{position:absolute;
                top:30px;
                left:0px;
                height:472px;
                width:600px;
                background-color:#ffffff;
                margin-left:0px;
                margin-top:0px;
                overflow:visible
                }
```

For Mac OS X, *dialogLayer_macosX.css* (shown in Example 6-7), the close box is on the left side of the titlebar, and minor dimensional differences are needed for the user interface elements.

Example 6-7. dialogLayer_macosX.css for Macintosh browsers in Mac OS X

```
#pseudoWindow {position:absolute;
                top:0px;
                left:0px;
                width:600px;
                height:502px;
                border:2px solid black;
                background-color:#ffffff;
                border-top:3px solid #cccccc;
                border-left:3px solid #cccccc;
                border-right:3px solid #666666;
                border-bottom:3px solid #666666;
                display:none
                }

#titlebar {position:absolute;
            top:0px;
```

```
        left:0px;
        height:16px;
        width:596px;
        background-image:url(titlebar_macosX.jpg);
        color:#000000;
        border-bottom:2px solid #666666;
        font-family:Charcoal;
        font-size:9pt;
        font-weight:normal;
        padding:2px;
        text-align:center
        }

#closebox {position:absolute;
        left:0px;
        top:0px;
        padding-left:5px
        }

#barTitle {padding-right:6px
        background-color:transparent
        padding-left:6px
        }

#contentFrame{position:absolute;
            top:22px;
            left:0px;
            height:480px;
            width:600px;
            background-color:#ffffff;
            margin-left:0px;
            margin-top:0px;
            overflow:visible
            }
```

One could also make a legitimate argument that attempting to simulate the user interface of the hosting operating system is not worth the effort. User interface details change over time, but a solid, independent design for all visitors may do the job equally well with less maintenance.

Perhaps the most significant advantage of using a positioned element as a pseudo-window is that no extraneous pop-up windows are spawned. Not only do some pop-up ad blockers prevent window.open( ) from working for some users, but multiple windows can get lost behind others, causing confusion among casual web surfers. Another, more philosophical, advantage is that the W3C DOM Level 2 pays only slight recognition to the window as an object. XHTML specifications recommend against the usage of multiple frames or windows (target attributes of form or a elements are not valid in strict XHTML 1.0, for example). Keeping everything in one browser window appeals to one-window designers.

At the same time, however, using a layer to simulate a window presents disadvantages over and above the dragging issue noted earlier. The foremost concern is that a layer is confined to the window or frame boundaries in which it resides. Unlike a true window, the user cannot drag the layer to a position such that it can be viewed beyond the main window or frame edges. If the main window's content is scrollable, the layer moves with the page when the user scrolls the main window while the pseudowindow is visible.

Although the example shown here is for a fixed-size pseudowindow, you could expand upon the existing code to let the openLayerDialog( ) function receive and operate on two more parameters that specify the layer size. This gets more complex in a version that needs to support the same range of operating-system user interfaces, as this example does. If you compare the style sheet settings that control div element widths and some div heights and top measures, you can see that you must account for a wide variety of tweaks for a number of UIs. For example, the height, width, and top style sheet properties for the iframe vary between the CSS- and backward-compatible versions of the Windows 9x specifications. If you are prepared to uncover the factors affecting various elements in this pseudowindow, as well as apply them to a fresh window size passed as parameters to openLayerDialog( ), you can make the function more malleable than shown here. The ideal scenario is deployment on an intranet where the browsers and operating systems that need supporting are strictly limited to a tolerable handful (or one!).

Another expansion on the pseudowindow is to fashion the equivalent of a modal window, where the user is blocked from clicking on underlying links or form controls. You can accomplish this by wrapping the current pseudoWindow div inside yet another div whose background is a transparent image. The tricky part is sizing the outer wrapper to the dimensions of the document so that it doesn't extend to such an arbitrarily large size that the browser window's scrollbars let users scroll the page into blank space. You must then position the pseudoWindow div within the outer wrapper, taking the page scrolling into account. Trap all events in the outer div, and assign the dragging event handlers to that div as well (instead of the base document). The more browser types you want to support for this kind of feature, the greater the challenge. But it's doable if you are persistent and patient.

See Also

Recipe 6.9 for proprietary IE modal and modeless dialog windows; Recipe 6.10 for a cross-browser simulated modal window using a subwindow; Recipe 11.5 for importing OS-specific style sheets; Recipe 13.3 for details of the DHTML API library; Recipe 13.7 for centering an element in a window; Recipe 13.11 for creating a draggable element; Recipe 14.15 for dynamically replacing a portion of body content; Recipe 9.1 and Recipe 9.3 for an event management library.

CHAPTER 7

Managing Multiple Frames

7.0 Introduction

As with multiple windows, multiple frames are controversial among experienced web designers. Some love them, others refuse to use them. Dislike for framesets has a couple of origins. One dates back many years, when not all browsers supported them. Many veteran designers refused to accept framesets then and the prejudice continues. More recently, however, the pure and strict XHTML implementations omit frames from the document markup vocabulary. Forms and hyperlinks in validating documents cannot even include a target attribute that loads the result of a form submission or a linked document into another frame.

But the frames concept is not disappearing into oblivion. The XHTML specification includes a frame-specific version, and future work at the W3C may provide a fresh, XML-based frame markup vocabulary (currently called XFrames). At the same time, virtually every graphical user interface browser in use today supports HTML frames, and will do so for a long time to come. By setting the frameset element's border attribute to zero to create a seamless space, users may not even be aware of your frame structure.

Frames are especially useful in a few specific instances. The most common application is dividing a page into a large content frame and a smaller frame that acts as an index, table of contents, or site navigation menu. Such small frames might be along the left or right edge of the window, or sometimes as a horizontal slice at the top of the window. As the user scrolls and navigates content in the large frame, the smaller frame remains fixed and in position, ready for the next action. With the navigation frame remaining stable as the larger frame moves from page to page, the user does not have to wait for the navigation frame content to reload at every content page refresh. Another advantage to this relative stability is that you can use the framesetting document or other frame as a temporary repository of JavaScript data that persists while content pages change.

Frames can also present user interface design challenges. For example, the browser's Back button steps backward through the history of individual frame changes, which is something the user may not expect. Also, the browser's titlebar description is governed by the `title` element of the frameset, and therefore does not change with each frame's navigation. This behavior might be an advantage for some UI designs, but not others. Users, unfamiliar with the context menu available within a frame, may also become frustrated trying to print the content of only one frame of a frameset. Weigh these considerations when looking at a frame-based application.

Frames As Window Objects

Since the days of the earliest scriptable browsers, the browser's object model exposed frames to scripts, but not in the supplemental way that the latest W3C DOM does. Each frame in the original system (still very valid in today's browsers) is treated as a window. After all, a frame contains a document just like a regular browser window. If you can gain scriptable access to the frame, most `window` object properties and methods apply directly to the frame as well.

The model for visualizing the relationships between frames in this manner uses a parent-child metaphor. The initial document that loads into the browser—the one containing the `frameset` element and all specifications for the frameset's makeup—is the parent of the frames containing documents that the user sees. Parent and individual child frames are all treated as `window` objects.

A script running in the framesetting document can reference any of the child frames, and thus their documents, via the `frames` property of the parent window. The `frames` property contains a collection (array) of `frame` elements belonging to the parent:

```
window.frames[i]
window.frames["frameName"]
window.frameName
```

Two of the reference syntaxes rely on the `name` attribute of the `frame` elements being set. As for the numeric index, it is zero-based and follows the source code order of the `frame` elements, even if the frames are nested deeply in framesets defined in the same top-level frameset document. In other words, regardless of the number of `frameset` elements defined in a framesetting document, there is only one parent, and as many child frames as there are `frame` elements defined in the document.

A more complex relationship exists, however, if one of the documents assigned to a frame's `src` attribute is, itself, another frameset. A script in the top-level frameset accesses this kind of nested frame through the following hierarchy:

```
window.frames["anotherFramesetName"].frames["nestedFrameName"]
```

Scripts operating inside a frame can reference both the `parent` frameset as well as sibling frames, but references must follow the hierarchy rather strictly. The `parent` keyword is the gateway to the parent framesetting document. For example, if the framesetting document contains a global variable named `allLoaded`, a script in one of the frames can read that value this way:

```
parent.allLoaded
```

For a script to access one of its siblings, the reference must include a parent frameset that both siblings have in common. For example, consider the following simple frameset:

```
<frameset cols="90, *">
    <frame name="navigation" src="navbar.html">
    <frame name="content" src="frameHome.html">
</frameset>
```

A script in the navigation frame can access the content frame with any of the following references:

```
parent.frames[1]
parent.frames["content"]
parent.content
```

Thus, a script in the navigation frame can instruct the content frame to scroll to the top as follows:

```
parent.frames["content"].scrollTo(0,0);
```

If the document loaded into the content frame was, itself, a framesetting document, the reference lengthens to include the pathway to one of its nested frames:

```
parent.frames["content"].frames["main"].scrollTo(0, 0);
```

To simplify references between frames within deeply nested framesets, you can always begin a reference from the topmost frameset, and then work your way down to the desired frame. That's where the top keyword is most useful:

```
top.frames["content"].frames["main"].scrollTo(0, 0);
```

A script in the deeply nested main frame can gain ready access to the highest navigation frame as follows:

```
top.frames["navigation"]
```

Perhaps more important than all of these referencing scenarios is the concept that referencing frames as windows gives you immediate access to the document of that window. For example, if a script in one frame wants to read the value of a text box in a sibling frame, the following backward-compatible syntax uses all original Java-Script and DOM Level 0 conventions:

```
var val = parent.frames["content"].document.entryForm.entryField.value;
```

Don't forget to include the document reference after the frame reference (a common mistake).

Framesets and Frames As Elements

In contrast to the frame-as-window scenario, the Internet Explorer and W3C object models allow scripts to reference the elements that create the framesets and frames. These objects have nothing to do with windows, per se, but everything to do with the ways the object models treat elements. Thus, these objects grant your scripts access to properties that mirror the tag attributes, such as a frameset's cols and rows properties and a frame's src and noResize properties. Access to these properties is handy when your scripts need to read or modify the attribute values. For example, Recipes 7.7 and 7.9 demonstrate how to adjust the dimensions of frames and even the column and row makeup of a frameset under script control.

The question that arises, however, is how a script that has a reference to a frame element can reach the document inside the frame. For this, you need to access a special property of the frame element—more accurately, one of two possible properties, depending on the object model you are using. The IE 5.5 and later model features a contentWindow property of a frame element, through which you can get to the document. For the W3C DOM, the contentDocument property references the document object inside the frame. Mozilla, Safari, and Opera have implemented both properties, but if you need solid cross-browser support including IE 4, use the following equalizer utility function:

```
function getFrameDoc(frameElem) {
    var doc = (frameElem.contentDocument) ? frameElem.contentDocument :
        ((frameElem.contentWindow) ? frameElem.contentWindow.document : null);
    return doc;
}
```

Frames and Events

One common problem facing scripters who are new to frames is that cross-frame scripts almost always rely on the other frame being loaded to operate correctly. If one frame loads quickly and references a form in a sibling frame but that form's document has not yet loaded, a script error greets the user. To compensate for this behavior, you must be mindful of the load event handler characteristics for frames and framesets.

Just like a window, each frame element can have a load event handler. The load event for a frame fires when the complete contents of that frame's document have reached the browser. The frameset element, too, receives a load event, but only after all of the nested frames' documents have loaded (and each of their load events has fired). Therefore, the only sure way to trigger functions that operate across frames is to do so via the frameset's load event handler (which you can bind as an attribute to the actual <frameset> tag).

Don't confuse this behavior with the kind of event bubbling that graces the IE and W3C DOM event models. The frameset element's load event handler fires only the first time the frameset and its child frames load. If the user or a script changes the URL of one of the frames, that frame's load event fires, but the frameset's load event does not fire again. If you assign a load event handler to the <frame> tag in the frame-setting document, it executes each time the content of that frame changes (but only in IE 5.5 or later and other modern browsers). For older browsers, the load event handler must be defined in the body of the loaded document.

When documents in your framesets change a lot, and when they have substantial dependence on each other's scripting, you can also use another less elegant, but effective, technique to poll for the availability of another frame's document. Assuming that each document is served from the same domain and server (to satisfy the same-origin security policy), the `load` event handler in each document sets a global Boolean variable, which acts as a flag for other frames' access. The variable is initialized at the top of the script as `false`, but the `load` event handler sets it to `true`:

```
<script type="text/javascript">
var loaded = false;
...
</script>
...
<body onload="loaded = true">
```

Any script that needs to access content or scripts in this document can check first for the value of the `loaded` variable, and check it every second or so until it is `true` or the number of permitted attempts reaches your maximum tolerance level:

```
// count attempts to reach other frame
var tries = 0;
// the function that needs info from the other frame
function someFunc( ) {
    if (parent.otherFrameName.loaded) {
        // OK, other frame is ready; use it in this branch
        tries = 0;     // prepare for next access
        ...
    } else if (tries < 5) {
        tries++;
        // try again in 1 second
        setTimeout("someFunc( )", 1000);
    } else {
        tries = 0;
        alert("Sorry, we could not complete this task.");
    }
}
```

Frame No-Nos

Just as windows and `window` objects could expose users to unscrupulous sites if security precautions were not in place, frames could offer a similar range of holes. But those, too, are blocked. Because frames are not as rich as windows with respect to their impact on the browser application, the list of things you can't do with frames is much shorter than for windows. Regardless of your good intentions, you cannot do the following things with frames:

Access document properties from other frames served by other domains
   It could be potentially nasty business if a script in one frame could look into another frame and retrieve its URL or any of the HTML content. Browsers implement what is known as a same-origin security policy, which means that a script in one frame (or window) cannot access critical details (URL, DOM structure, form

control settings, text content) from another frame (or window) unless both pages are delivered by the same domain and server, and arrived via the same protocol (such as HTTP or HTTPS, but not both).

Change the content of the Address/Location text field
The URL shown in the field is of the framesetting document. You cannot place, say, the main content frame's URL in the field.

Set a Favorites/Bookmarks entry to maintain the precise frameset composition
If a user navigates through your framed web site, the browser's own bookmarking facilities will preserve either the frameset or (through a contextual menu) a single frame's document. See Recipe 7.6 to assist in reconstructing a frameset from one frame's bookmark.

7.1   Creating a Blank Frame in a New Frameset

Problem

You want a frameset definition to include a blank frame (as a clean slate, awaiting a menu selection), but without having to create a blank HTML document on the server.

Solution

The following framesetting page demonstrates the technique of using a script-generated blank page in one of two frames:

```
<html>
<head>
<script type="text/javascript">
function blankFrame( ) {
    return "<html><body></body></html>";
}
</script>
</head>
<frameset rows="50, *">
    <frame name="frame1" id="frame1" src="navSlice.html">
    <frame name="frame2" id="frame2" src="javascript:parent.blankFrame( )">
</frameset>
</html>
```

You can apply the javascript: pseudo-URL to the src attribute of any frame element.

Discussion

As you can probably deduce from the example in the Solution, you can use JavaScript to create any HTML as the initial content of a frame. For example, if you wanted to use a special background color of the blank frame to be the same as your HTML pages in the frameset, you could include the bgcolor attribute of the <body> tag inside the blankFrame( ) function:

```
function blankFrame( ) {
    return "<html><body bgcolor='#ccee99'></body></html>";
}
```

Using the javascript: protocol with a src attribute is a somewhat controversial sub-ject. On the one hand, it is the only backward-compatible way to let dynamic con-tent fill an element that normally gets its content from a file or CGI process on the server. But this kind of URL fails if the user has JavaScript disabled or the browser doesn't support JavaScript. Most browsers with JavaScript disabled will simply leave the frame area blank, but the browser may be in an unstable state. Therefore, deploy this technique only if you know your audience has script-enabled browsers.

Notice that the reference to the function points to the parent frame. This is required because the execution of the javascript: pseudo-URL occurs inside the context of the frame. In the frame's eyes, the function is located in the parent, and the refer-ence must include that pointer.

As an aside, a common mistake for scripting beginners is to replicate the javascript: URL in event handler tag attributes. I don't know where this came from, but it is wrong, redundant, and sometimes disastrous. The javascript: protocol belongs only where a URL is normally assigned. Thus, it is appropriate in assignments to src and href attributes in tags. Do not use it in event handler assignments. Period.

See Also

Recipe 7.2 for modifying a frame's content after the frameset loads; Recipe 14.1 for creating dynamic content during the loading of a single page.

7.2   Changing the Content of One Frame from Another

Problem

You want a script in one frame to change the document in another frame.

Solution

Assign the URL to the location.href property of the sibling frame with the follow-ing syntax:

```
parent.otherFrameName.location.href = "newPage.html";
```

Replace otherFrameName with the name assigned to the name attribute of the <frame> tag designated for that other frame in the framesetting document.

Discussion

You don't need JavaScript at all to load a page into another frame if the user is clicking on a hyperlink. Instead, assign the frame's name to the `target` attribute of the `<a>` tag, and let the `href` assignment handle the navigation part:

```
<a href="products.html" target="content">Product Catalog</a>
```

On the other hand, if you want your pages to validate under strict XHTML, the `target` attribute is not allowed for hyperlink elements (your framesetting document also wouldn't validate under strict XHTML, but you might be satisfied with letting that document validate under the frameset version of XHTML 1.0).

If you need a `target` attribute but can't use it due to validation conflicts, you can use scripts to fill in the `target` attribute values after the page loads. Assign a `load` event handler to the page so that a function assigns frame names to the `target` properties of all links on the page. Thanks to the `document.links` collection found in every HTML page, a script can easily loop through them all and assign the values as needed. You can even segregate links that are to be loaded into another frame from those that are to replace the current frame: use the `class` attribute of the a elements to divide the elements into two classes. The following function assigns the `content` frame target to those links whose `class` attributes are set to other:

```
function setLinkTargets( ) {
    for (var i = 0; i < document.links.length; i++) {
        if (document.links[i].className == "other") {
            document.links[i].target = "content";
        }
    }
}
```

Bear in mind that client-side image map `area` elements are also counted among the `document.links` collection. Include them or not in this scripted assignment task, as your design requires, by choosing which `area` elements have their `class` attributes assigned in the HTML code.

Technically speaking, using scripts to add invalid attributes to XHTML-strict source code breaks the page's validation. It's just that validators typically do not execute JavaScript, and therefore see only the markup delivered by the server. You'll have to determine whether such workarounds violate validation policies (if any) imposed by the site and application design.

See Also

Recipe 7.3 to change multiple frames from one user action; Recipe 7.4 for replacing the current frameset with an entirely new document or frameset.

7.3 Changing the Content of Multiple Frames at Once

Problem

You want a single button or hyperlink to change the content of two or more frames of the frameset.

Solution

Scripting is required for two frame changes at once. It is best to define a generalized function that performs the navigation, and invoke that function from a click event handler of a button or hyperlink. A function format that works for both interface elements is like the following:

```
function loadFrames(url1, url2) {
    parent.otherFrameName.location.href = url1;
    location.href = url2;
    return false;
}
```

The hyperlink tag that invokes this function looks as follows:

```
<a href="content12.html" target="content" onclick="return
loadFrames('content12.html', 'navbar12.html')">...</a>
```

A default navigation path for the link is provided to accommodate visitors who have scripting disabled.

Discussion

There are numerous variations on the solution script. Your choice depends on your design and the audience for the pages. Let's examine some other scenarios and alternate approaches.

As indicated in Recipe 5.13, your site design can allow for nonscripted access to be controlled strictly by the standard hyperlink href and target attributes, but a script-enhanced presentation takes advantage of the click event handler of the link to supplement or replace the default hyperlink action. You can even go so far as to have the default action navigate to one part of your web site, while the scripted action goes down an entirely different path suited to scriptable browsers.

The example shown in the Solution is tailored to a link that changes documents in both the current frame and one other. You aren't limited to this combination. If you'd rather keep the current frame intact (perhaps it is a static navigation bar), but multiple other frames are to be updated with each navigation bar click, change the references in the loadFrames( ) function to point to the desired frames in the order the URLs arrive from the event handler calls. When using hyperlinks as the user interface element, however, be sure to use the technique shown in the example so that the click event handler ultimately evaluates to return false to prevent the default link action from operating.

If access by nonscriptable browsers is a significant issue for your design, and you have a complex frameset consisting of several frames, you can still offer the equivalent of changing multiple frames, but do it for scriptable browsers more quickly. For nonscriptable browser users, you have to define a different framesetting document for each combination of frame content you offer from your navigation menu. Assign the framesetting document to the href attribute of a link, with the target pointing to the special _top window. Continue to use the loadFrames() function for the click event handler of the link:

```
<a href="frameset12.html" target="_top" onclick="return
loadFrames('content12.html', 'navbar12.html')">...</a>
```

The advantage for the scriptable browser user is that the frames that don't have to change stay right where they are, and the browser doesn't have to compare the cache for those frames against the server's document. Thus, navigation is faster for scriptable browsers, but just as complete for nonscriptable browsers. This is the ideal value-added proposition that DHTML brings to a web page.

See Also

Recipe 7.2 for changing the content of one sibling frame.

7.4   Replacing a Frameset with a Single Page

Problem

You want a script statement in one frame to replace the frameset with a new document, such as removing your frameset to make way for an entirely different web site.

Solution

Assign the URL to the topmost parent of the frame hierarchy:

```
top.location.href = "newPage.html";
```

This is the scripted equivalent of the following hyperlink specification:

```
<a href="newPage.html" target="_top">...</a>
```

Use the scripted version only if you are performing some other script activity leading up to the replacement, or you need your page to validate to the XHTML strict DTD, which forbids the target attribute.

Discussion

You could reference the parent frameset instead of the top in a simple frameset. In this instance, a reference to the top and parent framesets points to the same object.

But if you specify the topmost frameset, you are guaranteed removal of any vestiges of earlier framesets, especially if the script is potentially running within a nested frameset. That includes a frameset from an origin other than your own domain and server.

Be aware that if your frameset should be embedded within another site's frameset, the top reference points to the other site's frameset. To limit the scope of your calls to only your frames, use parent references.

See Also

Recipe 7.5 for how to use this technique to prevent your site from being displayed in another site's frameset.

7.5   Avoiding Being "Framed" by Another Site

Problem

You want to prevent your site from appearing within another site's frameset.

Solution

Include the following script statements at the very top of a script appearing in the head portion of the document:

```
if (top != self) {
    top.location.href = location.href;
}
```

If you are using a frameset, include this script only in the framesetting document's script, and not in the documents that appear in the frames.

Discussion

The act of framing someone else's site is less prevalent than it was some years ago, but it can still happen. Sometimes it occurs innocently enough, when another site includes a pointer to your site but the link is part of a frameset navigation system, where all link destinations are loaded into a content frame of the site. Whether you are concerned that your site appears in a frame of someone else's site is a personal issue. A corporate site usually desires control of the user's experience at the site, and doesn't wish to have someone else's banner advertising appear in the same browser window as its own pages. Also, being in someone else's frameset makes it less likely that the visitor will correctly bookmark your site. Not all users—especially nontechnical casual web surfers—know that the browser's contextual menu includes an option to bookmark just one frame.

The script in this recipe compares the current window object against whatever window object is reflected by the top window reference. A window object has four different ways to be referenced: window, self, parent, and top. There is no difference between window and self: they always refer to the current window regardless of the window's relationship among frames and framesets. Sometimes, as in this case, using self is more descriptive when you read the script. When the browser window contains no framesets, the current window object is also the parent and top object. If that condition isn't met when the page with the script shown in the Solution loads, the frameset gets replaced by the page running the script.

Because the unknown outer frame is undoubtedly originating from another domain and server, you cannot dig too deeply into the details of the top window, such as its URL. Security restrictions prevent that. But comparing the window object references does not violate the same origin policy.

See Also

Recipe 7.6 for a way to guarantee that a URL to one of your framed documents loads in its frameset.

7.6 Ensuring a Page Loads in Its Frameset

Problem

You want a page bookmarked from a frame within a frameset to load within its frameset.

Solution

For a frameset that always consists of the same framed documents, include a script patterned on the one below in each frame's document. This solution includes a test for a peculiarity of the Netscape Navigator 4 browser described in the Discussion section:

```
var isNav4 = (navigator.appName == "Netscape" &&
    parseInt(navigator.appVersion) == 4);
if (top.location.href == self.location.href) {
    if (isNav4) {
        if (window.innerWidth != 0) {
            top.location.href = "frameset12.html";
        }
    } else {
        top.location.href = "frameset12.html";
    }
}
```

If a user has bookmarked a page with the previous script in it, the page will begin to load, but will then load the frameset that normally houses the page.

Discussion

The Navigator 4 issue affects the Windows version in particular. In that browser, when a user prints a frame, the page is automatically loaded into a temporary window of zero width. Scripts run when the page loads into that invisible window, so it's important to bypass the frameset-loading routine when the page is being printed or else you'll land in an infinite loop. If Navigator 4 is not used among your target audience, you can simplify the script to just one branch:

```
if (top.location.href == self.location.href) {
    top.location.href = "frameset12.html";
}
```

This script compares the URLs of the windows referred to as top and self. If they are the same, it means that the document is loading as the only one in the browser window. You'll have to tailor the URL assignment for each document containing this script so that the desired frameset loads.

For a more fluid frameset, where one or more frames change in response to user action, you need more intelligence built into the scripts and documents. At the core, each page's document needs a script not only to load the frameset, but to convey the URL of the page that needs loading into one of the frames. For example, if a frameset contains a fixed navigation frame through a product catalog, and the content frame's document changes with each menu choice, you want a bookmark to one of the product frames to load the frameset with that product showing.

To make this intelligent frame loading proceed correctly requires scripts in each bookmarkable page and one in the frameset. Each page sends information about itself by way of a search string appended to the frameset page's URL; the frameset's script receives that information and loads the content frame accordingly.

Let's start with a content document. The script gets all of its information from the page itself, so you can write this script once as an external library and link it into each content page. Here is the library script, which runs as the page loads:

```
var isNav4 = (navigator.appName == "Netscape" &&
    parseInt(navigator.appVersion) == 4);
if (parent == window) {
    // Don't do anything if NN4 is printing frame
    if (!isNav4 || (isNav4 && window.innerWidth != 0)) {
        if (location.replace) {
            // Use replace(), if available, to keep current page out of history
            location.replace("masterFrameset.html?content=" + escape(location.href));
        } else {
            location.href = "masterFrameset.html?content=" + escape(location.href);
        }
    }
}
```

The current page's URL is attached to the URL of the frameset in the form of a name/value pair, just like a typical form submission search string. All browsers except some early ones apply the location.replace() method so that the current page won't be added to the browser's history. If the page were to be part of the history, a user clicking the Back button could get into an infinite backward loop because the button would never be able to go any earlier than this page.

Code for the frameset consists of two functions, one of which is triggered by the load event handler of the <frameset> tag. The key supporting function converts the search string from the URL into an object whose property name is the name part of the name/value pair passed in the search string. The function also accommodates multiple name/value pairs embedded in the search string in case you wish to pass additional information to the frameset:

```
function getSearchData() {
    var results = new Object();
    if (location.search.substr) {
        var input = unescape(location.search.substr(1));
        if (input) {
            var srchArray = input.split("&");
            var tempArray = new Array();
            for (var i = 0; i < srchArray.length; i++) {
                tempArray = srchArray[i].split("=");
                results[tempArray[0]] = tempArray[1];
            }
        }
    }
    return results;
}
```

The load event handler of the frameset invokes the following loadFrame() function, which reads the search string data and applies the URL to the content frame:

```
function loadFrame() {
    if (location.search) {
        var srchArray = getSearchData();
        if (srchArray["content"]) {
            self.content.location.href = srchArray["content"];
        }
    }
}
```

This example uses the same frame name (content) as the property name in the name/value pair of the search string. Theoretically, you could generalize the loadFrame() function to assign the URL to the frame whose name arrives in the name/value pair. That design choice, however, places the burden of knowing the destination frame at the individual frame level. By leaving the specification to the frameset script, the destination frame's name is kept within the context of the affected frameset.

Assuming that the framesetting document contains a default URL for the content frameset (i.e., for when the visitor first arrives to the frameset), that default page stays in place if no search string containing a content property name arrives with the frameset URL. If a search string accompanies the URL, the default page appears momentarily, until the passed URL is loaded into the frame.

See Also

Recipe 7.5 for a script that keeps your site from being encapsulated in someone else's frameset; Recipe 10.6 for more examples of passing data between pages via URLs.

7.7 Reading a Frame's Dimensions

Problem

You want to know the precise pixel dimensions of a frame after the frameset is rendered.

Solution

Because it is not uncommon to specify a percentage or * wildcard character for one or more frame size specifications, the actual rendered size is unknown until the browser completes all of its calculations for rendering. A script running in one of the frames can access the interior dimensions of any sibling frame (and its own frame) with the following function:

```
function getFrameSize(frameID) {
    var result = {height:0, width:0};
    if (document.getElementById) {
        var frame = parent.document.getElementById(frameID);
        if (frame.scrollWidth) {
            result.height = frame.scrollHeight;
            result.width = frame.scrollWidth;
        }
    }
    return result;
}
```

The function returns an object with height and width properties containing the rendered pixel measures of the frame whose ID is passed as a parameter. You get accurate readings in IE 4 or later for Windows, Mozilla, Safari, and Opera. IE for Macintosh through version 5.x provides accurate readings when the frame in question does not have scrollbars. When scrollbars are present, the returned sizes are reduced by the thickness of the scrollbars. Unfortunately, no property reveals whether a scrollbar is visible in the frame if the frame's scroll attribute defaults to the auto setting.

Discussion

The keys to making the function work include referencing the parent (or top) of the individual frames and the actual frame element as opposed to the frame-as-window object. Thus, the more common parent.*frameName* or parent.frames["*frameName*"] type of reference will not suffice. By referencing the frame element directly, you get the browser to report the rendered size of the element, irrespective of the content of the frame.

You can also install this function inside the frameset document's script. But you must then remove the reference to the parent in the fourth line of the function. Because the script already operates in the parent, its own element collection includes the frame elements. You can install this function in the frameset, yet still invoke it from one of the frames, as in:

```
var frameSize = parent.getFrameSize("myFrame4");
```

The parent window is part of the equation in one form or another.

See Also

Recipe 7.8 for resizing a frame under script control.

7.8   Resizing Frames

Problem

You want a script to adjust the size of one or more frames in a frameset, including resizing a frame to zero width or height to hide a frame.

Solution

Apply a variation of the script shown in Example 7-1 in the Discussion to your frameset (customized with your frameset element's ID). The script goes in the frame-setting document and is invoked by a user interface element in one of the frames. For example, a button specification in one of the frames invokes the toggleFrame( ) function as follows:

```
<button onclick="parent.toggleFrame( )">Hide/Show Navbar</button>
```

You could also use hyperlinks or linked images to act as clickable triggers for the action.

Discussion

In browsers whose object models support access to all element types (IE 4 and later, Mozilla, Safari, and Opera), you can control the values of the cols and rows attributes of the frameset element via properties of the same names. The *frameResize.js* code library shown in Example 7-1 adjusts only the cols property of a typical two-column frameset. In this case, the width of the lefthand frame is set to zero, effectively hiding the frame from view.

Example 7-1. Frame-resizing functions in frameResize.js

```
// global to save previous setting
var origCols;

// resize lefthand frame
function resizeLeftFrame(left) {
```

Example 7-1. Frame-resizing functions in frameResize.js (continued)

```
    var frameset = document.getElementById("masterFrameset");
    origCols = frameset.cols;
    frameset.cols = left + ", *";
}
function restoreFrame( ) {
    document.getElementById("masterFrameset").cols = origCols;
    origCols = null;
}
function toggleFrame( ) {
    if (origCols) {
        restoreFrame( );
    } else {
        resizeLeftFrame(0);
    }
}
```

The code begins by declaring a global variable, origCols, that preserves the original cols attribute setting so it can be used later to restore the previous setting. Next, the resizeLeft( ) function is wired to apply a numeric value (arriving as an argument) to the first of two values of the frameset's cols property. Before doing so, the function stores a copy of the property value in the origCols variable. To return the frameset to its previous state, invoke the restoreFrame( ) function. These two functions are controlled through a master function, toggleFrame( ), invoked from user interface elements located in one or more of the visible frames.

A logical user interface idea behind the frame toggle is to change the text or image signifying the purpose of the click action. For example, when the frame is showing, the label says something like "Hide Navbar"; when the bar is invisible, the label says "Show Navbar." You can do this quite easily on IE browsers, but not some early Mozilla versions. Here's how to implement the toggleFrame( ) function to work this IE magic:

```
function toggleFrame(elem) {
    if (origCols) {
        restoreFrame( );
        elem.innerHTML = "&lt;&lt;Hide Navbar";
    } else {
        resizeLeftFrame(0);
        elem.innerHTML = "Show Navbar&gt;&gt;";
    }
}
```

The button in the frame is:

```
<button onclick="parent.toggleFrame(this)">&lt;&lt;Hide Navbar</button>
```

Figure 7-1 shows the two states of the button with respect to the frameset.

The reason some early Mozilla-based browsers won't let you handle the UI portion so elegantly is that when the frameset resizes itself to the new specifications, the browser automatically reloads the pages (needlessly, in my opinion). Thus, the default value for the UI element reverts to the value as delivered from the server.

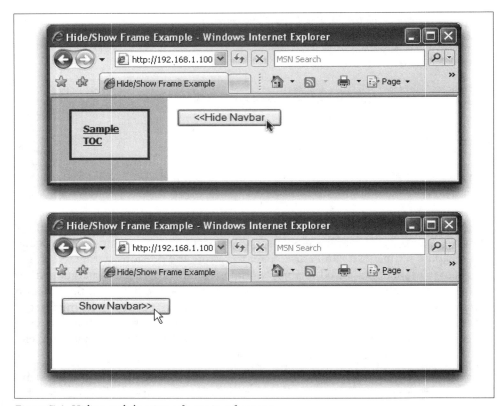

Figure 7-1. Hiding and showing a frame in a frameset

To counteract the problem—and provide a cross-browser service to all users—you can preserve the state of the frame's visibility in a cookie, and use the cookie to determine the text of the button (or image URL if you prefer) each time the frame loads. This added work lets the user's preference persist from session to session, thus enhancing the visitor's enjoyment of the site.

Coding for this enhancement has to work around an unfriendly bug in some versions of IE, where an event handler invoking a function in the parent provides incorrect information about the actual target of the event. The solution requires a little bit of indirection, but the result works in all browsers that support W3C DOM syntax.

The page in the frame that always stays visible defines a placeholder span element whose content is filled only if the browser is of a required minimum scriptability:

```
<span id="togglePlaceholder"></span>
```

Scripts include a linked *cookieManager.js* library (see Recipes 1.10 and 3.14):

```
<script src="cookieManager.js"></script>
```

A load event handler in that frame's page initiates the creation of the UI element for the frame state toggle:

```
function setToggleUI( ) {
    var label = "<<Hide Navbar";
    if (document.getElementById) {
        if (cookieMgr.getCookie("frameHidden") == "true") {
            label = "Show Navbar>>";
        }
        var newElem = document.createElement("button");
        newElem.onclick = initiateToggle;
        var newText = document.createTextNode(label);
        newElem.appendChild(newText);
        document.getElementById("togglePlaceholder").appendChild(newElem);
    }
}
```

Notice that the button element's click event handler invokes the local function initiateToggle( ) in the same frame. This indirection allows the accurate event target to be reported in IE. That function reads the target and sends it along to the revised toggleFrame( ) function in the parent frame:

```
function initiateToggle(evt) {
    evt = (evt) ? evt : event;
    var elem = (evt.target) ? evt.target : evt.srcElement;
    if (elem.nodeType == 3) {
        elem = elem.parentNode;
    }
    parent.toggleFrame(elem);
}
```

In the parent frame (which must also link in the *cookieManager.js* library from Recipe 3.14), the toggleFrame( ) function now not only adjusts the cols setting of the frameset, but it also saves the current state value to a cookie and sets the button's label to the new version (since IE doesn't reload the frameset, it needs the new values directly):

```
function toggleFrame(elem) {
    if (origCols) {
        elem.firstChild.nodeValue = "<<Hide Navbar";
        cookieMgr.setCookie("frameHidden", "false", cookieMgr.getExpDate(180, 0, 0));
        restoreFrame( );
    } else {
        elem.firstChild.nodeValue = "Show Navbar>>";
        cookieMgr.setCookie("frameHidden", "true", cookieMgr.getExpDate(180, 0, 0));
        resizeLeftFrame(0);
    }
}
```

All other functions in the parent stay the same as in the original solution.

See Also

Recipe 7.7 for reading the current pixel dimensions of a frame; Recipe 1.10 and Recipe 3.14 for details on the *cookieManager.js* library.

7.9   Setting Frameset Specifications Dynamically

Problem

You want to use a script to build an entirely new set of frames within the current frameset.

Solution

Use either of the makeNewFrameset( ) functions described in the Discussion to empty the current set of frames and install a new set. The current framesetting document's scripts and variables remain intact throughout the process. Invoke the function from a user interface element (button or link) or from any other function in one of the frames:

```
parent.makeNewFrameset( );
```

This solution works only with IE 5.5 or later and Mozilla 1.7 or later (but see the Discussion for a workaround in older browsers).

Discussion

The makeNewFrameset( ) function shown in Example 7-2 converts a frameset that is initially delivered as one set up in two columns to a frameset with different documents in a two-row frameset.

Example 7-2. A function to generate a new frameset for IE 5.5 or later

```
function makeNewFrameset( ) {
    var newFrame1 = document.createElement("frame");
    newFrame1.id = "newFrame1";
    newFrame1.name = "newFrame1";
    newFrame1.src = "altNavBar.html"
    var newFrame2 = document.createElement("frame");
    newFrame2.id = "newFrame2";
    newFrame2.name = "newFrame2";
    newFrame2.src = "altHome.html"

    var frameset = document.getElementById("masterFrameset");
    while (frameset.childNodes.length > 0) {
        frameset.removeChild(frameset.firstChild);
    }
    frameset.cols = null;
    frameset.rows = "80, *";
    frameset.appendChild(newFrame1);
    frameset.appendChild(newFrame2);
}
```

It is important to clean out the existing node tree and associated properties before repopulating it with new elements. In this function, the new frame elements are created in memory only. While they stand by, the original frameset is first cleansed of its previous child nodes. Thus, even if the main frameset has a more complex frame construction inside it, everything is gone after the while loop does its job. Because we're changing the main frameset from a column- to row-oriented frameset, the original setting for the cols attribute is cleared out before assigning fresh values to the rows property. At last, the new frame elements are appended to the frameset.

If IE 6 and Mozilla are your only target browsers for this kind of application, you might consider using a W3C DOM DocumentFragment object as a temporary container for the frame elements. The revised function is shown in Example 7-3.

Example 7-3. A function to generate a new frameset for W3C browsers and IE 6 or later

```
function makeNewFrameset( ) {
    var frag = document.createDocumentFragment( );
    var newFrame= document.createElement("frame");
    newFrame.id = "newFrame1";
    newFrame.name = "newFrame1";
    newFrame.src = "altNavBar.html"
    frag.appendChild(newFrame);
    newFrame = document.createElement("frame");
    newFrame.id = "newFrame2";
    newFrame.name = "newFrame2";
    newFrame.src = "altHome.html"
    frag.appendChild(newFrame);

    var frameset = document.getElementById("masterFrameset");
    while (frameset.childNodes.length > 0) {
        frameset.removeChild(frameset.firstChild);
    }
    frameset.cols = null;
    frameset.rows = "30%, *";
    frameset.appendChild(frag);
}
```

For a backward-compatible solution, you can always fall back on the document. write( ) method of the parent or top frame. Assemble the entire contents of a new framesetting document as one string. Then issue one top.document.write( ) method followed by a top.document.close( ) method. All vestiges of the original frameset (including script variables in the frameset and frames) disappear and are replaced by the new frameset.

See Also

Recipe 7.8 for resizing frames; Recipe 14.2 for using document.write( ) to generate a new page (and techniques for including script libraries in such a page).

CHAPTER 8

Dynamic Forms

8.0   Introduction

Giving scripted intelligence to web forms was the impetus that led to the development of the JavaScript language and the notion of a document object model. While a lot has happened to scripting in the meantime, forms still make frequent use of scripts to assist with user-friendly instantaneous interaction that otherwise requires a two-way trip to the server (and delays for the user) to accomplish.

Because of the comparatively long history of scriptable forms and form controls, it is comforting to know that most such scripts work with a wide range of browsers, and not just those that implement the W3C DOM. Even so, there are some misunderstandings about the combination of scripts and forms that I'll attempt to clear up in this chapter.

Referencing Forms and Controls

Before the W3C DOM, scripts used what is now known as DOM Level 0 syntax to reference `form` objects and the form controls (`input` and `textarea` elements) within them. This long-time convention relies for the most part on the form and controls having `name` attributes assigned to them. In fact, even today's browsers won't submit form control values to the server unless the elements have names assigned to them (independent of the now ubiquitous `id` attribute). At the same time, however, the object model provides arrays of forms and form elements, which can be accessed through JavaScript array syntax and numerical index values. For example, if a document contains a single form whose name is `userInfo`, backward-compatible scripts can reference the `form` object in any of the following ways:

```
document.forms[0]
document.forms["userInfo"]
document.userInfo
```

Each `form` element object also contains an `elements` array that contains references to all of the recognized form controls nested inside the form. For example, if the second input element of the userInfo form is a text box named age, you have three ways to reference that text box for each of the three ways you can use to reference the containing form. Using just one containing form reference, here is an example of three equivalent references to the age text box:

```
document.userInfo.elements[1]
document.userInfo.elements["age"]
document.userInfo.age
```

Notice how this syntax follows the element containment hierarchy: document to form to control. This allows for the possibility of a form control's name being reused in multiple forms on the page—something not possible (or at least not encouraged) with id attributes.

In browsers supporting scriptable id attributes of elements, you can also reference a form directly by way of the object model syntax(es) supported by the browser. For example, in IE 4 and later, you can use the Microsoft DOM reference syntax:

```
document.all.formID
document.all.formControlID
```

For W3C DOM syntax (IE 5 or later, Mozilla, and Safari), use the regular element-referencing syntax:

```
document.getElementById("formID")
document.getElementById("formControlID")
```

Even though your scripts can use only the ID to build references, you'll want to assign an identifier to both the name and id attributes of each element if the form is to be submitted to the server. You can use the same identifier for both attributes of an element and not risk collisions:

```
<input type="text" id="firstName" name="firstName" />
```

Browser versions that you need to support with your scripts should dictate the syntax you use to address forms and controls. If backward-compatibility is of any concern with your audience (including the now ancient Navigator 4), stick with the DOM Level 0 syntax. It will continue to be supported in new mainstream browsers for a long time to come. This book uses DOM Level 0 syntax in numerous examples to remind you that we're addressing form controls.

Form Validation Strategies

Client-side form validation is a helpful service that speeds the correction of potential errors in forms before they ever reach the server. That is not meant to imply that client-side validation can replace server-side validation. Far from it. But, like most DHTML applications, client-side validation helps your users be more efficient when filling out complex forms.

Even on the client, however, you have two types of validation strategies to consider: real-time and batch mode. In real-time validation, a script looks for signs of activity—such as change events in text boxes—to immediately validate an entry against whatever data restrictions apply to the field. The advantage of instantaneous validation feedback is that the user's mind is still fresh about the information filled into a field. In other words, when the user has just entered an address into an email address field, it's more helpful to bring the user immediately back to that field and correct the error, rather than wait until later. On the other hand, in most situations, you should not be so dogmatic as to absolutely require that a form be filled out in order, which can happen when you use blur events of text boxes to trigger validation. Give the user a chance to tab through and skip over a text box while filling out a form.

But then be sure to catch any missed or passed text boxes with a batch validation right before the form gets submitted. This offers a last-chance review of data before sending it to the server. In most cases, the same routines you use for the real-time field checking can be reused by the batch validation routines triggered either by the submit event of the form object or by a regular button-type input element that invokes validation routines and form submission.

Additionally, you will have to decide whether your text box inspections will use old-fashioned string parsing or the more modern regular expression facilities of JavaScript. Regular expressions provide powerful and quick ways of looking for patterns in a text box entry, but the syntax for using regular expressions is rather terse and cryptic. You will see some examples of both forms in Recipe 8.2. The introduction to Chapter 1 presents a brief overview of regular expressions in JavaScript, but you'll need a solid JavaScript tutorial or reference to understand the full scope of regular expressions.

Email Submissions and Return Pages

A traditional HTML form submits its data to a program running on the server. That program can be in a variety of languages (Perl, Java, Visual Basic, C, C++, C#, Tcl, and more), but the client never knows or cares what happens on the server. In typical operation, the server program receives the data, tears it apart, stuffs it into database tables, or otherwise manipulates the data for storage on the server. When the data is processed correctly, the server then returns an HTML page back to the client. By default, that return page displays in the same window or frame as the form. There's nothing particularly special about this transaction.

But many scripters don't have access to server scripting, either because they host on closed systems, or the technology is beyond their field of expertise. To fill in the gap and still capture the data submitted by a form, they have resorted to assigning a mailto: URL to the action attribute of a form element. When this approach first appeared in browsers, the form's data was quietly emailed to the address assigned to the mailto: URL. But as security consciousness overtook the Web (especially with the advent of scripting), such surreptitious emailing came to an end. Instead, a more explicit email process took hold, whereby the user with a properly configured browser and email client sees the email message before it is sent.

A problem with this scenario is that a significant number of users either don't have their email clients configured correctly and matched to their browser, or they are intimidated by the appearance of the email window. The result is that using a `mailto:` URL to submit forms is less likely to capture all submissions that you might otherwise receive.

However, should you persist with your usage of the `mailto:` URL, be aware that this kind of submission does not return any kind of page to the browser. There is no confirmation that the mail was submitted correctly or completely. Moreover, there is no absolutely reliable way to script a dummy confirmation page. To do so reliably requires that the browser receive some notification of completion so that the page could be displayed in place of the form's page. If you or a script removes the form's page before the actual submission completes its task, the submission may be aborted on the network—losing even more potential submissions before they reach you.

The solution is to search the Web for a third-party host for a Unix program called FormMail. This program lets you submit a form to a genuine server program that forwards the content to a mail address you supply in the setup process.

 Many examples in this chapter show event handlers being bound to form and form control elements by way of inline attributes (e.g., onchange). This approach simplifies the demonstrations—you can clearly see what events and functions are being assigned to an element. In practice, however, it is better to remove these event bindings from inside elements and employ scripted event bindings, as shown in Recipes 9.1 and 9.3 (built into the *eventsManager.js* library described in those recipes).

8.1 Auto-Focusing the First Text Field

Problem

You want the user to begin typing into the first text box of a form without having to physically bring focus to the box.

Solution

Assuming that the page always contains a form and text field with the same names, use an onload event handler to invoke the focus( ) method of the text box:

```
<body onload="document.formName.fieldName.focus( )">
```

Substitute the name of your form and text box for the two placeholders in this code.

Discussion

As simple as this solution is, you'll be amazed how much it helps casual users get faster results from a page's form. The Google search form uses a similar technique so that all a user needs to do is select the *Google.com* site from the Favorites/Bookmarks list and start typing the query string. Without this scripted assistance, users of most browsers have to click on the text box or press the Tab key a couple of times to bring focus to the text box. You must wait for the page to complete its loading process before giving the text box focus, or some browsers will grab focus away from the box.

If you deliver the text box with default or sample text that is to be replaced by the user, you should also invoke the select( ) method of the box:

```
<body onload=
    "document.formName.fieldName.focus( );document.formName.fieldName.select( )">
```

This action also selects the text in the box, such that the next keyboard key that gets pressed removes the default text.

See Also

Recipe 8.4 for auto-selecting a form field that fails validation; Recipe 8.10 for auto-tabbing between text boxes with fixed-length entries.

8.2   Performing Common Text Field Validations

Problem

You want to verify that a text box contains one of the following: any text, a number, a string of a fixed length, or an email address.

Solution

Apply the library of text field validation routines shown in the Discussion (Examples 8-1 and 8-2) to your form. The library includes the following functions:

isNotEmpty( )
:   The field has one or more characters in it.

isNumber( )
:   The value is a number.

isLen16( )
:   The field contains exactly 16 characters.

isEMailAddr( )
:   The field contains a likely email address.

For real-time validation of text box entries, use a change event handler in the input element and pass a reference to the element by way of the this keyword. For example, the following input element could be used for an email address:

```
<input type="text" size="30" name="eMail" id="eMail"
    onchange="isEMailAddr(this)" />
```

See Recipe 8.3 for an example of how these validation functions can be linked together in batch validation prior to submitting the form. The return values from the validation functions are vital for successful operation triggered by the form's submit event handler.

Discussion

Example 8-1 shows a set of fully backward-compatible text validation functions. All of these functions are to be invoked by both the change event handler of the text box and a batch validation function triggered by the submit event handler of the enclosing form. All functions are passed references to the form control invoking the event handler.

Example 8-1. Backward-compatible text field validation functions

```
// validates that the field value string has one or more characters in it
function isNotEmpty(elem) {
    var str = elem.value;
    if(str == null || str.length == 0) {
        alert("Please fill in the required field.");
        return false;
    } else {
        return true;
    }
}

// validates that the entry is a positive or negative number
function isNumber(elem) {
    var str = elem.value;
    var oneDecimal = false;
    var oneChar = 0;
    // make sure value hasn't cast to a number data type
    str = str.toString();
    for (var i = 0; i < str.length; i++) {
        oneChar = str.charAt(i).charCodeAt(0);
        // OK for minus sign as first character
        if (oneChar == 45) {
            if (i == 0) {
                continue;
            } else {
                alert("Only the first character may be a minus sign.");
                return false;
            }
        }
        // OK for one decimal point
```

Example 8-1. Backward-compatible text field validation functions (continued)

```
            if (oneChar == 46) {
                if (!oneDecimal) {
                    oneDecimal = true;
                    continue;
                } else {
                    alert("Only one decimal is allowed in a number.");
                    return false;
                }
            }
            // characters outside of 0 through 9 not OK
            if (oneChar < 48 || oneChar > 57) {
                alert("Enter only numbers into the field.");
                return false;
            }
        }
    }
    return true;
}

// validates that the entry is 16 characters long
function isLen16(elem) {
    var str = elem.value;
    if (str.length != 16) {
        alert("Entry does not contain the required 16 characters.");
        return false;
    } else {
        return true;
    }
}

// validates that the entry is formatted as an email address
function isEMailAddr(elem) {
    var str = elem.value;
    str = str.toLowerCase();
    if (str.indexOf("@") > 1) {
        var addr = str.substring(0, str.indexOf("@"));
        var domain = str.substring(str.indexOf("@") + 1, str.length);
        // at least one top level domain required
        if (domain.indexOf(".") == -1) {
            alert("Verify the domain portion of the email address.");
            return false;
        }
        // parse address portion first, character by character
        for (var i = 0; i < addr.length; i++) {
            oneChar = addr.charAt(i).charCodeAt(0);
            // dot or hyphen not allowed in first position; dot in last
            if ((i == 0 && (oneChar == 45 || oneChar == 46)) ||
                (i == addr.length - 1 && oneChar == 46)) {
                alert("Verify the user name portion of the email address.");
                return false;
            }
            // acceptable characters (- . _ 0-9 a-z)
            if (oneChar == 45 || oneChar == 46 || oneChar == 95 ||
```

```
                (oneChar > 47 && oneChar < 58) || (oneChar > 96 && oneChar < 123)) {
                continue;
            } else {
                alert("Verify the user name portion of the email address.");
                return false;
            }
        }
        for (i = 0; i < domain.length; i++) {
            oneChar = domain.charAt(i).charCodeAt(0);
            if ((i == 0 && (oneChar == 45 || oneChar == 46)) ||
                ((i == domain.length - 1  || i == domain.length - 2) && oneChar == 46)) {
                alert("Verify the domain portion of the email address.");
                return false;
            }
            if (oneChar == 45 || oneChar == 46 || oneChar == 95 ||
                (oneChar > 47 && oneChar < 58) || (oneChar > 96 && oneChar < 123)) {
                continue;
            } else {
                alert("Verify the domain portion of the email address.");
                return false;
            }
        }
        return true;
    }
    alert("The email address may not be formatted correctly. Please verify.");
    return false;
}
```

Regular expression versions of the validation functions are more compact when the validation is complex (as in the case of email addresses), but they require great care and stress testing to make sure they are doing what you expect. Example 8-2 shows the equivalent validation functions using regular expressions.

Example 8-2. Text field validation functions with regular expressions

```
// validates that the field value string has one or more characters in it
function isNotEmpty(elem) {
    var str = elem.value;
    var re = /.+/;
    if(!str.match(re)) {
        alert("Please fill in the required field.");
        return false;
    } else {
        return true;
    }
}

//validates that the entry is a positive or negative number
function isNumber(elem) {
    var str = elem.value;
    var re = /^[-]?\d*\.?\d*$/;
    str = str.toString();
```

```
    if (!str.match(re)) {
        alert("Enter only numbers into the field.");
        return false;
    }
    return true;
}

// validates that the entry is 16 characters long when
// input field's maxlength attribute is set to 16
function isLen16(elem) {
    var str = elem.value;
    var re = /\b.{16}\b/;
    if (!str.match(re)) {
        alert("Entry does not contain the required 16 characters.");
        return false;
    } else {
        return true;
    }
}

// validates that the entry is formatted as an email address
function isEMailAddr(elem) {
    var str = elem.value;
    var re = /^[\w-]+(\.[\w-]+)*@([\w-]+\.)+[a-zA-Z]{2,7}$/;
    if (!str.match(re)) {
        alert("Verify the email address format.");
        return false;
    } else {
        return true;
    }
}
```

Notice that the validation done in these functions provides the user with less detailed information about the more complex data entries than the backward-compatible versions. It is possible to provide more information, but this involves pulling apart the regular expressions to test for subsets of matches. In the first one, isNotEmpty( ), the regular expression pattern looks for a string with one or more characters of any kind (.+). To test for a number in isNumber( ), the pattern looks for a string that begins with (^) zero or one minus sign ([-]?), followed by zero or more numerals (\d*), zero or one decimal (\.?), and zero or more numerals (\d*) on the tail end ($). A fixed-length string pattern in isLen16( ) looks for word boundaries on both ends (\b) and any characters (.) appearing exactly 16 times ({16}). To ensure the user keeps to the 16-character length, limit the text-type input element to a maximum length of 16.

The gnarled email pattern inside isEMailAddr( ) looks for a match that begins (^) with one or more letters, numerals, underscores, or hyphens ([\w-]), followed by zero or more combinations of a period, letter, numeral, underscore, or hyphen ((\.[\w-]+)*), followed by the @ sign, followed by one or more computer or domains (([\w-]+\.)+), followed by two to seven upper- or lowercase letters for the top-level domain name ([a-zA-Z]{2,7}) on the tail end ($). The pattern does not match the use of straight IP addresses for the portion after the @ sign, but the email message specification (Internet Engineering Task Force RFC 822) frowns on such usage anyway.

In addition to individual validation routines, you sometimes need to cascade them. For example, none of the functions that validate numbers, fixed-length strings, or email addresses performs any checking that ensures the field has something in it. For example, if the email address field is a required field in the form, you would wire the change event handler for that input element to pass the values first to the isNotEmpty() function and then the isEMailAddr() function—but in such a way that if the first fails, the second one does not execute. That's where the returned Boolean values of the functions come into play:

```
<input type="text" size="30" name="eMail" id="eMail"
    onchange="if (isNotEmpty(this)) {isEMailAddr(this)}" />
```

Not shown among the text field validation routines here is one that validates a date entry. Validating date entries is tricky business due to the wide range of date formats and sequences of numbers used around the world. Except for intranet applications where everyone standardizes on a single date format, I recommend implementing date input as three distinct fields (or select elements) for entry of month, date, and year. Use the submit event handler to combine the values into a single string for a hidden input element whose value the server can pass directly to the database. You can also use the pop-up calendar shown in Recipe 15.10 to help a user select a date, leaving the formatting up to your scripts. Or if all of your users follow a fixed date format, you can try the date validation techniques described in Recipe 2.12.

Although in general I advocate binding event handler functions to HTML elements away from the HTML markup, I find the opposite to be more easily maintainable for form validations. Each form control has its own validation needs, served by one or more generic validation routines, such as those shown in this recipe. It seems more logical to me to encapsulate the calls to the required validation behaviors within the element markup (e.g., via an onchange event attribute). If you add or delete elements in the form design, you don't have to go hunting around your scripts to insert or remove event assignments—they're right there, in plain view of the element source code. It also simplifies cascading multiple validations for a field, as you have just seen.

If you evolve into a large set of validation functions, it is a good idea to wrap them up in a custom JavaScript validation object (see Recipe 8.5). The functions become methods of the custom object, and are invoked throughout that object, as follows:

```
<input type="text" size="30" name="eMail" id="eMail"
    onchange="if (validator.isNotEmpty(this)) {validator.isEMailAddr(this)}" />
```

See Also

Recipe 8.3 for a batch validation structure that uses the functions just described; Recipe 8.1 for automatically focusing and selecting a text field that fails validation; Recipe 2.12 for date validation ideas; Recipe 8.5 for design ideas for a custom validation object.

8.3 Preventing Form Submission upon Validation Failure

Problem

You want a validation function that detects incorrect data entry to halt the submission of the form until the user corrects the data entry.

Solution

Batch validation checking typically operates from the submit event handler of the form element. Submission is aborted if the event handler evaluates to return false. Include the return statement in the event handler assignment, and let the validation function supply the Boolean value based on its findings:

```
<form ... onsubmit="return validateForm(this)">
```

Discussion

You can implement batch validation by way of a master function that calls the individual validation functions as needed. To demonstrate, let's create a small form with numerous control types in it. Text fields execute real-time validation, while the form's submit event handler performs the batch validation. Both validation types use the validation functions shown in Recipe 8.2 (either the string parsing or regular expression varieties). Here's the form's HTML:

```
<form method="GET" action="cgi-bin/register.pl"
    name="sampleForm" onsubmit="return validateForm(this)">
First Name: <input type="text" size="30" name="name1" id="name1"
    onchange="isNotEmpty(this)" /><br />
Last Name: <input type="text" size="30" name="name2" id="name2"
    onchange="isNotEmpty(this)" /><br />
Email Address: <input type="text" size="30" name="eMail" id="eMail"
    onchange="if (isNotEmpty(this)) {isEMailAddr(this)}" /><br />
Your Region: <select name="continent" id="continent">
    <option value="" selected>Choose One:</option>
    <option value="Africa">Africa</option>
    <option value="Asia">Asia</option>
    <option value="Australia">Australia/Pacific</option>
```

```
                <option value="Europe">Europe</option>
                <option value="North America">North America</option>
                <option value="South America">South America</option>
        </select><br />
        Licensing Terms:
                <input type="radio" name="accept" id="accept1" value="agree" />I agree
                <input type="radio" name="accept" id="accept2" value="refuse" />I do not agree
        <br />
        <input type="reset" /> <input type="submit" />
        </form>
```

You can see the form in Figure 8-1. As the user tabs and clicks through the form, typically the only validation taking place is in the email text box. Tabbing through the empty name fields without making any changes won't trigger the change event handlers there (another reason why batch validation is needed). In this form, we also want to make sure that a choice is made from a select element, and that a member of the radio button group is clicked (some designers might question delivering radio buttons without a default selection, but this example requires no initial selection).

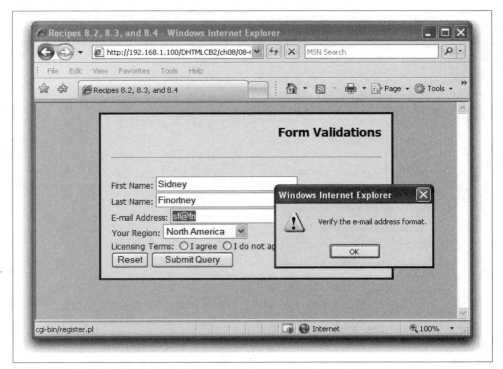

Figure 8-1. A form of mixed input types

When the user clicks the Submit button, the validateForm( ) function executes to perform validations of all required form controls. The calls to the validations are cascaded so that if there are multiple errors and the user corrects the first one to be reported, subsequent clicks of the Submit button find an error lower in the form than a previous one:

```
function validateForm(form) {
    if (isNotEmpty(form.name1)) {
        if (isNotEmpty(form.name2)) {
            if (isNotEmpty(form.eMail)) {
                if (isEMailAddr(form.eMail)) {
                    if (isChosen(form.continent)) {
                        if (isValidRadio(form.accept)) {
                            return true;
                        }
                    }
                }
            }
        }
    }
    return false;
}
```

Validation functions for a select element and radio button group are not among routines in Recipe 8.2, but are shown here:

```
// validate that the user made a selection other than default
function isChosen(select) {
    if (select.selectedIndex == 0) {
        alert("Please make a choice from the list.");
        return false;
    } else {
        return true;
    }
}

// validate that the user has checked one of the radio buttons
function isValidRadio(radio) {
    var valid = false;
    for (var i = 0; i < radio.length; i++) {
        if (radio[i].checked) {
            return true;
        }
    }
    alert("Make a choice from the radio buttons.");
    return false;
}
```

Note that the select element design assumes that the first item is an invalid choice.

All of the functions feed back to the main dispatching function. If any one validation fails, the dispatching function returns false to the submit event handler, forcing it to evaluate to return false and thus aborting the submission. But if all validations return true, the dispatching function also returns true to the event handler, allowing the submission to continue normally.

Relying on the submit event handler means that the user could disable JavaScript in the client to bypass client-side validation. This is a good reason to duplicate validation on the server. But if you'd rather perform all validation on the client and you know that all users have scriptable browsers, consider using a button-type input element instead of a true submit-type input element. Let the button's click event handler invoke the batch validation function and (if validation succeeds) the submit( ) method of the form object. Under these conditions, the user can't submit the form with JavaScript turned off.

See Also

Recipe 8.2 for individual data validation functions; Recipe 8.4 for focusing and selecting text in an invalid text field; Recipe 2.12 for date field validation suggestions.

8.4 Auto-Focusing an Invalid Text Field Entry

Problem

You want to bring focus to an errant or missing text field entry and select all text in the text field for quick replacement.

Solution

The basic solution is to invoke the focus( ) and select( ) methods of the text box under inspection. An unfortunate timing bug (primarily affecting IE for Windows) prevents these calls from occurring immediately in the validation function. An arbitrary time-out is needed to let the failed validation alert window disappear and the rest of the page to settle down before focusing and selecting the text box.

Here's a generic function that can handle any field:

```
function focusElement(formName, elemName) {
    var elem = document.forms[formName].elements[elemName];
    elem.focus( );
    elem.select( );
}
```

Next, modify each text field validation routine so that immediately after the error-reporting alert dialog—but before the return false statement—you invoke the above function through a setTimeout( ) call. Here is the regular expression version of the email address validation function (from Recipe 8.2) with the modification installed and highlighted in bold:

```
function isEMailAddr(elem) {
    var str = elem.value;
    var re = /^[\w-]+(\.[\w-]+)*@([\w-]+\.)+[a-zA-Z]{2,7}$/;
    if (!str.match(re)) {
        alert("Verify the email address format.");
        setTimeout("focusElement('" + elem.form.name + "', '" + elem.name + "')", 0);
        return false;
```

```
        } else {
            return true;
        }
    }
```

Because the first parameter of the setTimeout( ) function is a string, you can pass the necessary information about the form and input elements by way of their string names.

Discussion

You can also invoke the focus( ) (but not the select( )) method on other types of input elements, such as radio buttons and selects, but you'll have to make sure you are invoking the method on the correct element. In the case of a radio button group, the name attribute is the same for all related buttons. You can give focus to only one radio button, so you will need to reference one of the radio buttons of the group by array index (or via unique ID if your scripts have that information).

To differentiate among the different form control types, you can use the type property. For input elements, the type property can return any of the following: button, checkbox, file, hidden, image, password, radio, reset, submit, or text (older browsers do not treat the image type as a scriptable object). A select element can return select-multiple or select-one. Therefore, you can branch a function such as focusElement( ) to invoke the focus( ) method only on those element types that don't provide text input.

See Also

Recipe 8.2 for validation functions that can be adapted to the auto-focus technique; Recipe 8.3 for batch validation techniques that automatically employ the focusing embedded in the individual validation functions.

8.5   Using a Custom Validation Object

Problem

You want to encapsulate a large set of reusable form validation routines into a global object.

Solution

Use the code in Example 8-3 (shown in the Discussion section) as a model for designing a single object that contains methods for each of your validation routines. The example goes one step further in using modern event techniques for the form element's submit event binding and processing. With the help of the *eventsManager.js* library from Recipes 9.1 and 9.3, you can create a handy validation dispatching mechanism that can easily accommodate multiple forms on the same page.

Discussion

Example 8-3 is a revised version of various components shown in recipes earlier in this chapter, bringing together all of the operations you would typically perform on a form for client-side validation. Two primary differences are: 1) creation of a single validator object whose methods take the place of the individual validation functions described in Recipe 8.2; and 2) binding the submit event handler to the form element via modern event model practices. Similarly, the modern event model is taken into account during the validation process.

Example 8-3. Validation via a global object

```
<html>
<head>
<title>Recipe 8.5</title>
<link rel="stylesheet" id="mainStyle" href="../css/cookbook.css" type="text/css" />
<script src="../js/eventsManager.js"></script>
<script type="text/javascript">
// global validation object encapsulates validation routines
var validator = {
    // validates that the field value string has one or more characters in it
    isNotEmpty : function(elem) {
        var str = elem.value;
        var re = /.+/;
        if(!str.match(re)) {
            alert("Please fill in the required field.");
            setTimeout("validator.focusElement('" + elem.form.name +
                "', '" + elem.name + "')", 0);
            return false;
        } else {
            return true;
        }
    },
    //validates that the entry is a positive or negative number
    isNumber : function(elem) {
        var str = elem.value;
        var re = /^[-]?\d*\.?\d*$/;
        str = str.toString();
        if (!str.match(re)) {
            alert("Enter only numbers into the field.");
            setTimeout("validator.focusElement('" + elem.form.name +
                "', '" + elem.name + "')", 0);
            return false;
        }
        return true;
    },
    // validates that the entry is 16 characters long
    isLen16 : function(elem) {
        var str = elem.value;
        var re = /\b.{16}\b/;
        if (!str.match(re)) {
            alert("Entry does not contain the required 16 characters.");
```

Example 8-3. Validation via a global object (continued)

```
            setTimeout("validator.focusElement('" + elem.form.name +
                "', '" + elem.name + "')", 0);
            return false;
        } else {
            return true;
        }
    },
    // validates that the entry is formatted as an e-mail address
    isEMailAddr : function(elem) {
        var str = elem.value;
        var re = /^[\w-]+(\.[\w-]+)*@([\w-]+\.)+[a-zA-Z]{2,7}$/;
        if (!str.match(re)) {
            alert("Verify the e-mail address format.");
            setTimeout("validator.focusElement('" + elem.form.name +
                "', '" + elem.name + "')", 0);
            return false;
        } else {
            return true;
        }
    },
    // validate that the user made a selection other than default
    isChosen : function(select) {
        if (select.selectedIndex == 0) {
            alert("Please make a choice from the list.");
            return false;
        } else {
            return true;
        }
    },
    // validate that the user has checked one of the radio buttons
    isValidRadio : function(radio) {
        var valid = false;
        for (var i = 0; i < radio.length; i++) {
            if (radio[i].checked) {
                return true;
            }
        }
        alert("Make a choice from the radio buttons.");
        return false;
    },
    focusElement : function(formName, elemName) {
        var elem = document.forms[formName].elements[elemName];
        elem.focus();
        elem.select();
    }
}

// batch validation router tailored for "sampleForm"
function validateSampleForm(form, evt) {
    if (validator.isNotEmpty(form.name1)) {
        if (validator.isNotEmpty(form.name2)) {
            if (validator.isNotEmpty(form.eMail)) {
```

Example 8-3. Validation via a global object (continued)

```
                if (validator.isEMailAddr(form.eMail)) {
                    if (validator.isChosen(form.continent)) {
                        if (validator.isValidRadio(form.accept)) {
                            return true;
                        }
                    }
                }
            }
        }
    }
    if (evt.preventDefault) {
        evt.preventDefault();
    }
    evt.returnValue = false;
    return false;
}

// dispatcher, in case of multiple forms
function dispatchValidation(evt) {
    evt = (evt) ? evt : window.event;
    if (evt) {
        var elem = (evt.target) ? evt.target : evt.srcElement;
        if (elem.name == "sampleForm") {
            validateSampleForm(elem, evt);
        }
    }
}

function setElementEvents() {
    addEvent(document.getElementById("sampleForm"), "submit", dispatchValidation, false);
    // set more element events here, if needed
}
// from eventsManager.js
addOnLoadEvent(setElementEvents);
</script>
</head>
<body>
<h1>Form Validations</h1>
<hr />
<form method="GET" action="cgi-bin/register.pl"
    name="sampleForm" id="sampleForm">
First Name: <input type="text" size="30" name="name1" id="name1"
    onchange="validator.isNotEmpty(this)" /><br />
Last Name: <input type="text" size="30" name="name2" id="name2"
    onchange="validator.isNotEmpty(this)" /><br />
E-mail Address: <input type="text" size="30" name="eMail" id="eMail"
    onchange="if (validator.isNotEmpty(this)) {validator.isEMailAddr(this)}" /><br />
Your Region: <select name="continent" id="continent">
    <option value="" selected>Choose One:</option>
    <option value="Africa">Africa</option>
    <option value="Asia">Asia</option>
    <option value="Australia">Australia/Pacific</option>
```

Example 8-3. Validation via a global object (continued)

```
    <option value="Europe">Europe</option>
    <option value="North America">North America</option>
    <option value="South America">South America</option>
</select><br />
Licensing Terms:
    <input type="radio" name="accept" id="accept1" value="agree" />I agree
    <input type="radio" name="accept" id="accept2" value="refuse" />I do not agree
<br />
<input type="reset" /> <input type="submit" />
</form>
</body>
</html>
```

Because the specific validation routines are discussed in Recipe 8.2, I will focus here on the differences between Example 8-3 and the component pieces described in Recipes 8.2 through 8.4. The individual validation routines are now methods of the `validator` object. There are no changes to the internal workings of the validations.

At the bottom of the script, the `addOnLoadEvent( )` function (from Recipe 9.3) forces the page's `load` event to invoke the `setElementEvents( )` function. In this example, we assign only one event to a single element, a call to `dispatchValidation( )` for the `submit` event of the form named `sampleForm`. This is where other scripted event bindings should be placed.

The `dispatchValidation( )` function uses modern event processing (see Recipe 9.1) to derive a reference to the form from which the `submit` event fired. There is only one form in this page, but the function accommodates additional forms by branching code to a specific validation router customized for the details of a particular form. Notice that a reference to the event object is passed to the validation router, along with a reference to the form element.

For this example, the form named `sampleForm` is validated through the `validateSampleForm( )` function. The function is identical to the one shown in Recipe 8.3 until we get to the end, where the function, upon finding a problem with one of the form controls, prevents the form from submitting itself. Because this version uses modern event binding and processing, it includes both the W3C DOM and IE event model ways of preventing the form's default action from occurring. This is different from the way shown in Recipe 8.2, which relied on the `onsubmit` attribute of the `<form>` tag to evaluate to `return false`. Binding events away from the element requires the slightly more cumbersome (and not cross-browser compatible) syntax.

See Also

Recipe 8.2 for the operations occurring inside the individual validation routines; Recipe 8.3 for validation routing discussions; Recipes 9.1 and 9.3 for using modern event binding and processing practices; Recipe 3.14 for converting related functions into methods of a custom object.

8.6   Changing a Form's Action

Problem

You want to submit a form to a different action depending on user activity in the page.

Solution

The most common scenario is a form with two or more buttons that submit the form, but each button directs the form to a different CGI program on the server. If you use submit-type input elements, use the click event handlers to assign the desired CGI URL to the action property of the form:

```
<input type="submit" value="Send To HeadQuarters"
onclick="this.form.action='http://main.megacorp.com/submitSpecs.asp'" />
<input type="submit" value="Send For Peer Review"
onclick="this.form.action='http://eng.megacorp.com/reviewComm.asp'" />
```

Any function executing before the form submits itself can assign a URL to the form element's action property to influence where the form goes.

Discussion

Deploying this solution to a browser base that may include nonscriptable browsers (including browsers with scripting turned off) should be done with care. Your first inclination might be to assign a default action URL in the form that receives the form if scripting is not available. But if you use two submit-type input elements, as shown in the example, both buttons will submit the form to the default action, regardless of the label in the button. This could mislead your scriptless visitors.

You aren't limited to using submit-type input elements, of course. For example, your form may contain a checkbox that acts as a signal for which action the form should follow. In this case, the submit event handler of the form can inspect the checked property of the checkbox button, and set the action property's URL before allowing the submission to continue:

```
form.action = (form.myCheckbox.checked) ? "cgi-bin/special.pl" : "normal.jsp";
```

With modern W3C DOM-capable browsers, it is also feasible to use scripting to replace entire elements after the page has loaded. For example, if a web site contact page gets hammered by blog spammers who harvest form action URLs to send automated guestbook or blog comment spam, you can serve up the page initially without a Submit button. If a human visitor has scripting enabled, the load event can insert a script-generated Submit button and assign the URL to the form element's action property. If the script is loaded from an external *.js* file, the spammer's web crawlers won't find your form's URL.

Bear in mind that the action attribute is required in a form element under all recent HTML and XHTML validation scenarios.

See Also

Recipe 8.3 for using the submit event handler to perform last-instant processing before form submission.

8.7   Blocking Submissions from the Enter Key

Problem

You want to prevent a press of the Enter/Return key from submitting the form.

Solution

The default behavior of IE and Mozilla browsers (but this is not specified in any HTML standard) is that a form consisting of a single text input element submits the form when the field has focus and the user presses the Enter/Return key. Although this behavior is a convenience for some forms, it may prematurely submit a form that has other kinds of elements that need attention. Other major browsers don't exhibit the same behavior. Safari submits with the Enter key regardless of the number of text fields; Opera never submits from a text field.

To prevent premature submission, you can block any standard form submission by short-circuiting the submit event handler in the <form> tag:

```
onsubmit="return false"
```

This means, however, that you need to script the submission in a button or link that inovkes the form's submit( ) method:

```
<input type="button" value="Submit" onclick="if (validateForm(this.form))
{this.form.submit( )}" />
```

Discussion

Using a form object's submit( ) method does not trigger the submit event of the form. If additional scripting must execute prior to the form being submitted, invoke those script statements before calling submit( ).

Blocking sumissions comes in handy when you are using JavaScript for some strictly client-side calculations that rely on text field input (e.g., a mortgage calculator). If the form has no action attribute value, a submission reloads the current page, ruining any client-side calculations you intend to carry out.

See Also

Recipe 8.8 for using the Enter key to advance focus to the next field in sequence; Recipe 8.13 for automatically advancing focus to an adjacent text box in fixed-length fields.

8.8 Advancing Text Field Focus with the Enter Key

Problem

You want to use the Enter/Return key in a text field to give focus to the next text field in the form.

Solution

Include a keypress event handler in each field that needs to advance focus to another field in the form. The event handler should invoke the focusNext( ) function described in the Discussion. The event handler must pass arguments for the form reference, the name of the next field in sequence, and (for the W3C event model in NN) the event object. For example, the event handler in a field called name1 directs focus to field name2 in the following:

```
<input type="text" name="name1" id="name1"
    onkeypress="return focusNext(this.form, 'name2', event)">
```

Discussion

Although HTML forms don't normally follow the user interface behavior of stand-alone database form programs, you can script text input fields to advance focus to the next field when the user presses the Enter/Return key. The scripting task is a bit tedious because each event handler must be tailored to focus a specific field that is next in the sequence. First, block all submissions using onsubmit="return false" in the <form> tag. The following function is invoked from each text field:

```
function focusNext(form, elemName, evt) {
    evt = (evt) ? evt : event;
    var charCode = (evt.charCode) ? evt.charCode :
        ((evt.which) ? evt.which : evt.keyCode);
    if (charCode == 13 || charCode == 3) {
        form.elements[elemName].focus( );
        return false;
    }
    return true;
}
```

Continue to use the change event handlers in the text boxes to perform real-time validations as well as the auto-focusing via keypress. Note that you are not restricted to advancing to text fields in source code order. If a form is laid out such that it is more efficient to enter data out of source code order, this solution does the trick.

See Also

Recipe 8.13 for automatically advancing focus to an adjacent text box in fixed-length fields.

8.9 Submitting a Form by an Enter Key Press in Any Text Box

Problem

You want a press of the Return/Enter key in one or more text fields to submit the form.

Solution

To simulate a standalone database entry form, you might implement the auto-focusing technique in Recipe 8.8 for all but the last test box, which instead uses the keypress event handler to invoke the following function:

```
function submitViaEnter(evt) {
    evt = (evt) ? evt : event;
    var target = (evt.target) ? evt.target : evt.srcElement;
    var form = target.form;
    var charCode = (evt.charCode) ? evt.charCode :
        ((evt.which) ? evt.which : evt.keyCode);
    if (charCode == 13 || charCode == 3) {
        if (validateForm(form)) {
            form.submit( );
            return false;
        }
    }
    return true;
}
```

Omit the change event handler that performs real-time validation. The above function triggers the batch validation (which alerts the user to any problems in the last field) and submits the form via the submit( ) method. The event handler of the last field of the form looks like the following:

```
onkeypress="return submitViaEnter(event)"
```

This technique also assumes that the form element has the onsubmit="return false" event handler in place so that only the scripted submit( ) method submits the form (as discussed in Recipe 8.7).

Discussion

To help summarize some of the form enhancements described in Recipes 8.7 and 8.8, as well as this recipe, the following text field form incorporates event handlers that invoke several functions described earlier in this chapter. Guiding the design of this form are requirements that the Return key advance focus to the next text field until the last field is reached, where Return submits the form:

```
<form action="..." method="GET" name="sampleForm" onsubmit="return false">
First Name: <input type="text" size="30" name="name1" id="name1"
    onkeypress="return focusNext(this.form, 'name2', event)"
    onchange="isNotEmpty(this)" /><br />
Last Name: <input type="text" size="30" name="name2" id="name2"
    onkeypress="return focusNext(this.form, 'eMail', event)"
    onchange="isNotEmpty(this)" /><br />
Email Address: <input type="text" size="30" name="eMail" id="eMail"
    onkeypress="return submitViaEnter(event)" /><br />
<input type="reset" /> <input type="button" value="Submit"
    onclick="if (validateForm(this.form)) {this.form.submit()}" />
</form>
```

Notice that the Submit button is a regular button-type input element. This prevents nonscriptable browsers from submitting the form. If you'd like nonscriptable browsers to be able to submit the form (presumably to let server-side validation catch any errors), use a modified submit-type input element as follows:

```
<input type="submit"  onclick="if (validateForm(this.form)) {this.form.submit()}" />
```

For scripted browsers, the default action of the submit-type input element is cancelled by the form's submit event handler, but nonscriptable browsers will submit the form like an ordinary form.

See Also

Recipe 8.7 for blocking unintended form submission through the press of the Return/Enter key; Recipe 8.8 for using the Enter key to advance focus to the next field in the sequence.

8.10   Disabling Form Controls

Problem

You want to temporarily lock down a form control to prevent user access to the control.

Solution

In IE 4 or later and modern browsers, form controls provide a Boolean disabled property that scripts can change at any time. Use any valid reference to the form control to set its disabled property to true:

```
document.myForm.myFirstTextBox.disabled = true;
```

To restore functionality to the control, set its disabled property to false:

```
document.myForm.myFirstTextBox.disabled = false;
```

A disabled form control generally displays a grayed-out appearance and does not permit user modification of the setting.

Discussion

Figure 8-2 shows the form from Figure 8-1 with form controls disabled. While scripts can still read and write values in disabled controls, a disabled form control's name/value pair does not submit to the server at submission time.

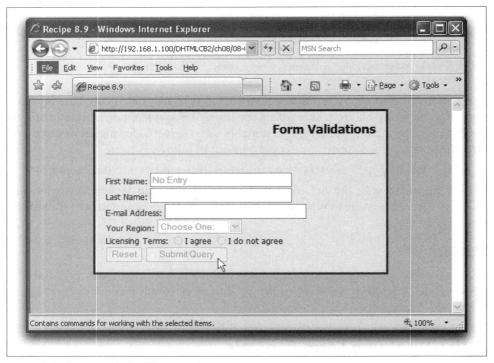

Figure 8-2. A form with disabled controls

IE 4 and later for Windows provides a more pervasive `disabled` property, available to all renderable element objects. But the property is not fully inheritable. For example, if you set the `disabled` property of a `form` element object to `true`, the nested controls might look disabled (as will their text labels), but users can still access the controls to modify their content. If you want to disable both the labels and controls in IE for Windows, disable the controls and the containing form at the same time. Mozilla, Safari, and Opera do not support disabling of nonform rendered elements.

See Also

Recipe 8.11 for hiding portions of a form until they're needed; Recipe 12.10 for hiding and showing elements.

8.11   Hiding and Showing Form Controls

Problem

You want to keep subsidiary form controls hidden until they are needed in response to other control settings.

Solution

You can keep more detailed controls hidden from view until a user chooses an item in a select element or turns on a checkbox using a function that is similar to the togglePurDec( ) function shown in the Discussion to hide and show a relevant group of form controls.

Discussion

An alternative to disabling form controls (Recipe 8.10) is to hide subsidiary groups of controls until they are needed. For example, the following excerpt from a magazine subscription form has nested controls that remain hidden until the user answers Yes to question number 3:

```
<form name="survey" ...>
...
<p>3. Do you make purchase decisions for your company?<br />
<input type="radio" id="purDecFlag0" name="purchaseDecision"
    onclick="togglePurDec(event)" />No
<input type="radio" id="purDecFlag1" name="purchaseDecision"
    onclick="togglePurDec(event)" />Yes
<div id="purchaseDecisionData" style="display:none; margin-left:20px">
</p>
<p>
3a. What is your purchase budget for the current fiscal year?
<select name="PurBudget">
    <option value="">Choose One:</option>
    <option value="1">Less than $50,000</option>
    <option value="2">$50,000-100,000</option>
    <option value="3">$100,000-500,000</option>
    <option value="4">$500,000+</option>
</select>
</p>
<p>
3b. What role do you play in purchase decisions? (check all that apply)<br />
<input type="checkbox" name="purRole1" />Research<br />
<input type="checkbox" name="purRole2" />Recommend<br />
<input type="checkbox" name="purRole3" />Review Recommendations of Others<br />
<input type="checkbox" name="purRole4" />Sign Purchase Orders<br />
<input type="checkbox" name="purRole5" />None of the above<br />
</p>
</div>
</p>
<p>4. How long have you been at your current employment position?
```

```
<select name="emplLen">
    <option value="">Choose One:</option>
    <option value="1">Less than 6 months</option>
    <option value="2">6-12 months</option>
    <option value="3">1-2 years</option>
    <option value="4">2+ years</option>
</select>
</p>
...
</form>
```

Figure 8-3 shows the two states of this segment of the form.

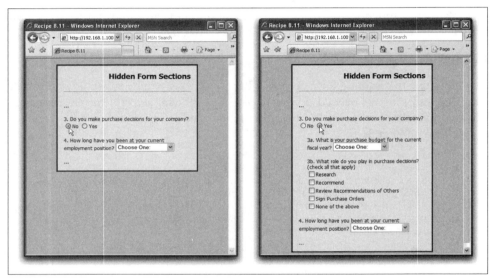

Figure 8-3. Hiding and showing subsidiary form controls

The click event handlers of the two radio buttons insert or remove the optional block from the renderable content as needed, using the following togglePurDec( ) function:

```
function togglePurDec(evt) {
    evt = (evt) ? evt : event;
    var target = (evt.target) ? evt.target : evt.srcElement;
    var block = document.getElementById("purchaseDecisionData");
    if (target.id == "purDecFlag1") {
        block.style.display = "block";
    } else {
        block.style.display = "none";
    }
}
```

See Also

Recipe 8.10 for disabling form controls; Recipe 12.10 for more examples of hiding and showing elements.

8.12 Allowing Only Numbers (or Letters) in a Text Box

Problem

You want to restrict a text field's data entry to numbers only, letters only, or characters from a fixed set.

Solution

You can allow keypress events to succeed only if the desired character keys are pressed. The following function, invoked from a text field's keypress event, allows only numerals 0 through 9 (no decimals or minus signs):

```
function numeralsOnly(evt) {
    evt = (evt) ? evt : event;
    var charCode = (evt.charCode) ? evt.charCode : ((evt.keyCode) ? evt.keyCode :
        ((evt.which) ? evt.which : 0));
    if (charCode > 31 && (charCode < 48 || charCode > 57)) {
        alert("Enter numerals only in this field.");
        return false;
    }
    return true;
}
```

The field's event handler would be configured like the following:

```
onkeypress="return numeralsOnly(event)"
```

Use the charCode values derived in the numeralsOnly( ) function just shown to make your own variations that permit your desired characters to be entered into the field.

Discussion

Observe the logic of the if condition in the numeralsOnly( ) function just shown. Restated in English, it blocks any character code greater than 31 and any code that is outside the ASCII value of the 10 numerals. It's important to allow ASCII values below 32 to pass through the field for most entries. All characters below 32 are non-alphanumeric characters, including the Backspace (8), Tab (9), and Return (13) keys. You usually don't want to block users from editing their entries.

You can cascade more character value comparisons as needed. For example, if you want to allow a decimal in the number, you'd add one more condition to the expression to block characters that met earlier conditions and were not the period's value of 46:

```
if (charCode > 31 && (charCode < 48 || charCode > 57) && charCode != 46) {...}
```

You should still perform validation on the entry to make sure the user hasn't entered more than one decimal.

When it comes to text box filtering that permits one or more letters, you must take upper- and lowercase letters into account. Upper- and lowercase versions of a character have their own ASCII values, and the two ranges are not contiguous (see Appendix A). Although you can go to great lengths to convert the ASCII value to a character and force its evaluation in strictly upper- or lowercase characters, it's easier to run your comparisons against two ranges of ASCII values. The following function permits letters of both cases (but no punctuation) to pass to the text box:

```
function lettersOnly(evt) {
    evt = (evt) ? evt : event;
    var charCode = (evt.charCode) ? evt.charCode : ((evt.keyCode) ? evt.keyCode :
        ((evt.which) ? evt.which : 0));
    if (charCode > 31 && (charCode < 65 || charCode > 90) &&
        (charCode < 97 || charCode > 122)) {
        alert("Enter letters only.");
        return false;
    }
    return true;
}
```

Recipe 9.9 contains a function that works only in IE to convert characters that are typed as lowercase Latin letters to uppercase Latin characters by the time they reach the text box. If your database requires uppercase characters, you can also consider using the field's client-side validation routine to change the value of the text box to a string of all uppercase letters:

```
form.field.value = form.field.value.toUpperCase();
```

Finally, here's a function that allows only a limited list of characters to be entered. For example, a database table may be set up to require a string entry of Y or N (for Yes or No). To make sure only those characters are entered into the field, the key filtering function (allowing upper- and lowercase letters) looks like the following:

```
function ynOnly(evt) {
    evt = (evt) ? evt : event;
    var charCode = (evt.charCode) ? evt.charCode : ((evt.keyCode) ? evt.keyCode :
        ((evt.which) ? evt.which : 0));
    if (charCode > 31 && charCode != 78 && charCode != 89 &&
        charCode != 110 && charCode != 121) {
        alert("Enter \"Y\" or \"N\" only.");
        return false;
    }
    return true;
}
```

In this case, you could add some more protection against incorrect entries by limiting the text box to a single character:

```
Signature Present: <input type="text" name="signature" size="2" maxlength="1"
onkeypress="return ynOnly(event)" /> (Y/N)
```

See Also

Recipe 9.9 for tips on examining the character the user typed before the character reaches the text field.

8.13 Auto-Tabbing for Fixed-Length Text Boxes

Problem

You want to advance the text cursor from one field to the next in a sequence of fixed-length boxes.

Solution

The following form excerpt requests the customer's credit card number in four segments of four characters each:

```
Credit Card Number:
<input type="text" name="cc1" size="5" maxlength="4"
    onkeypress="return numeralsOnly(event)"
    onkeyup="autofocus(this, 'cc2', event)" />  
<input type="text" name="cc2" size="5" maxlength="4"
    onkeypress="return numeralsOnly(event)"
    onkeyup="autofocus(this, 'cc3', event)" />  
<input type="text" name="cc3" size="5" maxlength="4"
    onkeypress="return numeralsOnly(event)"
    onkeyup="autofocus(this, 'cc4', event) /">  
<input type="text" name="cc4" size="5" maxlength="4"
    onkeypress="return numeralsOnly(event)" />
```

The keypress event handler for each field restricts entry to numerals (see Recipe 8.12), while the keyup event handlers invoke the following function, which advances focus to a named form field after a set number of characters:

```
function autofocus(field, next, evt) {
    evt = (evt) ? evt : event;
    var charCode = (evt.charCode) ? evt.charCode : ((evt.keyCode) ? evt.keyCode :
        ((evt.which) ? evt.which : 0));
    if (charCode > 31 && field.value.length == field.maxLength) {
        field.form.elements[next].focus();
    }
}
```

In this example, the final field does not advance focus, but you can add a keyup event handler that passes the name of the next form field to the autofocus( ) function.

Discussion

Many variations on the themes presented in the autofocus( ) function are possible with this application. While it could be customized to work with a known set of fields (tearing apart the name of the event-processing field and incrementing the numeral portion to derive the name of the next field—cc1, cc2, etc.), it is usually best to generalize the function so that it may be reused with other field sets on the same page or some other application later on. Thus, the second argument to autofocus( ) is the number of characters to act as the upper limit of acceptable length. The same function could be used for the segments of a U.S. Social Security number, which is in segment lengths of three, two, and four.

The reason for the initial character code analysis (charCode > 31) is to allow Shift-Tab to move focus in the reverse direction through these fields for the user's convenience. If you include the low-order ASCII characters in the four-character limit, the user could become lost in a frustrating focus circle.

See Also

Recipe 8.12 for limiting real-time text field entries to a subset of characters.

8.14   Changing select Element Content

Problem

You want to change the options in a select element in response to other form control settings.

Solution

Begin by removing all option elements from the desired select element:

```
document.myForm.mySelect.options.length = 0;
```

Then repopulate the option elements with new option objects:

```
document.myForm.mySelect.options[0] = new Option("Extra Fine", "xf", false, false);
document.myForm.mySelect.options[1] = new Option("Fine", "f", false, false);
document.myForm.mySelect.options[2] = new Option("Medium", "m", false, false);
```

This syntax works for all browsers back to IE 4 and even NN 4 (but Navigator 4 does not resize the width of the select element to fit new, wider option text, and generally requires a call to history.go(0) to force the revised options to appear).

Discussion

The constructor function syntax for the option object is as follows:

```
var newOpt = new Option("text", "value", isDefaultSelectedFlag, isSelectedFlag);
```

The *text* parameter is a string containing the item's label as seen by the user in the select list, while the *value* parameter is the otherwise hidden string that is submitted with the form if the option is selected. The two Boolean parameters let you set whether the option is the default selected option (i.e., the equivalent of having the selected attribute set in the HTML for the option element), and whether the option is currently selected.

You can replace individual options by assigning a new option object to one of the elements in the options array. But if you need to change multiple items, it's cleaner to remove all of the old ones and start the list fresh.

Data for the new option elements can come from sources such as JavaScript custom objects embedded within the page's script. This means that you have to include all possible data choices within the page's scripts. You'll also have to devise a data structure that works for the kind of data you want to convey via the select element. For example, consider a page that displays two select elements, from which users select the nearest city around the world to which to submit a form. The first select element lists regions of the world. With the choice of each region, the second select element lists the cities belonging only to that region. The HTML for the two select elements is as follows:

```html
Submit Request to: <select name="continent" onchange="setCities(this)">
    <option value="" selected>Choose a Region:</option>
    <option value="africa">Africa</option>
    <option value="asia">Asia</option>
    <option value="australia">Australia/Pacific</option>
    <option value="europe">Europe</option>
    <option value="noamer">North America</option>
    <option value="soamer">South America</option>
</select> 
<select name="city">
    <option value="" selected>Choose a City:</option>
</select>
```

A custom object contains all of the data required for the setCities( ) event handler function to modify the contents of the second select element. Here is the data structure for the data, delivered as a custom JavaScript object:

```javascript
var regiondb = new Object( )
regiondb["africa"] = [{value:"102", text:"Cairo"},
                      {value:"88", text:"Lagos"},
                      {value:"80", text:"Nairobi"},
                      {value:"55", text:"Pretoria"}];
regiondb["asia"] = [{value:"30", text:"Ankara"},
                    {value:"21", text:"Bangkok"},
                    {value:"49", text:"Beijing"},
                    {value:"76", text:"New Delhi"},
                    {value:"14", text:"Tokyo"}];
regiondb["australia"] = [{value:"64", text:"Suva"},
                         {value:"12", text:"Sydney"}];
regiondb["europe"] = [{value:"11", text:"Athens"},
                      {value:"35", text:"Frankfurt"},
                      {value:"3", text:"London"},
                      {value:"15", text:"Madrid"},
                      {value:"1", text:"Paris"},
                      {value:"10", text:"Rome"},
                      {value:"6", text:"Stockholm"},
                      {value:"97", text:"St. Petersburg"}];
regiondb["noamer"] = [{value:"73", text:"Dallas"},
                      {value:"71", text:"Los Angeles"},
```

```
                              {value:"5", text:"New York"},
                              {value:"37", text:"Toronto"}];
     regiondb["soamer"] = [{value:"65", text:"Buenos Aires"},
                              {value:"31", text:"Caracas"},
                              {value:"66", text:"Rio di Janeiro"}];
```

Each time the user makes a new selection from the first select element, the onchange event handler triggers the following function that repopulates the second select element:

```
function setCities(chooser) {
    var cityChooser = chooser.form.elements["city"];
    // empty previous settings
    cityChooser.options.length = 0;
    // get chosen value to act as index to regiondb hash table
    var choice = chooser.options[chooser.selectedIndex].value;
    var db = regiondb[choice];
    // insert default first item
    cityChooser.options[0] = new Option("Choose a City:", "", true, false);
    if (choice != "") {
        // loop through array of the hash table entry, and populate options
        for (var i = 0; i < db.length; i++) {
            cityChooser.options[i + 1] = new Option(db[i].text, db[i].value);
        }
    }
}
```

You can use the XMLHttpRequest object to retrieve data in XML or JSON format from the server. In the case of JSON, the string data would be structured so that an eval( ) method applied to the string creates a JavaScript object such as the regiondb example object shown earlier. This type of Ajax call makes the most sense when the possible choices for the second select element are lengthy.

In place of the DOM Level 0 syntax shown thus far, you may instead use the W3C DOM style of node tree modification syntax. You are free to use it for option element modification, but an inconsistency in the implementations between IE (through version 6) and the W3C DOM (as implemented in Mozilla) complicates the matter. The W3C DOM provides two methods of the select element, add( ) and remove( ), that slightly simplify the usual node tree modification sequence for this element. The following function is a W3C DOM version of the setCities( ) function shown earlier. It accounts for the browser differences in the second parameter of the add( ) method:

```
function setCities(chooser) {
    var newElem;
    var where = (navigator.appName == "Microsoft Internet Explorer") ? -1 : null;
    var cityChooser = chooser.form.elements["city"];
    while (cityChooser.options.length) {
        cityChooser.remove(0);
    }
    var choice = chooser.options[chooser.selectedIndex].value;
    var db = regiondb[choice];
    newElem = document.createElement("option");
```

```
newElem.text = "Choose a City:";
newElem.value = "";
cityChooser.add(newElem, where);
if (choice != "") {
    for (var i = 0; i < db.length; i++) {
        newElem = document.createElement("option");
        newElem.text = db[i].text;
        newElem.value = db[i].value;
        cityChooser.add(newElem, where);
    }
}
}
```

The second parameter of the `add( )` method determines the location of the added
option element. The W3C DOM expects either a reference to an existing `option` element or `null`. The latter signifies that the added element goes to the end of the list.
IE's second parameter is optional, but when supplied, it is supposed to be an integer
pointing to the zero-based index of the options array where the added element is to
go. If you omit the second parameter or supply a `-1`, the new option goes to the end
of the list. That is the reason for the brief browser sniffing near the beginning of the
function to set the second parameter value.

See Also

Recipe 3.8 for creating custom object data structures.

8.15 Copying Form Data Between Pages

Problem

You want to convey all form control settings from one page to another.

Solution

Use the *stringForms.js* library shown in the Discussion to convert all values in a form
to a string that can be passed to another page via URLs or cookies. Invoke the
`form2ArrayString( )` function, passing as an argument a reference to the form in need
of conversion. The function returns a string whose format is of a shortcut constructor
of an array of objects. Each object represents a form control in the following format:

    {name:'*elemName*',id:'*elemID*',type:'*elemType*',value:*value*}

To distribute the values to a form with the same control structure, invoke
`string2FormObj( )`, passing parameters for a reference to the destination form and to
the string originally created by the `form2ArrayString( )` function.

Discussion

Example 8-4 shows the code for the *stringForms.js* library (applied in Recipe 10.6).
The library provides two main functions that your scripts invoke: `form2ArrayString( )`,

which converts a form's content to a string formatted like a JavaScript array of objects, and `string2FormObj( )`, which copies values from the array to form controls in another page that have the same names or IDs.

Example 8-4. The stringForms.js library

```
// Read the name, id, type, and value of one form control element
// as requested by form2ArrayString( )
function formObj2String(obj) {
    var output = "{";
    if (obj.name) {
        output += "name:'" + obj.name + "',";
    }
    if (obj.id) {
        output += "id:'" + obj.id + "',";
    }
    output += "type:'" + obj.type + "',";
    switch (obj.type) {
        case "radio":
            if (obj.name) {
                obj = document.forms[0].elements[obj.name];
                var radioVal = "value:false,index:-1";
                for (var i = 0; i < obj.length; i++) {
                    if (obj[i].checked) {
                        radioVal = "value:true,index:" + i;
                        i = obj.length;
                    }
                }
                output += radioVal;
            } else {
                output += "value:" + obj.checked;
            }
            break;
        case "checkbox":
            output += "value:" + obj.checked;
            break;
        case "select-one":
            output += "value:" + obj.selectedIndex;
            break;
        case "select-multiple":
            output += "value:" + obj.selectedIndex;
            break;
        case "text":
            output += "value:'" + escape(obj.value) + "'";
            break;
        case "textarea":
            output += "value:'" + escape(obj.value) + "'";
            break;
        case "password":
            output += "value:'" + escape(obj.value) + "'";
            break;
        case "hidden":
            output += "value:'" + escape(obj.value) + "'";
            break;
```

Example 8-4. The stringForms.js library (continued)

```
            default:
                output += "";
        }
        output += "}"
        return output;
    }
// Convert a passed form reference to a string formatted like
// a JavaScript array of objects
function form2ArrayString(form) {
    var elem, lastName = "";
    var output = "[";
    for (var i = 0; i < form.elements.length; i++) {
        elem = form.elements[i];
        if (elem.name && (elem.name != lastName)) {
            output += formObj2String(form.elements[i]) + ",";
            lastName = elem.name;
        }
    }
    output = output.substring(0, output.length-1) + "]";
    return output;
}


// Distribute form control values from another source to the
// controls in this page's form, whose names/ids match those
// of the original form controls
function string2FormObj(form, str) {
    var elem, objArray = eval(str);
    for (var i = 0; i < objArray.length; i++) {
        elem = (objArray[i].name) ? form.elements[objArray[i].name] :
            document.getElementById(objArray[i].id);
        switch (objArray[i].type) {
            case "radio":
                if (objArray[i].name && objArray[i].value && objArray[i].index >= 0) {
                    elem = elem[objArray[i].index];
                }
                elem.checked = objArray[i].value;
                break;
            case "checkbox":
                elem.checked = objArray[i].value;
                break;
            case "select-one":
                elem.selectedIndex = objArray[i].value;
                break;
            case "select-multiple":
                elem.selectedIndex = objArray[i].value;
                break;
            default:
                elem.value = unescape(objArray[i].value);
        }
    }
}
```

The `form2ArrayString()` function manages the conversion process by iterating through all elements of a form. For each element, it invokes the support function, `formObj2String()`, which does the hard work of this library. The purpose of the `formObj2String()` function is to convert basic specifications about a passed form control element to a string formatted as a shortcut object creation sequence. Each of these objects contains four properties: `name`, `id`, `type`, and `value`. Each control type that accepts user input and can be read without security violations is accounted for.

Your scripts invoke the `form2ArrayString()` function to obtain the string specification of the form's controls. Pass a reference to the form on the source page whose values you want to preserve. The function returns a string that looks like shortcut array notation. Each array entry is a string representation of an object whose properties define a single form control. This string may be passed as a search string in a URL or saved as a cookie for reading by another page from the same server and domain.

When it's time to reapply the values to a form on another page, use the `string2FormObj()` function of this library. Pass to this function a reference to the form on the current page and the string containing the array syntax. Although normally avoided for performance reasons, you need the `eval()` function here to convert the array string into an actual array object. Form controls with the same name (or, lacking a name, the ID) of the original form are populated with the same values reported previously. Other form controls with unique names are not disturbed.

While the *stringForms.js* library takes into account the peculiar ways that radio buttons share the same name, it does not preserve multiple selection values of a `select-multiple` type of `select` element. Instead, the function relies exclusively on the `selectedIndex` property of the element. You could modify the library to accommodate multiple selections by preserving the value as an array (in string format, of course) of options whose `selected` property is `true`.

The importance of preserving form specifications in string format becomes evident when you need to convey the data across pages. As described in Recipe 10.4 and Recipe 10.6, two of the three ways to pass data from one page to the next (URLs and cookies) require that the data be in string format. The JavaScript shortcut syntax for creating arrays and objects comes in very handy here, because the strings are very compact (compared to other kinds of formats), making it less likely that you'll overrun the 512-character limit of URLs, or the practical 2 KB limit of a single cookie value.

See Also

Recipes 3.1 and 3.8 for more about shortcut array and object creation syntax; Recipe 3.13 for a similar type of object-to-string conversion for custom objects; Recipe 10.4 for passing string data between pages via cookies; Recipe 10.6 for data passing via URL search strings.

CHAPTER 9

Managing Events

9.0   Introduction

Without events, there would be no Dynamic HTML. A strong statement, perhaps, but given the kinds of document object models we have inherited, it's true. For any dynamism to occur in an HTML page, some kind of trigger is needed.

Two categories of triggers are available: user-generated actions and system-generated actions. Direct *user-generated actions* are those caused by mouse and keyboard activity. *System-generated actions* occur when something significant occurs in the browser, such as the document completing its loading into the browser or an image failing to retrieve its data from the server.

One of your jobs as a DHTML scripter is to determine which events on which elements or objects should trigger scripted actions. Any kind of form button, for example, will usually have some script action associated with it (unless it is just the default actions of submit and reset input element types). Less obvious, perhaps, are events that inspect the characters being typed into a text box, to make sure only allowed characters are permitted to pass. Very common mouse-oriented events detect when the cursor rolls atop an image element (or an a hyperlink element surrounding the image) so that a script can change the image to a highlighted version during this "rollover." A corresponding event for when the cursor rolls off the image reverts the image back to its default version. Even the background processing of the `XMLHttpRequest` object fires events while it is in the process of receiving data from a server.

The Event-Scripting Process

In scripting terms, you need a way to connect the occurrence of an event to some function that carries out tasks for that event. Events are said to be *bound* to an element or object. You instruct an element or object to be on the lookout for an event of a particular type that comes its way. For example, you can instruct a button to respond to a mouse click on it, while all surrounding elements ignore clicks on them.

Syntax for event binding takes on many forms (see the Discussion for Recipe 9.1), but the basic task for the scripter is to assign a function to a particular event of a particular element or object. The assignment statement is sometimes called an *event handler*, and the function assigned to the event handler is called an *event handler function*. Thus, when the user clicks on a button that has pre-assigned the handleClick( ) function to the click event, that event handler function runs whenever the user clicks on the button.

You can assign functions to as many event types on as many elements and objects as your content and interface design require. For example, you can instruct an image to change its picture to a highlighted version when the user rolls the cursor atop the img element on the page, and then change to a concave image of itself when the user presses down on the image via the mouse button. Upon release of the mouse button, the image goes back to the rollover highlight color. When the cursor leaves the rectangle of the image, the image reverts to its original file. In this case, the img element might have four event handlers assigned to it (for the mouseover, mousedown, mouseup, and mouseout events, respectively) and a different event handler function assigned to each event.

Event Types

Knowledge of the range of event types available to you will have a substantial impact on the amount and kind of user interaction you design into your pages. Several event types have been around since at least the days of IE 4 and NN 4 browsers. These generic events act as a lowest common denominator of events that do not depend on any particular browser or operating system. Table 9-1 lists these event types and their browser compatibility ratings, as well as whether the HTML 4 standard recognizes the event handler as a tag attribute (the event type with the "on" prefix). Modern browsers (Mozilla, Safari, and Opera) support all of the types shown in Table 9-1. While most of these event types can be bound to any rendered element in the latest browsers, events in earlier browsers (especially IE 3 and Navigator through version 4) were limited to a handful of elements.

Table 9-1. Event types for early DHTML browsers

Event type	NN	IE/ Win	IE/ Mac	HTML	Description
abort	3	4	3.01	n/a	The user has interrupted the transfer of an image to the client.
blur	2	3	3.01	4	An element has lost the input focus because the user clicked out of the element or pressed the Tab key.
change	2	3	3.01	4	An element has lost focus and the content of the element has changed since it gained focus.
click	2	3	3.01	4	The user has pressed and released a mouse button (or keyboard equivalent) on an element.

Table 9-1. Event types for early DHTML browsers (continued)

Event type	NN	IE/ Win	IE/ Mac	HTML	Description
dblclick	4	4	3.01	4	The user has double-clicked a mouse button on an element.
error	3	4	4	n/a	An error has occurred in a script or during the loading of some external data.
focus	2	3	3.01	4	An element has received the input focus.
keydown	4	4	4	4	The user has begun pressing a keyboard character key.
keypress	4	4	4	4	The user has pressed and released a keyboard character key.
keyup	4	4	4	4	The user has released a keyboard character key.
load	2	3	3.01	4	A document or other external element has completed downloading all data into the browser.
mousedown	4	4	4	4	The user has begun pressing a mouse button.
mousemove	4	4	4	4	The user has rolled the mouse (irrespective of mouse button state).
mouseout	3	3	3.01	4	The user has rolled the mouse out of an element.
mouseover	2	3	3.01	4	The user has rolled the mouse atop an element.
mouseup	4	4	4	4	The user has released the mouse button.
move	4	3	4	n/a	The user has moved the browser window.
reset	3	4	4	4	The user has clicked a Reset button in a form.
resize	4	4	4	n/a	The user has resized a window or object.
select	2	3	3	4	The user is selecting text in an input or textarea element.
submit	2	3	3.01	4	A form is about to be submitted.
unload	2	3	3.01	4	A document is about to be unloaded from a window or frame.

Beyond the cross-browser events in Table 9-1, Microsoft implements an additional set that allows DHTML scripts to react to more specific user and system actions. Table 9-2 lists the IE events that may assist a DHTML application—almost all of them assist only the Windows version because of IE's tight integration with the operating system. Apple has implemented several of these events in recent versions of Safari, as shown. Not listed in Table 9-2 are the many event types that apply only to Internet Explorer's data binding facilities, which allow form elements to be bound to server database sources.

Table 9-2. Internet Explorer DHTML events

Event type	IE/ Win	IE/ Mac	Safari	Description
activate	5.5	n/a	n/a	An object has become active (but not necessarily focused).
afterprint	5	n/a	n/a	Data has been sent to the pringer.
beforeactivate	6	n/a	n/a	An object is about to become the active object.
beforecopy	5	n/a	1.3/2	The user has issued a Copy command, but the operation has not yet begun.
beforecut	5	n/a	1.3/2	The user has issued a Cut command, but the operation has not yet begun.
beforedeactivate	5.5	n/a	n/a	The active object is about to yield to a different object.
beforepaste	5	n/a	1.3/2	The user has issued a Paste command, but the operation has not yet begun.
beforeprint	5	n/a	n/a	The user has issued a Print command, but the document has not yet been sent to the printer.
contextmenu	5	n/a	all	The user has pressed the context menu (i.e., "right-click") mouse button.
copy	5	n/a	1.3/2	The user has initiated a Copy command, but the operation has not yet begun.
cut	5	n/a	1.3/2	The user has issued a Cut command, but the operation has not yet begun.
deactivate	5.5	n/a	n/a	An object has yielded to another active object.
drag	5	n/a	1.3/2	The user is dragging the element.
dragend	5	n/a	1.3/2	The user has completed dragging the element.
dragenter	5	n/a	1.3/2	The user has dragged an element into the space of the current element.
dragleave	5	n/a	1.3/2	The user has dragged an element out of the space of the current element.
dragover	5	n/a	1.3/2	The user is dragging an element through the space of the current element.
dragstart	5	n/a	1.3/2	The user has begun dragging a selection.
drop	5	n/a	1.3/2	The user has dropped a dragged element atop the current element.
focusin	6	n/a	n/a	The user has acted to give focus to the element, but the actual focus has not yet occurred; the event fires before onfocus.
focusout	6	n/a	n/a	The user has given focus to another element; the event fires before onblur.
help	4	4	n/a	The user has pressed the F1 key or chosen Help from the browser menu.
mouseenter	5.5	n/a	n/a	The user has moved the cursor into the space of the element.
mouseleave	5.5	n/a	n/a	The user has moved the cursor to outside the space of the element.
mousewheel	6	n/a	n/a	The user is rolling the mouse wheel.

Table 9-2. Internet Explorer DHTML events (continued)

Event type	IE/ Win	IE/ Mac	Safari	Description
moveend	5.5	n/a	n/a	A positioned element has completed its motion.
movestart	5.5	n/a	n/a	A positioned element is starting its motion.
paste	5	n/a	1.3/2	The user has issued a Paste command, but the operation has not yet begun.
scroll	4	4	n/a	The user has adjusted an element's scrollbar.
selectstart	4	4	1.3/2	The user is beginning to select an element.

Keeping all of these events and their idiosyncrasies straight is not an easy task. To get into the depths of the more esoteric events, find a good DHTML reference (such as my book *Dynamic HTML: The Definitive Reference* [O'Reilly]).

Event Models

The key to working with events over the long term is knowing how to take advantage of the abstract event object that is created each time an event registers with the browser. An event object contains numerous properties that describe the details of the event, such as the identity of the element receiving the event, mouse coordinates, keyboard characters, and even a self-descriptive property revealing the type of the event. The purpose of this event object is to let event handler functions derive details that could be useful for processing the event. For example, if a mousemove event handler is being programmed to reposition an element along with the cursor, the event handler function needs to know the coordinates of the mouse at each firing of the mousemove event.

Complicating matters, however, is the fact that the event model that defines what an event object should be and how it should behave is not the same across all DHTML browsers. As of Internet Explorer 7, Microsoft has not yet implemented the W3C DOM Level 2 event model. Mozilla, Safari, and Opera, however, have followed the W3C DOM event model, adopting only a couple of IE convenience properties along the way. Each model supports a different way of communicating the event object to an event handler function, so Recipe 9.1 demonstrates how to equalize that discrepancy. You may also need to equalize the properties of the two event objects to make one function operate in both worlds. Table 9-3 provides an overview of the comparative event object properties in the two object models.

Table 9-3. Equivalent properties of the IE and W3C DOM event objects

IE property	Description	W3C property or method
altKey	The Alt key was pressed during the event (Boolean).	altKey
button	The mouse button was pressed in the mouse event (integer, but different numbering systems per model).	button
cancelBubble[a]	Whether the event should bubble further.	stopPropagation()

IE property	Description	W3C property or method
clientX, clientY	The horizontal and vertical coordinates of the event in the content region of the browser window.	clientX, clientY
ctrlKey	The Ctrl key was pressed during the event (Boolean).	ctrlKey
fromElement	The object or element from which the pointer moved for a mouseover or mouseout event.	relatedTarget
keyCode	The keyboard character code of a keyboard event (integer).	keyCode
offsetX, offsetY	The horizontal and vertical coordinates of the event within the element space.	(calculated from other properties)
(calculated from other properties)	The horizontal and vertical coordinates of the event within the document space.	pageX, pageY[b]
returnValue	The value returned to the system by the event (used to prevent default action in IE).	preventDefault( )
screenX, screenY	The horizontal and vertical coordinates of the event relative to the screen.	screenX, screenY
shiftKey	The Shift key was pressed during the event (Boolean).	shiftKey
srcElement	The object or element intended to receive the event.	target
toElement	The object or element to which the pointer moved for a mouseover or mouseout event.	relatedTarget
type	The name of the event (without "on" prefix).	type
x, y	The horizontal and vertical coordinates of the event within the body element (for unpositioned target) or the positioned element.	layerX, layerY[c]

[a] Supported in Mozilla-based browsers for convenience.
[b] Not part of the W3C DOM spec, but supported by Mozilla, Safari, and Opera.
[c] Not part of the W3C DOM spec, but supported by Mozilla and Safari.

A few of the recipes in this chapter demonstrate how to equalize the most commonly accessed properties of the IE and W3C DOM event objects.

9.1 Equalizing the IE and W3C Event Models

Problem

You want a script to inspect details about a particular event when the page is loaded in Internet Explorer and in a W3C DOM browser that supports only the W3C DOM event model.

Solution

Because Internet Explorer (at least through version 7) does not implement the W3C DOM event model, and because pure W3C DOM browsers such as Mozilla and

Safari implement only the W3C DOM event model, you must use model-specific ways to derive a common reference to the event to assist further processing.

Event handlers receive a reference to the W3C DOM event object as a parameter (see the Discussion), whereas the IE event object is a property of the window object. To accommodate both and end up with a single reference that subsequent statements can use to examine the event object, use the following skeletal structure in every event-invoked function:

```
function functionName(evt) {
    evt = (evt) ? evt : ((window.event) ? event : null);
    if (evt) {
        // perform processing here
    }
}
```

This structure uses object detection, rather than browser version sniffing, to not only extract the event model-specific reference, but also guard against script errors if the browser does not support either event model (i.e., much older browsers responding to simple events).

If your script structure prevents older browsers from invoking event handler functions (e.g., you use object detection to make sure only newer browsers bind events to elements), the first statement of the handler function can use shortcut notation—via the OR (||) JavaScript operator—to assign the browser-supported event object to the evt variable, as follows:

```
function functionName(evt) {
    evt = (evt) || window.event;
    // perform processing here
}
```

You will see this notation used in several scripts later in this book.

Discussion

Getting a non-IE event model browser to pass the event object to the event handler function requires either a little planning ahead or none whatsoever, depending on the way you bind your event handlers to element objects. The W3C DOM specification formally supports event binding only via the addEventListener( ) method of any element, as in the following example:

```
document.getElementById("myButton").addEventListener("click", processClick, false);
```

A function triggered by an event bound to the element in this fashion automatically passes the event object as the sole parameter to the function. All you need to do is catch the parameter by assigning a function parameter variable at the start of the function definition (i.e., the evt inside parentheses in the skeletal structure shown in the Solution).

IE's preferred event binding is through the attachEvent( ) method. Its syntax, however, is different from that of the W3C's addEventListener( ) method. In a moment, you'll see how to reconcile the differences.

Fortunately for cross-platform developers, two pre-W3C DOM ways of binding events to elements work without a problem in all modern browsers—and will likely do so for a long time to come. Those two approaches are assigned as element object properties, and assigned the original way, as attributes inside the element's tag.

Assigning an event as a property of an object is performed in one JavaScript statement. The left side of the statement is a reference to the element object and a property consisting of the event handler name (with the "on" prefix) in lowercase letters; the right side is a reference to the function to be invoked when that element receives the event. A function reference is just the function's name without parentheses, as in:

```
document.getElementById("myButton").onclick = processClick;
```

Events bound this way in browsers such as Mozilla automatically pass the event object as the sole parameter to the function.

Although at first the event property binding technique appears to preclude passing parameters, you can use an anonymous function (Recipe 4.4) to fill the gap. The following example passes both the W3C DOM event object and a timestamp of the event to the processClick( ) function:

```
document.getElementById("myButton").onclick = function(evt) {processClick(new Date( ),
evt);};
```

You can pass any literal values or variables within the scope of the assignment statement (e.g., a local variable if this statement appears inside a function).

Despite the number of competing binding techniques, save yourself a lot of anguish by combining three techniques (W3C standard, IE proprietary, and event properties) into a library, such as *eventsManager.js*. Two of the library's three functions (the third is described in Recipe 9.3) are as follows:

```
function addEvent(elem, evtType, func, capture) {
   capture = (capture) ? capture : false;
   if (elem.addEventListener) {
      elem.addEventListener(evtType, func, capture);
   } else if (elem.attachEvent) {
      elem.attachEvent("on" + evtType, func);
   } else {
      // for IE/Mac, NN4, and older
      elem["on" + evtType] = func;
   }
}

function removeEvent(elem, evtType, func, capture) {
   capture = (capture) ? capture : false;
   if (elem.removeEventListener) {
      elem.removeEventListener(evtType, func, capture);
```

```
        } else if (elem.attachEvent) {
            elem.detachEvent("on" + evtType, func);
        } else {
            // for IE/Mac, NN4, and older
            elem["on" + evtType] = null;
        }
    }
```

These two functions offer a simple interface for your code to bind and unbind events to element objects. For example, the button event example used so far would be handled by the following:

```
addEvent(document.getElementById("myButton"), "click", processClick, false);
```

The library applies the preferred binding syntax to each browser class, including a version for older browsers.

One other cross-platform (and fully backward-compatible) event binding mechanism is through an attribute embedded in the element's tag. You see a lot of this in code around the Internet because it was the original way event binding took place when scripting started. It is also a convenient way to pass one or more parameters of your choosing to the function. Therefore, it's common to see input form controls pass a reference to the element itself (this) or the containing form element (this. form) to make it easier for the function to work directly with the element's value or other controls in the form. But to convey the W3C DOM event object to the handler function, events bound this way must also explicitly include the keyword event as one of the parameters:

```
<input type="button" name="myButton" id="myButton" value="Process"
onclick="processClick(event)" />
```

You can pass multiple parameters if you like, but the position of the parameters being passed must be the same in the parameter variable definitions in the function. For example, the event handler defined as:

```
onclick="processClick(this.form, event)"
```

must have a function defined with two parameter variables to catch the passed arguments:

```
function processClick(form, evt) {...}
```

When you include the explicit event object as a parameter, IE also passes its version of the event object, so the syntax does double duty. But the trend in scripting and document markup in general is to get away from this in-tag event binding and gravitate toward other approaches exemplified by the *eventsManager.js* library, earlier—all in the name of separating content from style and processing.

Binding events by a process other than in-tag attributes, however, has its own gotchas to be aware of. The most significant is that you cannot simply bind events to objects while the page loads but before the objects are loaded into the browser. The Java-Script interpreter attempts to resolve all assignment statements when they execute. If the object is not yet known to the object model, the assignment fails (with a script error). This goes even for the body element: assigning an event handler property to document.body in the head portion of the document triggers script errors in some browsers.

To work around this conundrum, you can place (almost) all of your event assignments in a function that gets invoked after the entire page has loaded. See Recipes 9.2 and 9.3 for more details.

If you use the event object equalization routine shown in the Solution, you may still have to perform additional platform-specific equalizations in your handler function. This occurs whenever the property you're looking for is known by different names (see Recipes 9.4 and 9.7 for examples). But there is also a sufficient amount of similarity between the two objects' properties that they are quite useful blended into a single event handler function.

See Also

Table 9-3 in the introduction of this chapter for a comparative list of event object properties; all other recipes throughout this book that process events using the event object equalization technique shown here; Recipe 9.2 for triggering a function (for event handler property assignments) after the page loads; Recipes 9.4 and 9.7 for equalizing disparate event object properties.

9.2   Initiating a Process After the Page Loads

Problem

When a new page loads into the browser, you want to execute script statements requiring that all content, including images and plug-ins or ActiveX controls, be loaded and ready to go.

Solution

The load event of the window object fires after all content and processes coded in the HTML have finished loading and self-initializing. Use this event to trigger the function(s) needed to complete the initialization of your scripted objects. All scriptable browsers support the following syntax:

```
<body onload="myInitFunction( )"> ... </body>
```

All browsers back to Navigator 3 and Internet Explorer 4 support the following script syntax, which may be included in a script located in the head portion of the document:

```
window.onload = myInitFunction;
```

In this latter case, make sure the myInitFunction( ) is defined earlier in the script code than the event assignment statement.

Discussion

Do not, under any circumstances, bind load events both by script and onload attribute in the <body> tag. If the scripts execute in the head, the attribute binding overwrites the earlier property assignments.

Event binding via property assignment does not allow multiple function assignments to the same event. If you include a second statement for the same object and event, it overrides the first. Therefore, if you need multiple functions initialized for window. onload, direct the event to fire a dispatcher-like function that then invokes each of your detailed initialization functions in the desired sequence:

```
function startup( ) {
    initDHTMLAPI( );
    setHeights( );
}
window.onload = startup;
```

Recipe 9.3 shows an even more flexible way to handle multiple initializations.

Initializing event handlers after the document has loaded brings you and your users one extra benefit: events do nothing until all of the page's content is loaded into the browser. This is especially helpful if your page includes scripts that communicate with plug-ins or ActiveX controls. If a user clicks on a button that triggers a script before the ancillary machinery is in place, script errors will occur.

Using the load event handler as a trigger for scripted event binding offers some intriguing benefits. First of all, you automatically ensure that very old browsers won't respond to events because they don't understand the event name properties. The result is that you filter out browsers that choke on function handlers intended for more modern browsers. Second, you can filter out even more browsers with the help of object detection. For example, if you wish to limit event function access to browsers that support the basic W3C DOM element object reference syntax, you can surround the event assignment statements by conditional statements that validate browser support for your requirements:

```
function initEvents( ) {
    // these events OK with all but NN2 and IE3
    document.forms[0].onsubmit = validateMainForm;
    document.forms[0].elements["email"].onchange = validateEmail;
    if (document.getElementById) {
        // these work only when W3C DOM is supported
        document.getElementById("logo").onclick = goHome;
        document.body.onclick = blockEvent;
    }
}
window.onload = initEvents;
```

This approach is far superior to wrapping script statement blocks in <script> tags that define the JavaScript version through the language attribute (e.g., language="JavaScript1.2"). Using the core JavaScript language versions as a predictor of things such as document object model version and support is foolhardy. Use object detection instead.

See Also

The Discussion in Recipe 9.1 on event binding types; Recipe 9.3 for managing multiple load events, even when they are specified in multiple library files.

9.3   Appending Multiple Load Event Handlers

Problem

You have multiple .js library or other initializations that need to execute after the page loads.

Solution

Use a generic load event queue manager as part of the *eventsManager.js* file introduced in Recipe 9.1. Each library can self-initialize itself by including a call to the addOnLoadEvent( ) function of the library, such as the following:

```
addOnLoadEvent(initMyLib);
```

Because succeeding calls to addOnLoadEvent( ) append the passed function to the end of the load event queue, you can invoke addOnLoadEvent( ) as often as needed in external libraries and main page scripts.

Discussion

The addOnLoadEvent( ) function relies on the addEvent( ) function from the *eventsManager.js* library shown in Recipe 9.1. Therefore, it makes sense to band all of these functions into the *eventsManager.js* library.

The code for addOnLoadEvent( ) is as follows:

```
function addOnLoadEvent(func) {
    if (window.addEventListener || window.attachEvent) {
        addEvent(window, "load", func, false);
    } else {
        var oldQueue = (window.onload) ? window.onload : function() {};
        window.onload = function() {
            oldQueue();
            func();
        }
    }
}
```

For browsers that support either the W3C DOM event model or IE proprietary model, the function invokes addEvent( ) from Recipe 9.1. This recipe uses the object-model-appropriate syntax for binding the function reference to the event type. Both the addEventListener( ) and attachEvent( ) methods accept multiple invocations on the same element and event type, keeping each event binding (event type-to-function) separate.

If the order of initializations is critical to the successful operation of your systems, be aware of a significant difference between the addEventListener( ) and attachEvent( ) methods. Functions bound via addEventListener( ) are invoked in the order in which they were bound (first in, first executed); functions bound via attachEvent( ) are invoked in the reverse order (last in, first executed) when the load event fires.

For older browsers that don't support the advanced event binding syntax, the addOnLoadEvent( ) function creates its own queue of load event function calls. The queue is built by assembling a chain of nested anonymous function calls (facilitated by JavaScript closures).

Initialization methods of custom objects exhibit what may appear to be odd behavior when they are invoked from the load event. For example, consider the *DHTML3API.js* library described in Recipe 13.3. This library creates a single object, named DHTMLAPI, whose definition includes an init( ) method. The init( ) method sets some property names that other methods of the object rely on later. The normal way of referring to properties within the DHTMLAPI object is via the this keyword. The keyword points to the context in which the current object runs. During initialization triggered by the load event, however, the context is the window object, not the DHTMLAPI object. References to this.*propertyName* fail to refer to properties within the custom object.

To circumvent this potential problem, you can, in a sense, decouple the object from the window object whose load event invokes the init( ) method. Do so by defining the function parameter of addOnLoadEvent( ) as an anonymous function that wraps around the call to the init( ) method:

```
addOnLoadEvent(function() {DHTMLAPI.init( )});
```

This syntax forces the DHTMLAPI.init( ) method to execute within the context of the DHTMLAPI object. References to the this keyword point to the object, and not the window whose load event causes the method to execute.

See Also

Recipe 9.1 for other parts of the *eventsManager.js* library; Recipe 3.8 for creating custom objects; Recipe 4.4 for more on anonymous functions.

9.4 Determining the Coordinates of a Click Event

Problem

You want to read the x,y coordinates of a click (or other) event with respect to the coordinate plane of the entire page or just the element being clicked.

Solution

This recipe presents solutions for two situations because each has its own idiosyncrasies when trying to merge event coordinates with page coordinates typically used for positioning elements. The same scenario is assumed: a user clicks somewhere on the page to point to a location where a positioned element is to be placed. Imagine the user clicking on a map to position an arrow graphic. Differences accrue as to whether the positioning is relative to the page or to the rectangle occupied by a positioned element. Use one of two functions described in the Discussion, getPageEventCoords( ) or getPositionedEventCoords( ), to obtain coordinates that coincide with the event's coordinates. Both functions return an object with left and top properties whose values represent position coordinates.

The basis for this example's user interface is one of two versions of the moveToClick( ) function, which relies on the moveTo( ) method of the DHTML API (Recipe 13.3). When the user clicks anywhere within the scope of the event binding with the Shift key down, the top-left corner of a positioned element is brought to the click spot.

The first case we'll cover obtains coordinates relative to the space occupied by the entire page, so you can position the top-left corner of a first-level (i.e., nonnested) positioned element at the spot of a user click. The event binding can be assigned to the document object:

```
document.onmousedown = moveToClick;
```

For this version, the moveToClick( ) function calls upon getPageEventCoords( ). Returned values are applied as arguments to the shiftTo( ) function:

```
function moveToClick(evt) {
    evt = (evt) ? evt : event;
    if (evt.shiftKey) {
        var coords = getPageEventCoords(evt);
        DHTMLAPI.moveTo("mapArrow", coords.left, coords.top);
    }
}
```

For the second click-positioning case, the task is to locate a nested-positioned element inside its parent-positioned element. In other words, the goal is to get the coordinates of the click within the outer-positioned element because the outer element defines its own rectangle as the coordinate plane for its children. It's best in this situation to bind the event handler to the outer-positioned element, although it's not a requirement. It just makes it easier to confine processing to clicks on that element

---

rather than the entire document. In an initialization routine triggered by the load event, bind the event accordingly:

```
document.getElementById("myMap").onmousedown = moveToClick;
```

moveToClick( ) calls upon getPositionedEventCoords( ) to read the nested coordinates:

```
function moveToClick(evt) {
    evt = (evt) ? evt : event;
    if (evt.shiftKey) {
        var coords = getPositionedEventCoords(evt);
        DHTMLAPI.moveTo("mapArrow", coords.left, coords.top);
    }
}
```

Discussion

To determine the mouse event location in the coordinate plane of the entire document, the getPageEventCoords( ) function shown in the following example has two main branches. The first gets the simpler pageX and pageY properties of the event object supported in Mozilla, Safari, and Opera. For IE, many more calculations need to be carried out to derive the coordinates to accurately position an element at the specified location. The clientX and clientY properties need additional factors for any scrolling of the body content and some small padding that IE automatically adds to the body (normally two pixels along both axes). In the case of IE 6 or later running in CSS-compatibility mode, the html element's small padding must also be factored out of the equation.

```
function getPageEventCoords(evt) {
    var coords = {left:0, top:0};
    if (evt.pageX) {
        coords.left = evt.pageX;
        coords.top = evt.pageY;
    } else if (evt.clientX) {
        coords.left =
            evt.clientX + document.body.scrollLeft - document.body.clientLeft;
        coords.top =
            evt.clientY + document.body.scrollTop - document.body.clientTop;
        // include html element space, if applicable
        if (document.body.parentElement && document.body.parentElement.clientLeft) {
            var bodParent = document.body.parentElement;
            coords.left += bodParent.scrollLeft - bodParent.clientLeft;
            coords.top += bodParent.scrollTop - bodParent.clientTop;
        }
    }
    return coords;
}
```

Deriving the event coordinates inside a positioned element is the job of the getPositionedEventCoords( ) function, shown in the following code listing. Mozilla and Safari provide special event object properties (layerX and layerY) which provide the desired offset values within a positioned element. Adjustments are needed, however, if the positioned element has borders. The IE branch (for Opera, too), which supports the offsetX and offsetY properties of the event object, is the easy one here. Those values are relative to the coordinate plane of the positioned element target. To prevent the event from propagating any further (and possibly conflicting with other mousedown event targets), the event's cancelBubble property is set to true:

```
function getPositionedEventCoords(evt) {
    var elem = (evt.target) ? evt.target : evt.srcElement;
    var coords = {left:0, top:0};
    if (evt.layerX) {
        var borders = {left:parseInt(DHTMLAPI.getComputedStyle("progressBar",
                        "border-left-width")),
                       top:parseInt(getElementStyle("progressBar",
                        "border-top-width"))};
        coords.left = evt.layerX - borders.left;
        coords.top = evt.layerY - borders.top;
    } else if (evt.offsetX) {
        coords.left = evt.offsetX;
        coords.top = evt.offsetY;
    }
    evt.cancelBubble = true;
    return coords;
}
```

A compatibility complication must be accounted for, however. If the outer element has a CSS border assigned to it, Mozilla and IE (in any mode) disagree whether the coordinate plane begins where the border starts or where the content rectangle starts. Mozilla includes the border; IE does not. Therefore, along the way, the situation is equalized by factoring out the border in the Mozilla calculations. This is done with the help of the getComputedStyle( ) method from Recipe 13.3:

```
// return computed value for an element's style property
getComputedStyle : function (elemRef, CSSStyleProp) {
    var elem = this.getRawObject(elemRef);
    var styleValue, camel;
    if (elem) {
        if (document.defaultView && document.defaultView.getComputedStyle) {
            // W3C DOM version
            var compStyle = document.defaultView.getComputedStyle(elem, "");
            styleValue = compStyle.getPropertyValue(CSSStyleProp);
        } else if (elem.currentStyle) {
            // make IE style property camelCase name from CSS version
            var IEStyleProp = CSSStyleProp;
            var re = /-\D/;
            while (re.test(IEStyleProp)) {
                camel = IEStyleProp.match(re)[0].charAt(1).toUpperCase( );
                IEStyleProp = IEStyleProp.replace(re, camel);
            }
            styleValue = elem.currentStyle[IEStyleProp];
        }
    }
    return (styleValue) ? styleValue : null;
}
```

It may seem odd that deriving these kinds of event coordinates should be so laborious in one circumstance or the other. There is little justification for this, except perhaps that those who designed the event object and content-coordinate systems didn't envision how DHTML designers might utilize these features. The W3C DOM Level 2 event model is only partially helpful by defining two pairs of coordinate-related properties of the event object: clientX/clientY and screenX/screenY. But even then, the formal descriptions of the clientX and clientY properties—a coordinate at which the event occurred relative to the DOM implementation's client area—leave a lot to interpretation. Is the "client area" the page or just the visible portion of the page? Mozilla, Safari, and Opera interpret it as being the entire page, but IE's clientX and clientY properties (admittedly not based on the W3C DOM event model) are measures within the visible space of the document, thus requiring adjustments for document scrolling.

The W3C DOM Level 2 is mum on event coordinates within a positioned element. Of course, with some more arithmetic and element inspection, you can figure out those values from the style properties of the element and the event's clientX and clientY properties. The proprietary properties for offsetX/offsetY in IE and layerX/layerY in Mozilla (a convenience holdover from Navigator 4) partially pick up the slack, but as you've seen, they're not universally perfect.

Even with the adjustments shown in the examples for this recipe, you may still encounter combinations of CSS borders, margins, and padding that throw off these careful calculations. If these CSS-style touches are part of the body element or the element you're positioning, you will probably have to experiment with adjustment values that work for the particular design situation of the page. In particular, inspect the offsetLeft, offsetTop, clientLeft, and clientTop properties of not only the direct elements you're working with, but also those within the containers that impact elements' offset measures (usually reachable through the offsetParent property, and further offsetParent chains outward to the html element). Also, don't overlook CSS border, margin, and padding thicknesses that might impact coordinate measures of the elements. Look for values that represent the number of pixels that your calculations miss. It's a tedious process, so be prepared to spend some time figuring it out. One size does not fit all.

See Also

Recipe 9.5 for cancelling event bubbling; Recipe 11.12 for a utility function that reveals values from imported style sheets; Recipe 13.8 for determining the pixel position of an element within the normal flow of a document.

9.5 Preventing an Event from Performing Its Default Behavior

Problem

You want to prevent an event from triggering its default behavior.

Solution

Although it is a fruitless endeavor to use scripts to block users from, say, right-clicking on an image to save a copy of the image on the local hard disk, this recipe shows how to use event blocking to discourage casual users who may be dissuaded by an alert message.

The primary event to block in this case is the `contextmenu` event, which is implemented in IE 5 or later for Windows, Mozilla, and Safari. Assign a function to the event at the document level. The following function blocks the event for all `img` elements:

```
function blockEvents(evt) {
    evt = (evt) ? evt : event;
    var elem = (evt.target) ? evt.target : ((evt.srcElement) ?
        evt.srcElement : null);
    if (elem && elem.tagName && elem.tagName.toLowerCase() == "img") {
        if (evt.cancelBubble) {
            evt.cancelBubble = true;
        }
        alert("Sorry, feature not available.");
        return false;
    }
}
document.oncontextmenu = blockEvents;
```

Discussion

Inhibiting an event's default action can give your dynamic pages powers they couldn't have on their own. For example, if you want to limit text field entry to numbers only, examine the event object details and block nonnumeric characters from reaching the field. Similarly, if you are performing client-side form validation (see Chapter 8) when the user submits the form, you want to block the `submit` event from carrying out its default behavior if the validation fails.

Before browsers had the sophisticated event models of today, events could be blocked, although on a more limited basis. The basic technique was to make sure that the event handler's last in-line statement evaluated to the expression:

```
return false;
```

For example, in Recipe 5.13, you see how an a element can link to one document through its traditional href reference when the browser isn't scriptable, but navigate to another page when scripting is available:

```
<a href="std/newProds.html" title="To New Products"
    onclick="return linkTo('ieWin/newProds.html', 'w3/newProds.html')">New
    Products</a>
```

In this case, the linkTo( ) function returns a value of false so that the click event handler evaluates to return false. The a element never acts on the href link when scripting is enabled because as far as the element is concerned, the click never happened. You could also format the click event handler as two separate statements in a series:

```
onclick="linkTo('ieWin/newProds.html', 'w3/newProds.html'); return false"
```

The first format is ideal when the function invoked by the event handler processes the event with the goal of discovering whether the default action of the event should be permitted to pass to the element. See Recipe 8.3 for this technique to be used with form validation and Recipe 8.12 to allow only desired characters in a text field.

As the event models increased in sophistication, the old ways still worked (and still do), but events were also being bound to elements in ways that did not permit the direct inclusion of a return false statement in the binding assignment. Instead, when events are bound to an element by way of property assignment, the last executing statement of the handler function dictates whether the default action of the event passes to the element. Therefore, if the last statement of the function is return true, the default action is processed normally; a final return false prevents the default action.

This technique was improved syntactically in the IE 4 event model with the addition of the event object's returnValue property. You can set this property to true or false to direct the target element to process or ignore the default behavior, respectively. A side benefit of this extra property is that you can return something other than a Boolean value from the function, yet the default behavior is controlled independently.

Comparable capabilities are built into the W3C DOM event model by way of a method of the event object passed to the handler function. Invoke the event object's preventDefault( ) method (no parameters) to tell the target element to ignore the event. Calling this method in Mozilla, for instance, is the same as setting the event. returnValue property to false in IE 4 or later. Of course, the cross-browser choice is the old-fashioned return false approach if it's applicable to your coding style.

Consider event propagation in your event processing. The IE 4 and W3C DOM event models allow events to propagate up the document node tree. For example, a click event on a form's button fires on the button, on the form element, on the body element, and on the root document node. You might wish to take advantage of this feature if you have a series of similar objects and want a single event handler to process a particular event on all of those elements—let the events from the individual elements bubble up to a container node, whose event handler for that event type triggers a function.

Event propagation in the direction of the document node is called *event bubbling* (i.e., the event "bubbles" upward through the node tree). If you have event handler definitions assigned for nodes high up on the tree, you may need to block events of the same type from bubbling beyond the elements in which they do their work. Otherwise, the events will trigger those higher-up event handler functions and mess up your processing goals.

To help control event bubbling, IE 4 implemented the cancelBubble property of the event object. Mozilla, Safari, and Opera implement this property, too, as a cross-browser convenience (it's not part of the W3C DOM Level 2 event model). If you set this property to true, the event does not bubble beyond the node that is processing the event at the time. The W3C DOM version of this feature is the stopPropagation( ) method of the event object. This method is implemented only in Mozilla, Safari, and Opera.

Here's an object model-specific revised version of the blockEvents( ) function for IE:

```
function blockEvents( ) {
    var elem = event.srcElement;
    if (elem && elem.tagName && elem.tagName.toLowerCase( ) == "img") {
        event.cancelBubble = true;
        event.returnValue = false;
        alert("Sorry, feature not available.");
    }
}
```

In pure W3C DOM syntax, the function becomes:

```
function blockEvents(evt) {
    var elem = (evt.target) ;
    if (elem && elem.tagName && elem.tagName.toLowerCase( ) == "img") {
        evt.preventDefault( );
        evt.stopPropagation( );
        alert("Sorry, feature not available.");
    }
}
```

Despite all the best efforts of web content developers, there is no defense against the determined page visitor who wants to view your page source code (including linked JavaScript libraries and CSS style sheets) or capture a copy of an image file showing in the page. That's not the only reason to block events, but it is perhaps the most common request among content providers. Any scripted technique is immediately defeatable by the user turning off scripting in the browser. Even if you try to disguise things by opening the page in a menu bar-less window, the URL to that page is accessible in the loading page so that the URL can be opened manually in a regular browser window. As weak as this level of "right-click" protection is, plenty of content developers observe the technique on other pages and are convinced it offers genuine blockage. They frequently inquire in online forums for guidance in implementing what they've seen. This provides anecdotal evidence that even many experienced developers can be dissuaded by this simple event trick.

See Also

Other recipes that control event propagation or default actions: Recipe 5.13 for hyperlinks; Recipe 8.3 for form submissions; Recipe 8.12 for text boxes.

9.6   Blocking Duplicate Clicks

Problem

You want to prevent a second click on a button or link.

Solution

Use the `click` event handler of the button or link to carry out the intended single-click action, and then redirect the event handler for any subsequent click. For example, the following link submits a form by way of the `submitForm( )` function:

```
<a href="#" onclick="return submitForm( )">Submit</a>
```

In the event handler function, reassign the function to a second function that performs no action:

```
function submitForm( ) {
    document.forms["myForm"].submit( );
    submitForm = blockIt;
    return false;
}
function blockIt( ) {
    return false;
}
```

Discussion

Notice that this recipe makes no mention of the `doubleclick` event handler. That's because the event is irrelevant for this kind of blocking operation. If you don't script a `doubleclick` event handler, nothing happens when that event fires. You want to prevent a subsequent `click` event. This is especially important for form submissions in applications such as e-commerce transactions. If the user clicks the Submit button a second time while the form page is still visible, the server may process both submissions and store the order in the database twice.

The technique shown in the Solution is deceptively simple. The second statement of the `submitForm( )` function equates the `submitForm( )` function with the `blockIt( )` function. The next time that `submitForm( )` is invoked, the `blockIt( )` function is invoked in its place. Bear in mind that this function reassignment stays in force unless the page reloads.

If you wish to script an action to occur upon double-clicking an element, you can use the doubleclick event handler. But attempting to script both the click and doubleclick event handlers for the same element will lead to unsatisfactory results. At best, you can combine doubleclick event handlers with mousedown or mouseup event handlers, just like real applications do.

See Also

Recipe 9.5 for blocking the default behavior of an event.

9.7 Determining Which Element Received an Event

Problem

You want to obtain a reference to the element receiving the most recent event.

Solution

The IE and W3C DOM event models offer properties of their respective event objects that return a reference to the element initially receiving an event. Although the syntax is different, you can equalize IE's srcElement and the W3C DOM's target event properties to achieve a single reference valid in both browser classes. The technique also requires equalizing the event objects, as shown in Recipe 9.1.

A typical event handler function that degrades gracefully in older browsers starts this way:

```
function myFunction(evt) {
    evt = (evt) ? evt : ((window.event) ? event : null);
    if (evt) {
      var elem = (evt.target) ? evt.target :
         ((evt.srcElement) ? evt.srcElement : null);
      if (elem ) {
          // perform all event processing here
      }
    }
}
```

Discussion

The W3C DOM event model presents one extra wrinkle to the solution if the target element acts as an HTML container of one or more text nodes. In the W3C DOM, text nodes can be targets. Therefore, if you bind a click event handler to an a element that surrounds hyperlinked text, the event object passed to the handler function regards the text node nested inside the a element as the target. More than likely, however, your function is interested in the surrounding a element and its properties.

If the elements you're assigning events to are containers, and if your function must obtain a reference to the element containing that text, modify the template shown in the Solution to the following:

```
function myFunction(evt) {
    evt = (evt) ? evt : ((window.event) ? event : null);
    if (evt) {
       var elem = (evt.target) ? evt.target :
          ((evt.srcElement) ? evt.srcElement : null);
       if (elem.nodeType == 3) {
           elem = elem.parentNode;
       }
       if (elem) {
           // perform all event processing here
       }
    }
}
```

Acknowledging the potential headache that can accrue to text nodes being the target of events, Mozilla (starting with version 1.4) and Safari (starting with version 2.02) changed their behaviors so that an event initially targeting a text node is automatically redirected to the element containing the text node—and the target property changes accordingly. If, on the other hand, you really want to know the text node that was the actual target, Mozilla 1.4 and later provide the explicitOriginalTarget property of the event object to obtain that information.

Not all event functions need a reference to the target element, but the technique is important if you are using event handler property binding techniques for elements that normally need some kind of connection to the context of the event. For example, say you assign a change event handler to a text input field through property syntax such as:

```
document.getElementById("emailAddress").onchange = validateEmail;
```

In this case, the function needs to get information from the element to complete its job. In the following fragment, the value and form properties of a text input box are retrieved as properties of the target element:

```
function validateEmail(evt) {
    evt = (evt) ? evt : ((window.event) ? event : null);
    if (evt) {
       var elem = (evt.target) ? evt.target :
          ((evt.srcElement) ? evt.srcElement : null);
       if (elem.nodeType == 3) {
           elem = elem.parentNode;
       }
       if (elem) {
           var val = elem.value;
           var form = elem.form;
           // perform more event processing here
       }
    }
}
```

Get to know these techniques of reading the event object for information about the target element. As the trend continues to move away from in-tag event handler binding, the element reference becomes increasingly important for effective event handler functions.

See Also

Recipe 9.1 for equalizing IE and W3C DOM event objects in event handler functions.

9.8   Determining Which Mouse Button Was Pressed

Problem

You want your event handler function to read which mouse button or button combination was used for a click-related mouse event.

Solution

Both the IE and W3C DOM event models agree that the button property of the event object is the one that holds information about the button or buttons used to generate a mousedown event (button values don't always come with mouseup or click events). Unfortunately, this is where the similarity ends.

Some of the integer values associated with the button property differ between the two event models. But they do agree that a value of 2 means that the right (nondominant) mouse button was used for the event. Here is a template for an event handler function that branches into separate processing paths for the right button and all other buttons:

```
function myFunction(evt) {
    evt = (evt) ? evt : ((window.event) ? event : null);
    if (evt) {
        if (typeof evt.button != "undefined") {
            if (evt.button == 2) {
                // process right-click here
                return false;
            } else {
                // process all other clicks here
            }
        }
    }
}
```

Discussion

The reason that the example function tests for the presence of the button property is for the sake of graceful degrading with Navigator 4, which has an entirely different property and value range for the mouse button information. The property is called which, and the value for the right button is 3. If you need to support Navigator 4, you can rework the skeletal structure in the Solution to accommodate the differences:

```
function myFunction(evt) {
    evt = (evt) ? evt : ((window.event) ? event : null);
    if (evt) {
        var rightButton = false;
        if ((typeof evt.button != "undefined" && evt.button == 2) ||
            (evt.which && evt.which == 3)) {
            rightButton = true;
        }
        if (rightButton) {
            // process right-click here
            return false;
        } else {
            // process all other clicks here
        }
    }
}
```

Again, I cannot emphasize enough that checking for buttons is most reliably performed with mousedown events only.

As for all the possible values of the button property, Table 9-4 shows the possibilities, which are far more extensive in IE. Mozilla, Safari, and Opera 7 or later support the W3C DOM value.

Table 9-4. Possible values of button property

Button(s)	IE 4+	W3C DOM
No button	0	null
Left (primary)	1	0
Middle	4	1
Right	2	2
Left + Right	3	n/a
Left + Middle	5	n/a
Right + Middle	6	n/a
Left + Middle + Right	7	n/a

If Macintosh users are in your target audience, limit right-click actions to nonmission critical actions. Macs traditionally have used single-button mice, although this may change in the future. Although some browsers simulate the right-click when the user holds down one of the keyboard modifier keys (usually Ctrl) while pressing the mouse button, you cannot guarantee that users even know to do this. Additionally, only Mozilla sets the button property correctly to 2. Therefore, if you intend to offer some special action with a right-click for Windows and Unix users, be sure to offer a suitable alternative for Mac users. Otherwise, change your interface to make the extra functionality available by clicking while holding down one of the modifier keys for all operating systems.

See Also

Recipe 9.1 for equalizing the IE and W3C DOM event objects in event handler functions.

9.9 Reading Which Character Key Was Typed

Problem

You want to inspect each alphanumeric key typed by the user before the character reaches a form field.

Solution

The following function should be invoked by a keypress event handler bound to a text input field in which you want to limit characters to the digits 0 through 9, a minus sign, and a decimal:

```
function numberOnly(evt) {
    evt = (evt) ? evt : ((window.event) ? event : null);
    if (evt) {
        var elem = (evt.target) ? evt.target :
            ((evt.srcElement) ? evt.srcElement : null);
        if (elem) {
            var charCode = (evt.charCode) ? evt.charCode;
            if ((charCode < 32 ) ||
                (charCode > 44 && charCode < 47) ||
                (charCode > 47 && charCode < 58)) {
                return true;
            } else {
                evt.returnValue = false;
                if (evt.preventDefault) evt.preventDefault( );
                return false;
            }
        }
    }
}
```

Discussion

Of the three keyboard-related events—keydown, keyup, and keypress—the keypress event is used to examine a typed character. See Recipe 9.10 for using the other two events.

Details about the typed character are contained in event object properties of different names depending on the event model used in the browser. Internet Explorer 4 and later use only the keyCode property for all keyboard-related event details. In response to a keypress event, the keyCode property contains the Unicode integer value of the character being typed. Safari and Opera also support the keyCode property in this fashion. Mozilla, however, reserves the keyCode property for a different purpose (see Recipe 9.10), and presents the charCode property to return the same Unicode integer that IE's keyCode property returns. (The now defunct Navigator 4 event model uses the which property [the same one that reports mouse button numbers] to return the character value.)

For English-language characters, the Unicode values are the same as those of the ASCII-character set. Appendix A contains a list of ASCII characters and their corresponding codes. Notice that upper- and lowercase letters have different codes; standard punctuation symbols also have codes. In addition, some control character keys (Tab, Space, Backspace, and Enter/Return) have low number codes.

The complexity of the numberOnly( ) function is in the combination of comparison expressions in the if statement. The comparisons state that the function should allow the default action of the character reaching the field if its character code falls into any of these categories:

- It's below the first true typeable character (the Space character, with a value of 32).
- It's equal to 45 or 46 (the hyphen or period characters).
- It's one of the digits 0 through 9 (Unicode values 48 through 57, inclusive).

All other values force the function to block default behavior, which prevents the character from reaching the text field.

See Also

Recipe 9.10 for examining events of noncharacter keys; Recipe 9.11 for reading modifier keys used with other character keys; Recipe 8.12 for more about prefiltering characters typed into text boxes.

9.10   Reading Which Noncharacter Key Was Pressed

Problem

You want to initiate a script action based on whether the user pressed one of the noncharacter keyboard keys.

Solution

Use a keydown or keyup event handler to read the code number associated with the noncharacter key. You can read this value from the event object's keyCode property.

The following function (which also invokes the `getComputedStyle( )` function from Recipe 11.12) moves an absolute-positioned element in five-pixel increments in the direction of the keyboard arrow key that the user presses:

```
function handleArrowKeys(evt) {
    evt = (evt) ? evt : ((window.event) ? event : null);
    if (evt) {
        var top = DHTMLAPI.getComputedStyle("moveableElem", "top");
        var left = DHTMLAPI.getComputedStyle("moveableElem", "left");
        var elem = document.getElementById("moveableElem");
        switch (evt.keyCode) {
            case 37:
                elem.style.left = (parseInt(left) - 5) + "px";
                break;
            case 38:
                elem.style.top = (parseInt(top) - 5) + "px";
                break;
            case 39:
                elem.style.left = (parseInt(left) + 5) + "px";
                break;
            case 40:
                elem.style.top = (parseInt(top) + 5) + "px";
                break;
        }
    }
}

document.onkeyup = handleArrowKeys;
```

This example uses the keyup event handler because the keydown event was broken in Mozilla prior to version 1.4. If you can target Mozilla versions starting with 1.4 or later, you can use the keydown event, which may benefit IE users. In IE, holding the key down until it goes into auto-repeat causes the keydown event to fire repeatedly, moving the positioned element in the same direction over and over (a desirable user interface behavior).

Discussion

Key codes are different from character codes. Each physical key on the keyboard has a code associated with it. For example, while the "2" key in the top row of character keys and the "2" key on the numeric keypad generate the same character codes, each key creates a distinct key code during keydown and keyup events. Key codes for regular alphanumeric keys are the same regardless of whether the Shift key is down at the time. Appendix B lists the key codes for a typical English-language PC keyboard.

Designing an application around the noncharacter keys is tricky because each browser and operating system has its own default behavior for things like function and navigation keys. To prevent scripts from hijacking the application entirely, browsers do not let you block events that are native to the application or operating system. Thus, in the function shown in the Solution, where the four arrow navigation keys are used to move an element, if the page is scrollable at all, the default scrolling action also occurs in addition to the repositioning of the element. No amount of returning false or cancelling event bubbling prevents the normal action from taking place. (Although in this case, if you assign focus to an empty text input field, the default of moving the cursor has no apparent action, and the page doesn't scroll.)

If you wish to program a function key to initiate some action, you should plan to do so only on one browser platform on one operating system whose key behaviors you can predict. Even in just the Windows environment, you need to make sure that a function key you wish to program truly has no default action—something that isn't always apparent just by trolling through the browser's menus. Some function key assignments are implemented to perform actions not listed in any menu. Test, test, test!

These same kinds of cautions apply to attempts at scripting keyboard combinations to act as scripted shortcuts. You cannot override browser-defined keyboard short-cuts, and finding unused two-key combinations across browsers will be a challenge. It is easier to find accelerator combinations utilizing two or more modifier keys. For example, the following keyup event handler function invokes the runSpecial( ) function when the user holds down Ctrl-Alt and then presses and releases the "P" key:

```
function handleAccelerator(evt) {
    evt = (evt) ? evt : ((window.event) ? event : null);
    if (evt) {
        if (evt.keyCode == 80 && evt.ctrlKey && evt.altKey) {
            runSpecial( );
        }
    }
}
document.onkeyup = handleAccelerator;
```

When coding accelerator key behavior, it is best to bind the keyboard event to the document node because that node has the greatest scope across browsers. Keyboard events that occur inside nested nodes (such as text input fields or text areas) will bubble up to the document node unless cancelled along the way. If such an event occurs inside an editable text field, the target of the event is the text field element. Thus, you could create a context-sensitive help feature with Ctrl-Alt-F2 providing details about the field while the user is editing it:

```
function showHelp(elem) {
    var elemID = elem.id;
    switch (elemID) {
        case "name":
            alert("Enter your full name.");
            break;
        case "email":
            alert("We will be contacting you with your access code. \n" +
                "Make sure the address is accurate and up to date.");
```

```
            break;
        ...
    }
}

function handleAccelerator(evt) {
    evt = (evt) ? evt : ((window.event) ? event : null);
    var elem = (evt.target) ? evt.target :
        ((evt.srcElement) ? evt.srcElement : null);
    if (evt) {
        // for Ctrl+Alt+F2
        if (evt.keyCode == 113 && evt.ctrlKey && evt.altKey) {
            showHelp(elem);
        }
    }
}
document.onkeyup = handleAccelerator;
```

You can't use F1 in this case, because IE for Windows triggers the application help system with any keyboard combination involving the F1 function key.

See Also

Recipe 9.1 for equalizing disparate event model objects; Recipe 9.7 for equalizing event target references; Recipe 9.9 for reading character key values; Recipe 9.11 for reading modifier key status during keyboard-event processing.

9.11   Determining Which Modifier Keys Were Pressed During an Event

Problem

You want to know if the Ctrl, Alt, or Shift modifier keys were being held down during the last event.

Solution

Both the IE and W3C DOM event models use the same set of event object properties to report whether the modifier keys were pressed during the event. The property names are:

- altKey
- ctrlKey
- shiftKey

Another property, metaKey, is active on the Macintosh keyboard as the Command key (but is not supported by IE/Mac). Each property has a value of true or false when an event fires. If the property value is true, the corresponding key was held down at the instant the event fired. The following event function performs one set of actions during an unmodified click, and another action if the Shift key is held down during the click:

```
function handleClick(evt) {
    evt = (evt) ? evt : ((window.event) ? event : null);
    if (evt) {
        if (evt.shiftKey) {
            // process Shift-Click here
        } else {
            // process normal Click here
        }
    }
}
```

Discussion

Limiting event processing to cases in which multiple modifier keys are held down is as easy as increasing the test applied to the event object. For example, if you want a branch of your event handler function to operate only when the Shift and Ctrl keys are pressed, the if condition becomes:

```
if (evt.shiftKey && evt.ctrlKey) {...}
```

You can easily get carried away designing several possible execution branches based on combinations of modifier keys being held down during the event. From a user interface design point of view, however, it's best to limit the number of choices you offer to prevent the user from getting completely confused about what the event does. Because users have different experience with modifier keys from other programs, you might consider offering just one alternative execution branch, and let any modifier key act as the gateway to that branch. To accomplish this, use the Boolean OR (||) operator in your if condition, and include all modifier key properties:

```
if (evt.altKey || evt.ctrlKey || evt.metaKey || evt.shiftKey) {...}
```

The issue about the metaKey property for Macintosh keyboards is important to understand if you have not had experience on a Mac. Macintosh programs provide the same kind of accelerator keyboard combinations as in Windows and other platforms. But instead of the ubiquitous Ctrl-key combinations in Windows programs, the Macintosh uses the Command key (the one with the ⌘ symbol on it if you've ever seen it). In other words, as comfortable as a Windows or Unix user is with Ctrl-key combinations, Mac users are comfortable with Command-key combinations. The Alt key (called the Option key on a Mac) is also commonly used in programs and user interface tasks (such as Option-dragging on the desktop to move a copy of a file from one folder to another). Note that Windows browsers do not treat the Windows key (the one with the Windows logo on it) as a Meta key.

See Also

Recipe 9.8 for handling mouse events; Recipe 9.9 for reading the character key (perhaps in concert with a modifier key); Recipe 9.10 for reading navigation and function key event values.

9.12 Determining the Element the Cursor Rolled From/To

Problem

You want to know the element from which the cursor rolled into the current element or the element to which the user rolled the cursor.

Solution

The IE event model supplies two different property names—fromElement and toElement—to convey references to the relevant elements. In contrast, the W3C DOM event model lets one property—relatedTarget—handle both chores because the reference depends entirely upon which event is being processed. A mouseover event reveals the element from which the cursor came; a mouseout event reveals the element to which the cursor has gone. For example, the following element has mouse event handlers to invoke separate functions for cursor rolls into and out of the element:

```
<img src="myImg.jp" ... onmouseover="incoming(event)" onmouseout="outgoing(event") />
```

The following incoming( ) function applies event-property equalization to obtain a reference to the element from which the cursor rolled:

```
function incoming(evt) {
    evt = (evt) ? evt : ((window.event) ? event : null);
    if (evt) {
        var from = (evt.relatedTarget) ? evt.relatedTarget :
            ((evt.fromElement) ? evt.fromElement : null);
        if (from) {
            // work with adjacent "from" element
        }
    }
}
```

The parallel outgoing( ) function obtains a reference to the element to which the cursor has already rolled:

```
function outgoing(evt) {
    evt = (evt) ? evt : ((window.event) ? event : null);
    if (evt) {
        var to = (evt.relatedTarget) ? evt.relatedTarget :
            ((evt.toElement) ? evt.toElement : null);
```

```
        if (to) {
            // work with adjacent "to" element
        }
    }
}
```

Discussion

To provide a more concrete example of the interaction between the mouse events and the event properties, Figure 9-1 shows a table containing one central cell and four "hot" cells, one on each side. As you roll the cursor to the center cell, the page indicates which cell the cursor rolled from; conversely, if you roll the cursor out of the center cell, you get a reading of the cell to which the cursor rolled.

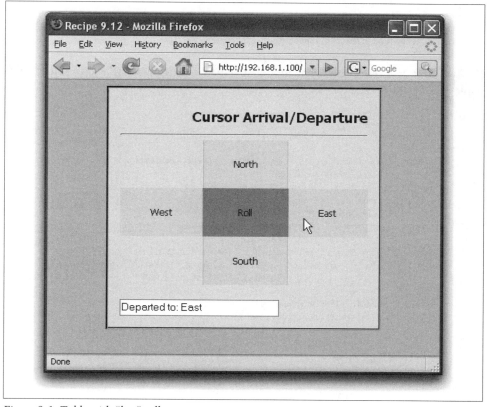

Figure 9-1. Table with "hot" cells

The HTML for the table, center cell event handlers, and the text box is as follows:

```
<table cellspacing="0" cellpadding="25">
<tr><td></td><td class="direction">North</td><td></td></tr>
<tr><td class="direction">West</td>
<td id="main" onmouseover="showArrival(event)"
```

```
                onmouseout="showDeparture(event)">Roll</td>
<td class="direction">East</td></tr>
<tr><td></td><td class="direction">South</td><td></td></tr>
</table>

<form name="output">
<input id="direction" type="text" size="30" />
</form>
```

A CSS style sheet sets cell background colors to distinguish the outer cells from the center one:

```
<style type="text/CSS">
.direction {background-color:#00ffff;
            width:100px;
            height:50px;
            text-align:center
            }
#main {background-color:#fff6666; text-align:center}
</style>
```

The two functions read the event model-specific properties of the event object, and display the results in the text box:

```
function showArrival(evt) {
    var direction = "";
    evt = (evt) ? evt : ((window.event) ? event : null);
    if (evt) {
        var elem = (evt.target) ? evt.target : ((evt.srcElement) ?
            evt.srcElement : null);
        if (elem) {
            // limit processing to element nodes
            if (elem.nodeType == 1) {
                // for W3C DOM property
                if (evt.relatedTarget) {
                    if (evt.relatedTarget != elem.firstChild) {
                        direction = (evt.relatedTarget.firstChild) ?
                            evt.relatedTarget.firstChild.nodeValue : "parts unknown";
                    }
                // for IE DOM property
                } else if (evt.fromElement) {
                    direction = (event.fromElement.innerText) ?
                        event.fromElement.innerText : "parts unknown";
                }
                // display results
                document.getElementById("direction").value = "Arrived from: " +
                    direction;
            }
        }
    }
}

function showDeparture(evt) {
    var direction = "";
    evt = (evt) ? evt : ((window.event) ? event : null);
```

```
            if (evt) {
                var elem = (evt.target) ? evt.target : ((evt.srcElement) ?
                    evt.srcElement : null);
                if (elem) {
                    // limit processing to element nodes
                    if (elem.nodeType == 1) {
                        // for W3C DOM property
                        if (evt.relatedTarget) {
                            if (evt.relatedTarget != elem.firstChild) {
                                direction = (evt.relatedTarget.firstChild) ?
                                    evt.relatedTarget.firstChild.nodeValue : "parts unknown";
                            }
                        // for IE DOM property
                        } else if (evt.toElement) {
                            direction = (event.toElement.innerText) ?
                                event.toElement.innerText : "parts unknown";
                        }
                        // display results
                        document.getElementById("direction").value = "Departed to: " +
                            direction;
                    }
                }
            }
        }
```

Because the W3C DOM event model processes events for text nodes in some browsers (see Recipe 9.7), the functions above limit their processing to the td element that contains the text label. If we do nothing to filter the event processing, the mouseover event of the text node bubbles up to the td element (assuming that no event handler is attached to the text node to cancel event bubbling), and the relatedTarget value points to the central td element itself. In other words, the text node's event regards the surrounding central td element as the node from which the cursor came. This is one case (in contrast to the example in Recipe 9.4) where automatically referencing the parent node of the text node doesn't work, since the event object properties for the two node types have different values for the relatedTarget property.

The complexity of the elements for which you're using this event object feature may have an impact on how successful you are in achieving your goal. This is especially true in the W3C DOM event model, but it isn't limited to there. If the container element has a lot of nested elements that don't supply sufficient padding or margin space to allow the mouseover or mouseout events to fire in a timely fashion, you may miss events that you believe should occur. The problem occurs when users are fast with the mouse, and the cursor skips over the container's exposed area so quickly that no event fires.

All of these cautions point to deployment of this technique in carefully controlled environments. The ideal situation has large elements abutting each other, and none with nested content. A table full of images acting as a rectangular mosaic, for example, should work well. Assuming, of course, that you have an application-specific need to capture adjacent element information during mouse events.

See Also

Recipe 9.1 for equalizing event objects of disparate event models.

9.13   Synchronizing Sounds to Events

Problem

You want to play a sound associated with the occurrence of an event on an element.

Solution

For the sake of simplicity, this solution works only in Internet Explorer for Windows, with its ability to control the Windows Media Player. The hard work goes in the HTML, making sure the object element has the correct information to load the player.

We'll add a pair of subtle sounds to the drop-down menu navigation interface described in Recipe 10.8. A higher tone sounds when the menu header is highlighted; a lower tone sounds when an item in the menu is highlighted. Browsers do not offer any built-in sounds, so this recipe assumes that you have recorded or acquired two short and small sound files, called *hi.wav* and *lo.wav*.

Starting with the HTML, add two <object> tags, one for each sound:

```
<object id="hiPing" width="1" height="1"
    classid="CLSID:22d6f312-b0f6-11d0-94ab-0080c74c7e95"
    codebase="#Version=6,0,0,0">
    <param name="FileName" value="hi.wav">
    <param name="AutoStart" value="false">
</object>

<object id="loPing" width="1" height="1"
    classid="CLSID:22d6f312-b0f6-11d0-94ab-0080c74c7e95"
    codebase="#Version=6,0,0,0">
    <param name="FileName" value="lo.wav">
    <param name="AutoStart" value="false">
</object>
```

Next, add the following function to the page's scripts:

```
function playSound(id) {
    if (document.all && document.all[id].FileName) {
        document.all[id].Play( );
    }
}
```

Finally, wherever you want one of the sounds to play, invoke the function and pass the ID of the sound object you wish to play:

```
playSound("hiPing");
```

In the case of the drop-down menu of Recipe 10.8, you should add `playSound("hiPing");` to the `swap( )` function just before the call to `showMenu( )`. Then add `playSound("loPing");` to the `toggleHighlight( )` function immediately before the `keepMenu( )` statement.

Discussion

Details in the `<object>` tag shown in the Solution are for a relatively early version of Windows Media Player (6.4), to ensure it works with IE 5 and later. The `Play( )` command is forward-compatible with newer versions of the player, but the `classid` attribute loads the old player anyway. By repeating the tag for each sound, you help preload both sounds as the page loads, minimizing any delay in the first utterance of both sounds.

It's tricky to truly synchronize a sound with a rapidly occurring event. First, the sound file must be of extremely short duration, with virtually no attack delay or decay to it. A short sound makes it more likely that the player is ready for the next command to play the sound while the user quickly rolls the mouse pointer through a menu list. Even so, you may still not achieve pinpoint precision in the attempted synchronicity. Controlling the Media Player adds some latency to the equation. That's why it's a good idea to issue the `Play( )` command prior to a visual change triggered by the event.

Adding sound of any kind is a controversial topic among web designers. Gratuitous background music that accompanies someone reading a web site may be distracting, and perhaps enough to get an employee in trouble for visiting your site during working hours. Treat sound like any DHTML enhancement: something that should add value to the presentation for those users equipped to take advantage of it. This frequently means giving the user the opportunity to turn off sound effects (or better yet, start with sound effects off, and provide a button to turn them on).

Controlling sounds through other plug-ins or ActiveX controls is also possible, but the range of browsers that support such activity is somewhat limited. IE for the Macintosh (through version 5.x) provides no connection between scripts and plug-ins. Mozilla browsers do provide such connections, but the mechanism for communicating with plug-ins is entirely different than shown in the Media Player example in the Solution.

See Also

Recipe 10.8 for the drop-down navigation menu used for this example.

CHAPTER 10
Page Navigation Techniques

10.0   Introduction

No web page is (or should be) an island. Just as there is a way to reach the page, so should there be one or more ways to navigate to other destinations, either within the same site or outside. The HTML hyperlink element—embedded in pages as the rather nondescript <a> tag—is the conventional, nonscripted way to provide a clickable avenue for the user to navigate to another page. But more sophisticated user interface designs frequently require Dynamic HTML to assist with the presentation of navigation options and the very act of navigating.

The location Object

Each window (and frame) object in every scriptable browser has a location object whose properties contain information about the URL of the page currently loaded into the browser. This is an abstract object, meaning that the object has no particular physical presence visible on the page—except perhaps the URL that appears in the browser's Location or Address field. But the location object does not control what the user sees in the Location/Address field unless the browser succeeds in navigating to a page you assign to the location object.

Properties of the location object are read/write. The individual properties reveal components of the URL (and even the entire URL) of the loaded page. Without any restrictions to this information, however, scripts could spy on your browser activity without you knowing it. For example, imagine entering an unscrupulous web site that looks like the Google search page. In fact, you could be viewing the actual Google search page within a frameset whose second frame is hidden from view. A script in the framesetting document or the other frame could inspect the location object of the visible frame every 10 seconds, accumulating a record of every page visited in that frame. The information could then be sent back to the spoofer's server without the user's knowledge or permission.

Despite the fact that, in some situations, knowing the URL of another frame or window could enhance the user experience, the potential for invasion of privacy has forced browser makers to clamp down on the reading power of location object properties. Browsers observe various types of security policies to help protect a user's privacy. The policy that applies to the location object is known as the *same origin policy*. If a script running in a page served by one server and domain wishes to inspect the location object of another frame or window, the document in the other frame or window must also be served by the same server and domain. If the user navigates in one of the frames to another domain or server, the same origin policy fails (even though the frameset is still served within the policy), and the location information is not accessible to the other frame.

Partially as a result of a variety of security holes in Internet Explorer for Windows, Microsoft occasionally clamps down so tightly on a potential threat that attempts to read location object properties of another window or frame—even from the same origin—resulting in a security-related script error (such as "Access denied."). From a reliability standpoint, reading the location object is best done in the same page as the script doing the reading. As you'll see in a few recipes in this chapter, there are some good reasons to do this.

All this security stuff, however, applies only to reading the location object's property values. You can assign new values to the properties across window and frame boundaries with impunity.

Passing Data Between Pages

A very common model in the web-application world is essentially a forms-based navigation system, in which virtually every page is a form whose values are submitted as a way to progress to the next page. When the submitted form reaches the server, programming on the server dissects the form controls' name/value pairs. Some of the pairs may get shunted off to a backend database. Other bits may be reformulated as values of hidden input elements in the page that get assembled for return as the next page. Once the second page is served up, the server doesn't know whether the user is still connected to the site or has perhaps navigated off somewhere else. In other words, the server simply reacts to requests from a browser, returning a page in response.

The server may be programmed to keep some temporary information about the user on hand, identified by a session ID. That session ID is passed down to the browser with each returned page so that when the next request arrives, the server program can tie together requests that come from a single browser. Some server programs that assemble pages on the fly for each visitor (such as *Amazon.com*) populate the href attributes of all intrasite links with the session ID so that the server can keep passing the ID along from page to page. It may sound a bit crude, but it is much more bandwidth-efficient than maintaining a full-time connection between server and browser (or between thousands of browsers at any instant for a popular public site).

However, not everyone has the requisite programming skills or server access to accomplish this server-based way of passing along live information from one page to another. By the same token, security restrictions in browsers prevent the random reading and writing of data to the local hard drive of users. Fortunately, with the help of JavaScript and various pieces of the object models, you do have a few different ways to get information from one page to another without having to involve the server. Recipes 10.4 through 10.6 show these approaches using cookies, frames, and URLs. For example, consider the case in which a user has bookmarked just one content page from a frameset whose other frames provide vital site navigation tools. If the user loads the bookmarked page into the browser, a simple script in that page can make sure that not only the complete frameset loads, but also that the bookmarked page appears in the content frame, rather than the default pages of the frameset.

Pop-Up/Drop-Down Navigation Menus

Navigation menus that pop up or drop down from some steady user interface element (such as a pseudo-menu bar or tab) are incredibly space-efficient. Rather than list dozens of choices in a navigation panel on a page, only top-level categories are visible by default. Rolling the mouse over one of the category names makes a nested list of relevant destinations suddenly appear out of the ether. This is a user interface concept that all Windows, Mac, and X Window System users can readily identify and know how to use.

Every DHTML guru and his cat has created a menuing system that takes advantage of element visibility and positioning in Version 4 browsers and later. I don't know if the world needs yet another pop-up menu system, but a DHTML cookbook would not be complete without one. One insurmountable hurdle is that a single design cannot fit all situations. Every site designer has a different look in mind when envisioning a menu system, and design requires far more fiddling with cookbook-style code than applying a different style sheet set. The goal, then, is not to create a be-all, end-all menuing system. Instead, focus on producing standards-compatible code for as simple a system as possible (using a DHTML library described more fully in Chapter 13), which is flexible enough to be tweaked for lots of different looks and situations.

Before you decide to deploy a pop-up menu system, especially in a public site, be sure to treat it as a value-added interface element, rather than as a mission-critical element. You should make it possible for a user with JavaScript disabled or unavailable to navigate through your site, even if it requires one or more extra page loads to reach the destinations listed in the pop-up menus. By relying on traditional links for nonscripted backup navigation, you also ensure that search engine spiders and bots will be able to reach the inner depths of your site and index those pages as well.

Default Data Delivery to a Page

Some of the recipes in this and subsequent chapters rely on a body of unseen data being accessible to the page's scripts. Depending on your specific application, the data may be static, or it may be dynamic data pulled from a database and assembled into a form suitable for download to the browser.

You now have two well-supported ways to get data into the hands of your browser scripts. The time-tested way is by embedding JavaScript objects or arrays (see Recipe 14.5) directly into *.html* pages on the server or blending them into server-generated page content on the fly.

But what's "all the rage" these days is to use the XMLHttpRequest object to create what are known as Ajax applications (see Recipe 14.4). This object can download XML data to the browser into an unseen virtual document without disturbing the current page. Scripts in the main page then access the XML data using DOM standards-based document tree-access techniques. With more and more database data being stored and easily delivered in XML format, this latter technique is undoubtedly one to consider for your applications.

10.1   Loading a New Page or Anchor

Problem

You want a script (instead of a hardwired link) to perform the navigation to another page or anchor.

Solution

To load a different page into the current window or frame, assign the new page's URL string to the location.href property:

```
location.href = "http://www.megacorp.com/products/framistan309.html";
```

To navigate to an anchor on the current page, assign the anchor's name string (the value assigned to the a element's name attribute) to the location.hash property:

```
location.hash = "section03";
```

Discussion

The URL value you assign to the location.href property can be a relative or complete URL, in string form. A relative URL is influenced by any <base> tag that may be delivered with the page (sometimes a server is configured to deliver this tag with all pages, and it is occasionally visible in a browser's source view). Because an assignment statement using location.href unloads the current page, you cannot count on any script statements below this one to execute before the page and all its variables and values disappear (although some browsers seem to operate a little bit ahead).

Knowing how popular scripted navigation could become, Brendan Eich (JavaScript's creator) built a shortcut into the location object that forces it to receive any string assigned to the object as being the equivalent of assigning the value to the href property. Thus, the following statements perform the same action:

```
location = "someplaceElse.html";
location.href = "someplaceElse.html";
```

Even so, it is good practice to utilize the location.href property approach to avoid any potential snafus in future implementations.

Some other ways to navigate via scripting have been supported in varying degrees in earlier browsers, presented here primarily for historical accuracy, but also to let you know what the code means if you encounter it in existing scripts. In addition to the location object, the document object was also, especially in the early days, an alternative object for navigation. The document object is more concrete than the abstract location object, which may have had some part in the document object's origin.

At one time, the document object also bore a location property (document.location), whose value is a relative or complete URL string. Due to potential internal semantic confusions with the location object, the document.location property was deprecated starting in Navigator 3. In its place came the read/write document.URL property. This property's value, too, is a URL string.

The structure of the W3C DOM, however, made it untenable for document.URL to act as a navigation device (in fact, there is explicitly no navigation mechanism in the DOM Level 2 specification). While the URL property is still included as a property of the HTMLDocument object (the root document node of an HTML document), the property is read-only in that specification. Thus, going forward, you can expect that property to be read-only (as it is in Mozilla-based browsers), and no longer usable as a navigation property.

One final bit of arcana on the subject is that Microsoft implemented a window. navigate( ) method in the earliest scriptable IE version, and it persists to this day in all platform versions of IE. The sole parameter to the method is a string of the URL. Don't use this method unless your code will be used forever in the future only by Internet Explorer.

When scripting navigation to an anchor in the current page via the location.hash property, do not include the # delimiter character that normally goes between the page URL and anchor name. This behavior differs from the location.search property, which requires the ? delimiter character that starts the search string portion of a URL. Navigation to an anchor on the same page should be nearly instantaneous. If you are seeing the browser (notably IE for Windows) hit the server each time you assign a value to the location.hash property, the server is most likely configured to convey page headers that expire the page immediately or don't cache the page. If you allow the page to cache, the anchor navigation should be speedy.

Also, be aware that you can navigate to any element on the page via the location. hash property. Simply assign the element's id attribute value (as a string) to the location.hash property:

```
location.hash="heading4";
```

The page scrolls as needed to bring the element into view.

See Also

Recipe 5.13 for navigating to different pages from a link based on browser capabilities; Recipes 7.2 and 7.3 for scripting the navigation of other frames in a frameset; Recipe 7.4 for navigating from a frameset to a page without a frameset.

10.2 Keeping a Page Out of the Browser History

Problem

You want to remove the current page from the browser history so that the Back button does not take the user back to the current page after a script navigates to some other page.

Solution

Navigate to the next page via the location.replace( ) method:

```
location.replace("http://www.megacorp.com/indexDHTML.html");
```

Discussion

The capability of keeping a page out of the browser's history can come in handy when your site contains a page that includes automatic forwarding under script control. Recipe 5.13 is a typical situation that benefits from keeping a temporary page out of the history. If the user reaches the real home page, a click of the browser's Back button normally brings the user back to the temporary page, and the user is essentially trapped in an infinite loop from which escape can only occur by going forward.

You can also use this technique if you do not want a user to come back to a form after submitting it. But in this case, you must assemble the form data yourself, appending it to the URL string passed with the replace( ) method. The page returned from your server program replaces the form page in the browser history. Be aware, however, that this works only for form submissions that can be accomplished with the GET method, rather than the POST method. Invoking the location. replace( ) method causes the browser to request a page through a GET method just like a regular web page.

See Also

Recipe 5.13 for a likely scenario for using `location.replace( )`; Recipe 10.6 to see how to assemble form data as part of a URL.

10.3   Using a select Element for Navigation

Problem

You want users to choose a destination from a pop-up list originating from a `<select>` tag.

Solution

You have a few scripting possibilities for this solution, depending on your design and scripting style, but they all rely on the select element having been outfitted with option elements containing the URL for each destination. You can display any text you like that is visible in the list, but assign the URL for each item to the value attribute of each option:

```
<select name="chooser" id="chooser">
    <option value="">Choose a Destination:</option>
    <option value="http://www.megacorp.com/index.html">Home</option>
    <option value="http://www.megacorp.com/products/index.html">Products</option>
    <option value="http://www.megacorp.com/support/index.html">Support</option>
    <option value="http://www.megacorp.com/contact.html">Contact Us</option>
</select>
```

Some event must trigger the navigation action. The most backward-compatible approach is to locate a clickable button or "Go" icon next to the select element. The click event handler of that button or link-surrounded image invokes a function that reads the selected option's value property:

```
function navigate( ) {
    var choice = document.forms[0].chooser;
    var url = choice.options[choice.selectedIndex].value;
    if (url) {
        location.href = url;
    }
}
```

Perhaps more convenient for users is to trigger the navigation by making the choice from the list in which case, you can create a generic (reusable) function that receives as an argument a reference to a select element:

```
function navigate(choice) {
    var url = choice.options[choice.selectedIndex].value;
    if (url) {
        location.href = url;
    }
}
```

The event handler in the select element should be as follows:

```
<select name="chooser" id="chooser" onchange="navigate(this)">...</select>
```

Discussion

The myriad ways to translate a select element's choice into a navigation command depend primarily on the browser versions you need to support and your coding style, particularly with respect to event processing. For example, in IE 4 or later and modern W3C DOM browsers, you can access the value property of the chosen option by simply retrieving the value property of the select element directly. This cuts down on all the options array referencing shown in the Solution. On the other hand, if you wish to bind the change (or other) event to the select element through other means, the event handler function cannot receive a reference to the select element as an argument. Instead, the function has to derive that information from the event object in a way that applies to both the IE and W3C DOM event models:

```
function navigate(evt) {
    evt = (evt) ? evt : ((event) ? event : null);
    if (evt) {
        var elem = (evt.target) ? evt.target : ((evt.srcElement) ?
            evt.srcElement : null);
        if (elem && elem.tagName.toLowerCase() == "select" && elem.value) {
            location.href = elem.value;
        }
    }
}
```

You can then bind the event handler within the tag:

```
<select name="chooser" id="chooser" onchange="navigate(event)">...</select>
```

Or in a script statement that executes after the page loads:

```
document.getElementById("chooser").onchange = navigate;
```

Or via the *eventsManager.js* library function:

```
addEvent(document.getElementById("chooser"), "change", navigate, false);
```

The scheme presented thus far has a significant flaw, however. If the user navigates from the current page to a choice in the select element and then returns to this page via the Back button, most browsers display the page just as it was the instant it unloaded—with the last choice preselected. The problem is that if the user wants to make the same selection again, the select element will not fire a change event (in most browsers). In other words, the user won't be able to duplicate the choice a second time without first making some other choice. You might think to bind any mouse-related events to trigger the navigation, but this is fraught with peril, because users can mouse down, mouse up, and click on a select element just to look through it, or (in some operating systems) keep a sticky list showing to view the list. Thus, mouse events are not suitable substitutes.

To force the user to make a selection that fires the change event, script the page to restore the select element (or perhaps all form controls) to its default state either via the load or unload event for the document or window objects. Either invoke the reset( ) method of the containing form element object, or set the selectedIndex property of the select element to zero. Notice that the select element shown in the Solution contains an initial choice that has no value—just a text label with instructions. All of the navigation event handler functions shown here assign a value to the location. href property only if there is, indeed, a value (other than an empty string) associated with the selected option.

You may wonder why, with the efficiency of the change event handler, a designer would include a "Go" button next to a select element. There are two primary reasons. First, some user interface designers don't like the idea of a select element triggering as drastic an action as navigating to another page. In other words, they intentionally separate the actions of choosing and going. Second, special browsers designed to assist vision- and motor skill-impaired visitors may work more predictably when the selection and "go" action are separate controls. Additionally, you can code the HTML and server to make this navigation queue workable for visitors with scripting turned off: The "Go" button submits the form containing the select element; the server reads the value and delivers the desired page. How much each of these reasons influences today's designs is hard to say. If I want to make a page that provides select list navigation, yet can also work with nonscriptable browsers, I would include a "Go" button, but use scripted feature detection and style sheets to hide the button in scriptable, CSS-capable browsers.

See Also

Recipes 7.2 and 7.3 for controlling navigation of other frames; Recipe 14.1 for ideas about using scripts to add content to a page dynamically during page loading.

10.4 Passing Data Between Pages via Cookies

Problem

You want to move user-influenced data from one of your pages to another without server intervention using browser cookies.

Solution

Using the *cookies.js* library from Recipe 1.10, you can use the unload event handler of one page to store from one to twenty name/value pairs on the user's machine. The following example captures a text input field's value and saves it to a cookie that stays on the visitor's computer for 180 days:

```
<script src="cookies.js"></script>
<script type="text/javascript" >
```

```
function saveData( ) {
    var data = document.forms[0].userName.value;
    var expDate = cookieMgr.getExpDate(180, 0, 0);
    cookieMgr.setCookie("userName", data, expDate);
}
</script>
...
<body onunload="saveData( )">
```

In the second document, a load event handler retrieves the cookie data and assigns the value to a text input field with the same name located on the second page:

```
<script src="cookies.js"></script>
<script type="text/javascript" >
function readData( ) {
    var data = cookieMgr.getCookie("userName");
    document.forms[0].userName.value = data;
}
</script>
...
<body onload="readData( )">
```

You can embed both event handlers and functions into all related pages to keep the data moving through all page visits.

Discussion

Unlike the other client-side persistence techniques described in this chapter, only the cookie approach preserves the data on the user's computer even after the user visits other sites and, if you assign an expiration date in the future, turns off the computer. If you don't specify an expiration date, the cookie remains in place only until the user quits the browser.

Cookie data may contain only strings. Therefore, if you wish to preserve information that your scripts have accumulated into arrays or custom objects, you must convert those items to strings (Recipes 3.3 and 3.13) before they may be saved as cookies. Upon reading the values, you may then re-create the arrays or objects from the string values.

To move all the data from a form containing multiple elements (and different types of elements) requires extracting the form control values individually. You can perform this task manually, assigning each control's value to a separate name/value pair for each cookie. Or you can use a utility script (Recipe 8.15) that systematically extracts all malleable form control names and values and combines them into a single string; a companion function extracts the data and repopulates an identical form in another page.

Carrying over data via cookies is an efficient procedure that is completely invisible to most users. They won't even know you're reading and writing cookies on their computers. But users can also modify the default behavior of cookies in their browsers, which can disrupt or ruin the silent data passage from page to page. For instance, users may set their browsers to alert them whenever a cookie is accessed. With cookie usage so high across the Web these days, there are not too many users likely have this annoying preference style in place. More common is the user who has turned off cookies entirely. Some organizations install browsers for their employees with cookies turned off by default. Use cookie detection (Recipe 5.12) to ensure that your scripts can use cookies for passing data.

Bear in mind that there are physical limits to cookie data, particularly in earlier browsers. No more than 20 name/value pairs may be saved from one server and domain. If you need to store the equivalent of more than 20 entries, you must devise a data structure that can be represented in string form. For example, you could create a custom object with 25 properties, and then use Recipe 3.13 as a model to convert that object to a string for storage in a single name/value pair cookie. Another limitation comes into play when storing a lot of data. The total storage space available per server and domain is 4,000 characters, and the safe range per name/value pair is less than 2,000 characters. When calculating data length, take into account that values go through the escape( ) function, which expands some characters to a total of three characters (e.g., a space becomes %20).

See Also

Recipe 1.10 for cookie utilities; Recipe 3.13 for converting custom objects to strings; Recipe 5.12 for detecting whether cookies are enabled; Recipe 8.15 for extracting all form control data for passage as string data.

10.5   Passing Data Between Pages via Frames

Problem

You want to move user-influenced data from one of your pages to another without server intervention while using a frameset.

Solution

The window object representing the frameset remains fixed while documents move in and out of child frames. This top window is capable of storing JavaScript data of all types in global variables. Use an unload event handler of a framed page to preserve the data in a global variable of the frameset's window. In the following example, a string from a text input element is stored in a global variable called userName:

```
<script type="text/javascript" >
function saveData( ) {
    top.userName = document.forms[0].userName.value;
}
</script>
...
<body onunload="saveData( )">
```

In the second document, an onload event handler retrieves the data and assigns the value to a text input field on the second page:

```
<script type="text/javascript" >
function readData( ) {
    if (typeof top.userName != "undefined") {
        document.forms[0].userName.value = top.userName;
    }
}
</script>
...
<body onload="readData( )">
```

You can embed both event handlers and functions into all related pages to keep the data moving through all page visits.

Discussion

Some significant benefits accrue to the frameset approach of passing data, but you should also be aware of potential downsides. One of the biggest benefits is that you can store any JavaScript data type in a variable. Conversion of objects or arrays to strings is not necessary. At the same time, the typical data-length limits that confine the amount of data transferable via cookies or URLs do not apply. You also don't have to predefine variables in the framesetting document. JavaScript automatically declares and initializes a global variable when you assign a value to a variable name as a property of a window (or frame) object.

A value assigned to a top window variable remains in effect as long as the framesetting document remains loaded in the browser. Therefore, if the site design allows users to navigate one of the frames to a destination outside of the frameset's server and domain, the value will still be there when navigation in that frame returns to the original server and domain. Scripts from outside the frameset's server and domain do not have access to the top window's variables because of blockades formed by the same-origin security policies in force in today's browsers.

Perhaps the most vulnerable aspect of using window global variables as temporary data stores is that they generally do not survive reloading of the page. If the user intentionally or accidentally clicks the Refresh or Reload button of the browser, the entire frameset reloads, causing all variable values to disappear. This is the reason the solution's readData( ) function checks for the existence of the variable in the framesetting window before accessing its value. By relying on the data to persist no longer than a change of documents in one frame, this potential problem does not loom so large.

Another consideration is that not every web designer is enamored with frames, for a variety of reasons. Users probably don't care one way or the other unless the frameset design (and navigation system within the frameset) makes Back and Forward button navigation confusing. One way to minimize this confusion while still deriving the advantage of a relatively stable framesetting window is to create a frameset consisting of two frames, one visible and the other invisible:

```
<frameset rows="100%, *" border="0">
    <frame name="main" src="content.html">
    <frame name="hidden" src="blank.html">
</frameset>
```

With this arrangement, you have two window objects to use as temporary data repositories: the top window and the hidden frame (parent.hidden). Some designers use this hidden frame scheme to let a faceless Java applet reside in the hidden frame, maintaining an open connection with the server, while the visible frame's document feeds off real-time data that arrives to the applet.

You can use this hidden frame scheme to further minimize the delicate state of variable data stored in a window object. Many (but not all) browsers preserve form control settings and values during page reloads. Therefore, instead of saving the data to window variables, save them as strings for text input or textarea elements. For example, if you are creating a shopping cart for a web site, you can accumulate ordered items in fields of a hidden frame as the user navigates the visible frame to various product pages. At checkout time, the visible shopping cart page retrieves the data from the hidden frame's form fields, and generates a nicely formatted page (perhaps using document.write( ) statements to assemble the HTML for the cart page). If you attempt this kind of persistence—especially for an e-commerce site—be sure to test the reliability of the hidden field data during reloads of the frameset on as many browsers and operating systems as possible. In your tests, include navigating out of the site via the browser's Back button, and then returning to the site via the Forward button. If the data in the hidden text boxes survives, that's a good sign.

See Also

Chapter 7 on managing frames and framesets.

10.6   Passing Data Between Pages via URLs

Problem

You want to move user-influenced data from one of your pages to another without server intervention, cookies, or frames.

Solution

Pass the data as a search string appended to the URL of the next page and include a script in the next page to read the search string to retrieve the data. As a simple case, the following code passes a single value retrieved from a text input field as a search string:

```
<script type="text/javascript">
function goNext(url) {
    var data = document.forms[0].userName.value;
    location.href = url + "?" + encodeURIComponent(data);
}
</script>
...
<a href="page3.html" onclick="goNext('page3.html'); return false">...</a>
```

In the second document, a load event handler retrieves the search string data and assigns the value to a text input field with the same name located on the second page:

```
<script type="text/javascript" >
function readData( ) {
    var srchString = decodeURIComponent(location.search.substring(1, location.search.
length));
    if (srchString.length > 0) {
        document.forms[0].userName.value = srchString;
    }
}
</script>
...
<body onload="readData( )">
```

You can embed both event handlers and functions into all related pages to keep the data moving through all page visits.

Discussion

The magic behind the URL scheme is that all modern browsers retain the search string that comes back from a server, even if the server doesn't use the information. A search string begins with a question mark delimiter following the address of the page. When assembling the URL for the next page, you must include this delimiter. At the same time, the function that reads the data must start with the first character following the delimiter.

Code shown in the Solution employs two global JavaScript methods—encodeURIComponent( ) and decodeURIComponent( )—which are available in IE 5.5 or later, as well as Mozilla, Safari, and Opera. For earlier browsers, you can substitute the escape( ) and unescape( ) methods, but they have been deprecated in the current ECMAScript standard (they also operate slightly differently from the newer versions).

The Solution demonstrates a very simple case of passing a single value from page to page. You can pass far more complex string data across pages. More typically, you assemble this data in the same kind of name/value pair format that browsers submit as form data, with an equals sign between the name and value and an ampersand character delimiting multiple name/value pairs:

```
pageURL?name1=value1&name2=value2&name3=value3
```

Take into account, however, that the purpose of passing data from page to page is to be able to use that data in the subsequent page. Since the name/value pair format of the typical search string is distinct from the syntax used by JavaScript, you'll need some conversion code that encodes JavaScript objects or arrays into the search string form prior to leaving the first page, and reconverts that search string into usable objects or arrays upon arriving at the second page.

For this purpose, you can use the same object-to-string library shown in Recipe 3.13. Both cookie data and search string data can (and some would say should) be formatted as name/value pairs that can then be reassembled in convenient JavaScript object form for distribution through form controls or just kept in global variables ready for other scripts to pluck their values. The following script segments demonstrate how a custom object's values can be passed and reassembled via URLs with the help of the *objectsArraysStrings.js* library from Recipe 3.13:

```
<script src="objectsArraysStrings.js">
</script>
<script type="text/javascript">
var customObject;
function goNext(url, obj) {
    srchString = object2String(obj);
    url += "?" + encodeURIComponent(srchString);
    location.href = url;
}
function readData() {
    var srchString = decodeURIComponent(location.search.substring(1, location.search.
length));
    if (srchString.length > 0) {
        customObject = string2Object(srchString);
    }
}
// other functions that create and/or modify
// customObject in response to user action...
</script>
...
<body onload="readData()">
...
<a href="page3.html" onclick="goNext('page3.html', customObject); return false">...
</a>
```

If your goal is to pass values of a form's entire control set from page to page, you can use the *stringForms.js* library from Recipe 8.15 to simplify the gathering and redeployment of form values on both ends:

```
<script src="stringForms.js">
</script>
<script type="text/javascript" >
function goNext(url, form) {
    srchString = form2ArrayString(form);
    url += "?" + encodeURIComponent(srchString);
    location.href = url;
}
```

```
function applyValues(form) {
    var srchString = decodeURIComponent(location.search.substring(1, location.search.
length));
    if (srchString.length > 0) {
        string2FormObj(form, srchString);
    }
}
// other functions that create and/or modify
// customObject in response to user action...
</script>
...
<body onload="applyValues(document.forms[1])">
...
<a href="page3.html" onclick="goNext('page3.html', document.forms[0]); return false">
...
</a>
```

Notice how both functions are generalized to accept form object references. This allows the invoking call to determine which of the page's forms (if there are more than one) are to be gathered or populated. Don't be fooled, however, by the apparent simplicity of the examples shown here; they rely on libraries that perform some heavy lifting with respect to converting objects to strings and manipulation of form data. Yet that's the purpose of a reusable utility library.

See Also

Recipe 3.13 for object and string conversions; Recipe 7.6 for an example of using URL data passing to ensure that a bookmarked page from a frameset always loads into that frameset; Recipe 8.15 for extracting all form control data for passage as string data.

10.7 Creating a Contextual (Right-Click) Menu

Problem

You want to display a customized menu of navigation or other options when the user right-clicks (Windows) or Ctrl-clicks (on the Mac)—actions that normally trigger the browser's internal context menu.

Solution

Use the contextmenu event handler that is part of modern browsers (except Opera through version 9) to intercept the normal browser action and display a menu of your own design. The example page described in the Discussion demonstrates one way to let scripts create a menu out of standard HTML elements and control each menu's visibility, positioning, and interactivity. Only browsers capable of displaying the context menus assign an identifiable style to the words featuring the menus. Figure 10-1 shows the finished results.

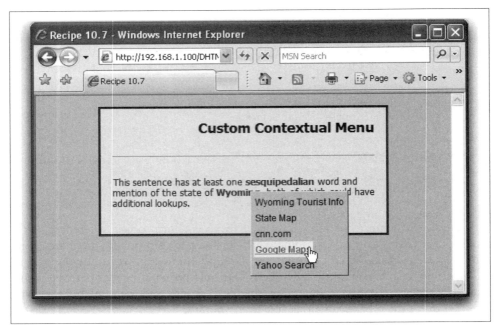

Figure 10-1. A context-sensitive pop-up menu

To deploy this recipe on a page of your own design, you need to customize the following items in the HTML page:

- A CSS class rule for the highlighted body text
- IDs for the span elements surrounding the words and phrases to be highlighted
- Data in the page-specific cMenu object, particularly the IDs you wish to assign to each menu and both the labels and link destinations for entries in each menu

All code for creating and managing the context menus is contained in the *contextMenus.js* library. A single library object, named cMenuMgr, holds all the methods that create the menus and make them run. The show gets started by a self-initialization statement in the library that relies on the *eventsManager.js* library from Recipe 9.3:

```
addOnLoadEvent(function() {cMenuMgr.initContextMenus()});
```

To simplify numerous references inside the object to other methods of the object, the load event utilizes an anonymous function call to the initialization routine.

Discussion

Example 10-1 shows the HTML page and embedded CSS style sheet that uses custom context menus powered by the scripts in Example 10-2. The page is designed around body text containing highlighted words or phrases for which you want to offer two or more navigation links per entry in a context-sensitive pop-up menu. Figure 10-1 shows a contextual menu for this solution.

Example 10-1. HTML and CSS portions of the contextual menu recipe

```
<html>
<head>
<title>Recipe 10.7</title>
<link rel="stylesheet" id="mainStyle" href="../css/cookbook.css" type="text/css" />

<style type="text/css">
.contextMenus {position:absolute; background-color:#cfcfcf;
               border-style:solid; border-width:1px;
               border-color:#efefef #505050 #505050 #efefef;
               display:block; padding:3px;
               visibility:hidden}
.menuItem {cursor:pointer; font-size:9pt;
           font-family:Arial, Helvetica, sans-serif;
           color:black; padding:2px;
           background-color:transparent;
           text-decoration:none;
           height:1.4em; display:block; line-height:1.4em}
.menuItemOn {cursor:pointer; font-size:9pt;
             font-family:Arial, Helvetica, sans-serif;
             color:red; padding:2px;
             background-color:yellow;
             text-decoration:underline;
             height:1.4em; display:block; line-height:1.4em}
.contextEntryLive {font-weight:bold; color:darkred; cursor:pointer}
</style>
<script src="../js/eventsManager.js"></script>
<script type="text/javascript">
// page-specific context menu data objects
var cMenu = new Object();
cMenu["lookup1"] = {menuID:"contextMenu1",
    menuItems:[{label:"Merriam-Webster Dictionary", href:"http://www.m-w.com/cgi-bin/
dictionary?book=Dictionary&va=sesquipedalian"},
              {label:"Merriam-Webster Thesaurus", href:"http://www.m-w.com/cgi-bin/
dictionary?book=Thesaurus&va=sesquipedalian"}]};

cMenu["lookup2"] = {menuID:"contextMenu2",
    menuItems:[{label:"Wyoming Tourist Info", href:"http://www.wyomingtourism.org/"},
              {label:"State Map", href:"http://www.pbs.org/weta/thewest/places/states/
wyoming/"},
              {label:"cnn.com", href:"http://cnn.looksmart.com/r_
search?l&izch&pin=020821x36b42f8a561537f36a1&qc=&col=cnni&qm=0&st=1&nh=10&rf=1&venue=all&
keyword=&qp=&search=0&key=wyoming"},
              {label:"Google Maps", href:"http://maps.google.com/
maps?f=q&hl=en&q=wyoming&layer=&ie=UTF8&z=7&ll=42.916206,-107.226562&spn=4.56153,10.
623779&om=1"},
              {label:"Yahoo Search", href:"http://search.yahoo.com"}]};
</script>
<script src="contextMenus.js"></script>
```

Example 10-1. HTML and CSS portions of the contextual menu recipe (continued)

```
</head>
<body>
<h1>Custom Contextual Menu</h1>
<hr />

<p>This sentence has at least one <span id="lookup1" class="contextEntry">sesquipedalian</
span> word and mention of the state of <span id="lookup2" class="contextEntry">Wyoming</
span>, both of which could have additional lookups.</p>

</body>
</html>
```

Note that no HTML for the context menus is included with the page. Those elements get created in supporting browsers based on data you supply to the cMenu custom JavaScript object delivered with the page. Each menu is defined as an object within the cMenu object, defined in the order in which the designated words or phrases appear in the source code. Names for these subobjects (lookup1 and lookup2 in the example) must match the IDs assigned to spans surrounding the words or phrases to be associated with a context menu. Each subobject, in turn, has two properties. The first, menuID, is the string value that will be assigned to the element that will contain the context menu's pieces; the second, menuItems, is an array of objects, each object pertaining to a choice in the context menu. Each choice has two properties associated with it. The label property is a string of the text to appear for that item in the context menu; the href property is a string of the URL destination when a user chooses that item in the menu.

Data from the cMenu object must be in place before the *contextMenu.js* library loads. Therefore, the <script> tag that loads the library comes after the cMenu object creation in source code order.

Scripts for the contextual menus are contained in the *contextMenus.js* library, shown in Example 10-2.

Example 10-2. contextMenus.js library

```
var cMenuMgr = {
    // position and display context menu
    showContextMenu : function(evt) {
        this.hideContextMenus();
        evt = (evt) ? evt : ((event) ? event : null);
        if (evt) {
            var elem = (evt.target) ? evt.target : evt.srcElement;
             if (elem.nodeType == 3) {
                elem = elem.parentNode;
            }
            if (elem.className == "contextEntryLive") {
                var menu = document.getElementById(cMenu[elem.id].menuID);
                // turn on IE mouse capture
```

Example 10-2. contextMenus.js library (continued)

```
                  if (menu.setCapture) {
                      menu.setCapture( );
                  }
                  // position menu at mouse event location
                  var coords = this.getPageEventCoords(evt);
                  menu.style.left = coords.left + "px";
                  menu.style.top = coords.top + "px";
                  menu.style.visibility = "visible";
                  if (evt.preventDefault) {
                      evt.preventDefault( );
                  }
                  evt.returnValue = false;
              }
          }
    },
    // hide all context menus
    hideContextMenus : function( ) {
        if (document.releaseCapture) {
            // turn off IE mouse event capture
            document.releaseCapture( );
        }
        for (var i in cMenu) {
            var menu = document.getElementById(cMenu[i].menuID)
            menu.style.visibility = "hidden";
        }
    },
    // rollover highlights of context menu items
    toggleHighlight : function(evt) {
        evt = (evt) ? evt : ((event) ? event : null);
        if (evt) {
            var elem = (evt.target) ? evt.target : evt.srcElement;
            if (elem.nodeType == 3) {
                elem = elem.parentNode;
            }
            if (elem.className.indexOf("menuItem") != -1) {
                elem.className = (evt.type == "mouseover") ? "menuItemOn" : "menuItem";
            }
        }
    },
    // navigate to chosen menu item
    execMenu : function(evt) {
        evt = (evt) ? evt : ((event) ? event : null);
        if (evt) {
            var elem = (evt.target) ? evt.target : evt.srcElement;
            if (elem.nodeType == 3) {
                elem = elem.parentNode;
            }
            if (elem.className == "menuItemOn") {
                location.href = this.getHref(elem);
            }
            this.hideContextMenus( );
        }
    },
```

Example 10-2. contextMenus.js library (continued)

```javascript
        // retrieve URL from cMenu object related to chosen item
        getHref : function(menuItemElem) {
            for (var i in cMenu) {
                // find the cMenu object
                if (cMenu[i].menuID == menuItemElem.parentNode.id) {
                    for (var j = 0; j < cMenu[i].menuItems.length; j++) {
                        // find the item whose label matches the menu item text
                        if (menuItemElem.firstChild.nodeValue == cMenu[i].menuItems[j].label) {
                            return cMenu[i].menuItems[j].href;
                        }
                    }
                }
            }
            return "";
        },
        // returns event coordinates on the page (for showContextMenu( ))
        getPageEventCoords : function(evt) {
            var coords = {left:0, top:0};
            if (evt.pageX) {
                coords.left = evt.pageX;
                coords.top = evt.pageY;
            } else if (evt.clientX) {
                coords.left =
                    evt.clientX + document.body.scrollLeft - document.body.clientLeft;
                coords.top =
                    evt.clientY + document.body.scrollTop - document.body.clientTop;
                // include html element space, if applicable
                if (document.body.parentElement && document.body.parentElement.clientLeft) {
                    var bodParent = document.body.parentElement;
                    coords.left += bodParent.scrollLeft - bodParent.clientLeft;
                    coords.top += bodParent.scrollTop - bodParent.clientTop;
                }
            }
            return coords;
        },
        // get all elements within document having a particular class name
        getElementsByClassName : function(className) {
            var allElements = (document.all) ? document.all :
                document.getElementsByTagName("*");
            var results = new Array();
            var re = new RegExp("\\b" + className + "\\b");
            for (var i = 0; i < allElements.length; i++) {
                if (re.test(allElements[i].className)) {
                    results.push(allElements[i]);
                }
            }
            return results;
        },
        // generate context menu elements associated with each "contextEntry" class element
        createContextMenus : function( ) {
            var hotItems = this.getElementsByClassName("contextEntry");
            for (var i = 0; i < hotItems.length; i++) {
```

Example 10-2. contextMenus.js library (continued)

```
                appendContextMenu(hotItems[i].id);
                hotItems[i].className = "contextEntryLive";
                var menuAction = (navigator.userAgent.indexOf("Mac") != -1) ? "Ctrl-click " :
                    "Right click ";
                hotItems[i].title = menuAction + "to view relevant links";
                addEvent(hotItems[i], "contextmenu",
                    function(evt) {cMenuMgr.showContextMenu(evt)}, false);
            }
            // build ul/li elements and put into body
            function appendContextMenu(id) {
                var cMenuData = cMenu[id];
                var ul = document.createElement("ul");
                var li;
                ul.id = cMenuData.menuID;
                ul.className = "contextMenus";
                for (var j = 0; j < cMenuData.menuItems.length; j++) {
                    li = document.createElement("li");
                    li.className = "menuItem";
                    li.appendChild(document.createTextNode(cMenuData.menuItems[j].label));
                    ul.appendChild(li);
                }
                document.body.appendChild(ul);
            }
        },
        // bind events and initialize tooltips
        initContextMenus : function() {
            var isNotOpera = navigator.userAgent.indexOf("Opera") == -1;
            if (cMenu && document.getElementById && isNotOpera) {
                // generate context menu elements
                this.createContextMenus();
                // click outside of context menu hides menu
                addEvent(window, "click", function() {cMenuMgr.hideContextMenus()}, false);
                // set events for items inside context menu
                var contextMenuList = this.getElementsByClassName("contextMenus");
                for (var i = 0; i < contextMenuList.length; i++) {
                    addEvent(contextMenuList[i], "click",
                        function() {cMenuMgr.hideContextMenus()}, false);
                    addEvent(contextMenuList[i], "mouseup",
                        function(evt) {cMenuMgr.execMenu(evt)}, false);
                    addEvent(contextMenuList[i], "mouseover", cMenuMgr.toggleHighlight, false);
                    addEvent(contextMenuList[i], "mouseout", cMenuMgr.toggleHighlight, false);
                }
            }
        }
    }
};

addOnLoadEvent(function() {cMenuMgr.initContextMenus()});
```

The cMenuMgr object consists of nine methods, divided into three categories:

Initialization	Operation	Support
initContextMenus( )	showContextMenu( )	getHref( )
createContextMenus( )	hideContextMenus( )	getPageEventCoords( )
	toggleHighlight( )	getElementsByClassName( )
	execMenu( )	

At load time, the initContextMenus( ) method filters out execution if the browser doesn't support basic W3C DOM element referencing terminology, if the HTML page doesn't define a cMenu object, and if the browser is Opera. Because Opera (at least through version 9) does not support the contextmenu event, the script will not highlight the designated words or phrases so as not to frustrate such users.

The first major task of the initContextMenus( ) method is to invoke createContextMenus( ). This method gathers a list of all HTML elements that have been designated menu-able items by their contextEntry class name. See Recipe 14.14 for details of the getElementsByClassName( ) method. In a loop through all menu-able elements, the script creates HTML elements (as ul and li elements) for the corresponding menu via the nested appendContextMenu( ) function. Details about each menu and item within the menu are captured from the cMenu object defined in the HTML page. Once the menu containers are appended to the body (their CSS rules make them positionable elements, so their source code placement is not important), the body text spans for the menuable elements are changed to the contextEntryLive class, which picks up the highlighted style sheet rule in the HTML page. As we continue the loop through menuable elements, we assign instructional titles to the elements for Windows and Mac users. Finally, each of these menuable items is bound to a contextmenu event handler, which invokes the showContextMenu( ) method of the cMenuMgr object.

The job of showing the context menu begins by hiding any other context menu that may be visible. Next, after verifying that the event target was one we're interested in (whose class name is contextEntryLive), we use the ID of that element (lookup1 and lookup2 in the example) to fetch the cMenu object associated with that element. That lets us grab the ID of the context menu ul element to help us position it in the vicinity of the contextmenu mouse event. We use the getPageEventCoords( ) function described in Recipe 9.4 to obtain the location.

For IE, we can limit event processing while a context menu is visible by temporarily turning on event capture (which works only for mouse events). In capture mode, mouse events are directed to the element for which the setCapture( ) method is invoked. The browser goes into a kind of modal state, during which the user cannot access other page elements by the mouse because the events on elements outside of the invoking element automatically go to the invoking element. Thus, each ul menu element has a click event handler assigned that hides the context menus. With a context menu showing, if the user clicks anywhere outside of the menus, they disappear, just like a browser-based context menu. Hiding the context menus disengages capture mode in IE, returning mouse activity to normal. For non-IE browsers, the click event bound to the window during initialization does the job.

As the user rolls the cursor up and down a context menu, mouseover and mouseout events trigger the toggleHighlight( ) method. This method simply switches the class name of the items between menuItem and menuItemOn (highlighted version) to act as visual feedback to the active choice in the menu.

If the user clicks on one of the choices in the menu, the mouseup event invokes the execMenu( ) method. With the help of the getHref( ) method, the script obtains the URL associated with that menu item from the cMenu object, and navigates to that page (see Recipe 10.1).

Just because the recipe shown here uses the contextmenu event handler to display the menu doesn't mean that you are limited to employing that event as the trigger. A rollover (mouseover event handler) for the highlighted entries works just as well.

See Also

Recipe 13.1 for positioning an element on the page; Recipe 12.10 for changing the visibility of an element; Recipe 3.14 for the benefits of encapsulating functions as custom object methods; Recipes 9.1 and 9.3 for details on the *eventsManager.js* library; Recipe 11.8 for toggling between style sheet rules.

10.8   Creating Drop-Down Navigation Menus

Problem

You want navigation menus to drop down from a menu bar on the page.

Solution

This solution demonstrates one of dozens of ways to implement drop-down menus. It relies on some simple images for the always visible menu headers, a single external style sheet called *menus.css* (shown in Example 10-3 in the Discussion), and an external JavaScript library called *menus.js* (shown in Example 10-4 in the Discussion). You can see the results in Figure 10-2.

To implement this solution, you must create (or borrow) menu header images for normal and highlighted versions. In several places within the *menus.js* library, you fill in the text and links for the menu items. The library does the rest to assemble the DHTML components for the menus, under guidance of the *menus.css* style sheets.

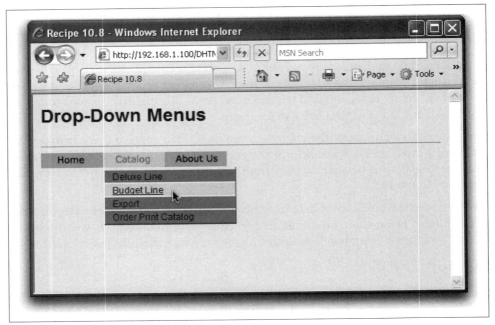

Figure 10-2. Drop-down menus in action

Discussion

The menu bar is hardwired into the page's HTML as a single div containing three img elements. Each img element is surrounded by a hyperlink (a) element containing basic navigation action for use by drop-down menu users and simple clicking. Mouse event handlers for the img elements are assigned later by a script:

```
<div id="menubar">
<a href="index.html"><img id="menuImg_1" class="menuImg"
src="home_off.jpg" border="0" height="20"
width="80"></a><a href="catalog.html"><img id="menuImg_2"
class="menuImg" src="catalog_off.jpg" border="0" height="20"
width="80"></a><a href="about.html"><img id="menuImg_3"
class="menuImg" src="about_off.jpg" border="0"
height="20" width="80"></a>
</div>
```

An imported style sheet, *menus.css*, shown in Example 10-3, contains specifications for the drop-down menu containers (class menuWrapper, which is assigned by script during initialization) and the individual items in the menus in both normal and highlighted states.

Example 10-3. menus.css style sheet

```
.menuWrapper {
          position:absolute;
          width:162px;
          background-color:#ff9933;
```

Example 10-3. menus.css style sheet (continued)

```
                visibility:hidden;
                border-style:solid;
                border-width:2px;
                border-color:#efefef #505050 #505050 #efefef;
                padding:3px;
                }
.menuItem      {
                cursor:pointer;
                font-size:16px;
                font-family:Arial, Helvetica, sans-serif;
                border-bottom:1px solid #505050;
                border-top:1px solid #efefef;
                padding-left:10px;
                color:black;
                background-color:#ff9933;
                text-decoration:none;
                position:absolute;
                left:0px;
                width:159px;
                height:22px;
                line-height:1.4em
                }
.menuItemOn    {
                cursor:pointer;
                font-size:16px;
                font-family:Arial, Helvetica, sans-serif;
                border-bottom:1px solid #505050;
                border-top:1px solid #efefef;
                padding-left:10px;
                color:#0099ff;
                background-color:#ffcc99;
                text-decoration:underline;
                position:absolute;
                left:0px;
                width:159px;
                height:22px;
                line-height:1.4em
                }
```

Example 10-4 shows the *menus.js* library for all the scripts used with the menus.

Example 10-4. menus.js drop-down menu library

```
// global menu state
var menuReady = false;

// pre-cache menubar image pairs
if (document.images) {
    var imagesNormal = new Array( );
    imagesNormal["home"] = new Image(20, 80);
    imagesNormal["home"].src = "home_off.jpg";
    imagesNormal["catalog"] = new Image(20, 80);
    imagesNormal["catalog"].src  = "catalog_off.jpg";
```

Example 10-4. menus.js drop-down menu library (continued)

```
        imagesNormal["about"] = new Image(20, 80);
        imagesNormal["about"].src  = "about_off.jpg";

        var imagesHilite = new Array( );
        imagesHilite["home"] = new Image(20, 80);
        imagesHilite["home"].src = "home_on.jpg";
        imagesHilite["catalog"] = new Image(20, 80);
        imagesHilite["catalog"].src  = "catalog_on.jpg";
        imagesHilite["about"] = new Image(20, 80);
        imagesHilite["about"].src  = "about_on.jpg";
}

function getElementStyle(elem, CSSStyleProp) {
    var styleValue, camel;
    if (elem) {
        if (document.defaultView && document.defaultView.getComputedStyle) {
            // W3C DOM version
            var compStyle = document.defaultView.getComputedStyle(elem, "");
            styleValue = compStyle.getPropertyValue(CSSStyleProp);
        } else if (elem.currentStyle) {
            // make IE style property camelCase name from CSS version
            var IEStyleProp = CSSStyleProp;
            var re = /-\D/;
            while (re.test(IEStyleProp)) {
                camel = IEStyleProp.match(re)[0].charAt(1).toUpperCase( );
                IEStyleProp = IEStyleProp.replace(re, camel);
            }
            styleValue = elem.currentStyle[IEStyleProp];
        }
    }
    return (styleValue) ? styleValue : null;
}

// carry over some critical menu style sheet attribute values
var CSSRuleValues = {menuItemHeight:"18px",
                     menuWrapperBorderWidth:"2px",
                     menuWrapperPadding:"3px",
                     defaultBodyFontSize:"12px"
                    };

// specifications for menu contents and menubar image associations
var menus = new Array( );
menus[0] = {mBarImgId:"menuImg_1",
            mBarImgNormal:imagesNormal["home"],
            mBarImgHilite:imagesHilite["home"],
            menuItems:[],
            elemId:""
           };
menus[1] = {mBarImgId:"menuImg_2",
            mBarImgNormal:imagesNormal["catalog"],
            mBarImgHilite:imagesHilite["catalog"],
            menuItems:[ {text:"Deluxe Line", href:"catalog_deluxe.html"},
```

Example 10-4. menus.js drop-down menu library (continued)

```
                        {text:"Budget Line", href:"catalog_budget.html"},
                        {text:"Export", href:"catalog_export.html"},
                        {text:"Order Print Catalog", href:"catalog_order.html"}
                        ],
            elemId:""
            };
menus[2] = {mBarImgId:"menuImg_3",
            mBarImgNormal:imagesNormal["about"],
            mBarImgHilite:imagesHilite["about"],
            menuItems:[ {text:"Press Releases", href:"press.html"},
                        {text:"Executive Staff", href:"staff.html"},
                        {text:"Map to Our Offices", href:"map.html"},
                        {text:"Company History", href:"history.html"},
                        {text:"Job Postings", href:"jobs.html"},
                        {text:"Contact Us", href:"contact.html"}
                        ],
            elemId:""
            };

// create hash table-like lookup for menu objects with id string indexes
function makeHashes() {
    for (var i = 0; i < menus.length; i++) {
        menus[menus[i].elemId] = menus[i];
        menus[menus[i].mBarImgId] = menus[i];
    }
}

// assign menu label image event handlers
function assignLabelEvents() {
    var elem;
    for (var i = 0; i < menus.length; i++) {
        elem = document.getElementById(menus[i].mBarImgId);
        elem.onmouseover = swap;
        elem.onmouseout = swap;
    }
}

// invoked from init(), generates the menu div elements and their contents.
// all this action is invisible to user during construction
function makeMenus() {
    var menuDiv, menuItem, itemLink, mbarImg, textNode, offsetLeft, offsetTop;

    // determine key adjustment factors for the total height of menu divs

    var menuItemH = 0;
    var bodyFontSize = parseInt(getElementStyle(document.body, "font-size"));
    // test to see if browser's font size has been adjusted by the user
    // and that the new size registers as an applied style property
    if (bodyFontSize == parseInt(CSSRuleValues.defaultBodyFontSize)) {
        menuItemH = (parseFloat(CSSRuleValues.menuItemHeight));
    } else {
        // works nicely in Mozilla
```

Example 10-4. menus.js drop-down menu library (continued)

```
        menuItemH = parseInt(parseFloat(CSSRuleValues.menuItemLineHeight) * bodyFontSize);
    }
    var heightAdjust = parseInt(CSSRuleValues.menuWrapperPadding) +
        parseInt(CSSRuleValues.menuWrapperBorderWidth);
    if (navigator.appName == "Microsoft Internet Explorer" &&
        navigator.userAgent.indexOf("Win") != -1 &&
        (typeof document.compatMode == "undefined" ||
        document.compatMode == "BackCompat")) {
        heightAdjust = -heightAdjust;
    }

    // use menus array to drive div creation loop
    for (var i = 0; i < menus.length; i++) {
        menuDiv = document.createElement("div");
        menuDiv.id = "popupmenu" + i;
        // preserve menu's ID as property of the menus array item
        menus[i].elemId = "popupmenu" + i;
        menuDiv.className = "menuWrapper";
        if (menus[i].menuItems.length > 0) {
            menuDiv.style.height = (menuItemH * menus[i].menuItems.length) -
            heightAdjust + "px";
        } else {
            // don't display any menu div lacking menu items
            menuDiv.style.display = "none";
        }
        // define event handlers
        menuDiv.onmouseover = keepMenu;
        menuDiv.onmouseout = requestHide;

        // set stacking order in case other layers are around the page
        menuDiv.style.zIndex = 1000;

        // assemble menu item elements for inside menu div
        for (var j = 0; j < menus[i].menuItems.length; j++) {
            menuItem = document.createElement("div");
            menuItem.id = "popupmenuItem_" + i + "_" + j;
            menuItem.className = "menuItem";
            menuItem.onmouseover = toggleHighlight;
            menuItem.onmouseout = toggleHighlight;
            menuItem.onclick = hideMenus;
            menuItem.style.top = menuItemH * j + "px";
            itemLink = document.createElement("a");
            itemLink.href = menus[i].menuItems[j].href;
            itemLink.className = "menuItem";
            itemLink.onmouseover = toggleHighlight;
            itemLink.onmouseout = toggleHighlight;
            textNode = document.createTextNode(menus[i].menuItems[j].text);
            itemLink.appendChild(textNode);
            menuItem.appendChild(itemLink);
            menuDiv.appendChild(menuItem);
        }
        // append each menu div to the body
```

Example 10-4. menus.js drop-down menu library (continued)

```
        document.body.appendChild(menuDiv);
    }
    makeHashes( );
    assignLabelEvents( );
    // pre-position menu
    for (i = 0; i < menus.length; i++) {
        positionMenu(menus[i].elemId);
    }
    menuReady = true;
}

// initialize global that helps manage menu hiding
var timer;

// invoked from mouseovers inside menus to cancel hide
// request from mouseout of menu bar image et al.
function keepMenu( ) {
    clearTimeout(timer);
}

function cancelAll( ) {
    keepMenu( );
    menuReady = false;
}

// invoked from mouseouts to request hiding all menus
// in 1/4 second, unless cancelled
function requestHide( ) {
    timer = setTimeout("hideMenus( )", 250);
}

// "brute force" hiding of all menus and restoration
// of normal menu bar images
function hideMenus( ) {
    for (var i = 0; i < menus.length; i++) {
        document.getElementById(menus[i].mBarImgId).src = menus[i].mBarImgNormal.src;
        var menu = document.getElementById(menus[i].elemId)
        menu.style.visibility = "hidden";
    }
}

// set menu position just before displaying it
function positionMenu(menuId){
    // use the menu bar image for position reference of related div
    var mBarImg = document.getElementById(menus[menuId].mBarImgId);
    var offsetTrail = mBarImg;
    var offsetLeft = 0;
    var offsetTop = 0;
    while (offsetTrail) {
        offsetLeft += offsetTrail.offsetLeft;
        offsetTop += offsetTrail.offsetTop;
        offsetTrail = offsetTrail.offsetParent;
```

Example 10-4. menus.js drop-down menu library (continued)

```
    }
    if (navigator.userAgent.indexOf("Mac") != -1 &&
        typeof document.body.leftMargin != "undefined") {
        offsetLeft += document.body.leftMargin;
        offsetTop += document.body.topMargin;
    }
    var menuDiv = document.getElementById(menuId);
    menuDiv.style.left = offsetLeft + "px";
    menuDiv.style.top = offsetTop + mBarImg.height + "px";
}

// display a particular menu div
function showMenu(menuId) {
    if (menuReady) {
        keepMenu( );
        hideMenus( );
        positionMenu(menuId);
        var menu = document.getElementById(menuId);
        menu.style.visibility = "visible";
    }
}

// menu bar image swapping, invoked from mouse events in menu bar
// swap style sheets for menu items during rollovers
function toggleHighlight(evt) {
    evt = (evt) ? evt : ((event) ? event : null);
    if (typeof menuReady != "undefined") {
        if (menuReady && evt) {
            var elem = (evt.target) ? evt.target : evt.srcElement;
            if (elem.nodeType == 3) {
                elem = elem.parentNode;
            }
            if (evt.type == "mouseover") {
                keepMenu( );
                elem.className ="menuItemOn";
            } else {
                elem.className ="menuItem";
                requestHide( );
            }
            evt.cancelBubble = true;
        }
    }
}

function swap(evt) {
    evt = (evt) ? evt : ((event) ? event : null);
    if (typeof menuReady != "undefined") {
        if (evt && (document.getElementById && document.styleSheets) && menuReady) {
            var elem = (evt.target) ? evt.target : evt.srcElement;
            if (elem.className == "menuImg") {
                if (evt.type == "mouseover") {
                    showMenu(menus[elem.id].elemId);
```

Example 10-4. menus.js drop-down menu library (continued)

```
                    elem.src = menus[elem.id].mBarImgHilite.src;
                } else if (evt.type == "mouseout") {
                    requestHide( );
                }
                evt.cancelBubble = true;
            }
        }
    }
}

// create menus only if key items are supported
function initMenus( ) {
    if (document.getElementById && document.styleSheets) {
        setTimeout("makeMenus( )", 5);
        window.onunload=cancelAll;
    }
}

addOnLoadEvent(initMenus);
```

Unlike some other related recipes (such as Recipe 10.7), this one does not encapsulate its functions within a custom object. It could be converted to that style without much difficulty.

Scripts begin with one global variable declaration, menuReady, that is ultimately used as a flag to let other functions know when the menus are available for animation. Next is code for precaching all menu button images in two states (à la Recipe 12.1). A utility function, getElementStyle( ), is a variation of the function from Recipe 11.12, which this script uses to keep menu item font sizes in sync with user-selected font sizes in Mozilla-based browsers.

Because browser security restrictions (at least in IE 6 and 7) prevent scripts from reading rule property values of style sheets, the script includes a global object that replicates some key style sheet values that the scripts use for help with menu positioning and sizing. You can get these values from the style sheet settings.

Next is the creation of objects (inside an array called menus) that contain vital menu details needed later when they are built. Each object has five properties, which are described in more detail later.

Scripts for hiding and showing the menus frequently require that a menu's reference be capable of pointing to the swappable image at the top of the menu, and vice versa. To speed this process along (i.e., to avoid looping through all of the menu's array items in search of properties that match either the image or menu IDs), it is more convenient during initialization to create a one time, simulated hash table (in the makeHashes( ) function), whose string index values consist of both the image and menu element IDs (see Recipe 3.9). The result is a hash table that has two pointers to each menus array entry—one for the image ID and one for the menu ID. Another function invoked during initialization, `assignLabelEvents( )`, assigns the mouse roll-over event handlers to the image elements at the top of each menu.

The biggest function of the recipe, `makeMenus( )`, assembles the menu elements, using W3C DOM node creation syntax. This routine is invoked at initialization time and depends on the `menus` array, defined earlier, to help populate each menu with the text and link for each menu item.

There are two rollover concerns for this application: the menu bar image swapping and the display of the menus. While their actions are different, the actions work with each other. But first, some support code to do the dirty work is needed. Because of the interaction between menu bar image and menus, a `setTimeout( )` timer is used to assist in cleaning up menus that are no longer necessary. The timer identifier (created when `setTimeout( )` is invoked) is preserved as a global variable called `timer`.

You can't just hide the menu when a `mouseout` event occurs in one of the menu bar images, since the mouse may be headed to the currently displayed menu and you want that menu to remain in place. To assist with this task is the `keepMenu( )` function, which cancels a timer set in the `requestHide( )` function, and thus makes sure the menu stays visible.

A related function, `cancelAll( )`, which is invoked by an `unload` event handler, guards against potential problems (particularly in Mozilla) in states between page loadings, while the cursor may still be rolling around a swappable image. Global variables are in transient states and may be valid when a function begins, but be gone by the time the value is needed. The `cancelAll( )` function puts the page in a quiet state during the transition.

All `mouseout` events from the menu bar and menus start the 1/4-second delay clock ticking in the `requestHide( )` function. If the timer is still valid in 1/4 second, the `hideMenus( )` function runs. The `hideMenus( )` function performs a blanket restoration of menu bar images and menu display.

A separate positioning function, `positionMenu( )`, is invoked before any menu is displayed. Therefore, if the menu bar changes position on the page (perhaps due to dynamic content or a resized browser window), the menu is displayed correctly with respect to the menu title image.

Invoked by all `mouseover` events in menu bar images and menu components, the `showMenu( )` function turns off the timer so that any pending `hideMenu( )` call won't occur. Then it immediately hides all menus (rather than waiting for the timer) and shows the menu `div` element whose ID is accessed from the `menus` array (index passed as a parameter) `elemId` property.

As the user rolls the mouse pointer over items within a displayed menu, the `mouseover` and `mouseout` events trigger style sheet changes to the entries (by changing the element's class assignment in the `toggleHighlight( )` function). In the case of a `mouseover`, the `keepMenu( )` function fires to make sure any pending menu hiding gets cancelled. For a mouseout, the hide request is made, in case the mouseout motion is toward some other region on the page.

The swap() function, invoked by the mouse event handlers of the menu bar images, is the main trigger to display a drop-down menu. In response to a mouseover event, the menu is displayed, and the menu bar image changes to the highlighted version. For a mouseout event, a hide request is made. If the hide timer isn't cancelled in time, the menu disappears and the menu bar image returns to its default image.

Invoked by the load event handler (via the addOnLoadEvent() function of *eventsManager.js* from Recipe 9.3), the initMenus() function certifies that the browser has the right stuff for the menuing system. It looks not only for basic W3C DOM support, but also for the more esoteric document.styleSheets property. If the browser supports the necessary facilities, the makeMenus() function generates the menu div elements. It also assigns an unload event handler to the window so that any pending menu-hide request is cancelled before the page goes away.

One of the goals of the design shown in this recipe is to minimize the amount of custom work needed to implement the drop-down menu in a variety of visual contexts. Most of the menuing libraries available from other sources go to even further extremes in this regard, building very complex and thorough systems of custom objects and dynamically written HTML. General-purpose libraries, especially those designed to work with outdated object models (e.g., the Navigator 4 DOM), need the extra complexity to accommodate as wide a range of deployment scenarios as possible. This example, on the other hand, is pared to a smaller size, and might require a bit more work to blend into your design (particularly around the images for the menu bar). But there should be plenty of ideas here that you can use as-is for a largely automatic menuing system compatible with IE 5 or later, Mozilla, Safari, and Opera 7 or later.

Reliance on style sheets for the visual aspects of the menus simplifies your experimentation with different looks, such as color combinations, font specifications, and sizes. The JavaScript code supporting the style sheets makes only a few assumptions:

- All drop-down menus are the same width, regardless of the widths of their menu title images (which may vary as you see fit).

- Widths of menu items are determined by subtracting the menu wrapper's padding from the wrapper's width (162 pixels for the wrapper and 159 pixels for menu items in this recipe).

- Style sheets for the two states of menu item (normal and highlighted) should specify the same dimensions and font sizes.

- Several menu item height and menu wrapper border style sheet properties must be replicated in the CSSRuleValues object defined in the menu JavaScript code. If you modify your style sheet, duplicate the changes in CSSRuleValues.

You need to customize a few parts of the JavaScript code to fit the menu system to your graphical menus. First, establish the image precaching for the individual graphics in your menu bar (your menu bar may be a vertical list of menu titles or other element arrangement). Image array string index values and src properties are set just like they are in Recipe 12.1.

Next are the specifications for the content of the menus. The menus array contains custom objects corresponding to the menus that get created elsewhere. Each custom object has numerous properties that get used through various stages of creating, displaying, and hiding the menus:

mBarImgId

> String containing the ID of the img element for the menu bar menu title image associated with this menu.

mBarImgNormal

> Reference to the precached image object for the normal state of the menu title image.

mBarImgHilite

> Reference to the precached image object for the highlighted state of the menu title image.

menuItems

> Array of objects, one for each item in the menu (or an empty array if the menu title has no drop-down menu items). Each object consists of two properties: one for the text that shows in the drop-down menu; the other with the URL to which the user will navigate when selecting the menu item.

elemId

> Initialized as an empty string, this property gets its value filled in automatically when the menus are created. Do nothing with this property.

The final item to customize is the menu bar. Each menu title must be its own img element (and have two states—normal and highlighted—as fed to the precaching code earlier). You must add mouseover and mouseout event handlers to each img element's HTML code. Both event handlers invoke the same method (swap( )), and pass as the first parameter the zero-based index integer corresponding to the index of the menus array entry bearing the menu specifications for this menu title.

Although it is not a requirement for the menuing system, I recommend that each menu title image also be surrounded by a hyperlink. This is so that underpowered browsers and search engines are able to follow paths to the next lower levels of your web site, even if the destinations of those links are simple pages offering traditional links to the same items in your drop-down menus. Users of your menus will be able to bypass those pages.

All of the other code in the recipe works on its own to build the menus and handle their display activities. Items in the menus are created as traditional links so that users who expect to see URLs of links in the status bar will be right at home.

Code in the makeMenus( ) function assumes that the menus are to be deployed as true drop-down menus by positioning the menus flush left and just below the images in the menu bar. If you need the menus to push to the right or upward, you'll need to adjust the statements that set values of the menuDiv.style.left and menuDiv.style. top properties. Notice that in the drop-down recipe, the left position is lined up with the mBarImg.offsetLeft value, and that the top is pushed to the bottom of the image by the addition of mBarImg.height. If you want to make the menu push to the right, the top would be flush with the mBarImg.offsetTop, and the left would be extended to the right by the amount of mBarImg.width. To make the menu appear to pop upward, the top of the menu would be at the mBarImg.offsetTop minus the height of the menuDiv (set earlier in this function). In all cases, leave the plain offsetLeft and offsetTop variable adjustments in the formulas because they take care of some non-standard position alignment behaviors of Internet Explorer.

It's unfortunate that misplaced security restrictions prevent scripts from reading style sheet rule attributes directly in IE 6 and 7. As a workaround, we have to duplicate some important values in the script code (in the CSSRuleValues global variable) to refer to them while sizing the menus. If, in the future, IE is able to access style sheet rules without offending security restrictions, you should be able to let the definitions in the style sheet rules govern the menu positioning and sizing. For future reference, the following function adheres to the W3C DOM (and IE syntax idiosyncrasies) to read individual rule values from a style sheet embedded in a style or link element bearing an ID. While the function works as-is from a local hard disk, it generates security-related errors when the page is accessed from a server in IE:

```
// utility function invoked from makeMenus( )
// returns style sheet attribute value.
// parameters are: ID of <style> element, selector name, and attribute name
function getCSSRuleValue(styleID, selector, attr) {
    var sheet, styleElem, i;
    for (i = 0; i < document.styleSheets.length; i++) {
        sheet = document.styleSheets[i];
        styleElem = (sheet.ownerNode) ? sheet.ownerNode :
            ((sheet.owningElement) ? sheet.owningElement : null);
        if (styleElem) {
            if (styleElem.id == styleID) {
                break;
            }
        }
    }
    var rules = (sheet.cssRules) ? sheet.cssRules : ((sheet.rules) ?
        sheet.rules : null);
    if (rules) {
        for (i = 0; i < rules.length; i++) {
            if (rules[i].selectorText == selector || rules[i].selectorText ==
                "*" +  selector) {
```

```
                return rules[i].style[attr];
            }
        }
    }
    return null;
}
```

If you design your menu bar to live in one frame and expect the pop-up menu to appear in another frame, you have some more coding to do because div elements exist within the context of a browser window and do not extend into adjacent frames. To begin, the code that generates the div elements in the changeable frame has to be incorporated into each document that loads into that other frame. But that code needs to be modified to look to the menu bar title images in the navigation frame for position information. You also have to take into account any possible scrolling that occurs in the changeable frame, since it influences the position of the menu within the page, even though the menu title is static. Additional cross-frame communication is needed to synchronize the image swapping and menu showing/hiding actions.

As a last note, you may be interested in the rationale behind the requestHide( ) function and the use of the setTimeout( ) method to hide a menu. Notice that two different elements' states change: the menu title image's src and the visibility of the associated menu. A simple mouseout event handler on the image to swap the image and hide the menu works only if the user moves the pointer in a direction other than downward into the menu. In the latter case, you don't want the menu title to change back to its original state or hide the menu. Instead, the image's mouseout event handler sets the timer to execute the restoration process in 250 milliseconds via setTimeout( ). However, the mouseover event handlers of menu components, which fire before the 250 milliseconds are up, clear the timer so that the state stays the same, all while the cursor is in the menu (or goes back up to the menu title).

If the user slides over to another menu title, the time-out timer is also cleared so that the hideMenus( ) method can restore initial state instantly (which is a little faster than 250 milliseconds, so response feels quicker). Only when the user slides the pointer out and away from the menu bar or a visible menu does the timer have a chance to invoke hideMenus( ), which puts everything back the way it was when the page loaded.

With the requestHide( ) function setting a timer to go off in the future (no matter how soon the future will be), you must set the unload event handler for the page to invoke cancelHide( ). Failure to do so will allow the hideMenus( ) function call in the timer queue to execute after the page has gone away—taking its scripts with it. The result is a script error. If your pages assign another unload event handler via script properties for other purposes, you need to define yet another function that invokes both cancelHide( ) and your other function, so that the unload event can invoke both functions (or use the *eventsManager.js* library to add events to the window object).

See Also

Recipe 3.9 for simulating a hash table; Recipe 12.1 for precaching images; Recipe 12.10 for hiding and showing elements; Recipe 13.1 for creating a positioned element.

10.9   Providing Navigation Trail Menus

Problem

You want the top of every page in a deep and highly structured site to display "bread crumb trails" of where the user is within a hierarchy path.

Solution

Customize and apply the *trail.js* library (shown in Example 10-5 in the Discussion) to a location on your pages where the menu trail is to appear. Figure 10-3 shows one example on a page that includes the following HTML and script call to the makeTrailMenu( ) function in the library:

```
<div id="trailMenu" style="position:absolute; left:200px; top:200px">
<script language="JavaScript" type="text/javascript">
document.write(makeTrailMenu( ));
</script>
</div>
```

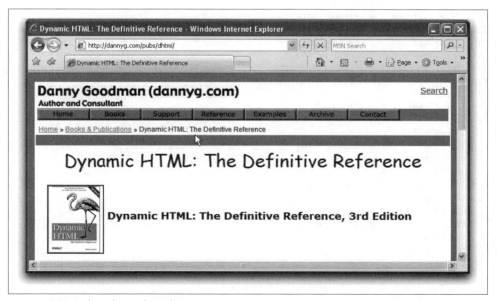

Figure 10-3. A "bread crumb trail" menu

Discussion

The sample code of this recipe assumes that the web documents on the server are structured in a directory hierarchy that matches the conceptual organization of the site. For example:

```
index.html (home at the root directory)
    catalog/
        index.html (intro to catalog and links to categories)
        economy/
            [many .html pages for this category]
        deluxe/
            [many .html pages for this category]
        export/
            [many .html pages for this category]
    support/
        index.html (intro to support and links to categories)
        contact.html
        faq/
        downloads/
        manuals/
```

Example 10-5 shows the code for the *trail.js* library, which should be linked into every page of the site that fits within the structural hierarchy.

Example 10-5. The trail.js library

```
var trailMenu = new Object( );
trailMenu["catalog"] = "Product Line";
trailMenu["economy"] = "Budget";
trailMenu["deluxe"] = "Luxury";
trailMenu["export"] = "Export Only";
trailMenu["support"] = "Product Support";
trailMenu["faq"] = "Frequently Asked Questions";
trailMenu["downloads"] = "Free Downloads";
trailMenu["manuals"] = "Manuals";

function makeTrailMenu( ) {
    for (var i = parseStart; i < parseEnd; i++) {volDelim, parseEnd;
    var output =
        "<span style='font-family:Arial, Helvetica, sans-serif; font-size:12px;" +
        "color:#000000; padding:4px'>";
    var linkStyle = "color:#339966";
    var path = location.pathname;
    var separator = " &raquo; ";
    var re = /\\/g;
    path = path.replace(re, "/");
    var trail = location.protocol + "//" + location.hostname;
    var leaves = path.split("/");
    if (location.protocol.indexOf("file") != -1) {
        parseStart = 1;
        volDelim = "/";
    } else {
        parseStart = 0;
```

Example 10-5. The trail.js library (continued)

```
            volDelim = "";
        }
        if (leaves[leaves.length-1] == "" || leaves[leaves.length-1] == "index.html" ||
            leaves[leaves.length-1] == "default.html") {
            parseEnd = leaves.length -1;
        } else {
            parseEnd = leaves.length;
        }
        for (var i = parseStart; i < parseEnd; i++) {
            if (i == parseStart) {
                trail += "/" + leaves[i] + volDelim;
                output += "<a href='" + trail + "' style='" + linkStyle + "'>";
                output += "Home";
            } else if (i == parseEnd - 1) {
                output += document.title;
            } else {
                trail += leaves[i] + "/";
                output += "<a href='" + trail + "' style='" + linkStyle + "'>";
                output += trailMenu[leaves[i]] += "</a>" + separator;
            }
        }
    }
}
```

The library begins by defining an object whose string property names are the various directory names of your site (in any order) and the corresponding plain language label you want to appear in the menus. Next is the makeTrailMenu( ) function, which assembles the HTML for the page's navigation trail menu, based on the path of the current document and its title. This example uses a guillemet character (») to act as arrows between levels.

This trail menu system works best on sites that serve up pages from *.html* files because the location.pathname property contains a lot of the information that the code uses to generate the menus. You can also make this work with sites served by server-side programs (*.pl*, *.asp*, *.jsp*, *.php*, and others), provided the directory structure is preserved. Of course, if you are using server programming to generate content for pages, you might as well use that programming power to assemble the menu trail before ever leaving the server.

The only implementation and maintenance necessities are as follows:

- Each page must have a descriptive <title> tag.
- Each directory must have a home page (such as *index.html* or *default.html*) served up when the URL points to the directory.
- Each file must include the *trail.js* library containing the data and routines.
- Changes or additions made to the site's directory structure need to be noted in the trailMenu object definition in the *trail.js* file.

Employing a custom object (trailMenu) for the lookup table of directory names and user-friendly labels offers a much faster way of performing the lookups than a more typical array. Items do not have to be in any particular order with respect to the directory structure, but keeping the structures aligned makes it easier to maintain over time as directories are added, removed, and renamed.

You have virtually unlimited flexibility in the stylesheet attributes that affect the appearance of the trail menu. It is also possible to remove the style sheet from the tag and link it into the page from a separate *.css* file if you prefer, provided you assign an ID or class identifier to the menu container and associate the container with the imported style rule. Additionally, the menu can be in the page's body, in a table, or, as shown in the recipe, a positioned element unto itself.

Slightly more challenging is implementing this kind of menu within a frameset, where the menu occupies its own frame and the content that changes is in another frame. The same algorithms apply, but you have to watch out for two points in particular. First, you need a way to trigger the rewriting of the menu each time a content page changes. The way to do this is through the load event of each page. It could invoke a function (loaded into each page from an external *.js* library) that assembles the menu (using the location property of the content window), and writes the content of the other frame. You also need to modify the links that surround each clickable item in the menu so that the target is the content-bearing frame.

In the recipe, the separator between hierarchy levels in the menu consists of a character that looks like an arrow (a guillemet character is actually a right-pointing double angle quotation mark). But the separator can be any HTML of your choice, including an image. Simply assign the HTML to the separator variable.

See Also

Recipe 1.1 for building long strings from bits and pieces; Recipe 14.1 for using document.write( ) while the page loads.

10.10 Creating Expandable Menus

Problem

You want to present a navigation menu that looks and operates like the expandable/collapsible hierarchy shown in the lefthand frame of many popular products (Windows Explorer, Outlook Express, Adobe Acrobat PDF bookmarks, and so on).

Solution

Use the *expandableMenu.js* library shown in Example 10-6 in the Discussion to populate an HTML container on your page with a collapsible menu like the one shown in Figure 10-4. A simple, empty div element is all you need in the HTML portion of the solution:

```
<div id="content"></div>
```

Bind the menu initialization function, initExpMenu( ), to the load event via the `<body>` tag, window.onload property, or the addOnLoadEvent( ) function of the *eventsManager.js* library (Recipe 9.3).

Other pieces that you need to provide or customize, as described in the Discussion, are the following:

- Images for the outline graphics
- A script global variable value for the outline item link target
- Outline data assigned to the olData object
- A pre-expansion state (optional)
- Style sheet rule dimensions to match your image designs and font specifications

This recipe works with Internet Explorer 5 or later and Netscape 6 or later. It does not operate as is in Opera, but see the Discussion section for more information.

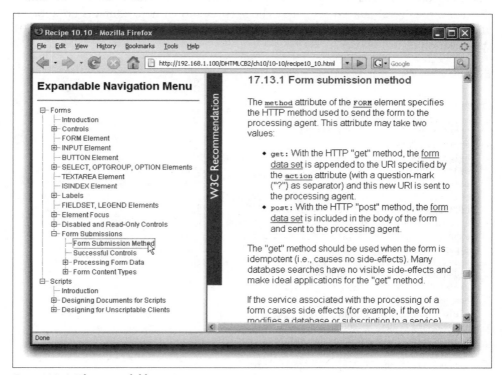

Figure 10-4. The expandable navigation menu

Discussion

Participating in this recipe are a few style sheet rules that control the appearance and layout of elements that scripts create on the fly. You may include them in the HTML page or import them:

```
<style type="text/css">
    .OLRow {vertical-align: middle;
            font-size: 12px;
            line-height: 11px;
            font-family: Arial,sans-serif
           }
    .OLBlock {display: none}
    .OLBlock a {text-decoration: none}
    img.widgetArt {vertical-align: text-top}
</style>
```

The *expandableMenu.js* library is shown in Example 10-6. It is a fairly large library divided into several labeled sections. The version shown here contains an abbreviated set of sample data for a menu that displays portions of the W3C HTML 4.01 specification.

Example 10-6. The expandableMenu.js library

```
/*********************************
        GLOBAL VARIABLES
*********************************/
var expMenuWidgets = {
    height : 16,
    width : 20,
    collapsedWidget : {src : "oplus.gif"},
    collapsedWidgetStart : {src : "oplusStart.gif"},
    collapsedWidgetEnd : {src : "oplusEnd.gif"},
    expandedWidget : {src : "ominus.gif"},
    expandedWidgetStart : {src : "ominusStart.gif"},
    expandedWidgetEnd : {src : "ominusEnd.gif"},
    nodeWidget : {src : "onode.gif"},
    nodeWidgetEnd : {src : "onodeEnd.gif"},
    emptySpace : {src : "oempty.gif"},
    chainSpace : {src : "ochain.gif"},
    preloadImages : function( ) {
        var img = new Image(this.height, this.width);
        img.src = this.collapsedWidget.src;
        img.src = this.collapsedWidgetStart.src;
        img.src = this.collapsedWidgetEnd.src;
        img.src = this.expandedWidget.src;
        img.src = this.expandedWidgetStart.src;
        img.src = this.expandedWidgetEnd.src;
        img.src = this.nodeWidget.src;
        img.src = this.nodeWidgetEnd.src;
        img.src = this.emptySpace.src;
        img.src = this.chainSpace.src;
```

Example 10-6. The expandableMenu.js library (continued)

```
    }
}
expMenuWidgets.preloadImages();

// miscellaneous globals
var currState = "";
var displayTarget = "contentFrame";

/**********************************
           DATA COLLECTIONS
**********************************/
var expansionState = "1,3,10";
// constructor for outline item objects
function outlineItem(text, uri) {
    this.text = text;
    this.uri = uri;
}
var olData = {childNodes:
            [{item:new outlineItem("Forms"),
              childNodes:
                  [{item:new outlineItem("Introduction",
                      "http://www.w3.org/.../forms.html#h-17.1")},
                   ...
                   {item:new outlineItem("INPUT Element",
                      "http://www.w3.org/.../forms.html#h-17.4"),
                    childNodes:
                        [{item:new outlineItem("INPUT Control Types",
                            "http://www.w3.org/.../forms.html#h-17.4.1")},
                         {item:new outlineItem("Examples",
                            "http://www.w3.org/.../forms.html#h-17.4.2")}
                        ]},
                   ...
                  ]},
             {item:new outlineItem("Scripts"),
              childNodes:
                  [{item:new outlineItem("Introduction",
                      "http://www.w3.org/.../scripts.html#h-18.1")},
                   {item:new outlineItem("Designing Documents for Scripts",
                      "http://www.w3.org/.../scripts.html#h-18.2"),
                    childNodes:
                        [{item:new outlineItem("SCRIPT Element",
                            "http://www.w3.org/.../scripts.html#h-18.2.1")},
                         {item:new outlineItem("Specifying the Scripting Language",
                            "http://www.w3.org/.../scripts.html#h-18.2.2"),
                          childNodes:
                              [{item:new outlineItem("Default Language",
                                  "http://www.w3.org/.../scripts.html#h-18.2.2.1")},
                               {item:new outlineItem("Local Language Declaration",
                                  "http://www.w3.org/.../scripts.html#h-18.2.2.2")},
                               {item:new outlineItem("References to HTML Elements",
                                  "http://www.w3.org/.../scripts.html#h-18.2.2.3")}
                              ]
```

Example 10-6. The expandableMenu.js library (continued)

```
                }
             ]
          ...
          }
       ]
    };
```

```
/*********************************
  TOGGLE DISPLAY AND ICONS
*********************************/
// invert item state (expanded to/from collapsed)
function swapState(currState, currVal, n) {
    var newState = currState.substring(0,n);
    newState += currVal ^ 1 // Bitwise XOR item n;
    newState += currState.substring(n+1,currState.length);
    return newState;
}

// retrieve matching version of 'minus' images
function getExpandedWidgetState(imgURL) {
    if (imgURL.indexOf("Start") != -1) {
        return expMenuWidgets.expandedWidgetStart.src;
    }
    if (imgURL.indexOf("End") != -1) {
        return expMenuWidgets.expandedWidgetEnd.src;
    }
    return expMenuWidgets.expandedWidget.src;
}

// retrieve matching version of 'plus' images
function getCollapsedWidgetState(imgURL) {
    if (imgURL.indexOf("Start") != -1) {
        return expMenuWidgets.collapsedWidgetStart.src;
    }
    if (imgURL.indexOf("End") != -1) {
        return expMenuWidgets.collapsedWidgetEnd.src;
    }
    return expMenuWidgets.collapsedWidget.src;
}

// toggle an outline mother entry, storing new state value;
// invoked by onclick event handlers of widget image elements
function toggle(img, blockNum) {
    var newString = "";
    var expanded, n;
    // modify state string based on parameters from IMG
    expanded = currState.charAt(blockNum);
    currState = swapState(currState, expanded, blockNum);
    // dynamically change display style
```

Example 10-6. The expandableMenu.js library (continued)

```
        if (expanded == "0") {
            document.getElementById("OLBlock" + blockNum).style.display = "block";
            img.src = getExpandedWidgetState(img.src);
        } else {
            document.getElementById("OLBlock" + blockNum).style.display = "none";
            img.src = getCollapsedWidgetState(img.src);
        }
    }

function expandAll( ) {
    var newState = "";
    while (newState.length < currState.length) {
        newState += "1";
    }
    currState = newState;
    var contentImages = document.getElementById("content").getElementsByTagName("img");
    var widgetNum, expanded;
    for (var i = 0; i < contentImages.length; i++) {
        if (contentImages[i].className == "collapsible") {
        widgetNum = contentImages[i].id.substring(6);
            contentImages[i].src = getExpandedWidgetState(contentImages[i].src);
        }
    }
    initExpand( );
}

function collapseAll( ) {
    var newState = "";
    while (newState.length < currState.length) {
        newState += "0";
    }
    currState = newState;
    var contentImages = document.getElementById("content").getElementsByTagName("img");
    var widgetNum, expanded;
    for (var i = 0; i < contentImages.length; i++) {
        if (contentImages[i].className == "collapsible") {
        widgetNum = contentImages[i].id.substring(6);
            contentImages[i].src = getCollapsedWidgetState(contentImages[i].src);
        }
    }
    initExpand( );
}

/********************************
   OUTLINE HTML GENERATION
********************************/
// apply default expansion state from outline's header
// info to the expanded state for one element to help
// initialize currState variable
function calcBlockState(n) {
    // get default expansionState data
    var expandedData = (expansionState.length > 0) ? expansionState.split(",") : null;
```

Example 10-6. The expandableMenu.js library (continued)

```
    if (expandedData) {
        for (var j = 0; j < expandedData.length; j++) {
            if (n == expandedData[j] - 1) {
                return "1";
            }
        }
    }
    return "0";
}

// counters for reflexive calls to drawOutline()
var currID = 0;
var blockID = 0;
// generate HTML for outline
function drawOutline(ol, prefix) {
    var output = "";
    var nestCount, link, nestPrefix, lastInnerNode;
    prefix = (prefix) ? prefix : "";
    for (var i = 0; i < ol.childNodes.length ; i++) {
        nestCount = (ol.childNodes[i].childNodes) ? ol.childNodes[i].childNodes.length : 0;
        output += "<div class='OLRow' id='line" + currID++ + "'>\n";
        if (nestCount > 0) {
            output += prefix;
            currState += calcBlockState(currID-1);
            if (currState.substr(currState.length-1) == "0") {
                output += "<img id='widget" + (currID-1) + "' class='collapsible' src='" +
                    ((i == ol.childNodes.length-1 && blockID != 0) ?
                    expMenuWidgets.collapsedWidgetEnd.src : (blockID == 0) ?
                    expMenuWidgets.collapsedWidgetStart.src :
                        expMenuWidgets collapsedWidget.src);
            } else {
                output += "<img id='widget" + (currID-1) + "' class='collapsible' src='" +
                    ((i == ol.childNodes.length-1 && blockID != 0) ?
                    expMenuWidgets.expandedWidgetEnd.src : (blockID == 0) ?
                    expMenuWidgets.expandedWidgetStart.src :
                        expMenuWidgets.expandedWidget.src);
            }
            output += "' height=" + expMenuWidgets.height + " width=" +
                expMenuWidgets.width;
            output += " title='Click to expand/collapse nested items.'" +
                "onClick='toggle(this," + blockID + ") '> ";
            link =  (ol.childNodes[i].item.uri) ? ol.childNodes[i].item.uri : "";
            if (link) {
                output += "<a href='" + link + "' class='itemTitle' title='" +
                link + "' target='" + displayTarget + "'>" ;
            } else {
                output += "<a class='itemTitle' title='" + link + "'>";
            }
            output += "<span style='position:relative; top:-3px; height:11px'>" +
                ol.childNodes[i].item.text + "</span></a>";
            output += "<span class='OLBlock' blocknum='" + blockID + "' id='OLBlock" +
                blockID++ + "'>";
```

Example 10-6. The expandableMenu.js library (continued)

```
                    nestPrefix = prefix;
                    nestPrefix += (i == ol.childNodes.length - 1) ?
                        "<img src='" + expMenuWidgets.emptySpace.src + "' height=" +
                        expMenuWidgets.height + " width=" + expMenuWidgets.width + ">" :
                        "<img src='" + expMenuWidgets.chainSpace.src + "' height=" +
                        expMenuWidgets.height + " width=" + expMenuWidgets.width + ">"
                    output += drawOutline(ol.childNodes[i], nestPrefix);
                    output += "</span></div>\n";
                } else {
                    output += prefix;
                    output += "<img id='widget" + (currID-1) + "' src='" +
                        ((i == ol.childNodes.length - 1) ? expMenuWidgets.nodeWidgetEnd.src :
                        expMenuWidgets.nodeWidget.src);
                    output += "' height=" + expMenuWidgets.height + " width=" +
                        expMenuWidgets.width + ">";
                    link = (ol.childNodes[i].item.uri) ? ol.childNodes[i].item.uri : "";
                    if (link) {
                        output += " <a href='" + link + "' class='itemTitle' title='" +
                        link + "' target='" + displayTarget + "'>";
                    } else {
                        output += " <a class='itemTitle' title='" + link + "'>";
                    }
                    output += "<span style='position:relative; top:-3px; height:11px'>" +
                        ol.childNodes[i].item.text + "</span></a>";
                    output += "</div>\n";
                }
            }
        }
        return output;
    }


    /*********************************
        OUTLINE INITIALIZATIONS
    *********************************/
    // expand items set in expansionState var, if any
    function initExpand( ) {
        for (var i = 0; i < currState.length; i++) {
            if (currState.charAt(i) == 1) {
                document.getElementById("OLBlock" + i).style.display = "block";
            } else {
                document.getElementById("OLBlock" + i).style.display = "none";
            }
        }
    }


    // initialize first time -- invoked onload
    function initExpMenu(xFile) {
        // wrap whole outline HTML in a span
        var olHTML = "<span id='renderedOL'>" + drawOutline(olData) + "</span>";
        // throw HTML into 'content' div for display
        document.getElementById("content").innerHTML = olHTML;
        initExpand( );
    }
```

This script begins by defining and precaching the small images that become components of the finished outline display (called *widgets* in this example). Images created for this solution are shown in Figure 10-5. All images are the same size.

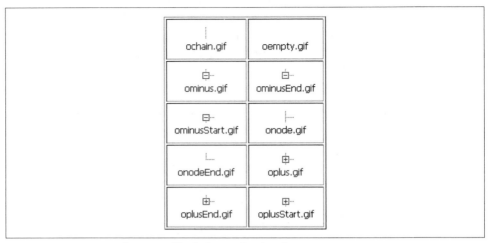

Figure 10-5. Images used to assemble the hierarchical path

Some global definitions come first. Images are specified (size and image file URLs) and preloaded into the expMenuWidgets global object. By assigning the URLs to an instance of the Image object, the script forces the browser to fetch all of the images during the page load. The script will use the currState variable to preserve a representation of the expanded and collapsed state of various items in the menu. For a framed layout, you should assign to the displayTarget variable the name of the frame where content linked from the menu items will appear.

The next code block contains the outline data and some supporting values. One global variable, expansionState, contains a comma-delimited list of line numbers (each entry of the outline is in its own line) of those entries that are to be displayed in their expanded state when first displayed. If only the top-level items are to be visible (i.e., the menus are fully collapsed), assign an empty string to this variable. The outlineItem( ) constructor function is invoked repeatedly when the custom JavaScript object code executes during page loading. Each outline entry has displayable text and an optional link URL.

Next is the definition of the object (named olData) containing the outline data. For this recipe, I chose a structure that ultimately simulates the kind of node structure that an XML data source provides. Thus, a sequence of nested objects and arrays define the outline. Only a portion of the example outline (links to sections of the W3C HTML 4.01 recommendation) is shown here. I'll have more to say about the formatting later.

The section marked "Toggle Display and Icons" includes functions that control the change of state between expanded and collapsed. A pair of functions named getExpandedWidgetState( ) and getCollapsedWidgetState( ) (both invoked by the toggle( ) function discussed later), retrieve one of three expanded or collapsed images depending on the name (specifically, a portion of the name) of the current widget image. The swapState( ) helper function (also invoked from toggle( )) performs binary arithmetic on the value of the currState variable to change a specific character from zero to one or vice versa (these characters represent the state of each branch node).

At the center of user interaction is the toggle( ) function, which is activated by click event handlers assigned to each clickable widget. Because the event handlers are assigned while a script builds the outline, the event handlers can include parameters that indicate which item is being clicked. Thus, toggle( ) receives the widget's current image URL (used to determine which image should take its place) and a numeric ID associated with the span containing nested items. Although the function is small, it uses some helper functions to do the job. The two basic tasks of this function are to change the clicked widget image and display style sheet setting of the element containing nested items below it.

Two more functions, expandAll( ) and collapseAll( ), stand ready to fully expand and collapse the entire outline, if your user interface design provides user control of that feature.

The next-to-last block of code devotes itself to the creation of the HTML for the outline menu content. One helper function, calcBlockState( ), is invoked repeatedly during the HTML construction, and looks to see if the particular line number of the outline is supposed to be expanded by default. The data for these settings consists of a comma-delimited list of line numbers for expanded items (assigned to global variable expansionState).

Assembly of the outline's HTML in the drawOutline( ) function iterates through the olData object. But a major part of that iteration entails recursive calls to the same drawOutline( ) function to build the nested items. Therefore, a pair of counting variables (used to compose unique IDs for elements) are declared in the global space as currID and blockID.

Now we reach the drawOutline( ) function, which acts like a whirling dervish to accumulate the HTML for the rendered outline. The content is assembled just once, while all subsequent adjustments to the expanded or collapsed states are controlled by style sheet settings. Layout of the various widget images is governed by the structure of the olData objects. Among the more complex tasks that the drawOutline( ) recursive code needs to keep track of is whether an image column position requires a vertical line to signify a later connection with an earlier item or just a blank space. The regularity of all widget image sizes lets the script build the widget image parts of each line as if the images were mosaic tiles.

The final code block performs all initializations and gets the ball rolling. First is a function (initExpand( )) that iterates through the currState variable to establish the expand/collapse state of each nested block. This function is invoked not only by the following initExpMenu( ) function, but also by the expandAll( ) and collapseAll( ) functions.

At last we reach the initExpMenu( ) function, invoked by the load event handler for the page. This is the driving force behind the creation of the rendered HTML, embedding it inside a dedicated span element, and then tucking it all into a pre-existing div element, as shown in the body's HTML.

To deploy this menu system successfully, you need to create your set of widget images, like the ones shown in Figure 10-5. All images must be the same size, and you may have to tweak the style sheet values for the text fonts to achieve a proportioned look with sizes other than those shown in the recipe.

Most code customizations take place at the top of the script area. Start by assigning URLs for the widget images, image sizes, and target frame for menu links. (This menuing system works best in framesets or with content iframes so that the outline remains unchanged during navigation.)

Perhaps the most complicated part of customizing this collapsible navigation menu is creating the olData object. Before you begin to plug in your own data, you need to have a solid hierarchy to map. It doesn't hurt to literally write it down so you can visualize the nesting of subjects. For example, the start of the outline shown in the recipe looks like the following when fully expanded:

```
Forms
    Introduction
    Controls
        Control Types
    FORM Element
    INPUT Element
        INPUT Types
        Examples
    BUTTON Element
```

Each line of the outline contains an item. Each item must have text associated with it, as well as an optional URL for a clickable link associated with the text. If you omit the URL, the text still appears in the outline, but its content does not link to any other destination.

To convert the written outline into an olData data set, you recreate the parent-child-sibling relationships among the entries. Schematically, the above outline fragment in olData form looks like the following:

```
olData =
  {childNodes:[{item:"Forms",
                childNodes:[{item:"Introduction"},
                            {item:"Controls", childNodes:[{item:"Control Types"}]},
                            {item:"FORM Element"},
```

```
                              {item:"INPUT Element", childNodes[{item:"INPUT Types"},
                                                         {item"Examples"}]},
                     {item:"BUTTON Element"}]
          }]
    };
```

The hard part is keeping all of the array and object containment (the open and close pairs of braces and square brackets) straight as the outline grows. The use of the childNodes property name for the nested entries has its roots in the XML version of this menu (see Recipe 10.11). You can use another name if you prefer. Also, the indented formatting shown in the recipe may be helpful in aligning the nestings correctly.

The line numbers of the fully expanded outline are significant if you wish the outline to be partially expanded when it first appears. You can convey a comma-delimited list of expanded lines in the expansionState global variable. The only line numbers you need to include here are those that act as branch nodes—items that contain further nested items. If you leave the variable an empty string (as shown in this recipe), only the top-level items appear by default.

Operating slightly differently is the currState variable. This value consists of ones and zeros in string form; it tracks the expansion state of branch nodes in the outline only. Thus, an outline consisting of five branch nodes and dozens of leaf nodes (items containing no further nested items) carries only a five-digit currState value. A numeric value of zero at any digit means that the corresponding branch node is collapsed, while a one means the branch is expanded. This mechanism makes it easy to switch the value of an individual branch node (in the swapState( ) function) in response to the click of its widget icon. It also means that the currState variable remembers when more deeply nested branches were expanded previously. If a branch closer to the top level collapses, any expanded nodes inside it remain expanded for the next time they're seen. Also, if you wish to preserve the expansion state between user visits to the page, the currState value (in string form) is what you'd preserve in a cookie and read during initialization to restore the previous settings. For first-time visitors, you need to supply a default currState value with the requisite number of zeros corresponding to branch nodes in your outline.

This recipe shows only text hyperlinks as visible nodes in the outline, but you are not limited to text. You can reconfigure the olData object's properties and the drawOutline( ) function to accumulate any HTML content you like in place of the text labels. Iteration through the olData object is still the governing loop control of drawOutline( ).

You may be wondering why the first call to drawOutline( ) from the initExpMenu( ) function passes a reference to the olData global variable. Due to the recursive nature of the drawOutline( ) function, which calls itself repeatedly, passing nested portions of olData where needed, it is convenient to let the function assume it will always receive a parameter containing a valid object from olData. At the start of the process, the object is the complete olData object. But as nested nodes are assembled in recursive calls, only groups of child nodes are passed. No other first-time flags or other loop-degrading tests get in the way.

If you prefer to deploy this outline so the outline is not dynamically generated but consists of hardcoded HTML (perhaps to allow search engines to see and follow its links), you can still perform your development with the olData object and its form of structuring the outline data. Then, load the page into a browser and capture the HTML for the entire outline. The quickest way to accomplish this is through a *bookmarklet*: a bookmark consisting of a javascript: URL that executes some Java-Script code. Or, you can simply enter the bookmarklet text into the Address/Location field of the browser:

```
javascript: "<textarea cols='120' rows='40'>" +
document.getElementById("content").innerHTML + "</textarea>"
```

You will then see a textarea element containing the entire outline HTML. Copy and paste this HTML into the outline page's div element whose ID is content. This technique is also a helpful way to examine the HTML generated by drawOutline( ), either for study or debugging. In the global variables, assign an initial zero-filled string value to the currState variable. You can delete the "Data Collections" and "Outline HTML Generation" code blocks, as well as all but the initExpand( ) function call from the initExpMenu( ) function. If your outline consists of hundreds of items (which may indicate an outline is too large), the hardwired HTML will render faster than the dynamically generated version.

See Also

Recipe 1.1 for building large strings from smaller segments; Recipe 10.11 for an XML-based outline data source; Recipe 12.1 for precaching images; Recipe 12.10 for hiding and showing elements.

10.11 Creating Collapsible XML Menus

Problem

You want to present a navigation menu that looks and operates like the collapsible hierarchy shown in the lefthand frame of many popular products (Windows Explorer, Outlook Express, Adobe Acrobat PDF bookmarks, and so on), but the data needs to come from an XML data source.

Solution

Use the *XMLoutline.js* library shown in Example 10-7 in the Discussion to convert a specially formatted XML outline document to an interactive collapsible menu like the one shown in Figure 10-4 of Recipe 10.10. Include a simple, empty div element in the HTML portion of your page where the outline is to appear:

```
<div id="content"></div>
```

Bind the menu initialization function, initXMLOutline( ), to the load event via the `<body>` tag, window.onload property, or addOnLoadEvent( ) function from the *eventsManager.js* library (Recipe 9.3), specifying the filename of the XML file:

```
onload="initXMLOutline('SpecOutline.xml')"
```

Other pieces that you need to provide or customize, as described in the Discussion, are the following:

- The OPML source for the data
- Images for the outline graphics
- A script global variable value for the outline item link target
- Style sheet rule dimensions to match your image designs and font specifications

This recipe works with Internet Explorer 5 or later for Windows, Mozilla, Safari 1.2 or later, and Opera 8 or later. Note that the code used in this recipe must be accessed via the HTTP protocol, not the file protocol.

Discussion

The recipe shown here is similar to the JavaScript data-based solution shown in Recipe 10.10. The difference is that the data is formatted in outline-flavored XML: OPML (Outline Processing Markup Language) designed by Dave Winer (*http://www.opml. org*). Thus, while all of the toggling and state-switching code is identical to Recipe 10. 10, the loading of the external OPML file and creation of the outline is different. For the sake of completeness and context, however, we treat this recipe separately.

Participating in this recipe are a few style sheet rules that control the appearance and layout of elements that scripts create on the fly. You may include them in the HTML page or import them:

```
.OLRow {vertical-align: middle;
        font-size: 12px;
        line-height: 11px;
        font-family: Arial,sans-serif
        }
.OLBlock {display: none}
.OLBlock a {text-decoration: none}
img.widgetArt {vertical-align: text-top}
```

The *XMLoutline.js* library is shown in Example 10-7. Because all of the data for the outline comes from a separate file, this library consists entirely of interactive code.

Example 10-7. The XMLoutline.js library

```
/*********************************
         GLOBAL VARIABLES
*********************************/
var expMenuWidgets = {
    height : 16,
    width : 20,
    collapsedWidget : {src : "oplus.gif"},
```

Example 10-7. The XMLoutline.js library (continued)

```
        collapsedWidgetStart : {src : "oplusStart.gif"},
        collapsedWidgetEnd : {src : "oplusEnd.gif"},
        expandedWidget : {src : "ominus.gif"},
        expandedWidgetStart : {src : "ominusStart.gif"},
        expandedWidgetEnd : {src : "ominusEnd.gif"},
        nodeWidget : {src : "onode.gif"},
        nodeWidgetEnd : {src : "onodeEnd.gif"},
        emptySpace : {src : "oempty.gif"},
        chainSpace : {src : "ochain.gif"},
        preloadImages : function( ) {
            var img = new Image(this.height, this.width);
            img.src = this.collapsedWidget.src;
            img.src = this.collapsedWidgetStart.src;
            img.src = this.collapsedWidgetEnd.src;
            img.src = this.expandedWidget.src;
            img.src = this.expandedWidgetStart.src;
            img.src = this.expandedWidgetEnd.src;
            img.src = this.nodeWidget.src;
            img.src = this.nodeWidgetEnd.src;
            img.src = this.emptySpace.src;
            img.src = this.chainSpace.src;
        }
    }
expMenuWidgets.preloadImages( );

// miscellaneous globals
var currState = "";
var displayTarget = "contentFrame";

/**********************************
  TOGGLE DISPLAY AND ICONS
**********************************/
// invert item state (expanded to/from collapsed)
function swapState(currState, currVal, n) {
    var newState = currState.substring(0,n);
    newState += currVal ^ 1 // Bitwise XOR item n;
    newState += currState.substring(n+1,currState.length);
    return newState;
}

// retrieve matching version of 'minus' images
function getExpandedWidgetState(imgURL) {
    if (imgURL.indexOf("Start") != -1) {
        return expMenuWidgets.expandedWidgetStart.src;
    }
    if (imgURL.indexOf("End") != -1) {
        return expMenuWidgets.expandedWidgetEnd.src;
    }
    return expMenuWidgets.expandedWidget.src;
}

// retrieve matching version of 'plus' images
function getCollapsedWidgetState(imgURL) {
```

Example 10-7. The XMLoutline.js library (continued)

```
    if (imgURL.indexOf("Start") != -1) {
        return expMenuWidgets.collapsedWidgetStart.src;
    }
    if (imgURL.indexOf("End") != -1) {
        return expMenuWidgets.collapsedWidgetEnd.src;
    }
    return expMenuWidgets.collapsedWidget.src;
}


// toggle an outline mother entry, storing new state value;
// invoked by onclick event handlers of widget image elements
function toggle(img, blockNum) {
    var newString = "";
    var expanded, n;
    // modify state string based on parameters from IMG
    expanded = currState.charAt(blockNum);
    currState = swapState(currState, expanded, blockNum);
    // dynamically change display style
    if (expanded == "0") {
        document.getElementById("OLBlock" + blockNum).style.display = "block";
        img.src = getExpandedWidgetState(img.src);
    } else {
        document.getElementById("OLBlock" + blockNum).style.display = "none";
        img.src = getCollapsedWidgetState(img.src);
    }
}

function expandAll( ) {
    var newState = "";
    while (newState.length < currState.length) {
        newState += "1";
    }
    currState = newState;
    var contentImages = document.getElementById("content").getElementsByTagName("img");
    var widgetNum, expanded;
    for (var i = 0; i < contentImages.length; i++) {
        if (contentImages[i].className == "collapsible") {
            widgetNum = contentImages[i].id.substring(6);
            contentImages[i].src = getExpandedWidgetState(contentImages[i].src);
        }
    }
    initExpand( );
}

function collapseAll( ) {
    var newState = "";
    while (newState.length < currState.length) {
        newState += "0";
    }
    currState = newState;
    var contentImages = document.getElementById("content").getElementsByTagName("img");
    var widgetNum, expanded;
```

Example 10-7. The XMLoutline.js library (continued)

```
    for (var i = 0; i < contentImages.length; i++) {
        if (contentImages[i].className == "collapsible") {
            widgetNum = contentImages[i].id.substring(6);
            contentImages[i].src = getCollapsedWidgetState(contentImages[i].src);
        }
    }
    initExpand( );
}


/********************************
   OUTLINE HTML GENERATION
********************************/
// apply default expansion state from outline's header
// info to the expanded state for one element to help
// initialize currState variable
function calcBlockState(ol, n, expandElem) {
    // get OPML expansionState data
    var expandedData = (expandElem && expandElem.childNodes.length) ?
        expandElem.firstChild.nodeValue.split(",") : null;
    if (expandedData) {
        for (var j = 0; j < expandedData.length; j++) {
            if (n == expandedData[j] - 1) {
                return "1";
            }
        }
    }
    return "0";
}

// counters for reflexive calls to drawOutline( )
var currID = 0;
var blockID = 0;
// generate HTML for outline
function drawOutline(ol, prefix, expState) {
    var output = "";
    var nestCount, link, nestPrefix, lastInnerNode;
    prefix = (prefix) ? prefix : "";
    if (ol.childNodes[ol.childNodes.length - 1].nodeType == 3) {
        ol.removeChild(ol.childNodes[ol.childNodes.length - 1]);
    }
    for (var i = 0; i < ol.childNodes.length ; i++) {
        if (ol.childNodes[i].nodeType == 3) {
            continue;
        }
        if (ol.childNodes[i].childNodes.length > 0 &&
            ol.childNodes[i].childNodes[ol.childNodes[i].childNodes.length - 1].nodeType
== 3) {
ol.childNodes[i].removeChild(ol.childNodes[i].childNodes[ol.childNodes[i].childNodes.
length - 1]);
        }
        nestCount = ol.childNodes[i].childNodes.length;
        output += "<div class='OLRow' id='line" + currID++ + "'>\n";
```

Example 10-7. The XMLoutline.js library (continued)

```
if (nestCount > 0) {
    output += prefix;
    currState += calcBlockState(ol, currID-1, expState);
    if (currState.substr(currState.length-1) == "0") {
        output += "<img id='widget" + (currID-1) + "' class='collapsible' src='" +
            ((i == ol.childNodes.length-1 && blockID != 0) ?
            expMenuWidgets.collapsedWidgetEnd.src : (blockID == 0) ?
            expMenuWidgets.collapsedWidgetStart.src :
                expMenuWidgets.collapsedWidget.src);
    } else {
        output += "<img id='widget" + (currID-1) + "' class='collapsible' src='" +
            ((i == ol.childNodes.length-1 && blockID != 0) ?
            expMenuWidgets.expandedWidgetEnd.src : (blockID == 0) ?
            expMenuWidgets.expandedWidgetStart.src :
                expMenuWidgets.expandedWidget.src);
    }
    output += "' height=" + expMenuWidgets.height + " width=" +
        expMenuWidgets.width;
    output += " title='Click to expand/collapse nested items.' " +
        "onClick='toggle(this," + blockID + ")'> ";
    link = (ol.childNodes[i].getAttribute("uri")) ?
        ol.childNodes[i].getAttribute("uri") : "";
    if (link) {
        output += "<a href='" + link + "' class='itemTitle' title='" +
        link + "' target='" + displayTarget + "'> ";
    } else {
        output += "<a class='itemTitle' title='" + link + "'>";
    }
    output += "<span style='position:relative; top:-3px; height:11px'>" +
        ol.childNodes[i].getAttribute("text") + "</span></a>";
    output += "<span class='OLBlock' blocknum='" + blockID + "' id='OLBlock" +
        blockID++ + "'>";
    nestPrefix = prefix;
    nestPrefix += (i == ol.childNodes.length - 1) ?
        "<img src='" + expMenuWidgets.emptySpace.src + "' height=" +
        expMenuWidgets.height + " width=" + expMenuWidgets.width + ">" :
        "<img src='" + expMenuWidgets.chainSpace.src + "' height=" +
        expMenuWidgets.height + " width=" + expMenuWidgets.width + ">"
    output += drawOutline(ol.childNodes[i], nestPrefix, expState);
    output += "</span></div>\n";
} else {
    output += prefix;
    output += "<img id='widget" + (currID-1) + "' src='" +
        ((i == ol.childNodes.length - 1) ? expMenuWidgets.nodeWidgetEnd.src :
        expMenuWidgets.nodeWidget.src);
    output += "' height=" + expMenuWidgets.height + " width=" +
        expMenuWidgets.width +
        ">";
    link = (ol.childNodes[i].getAttribute("uri")) ?
        ol.childNodes[i].getAttribute("uri") : "";
    if (link) {
        output += " <a href='" + link + "' class='itemTitle' title='" +
        link + "' target='" + displayTarget + "'>";
```

Example 10-7. The XMLoutline.js library (continued)

```
            } else {
                output += " <a class='itemTitle' title='" + link + "'>";
            }
            output +="<span style='position:relative; top:-3px; height:11px'>" +
                ol.childNodes[i].getAttribute("text") + "</span></a>";
            output += "</div>\n";
        }
    }
    return output;
}


/********************************
    OUTLINE INITIALIZATIONS
********************************/
// expand items set in expansionState OPML tag, if any
function initExpand( ) {
    for (var i = 0; i < currState.length; i++) {
        if (currState.charAt(i) == 1) {
            document.getElementById("OLBlock" + i).style.display = "block";
        } else {
            document.getElementById("OLBlock" + i).style.display = "none";
        }
    }
}

function insertOutline(req) {
    req = req.request;
    if (req.readyState == 4 && req.status == 200) {
        // get outline body elements for iteration and conversion to HTML
        var ol = req.responseXML.getElementsByTagName("body")[0];
        // wrap whole outline HTML in a span
        var olHTML = "<span id='renderedOL'>" + drawOutline(ol, "",
            req.responseXML.getElementsByTagName("expansionState")[0]) + "</span>";
        // throw HTML into 'content' div for display
        document.getElementById("content").innerHTML = olHTML;
        initExpand( );
    }
}

// constructor function for an XML request object;
function XMLDoc( ) {
    var me = this;
    var req = null;
    // branch for native XMLHttpRequest object
    if (window.XMLHttpRequest) {
        try {
            req = new XMLHttpRequest( );
        } catch(e) {
            req = null;
        }
    // branch for IE/Windows ActiveX version
    } else if (window.ActiveXObject) {
        try {
```

Example 10-7. The XMLoutline.js library (continued)

```
                req = new ActiveXObject("Msxml2.XMLHTTP");
        } catch(e) {
            try {
                req = new ActiveXObject("Microsoft.XMLHTTP");
            } catch(e) {
                req = null;
            }
        }
    } else {
        alert("This example requires a browser with XML support, such as IE5+/Windows,
Mozilla, Safari 1.2, or Opera 8.")
    }
    // preserve reference to request object for later
    this.request = req;
    // "public" method to be invoked whenever
    this.loadXMLDoc = function(url, loadHandler) {
        if (this.request) {
            this.request.open("GET", url, true);
            this.request.onreadystatechange = function () {loadHandler(me)};
            this.request.setRequestHeader("Content-Type", "text/xml");
            this.request.send("");
        }
    };
}

function initXML() {
    var outlineRequest = new XMLDoc();
    outlineRequest.loadXMLDoc("SpecOutline.xml", insertOutline);
}

addOnLoadEvent(initXML);
```

Some global definitions come first. Images are specified (size and image file URLs) and preloaded into the expMenuWidgets global object. Images created for this solution are shown in Figure 10-5 of Recipe 10.10. All images are the same size. The script will use the currState variable to preserve a representation of the expanded and collapsed state of various items in the menu. For a framed layout, you should assign to the displayTarget variable the name of the frame where content linked from the menu items will appear.

The section marked "Toggle Display and Icons" includes functions that control the change of state between expanded and collapsed. A pair of functions named getExpandedWidgetState() and getCollapsedWidgetState() (both invoked by the toggle() function) retrieve one of three expanded or collapsed images depending on the name (specifically, a portion of the name) of the current widget image. The swapState() helper function (also invoked from toggle()) performs binary arithmetic on the value of the currState variable to change a specific character from zero to one or vice versa (these characters represent the state of each branch node).

At the center of user interaction is the toggle( ) function, which is activated by click event handlers assigned to each clickable widget. Because the event handlers are assigned while a script builds the outline, they can include parameters that indicate which item is being clicked. Thus, toggle( ) receives the widget's current image URL (used to determine which image should take its place) and a numeric ID associated with the span containing nested items. Although the function is small, it uses some helper functions, specifically swapState( ), getExpandedWidget( ), and getCollapsedWidget( ). The two basic tasks of this function are to change the clicked widget image and display style sheet setting of the element containing nested items below it.

Two more functions, expandAll( ) and collapseAll( ), stand ready to fully expand and collapse the entire outline, if your user interface design provides user control of that feature.

The next-to-last block of code devotes itself to the creation of the HTML for the outline menu content. One helper function, calcBlockState( ), is invoked repeatedly during the HTML construction, and looks to see if the particular line number of the outline is supposed to be expanded by default. The data for these settings consists of a comma-delimited list of line numbers for expanded items read from the expansionState tag of the OPML data (e.g., <expansionState>1,3,8</expansionState>).

Assembly of the outline's HTML in the drawOutline( ) function iterates through the node tree of the XML data passed as the ol parameter (described later). But a major part of that iteration entails recursive calls to the same drawOutline( ) function to build the nested items. Therefore, a pair of counting variables (used to compose unique IDs for elements) are declared in the global space as currID and blockID.

The drawOutline( ) function accumulates the HTML for the rendered outline. The content is assembled just once, while all subsequent adjustments to the expanded or collapsed states get controlled by style sheet settings. Layout of the various widget images is governed by the structure of the XML document's element hierarchy. Among the more complex tasks that the drawOutline( ) recursive code needs to keep track of is whether an image column position requires a vertical line to signify a later connection with an earlier item or just a blank space. The regularity of all widget image sizes lets the script build the widget image parts of each line as if the images were mosaic tiles.

The final code block performs all initializations. First is a function (initExpand( )) that iterates through the currState variable to establish the expand/collapse state of each nested block. This function is invoked not only by the following verifyLoad( ) function, but also by the expandAll( ) and collapseAll( ) functions.

To assist with the XML document retrieval, we use the XMLDoc constructor function from Recipe 14.17. When invoked, this function creates an object that can retrieve XML (or a couple of other types of) data from a URL via the XMLHttpRequest object. The instance object's loadXMLDoc( ) method performs the retrieval and signifies the function to be invoked each time the XMLHttpRequest readyState property changes. For this example, we specify that insertOutline( ) be invoked.

The `insertOutline( )` function tests for the successful completion of the download. It then passes the `expansionState` and body elements of the OPML document to `drawOutline( )`, where the outline's HTML is assembled. The resulting HTML string is applied to the `innerHTML` property of the otherwise div element.

OPML is an extensible format for outline data. An OPML document is divided into two blocks, head and body. The body element contains all of the items that belong to the outline. Each item is called an `outline` element. Hierarchy (nesting) of outline items is determined entirely by the nesting of outline elements. You may add any attributes you like to an `outline` element and still conform to the format (provided the attribute/value syntax is well-formed XML). An excerpt of the OPML document that produces an outline like the one shown in Figure 10-4 (but with truncated URLs for space reasons) follows:

```
<?xml version="1.0"?>
<opml version="1.0">
    <head>
        <title>HTML Sections Outline</title>
        <dateCreated>Mon, 10 Sep 2002 03:40:00 GMT</dateCreated>
        <dateModified>Fri, 22 Sep 2002 19:35:00 GMT</dateModified>
        <ownerName>Danny Goodman</ownerName>
        <ownerEmail>dannyg@dannyg.com</ownerEmail>
        <expansionState></expansionState>
        <vertScrollState>1</vertScrollState>
        <windowTop></windowTop>
        <windowLeft></windowLeft>
        <windowBottom></windowBottom>
        <windowRight></windowRight>
    </head>
    <body>
        <outline text="Forms">
            <outline text="Introduction" uri="http://w3.org/.../forms.html#h-17.1"/>
            <outline text="Controls" uri="http://w3.org/.../forms.html#h-17.2">
                <outline text="Control Types"
                        uri="http://w3.org/.../forms.html#h-17.2.1"/>
            </outline>
            <outline text="FORM Element" uri="http://w3.org/.../forms.html#h-17.3"/>
            <outline text="INPUT Element" uri="http://w3.org/.../forms.html#h-17.4">
                <outline text="INPUT Control Types"
                        uri="http://w3.org/.../forms.html#h-17.4.1"/>
                <outline text="Examples"
                        uri="http://w3.org/.../forms.html#h-17.4.2"/>
            </outline>
            ...
        </outline>
        <outline text="Scripts">
            <outline text="Introduction"
                    uri="http://w3.org/.../scripts.html#h-18.1"/>
            <outline text="Designing Documents for Scripts"
                    uri="http://w3.org/.../scripts.html#h-18.2">
                <outline text="SCRIPT Element"
                        uri="http://w3.org/.../scripts.html#h-18.2.1"/>
                <outline text="Specifying the Scripting Language"
```

```
                          uri="http://w3.org/.../scripts.html#h-18.2.2">
                 <outline text="Default Language"
                          uri="http://w3.org/.../scripts.html#h-18.2.2.1"/>
                 <outline text="Local Language Declaration"
                          uri="http://w3.org/.../scripts.html#h-18.2.2.2"/>
                 <outline text="References to HTML Elements"
                          uri="http://w3.org/.../scripts.html#h-18.2.2.3"/>
            </outline>
            ...
        </outline>
        ...
    </outline>
  </body>
</opml>
```

Notice in the OPML document's structure that branch nodes contain other `outline` elements between their start and end tags, while leaf nodes contain no other `outline` elements.

If you issue the OPML content from a document on the server with an *.opml* extension, be sure that your server configuration maps that extension to the content type of `text/xml`. Similarly, any server-published content in this format should also be sent with a content type header of `text/xml`.

Parsing the XML document hierarchy (in the `drawOutline( )` function) takes advantage of the regularity of the `body` element of an OPML document. One nuisance arises, however, in Mozilla-based browsers. If the OPML document is transmitted with carriage returns between lines, these are treated as text nodes in the hierarchy. Thus, in the `drawOutline( )` code, you see a couple of instances where `for` loop execution is modified slightly when a node of type 3 is encountered. We're interested only in element nodes (`nodeType` of 1) because they contain attributes with the text and link URIs. The rest of the function operates with the same recursive calls to build nested lines of the outline as in Recipe 10.10.

Because attributes for OPML outline elements are extensible, you can add whatever information your outline needs for your version. This includes information about images (URIs, alternate text, and so on) if you prefer to use images rather than text as entries. Also, don't forget to look into the OPML elements in the head as sources of data that may be useful to render for the user, such as dates, title, and initial expansion state other than fully expanded or collapsed.

See Also

Recipe 14.17 for scripting the `XMLHttpRequest` object; Recipe 1.1 for building large strings from smaller segments; Recipe 10.10 for a comparable navigation outliner using a JavaScript data source; Recipe 12.1 for precaching images; Recipe 12.10 for hiding and showing elements.

CHAPTER 11

Managing Style Sheets

11.0 Introduction

The idea behind Cascading Style Sheets (CSS) is quite simple: separate the content from rules that govern how the content lays out on the page. In these days of specialization within web site authoring groups, writers can write and designers can design without stepping on each other's toes. There is perhaps an even simpler practical side as well. Rather than place design properties in HTML tags scattered around a document (or web site), the properties can be defined in just one place and automatically applied to every chunk of content that looks to the design rules for rendering instructions.

CSS is an evolving standard. It began with Level 1, which was partially implemented in Internet Explorer 3 and more fully in Internet Explorer 4 and Navigator 4. An extension to CSS, called CSS-Positioning, presented a standard for specifying the precise location of an element on the page (see Chapter 13). CSS and CSS-P were combined along with many new style facilities in CSS Level 2, which is implemented in varying stages of completeness starting with IE 5, Mozilla, and Opera 5. Various pieces of CSS Level 3 are implemented in the latest browsers.

Adding Styles to a Document

You have three ways to embed style sheet rules into a document:

- With the `<style>` tag
- Via the `style` attribute in an element
- By importing them from an external file (see Recipe 11.4)

The `<style>` tag requires you to specify the MIME type of the CSS source code you are using. These days, all style sheets use the standard CSS syntax, whose MIME type is `text/css`, specified in the `<style>` with the `type` attribute (`type="text/css"`).

While the syntax of style sheet rules lets you apply a rule to one or more elements, you also have the option of applying a style to a single element by including the style attribute in the element's tag. The value of the style attribute is a string of style property/value pairs in a format that differs from typical HTML attribute assignments.

Some page authors use the <style> tag technique exclusively, while other authors may use a combination of approaches. The former is easier to maintain over time, while the latter is more convenient during an ad-hoc authoring session. But if you intend to apply a style to lots of pages, importing a style sheet (Recipe 11.4) is the way to go.

Style Sheet Rule Syntax

When you define a style sheet rule within a <style> tag set, you must designate the recipient of the rule and the rule's properties. The recipient is designated by a *selector*, which may be an element tag name, an element class attribute value, or an element id attribute value. The style properties are placed inside curly braces according to the following schema:

```
selector {property1:value1; property2:value2; ...}
```

If the selector is a tag name, that name stands by itself:

```
h2 {property1:value1; property2:value2; ...}
```

Style property names are case-insensitive (although I tend to write them as all lowercase). Values typically do not need to be quoted unless a single value consists of more than one word. A colon (plus an optional space) separates the property name from its value. If two or more property/value pairs inhabit the rule, they are separated from each other by a semicolon (and an optional space).

When the style sheet rule is assigned via the style attribute within an element tag, the value of the attribute is a string of the property/value pairs that otherwise appear inside the curly braces of a <style> tag set, but without the curly braces in this case:

```
<h2 style="property1:value1; property2:value2; ...">...</h2>
```

Each property accepts specific types of values tailored for the property. Many properties specify a physical measurement of some kind on the page. Unless the value is zero, you should always include the measurement unit along with the numeric value. For example, if you want to set the font size of a paragraph to 14-point, the style rule looks like the following:

```
p {font-size:14pt}
```

Values are also commonly constant values. For example, to set the font style of a paragraph to italic, assign the italic value to the font-style property, as follows:

```
p {font-style:italic}
```

If a property accepts more than one value, the values should be comma-delimited, although space delimiting also works for some shortcut properties, such as border and font. For example, you can set many individual font properties via the shortcut font property and a space-delimited series of values for each of the specific properties:

```
p {font:12pt sans-serif bolder}
```

The browser knows how to parcel out the values to the individual implied properties because each value is acceptable by one specific font-related property only.

The Cascade and Specificity

CSS-enabled browsers follow well-defined guidelines for applying style sheets that appear in many places in a document. You may also see conflicting rules being applied to the same element. The cascade guidelines help the browser know which style definition to apply to each element.

At the root of the cascade guidelines is the fact that the more specifically a style sheet rule points to one element among all the elements on the page, the higher the priority that rule has for the element. For example, if you assign a style rule to all p elements on a page in the <style> tag and also assign a further (or conflicting) rule to one p element in its style attribute, any conflicts are settled in favor of the rule within the element's own style attribute. Unconflicting style properties from the more general rule are still applied to the p element (that is, global rules are inherited by an individual element, but an inherited rule can also be overridden with that element).

Additional details about Cascading Style Sheets and specificity guidelines can be found in my book *Dynamic HTML: The Definitive Reference* (O'Reilly).

11.1 Assigning Style Sheet Rules to an Element Globally

Problem

You want every instance of a given element in a document to be governed by the same style sheet rule.

Solution

Define a style sheet rule in the head portion of your document, assigning the rule to an HTML element name:

```
<style type="text/css">
tagName {styleProperty1:value1; styleProperty2:value2; ...}
</style>
```

For the *tagName*, specify the name of the tag without its angle brackets. The following example sets the font size and line height of every p element in a document to 14 points and 110 percent of normal, respectively:

```
<style type="text/css">
p {font-size:14pt; line-height:110%}
</style>
```

Discussion

Because global style definitions apply to every instance of a particular element in a document, you can essentially define custom appearances for a browser's default behavior. For example, if you don't like the way browsers render text surrounded by an <em> tag (signifying emphasis) as italic text, you could redefine this behavior by assigning a rule to all em elements that display the text in normal style but with a red color:

```
em {font-style:normal; color:red}
```

No change is needed in the actual <em> tags in the document. Browsers not capable of CSS display the element's content with their default italic style.

See Also

Recipes 11.2 and 11.3 to narrow a style's specificity to fewer than every element with a particular tag name.

11.2 Assigning Style Sheet Rules to a Subgroup of Elements

Problem

You want a mixed group of elements (of the same or different tag name) in a document to be governed by a single style sheet rule.

Solution

Use a class or contextual selector in your style sheet rule definition. If you use a class selector, the rule is applied to every element in the document (regardless of tag name) whose class attribute is assigned the arbitrary name you use for the class definition. A class selector name in the style sheet definition is preceded by a period, as in the following example:

```
.hot {color:red; text-decoration:underline}
```

But the period is not used in the class attribute assignment statement in the tag:

```
<p>And now for something <span class="hot">completely</span> different.</p>
```

A contextual selector lets you define a rule that applies to all instances of a given tag when they are nested inside another specific tag. For example, the following style sheet rule applies to all em elements that exist inside any p element in the document:

```
p em {font-size:16pt; font-style:normal}
```

If an em tag were embedded within, say, a li element, this rule would not be applied to it.

Discussion

Class and contextual selectors are rather powerful features of CSS. For example, you can limit a class selector name to apply to only a hand-picked group from a particular tag, as in:

```
p.narrow {margin-left:5em; margin-right:5em}
```

This rule is applied to all p elements only when those elements have the name narrow identifier assigned to their class attributes:

```
<p class="narrow">...</p>
```

You could then define a class selector of the same name that applies to all div elements whose class attributes are assigned the value narrow:

```
div.narrow {margin-left:7em; margin-right:7em}
```

You can also further refine the context of a contextual selector by specifying as deeply nested a context as your design calls for. In the following example, a style rule is defined for a span element whenever it appears nested inside an em tag, which, in turn, is nested inside a p element whose class selector is set to narrow:

```
p.narrow em span {background-color:yellow}
```

By virtue of style sheet inheritance, this rule also inherits any other style rules that are specified for p.narrow and em elements in the page.

Moreover, you can use the contextual selector to override a style rule for a portion of an element whose containing element has the same style rule properties set for it. The following example shows a rule defined for an em element within a p element, but then has one of the em element's attributes overridden when a span is located inside the em element:

```
p em {font-size:16pt; font-style:normal}
p em span {font-size:18pt}
...
<p>This is <span>all</span> 16pt <em>text except <span>this 18pt part</span></em></p>
```

The span element inside the em element inherits the normal font-style setting, but defines its own font-size setting just for the span content.

Class names (also called *identifiers*) that you create are entirely up to you. The only restrictions are as follows:

- Use one word only (no whitespace).
- Avoid punctuation symbols (underscores are OK).
- Do not use a numeral as the first character of the name.
- Do not use an ECMAScript reserved word (see Appendix C).

Not all of these restrictions are necessary for CSS, but if you also write client-side scripts that access objects by their IDs, you will stay out of trouble if you follow these rules.

See Also

Recipe 11.3 to define a rule for a single element; Recipe 11.9 to override a rule for just one element.

11.3 Assigning Style Sheet Rules to an Individual Element

Problem

You want a single element to stand out by having its own style sheet rule.

Solution

Define an ID selector for a style rule and assign that same selector name to the `id` attribute of an element. An ID selector name is preceded by a hash mark (#), as in the following example:

```
#special {border:5px; border-style:ridge; border-color:red}
```

This rule applies to the following element:

```
<div id="special>...</div>
```

When you create your HTML, assign an identifier to no more than one element on the page. Duplicate identifiers assigned to `id` attributes of multiple elements just confuse scripts.

Discussion

ID names are entirely up to you, but you should follow the same restrictions for these identifiers as those detailed for class names in Recipe 11.2. Be aware that if an element has both a `class` and `id` value assigned to it and those names have style rules associated with them, the style rule for the `id` takes precedence over the one for the `class` value wherever a conflict arises. This should be of concern to you only if the style rules for both the `class` and `id` values adjust the same style properties.

See Also

Recipe 11.3 for class selectors; Recipe 11.9 about overriding style rules; Recipe 4.1 for script identifier naming conventions that apply to `id` attributes.

11.4 Importing External Style Sheets

Problem

You want to implement a style sheet strategy across multiple HTML documents in a web site without embedding explicit CSS code in every document.

Solution

Define a style sheet (with one or more rules) as a separate .css file and import it into a document with the `<link>` tag:

```
<link rel="stylesheet" type="text/css" href="myStyleSheet.css" />
```

The contents of the style sheet file should consist solely of style sheet rules. Do not include the `<style>` tags or the usual nested HTML comments in this file.

Discussion

The Solution shows a cross-browser solution that works with all CSS-capable browsers. More current browsers that support the CSS2 specification can use an alternative "at-rule" inside the document's `<style>` tags. The at-rule version of the Solution is:

```
<style type="text/css">
@import url(myStyleSheet.css)
</style>
```

You can use the @import rule starting with Internet Explorer 4 and with all modern browsers. Some scripters use this import technique intentionally to exclude Navigator 4, which ignores the @import rule. You can combine the @import rule with other page-specific style sheet rules within the same `<style>` tag set on a page.

The filename extension for an external style sheet file should be .css. The server should also be configured to send the text/css MIME type with the file for Mozilla to process the file correctly (and to adhere to Internet standards).

It's not uncommon for external stylesheet files to be grouped in a separate subdirectory (typically named css). You should be aware, therefore, that if your CSS rules point to other sources (e.g., image files), the URLs specified in the rules must be either absolute URLs, or relative to the location of the .css file, not the HTML file into which the stylesheet is loaded. For example, if all CSS files are in a css subdirectory and all images are in an *images* directory (both sharing the same root parent directory), a CSS rule pointing to an image would look like the following:

```
.logo {background-image: url(../images/corpLogo.jpg)}
```

See Also

Recipe 11.5 for importing style sheets tailored to a particular browser or operating system; Recipe 11.6 for changing an imported style sheet after the page has loaded; Recipe 14.3 for importing HTML content into a page.

11.5   Importing Browser- or Operating System-Specific Style Sheets

Problem

You want to load separate external style sheet files for users on different kinds of computers.

Solution

Use JavaScript to write `<link>` tags within the head portion of the page, branching according to operating-system detection. The following example loads different style sheet files for Mac users and all other users:

```
<head>
...
<script type="text/javascript">
var cssFile = (navigator.userAgent.indexOf("Mac") != -1) ?
    "styles/macCSS.css" : "styles/pcCSS.css";
document.write("<link rel='stylesheet' type='text/css' href='" + cssFile + "'>");
</script>
...
</head>
```

You can combine the browser- or operating system-specific external style sheets with other fixed `<link>` elements in the same page, as well as other kinds of style sheet definitions or `@import` rules (where supported). If your content observes the strict version of XHTML, and you want dynamically generated code to also be in that form, you can use the following `document.write( )` call instead:

```
document.write("<link rel='stylesheet' type='text/css' href='" + cssFile + "' />");
```

To simplify the validation of your script under strict XHTML, you can move the CSS file loading statements to an external *.js* file.

Discussion

Employing multiple style sheets for different browsers or operating systems imposes the same maintenance headaches as multiple page implementations for different browsers. Any change you make to the design needs to be adapted for each version and tested thoroughly on the designated platforms. And yet, some applications of CSS styles may create an imperative for separate style sheet rules for Internet Explorer for Windows versions that are not fully CSS-compatible (see Recipe 11.13).

Starting with IE 5 for Windows, Microsoft added a special kind of HTML comment tag syntax that lets you define blocks of HTML that are to rendered for specific IE versions. Called *conditional comments*, they contain expressions that let you specify a single IE version or range of versions, such as all versions from IE 6 onward.

There are two types of conditional comments: *downlevel-hidden* and *downlevel-revealed*. The former allows you to supply HTML code that is rendered only in designated versions of IE 5 or later; the latter lets you supply HTML that is rendered *only* in browsers other than designated IE 5 or later versions. Each type has a slightly different syntax.

A downlevel-hidden conditional comment has the following syntax:

```
<!--[if expression]> HTMLContent <![endif]-->
```

IE 5 and later for Windows understand that the square brackets with if and endif directives are explicitly for conditional comments, and will render the *HTMLContent* portion if the *expression* evaluates to true. Other browsers treat the entire comment as a plain HTML comment, and won't render anything.

A downlevel-revealed conditional comment has the following syntax:

```
<![if expression]> HTMLContent <![endif]>
```

Note that there are no hyphens in this form. Browsers other than IE 5 or later will always render the *HTMLContent* portion. If you also want, say, IE 5 and 5.5 to render the content, but not IE 6 or later, you create an *expression* that tells IE to render the *HTMLContent* portion also for those IE browsers whose versions are less than 6, as in the following:

```
<![if lt IE 6]
<link type="text/css" rel="stylesheet" href="css/mainStyle_old.css" />
</script>
<![endif]>
```

An expression consists of a feature (IE is the only one supported to date), a comparison operator (omitting the operator means "equals"), and a version number (5 or later). Accepted comparison operators are lt (less than), gt (greater than), lte (less than or equal to), and gte (greater than or equal to). You can also negate the expression with a ! symbol in front of the feature (e.g., <![if !IE 7]>, meaning if IE is not version 7).

See Also

Recipe 11.3 about the impact on IE 6 for Windows by CSS-compatibility mode; Recipe 5.7 for detecting the browser's operating system.

11.6 Changing Imported Style Sheets After Loading

Problem

You want users to be able to select a different user interface "skin" for the page by loading a different *.css* file into a page already being viewed in the browser.

Solution

If you truly adhere to the spirit of separating content from rendering, the look and feel of a page can be controlled exclusively by style sheets. Designing different style sheets can transform the overall appearance of the page—background and foreground colors, margins, font specifications, and so on—even while the content remains the same. If you use a `<link>` element to import the default skin, you can assign a URL to a different *.css* file to import a different skin. Here is a sample `<link>` element:

```
<link id="basicStyle" rel="stylesheet" type="text/css" href="styles.normal.css" />
```

To load a new external style sheet into the link, use the following:

```
document.getElementById("basicStyle").href = "styles/crazySkin.css";
```

After the new file loads, Internet Explorer 5 or later and modern browsers automatically apply the new style definition to the document.

Discussion

There are other ways to refer to style sheets as objects (via the `document.styleSheets` collection, for example), but the `href` property of a `styleSheet` object referenced in this manner is not writable in all browsers.

If you allow users to set preferences such as design skins, you should preserve those settings so that they are employed automatically the next time they visit the site. The most efficient way to do this is to save the preference on the client machine in a cookie. For example, your page could include a group of radio buttons, each signifying a skin design choice. Each radio button's `value` attribute is the URL of the associated skin's *.css* file. Each button's `click` event handler invokes a function that both loads the new skin choice and preserves the setting in a cookie (with the help of a cookie utility, such as the one in Recipe 1.10):

```
function setSkin(evt) {
    // equalize IE and W3C event models
    evt = (evt) ? evt : ((window.event) ? window.event : null);
    if (evt) {
        var btn = (evt.srcElement) ? evt.srcElement : evt.target;
        document.getElementById("basicStyle").href = btn.value;
        cookieMgr.setCookie("skin", btn.value);
    }
}
```

Your scripts also then bear the responsibility of assigning the saved skin URL the next time the page loads. But you must also take into account browsers with cookies and/or scripting turned off. To do this, include the hardwired <link> element as before, but follow it with script statements in the head that retrieve cookie data and, if present, assign the preserved value to the href property of the link element:

```
var skin = cookieMgr.getCookie("skin");
if (skin) {
    document.getElementById("basicStyle").href = skin;
}
```

To complete the UI design, your page should also set the checked attribute of the radio button corresponding to the saved value. You can either use document.write( ) to generate the radio button HTML or a load event handler for the page to loop through the radio button set for a match between the saved skin value and the value property of one of the buttons.

See Also

Recipe 11.8 for scripts that toggle between already loaded style sheets; Recipe 1.10 for reading and writing cookies; Recipe 12.7 for a demonstration of using a cookie to set style preferences.

11.7 Enabling/Disabling Style Sheets

Problem

You want to activate or deactivate a style sheet in the page to change between style sheets dynamically.

Solution

To turn off a style sheet, assign the Boolean value true to a styleSheet object's disabled property:

```
document.styleSheets[1].disabled = true;
```

Conversely, to re-enable the style sheet, set its disabled property to false:

```
document.styleSheets[1].disabled = false;
```

You can disable and enable a link element object that has loaded a style sheet. A style element object has a disabled property supported by modern browsers.

Discussion

Enabling and disabling style sheets could be another way to implement a selectable "skin" interface for a page. The page could contain multiple <style> tags, each containing detailed specifications for a skin design. Radio button controls or clickable icons could disable all and enable one, along the lines demonstrated in Recipe 12.7.

See Also

Recipe 11.6 for loading a different external style sheet on the fly; Recipe 11.8 for switching between loaded style sheets; Recipe 12.7 for using cookies to preserve external style sheet choices between visits.

11.8 Toggling Between Style Sheets for an Element

Problem

You want to swap style sheets for an element based on user action, such as rolling the mouse over a hot spot or clicking on an arbitrary element.

Solution

First, define two style sheet rules, each with a different class selector. Then design an event handler for the element to change the element's `className` property to the desired class selector's identifier:

```
<style type="text/css">
.unhilited {background-color:white}
.hilited {background-color:yellow; text-decoration:underline}
</style>
...
<script src="eventsManager.js"></script>
<script type="text/javascript">
function setHilite(evt) {
    evt = (evt) ? evt : ((window.event) ? window.event : null);
    if (evt) {
        var elem = (evt.srcElement) ? evt.srcElement : evt.target;
        elem.className = "hilited";
    }
}
function setUnHilite(evt) {
    evt = (evt) ? evt : ((window.event) ? window.event : null);
    if (evt) {
        var elem = (evt.srcElement) ? evt.srcElement : evt.target;
        elem.className = "unhilited";
    }
}
// from eventsManager.js
function setEvents() {
    addEvent(document.getElementById("hotSpot"), "mouseover", setHilite, false);
    addEvent(document.getElementById("hotSpot"), "mouseour", setUnHilite, false);
}
addOnLoadEvent(setEvents);
...
<span id="hotSpot" class="unhilited">Some potentially hot spot text.</span>
```

Adjusting the `className` property of an element as shown here is perhaps the most widely used and supported way to implement dynamic styles.

Discussion

If you are toggling the style for just a single element, you might be tempted to use the id attribute and ID selector as your switch point, rather than the class attribute and selector. But an element's id attribute should not change unless absolutely necessary.

When a script reassigns a style sheet rule to an element, none of the CSS properties from the previous setting are inherited by the newly assigned rule. In the preceding example, the rule with the hilited class selector sets the text-decoration property to underline the element's text. But when the unhilited rule is reapplied to the element, the element automatically reverts to the previous value of the text-decoration property that the element inherited from the browser's default style sheet.

In the case of mouse rollovers, you can also use a CSS-only (i.e., no JavaScript required) solution, but with some limitations. CSS lets you define a rule that applies to what is called a pseudo-class. One of the CSS Level 2 pseudo-classes is called :hover. For example, you can define two rules for an element (or any other type of CSS selector), one for regular display, and one when the cursor hovers atop the element. Using the style rules from the code in the solution, the rules would be:

```
#hotSpot {background-color: white}
#hotSpot:hover {background-color: yellow; text-decoration: underline}
```

That's all you need for a rollover effect. The problem, however, is that IE implements :hover only for hyperlink (a) elements in IE 6 and earlier; in IE 7, you must be in CSS compatibility mode (Recipe 11.13) for :hover to work on other elements.

See Also

Recipe 11.7 for enabling or disabling a style sheet; Recipe 12.1 for swapping images with mouse rollovers.

11.9 Overriding a Style Sheet Rule

Problem

You want a single element to adhere to a global style sheet rule except for one or two style properties that are unique to the element.

Solution

There are two common ways to solve this problem. The first calls for creating a style rule with an ID selector tailored to the one element you wish to behave differently. That element can have both class and id attributes assigned to it. The style sheet rule associated with the class selector is applied first, but then the style rule associated with the ID selector can override any style properties needed for this element. An example of style rules and an element that applies those rules follows:

```
p.narrow {font-size:14pt; margin-left:2em; margin-right:2em}
#narrow_special {margin-left:2.5em; margin-right:2.5em; border:5px ridge red}
...
<p class="narrow" id="narrow_special">...</p>
```

Another approach is to assign the style properties that are unique to the element to the style attribute within the element's tag. The following shows the equivalent syntax for the previous example:

```
p.narrow {font-size:14pt; margin-left:2em; margin-right:2em}
...
<p class=narrow
style="margin-left:2.5em; margin-right:2.5em; border:5px ridge red">
...</p>
```

Discussion

Cascade-specificity rules give preference to styles that are assigned to an individual element. The one style sheet rule that cannot be overridden is the one assigned to the style attribute within the element's tag. Inheritance rules still apply, however. Therefore, an element with an assigned style attribute still observes other style rules assigned higher up the cascade precedence ladder, unless specifically overridden within the element.

Another CSS directive—!important—causes a CSS property setting to override any other settings, even those that traditionally have more weight in cascading rules. The directive goes after the property value in a rule:

```
p {font-size: 14px; margin-left: 2em !important; margin-right: 2em}
```

User style sheets (rules defined by the user to govern all browser activity) commonly use the !important directive to override page designers' CSS rules. For example, a vision-impaired visitor may require a large minimum font size for the page to be readable, regardless of the designer's wishes.

See Also

Recipes 11.1, 11.2, and 11.3 for basic style sheet rule bindings.

11.10 Turning Arbitrary Content into a Styled Element

Problem

You want to assign a style to a section of body content that is not currently delimited by HTML tags.

Solution

Wrap the content inside a `<span>` or `<div>` tag pair, and assign a style to that element type, class, or ID:

```
<p>And now for something <span class="hot">completely</span> different.</p>
```

Discussion

Despite the large number of contextual tags provided by HTML 4.0 (such as the `<address>` and `<blockquote>` tags), the tags don't necessarily have names that describe the true context within your document. Although you can use the XML capabilities of most modern browsers to fill this gap (by designing your own tags and namespace), you can also use HTML tags to define these contexts for you.

The `span` element is customarily used to wrap inline content, such as a sequence of text within a paragraph. A `div` element automatically defines a block-level entity, which means that the browser starts a `div` element's content on its own line while any content following the `div` element begins on a new line after the `div`. A `div` element is often used when the page needs to change alignment from, say, left to center. But a `div` is also a convenient container for content that is to be positioned on a page.

See Also

Recipes of Chapter 13 for using a `div` with CSS positioning; Recipe 15.2 for converting a user selection into an arbitrary element for styling.

11.11 Creating Center-Aligned Body Elements

Problem

You want paragraphs or other body content of a fixed width to be center-aligned within the page.

Solution

You have two approaches available to you. One is backward-compatible, while the other works in standards-compatibility mode for the newer browsers (see Recipe 11.13). The backward-compatible approach is to encase the element to be centered within an arbitrary `div` element, and then assign the `text-align` style sheet rule to the outermost block-level element. For example, to center a group of narrow paragraphs on a page, begin with the following style sheet rule for the paragraphs:

```
p.narrow {width:70%}
```

Then wrap those paragraphs with a `div` element whose style sheet rule reads:

```
div.centered {text-align:center}
```

In standards-compatible mode, you can do away with the `div` wrapper element, and specify left and right margin settings for the paragraphs:

```
p.narrow {width:70%; margin-left:auto; margin-right:auto}
```

In quirks mode, IE 6 and 7 ignore the margin settings and render the narrow paragraphs flush left.

Discussion

These style sheet techniques supplant the `center` element and the `align` attribute of numerous block elements—HTML terminology that is deprecated in HTML 4. Centering an element vertically in the browser window is not as simple, and typically requires the help of absolute-positioned elements, described in Chapter 13.

See Also

Recipe 11.13 for IE 6 and 7 compatibility modes; Recipe 13.7 for centering a positioned element in a window or frame.

11.12 Reading Effective Style Sheet Property Values

Problem

You want a script to ascertain the value of a style sheet property initially set via a `<style>` tag or imported style sheet.

Solution

The following getElementStyle( ) function works with browsers that support W3C DOM element referencing syntax, and either the IE currentStyle object or W3C DOM window.getComputedStyle( ) method:

```
function getElementStyle(elem, CSSStyleProp) {
    var styleValue, camel;
    if (elem) {
        if (document.defaultView && document.defaultView.getComputedStyle) {
            // W3C DOM version
            var compStyle = document.defaultView.getComputedStyle(elem, "");
            styleValue = compStyle.getPropertyValue(CSSStyleProp);
        } else if (elem.currentStyle) {
            // make IE style property camelCase name from CSS version
            var IEStyleProp = CSSStyleProp;
            var re = /-\D/;
            while (re.test(IEStyleProp)) {
                camel = IEStyleProp.match(re)[0].charAt(1).toUpperCase( );
                IEStyleProp = IEStyleProp.replace(re, camel);
            }
```

```
        styleValue = elem.currentStyle[IEStyleProp];
    }
  }
  return (styleValue) ? styleValue : null;
}
```

The function returns the value that the browser uses to govern the property whose name (in CSS form) is passed as a parameter.

Discussion

You might normally think of reading the value of an element's style sheet property by simply reading the style.*propertyName* property of the element. This works, however, only when the property is assigned via the style attribute of the element or the value is previously modified by script. But because it is more common (if not recommended) to bind style sheet rules to elements from a distance (in a <style> tag or imported through <link> tags or @import rules), this otherwise simple approach does not work. The value comes back as an empty string, even though there is a computed style sheet value being applied to the element at the time.

To read these distant style assignments requires help from the browser's DOM. Internet Explorer includes in its DOM an element object property called currentStyle. This object has most (but not all) of the same properties as an element's style property, but the values are read-only, and convey the effective style sheet property governing the element. This includes any default style property values (imposed from the browser's own default style sheet).

In contrast, the W3C DOM mechanism of the document.defaultView object's getComputedStyle( ) method returns an object that also contains properties similar to an element's style property (in Mozilla, the document.defaultView object is equivalent to a reference to the window object). Using this method, however, is a two-step process: first get the style object (technically, it's a CSSStyleDeclaration object in W3C DOM parlance), and then invoke the getPropertyValue( ) method on the style object.

As if the diverse models for this property inspection weren't enough, the two approaches frequently require different ways of referring to the style properties. In the case of the IE currentStyle object, references are made via the same object model syntax as is used for getting and setting style values. Therefore, hyphenated CSS property names must be referenced via the intercapitalization system (e.g., margin-left becomes marginLeft). But the property name for the W3C DOM getPropertyValue( ) method must be in the CSS property format (e.g., margin-left is margin-left). Fortunately for you, the getElementStyle( ) function shown in the recipe accepts only the W3C CSS version and internally handles the conversion for IE. For example, to retrieve the effective background color of an element named myDiv, the call is:

```
var divColor = getElementStyle("myDiv", "background-color");
```

Also be aware that for some CSS properties, different browser versions may return different value types—especially in colors that are specified by CSS syntax other than rgb(r,g,b). For example, if you set the color with a plain-language color name (e.g., orange), the value returned from the browsers may be in a different format. For the most part, if you specify colors in rgb(r,g,b) format, you'll get that back.

CSS values consisting of length measurements typically contain units (pixels, points, ems, and so on). If you intend to utilize the value of a style property for any math, such as adding five pixels to the left edge of a positioned element, be sure to extract the numeric portion of string values that include units. Use the parseInt( ) function for integers and the parseFloat( ) function for numeric values that may have digits to the right of the decimal (e.g., 0.5em).

Once you assign a value to a property of an element's style object, the value can be read subsequently through the style property. But for consistency's sake, you can continue to read a value through the getElementStyle( ) function because it returns the effective value applied to the element at any instant.

See Also

Recipe 9.4, Recipe 9.10, Recipe 13.12, and Recipe 13.13, where getElementStyle( ) (in a version embedded within the DHTML API from Recipe 13.3) is used.

11.13 Forcing Recent Browsers into Standards-Compatibility Mode

Problem

You want modern browsers to behave in keeping with the W3C specification for Cascading Style Sheets, rather than honoring old style behaviors now deemed to be out of standard.

Solution

Specify a DOCTYPE element as the first element of a document with any of the modern value sets. Some declarations require the URL portion to force the document into CSS-compatibility mode.

Use the following element if the document's markup generally follows the W3C HTML 4.0 recommendation, but also may include items deprecated from earlier versions (URL required for standards-compatible mode):

```
<!DOCTYPE HTML PUBLIC "-//W3C//DTD HTML 4.0 Transitional//EN"
        "http://www.w3.org/TR/REC-html40/loose.dtd">
```

The following element is for a framesetting document that follows the HTML 4.0 recommendation (URL required for standards-compatible mode):

```
<!DOCTYPE HTML PUBLIC "-//W3C//DTD HTML 4.0 Frameset//EN"
    "http://www.w3.org/TR/REC-html40/frameset.dtd">
```

Use this element if the document's markup strictly adheres to the W3C HTML 4.0 recommendation (URL not required for standards-compatible mode):

```
<!DOCTYPE HTML PUBLIC "-//W3C//DTD HTML 4.0//EN"
    "http://www.w3.org/TR/REC-html40/strict.dtd">
```

Use the following element if the document's markup generally follows the W3C XHTML 1.0 recommendation, but may also include items deprecated from HTML 4.0 (URL not required for standards-compatible mode):

```
<!DOCTYPE html PUBLIC "-//W3C//DTD XHTML 1.0 Transitional//EN"
    "http://www.w3.org/TR/xhtml1/DTD/xhtml1-transitional.dtd">
```

The following element is for a framesetting document that follows the W3C XHTML 1.0 recommendation with the addition of frame-related terminology (URL not required for standards-compatible mode):

```
<!DOCTYPE html PUBLIC "-//W3C//DTD XHTML 1.0 Frameset//EN"
    "http://www.w3.org/TR/xhtml1/DTD/xhtml1-frameset.dtd">
```

Use this element if the document's markup strictly adheres to the W3C XHTML 1.0 recommendation (URL not required for standards-compatible mode):

```
<!DOCTYPE html PUBLIC "-//W3C//DTD XHTML 1.0 Strict//EN"
    "http://www.w3.org/TR/xhtml1/DTD/xhtml1-strict.dtd">
```

Use the following element if the document's markup strictly adheres to the W3C XHTML 1.1 recommendation (URL not required for standards-compatible mode):

```
<!DOCTYPE html PUBLIC "-//W3C//DTD XHTML 1.1//EN"
    "http://www.w3.org/TR/xhtml11/DTD/xhtml11.dtd">
```

Including a DOCTYPE element for a particular HTML or XHTML level does not affect the browser's ability to recognize and render tags and attributes outside of the stated recommendation.

Discussion

The difference between standards-compatible mode and the earlier (sometimes called "quirks") mode varies by browser. You may notice a small difference in Mozilla between the two modes, except for an occasional variance in pixel spacing around form controls. The differences are more significant in IE 6 and 7, however. The W3C style sheet group adopted a different way of measuring element sizes with respect to borders, padding, and margins than the way Microsoft had originally implemented back in Internet Explorer 4. In many respects, IE 6 and 7 in standards-compatible mode is more predictable in the way it responds to dimensions, margins, and offset measures relative to other elements. The results more closely resemble those of Mozilla, Safari, and Opera using the same DOCTYPE specifications. For creating new content, you should utilize the standards-compatible mode for both browsers to get in the habit of operating according to the W3C specification (or at least as closely as the browsers interpret the standards). Earlier browsers do not alter their content rendering based on DOCTYPE declarations.

IE 6 or later, Mozilla, and Opera 7 or later provide a script-accessible property, document.compatMode, which reports the mode in which the document is operating. Property values are either BackCompat or CSS1Compat.

In theory, an XHTML page should also lead with an xml declaration, along with character set information:

```
<? xml version="1.0" encoding="UTF-8" ?>
```

But when IE 6 encounters this tag, it holds the browser in backward-compatible mode, regardless of the DOCTYPE declaration. To satisfy the XHTML validators, place your character set information in a meta element in the head portion of the document:

```
<meta http-equiv="Content-Type" content="text/html; charset=utf-8" />
```

See Also

Recipe 9.4, Recipe 11.11, Recipe 13.6, Recipe 13.7, Recipe 13.11, Recipe 13.13, Recipe 15.6, and Recipe 15.11 for examples of how scripts and style sheets frequently need to accommodate different CSS modes in IE 6 and 7.

CHAPTER 12

Visual Effects for Stationary Content

12.0 Introduction

The dynamic part of Dynamic HTML is not restricted to elements flying around the page, hierarchical menus popping up from the ether, and users dragging stuff around the page. An element that doesn't move one pixel during its lifetime can still be dynamic because a change to one or more properties can alter the appearance of the element's content. Such changes can be automatic or in response to user action.

Referencing Element Objects

If you intend to modify a characteristic of an element on the page, your script must be able to "talk" to the element. In the early days of client-side scripting, the browser exposed only a handful of elements as objects accessible to scripts. Those elements were generally the more interactive elements, such as form controls (buttons, text boxes, and the like). Syntax used to reference these elements followed a hierarchy of exposed elements, starting with the window object and then gradually narrowing the focus to the specific element. The window object is assumed for the current window, so references typically start with the document object. For example, if you assign an identifier to the name attribute of an a, form, or input element, references can employ those names:

```
document.linkName
document.formName
document.formName.controlName
```

When a document contains more than one type of exposed element, the group of elements of the same type can be referenced through an array (collection) of those items. Array index values can be either a zero-based integer (numbered in source code order) or the name attribute string:

```
document.links[i]
document.forms["formName"]
document.forms[2].elements["controlName"]
```

These old-fashioned element reference styles for the limited range of elements continue to be supported in scriptable browsers to maintain backward-compatibility with a gigantic universe of existing code that employs these referencing techniques.

Microsoft Internet Explorer 4 was the first scriptable browser to expose all HTML elements as scriptable objects in its document object model. Scripts could reference any element that had a name or, preferably, an id attribute value. The most common mechanism to address an element was by way of the document.all collection—an array of all elements in the document, regardless of element nesting or position in the document. Microsoft provided a variety of syntaxes to reference elements via this collection:

```
document.all.elementID
document.all["elementID"]
document.all("elementID")
```

The latter two versions were particularly helpful in processing a generic function that received a string of the ID of an element to operate on. Moreover, the IE object model let you omit the collection entirely and reference an element simply by its ID:

```
elementID
```

The effort to standardize document object models to encompass both HTML and XML documents took the form of the Document Object Model (DOM) recommendation from the World Wide Web Consortium (W3C). The W3C DOM working group elected to devise its own model and syntax for referencing elements as objects. The document object was still part of the equation, but a new method of the document object allowed a string of an element's ID to signify the specific element to reference:

```
document.getElementById("elementID")
```

This standards-based syntax is supported in IE 5 or later, as well as Mozilla, Safari, and Opera. Thus, it is supported by the vast majority of scriptable browsers in use today. Scripts for forms and form controls can utilize the original syntax, even if you use newer syntax in other portions of your scripts. Even so, you should gravitate to W3C DOM syntax where possible.

Recipes throughout this cookbook demonstrate the W3C DOM syntax except in the following cases:

- The recipe explicitly shows how to write code intended to work with multiple object models.
- Referenced elements are backward-compatible to browsers prior to IE 4 and Mozilla.

Small examples involving forms often use the old syntax primarily to help you understand that the example pertains to forms and form controls.

Referencing Elements from Events

If a function is defined as an event handler, the function very likely needs to devise a reference to the HTML element that was the target of the event. Internet Explorer and the W3C DOM have different event models and syntax, but they operate enough in parallel that you can equalize them to obtain a reference to the target element for further processing, as shown in the following function:

```
function myEventFunction(evt) {
    evt = (evt) ? evt : ((window.event) ? window.event : null);
    if (evt) {
        var elem = (evt.target) ? evt.target :
                    ((evt.srcElement) ? evt.srcElement : null);
        if (elem) {
            // process element here
        }
    }
}
```

See Chapter 9 for more details on processing events across incompatible event models.

Getting to an Element's Style

One constant you can count on (so far, anyway) is that if a browser supports referencing individual HTML elements of all types, every rendered element has a style property. The property is a reference to an object whose own properties are Cascading Style Sheet property names (occasionally contorted slightly to be in JavaScript-friendly format). A script reference to one of the style property values of an element follows the syntax:

elementReference.style.*stylePropertyName*

For example, using W3C DOM element referencing syntax for an element, the following statement assigns a new value to the color style sheet property for the element:

```
document.getElementById("mainHeading").style.color = "#ffff00";
```

The IE-only version is identical except for the element reference syntax:

```
document.all.mainHeading.style.color = "#ffff00";
```

When the CSS property name contains a hyphen, the DOM equivalent strips the hyphen and capitalizes the first character after each hyphen. This makes the reference compatible with the requirements of the JavaScript language (and others). Therefore, the following statement assigns a new value to the CSS font-size property of an element:

```
document.getElementById("link12").style.fontSize = "20px";
```

Changing an element's style sheet value is comparatively easy (there are multiple ways to do this, as shown in Recipes 11.7 and 11.8). But reading the current value applied to a particular property isn't always that easy, especially if the initial value is set via a style sheet definition outside of the element's style attribute. See Recipe 11.12 for more details.

12.1 Precaching Images

Problem

You want an image rollover to swap the image instantaneously the first time, rather than forcing the user to wait while the alternate image downloads from the server.

Solution

Begin by creating a custom object with a number of properties whose values apply to the rollover images you wish to precache for the current page. This solution assumes that all images are the same dimensions (purely optional) and you have a consistent naming system for your pairs of images (e.g., *homeNormal.jpg* and *homeHilite.jpg*):

```
var rolloverImageBank = {
    height : 20,
    width : 50,
    sharedImgURIs : ["img/home", "img/prod", "img/support", "img/contact"],
    normalSuffix : "Normal.jpg",
    hiliteSuffix : "Hilite.jpg",
    preloadImages : function() {
        var imgObj = new Image(this.height, this.width);
        for (var i = 0; i < this.sharedImgURIs.length; i++) {
            imgObj.src = this.sharedImgURIs[i] + this.normalSuffix;
            imgObj.src = this.sharedImgURIs[i] + this.hiliteSuffix;
        }
    }
};
rolloverImageBank.preloadImages();
```

When the custom object's preloadImages() method is invoked, the images are loaded into the browser's image cache but are not displayed. Recipe 12.2 shows how image rollover scripts access these cached images.

Discussion

Image caching in browsers occurs when a URI is assigned to the src property of either a visible image or an instance of an Image object. This object exists strictly in memory and never displays a picture. But this object has the same properties as the img element object, particularly the dimensions (height and width) and the URI (src). Passing the pixel height and width of the image to the Image() constructor function is not vital, but it can speed up the precaching slightly because the browser doesn't have to wait for the image to load to calculate its dimensions.

The real caching work occurs in the `preloadImage()` method of the custom object, when the statement assigning a URI to the `src` property executes. The browser immediately tries to resolve the URI, and downloads the image to the browser. Even though the URI is assigned to the same `Image` object instance over and over, it is not a factor in the precaching operation.

Although this solution is written for pairs of images, it can be modified for triplets (for `mouseover`, `mouseout`, and `mousedown` events) by adding one more property for the suffix used in the `mousedown` variety. Then add one more assignment statement in the `for` loop to precache that third variety. You can also modify the object to work with non-rollover images if you simply want to precache a bunch of images for quick display later. Assuming the images are of different sizes, you can omit the `height` and `width` properties, as well as the suffix-related properties. Then, in the `preloadImages()` method, eliminate the parameters from the `new Image()` constructor, and make only one `src` assignment per entry in the URI-related array.

If you encounter a situation in which the images do not appear to precache themselves (for instance, you experience download delays in image rollovers), look to the server configuration as the primary problem source. It is not uncommon for a web server (especially one that supplies frequently updated content) to be set to send HTTP headers for some or all MIME types that tell browsers to prevent content from caching in the browser. Make sure that headers for your image types do not declare an expiration date or "no-cache" instruction.

Users, too, may confound your efforts to precache images if they turn off browser caching in their Preferences settings. You cannot override this setting, but such users must already be accustomed to complete downloading of all content, no matter how frequently they visit a page.

With many browsers, you can verify that your images are in the cache. In IE for Windows, open the Tools → Internet Options window. In the General panel, click the Settings button in the Temporary Internet Files (IE 6) or Browsing history (IE 7) section. Click the View Files button to see a listing of all files currently in the browser's cache. IE for the Macintosh doesn't provide this direct access. For Mozilla-based browsers, enter the URL `about:cache`. Click on the links shown to view files in the memory and disk caches. The browser window fills with a list of items currently in the cache.

See Also

Recipe 12.2 for image rollovers; Recipes 10.9, 10.10, 10.11, and Recipe 15.9 to see examples of precached images in applications.

12.2 Swapping Images (Rollovers)

Problem

You want the picture displayed by an img or image-type input element to change
when the user rolls the mouse over the element.

Solution

This solution builds on Recipe 12.1, which handles precaching of pairs of images.
One additional method definition handles all image swapping when invoked by
mouseover and mouseout events in the img elements:

```
var rolloverImageBank = {
    height : 20,
    width : 50,
    sharedImgURIs : ["img/home", "img/prod", "img/support", "img/contact"],
    normalSuffix : "Normal.jpg",
    hiliteSuffix : "Hilite.jpg",
    preloadImages : function() {
        var imgObj = new Image(this.height, this.width);
        for (var i = 0; i < this.sharedImgURIs.length; i++) {
            imgObj.src = this.sharedImgURIs[i] + this.normalSuffix;
            imgObj.src = this.sharedImgURIs[i] + this.hiliteSuffix;
        }
    },
    toggleImage : function(evt) {
        evt = (evt) ? evt : event;
        var elem = (evt.target) ? evt.target : evt.srcElement;
        if (elem && elem.src) {
            var reOff = new RegExp("(.*)(" + this.normalSuffix + ")");
            var reOn = new RegExp("(.*)(" + this.hiliteSuffix + ")");
            if (reOff.test(elem.src)) {
                elem.src = reOff.exec(elem.src)[1] + this.hiliteSuffix;
            } else {
                elem.src = reOn.exec(elem.src)[1] + this.normalSuffix;
            }
        }
    }
};
rolloverImageBank.preloadImages();
```

The preloadImages() method is invoked immediately after the rolloverImageBank
object is created. You must also bind mouseover and mouseout events to the img elements in the document. Using the *eventsManager.js* library from Recipes 9.1 and 9.3,
the bindings look like the following (abbreviated to show only the first two images):

```
function setEvents() {
    addEvent(document.getElementById("home"), "mouseover",
        function(evt) {rolloverImageBank.toggleImage(evt)}, false);
    addEvent(document.getElementById("home"), "mouseout",
        function(evt) {rolloverImageBank.toggleImage(evt)}, false);
```

```
        addEvent(document.getElementById("products"), "mouseover",
            function(evt) {rolloverImageBank.toggleImage(evt)}, false);
        addEvent(document.getElementById("products"), "mouseout",
            function(evt) {rolloverImageBank.toggleImage(evt)}, false);
    ...
    }
    addOnLoadEvent(setEvents);
```

The function reference passed as the third parameter to addEvent( ) is an anonymous function, which lets the toggleImage( ) method of the rolloverImageBank object work within that object's context, rather than the img element's context.

In the HTML portion of the document, insert the img elements just as you would for any element:

```
    <img id="products" height="20" width="50" src="img/prodNormal.jpg" alt="Products"></a>
```

Feel free to surround the img element with a hyperlink (a) element to use the image as a site navigation tool.

Discussion

The design of this solution is intended to minimize the amount of setup work you need to do to prepare for the image caching and swapping. By creating pairs of image file names with consistent suffixes for the two image types (normal and highlighted), you can keep your image files straight easily, while facilitating a regularity that lets the preloading and toggling actions work compactly. In the case of the toggleImage( ) method, the suffixes specified in the rolloverImageBank properties help the script know (by testing a regular expression) which state the image is currently in before switching to the other.

Scripting isn't the only way to achieve mouse rollovers, however. In recent browsers, you can accomplish link rollovers without img elements via CSS. Instead use CSS to define style rules for a block-level a element for both normal display and highlighted display, the latter occurring during what CSS calls a "hover" of the cursor over a link. The style rules for a "Products" image link look as follows:

```
    a#products {background:url(img/prodNormal.jpg); display:block; height:20px;
    width:50px}
    a#products:hover {background:url(img/prodHilite.jpg)}
```

In the HTML, all you need is the a element set with an ID associated with the style sheet rules:

```
    <a id="products" href="products.html">...</a>
```

You need a pair of style sheet rules for all the a elements, each with a unique ID. The key to making this work is the display style sheet property for the a element. This forces the empty link to open to the block size specified in the rule. This approach, however, does not precache images, so you may wish to combine the CSS rollover technique with the image caching script from Recipe 12.1.

See Also

Recipe 12.1 for precaching images; Recipe 3.8 for working with custom objects; Recipe 9.1 for cross-browser event handling.

12.3 Reducing Rollover Image Downloads with JavaScript

Problem

You want to reduce the number of individual image files downloaded to the browser to accomplish three-state image rollovers.

Solution

The solution is a combination of traditional HTML techniques plus a small Java-Script library shown in the Discussion section. The script library makes some minor assumptions about identifiers assigned to the id attributes of the <img> tags and name attribute of the <map> tag, but takes most of its cues from HTML attribute values.

Begin by creating one large image for the entire rollover area in each of the visual states of the buttons or controls. Include graphical borders or other static artifacts associated with the active region. The script described here accommodates three states (normal, mouseover, mousedown), which means you should create three images, each one displaying all of the buttons in the same state. Figure 12-1 shows all three images used in this example.

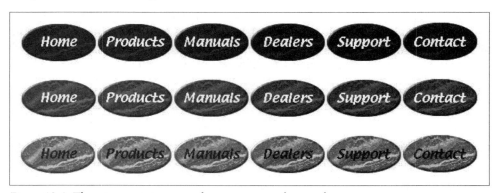

Figure 12-1. Three image states: normal, mouseover, and mousedown

The names you assign to the three image files are not critical. It may be helpful for development purposes to establish a system that clearly identifies each image's purpose and state. For example, the following sample file names readily identify the three states of a menubar image:

- *menubarUp.jpg*
- *menubarOver.jpg*
- *menubarDown.jpg*

Place the images in your page's HTML as absolute-positioned elements (stacked atop each other) nested inside another relative- or absolute-positioned container (such as a div element). Assign unique identifiers to each img element's id attribute so that the three share the same prefix of your choice and end with the suffixes Up, Over, and Down. Insert the <img> tags into the page with the normal (up) version occurring first in source code order. Assign style sheet rules that make the normal version visible by default, but the other two hidden by default, as shown in the following example:

```
<style type="text/css">
.menuImages {
            height: 110px;
            width: 680px;
            border: 0;
            position: absolute;
            top: 0px;
            left: 0px;
            visibility: hidden;
            }
#menubarUp {visibility: visible}
</style>
...
<div style="position:relative">
<img id="menubarUp" class="menuImages" src="menubarUp.jpg" alt="menubar"
usemap="#menubar" />
<img id="menubarOver" class="menuImages" src="menubarOver.jpg" alt="menubar"
usemap="#menubar" />
<img id="menubarDown" class="menuImages" src="menubarDown.jpg" alt="menubar"
usemap="#menubar" />
</div>
```

Define client-side image map elements (via <map> and <area> elements). Use the prefix of the id attribute values from the img elements as the value for the name attribute of the map element. Also assign a unique identifier of your choice to the id attribute of the <map> tag. Set the rectangular coordinates of the "hot spots" in the image as you normally would for an image map. For example:

```
<map id="menubarMap" name="menubar">
    <area shape="rect" coords="8,22,117,86" href="index.html" alt="home"
        title="home" />
    <area shape="rect" coords="120,22,227,86" href="products.html" alt="products"
        title="view products" />
    <area shape="rect" coords="230,22,337,86" href="manuals.html" alt="manuals"
        title="download manuals" />
    <area shape="rect" coords="340,22,447,86" href="dealers.html" alt="dealers"
        title="find a dealer" />
    <area shape="rect" coords="450,22,557,86" href="support.html" alt="support"
        title="get support" />
```

```
    <area shape="rect" coords="560,22,667,86" href="contact.html" alt="contact"
        title="contact us" />
</map>
```

Include the JavaScript code from the Discussion section in your page, either inside a
<script> tag or linked in from an external *.js* file. Initialize the code from the page's
load event handler, but do it in a way that lets you pass as a parameter the string ID
of the map element you wish to initialize. If you have multiple image maps, pass their
IDs as comma-delimited arguments in the call to the initMaps( ) function.

Discussion

Reducing the number of image retrievals at load time can substantially improve the
perceived performance of a web page. In the past, the menu whose pieces are shown
in Figure 12-1 would have been implemented through 18 individual image files, three
images for each button. But the solution shown here reduces the retrieval to only
three downloads. While it's true that each of the three images is larger than any of
the original smaller images, the real bottleneck is in the number of simultaneous connections—two, at best—that the browser can make to the server while loading the
page. Each request also has a fair amount of overhead (headers and such) that bogs
down a page's response if not kept in check.

The JavaScript portion of this recipe follows:

```
<script src="../js/eventsManager.js"></script>
<script type="text/javascript">
function initMaps( ) {
    if (document.getElementById) {
        var mapIds = initMaps.arguments; // pass string IDs of containing map elements
        var i, j, area, areas;
        for (i = 0; i < mapIds.length; i++) {
            areas = document.getElementById(mapIds[i]).getElementsByTagName("area");

            for (j = 0; j < areas.length; j++) {    // loop thru img elements
                area = areas[j];
                // from eventsManager.js
                addEvent(area, "mousedown", imgSwap, false);
                addEvent(area, "mouseout", imgSwap, false);
                addEvent(area, "mouseover", imgSwap, false);
                addEvent(area, "mouseup", imgSwap, false);
            }
        }
    }
}
// from eventsManager.js
addOnLoadEvent(function( ) {initMaps("menubarMap")});

// image swapping event handling
function imgSwap(evt) {
    evt = (evt) ? evt : event;
    var elem = (evt.target) ? evt.target : evt.srcElement;
    var imgClass = elem.parentNode.name;
```

```
var coords = elem.coords.split(",");
var clipVal = "rect(" + coords[1] + "px " +
                        coords[2] + "px " +
                        coords[3] + "px " +
                        coords[0] + "px)";
var imgStyle;

switch (evt.type) {
    case "mousedown" :
        imgStyle = document.getElementById(imgClass + "Down").style;
        imgStyle.clip = clipVal;
        imgStyle.visibility = "visible";
        break;
    case "mouseout" :
        document.getElementById(imgClass + "Over").style.visibility = "hidden";
        document.getElementById(imgClass + "Down").style.visibility = "hidden";
        break;
    case "mouseover" :
        imgStyle = document.getElementById(imgClass + "Over").style;
        imgStyle.clip = clipVal;
        imgStyle.visibility = "visible";
        break
    case "mouseup" :
        document.getElementById(imgClass + "Down").style.visibility = "hidden";
        // guarantee click in IE
        if (elem.click) {
            elem.click();
        }
        break;
    }
    evt.cancelBubble = true;
    return false;
}

</script>
```

After the page loads, the initMaps( ) function assigns four mouse-related event handlers to each of the area elements within the map elements whose IDs arrive in the initialization function's arguments. All four mouse events—mouseover, mouseout, mousedown, and mouseup—invoke the same event handler function, imgSwap( ). Event handlers are assigned only if the browser supports at least the basic W3C DOM capabilities needed for the rest of the image handling.

The lone event handler function, imgSwap( ), performs a lot of work but in a speedy and efficient manner. The function's primary jobs are: 1) to determine which of the three images needs to be visible or hidden (depending on event type); and 2) to adjust the clipping rectangle of the visible image to the dimensions of the specific area element being activated by the event.

The imgSwap( ) function begins by equalizing the Internet Explorer and W3C DOM event models to obtain a single reference to the event object (see Recipe 9.1) as well as a reference to the area element that received the event. The area element's parent node (the map element container) has a name that becomes an important part of the image visibility swapping later in the function. It's economical to grab that property just once and assign it to a local variable (imgClass) for use later.

Next, the function extracts the area element's coordinate values. These values are to be assigned to a clipping rectangle, but because the coords and style.clip property values are in different sequences and formats, the function needs to convert from one format to the other. For example, the first area element's coords value must transform from:

```
8, 22, 117, 86
```

to the clip style property value of:

```
rect(22px 117px 86px 8px)
```

With the essential variable values loaded for action, the imgSwap( ) function then branches execution based on the specific mouse event type. This is where the naming conventions for the id attributes of the img elements come into play. For example, during a mouseover event, the "menubarOver" image is clipped to the target element's coordinates, and then made visible; during a mouseout event, both of the secondary images are hidden from view.

Note that the same two functions shown above can be used with any number of three-image sets of rollover graphics on the same page. Simply add the name of the surrounding map elements as arguments to the initMaps( ) function call. The scripts pick up the clipping values from the coords attribute values of your area elements. If you or the page's graphic designer change the menubar art or image map coordinates, the scripts automatically pick up the changes from the revised HTML.

Not only does this solution significantly reduce the number of HTTP requests to the server for each group of rollover images, but it also eliminates the need to pre-cache images explicitly. All necessary images are included in the document's body, forcing all images to download with the page without any script intervention.

See Also

Recipe 9.1 for equalizing the incompatible Internet Explorer and W3C DOM event models; Recipe 4.8 for other techniques to improve script performance.

12.4   Reducing Rollover Image Downloads with CSS

Problem

You want to reduce the number of individual image files downloaded to the browser to accomplish image rollovers, but without JavaScript.

Solution

Using the same set of images from Recipe 12.3, this solution has minimal HTML involved—merely the hyperlink (a) elements, contained by a div element:

```
<div id="menuWrap">
<a id="homeArea" href="index.html"></a>
<a id="productsArea" href="products.html"></a>
<a id="manualsArea" href="manuals.html"></a>
<a id="dealersArea" href="dealers.html"></a>
<a id="supportArea" href="support.html"></a>
<a id="contactArea" href="contact.html"></a>
</div>
```

Layout, dimensions, and behaviors are all handled by the Cascading Style Sheet specifications, explained in the Discussion section.

Discussion

The CSS code is extensive, but pretty repetitive, with differences between sets of rules consisting of slightly different position adjustments. Example 12-1 shows the CSS portion.

Example 12-1. CSS code for efficient image swapping

```
#menuWrap {
        position: relative;
        background-image: url(menubarUp.jpg);
        width: 680px;
        height: 110px;
        }

#menuWrap a {
        display: block;
        position: absolute;
        visibility: visible;
        top: 0px;
        height: 110px;
        outline: none
        }
#homeArea {
        left: 0px;
        width: 117px;
        background-image: none;
        }
#homeArea:hover {
        background-image: url(menubarOver.jpg);
        background-position: 0px 0px
        }
#homeArea:active {
        background-image: url(menubarDown.jpg);
        background-position: 0px 0px
        }
```

Example 12-1. CSS code for efficient image swapping (continued)

```
#productsArea {
            left: 117px;
            width: 110px;
            background-image: none;
            }
#productsArea:hover {
            background-image: url(menubarOver.jpg);
            background-position: -117px 0px
            }
#productsArea:active {
            background-image: url(menubarDown.jpg);
            background-position: -117px 0px
            }
#manualsArea {
            left: 227px;
            width: 110px;
            background-image: none
            }
#manualsArea:hover {
            background-image: url(menubarOver.jpg);
            background-position: -227px 0px
            }
#manualsArea:active {
            background-image: url(menubarDown.jpg);
            background-position: -227px 0px
            }
#dealersArea {
            left: 337px;
            width: 110px;
            background-image: none
            }
#dealersArea:hover {
            background-image: url(menubarOver.jpg);
            background-position: -337px 0px
            }
#dealersArea:active {
            background-image: url(menubarDown.jpg);
            background-position: -337px 0px
            }
#supportArea {
            left: 447px;
            width: 110px;
            background-image: none
            }
#supportArea:hover {
            background-image: url(menubarOver.jpg);
            background-position: -447px 0px
            }
#supportArea:active {
            background-image: url(menubarDown.jpg);
            background-position: -447px 0px
            }
```

Example 12-1. CSS code for efficient image swapping (continued)

```
#contactArea {
          left: 557px;
          width: 110px;
          background-image: none
          }
#contactArea:hover {
          background-image: url(menubarOver.jpg);
          background-position: -557px 0px
          }
#contactArea:active {
          background-image: url(menubarDown.jpg);
          background-position: -557px 0px
          }
```

The menuWrap div element is set up as a relative-positioned element to provide a positioning context for the nested hyperlink elements, each of which will be absolute-positioned within that context. This allows the entire menu to flow naturally on the page, without further adjustments to the nested hyperlink positions. The background image for the wrapper is the normal version of the entire menu. It becomes the substrate for the menuing system.

All of the hyperlink elements have a number of CSS property values in common. Those values are assigned to all of them in one rule aimed at a elements nested inside the menuWrap element.

Next come three rules for the first "button" in the menu, the one labeled "Home." The hyperlink element is positioned at the left edge of the container, and its background image is set to none, meaning that the background is transparent, allowing the substrate image to show through. When the cursor hovers atop the "Home" link, the background image for that element is changed to the highlighted version. Because this button is at the left edge of the container, its left background-position property is set to 0px. When the user clicks down on the element, it is in the active state, which changes the background image to the third state, likewise positioned at 0px.

This set of three states (normal, hover, active) is repeated for each of the hyperlink elements. The differences are all in the left position of the hyperlink element, and the corresponding negative shift of the hover and active background images to the left.

Due to a couple of rendering irregularities in a couple of browsers, this solution may not be as flexible as you like. For example, IE 6 and IE 7 have difficulty restoring the background image to none after the element has been in the active state. A two-state rollover (normal and hover) appears to work well, however. In Mozilla, if a user navigates to a page in the menu and clicks the Back button, the clicked menu item may still be in the hover state until the cursor reaches the content region of the browser window. This could be disconcerting to some users. A div element, rather than a hyperlink, might work better, but IE 6 does not recognize the hover or active CSS states for the div element. None of these problems affect the JavaScript version, shown in Recipe 12.3.

See Also

Chapter 11 on applying CSS; Recipe 12.3 for a JavaScript version of this recipe.

12.5 Dynamically Changing Image Sizes

Problem

You want to offer a user option on your web page to enlarge or reduce the dimensions of one or more images, such as enlarging a thumbnail to a more viewable size.

Solution

Modern browsers scale an original image to whatever size is assigned to the img tag, either by the height and width attributes/properties or through CSS rule settings. This solution provides code for the latter method and assumes that all resizable images have the same original size.

This solution relies on three style sheet rules assigned to class names, as follows:

```
.largesize {height: 384px; width: 512px}
.mediumsize {height: 192px; width: 256px}
.smallsize {height: 77px; width: 102px}
```

The original image is 1024 pixels wide by 768 pixels high, and the display options are at 50 percent, 25 percent, and 10 percent of original size. Those values are precalculated and hardcoded into the style sheet rules.

HTML for this example consists of three radio button choices and an img element:

```
<form>
<p id="scale">Scale: <input id="smallScale" type="radio" name="scaler" value="small">
10%
<input id="mediumScale" type="radio" name="scaler" value="medium">25%
<input id="largeScale" type="radio" name="scaler" value="large" checked>50%
</p>
</form>
<img id="seascape" class="largesize" src="pointlobos.jpg" />
```

With the help of the *eventsManager.js* library from Recipes 9.1 and 9.3, the scripts in this example bind a click event handler to the p element that contains the three radio buttons. Click events from the radio buttons will bubble up to the container, but the event targets will be the radio buttons. The following script then reads the value of the clicked radio button to determine which class name should be assigned to the img element:

```
function setImgSize(evt) {
    evt = (evt) ? evt : window.event;
```

```
        var elem = (evt.target) ? evt.target : evt.srcElement;
        document.getElementById("seascape").className = elem.value + "size";
    }

    function setEvents() {
        addEvent(document.getElementById("scale"), "click", setImgSize, false);
    }
    addOnLoadEvent(setEvents);
```

Upon changing the `className` property of the `img` element, the chosen style is immediately applied to the image.

Discussion

Notice in the Solution that there is a link between the values assigned to each of the radio buttons and the class names used for the CSS rules. This relationship simplifies the assignment statement in the `setImgSize()` function because the new name is a combination of the chosen radio button's value and the string "size."

There are numerous ways to enhance this solution to take into account images of varying sizes. One characteristic to watch out for is that once an image is resized, you cannot obtain the original size of the image (except in Mozilla, which offers a proprietary pair of `img` element object properties, `naturalHeight` and `naturalWidth`). If you wish to use scripts to perform calculations on images whose dimensions are not the same throughout the page, you may want to use a load event handler function to capture an array of image sizes to use as a reference for subsequent calculated resizing operations.

Browsers won't keep the aspect ratio of your images intact—your calculations will have to do that. But if you multiply the height and width by the same factor, and round results to the nearest integer, you'll get decent results. Of course, you are at the mercy of the browser's rendering engine when it comes to the quality of thumbnails or enlargements. This isn't Adobe Photoshop.

See Also

Recipe 11.2 for using CSS with subgroups of elements; Recipe 11.8 for changing style sheet rules assigned to an element; Recipes 9.1 and 9.3 for the workings of the *eventsManager.js* library.

12.6   Changing Text Style Properties

Problem

You want to alter the style of some text already displayed on the page.

Solution

Change one or more of the associated style properties of the element containing the text, as in these examples:

```
elementReference.style.color = "00ff00";
elementReference.style.font =
    "bolder small-caps 16px 'Andale Mono', Arial, sans-serif";
elementReference.style.fontFamily = "'Century Schoolbook', Times, serif";
elementReference.style.fontSize = "22px";
elementReference.style.fontStretch = "narrower";
elementReference.style.fontStyle = "italic";
elementReference.style.fontVariant = "small-caps";
elementReference.style.fontWeight = "bolder";
elementReference.style.textDecoration = "line-through";
elementReference.style.textTransform = "uppercase";
```

Discussion

Many CSS properties affect the appearance of text on the page. Because all implemented CSS properties can be controlled via properties of the style object associated with an element, those CSS properties can be modified after the page has loaded.

Before you can modify the appearance of text, that text must be its own element, even if it is merely an arbitrary span within a larger element. See Recipe 15.2 for an example of converting a user text selection into an element ready for text style modification.

Note that to comply with JavaScript (and other) language rules, the CSS property names that contain hyphens are converted to intercapitalized style words. Thus, the DOM reference for the font-weight CSS property is fontWeight. Values assigned to these properties are always strings, and the constant values (such as none or xx-small) are identical to those assigned to CSS properties, including those with hyphens. Values that denote length, such as the fontSize value, must also include the units (e.g., 22px). Table 12-1 lists each CSS Level 2 text style property and the types of accepted values.

Table 12-1. CSS Level 2 text style properties and values

Property	Description
color	Foreground color specified as hexadecimal triplet (e.g., #ff00ff), CSS RGB value (e.g., rgb(255,0,255) or rgb(100%,0%,100%)), or color constant (e.g., green)
font	Combination property with one or more of fontFamily, fontSize, lineHeight (which must be preceded by a / symbol in this property), fontStyle, fontVariant, and fontWeight or a constant: caption, icon, menu, message-box, small-caption, or status-bar
fontFamily	Comma-delimited list of font families in decreasing priority; multiple-word family names must be quoted inside the string value
fontSize	Length value representing the height of the characters (fixed size with unit measure or percentage), relative size (larger or smaller), or constant: xx-small, x-small, small, medium, large, x-large, or xx-large

Table 12-1. CSS Level 2 text style properties and values (continued)

Property	Description
fontStretch	Character spacing governed by a constant: normal, wider, narrower, ultra-condensed, extra-condensed, condensed, semi-condensed, semi-expanded, expanded, extra-expanded, ultra-expanded, or none
fontStyle	Slant of text characters governed by a constant: normal, italic, or oblique
fontVariant	Small-caps version of font: normal or small-caps
fontWeight	Boldness of the characters: bold, bolder, lighter, normal, 100, 200, 300, 400, 500, 600, 700, 800, or 900
textDecoration	Extra ornament for the text: blink, line-through, none, overline, or underline
textTransform	Case transformations of the text: capitalize, lowercase, none, or uppercase

Additional style properties can also affect the overall appearance of a text-centric element. The element's background color (backgroundColor style property) can have a significant impact on the view and readability of a text span. Other text-related style properties, such as textAlign and textIndent, operate in block-level elements that contain text.

If you want to animate the transitions between states in any way, including alternating between states, you need to use setTimeout( ) or setInterval( ) to allow the animation to be visible. If, instead, you simply script a sequence of style changes, be aware that the browsers tend to delay refreshing the screen until the current script thread finishes. This speeds up the rendering of multiple style property changes and makes them appear all at once, rather than seeing each property change individually. For example, if you wish to momentarily alternate the background color of an element to bring the viewer's attention to it, you can set up a function that invokes itself several times through the setTimeout( ) mechanism. Each time the function runs, it changes the background color of the element whose ID is initially passed as a sole parameter to the function:

```
function flashBkgnd(elemID, count) {
    // if counter is null, initialize at zero
    count = count || 0;
    // execute reference just once
    var elem = document.getElementById(elemID);
    // grab value once for multiple comparisons
    var currColor = elem.style.backgroundColor;
    if (currColor == "rgb(255, 255, 0)" || currColor ==  "#ffff00") {
        elem.style.backgroundColor = "#ff0000";
    } else {
        elem.style.backgroundColor = "#ffff00";
    }
    if (count < 10) {
        // call this function again in 1/10 sec., with incremented counter value
        setTimeout(function( ) {flashBkgnd(elemID, ++count)}, 100);
    } else {
        // assumes a white body background
```

```
            elem.style.backgroundColor = "#ffffff";
        }
    }
```

This function maintains its own internal counter, passing the incremented value as a second parameter to the function for subsequent function calls. Once the counter reaches its maximum value, the background color of the element returns to a default value. You could also use a version of Recipe 11.2 to determine the effective background color of the body element, and set the flashing element's background color to that value upon exiting the function the final time.

Note, too, that in the flashBkgnd( ) function, the current color is tested in two forms: a CSS rgb(x,y,z) value and a hexadecimal triplet value. This is necessary because some browsers (Mozilla and Safari in particular) report color values in the RGB format, regardless of the value assigned to the property elsewhere.

See Also

Recipe 12.2 for special hover behaviors for hyperlinks; Recipe 4.5 for usage of setTimeout( ) as a delay mechanism; Recipe 11.2 for reading effective style sheet values; Recipe 15.2 for converting a user selection into a style-modifiable arbitrary element.

12.7   Offering Body Text Size Choices to Users

Problem

You want to let users choose the relative font size for the content of the page.

Solution

Create a user interface element that lets users select from three or four different font sizes. Each choice invokes the changeSizeStyle( ) function shown in the Discussion. This function enables a style sheet whose ID is passed as an argument and disables the rest. All of the related style sheets apply themselves to the body element. As an added bonus, the changeSizeStyle( ) function calls upon the *cookies.js* library (Recipe 1.10) to preserve the setting to be applied to the page the next time the user visits.

Discussion

This is a three-part solution, involving HTML for the font size controller, style sheets, and scripts. The result is a small controller on the page that lets users select from three font size bases upon which the rest of the page renders, as shown in Figure 12-2.

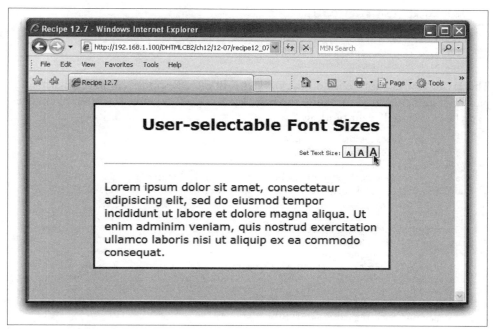

Figure 12-2. Text size controller for users

The HTML for the controller defines one surrounding div element and several nested img elements, each of which acts as a clickable button to change the body text size. To prevent blank space from occurring between the images, avoid source code line breaks between elements. The following HTML code inserts line breaks inside element tags:

```
<div id="textSizer">
<img src="fontSizer.jpg" height="18" width="72" alt="Font Sizer"><img
id="smallStyler" class="textSize" src="fontSmall.jpg" height="18" width="18"
alt="Smallest" /><img id="mediumStyler" class="textSize" src="fontMedium.jpg"
height="18" width="18" alt="Default" /><img id="largeStyler"
class="textSize" src="fontLarge.jpg" height="18" width="18" alt="Biggest" />
</div>
```

The stylesheet portion of this solution consists of several rules. Three (.smallText, .mediumText, and .largeText) indicate the class names that can be applied to the body element to influence the display. Three other rules control the rendering of the buttons' container and individual buttons. The :hover rule here is applied to img elements, a tactic that won't work in IE 6 unless you wrap the images in hyperlink (a) elements and assign the style rule to those elements (and cancel the default click behavior of the hyperlinks). By default, the controller is not rendered, but scripts take care of this, as discussed shortly:

```
body {font-family: Verdana, Helvetica, sans-serif; background-color: #ffffff}
.smallText {font-size: xx-small}
```

```css
.mediumText {font-size: small}
.largeText {font-size: large}
#textSizer {text-align: right; display: none}
.textSize {border: 1px solid black}
.textSize:hover {cursor: pointer}
```

The JavaScript portion relies on the *cookies.js* library (Recipe 1.10) and consists of a pair of statements that run while the page loads, two functions that control changes to styles and initial event binding:

```javascript
<script src="cookies.js"></script>
<script type="text/javascript">
// write style sheet link
var styleCookie = cookieMgr.getCookie("fontSize") || "medium";
document.write("<link rel='stylesheet' type='text/css' href='" + styleCookie +
    "Font.css' />");

// invoked by clicking on sizer icons
function changeSizeStyle(evt) {
    evt = evt || window.event;
    var elem = evt.target || evt.srcElement;
    var re = /(.*)(Styler\b)/;
    var sizeStyle = re.exec(elem.id)[1];
    cookieMgr.setCookie("fontSize", sizeStyle, cookieMgr.getExpDate(120, 0, 0));
    document.body.className=sizeStyle + "Text";
    setIconBorder(elem.id);
}
function setIconBorder(elemID) {
    elemID = (elemID) ? elemID :
        (cookieMgr.getCookie("fontSize") ?
        cookieMgr.getCookie("fontSize") + "Styler" : "mediumStyler");
    var iconIDs = ["smallStyler", "mediumStyler", "largeStyler"];
    for (var i = 0; i < iconIDs.length; i++) {
        document.getElementById(iconIDs[i]).style.borderColor = "black";
    }
    document.getElementById(elemID).style.borderColor = "red";
}
function setEvents() {
    addEvent(document.getElementById("smallStyler"), "click", changeSizeStyle,
false);
    addEvent(document.getElementById("mediumStyler"), "click", changeSizeStyle,
false);
    addEvent(document.getElementById("largeStyler"), "click", changeSizeStyle,
false);
}
addOnLoadEvent(function() {setIconBorder()});
addOnLoadEvent(setEvents);
</script>
```

Users' choices are preserved as a cookie value (in the changeSizeStyle( ) function) so that the previous setting is applied on the next visit to the page. The application occurs in the writing of a <link> element to load the desired *.css* file (see Recipe 11.5). Each of the *.css* files includes a rule that sets the display property of the textSizer

---

control container to block. In other words, the controls don't appear on the page unless the user has scripting enabled.

The controller consists entirely of images so that even as the body font size is adjusted, the label's text won't change as well. While the label could be given an inline style attribute to override the more remote style settings, using an image is easier. If the label text were allowed to resize, the position of the clickable images would shift with each click, driving users crazy. While the example here uses a non-positioned element and a percentage length for the left margin, you might find it more appealing to turn it into an absolute-positioned element that is keyed to some other relative-positioned wrapper element in your design.

Notice that this example does not specify a specific font size in any unit. Font sizing is always a problem in browsers due to their quirky behavior with regard to user settings in the browser and operating system. Using relative sizes suggests that we let users determine their default sizes outside of our application, and they can choose to display your font sets either in a smaller or larger font than the default. This also assumes that more detailed font size settings throughout each page's document are also relative, rather than absolute. Thus, top-level headlines may be specified in em units to derive the desired larger size, but always relative to the surrounding body element's current size. In a way, this approach embraces the flaws of the browser world, leaving the precise display up to the user. Your job as a designer is to make sure the content flows appropriately in a variety of sizes.

One of the challenges of this application is preventing the page from initially loading and displaying the default font sizes, and then having the page redraw itself with the previously selected size. Remember that scripts cannot assign a value to the style property of the body element in most browsers until the element has completely rendered. Waiting until the load event is too late because the body will have already begun to render in the default size. Thus, this solution dynamically writes the <link> tag in the head portion of the file so that it applies to the body element as it initially renders.

Names of the controller images are critical in this solution. A regular expression in the changeSizeStyle( ) function assumes that the first part of the name indicates the size (small, medium, or large) and the last part is Styler (although you can change the components to meet your design criteria). This allows the script to extract the size, which can then be used to assemble either the name of the class to be assigned to the body element or the name of the .css file to be loaded when the page arrives.

One final visual touch is that the border of the currently selected control button is set to a red color. This provides visual feedback to the user to see where the current size lies in respect to other choices. It's important for such a device to also signal the size at load time. Therefore, a load event handler invokes the setIconBorder( ) function. The assignment (in addOnLoadEvent( ) from *eventsManager.js* of Recipe 9.1 and Recipe 9.3) occurs as an anonymous function so that the W3C event object is not automatically passed as a parameter to the function. If no cookie had been previously saved, the medium control is highlighted (and the *mediumFont.css* style sheet will have already been written to the dynamically generated <link> element, earlier.

See Also

Recipe 1.10 for cookie utilities; Recipe 11.4 for importing style sheets; Recipe 11.5 for dynamically importing style sheets; Recipes 9.1 and 9.3 for event management.

12.8   Creating Custom Link Styles

Problem

You want links on the page to respond to rollovers and clicks differently than the default browser behavior.

Solution

Take advantage of CSS pseudoclasses for a elements that let you define separate style sheet rules for various states of a link. The following example displays the text of an a element in a dark reddish-brown except when the user clicks down on the link, at which point the background and text color invert. Also, the link does not display the traditional underline except while the cursor passes atop the link:

```
<style type="text/css">
a:link {color:#993300; background-color:#ffffff; text-decoration:none}
a:visited {color:#993300; background-color:#ffffff; text-decoration:none}
a:active {color:#ffffff; background-color:#993300; text-decoration:none}
a:hover {text-decoration:underline}
</style>
```

Discussion

The a:link, a:visited, and a:active CSS pseudoclasses for a elements are modern versions of old attributes of the <body> tag. The old attributes controlled nothing more than the color of a link in each of the three states. But the CSS version allows far more control over the appearance of the link's text and other environment factors.

The state, represented by the a:hover pseudoclass, is a simplified way of implementing style changes during what scripters might consider to be a mouseover event. But no scripting is needed. It's this same behavior that allows unscripted image rollovers in some situations (as described in Recipe 12.2). The only imperative for using genuine mouseover event handlers is that they work in older browsers than those that support the CSS pseudoclasses and they can perform other scripting tasks, such as retrieving data via the XMLHttpRequest object.

Note a peculiarity with IE for Windows and the a:active pseudoclass. This browser has a different meaning for active. While other browsers treat this state as meaning only while the mouse button is pressed on the element, IE for Windows considers an a element that has focus to be active. Therefore, if a user clicks on a hyperlink, the a:active style rule remains in effect until the link loses focus. It also means that if a user presses the Tab key enough times to bring focus to the link, the link's appearance is under the a:active style rule.

A valid user interface question occurs when contemplating the hiding of a link's traditional underline decoration. Some page designers object to the default appearance on aesthetic grounds in that the bold color and underline distract the user from the content, destroy the designer's other color schemes, and may encourage users to jump out of the site too quickly. Rather than omit external links (at the risk of giving the appearance of not being a good Net citizen), designers can, in a sense, disguise the links.

Your decision about link styles will most likely be influenced by the nature of your audience. An unsophisticated audience for a very public web site may not catch on quickly enough that your subtly hued, nonunderlined text segments are links, and may not even find some of your own site's gems. A web-savvy audience, on the other hand, may instinctively know where to expect links and will catch on quickly to your style scheme. In the end, consistency in your approach—throughout the site—is an important step toward users accepting your design.

The :hover pseudo-class works with elements other than hyperlinks in Mozilla, Safari, Opera 7 or later, and IE 7 (only in standards-compatibility mode). Other IE versions recognize :hover only for hyperlinks.

See Also

Recipe 12.2 for mouseover image swapping; Recipe 12.7 for an example of the :hover pseudoclass in use.

12.9   Changing Page Background Colors and Images

Problem

You want to give users an opportunity to select a background color or background image for the current page or site.

Solution

Change one or more of the background-related style properties of the body element. The following examples demonstrate the range of options:

```
document.body.background = "url(watermark.jpg) repeat fixed";
document.body.backgroundAttachment = "fixed";
document.body.backgroundColor = "rgb(255, 255, 204)";
```

```
document.body.backgroundImage = "url(corp%20watermark.jpg)";
document.body.backgroundPosition = "5% 5%";
document.body.backgroundRepeat = "repeat-y";
```

Discussion

Several CSS style properties control aspects of element backgrounds. When applied to the body element, the background properties affect the entire page. Table 12-2 lists the scriptable properties and the types of values they accept.

Table 12-2. Background style properties and values

Property	Description
background	Combination of several background styles in one specification, consisting of a space-delimited list of values for *backgroundAttachment*, *backgroundColor*, *backgroundImage*, *backgroundPosition*, and *backgroundRepeat* property values.
backgroundAttachment	How a background image clings to content during scrolling, controlled by the constants fixed and scroll.
backgroundColor	Color specified as hexadecimal triplet (e.g., #ff00ff), CSS RGB value (e.g., rgb(255,0,255) or rgb(100%,0%,100%)), or color constant (e.g., green).
backgroundImage	URI of an external background image in CSS format (e.g., url(logo.jpg)).
backgroundPosition	Offset of a background image relative to the edges of the (body) element. Values are a space-delimited pair of length or percentage values (horizontal and vertical measures) or a pair of combinations of constants: bottom, center, left, right, or top. A single value can also be applied to both dimensions.
backgroundRepeat	Controls whether the image is to be repeated and whether the repeat is along a single axis, according to the constants: no-repeat, repeat, repeat-x, or repeat-y.

If you set both a background color and image, the image overlays the color and the background color shows through any transparent pixels in the image.

Providing users with a choice in background style (perhaps by way of a select element somewhere on the page) adds an extra burden if you want a user-friendly web site. You should preserve the setting so that the next time the user visits, the earlier choice applies to the current visit. While you can save this information in a database if you like, it is probably more convenient to preserve the setting in a client cookie. This obviates the need for a user to register and log into your site just to have a previously chosen skin applied to the site's look and feel.

Recipe 1.10 contains a generic cookie reading and writing library, which the following description assumes is loaded in the page (providing you with the setCookie( ) and getCookie( ) functions). In the following example, the user can select from a list of images located in a select element whose ID is bgChooser. The cookie preserves the URI of the most recently chosen image, and applies that to the body's background after the page loads (via an onload event handler in the <body> tag). The core of the routine is a function that reads the cookie and applies the value to the backgroundImage property. If the cookie is empty, the first item in the select list is used as a default:

```
// save user choice in cookie and set the style value
function savebgImage(evt) {
    evt = (evt) ? evt : ((event) ? event : null);
    if (evt) {
        var elem = (evt.target) ? evt.target : evt.srcElement;
        cookieMgr.setCookie("bgImage", elem.value, getExpDate(120, 0, 0));
        // invoke function to change the visible image
        setbgImage();
    }
}

// change bkgnd image after user selection or onload
function setbgImage() {
    var uri = cookieMgr.getCookie("bgImage");
    // get reference to select element
    var selector = document.getElementById("bgChooser");
    if (uri) {
        // apply cookie value to background image
        document.body.style.backgroundImage = "url(" + uri + ")";
        // for onload, set select to the cookie value
        for (var i = 0; i < selector.options.length; i++) {
            if (uri == selector.options[i].value) {
                selector.options[i].selected = true;
                break;
            }
        }
    } else {
        // if no cookie, set to whatever is selected by default
        document.body.style.backgroundImage = "url(" + selector.value + ")";
    }
}
addOnLoadEvent(setbgImage);
...
<body>
...
<select id="bgChooser" onchange="savebgImage(event)">
    <option value="desk1.gif">Desk 1</option>
    <option value="desk2.gif">Desk 2</option>
    <option value="desk3.gif">Desk 3</option>
    <option value="desk4.gif">Desk 4</option>
</select>
```

Notice a subtle but important part of the setbgImage() function. The selected item in the select element should always echo the cookie value. A loop looks through all options of the select element to find a match between option and cookie values. When the loop locates a match, the option is set to be the selected item.

See Also

Recipe 12.7 for an alternative way of preserving and restoring style preferences by way of style sheets; Recipe 1.10 for a cookie library.

12.10 Hiding and Showing Elements

Problem

You want to hide a currently visible element or show a currently hidden element.

Solution

Two CSS style properties (and their corresponding scripted properties) influence the visibility of an element, but your choice of usage has a big impact on the results of showing or hiding an element. The less-intrusive property is `style.visibility`, whose fully supported values are `hidden`, `inherit`, or `visible`, as in the following example that hides an element:

```
document.getElementById("warning").style.visibility = "hidden";
```

Changing this value has no effect on surrounding content. The other relevant property, `style.display`, when set to `none`, removes the element from rendering flow of the page, forcing surrounding content to cinch up to fill the space formerly occupied by the element:

```
document.getElementById("warning").style.display = "none";
```

Restoring the `display` property value to its applicable display mode (typically `block` or `inline`) reinserts the element into rendering flow, and the content adjusts itself to accommodate the inserted content.

Discussion

CSS property inheritance plays a significant role in the resulting effect of your hiding and showing of elements. The default `visibility` property value is `inherit`, which means that an element's visibility is governed by its parent containing element. Therefore, if you hide a container, all nested elements are hidden as well. But each element can also be the master of its own visibility in most browsers. For example, if you set the visibility of a container element to `hidden` and one of the container's children to `visible`, the child element will be visible even though its parent is not. By and large, the `visibility` style property is most reliably used on either block-level elements or absolute-positioned elements.

Adjusting the `display` style property is a more substantial act in the eyes of the CSS model. This property has a large range of possible values, some of which are dedicated to the way browsers render tables, table components, and list items. It even has the power to override default element characteristics such that an inline element is treated instead as a block-level element. Therefore, when you set the property to none, the action does far more than just hide the element. You're telling the browser to shrink the element's renderable space to zero height and width, and to adjust the rendering of surrounding elements. The element, however, is not removed from its place in the document node tree.

See Also

Several recipes in Chapter 10 that hide and show elements in dynamic navigation menus.

12.11 Adjusting Element Transparency

Problem

You want an element to be partially transparent so that background content bleeds through.

Solution

The formal W3C CSS specification didn't get around to offering an opacity property until CSS Level 3. It is supported starting with Mozilla 1.7.2, Safari 1.2, and Opera 9. Even so, Internet Explorer for Windows and earlier Mozilla versions have different proprietary approaches to specifying opacity on any element in CSS-like syntax. In fact, IE has two different systems, one of which works only in IE 5.5 for Windows or later.

The IE style sheet syntax that works with versions as early as IE 4 (for Windows only) relies upon a proprietary `filter` property. The following example makes an element whose ID is `watermark` appear with 25 percent opacity:

```
#watermark {filter:alpha(opacity=25)}
```

The newer syntax utilizes an ActiveX control that is delivered with IE 5.5 or later for Windows and requires a more explicit reference:

```
#watermark {filter:progid:DXImageTransform.Microsoft.Alpha(opacity=25)}
```

For all Mozilla versions, use the Mozilla proprietary opacity style control, `-moz-opacity`:

```
#watermark {-moz-opacity:0.25}
```

The leading hyphen of the property name is intentional so that it won't be confused or conflict with the W3C opacity property.

For Mozilla 1.7.2 or later, Safari 1.2 or later, and Opera 9 or later, use the CSS3 opacity style property:

```
#watermark {opacity:0.25}
```

Discussion

Internet Explorer filter styles are an extensive set of transforms intended primarily for text. All filters are specified as CSS-like style rules whose property is `filter`. For the backward-compatible version, the property value consists of one of the filter's names followed by a pair of parentheses. Some filters, such as the `alpha` filter that controls opacity, have one or more additional properties that are set via equality symbol assignments inside the parentheses. Multiple property/value pairs are comma-delimited.

Possible properties for the `alpha` filter include not only a straight opacity level (specified within a range of 0 to 100, with 100 being completely opaque), but also additional opacity styles, such as an opacity gradient where the opacity varies across the area of the element. Possible gradient styles are uniform (value of 0, the default), linear (value of 1), radial (value of 2), or rectangular (value of 3). You can then use the `opacity` property to specify the opacity level for the start of the gradient and `finishopacity` for the end of the gradient:

```
{filter:alpha(opacity=25, finishopacity=75, style=2)}
```

Additional properties let you define the x,y coordinates for both the start and end points of the gradient (the `startX`, `startY`, `finishX`, and `finishY` properties).

To modify a filter's setting under script control, reference the filter just like any style property and assign its value as a string containing the entire filter name, parentheses, and extra properties:

```
document.getElementById("myBox").style.filter = "alpha(opacity=80)";
```

If you are using the newer ActiveX control for filtering in IE 5.5 and later, all references must include the control's internal object path, as shown in the Solution. Even script references must include this information, but access is through the `filters` collection of the element object (not the `style` object):

```
document.getElementById("myBox").
    filters["DXImageTransform.Microsoft.Alpha"].Opacity=80;
```

Be aware, however, that to modify a value of this newer version, the named filter must be declared in a CSS style sheet or in the element's `style` attribute. You cannot introduce a `DXImageTransform` opacity filter to an element that does not have one defined for it via CSS syntax.

Scripting the proprietary Mozilla opacity filter is accomplished through the `style.MozOpacity` property. A value for this property must be a string representing a number between 0 (transparent) and 1 (opaque). Note that the property has a leading uppercase letter. The Mozilla opacity filter is a uniform type without any gradients.

The CSS3 `opacity` property takes the same values as the `MozOpacity` property. Without any IE support through IE 7, and only recent browsers of other brands, it will be awhile before you can deploy the CSS3 `opacity` property with the expectation that users will observe any transparency.

See Also

Recipe 12.10 for hiding elements entirely.

12.12 Creating Transition Visual Effects

Problem

You want elements that change their visual characteristics (e.g., hiding, showing, image swapping) to reveal the new state by way of a visual effect such as a wipe, barn door, checkerboard, or dissolve.

Solution

Transitions in IE for Windows are part of the proprietary filter extensions to CSS (not implemented in IE for Macintosh, Mozilla, Safari, or Opera). Two filter syntaxes are available. One is backward-compatible all the way to IE 4; the other requires IE 5.5 or later. I'll demonstrate a solution that applies a dissolve transition between image swaps from Recipe 12.2.

Transitions have two components. The first is a filter definition applied via style sheet rules. The following modification of the <img> tag for Recipe 12.2 adds a one-half second dissolve (fade) transition filter in the backward-compatible syntax:

```
<img name="products" height="20" width="50" border="0" src="img/prodNormal.jpg"
style="filter:blendTrans(duration=0.5)" alt="Products">
```

Here's the newer syntax, which utilizes a more powerful ActiveX control delivered with IE 5.5 for Windows or later:

```
<img name="products" height="20" width="50" border="0" src="img/prodNormal.jpg"
style="filter:progid:DXImageTransform.Microsoft.Fade(duration=0.5)"
alt="Products">
```

The second component of an element transition consists of two scripted methods of the filter object: apply( ) and play( ). The apply( ) method freezes the view of the element whose filter you address. This gives you the opportunity to make the change(s) to the element out of view. Then the play( ) method lets the transition filter execute the transition between the original and modified states. Modifying the image-swapping function of Recipe 12.2 to accommodate the newer filter syntax causes the function to become:

```
var rolloverImageBank = {
    height : 20,
    width : 50,
    sharedImgURIs : ["img/home", "img/prod", "img/support", "img/contact"],
    normalSuffix : "Normal.jpg",
    hiliteSuffix : "Hilite.jpg",
    preloadImages : function( ) {
        var imgObj = new Image(this.height, this.width);
```

```
            for (var i = 0; i < this.sharedImgURIs.length; i++) {
                imgObj.src = this.sharedImgURIs[i] + this.normalSuffix;
                imgObj.src = this.sharedImgURIs[i] + this.hiliteSuffix;
            }
        },
    toggleImage : function(evt) {
        evt = (evt) ? evt : event;
        var elem = (evt.target) ? evt.target : evt.srcElement;
        if (elem && elem.src) {
            if (elem.filters) {
                elem.filters["DXImageTransform.Microsoft.Fade"].apply( );
            }
            var reOff = new RegExp("(.*)(" + this.normalSuffix + ")");
            var reOn = new RegExp("(.*)(" + this.hiliteSuffix + ")");
            if (reOff.test(elem.src)) {
                elem.src = reOff.exec(elem.src)[1] + this.hiliteSuffix;
            } else {
                elem.src = reOn.exec(elem.src)[1] + this.normalSuffix;
            }
            if (elem.filters) {
                elem.filters["DXImageTransform.Microsoft.Fade"].play( );
            }
        }
    }
};
```

Discussion

The two generations of CSS filters in IE for Windows present very different ways of referencing specific transition effects. Transitions in the backward-compatible form are divided into two families: the blend (dissolve) and reveal (numerous types). Assign a blend via the blendTrans( ) filter, with one parameter for the duration in seconds:

```
img.blends {filter:blendTrans(duration=0.5)}
```

A reveal transition (revealTrans( )) definition includes two parameters: transition, which requires an integer value corresponding to the type of shape used in the transition, and duration, which controls the speed:

```
div.wipe {filter:revealTrans(transition=7, duration=1.5)}
```

Transition types are listed in Table 12-3.

Table 12-3. IE backward-compatible transition types

Type	Meaning	Type	Meaning
0	Box in	12	Random dissolve
1	Box out	13	Split vertical in
2	Circle in	14	Split vertical out
3	Circle out	15	Split horizontal in
4	Wipe up	16	Split horizontal out
5	Wipe down	17	Strips left down

Table 12-3. IE backward-compatible transition types (continued)

Type	Meaning	Type	Meaning
6	Wipe right	18	Strips left up
7	Wipe left	19	Strips right down
8	Vertical blinds	20	Strips right up
9	Horizontal blinds	21	Random bars horizontal
10	Checkerboard across	22	Random bars vertical
11	Checkerboard down	23	Random

You can modify the properties of a particular filter by script. For example, if you want to change an element's transition filter from a wipe to a circle in style, reference the filter's transition property as follows:

```
elementReference.filters["revealTrans"].transition = 2;
```

In the newer filter syntax, each transition type has its own filter (see Table 12-4).

Table 12-4. IE new-style transition filters

Filter name	Description
Barn( )	A barn-door transition effect, with properties for duration, motion, and orientation
Blinds( )	A Venetian-blind transition effect, with properties for direction, duration, and thickness (bands) of the slats
Checkerboard( )	A checkerboard transition effect with properties for direction, duration, and square sizes (squaresX, squaresY)
Fade( )	A blended transition between views, with properties for duration and the degree of overlap of both views
GradientWipe( )	A wipe transition using a gradient blend at the wipe line, with properties for duration, thickness of the gradient (gradientSize), and direction (wipeStyle)
Inset( )	A wipe transition that works along horizontal and vertical axes, but diagonally from one corner to its opposite, with duration property
Iris( )	A zoom-style transition with properties for duration, motion (in or out), and irisStyle (e.g., circle, cross, diamond, plus, square, star)
Pixelate( )	Blends between views via an expansion/contraction and blurring/focusing of the content, with properties for duration and maximum pixel size (maxSquare)
RadialWipe( )	Blends between views via your choice of duration and wipeStyle (clock, wedge, radial)
RandomBars( )	Blends between views via expanding/contracting bars, with properties for orientation and duration
RandomDissolve( )	Blends between views through random pixel changes, with duration property
Slide( )	Blends between views through banded sliding of various types, with properties for band thickness (bands), duration, and slideStyle (hide, push, swap)
Spiral( )	Blends between views through spiral reveals, with properties for duration and spiral size (gridSizeX, gridSizeY)

Table 12-4. IE new-style transition filters (continued)

Filter name	Description
Stretch( )	Blends between views through various stretch-style reveals, with properties for duration and stretchStyle (hide, push, spin)
Strips( )	Blends between views with striped effect, with properties for duration and motion
Wheel( )	Blends between views via wheel spokes emanating from the element center, with properties for duration and spoke size (spokes)
ZigZag( )	Blends between views via removal of rows of bricks, with properties for duration and size (gridSizeX, gridSizeY)

The newer filter mechanism is obviously more powerful than the backward-compatible version, although it is also considerably more verbose because you must reference the ActiveX control in references to the filter:

```
document.images[imgName].filters["DXImageTransform.Microsoft.Fade"].apply( );
```

If you want to change the transition type after a page has loaded, you can assign a new filter string to the style.filter property:

```
elementRef.style.filter = "progid:DXImageTransform.Microsoft.Iris(duration=1.0)";
```

References to filter styles can get tricky because the reference syntax varies with your intention. To control an existing filter type (to invoke one of its methods or alter one of its properties), use the filters array of the element itself (not the element's style property). The index to the array can be either an integer (corresponding to the source code order of the filters assigned to the element) or a string name of the specific filter. To control the filter type, assign a complete filter specification to the element's style.filter property.

Using the apply( ) and play( ) methods of a filter object works within the same page when you alter some visible characteristic of an element. But if you want to use these transitions for slide shows when the slides are different HTML pages, you must assign the transition filters to <meta> tags of the pages. Proprietary attribute values instruct IE for Windows to apply the defined transition to the page upon entry and exit. Usually you need a transition on either entry or exit, but not both. The exception might be if you also have an intervening blank or black page between slides to emphasize two different effects, such as an iris-in when entering the blank page and an iris-out when leaving the blank page. The <meta> tags for the blank page in this scenario look like the following:

```
<meta http-equiv="Page-Enter"
content="progid:DXImageTransform.Microsoft.Iris(Motion='in', IrisStyle='circle')">
<meta http-equiv="Page-Exit"
content="progid:DXImageTransform.Microsoft.Iris(Motion='out', IrisStyle='circle')">
```

By placing these transitions in the blank pages, you don't need to specify page transitions in the content slides. Nor is any scripting required for the transitions. But you still use a script to assemble the URL of the next content slide and pass that data as a search string to the blank page (see Recipe 10.6). A script in the blank page parses the location.search data to navigate to the next content slide, causing the exit transition to fire en route.

See Also

Recipe 10.6 for passing data between pages via URLs; Recipe 15.5 for a DHTML slide show; for complete details on IE transition types and their properties, visit *http://msdn.microsoft.com/workshop/author/filter/filters.asp*.

12.13 Drawing Charts in the Canvas Element

Problem

You want to draw circles, lines, and filled shapes on the client without resorting to server programming.

Solution

Use the canvas element in Mozilla 1.8 or later, Safari 2 or later, and Opera 9 or later to provide a rectangular space on the page in which scripts can draw freeform. Only a minimal amount of HTML is needed to plant the element where you want it:

```
<canvas id="myCanvas" height="400" width="500"></canvas>
```

All the work of drawing inside the element is controlled by scriptable methods of the rendering context object within the element:

```
function draw( ) {
    var canvas = document.getElementById("myCanvas");
    var ctxt = canvas.getContext("2d");
    // invoke methods on ctxt object here
}
```

Thus far, only a two-dimensional context has been implemented in supporting browsers.

Discussion

The canvas mechanism is documented in a recommended standard authored by the Web Hypertext Application Technology Working Group (WHATWG). It offers a wide range of drawing capabilities, but it helps to have a good grounding in algebra and geometry to understand how the more complex operations work. Table 12-5 lists the properties and methods of the rendering context object.

Table 12-5. Properties and methods of the canvas context object

Property/Method	Description
canvas	Reference to current canvas object
fillStyle	Color, gradient, or pattern for shape fill

Table 12-5. Properties and methods of the canvas context object (continued)

Property/Method	Description
globalAlpha	Transparency level for all items
globalCompositeOperation	Masking type
lineCap	Line end point style
lineJoin	Style of line joints at meeting point
lineWidth	Line thickness
miterLimit	Miter line joint ratio
shadowBlur	Shadow depth
shadowColor	Shadow color
shadowOffsetX	Horizontal shadow width
shadowOffsetY	Vertical shadow width
strokeStyle	Color, gradient, or pattern for shape outline
arc(*x, y, radius, startAngle, endAngle, counterClockwiseFlag*)	Specifies an arc path
arcTo(*x1, y1, x2, y2, radius*)	Specifies arc path from current point
beginPath( )	Resets context path
bezierCurveTo(*cp1x, cp1y, cp2x, cp2y, x, y*)	Specifies cubic Bézier curve path
clearRect(*x, y, width, height*)	Erases rectangular region
clip( )	Creates clipping region of current path
closePath( )	Adds straight line from current point to first path point
createLinearGradient(*x0, y0, x1, y1*)	Generates CanvasGradient object for fillStyle
createPattern(*imageObjectRef*, "*repeatStyle*")	Generates CanvasPattern object for fillStyle
createRadialGradient(*x0, y0, r0, x1, y1, r1*)	Generates CanvasGradient object for fillStyle
drawImage(*imageOrCanvas, sx, sy, sw, sh, dx, dy, dw, dh*)	Copies imported image to context
fill( )	Fills current path space with fillStyle specs
fillRect(*x, y, width, height*)	Fills rectangle with fillStyle specs
lineTo(*x, y*)	Adds line to path from current point
moveTo(*x, y*)	Moves point to specific location
quadraticCurveTo(*cp1x, cp1y, x, y*)	Specifies quadratic Bézier curve path
rect(*x, y, width, height*)	Creates path for a rectangle
restore( )	Pops topmost state from internal stack
rotate(*angle*)	Rotates context within canvas
save( )	Pushes current state onto internal stack
scale(*x, y*)	Adjusts scale of context
stroke( )	Draws current path
strokeRect(*x, y, width, height*)	Draws rectangle
translate(*x, y*)	Moves origin point of context

The basic operation of drawing starts with a new path (beginPath( )), which sets the current point to 0,0 within the canvas context. You then move the point to a starting coordinate for your drawing, specify a series of movements of the point (either to draw arcs, lines, or shapes), and then cause the specified path to be drawn in the canvas (stroke( )). For example, the following function draws a yellow-filled smiley face inside a canvas element whose ID is myCanvas:

```
function drawSmiley( ) {
    var canvas = document.getElementById("myCanvas");
    var ctxt = canvas.getContext("2d");
    // set fill color to yellow
    ctxt.fillStyle = "rgb(255,225,0)";
    // reset current point to 0,0
    ctxt.beginPath( );
    // two-pixel thick line to start
    ctxt.lineWidth = 2;
    // move current point to starting point for big circle
    ctxt.moveTo(125, 75);
    // specify path for big head with a 50-pixel radius
    ctxt.arc(75,75,50,0,Math.PI*2,true);
    // fill it with fillStyle (yellow) and render
    ctxt.fill( );
    // move current point to start left eye
    ctxt.moveTo(65,65);
    // specify path for left eye with 5-pixel radius
    ctxt.arc(60,65,5,0,Math.PI*2,true);
    // and now to the right eye
    ctxt.moveTo(95,65);
    ctxt.arc(90,65,5,0,Math.PI*2,true);
     // render the two eye circles
    ctxt.stroke( );
    // start a new path
    ctxt.beginPath( );
    // move point to begin smile arc
    ctxt.moveTo(110,75);
    // make it wider than other lines thus far
    ctxt.lineWidth = 4;
    // specify arc for smile
    ctxt.arc(75,75,35,0,Math.PI,false);
    // render it
    ctxt.stroke( );
}
```

A smiley face may be cute, but there are more formal uses for drawing, such as creating a dynamic pie chart on a web page. For this example, we'll create a 200 × 200 canvas and provide four select elements to allow the user to change value for each of four pie chart wedges. Figure 12-3 shows the result.

The HTML portion is simplicity itself, consisting of nothing more than the canvas element and the "controller" holding the four select elements. I chose arbitrary values for each control. The four values don't have to add up to 100 because the scripts calculate the relative proportions from the total.

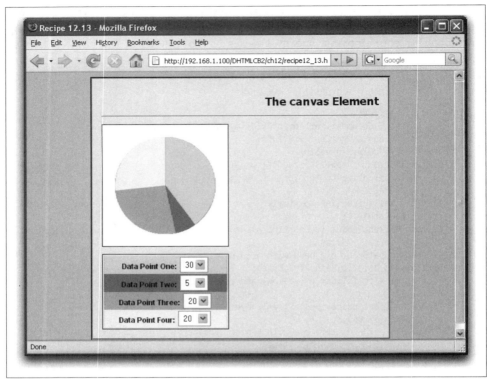

Figure 12-3. Dynamic pie chart and controller

```
<p>
<canvas id="myCanvas" height="200" width="200"></canvas>
</p>
<div id="pieController">
<form>
<div id="data1">Data Point One: <select id="select1" class="selector">
<option value="10">10</option>
<option value="30">30</option>
<option value="50">50</option>
<option value="70">70</option></select></div>
<div id="data2">Data Point Two: <select id="select2" class="selector">
<option value="5">5</option>
<option value="25">25</option>
<option value="50">50</option>
<option value="88">88</option></select></div>
<div id="data3">Data Point Three: <select id="select3" class="selector">
<option value="20">20</option>
<option value="40">40</option>
<option value="60">60</option>
<option value="80">80</option></select></div>
<div id="data4">Data Point Four: <select id="select4" class="selector">
<option value="10">10</option>
<option value="20">20</option>
```

```
<option value="50">50</option>
<option value="100">100</option></select></div>
</form>
</div>
```

Some style sheet rules apply background colors to each control to match the color to be rendered for that controller's value in the pie chart. I also surround the canvas with a one-pixel border and specify a white background. Without a border or background specification, the canvas element blends into the background (making whatever content is drawn within it to appear as if it is part of the HTML document).

```
canvas {border: 1px black solid; background-color: white}
#pieController {width: 196px;
                border: 1px solid black;
                padding: 2px;
                font-family: Arial;
                font-weight: bold;
                text-align: center
                }
.selector {padding: 2px; margin: 2px}
#data1 {background-color: rgb(51, 255, 0)}
#data2 {background-color: rgb(255, 51, 51)}
#data3 {background-color: rgb(51, 204, 255)}
#data4 {background-color: rgb(255, 255, 0)}
```

With the help of the *eventsManager.js* library, the script binds an event handler function (preparePie( )) to each of the select elements (for the change event) and also immediately draws a pie chart using default values, as you'll see in a moment:

```
function setEvents( ) {
    addEvent(document.getElementById("select1"), "change",
        preparePie, false);
    addEvent(document.getElementById("select2"), "change",
        preparePie, false);
    addEvent(document.getElementById("select3"), "change",
        preparePie, false);
    addEvent(document.getElementById("select4"), "change",
        preparePie, false);
}

addOnLoadEvent(setEvents);
addOnLoadEvent(function() {drawPie( )});
```

Specifying and drawing the pie chart are divided into two functions. The first, preparePie( ), is the one that is invoked by the select elements. This function extracts all the currently chosen values, and packages them into an array that gets sent to the actual drawing function, drawPie( ). By separating the drawing operation from the form extraction, I allow the drawing function to be invoked from other sources, such as the load event.

```
function preparePie(evt) {
    evt = evt || window.event;
    var elem = evt.target || evt.srcElement;
```

```
        var form = elem.form;
        var data = new Array( );
        for (var i = 0; i < form.elements.length; i++) {
            data.push(form.elements[i].value);
        }
        drawPie(data);
    }
```

The drawing function makes a few assumptions for this example. First, there are always four wedges to this pie, each of which has a unique color. Second, the size of the canvas is 200×200, meaning that the center point will be at 100,100, offering enough space for an 80-pixel radius pie chart to be drawn. Of course, all of these aspects can be algorithmically determined for a more flexible version, but there is enough going on in this example that it's best to simplify peripheral items. With those notions in mind, the drawPie( ) function follows:

```
function drawPie(data) {
    var ctxt = document.getElementById("myCanvas").getContext("2d");
    var data = data || [10, 5, 20, 10];
    var total = sumData(data);
    var colors = ["rgb(51, 255, 0)", "rgb(255, 51, 51)", "rgb(51, 204, 255)",
"rgb(255, 255, 0)"];
    var wedges = new Array( );
    var currAngle = 0;
    var centerX = 100;
    var centerY = 100;
    var radius = 80;
    var pct;

    // accumulate pie wedge parameters
    for (var i = 0; i < data.length; i++) {
        pct = data[i]/total;
        wedges[i] = {
            startAngle : currAngle * Math.PI * 2,
            endAngle : (currAngle += pct) * Math.PI * 2
        };
    }
    // draw pie wedges
    ctxt.save( );
    for (i = 0; i < wedges.length; i++) {
        ctxt.fillStyle = colors[i];
        ctxt.beginPath( );
        ctxt.moveTo(centerX, centerY);
        ctxt.arc(centerX, centerY, radius, wedges[i].startAngle - Math.PI/2,
            wedges[i].endAngle - Math.PI/2, false);
        ctxt.closePath( );
        ctxt.fill( );
    }
    ctxt.restore( );
}
```

Numerous local variables are initialized at the top of the function. The most important of all is obtaining a reference to the rendering context object (ctxt), whose methods make the drawing possible later. If there is any incoming data, it arrives as an array. Because we use the sum of those values as our "100%," the task of getting that total is passed to an external function, sumData( ):

```
function sumData(array) {
    var result = 0;
    for (var i = 0; i < array.length; i++) {
        result += parseFloat(array[i]);
    }
    return result;
}
```

The focus of the drawPie( ) function is to provide parameters for the canvas context's arc( ) method. The method specifies an arc within the context anchored to a point that would be the center of a circle if the arc continued to complete a circle. For the pie chart, that is the center of the pie. Also needed is the distance from the center—the radius—at which the arc path is made. The arc extends around the circle between two points represented as the start and end angles, with an angle of 0 being straight up from the center point.

After the local variables are defined in drawPie( ), the data is used to calculate the start and end angles of each wedge of the pie (assuming the total comes to a full circle). These values for each wedge are stored as properties of a custom object, and the wedge objects are collected in the wedges array.

With the angles in hand, the drawing begins by pushing the current context onto an internal canvas context stack (in case you interrupt some other context path to draw the pie chart wedges). Then, while iterating through the array of wedge objects, the script assigns a fill color and starts specifying the path for each wedge, beginning by moving the current point to the chart's center, defining the arc's path, and closing the path (which finds its way back to the path's start point in the center. The fill( ) method renders the wedge. After all the wedges are rendered, the earlier context is popped from the internal stack.

Despite what seems to be an onerous process, it operates very quickly. Changes to the pie chart in response to selections are almost instantaneous, even though the entire chart is being redrawn.

If you want to add a legend or other labels to the chart, you can do so with absolute-positioned HTML elements in front of the canvas element. As you can tell from the range of properties and methods in Table 12-5, you can create all types of bar and line charts, including those with smooth curves. Some designers have created gauges and dials, as well as analog clocks with ticking second hands. Making the leap from artistic design to the math needed to draw those designs is perhaps the biggest challenge.

For more details about the canvas element, visit Mozilla's tutorial on the subject at *http://developer.mozilla.org/en/docs/Canvas_tutorial*.

CHAPTER 13

Positioning HTML Elements

13.0 Introduction

When a typical HTML page loads, the browser flows the content according to its interpretation of how each element should appear on the page. Some elements have attributes that control various dimensions, either in terms of pixels or percentages of the available space, but again, the designer is at the mercy of the rendering engine of the browser. The tradition of HTML as a passive publishing medium is much cruder than print publishing, where the designer is in total control of every millimeter of space on the page.

Precise HTML content layout is often left up to twisting HTML tables and transparent images inside table cells to make sure the position relationships, say, between an image and its caption, meet the designer's expectations. In fact, if you play with WYSIWYG (What You See is What You Get) web page layout programs the same way you use print publishing layout tools (such as PageMaker or QuarkXPress), a mass of HTML table-related code frequently accrues behind the pretty page. Manually tweaking that gnarled code can sometimes lead to tears.

To fill the gap by providing publishing-quality control over content appearance, the style sheet concept has gained a strong footing in web publishing, particularly with the W3C-sponsored Cascading Style Sheets (CSS) recommendation. Not only is the raw content—the words and images, primarily—separated from the specifications of how the content is rendered, but the publishing world has contributed to mapping out the nature and breadth of CSS properties that can be applied to content.

Not long after the first release of a CSS recommendation, a supplementary standard appeared, covering the notion of positioning HTML content. Element positioning became part of the main CSS Level 2 recommendation. At its root, CSS positioning lets you specify the exact coordinates of an element within the document space. A positioned element exists in its own plane above the page, much like the acetate sheet that cartoon animators once used to create characters that moved (in succeeding acetate cels) in front of a fixed background. Before CSS positioning, each rendered

HTML element occupied its own rectangular space on the page. With CSS positioning, you may overlap elements, which means that stacking order is also controllable. And since each positioned element lives in its own plane, positioned elements may also hide themselves and reappear without disturbing the layout of other elements.

When you add the scripting capabilities of modern browsers to element positioning concepts, you open up a door to a wide array of user interface possibilities—page features that extend far beyond the Web's original publishing concepts. Scripts can make an element jump from one position to another or glide slowly along a path (albeit not with the same level of speed control as is possible in dedicated animation technologies, such as Macromedia Flash). Interaction with mouse events allows scripts to track the location of an element along with the position of the mouse cursor on the screen for actual element dragging on the page. Another kind of positioning animation lets you create blocks of body text that automatically scroll for page visitors.

Positioning Scope

As you determine how you might wish to employ element positioning on your page, you have to consider the range of options you have with regard to the positioning context you wish to use. The most common positioning context is that of the entire space occupied by the web page inside the browser window. In this scenario, treat the area occupied by the page's content as your layout space, within which you can define the location of one or more elements, each residing in its own plane. This space has a two-dimensional coordinate system, with point 0,0 being the very top left of the page (the top-left corner of the browser's content region if the page is scrolled all the way to the top and left). Numbers for the coordinates increase as you move to the right and downward.

Another positioning context can be an already-positioned element. In other words, you can position an element inside another positioned element. In this case, the more nested element uses the layout space of the outer element as its context. The outer element presents its own coordinate system, with point 0,0 being the top-left corner of the element. If the outer element is moved, the inner nested element moves right along with it, maintaining its interior coordinates relative to its positioning context.

An important design consideration to keep in mind is that even though a positioned element seems to float in front of all other content, it does not act like a browser window. If you position an element so that some of its area extends beyond the visible area of a web page, the positioned element is clipped to the edge of the window, rather than overlapping the browser's scrollbars or other window chrome. In fact, positioning an element outside of the regular document flow is likely to force the browser to resize the page, extending it in such a way as to display browser scrollbars where none existed before. This kind of clipping, however, does not occur when you position an element within another positioned element, unless you explicitly set the clipping rectangle of the outer container.

Positioning Types

You have a few positioning types to choose from. A helpful type, which is not implemented in IE for Windows through version 6, is *fixed positioning*. This style allows an element to remain in a constant location in the content region of the browser window, regardless of page scrolling. Typical applications for a fixed element include floating control panels and page watermarks (similar to the network symbols that occupy the corners of many television channel screens). More common are two other types, whose names do not always convey their meaning: *absolute positioning* and *relative positioning*. Keeping the characteristics of these two types straight is important.

An absolute-positioned element is removed from the rest of the page's rendering flow, regardless of its location within the source code. A nonnested, absolute-positioned element uses the page coordinate space as its positioning context (more about this in a moment, because it's not exactly that simple). Any other HTML in the source code flows on the page as if the positioned element were not there. In fact, if you instruct an element to be positioned but fail to give it coordinates to follow, the positioned element appears at the top-left corner of the page, on top of whatever other content happens to be in that location. And yet, the element containment hierarchy with respect to nodes and their children in the document's object model still exists.

In contrast to the absolute-positioned element is the relative-positioned element. A significant difference between absolute- and relative-positioned elements is that a relative-positioned element influences the rendering flow of the main document content. The positioning context of a relative-positioned element is the location in the main document where the element normally appears if it is not positioned. In fact, if you specify an element as being relative-positioned and don't supply any coordinates (defaulting to 0,0), the element looks no different than if it were a non-positioned element. The difference, however, comes when you assign coordinates to the element. It moves (relative to its original position), and the surrounding content does not cinch up around the unused space.

A valuable application of a relative-positioned element is to provide a positioning context for some other absolute-positioned element. This lets the relative-positioned element flow into the page as normal (influenced by the browser window size, style sheet settings, and the like). But then a nested absolute-positioned element can define its location relative to that positioning context, such as 20 pixels below the end of a paragraph whose final period is a relative-positioned span element (see Recipe 13.2).

Evolving Contexts

In the first versions of Internet Explorer for Windows that permitted element positioning, Microsoft designed parts of its system in a way that ultimately was not adopted by the W3C in its CSS recommendation. To get back on the standards track, IE 6 implemented CSS more in line with the standard. But some of these changes could make older content—which looked and operated fine in IE 4 through 5.5—render in unexpected ways.

To bridge the gap, IE 6 (and now IE 7) includes two modes, one for backward compatibility and one for CSS compatibility. By default, IE 6 and 7 operate in backward-compatibility mode. But to switch them into CSS-compatibility mode, you need to define a DOCTYPE element at the top of the document with certain characteristics. Other modern browsers similarly have two modes, although the differences between the two are less apparent for typical positioning tasks. See Recipe 11.13 for details about defining an appropriate DOCTYPE element.

One important difference between the two modes in IE 6 and 7 is that the primary positioning context for an unnested element moves outward from the body element (as in IE 4 through 5.5) to the html element, which represents the full rendered document context. The difference is more than just symbolic because the body element in IE has some built-in margins that can affect precise positioning when trying to align positioned and non-positioned elements (see Recipe 13.6).

Incompatibility Hazards

Although far less of an issue than it once was, you need to be aware of potential problems with older and underpowered browsers (e.g., in some cell phones) when you include positioned elements in the page. If a browser doesn't support the CSS positioning properties, the elements you have set aside as positioned elements render on the page in their source code order. Not only will your carefully positioned elements not be where you want them to be, but they will likely confuse the visitor.

Counteracting this problem results in a variety of compromises, depending on your solution. One choice is to limit page access to browsers that support CSS positioning.

Another possibility is to use scripts to generate the HTML for positioned content dynamically while the page loads. The script can verify that the browser supports CSS and basic W3C DOM syntax, and then use DOM element creation techniques to create the HTML. Of course, your page must be able to stand on its own without the positioned content to be meaningful to users of other older browsers. A potential downside to this technique is that search engines will not detect any links in the dynamically generated content.

Units of Measure

Designers from the publishing world are accustomed to laying out content in a variety of units of measure, such as inches, centimeters, picas, points, and ems. CSS supports all of these units of measure for length values, but for the most part, they are difficult to work with in a medium that most commonly outputs to a video screen. In computer monitors, the pixel is king. It is also indivisible, so that any measure that attempts to split hairs in units other than pixels is likely doomed to failure.

Even if you intend the output to go to a printer, you may not get the results you expect if you specify units other than pixels. Browsers perform a lot of estimations, conversions, and interpolations between the screen-rendered output and what they send to a printer. It's true that you might get lucky with a design template in other units on a particular browser, but such results are the exception rather than the rule.

The Erstwhile <layer> Tag

Navigator 4 was the first browser to implement the notion of positioned elements, which it did via a then-new element called the layer. This effort pre-dated the W3C's effort to codify CSS positioning. When the standards body finished its work, it decided to steer clear of the <layer> tag and all associated coding. The Navigator 4 browser was a popular version, and developers created a lot of content that not only used the proprietary <layer> tag, but also the required Navigator 4 DOM syntax for referencing such elements to adjust their properties (e.g., to move or hide an element). In the meantime, Microsoft came up with its own referencing scheme, whereby any element (positioned or otherwise) could be referenced through the document.all collection. Equalizing references to the positioned-element properties of IE and NN 4 browsers was a part of any DHTML page at the time.

With the layer element eliminated from the standardized HTML grammar before it ever got there, developers of the next generation of Netscape browser made the difficult but ultimately correct decision to drop support for the <layer> tag and DOM reference scheme from the Mozilla browser. Lots of Netscape-specific scripts broke during the transition, but thanks to the W3C DOM and support for it in current browsers, it is now possible to use the same HTML- and DOM-referencing syntax to produce and manipulate positioned elements on a wide range of browsers, including IE 5 or later. The W3C syntax is a stable development platform going forward.

One legacy of the Navigator 4 effort, however, is that positioned elements are frequently called *layers*, regardless of the browser platform. It is a convenient metaphor for the way these positionable, floating elements behave, and you will find this usage in this book as well.

13.1 Making an Element Positionable in the Document Space

Problem

You want one or more elements in your page to overlap other elements or appear in a specific location on the page out of rendering order.

Solution

Assign the absolute value to the position CSS property. You can do this in a separate style declaration:

```
<style type="text/css">
#someElementID {position: absolute; left: 100px; top: 100px}
</style>
```

Or you can include the style declaration as an attribute to an element:

```
<div id="myDIV" style="position:absolute; left:100px; top:100px">Content Here</div>
```

Give coordinates for the top-left corner of the element relative to the top-left corner of the document.

Discussion

There is nothing particularly dynamic about a positioned element, except that it is loaded with potential for scripting activity in motion, visibility, stacking, and clipping. In today's browsers the positioned element itself can be of any renderable HTML element, and may thus have event handler assignments (perhaps for mouse dragging) and any HTML content. Even an inline element (such as a span element) becomes a block-level element when it is positioned (even if the display style property value doesn't necessarily change to reflect its behavior).

As you will see in Recipe 13.3, scripted modifications to the position of an element are performed via the style property of the element. Using W3C DOM element referencing, for example, allows you to adjust the top coordinate of the example as follows:

```
document.getElementById("myDIV").style.top = "200px";
```

Note that the position property of the style object is read-only, which means that once an element renders according to its associated position CSS property, the value cannot be changed. Therefore, you cannot turn an inline element into a positioned element simply by altering the value assigned to the style.position property.

See Also

Recipe 13.3 for a script library of functions to control positioned elements; Chapter 11 for style sheet assignment syntax.

13.2 Connecting a Positioned Element to a Body Element

Problem

You want an element to render on the page a fixed number of pixels vertically and/or horizontally distant from an element that flows in the main document.

Solution

Create a positioning context with a relative-positioned container around the primary element, and embed an absolute-positioned element within the container. The following code binds an absolute-positioned photo copyright image to the photo image:

```
<div style="position:relative; margin-left:20%">
    <img src="kitty.jpg" height="511" width="383" style="border:4px groove darkred"
        alt="My Kitty" />
    <img src="photoCopyright.jpg" style="position:absolute; top:519px; left:263px"
        alt="Copyright 2003 Snaps McGraw" />
</div>
```

Discussion

The result appears in Figure 13-1. The relative-positioned container has a percentage value for its margin, so its precise horizontal position varies with the width of the browser window. But no matter where the photo image appears on the page, the copyright image will appear immediately below it and flush right.

In the Solution, the coordinates of the absolute-positioned element need to be adjusted for each inline image because the coordinates depend on the size of the image. The 0,0 point of the coordinate system is determined by the location of the first element encased in the relative-positioned div element. Although the main image has a height of 511 pixels, the image has a four-pixel wide border around it. For the copyright image to be clear of the border, its top coordinate must be 511 plus the width of the top and bottom borders, for a total of 519 pixels. The left position is determined by the width of the main image (383 pixels) minus the width of the copyright image (120 pixels).

The choice of the div element as a container is driven by the block-level nature of the image in the layout. A div element is a convenient block-level container that lets you create an arbitrary HTML container wherever one is needed (see Recipe 13.4). Because an img element is not a container, it cannot be made a relative-positioned element that can contain an absolute-positioned element—thus the need for the div container.

Figure 13-1. Binding an absolute-positioned element (copyright notice) to a relative-positioned element (photo)

This technique is also useful for overlapping elements. For example, instead of a copyright image, the page owner might prefer to overlay a transparent image that includes a subtle watermark-looking credit line. If the credit image is the same height and width as the underlying image, its absolute-positioned coordinates can be set to 0,0, corresponding to the top-left corner of the main image. However, if the water-mark is a smaller image, it can be positioned anywhere on the image so that it is readable, yet doesn't detract from the view of the image.

See Also

The introduction to this chapter to understand the differences between absolute- and relative-positioned elements; Recipe 13.4 to help you know when to use a div or span element for positioning.

13.3   Controlling Positioning via a DHTML JavaScript Library

Problem

You want a reusable library of routines that ease the scripted positioning of elements in a page.

Solution

Use the DHTML library, *DHTML3API.js* (shown in Example 13-1 in the Discussion), to simplify cross-browser scripting of positionable elements. The library is compatible with IE 4 or later and Navigator 4 or later. The library creates one global object, called DHTMLAPI, which has numerous methods your scripts invoke for common positioning tasks. It provides API routines for moving, hiding/showing, and modifying the stacking order of positioned elements. For example, you can move an absolute-positioned element whose ID is helpWindow to a location 300 pixels to the right and 200 pixels down from the top-left corner of the document with the following function call:

```
DHTMLAPI.moveTo("helpWindow", 300, 200);
```

Additional utility routines in the library retrieve object references given an element's ID, dimensions, and positions, rendered style values, and some browser window dimensions.

If you save this library under the name *DHTM3LAPI.js*, you can link it into any document with the following tag:

```
<script src="DHTML3API.js"></script>
```

The library is self-initializing if you load the *eventsManager.js* external library before this library. Do not insert load event handlers into the <body> tag, as discussed in Recipe 9.3.

Discussion

Example 13-1 shows the full *DHTML3API.js* library. In addition to providing a set of cross-browser tools for controlling positioned elements, it also defines five Boolean properties about the browser environment that your other scripts may use.

Example 13-1. The DHTML3API.js library

```
// DHTML3API.js custom API for cross-platform
// object positioning by Danny Goodman (http://www.dannyg.com).
// Release 3.0. Supports NN4, IE, and W3C DOMs.

var DHTMLAPI = {
    browserClass : new Object(),
```

Example 13-1. The DHTML3API.js library (continued)

```
    init : function () {
        this.browserClass.isCSS = ((document.body && document.body.style) ? true : false);
        this.browserClass.isW3C = ((this.browserClass.isCSS && document.getElementById) ?
            true : false),
        this.browserClass.isIE4 = ((this.browserClass.isCSS && document.all) ?
            true : false),
        this.browserClass.isNN4 = ((document.layers) ? true : false),
        this.browserClass.isIECSSCompat = ((document.compatMode &&
            document.compatMode.indexOf("CSS1") >= 0) ? true : false)
    },
    // Seek nested NN4 layer from string name
    seekLayer : function (doc, name) {
        var elem;
        for (var i = 0; i < doc.layers.length; i++) {
            if (doc.layers[i].name == name) {
                elem = doc.layers[i];
                break;
            }
            // dive into nested layers if necessary
            if (doc.layers[i].document.layers.length > 0) {
                elem = this.seekLayer(doc.layers[i].document, name);
                if (elem) {break;}
            }
        }
        return elem;
    },

    // Convert element name string or object reference
    // into a valid element object reference
    getRawObject : function (elemRef) {
        var elem;
        if (typeof elemRef == "string") {
            if (this.browserClass.isW3C) {
                elem = document.getElementById(elemRef);
            } else if (this.browserClass.isIE4) {
                elem = document.all(elemRef);
            } else if (this.browserClass.isNN4) {
                elem = this.seekLayer(document, elemRef);
            }
        } else {
            // pass through object reference
            elem = elemRef;
        }
        return elem;
    },
    // Convert element name string or object reference
    // into a valid style (or NN4 layer) object reference
    getStyleObject : function (elemRef) {
        var elem = this.getRawObject(elemRef);
        if (elem && this.browserClass.isCSS) {
            elem = elem.style;
        }
        return elem;
    },
```

Example 13-1. The DHTML3API.js library (continued)

```
// Position an element at a specific pixel coordinate
moveTo : function (elemRef, x, y) {
    var elem = this.getStyleObject(elemRef);
    if (elem) {
        if (this.browserClass.isCSS) {
            // equalize incorrect numeric value type
            var units = (typeof elem.left == "string") ? "px" : 0;
            elem.left = x + units;
            elem.top = y + units;
        } else if (this.browserClass.isNN4) {
            elem.moveTo(x,y);
        }
    }
},

// Move an element by x and/or y pixels
moveBy : function (elemRef, deltaX, deltaY) {
    var elem = this.getStyleObject(elemRef);
    if (elem) {
        if (this.browserClass.isCSS) {
            // equalize incorrect numeric value type
            var units = (typeof elem.left == "string") ? "px" : 0;
            if (!isNaN(this.getElementLeft(elemRef))) {
                elem.left = this.getElementLeft(elemRef) + deltaX + units;
                elem.top = this.getElementTop(elemRef) + deltaY + units;
            }
        } else if (this.browserClass.isNN4) {
            elem.moveBy(deltaX, deltaY);
        }
    }
},

// Set the z-order of an object
setZIndex : function (obj, zOrder) {
    var elem = this.getStyleObject(obj);
    if (elem) {
        elem.zIndex = zOrder;
    }
},

// Set the background color of an object
setBGColor : function (obj, color) {
    var elem = this.getStyleObject(obj);
    if (elem) {
        if (this.browserClass.isCSS) {
            elem.backgroundColor = color;
        } else if (this.browserClass.isNN4) {
            elem.bgColor = color;
        }
    }
},
```

Example 13-1. The DHTML3API.js library (continued)

```
    // Set the visibility of an object to visible
    show : function (obj) {
        var elem = this.getStyleObject(obj);
        if (elem) {
            elem.visibility = "visible";
        }
    },

    // Set the visibility of an object to hidden
    hide : function (obj) {
        var elem = this.getStyleObject(obj);
        if (elem) {
            elem.visibility = "hidden";
        }
    },

    // return computed value for an element's style property
    getComputedStyle : function (elemRef, CSSStyleProp) {
        var elem = this.getRawObject(elemRef);
        var styleValue, camel;
        if (elem) {
            if (document.defaultView && document.defaultView.getComputedStyle) {
                // W3C DOM version
                var compStyle = document.defaultView.getComputedStyle(elem, "");
                styleValue = compStyle.getPropertyValue(CSSStyleProp);
            } else if (elem.currentStyle) {
                // make IE style property camelCase name from CSS version
                var IEStyleProp = CSSStyleProp;
                var re = /-\D/;
                while (re.test(IEStyleProp)) {
                    camel = IEStyleProp.match(re)[0].charAt(1).toUpperCase( );
                    IEStyleProp = IEStyleProp.replace(re, camel);
                }
                styleValue = elem.currentStyle[IEStyleProp];
            }
        }
        return (styleValue) ? styleValue : null;
    },

    // Retrieve the x coordinate of a positionable object
    getElementLeft : function (elemRef)  {
        var elem = this.getRawObject(elemRef);
        var result = null;
        if (this.browserClass.isCSS || this.browserClass.isW3C) {
            result = parseInt(this.getComputedStyle(elem, "left"));
        } else if (this.browserClass.isNN4) {
            result = elem.left;
        }
        return result;
    },
```

Example 13-1. The DHTML3API.js library (continued)

```
    // Retrieve the y coordinate of a positionable object
    getElementTop : function (elemRef)  {
        var elem = this.getRawObject(elemRef);
        var result = null;
        if (this.browserClass.isCSS || this.browserClass.isW3C) {
            result = parseInt(this.getComputedStyle(elem, "top"));
        } else if (this.browserClass.isNN4) {
            result = elem.top;
        }
        return result;
    },

    // Retrieve the rendered width of an element
    getElementWidth : function (elemRef)  {
        var result = null;
        var elem = this.getRawObject(elemRef);
        if (elem) {
            if (elem.offsetWidth) {
                if (elem.scrollWidth && (elem.offsetWidth != elem.scrollWidth)) {
                    result = elem.scrollWidth;
                } else {
                    result = elem.offsetWidth;
                }
            } else if (elem.clip && elem.clip.width) {
                // Netscape 4 positioned elements
                result = elem.clip.width;
            }
        }
        return result;
    },

    // Retrieve the rendered height of an element
    getElementHeight : function (elemRef)  {
        var result = null;
        var elem = this.getRawObject(elemRef);
        if (elem) {
            if (elem.offsetHeight) {
                result = elem.offsetHeight;
            } else if (elem.clip && elem.clip.height) {
                result = elem.clip.height;
            }
        }
        return result;
    },

    // Return the available content width space in browser window
    getInsideWindowWidth : function () {
        if (window.innerWidth) {
            return window.innerWidth;
        } else if (this.browserClass.isIECSSCompat) {
            // measure the html element's clientWidth
            return document.body.parentElement.clientWidth;
```

Example 13-1. The DHTML3API.js library (continued)

```
            } else if (document.body && document.body.clientWidth) {
                return document.body.clientWidth;
            }
            return null;
        },

        // Return the available content height space in browser window
        getInsideWindowHeight : function () {
            if (window.innerHeight) {
                return window.innerHeight;
            } else {
                if (document.body.clientHeight != document.body.parentNode.clientHeight) {
                    // measure the html element's clientHeight
                    return document.body.parentNode.clientHeight;
                } else {
                    return document.body.clientHeight;
                }
            }
            return null;
        }
    }
}

addOnLoadEvent(function() {DHTMLAPI.init()});
```

The purpose of this API is to present a single script interface for what can be nightmarish compatibility issues when trying to address three position-aware document object models: IE 4, NN 4, and W3C DOM. Your scripts invoke simple, one-size-fits-all functions, and the library takes care of the syntactic and conceptual differences among the three object models.

The DHTML library shown here first appeared in bonus downloads for *Dynamic HTML: The Definitive Reference* (O'Reilly). It contains numerous functions that may be invoked from other JavaScript code loaded in the same page. The utility functions you are most likely to invoke directly are:

DHTMLAPI.moveTo(*obj,x,y*)
> Moves an object to a coordinate point within its positioning context

DHTMLAPI.moveBy(*obj,deltaX,deltaY*)
> Moves an object by the specified number of pixels along the x and y axes of the object's positioning context

DHTMLAPI.setZIndex(*obj,zOrder*)
> Sets the z-index value of the object

DHTMLAPI.show(*obj*)
> Makes the object visible

DHTMLAPI.hide(*obj*)
> Makes the object invisible

All functions require as a parameter something to let the function know which element to operate on. Because the library cannot predict how your scripts may be referencing an element when the functions are needed, all functions welcome either full-fledged object references or just the ID of the element (as a string). If you supply only the ID, other internal functions obtain the correct reference needed to modify the desired style properties. This works even for the peculiar way that Navigator 4 requires references to layer objects, rather than style properties.

To move a positioned element to a coordinate within its positioning context, simply invoke the DHTMLAPI.moveTo( ) method, passing as parameters a reference to the element (or just its ID) and the left and top (x and y) coordinate points of the destination:

```
DHTMLAPI.moveTo("moveableFeast", 340, 500);
```

To increment the location along one or both axes, you can use the moveBy( ) method. For example, to move an element three pixels across and five pixels up, the statement is as follows:

```
DHTMLAPI.moveBy("moveableFeast", 3, -5);
```

In the moveBy( ) method, positive values move the element to the right or downward; negative values move the element to the left or upward.

Your scripts, of course, may invoke any of the functions of the library if they help the cause. For example, two utility functions at the end of the library return the height and width of the browser window's content region. These values may be useful in positioning or sizing an element under script control to the current browser window size or proportion.

This library includes a self-initializing load event handler via the addOnLoadEvent( ) mechanism of Recipe 9.3. You can have other libraries and scripts in the page add other load event handlers to the queue in the same fashion without fear of collisions.

As with many .js libraries, you can eliminate the methods that you don't use, and even extract some methods as free-standing functions if you like. Loading a big library to use only a few functions is a waste of bandwidth. Just exercise care that you don't remove helper methods invoked by the main methods you call directly. For example, if you wanted to use only the moveBy( ) method, you also need the init( ), getStyleObject( ), getRawObject( ), getElementLeft( ), and getElementTop( ) methods as a supporting cast.

Browsers tend to restrict rendering of repositioned content until an execution sequence completes execution. Therefore, even though repositioning an element requires adjustments along two different axes, the user sees a single jump from one position to another. For animation, you need to use the setInterval( ) mechanism to force the browser to continually redraw the position along a path (see Recipes 13.9 and 13.10).

See Also

Most recipes later in this chapter and many recipes in later chapters utilize this API for positioning tasks.

13.4   Deciding Between div and span Containers

Problem

You want to choose the optimum generic container for a positioned element.

Solution

Any container defined as an absolute- or fixed-position element becomes, for all practical purposes, a block-level element. Therefore, it makes little difference in most browsers whether you use div or span elements as arbitrary containers for positioned content. Conceptually, however, it may help you identify positioned code in your HTML if you use div elements for absolute- and fixed-position elements.

One significant exception is when you use a relative-positioned container around inline content to create a positioning context for some other nested and positioned content. The following example turns the trailing period of a paragraph into a positioning context so that some other, absolute-positioned content can maintain its position relative to that period, regardless of the content flow of the page:

```
<p>Lorem ipsum dolor sit amet, consectetaur adipisicing elit, sed do eiusmod tempor
incididunt ut labore et dolore magna aliqua. Ut enim adminim veniam, quis nostrud
exercitation ullamco laboris nisi ut aliquip ex ea commodo
consequat<span id="someSpan" style="position:relative">.
<span id="anotherSpan" style="position:absolute; top:20px; left:0px; width:80px">
-- Greek text in Latin.
</span>
</span>
</p>
```

Discussion

Figure 13-2 shows the results of the Solution in two different browser windows, so you can see how the absolute-positioned content maintains it position relative to the trailing period.

The default behavior of a block-level element in HTML (such as a p or div element) is to render the element at the start of the next line of content on the page; any subsequent element starts on the next line following the block-level element. This is why a standard p element starts flush left on its own line in left-to-right language systems. An inline element (such as an em or span element) does not affect the layout flow of its own or surrounding content.

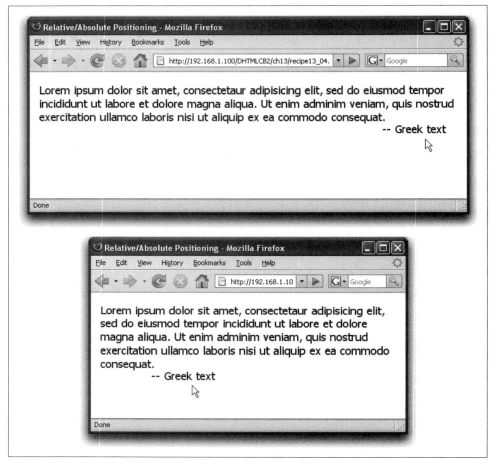

Figure 13-2. An absolute-positioned element inside a relative-positioned span element

If you use a span element as a container for an absolute- or fixed-position element, the content removes itself from the regular document flow entirely and starts its own block. But the CSS display property, which governs the rendering characteristics of elements (with values such as block, inline, none, and so on), remains set to inline, even though the positioned element has a lot of "blockness" about it.

By altering the value of an element's style.display property, you can control the flow characteristics of the element, over and above the default behavior. Typically, this approach is used to give the appearance of inserting and/or removing an element from the page. But you can turn a typically inline element into a truly block-level element by assigning the value block to the style.display property.

See Also

Recipe 13.2 for the use of a relative-positioned container as a positioning context.

13.5 Adjusting Positioned Element Stacking Order (Z-order)

Problem

You want to control the way an overlapping element appears in front of or behind another element.

Solution

You can either use the `DHTMLAPI.setZIndex( )` method from the DHTML library (Recipe 13.3) for backward-compatibility or, for all browsers that support the `style` property of elements, adjust the `style.zIndex` property directly:

```
document.getElementById("myLayer").style.zIndex = "100";
```

Discussion

Turning an element into a positioned element automatically raises it to a layer in front of the main document content. Unless the background of a layer is set to a color or image, the element's background is transparent by default, allowing content underneath to be visible in the blank spaces.

If the stacking order of a positioned element doesn't have to change during user interaction with the page, you can simply set the initial value via the CSS z-index property and be done with it. But there are times when scripts need to adjust the stacking order. For example, if you have multiple draggable elements on the page (see Recipe 13.11), you must ensure that the element being dragged is in front of all other elements, including other positioned elements. Otherwise, the dragged item will submarine beneath other positioned elements and befuddle the user. Once dropped behind other items, the element may be lost.

Stacking rules are pretty simple. If any two elements have the same z-index value, the elements stack in source code order, with the element that comes later in the source code appearing in front of the earlier item. The default CSS z-index value for a positioned element is auto, which equates to zero. A negative value does not layer the element behind the main content. An element with a higher z-index value appears in front of elements with lower numbers. Thus, you can control the layering regardless of source code order.

In the drag scenario just mentioned (and demonstrated in Recipe 13.11), the script that responds to the mouse event signaling the activation of a draggable element should raise the zIndex property value of the dragged element to a number guaranteed to be higher than all others. There is no practical limit to the value you assign. Therefore, it's not uncommon to assign an arbitrarily high number, such as 100 or 1,000, to an item that must be in front of all others. But once the user releases the dragged element, you need to restore the original value (which you should have preserved in a variable or custom property for later recall). This leaves room for the next dragged item to be assigned that high number so it appears in front of all others.

Beware, however, of mixing positioned elements and form controls. Except in the most recent browsers, you will encounter rendering conflicts between layers and several types of form controls when the layers are intended to overlap those controls. The most common offenders are text-based controls, such as text input elements, textarea elements, and select elements (which frequently use text-editing innards to display their content).

Unfortunately, when these conflicts arise, you can do nothing to make the layer display in front of the form control. Even the biggest number assigned to the zIndex style property won't help. If you cannot rework the design so that the overlap does not occur, the only workaround is to hide the form controls whenever the layer is visible. The best way to do this is to wrap the affected form in a relative-positioned span, and then change its style.visibility property as needed. This keeps the rest of the page from shifting around when the controls hide or show themselves.

See Also

Recipe 13.3 and its utility library for changing stacking order, among other DHTML tasks.

13.6   Centering an Element on Top of Another Element

Problem

You want to position an element so that it is vertically and horizontally centered in front of an element in the main document flow.

Solution

The following centerOnElement( ) function takes two arguments: the ID of the main document element and ID of the positioned element to be placed there. The function is compatible with browsers that support W3C DOM element reference syntax:

```
function centerOnElement(baseElemID, posElemID) {
    baseElem = document.getElementById(baseElemID);
    posElem = document.getElementById(posElemID);

    var offsetTrail = baseElem;
    var offsetLeft = 0;
    var offsetTop = 0;
    // accumulate offset values
    while (offsetTrail) {
        offsetLeft += offsetTrail.offsetLeft;
        offsetTop += offsetTrail.offsetTop;
```

```
        offsetTrail = offsetTrail.offsetParent;
    }

    posElem.style.left = offsetLeft + parseInt(baseElem.offsetWidth/2) -
        parseInt(posElem.offsetWidth/2) + "px"
    posElem.style.top = offsetTop + parseInt(baseElem.offsetHeight/2) -
        parseInt(posElem.offsetHeight/2)+ "px"
}
```

Discussion

As simple as this operation may sound in theory, the code that accomplishes it must compensate for issues affecting compatibility modes of Internet Explorer. Another key point that makes this function generalizable is that it bases its measurements on the rendered dimensions of both the static and positioned elements. If the elements contain content that flows (such as text), the dimensions will likely differ with browser window size and, in some browsers, font preferences that aren't overridden by document style sheets. This function reads the rendered dimensions before calculating sizes and locations.

The first part of the calculations obtains the absolute position of the non-positioned base element, wherever it may render in the document. This is an iterative process that accumulates the offsetLeft and offsetTop measures of the base element and any elements that report in as offset parent elements. For many browsers, the base element's offset measures are sufficient. But IE 6 and 7 in CSS-compatibility mode need to add the offset parent's dimensions to get accurate coordinates. Looping through the offsetParent trail takes care of the problem.

With the absolute location of the base element in hand, the final calculations establish the coordinates of the positioned element. To arrive at the value along any one axis, the inset dimension is calculated by subtracting half the size of the positioned element from half the size of the base element. Adding that difference to the absolute coordinate of the base element provides the absolute coordinate of the centered, positioned element.

Note that the function reads rendered data about both elements. This is possible only after the page has loaded. If you want an item centered without user interaction, invoke the function via a load handler.

You must also take into account the possibility that the user might resize the browser window in such a way that the flow of the base content changes—along with the position of the underlying element. Because there is no inherent connection between the elements (as there is with nested relative- and absolute-positioned elements, as in Recipe 13.2), you need to provide a resize event handler for the window that reinvokes the centering function. If multiple positioned elements are centered on multiple base elements, the resize event handler can invoke a function that makes repeated calls to centerOnElement( ), each with the necessary pair of arguments.

Bear in mind that the offset properties used in the centerOnElement( ) function are not part of the W3C DOM. But nothing in DOM Level 2 provides the kind of vital information needed for this kind of operation (and many other positioning tasks). Although the properties were Microsoft inventions (first used in IE 4), Mozilla-based browsers, Safari, and Opera also implement them.

See Also

Recipe 11.13 for IE 6 CSS-compatibility issues and how to govern which mode the browser follows; Recipe 9.3 for setting up load event handlers.

13.7   Centering an Element in a Window or Frame

Problem

You want to center an element within the browser window or a frame of a frameset.

Solution

For optimum backward-compatibility, use the *DHTML3API.js* library described in Recipe 13.3 to support the following generalizable centerOnWindow( ) function in IE 4 or later and Navigator 4 or later:

```
// Center a positionable element whose ID is passed as
// a parameter in the current window/frame, and show it
function centerOnWindow(elemID) {
    // 'obj' is the positionable object
    var obj = DHTMLAPI.getRawObject(elemID);
    // window scroll factors
    var scrollX = 0, scrollY = 0;
    if (document.body && typeof document.body.scrollTop != "undefined") {
        scrollX += document.body.scrollLeft;
        scrollY += document.body.scrollTop;
        if (document.body.parentNode &&
            typeof document.body.parentNode.scrollTop != "undefined" &&
            (document.body.scrollTop != document.body.parentNode.scrollTop)) {
            scrollX += document.body.parentNode.scrollLeft;
            scrollY += document.body.parentNode.scrollTop;
        }
    } else if (typeof window.pageXOffset != "undefined") {
        scrollX += window.pageXOffset;
        scrollY += window.pageYOffset;
    }
    var x = Math.round((DHTMLAPI.getInsideWindowWidth( )/2) -
        (DHTMLAPI.getElementWidth(obj)/2)) + scrollX;
    var y = Math.round((DHTMLAPI.getInsideWindowHeight( )/2) -
        (DHTMLAPI.getElementHeight(obj)/2)) + scrollY;
    DHTMLAPI.moveTo(obj, x, y);
    DHTMLAPI.show(obj);
}
```

Discussion

The primary challenge of centering an element in the browser window occurs in Internet Explorer, which provides no direct window object property for the window's size, inside or out. Thus, we must turn to other document-level objects and their measurements for clues about the content region of the browser window.

All of this negotiation takes place in the DHTML API library with the getInsideWindowWidth( ) and getInsideWindowHeight( ) methods. Although the process for obtaining these measurements is the same for either axis, a small document—which isn't as wide or as tall as the window—might convey incorrect dimensions. Internet Explorer provides clientHeight and clientWidth properties for all elements, which, for the body element, reveal the dimensions of the body space that is immediately visible through the browser window. For IE 5 and later (including IE 6 and 7 in backward-compatible mode), these dimensions for the body element supply the full interior window dimension, even for a small document. This changes, however, in CSS-compatibility mode for IE 6 and 7, where the window space is revealed by the html element (the parent element of the body). Thus, for browsers that do not support the Netscape window.innerHeight property (which pre-dates the IE client properties), the two similar API support methods derive the measures from the most revealing element, as in the one for window height from Recipe 13.3:

```
// Return the available content height space in browser window
getInsideWindowHeight : function ( ) {
    if (window.innerHeight) {
        return window.innerHeight;
    } else if (this.browserClass.isIECSSCompat) {
        // measure the html element's clientHeight
        return document.body.parentElement.clientHeight;
    } else if (document.body && document.body.clientHeight) {
        return document.body.clientHeight;
    }
    return null;
}
```

Another factor to be concerned about is whether the document whose positioning context you're using is scrolled along either the horizontal or vertical axis. For example, as the user scrolls the page downward, the 0,0 point of the positioning context moves up, meaning that the y coordinate of the positioned element must be increased by the number of pixels that the page has scrolled in that direction.

As with most window-oriented properties, the W3C DOM Level 2 does not offer properties for items such as document scrolling. Back in the version 4 browser days, Microsoft and Netscape developed their own vocabularies and ways to access the scrolled position of a window. Although most browsers implement the Microsoft properties (scrollLeft and scrollTop) for the sake of convenience, you can get more compatibility by branching the scroll-awareness code for syntactical support for either the Microsoft or Netscape way. The majority of lines in the `centerOnWindow( )` function in this recipe deal with reading those factors, which are then applied to the final coordinate values passed to the `moveTo( )` method of the DHTML API.

Rendering anomalies appear in IE and Safari when the user reloads a scrolled page. When the script reads the scrolling values, the browsers are in a temporary unscrolled position. To counteract the problem, bind the `load` event handler via `setTimeout( )`, as follows:

```
addOnLoadEvent(function() {setTimeout(function( ) {centerOnWindow("someElementID"),
0})});
```

Centering an element once, however, won't keep it centered if the user scrolls the page or resizes the window. To compensate for these typical user actions, you need event handlers that respond to both window resizing and scrolling. A window-resizing event is supported by all browsers capable of working with the DHTML API; a scrolling event is available in IE 4 or later, Mozilla, Safari, and Opera. For these event handlers to work most smoothly, assign them as event handler properties of the `window` object, as in the following *eventsManager.js* (Recipe 9.1) binding:

```
addEvent(window, "scroll", function( ) {centerOnWindow("someElementID")}, false);
```

Notice the use of an anonymous function to facilitate passing the ID of the positionable element to `centerOnWindow( )`.

To maintain a positioned element in a fixed-window position at all times, the best solution is to make the element a fixed-position element. You must still assign initial coordinates of the element when the page loads because every browser window can be a different size. Unfortunately, IE supports the `fixed` CSS position type only starting in IE 7 when switched into CSS compatibility mode.

See Also

Recipe 11.13 for controlling IE 6 and 7 CSS-compatibility modes.

13.8 Determining the Location of a Nonpositioned Element

Problem

You want to ascertain the pixel coordinates of an element that the browser has placed during normal page flow.

Solution

The following `getElementPosition( )` function returns an object with properties for the left and top absolute coordinates of the element whose ID is passed as an argument:

```
function getElementPosition(elemID) {
    var offsetTrail = document.getElementById(elemID);
    var offsetLeft = 0;
    var offsetTop = 0;
    while (offsetTrail) {
        offsetLeft += offsetTrail.offsetLeft;
        offsetTop += offsetTrail.offsetTop;
        offsetTrail = offsetTrail.offsetParent;
    }
    return {left:offsetLeft, top:offsetTop};
}
```

This function is compatible with browsers that support W3C DOM element referencing syntax.

Discussion

The typical purpose of establishing the absolute location of an element on the page is to position some other element on it or in relation to it. Because the location of inline elements can vary widely with the browser window size and font situation, the values need to be calculated after the page has loaded, the page is reflowed in response to other dynamic content additions and deletions, or the window is resized.

Although some browser versions report the accurate value simply via the offsetLeft and offsetTop properties of an element, others require the addition of any offsets imposed by parent elements offering positioning contexts (the element indicated by the offsetParent property). Therefore, this function includes a loop that iterates through the offsetParent hierarchy of the element passed as an argument to the function, accumulating additional coordinate offsets if they exist.

This function is not needed for CSS-type absolute-positioned elements because you can obtain the correct coordinates directly via the style.left and style.top properties (or via the effective style property, as retrieved through the script shown in Recipe 11.12).

See Also

Recipe 11.12 for reading initial style properties set in <style> and <link> tags.

13.9 Animating Straight-Line Element Paths

Problem

You want to animate the position of an element from one coordinate to another on the page along a straight-line path.

Solution

To animate a positioned element along a straight-line path, link the *animeLine.js* library (Example 13-2 in the Discussion) to your page and invoke the `initSLAnime()` function with at least the first five parameters in the following sequence:

1. ID of the positioned element (as a string)
2. x coordinate of the starting position
3. y coordinate of the starting position
4. x coordinate of the ending position
5. y coordinate of the ending position

For example:

```
initSLAnime("floater", 100, 100, 400, 360);
```

Discussion

While you can move a positioned element along a hardwired straight-line path in far less code than shown in this recipe, the *animeLine.js* library shown in Example 13-2 provides a generalizable solution, in which you specify the ID of the element to move, the start and end coordinates, and the relative speed. The custom objects and functions perform all of the necessary math to accomplish the job, regardless of direction or length of travel.

Example 13-2. The animeLine.js library for straight-line animation

```
// animation object holds numerous properties related to motion
var anime;

// initialize default anime object
function initAnime( ) {
    anime = {elemID:"",
            xCurr:0,
            yCurr:0,
            xTarg:0,
            yTarg:0,
            xStep:0,
            yStep:0,
            xDelta:0,
            yDelta:0,
            xTravel:0,
            yTravel:0,
            vel:1,
            pathLen:1,
            interval:null
            };
}

// stuff animation object with necessary explicit and calculated values
function initSLAnime(elemID, startX, startY, endX, endY, speed) {
```

```
        initAnime( );
        anime.elemID = elemID;
        anime.xCurr = startX;
        anime.yCurr = startY;
        anime.xTarg = endX;
        anime.yTarg = endY;
        anime.xDelta = Math.abs(endX - startX);
        anime.yDelta = Math.abs(endY - startY);
        anime.vel = (speed) ? speed : 1;
        // set element's start position
        document.getElementById(elemID).style.left = startX + "px";
        document.getElementById(elemID).style.top = startY + "px";
        // the length of the line between start and end points
        anime.pathLen = Math.sqrt((Math.pow((startX - endX), 2)) +
        (Math.pow((startY - endY), 2)));
        // how big the pixel steps are along each axis
        anime.xStep = parseInt(((anime.xTarg - anime.xCurr) / anime.pathLen) * anime.vel);
        anime.yStep = parseInt(((anime.yTarg - anime.yCurr) / anime.pathLen) * anime.vel);
        // start the repeated invocation of the animation
        anime.interval = setInterval("doSLAnimation( )", 10);
}

// calculate next steps and assign to style properties
function doSLAnimation( ) {
        if ((anime.xTravel + anime.xStep) <= anime.xDelta &&
            (anime.yTravel + anime.yStep) <= anime.yDelta) {
            var x = anime.xCurr + anime.xStep;
            var y = anime.yCurr + anime.yStep;
            document.getElementById(anime.elemID).style.left = x + "px";
            document.getElementById(anime.elemID).style.top = y + "px";
            anime.xTravel += Math.abs(anime.xStep);
            anime.yTravel += Math.abs(anime.yStep);
            anime.xCurr = x;
            anime.yCurr = y;
        } else {
            document.getElementById(anime.elemID).style.left = anime.xTarg + "px";
            document.getElementById(anime.elemID).style.top = anime.yTarg + "px";
            clearInterval(anime.interval);
        }
}
// using eventsManager.js library
addOnLoadEvent(initAnime);
```

The library begins by defining a blank anime object, which becomes the holding place for each animation you invoke. Each invocation of the main initSLAnime( ) function sets initial values of the anime object to zero, and then populates the properties with values passed as parameters or values calculated from the parameters. The final act of this intermediate initialization of the straight-line animation process ends with a setInterval( ) function, which invokes the actual animation function repeatedly.

The interval identifier is also preserved as a property of the animation object, rather than having an extra global variable cluttering up the document.

The repeated doSLAnimation( ) function moves the visible object toward its destination until the element approaches or reaches the target coordinates. When it can go no further, the element is explicitly positioned at the destination, and the interval identifier is cleared to stop the iterations.

All coordinate values are in the page-absolute coordinate system, as these values are ultimately assigned to the positioned element to start and end the animation. If you wish to align the start and/or end points of the animated element with a body content element, use Recipe 13.8 to determine the absolute position of the fixed-location element, and then use those values as parameters to initSLAnime( ). The straight-line path can be at any angle (including perfectly vertical or horizontal) and in any direction. But be careful about specifying coordinates that are beyond the browser window's width: you can lose an element that is off the page and out of view.

If you want to animate an element to follow a more complex path, you can string together invocations of the initSLAnime( ) function, but be sure to allow each setInterval( ) iteration to complete its task. The simplest way to begin is to assign one more property to the anime object, called next, and initialize it to zero. Because the initAnime( ) function is called from a different place in the script (and repeatedly), this new property value must preserve its value from one leg to the next. Thus, the object property assignment statement lets an existing value persist into the next initialization:

```
...
next: (anime.next) ? anime.next : 0,
...
```

Next, create a controlling function that contains an array of coordinate pairs for the start and end positions of each straight line comprising your complex path. For example, here is a version that provides three paths to make up a triangle:

```
function animatePolygon(elemID) {
    // prepare anime object for next leg
    initAnime( );
    // create array of coordinate points
    var coords = new Array( )
    coords[0] = [200, 200, 100, 400];
    coords[1] = [100, 400, 300, 400];
    coords[2] = [300, 400, 200, 200];
    // pass next coordinate group in sequence based on anime.next value
    if (anime.next < coords.length) {
        initSLAnime(elemID, coords[anime.next][0], coords[anime.next][1],
        coords[anime.next][2], coords[anime.next][3], 10);
        // increment for next leg
        anime.next++;
    } else {
```

```
                // reset 'next' counter after all legs complete
                anime.next = 0;
            }
        }
    }
```

Other changes include moving the `initAnime()` function call from `initSLAnime()` to the new `animatePolygon()` function. Finally, in `doSLAnimation()`, after the interval is cleared following a completion of one leg, invoke the `animatePolygon()` function again to get the next leg going, passing the element ID from the current anime object:

```
        animatePolygon(anime.elemID);
```

Employ as many coordinate points as you like to provide the animation path. You do not have to return the element to its original position if you don't want to.

An optional sixth parameter, an integer, represents the relative velocity of the animation. Speed is influenced by the size of the jump during each iteration of the `doSLAnimation()` function. The default value is 1, which is pretty slow. Users may expect a little more animated motion, for which a value of 10 works nicely. But you can experiment with your content and layout to find the optimum speed. As well as experiment with the second parameter of the `setInterval()` method (with much higher numbers than shown in the solution) to move in small steps at even slower speeds.

Be aware that the perceived speed of the animated element will not be constant across all browsers or computers. This is not animation in the same sense as time-based media displayed in dedicated environments such as Flash. The trade-off over the lack of temporal precision is that you can animate standard HTML elements and have the animated elements overlay other content anywhere on the page—you're not limited to the embedded Flash rectangle.

See Also

Recipe 13.8 for obtaining coordinates of elements within the body; Recipe 3.7 for creating a custom object; Recipe 13.10 for animation in a circular path.

13.10 Animating Circular Element Paths

Problem

You want to animate the position of an element in a circular path.

Solution

To animate a positioned element along a circular path, link the *animeCirc.js* library (Example 13-3 in the Discussion) to your page and invoke the `initCircAnime()` function with five parameters in the following sequence:

1. ID of animated element (as string)
2. x coordinate of start/end point of circle

3. y coordinate of start/end point of circle

4. Even integer value specifying the number of render points in the circle

5. Integer value of relative radius of the circle

A typical set of values to put an element into motion might be as follows:

```
initCircAnime("rounder", 200, 200, 36, 10);
```

Discussion

The process for circular animation is similar to the straight-line animation of Recipe 13.9, but trigonometry assists in prescribing the path for the element. Example 13-3 shows the *animeCirc.js* library containing the code that performs the animation.

Example 13-3. The animeCirc.js library for circular animation

```
// animation object holds numerous properties related to motion
var anime = new Object();

// initialize default anime object
function initAnime() {
    anime = {elemID:"",
            xStart:0,
            yStart:0,
            xCurr:0,
            yCurr:0,
            next:1,
            pts:1,
            radius:1,
            interval:null
            };
}

// stuff animation object with necessary explicit and calculated values
function initCircAnime(elemID, startX, startY, pts, radius) {
    initAnime();
    anime.elemID = elemID;
    anime.xCurr = anime.xStart = startX;
    anime.yCurr = anime.yStart = startY;
    anime.pts = pts;
    anime.radius = radius;
    // set element's start position
    document.getElementById(elemID).style.left = startX + "px";
    document.getElementById(elemID).style.top = startY + "px";
    // start the repeated invocation of the animation
    anime.interval = setInterval("doCircAnimation()", 10);
}

function doCircAnimation() {
    if (anime.next < anime.pts) {
        var x = anime.xCurr +
            Math.round(Math.cos(anime.next * (Math.PI/(anime.pts/2))) * anime.radius);
        var y = anime.yCurr +
```

Example 13-3. The animeCirc.js library for circular animation (continued)

```
        Math.round(Math.sin(anime.next * (Math.PI/(anime.pts/2)))) * anime.radius);
      document.getElementById(anime.elemID). style.left = x + "px";
      document.getElementById(anime.elemID). style.top = y + "px";
      anime.xCurr = x;
      anime.yCurr = y;
      anime.next++;
   } else {
      document.getElementById(anime.elemID).style.left = anime.xStart + "px";
      document.getElementById(anime.elemID).style.top = anime.yStart + "px";
      clearInterval(anime.interval);
   }
}
// using eventsManager.js library
addOnLoadEvent(initAnime);
```

The library begins by defining an abstract animation object that gets initialized each time a circular path runs. Your scripts invoke the `initCircAnime( )` function, which assigns parameter values to the anime object's properties. The function that executes repeatedly in response to `setInterval( )` comes at the library's end.

The smoothness of the circular motion is controlled by the number of points along the circle at which the display should be updated. This value becomes the upper limit of `anime.next` in the `if` clause of `doCircAnimation( )`. To accomplish a full circle, the value by which `Math.PI` is divided in the next two lines must be one-half the maximum value in the condition. For any given combination of values, the radius of the circle is controlled by the multiplier at the end of the two statements containing `Math.PI`. The value (preserved as `anime.radius`) is not a straight pixel measure, but rather a factor that governs the radius. The larger the number, the larger the radius.

If you assign larger values for `anime.pts` (such as 72), the animation is smoother because the arcs between refresh points are much smaller. This also means that the motion is slower because the interval time (at 10 milliseconds) is essentially whirling as quickly as it can. On the other hand, too few refresh points, while faster, may appear too jerky for your users.

See Also

Recipe 13.9 for straight-line animation; Recipe 3.7 for creating a custom object.

13.11 Creating a Draggable Element

Problem

You want a user to be able to click on and drag an element from one location on the page to another.

Solution

Use the load event queue manager from Recipe 9.2, the DHTML API from Recipe 13.3 and the *dragManager.js* library (Example 13-4 in the Discussion) to set up elements to drag around the page. The *dragManager.js* library is wired to expect one or more absolute-positioned elements whose class attribute is set to draggable. For example, here is the HTML for a pair of images that are set to be draggable:

```
<img id="imgA" class="draggable" src="widget1.jpg"
width="120" height="90" border="0" alt="Primary draggable widget">
<img id="imgB" class="draggable" src="widget2.jpg"
width="120" height="90" border="0" alt="Secondary draggable widget">
```

Set up the positioned elements by way of style sheet definitions. For example, the style sheets for the two img elements shown here are as follows:

```
<style type="text/css">
#imgA {position:absolute;
        left: 35%;
        top: 20%;
        width: 230px;
        height: 102px;
        border: solid black 1px;
        z-index: 0
       }
#imgB {
        position: absolute;
        left: 40%;
        top: 25%;
        width: 281px;
        height: 100px;
        border: solid black 1px;
        z-index: 0
       }
.draggable:hover {cursor: pointer}
</style>
```

All other initializations and event handler assignments are performed by the self-initializing libraries.

Discussion

Example 13-4 shows the *dragManager.js* library code. It should be linked into your page following the events and DHTML API libraries, as follows:

```
<script src="eventsManager.js"></script>
<script src="DHTML3API.js"></script>
<script src="dragManager.js"></script>
```

The library accommodates as many draggable elements as you like on the page, without conflicting with static items.

Example 13-4. The dragManager.js library for dragging elements on the page

```
// dragObject contains data for currently dragged element
var dragObject = {
    selectedObject : null,
    offsetX : 0,
    offsetY : 0,
    // invoked onmousedown
    engageDrag : function(evt) {
        evt = (evt) ? evt : window.event;
        dragObject.selectedObject = (evt.target) ? evt.target : evt.srcElement;
        var target = (evt.target) ? evt.target : evt.srcElement;
        var dragContainer = target;
        // in case event target is nested in draggable container
        while (target.className != "draggable" && target.parentNode) {
            target = dragContainer = target.parentNode;
        }
        if (dragContainer) {
            dragObject.selectedObject = dragContainer;
            DHTMLAPI.setZIndex(dragContainer, 100);
            dragObject.setOffsets(evt, dragContainer);
            dragObject.setDragEvents();
            evt.cancelBubble = true;
            evt.returnValue = false;
            if (evt.stopPropagation) {
                evt.stopPropagation();
                evt.preventDefault();
            }
        }
        return false;
    },
    // calculate offset of mousedown within draggable element
    setOffsets : function (evt, dragContainer) {
        if (evt.pageX) {
            dragObject.offsetX = evt.pageX - ((dragContainer.offsetLeft) ?
                    dragContainer.offsetLeft : dragContainer.left);
            dragObject.offsetY = evt.pageY - ((dragContainer.offsetTop) ?
                    dragContainer.offsetTop : dragContainer.top);
        } else if (evt.offsetX || evt.offsetY) {
            dragObject.offsetX = evt.offsetX - ((evt.offsetX < -2) ?
                    0 : document.body.scrollLeft);
            dragObject.offsetY = evt.offsetY - ((evt.offsetY < -2) ?
                    0 : document.body.scrollTop);
        }
    },
    // invoked onmousemove
    dragIt : function (evt) {
        evt = (evt) ? evt : window.event;
        var obj = dragObject;
        if (evt.pageX) {
            DHTMLAPI.moveTo(obj.selectedObject, (evt.pageX - obj.offsetX),
                (evt.pageY - obj.offsetY));
        } else if (evt.clientX || evt.clientY) {
            DHTMLAPI.moveTo(obj.selectedObject, (evt.clientX - obj.offsetX),
```

```
                (evt.clientY - obj.offsetY));
        }
        evt.cancelBubble = true;
        evt.returnValue = false;
    },
    // invoked onmouseup
    releaseDrag : function (evt) {
        DHTMLAPI.setZIndex(dragObject.selectedObject, 0);
        dragObject.clearDragEvents();
        dragObject.selectedObject = null;
    },
    // set temporary events
    setDragEvents : function () {
        addEvent(document, "mousemove", dragObject.dragIt, false);
        addEvent(document, "mouseup", dragObject.releaseDrag, false);
    },
    // remove temporary events
    clearDragEvents : function () {
        removeEvent(document, "mousemove", dragObject.dragIt, false);
        removeEvent(document, "mouseup", dragObject.releaseDrag, false);
    },
    // initialize, assigning mousedown events to all
    // elements with class="draggable" attributes
    init : function () {
        var elems = [];
        if (document.all) {
            // IE 5 & 5.5 don't know wildcard for getElementsByTagName
            // so use document.body.all, which lets IE 4 work OK
            elems = document.body.all;
        } else if (document.body && document.body.getElementsByTagName) {
            elems = document.body.getElementsByTagName("*");
        }
        for (var i = 0; i < elems.length; i++) {
            if (elems[i].className.match(/draggable/)) {
                addEvent(elems[i], "mousedown", dragObject.engageDrag, false);
            }
        }
    }
};
// set onload event via eventsManager.js
addOnLoadEvent(dragObject.init);
```

This library is designed to be encapsulated in one global object, named dragObject. Because only one element can be dragged at a time with this library, the global object has a one-to-one relationship with the element being dragged. You will see numerous references within the code to the global object. This because many methods are invoked by events from elements—elements that provide the context for the method execution. Therefore, this references won't point to dragObject to help us read and write properties or invoke internal methods. We supply that reference explicitly.

The library begins by declaring a few properties that convey information between initial activation of the drag and the actual drag operation. One, selectedObj, maintains a reference of the element being dragged. The offsetX and offsetY pair get set in the engage( ) method, and are used constantly during the positioning tasks while dragging.

Jumping down for a moment to the end of the library, you find the init( ) method. Its job is to bind mousedown event handler functions (the dragObject.engageDrag( ) method call) to all elements on the page whose class attribute has "draggable" assigned to it. This works even if an element has multiple class names assigned to it (through the regular expression matching technique).

It is the engageDrag( ) method (back at the top of the library) that gets the ball rolling. In addition to obtaining a reference to the draggable element (including finding the actual draggable element in case a mousedown event fired on one of its child nodes), it also performs the following tasks:

- Sets the z-index CSS property to an arbitrarily high value to make sure the element will be layered above other draggable elements
- Determines the number of pixels offset from the top-left corner of the element where the mousedown event occurred so that when the element is dragged, the offset stays constant
- Binds mousemove and mouseup events to the element about to be dragged
- Prevents any further propagation or action of the mousedown event (needed primarily for Macintosh browsers)

The mousemove event is bound to the dragIt( ) method. As the method is repeatedly invoked by the rapidly-firing event, the DHTML API library repositions the element accordingly to event properties that report the coordinates of the events. Corrections for the offsets are taken into account.

When the mouseup event fires, it means that the user has stopped dragging the element. It's time to clean up in the releaseDrag( ) method. First the z-index value is reset to zero. Then the temporarily set mousemove and mouseup events are unbound from the dragged element. Finally, the pointer to the dragged element (selectedObject) is nulled out.

The last statement of the library self-initializes the library with the help of the *eventsManager.js* library (Recipe 9.3), which, like the *DHTML3API.js* library, must be loaded ahead of the *dragManager.js* library. No preparations (beyond the class naming of draggable items) are necessary.

If you want to limit the region within which an element can be dragged, you can define a rectangular boundary and keep the element within that zone. To accomplish this, first define a dragObject property with coordinate points of the space:

```
zone: {left:120, top:120, right:400, bottom:400},
```

Then modify the dragIt( ) method in Example 13-4 so that it won't allow dragging outside of the zone:

```
dragIt : function (evt) {
    evt = (evt) ? evt : window.event;
    var x, y, width, height;
    var obj = dragObject;
    if (evt.pageX) {
        x = evt.pageX - obj.offsetX;
        y = evt.pageY - obj.offsetY;
    } else if (evt.clientX || evt.clientY) {
        x = evt.clientX - obj.offsetX;
        y = evt.clientY - obj.offsetY;
    }
    width = DHTMLAPI.getElementWidth(obj.selectedObj);
    height = DHTMLAPI.getElementHeight(obj.selectedObj);
    x = (x < obj.zone.left) ? obj.zone.left :
        ((x + width > obj.zone.right) ? obj.zone.right - width : x);
    y = (y < obj.zone.top) ? obj.zone.top :
        ((y + height > obj.zone.bottom) ? obj.zone.bottom - height : y);
    DHTMLAPI.moveTo(obj.selectedObject, x, y);
    evt.cancelBubble = true;
    evt.returnValue = false;
},
```

The modifications take advantage of the DHTML API's functions that easily obtain the width and height of the positioned element. Then the values of the intended coordinates are tested against the zone's points. If the intended position is outside the box, the coordinate value is set to the maximum value along the edge. This allows an element to reach an edge in one axis and still be draggable up and down along the edge.

See Also

Recipe 13.3 for the required DHTML API library; Recipe 11.13 for IE 6 and 7 CSS-compatibility mode issues.

13.12 Scrolling div Content

Problem

You want to let users scroll up and down through content located in a separate positioned viewable area on the page, without resorting to system (overflow) scrollbars.

Solution

This solution requires some HTML elements that are used as both scrollable content containers and the buttons that control the scrolling. You can see the HTML portion in Example 13-5 of the Discussion. You then use the *scrollButtons.js* library, shown in Example 13-6 of the Discussion, as the script basis for controlling scrollable regions on your page.

Your HTML page needs to link in three JavaScript libraries: *eventsManager.js* from Recipe 9.3, *DHTML3API.js* from Recipe 13.3 and *scrollButtons.js*. Although the DHTML API library is self-initializing, you can feed specifics to *scrollButtons.js* via a load event handler in the HTML page. Due to a "race" condition in IE, the scroll initialization must start in its own thread via setTimeout():

```
addOnLoadEvent(function() {setTimeout("initScrollers()",0)});
```

The initScrollers() function invokes an object constructor specifying HTML details of each instance of a scrollable region on the page. For example, the following initScrollers() function creates a JavaScript object that governs the scrolling activity for one region:

```
function initScrollers() {
    scrollBars[0] = new scrollBar("outerWrapper0", "innerWrapper0", "lineup0",
        "linedown0");
}
```

Discussion

The vital HTML portion of this recipe is shown in Example 13-5. The scrolling region consists of a series of nested div elements. The content container is a pair of nested containers. The outer wrapper defines the rectangular boundaries of the viewport through which the content is visible, while the second positioned container, innerWrapper0, holds the actual content to scroll. The trailing number of the IDs in this example helps illustrate that you can have multiple scrolling regions on the same page, and they will not collide as long as you use unique IDs for the components.

Example 13-5. HTML scrolling region and controller

```css
<style type="text/css">
body {height: 400px}
#pseudoWindow0 {
            position: absolute;
            top: 200px;
            left: 45%
            }
#outerWrapper0 {
            position: absolute;
            top: 0px;
            left: 0px;
            height: 150px;
            width: 100px;
            overflow: hidden;
            border-top: 4px solid #666666;
            border-left: 4px solid #666666;
            border-right: 4px solid #cccccc;
            border-bottom: 4px solid #cccccc;
            background-color: #ffffff
            }
#innerWrapper0 {
```

Example 13-5. HTML scrolling region and controller (continued)

```
                position: absolute;
                top: 0px;
                left: 0px;
                padding: 5px;
                font: 10px Arial, Helvetica, sans-serif}
</style>
...
<div id="pseudoWindow0">
    <div id="outerWrapper0">
        <div id="innerWrapper0">
            <p style="margin-top:0em"> Lorem ipsum dolor sit amet, consectetaur ...</p>
        </div>
    </div>
    <img id="lineup0" class="lineup" src="scrollUp.gif" height="16" width="16"
        alt="Scroll Up" style="position:absolute; top:10px; left:112px" />
    <img id="linedown0" class="linedown" src="scrollDn.gif" height="16" width="16"
        alt="Scroll Down"  style="position:absolute; top:128px; left:112px" />
</div>
```

Figure 13-3 illustrates the look of the scrolling pseudowindow assembly based on the HTML of Example 13-5.

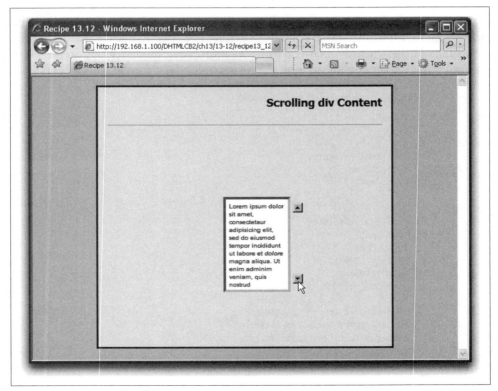

Figure 13-3. A custom scrolling container

Buttons that perform the scrolling (vertical scrolling in this case) are simple img elements. The arrow img elements are absolute-positioned within the context of the outermost div element (pseudoWindow0). If some other scripting needs to move the outermost div element, the buttons keep their positions relative to the whole set of components. The job of the associated script library, *scrollButtons.js* (shown in Example 13-6), is to slide the inner wrapper element up or down. Its content is clipped by the outer wrapper element, whose overflow style property is set to hidden.

Example 13-6. The scrollButtons.js library

```
var scrollEngaged = false;
var scrollInterval;
var scrollBars = new Array( );

function scrollBar(ownerID, ownerContentID, upID, dnID) {
    this.ownerID = ownerID;
    this.ownerContentID = ownerContentID;
    this.index = scrollBars.length;
    this.upButton = document.getElementById(upID);
    this.dnButton = document.getElementById(dnID);
    this.upButton.index = this.index;
    this.dnButton.index = this.index;

    this.ownerHeight = parseInt(DHTMLAPI.getComputedStyle(this.ownerID, "height"));

    this.contentElem = document.getElementById(ownerContentID);
    this.contentFontSize = parseInt(DHTMLAPI.getComputedStyle(this.ownerContentID,
        "font-size"));
    this.contentScrollHeight = (this.contentElem.scrollHeight) ?
        this.contentElem.scrollHeight : this.contentElem.offsetHeight;
    setScrollEvents(this.upButton, this.dnButton);
}

function setScrollEvents(upButton, dnButton) {
    addEvent(upButton, "mousedown", handleScrollClick, false);
    addEvent(upButton, "mouseup", handleScrollStop, false);
    addEvent(upButton, "contextmenu", blockEvent, false);

    addEvent(dnButton, "mousedown", handleScrollClick, false);
    addEvent(dnButton, "mouseup", handleScrollStop, false);
    addEvent(dnButton, "contextmenu", blockEvent, false);
}

function handleScrollStop( ) {
    scrollEngaged = false;
}

function blockEvent(evt) {
    evt = (evt) ? evt : event;
    evt.cancelBubble = true;
    return false;
}
```

Example 13-6. The scrollButtons.js library (continued)

```
function handleScrollClick(evt) {
    var fontSize;
    evt = (evt) ? evt : event;
    var target = (evt.target) ? evt.target : evt.srcElement;
    var index = target.index;
    fontSize = scrollBars[index].contentFontSize;
    fontSize = (target.className == "lineup") ? fontSize : -fontSize;
    scrollEngaged = true;
    scrollBy(index, parseInt(fontSize));
    scrollInterval = setInterval("scrollBy(" + index + ", " +
        parseInt(fontSize) + ")", 100);
    evt.cancelBubble = true;
    return false;
}

function scrollBy(index, px) {
    var scroller = scrollBars[index];
    var elem = document.getElementById(scroller.ownerContentID);
    var top = parseInt(DHTMLAPI.getComputedStyle(elem, "top"));
    var scrollHeight = parseInt(scroller.contentScrollHeight);
    var height = scroller.ownerHeight;
    if (scrollEngaged && top + px >= -scrollHeight + height && top + px <= 0) {
        DHTMLAPI.moveBy(elem, 0, px);
    } else {
        clearInterval(scrollInterval);
    }
}
```

The library employs an object-oriented approach by creating an abstract object that holds information about a pair of scroll buttons and the content containers. This simplifies an implementation that employs multiple scrolling boxes. At the start of the library, a few global variables are defined that preserve the collection of scroller objects and important state values during scrolling.

The scrollBar( ) constructor function for the scroller objects receives four string parameters: the IDs for the outer wrapper, the inner wrapper, and the two scroll buttons. The purpose of this constructor is to perform some one-time calculations and initializations per scroller, facilitating the click-and-hold scroll action later on. To help the buttons' event handlers know which set of scrollers is operating, an index value, corresponding to the position within the scrollBars array, is assigned to index properties of the two button elements. The scrollBars.length value represents the numeric index of the scrollBars item being generated because the scrollBars array has not yet been assigned the finished object, meaning that the array length is one less than it will be after the object finishes its construction.

Each scroller object invokes the setScrollEvents( ) function, right after the scroller object is created. The function assigns event handlers to the button images, including one that prevents a click-and-hold action from displaying the context menu (on the Macintosh).

Next come a group of event handler functions. All that handleScrollStop( ) does is turn off the flag that other functions use to permit repeated scrolling, while blockEvent( ) stops the contextmenu event from carrying out its default action. At the heart of this application is the handleScrollClick( ) event handler, which takes care of scrolling in both directions. Scrolling for this example is line-by-line, so the content's font size is the approximation used to determine the scroll jump size. The event targets are img elements, each of which is assigned an index value property corresponding to the scroller object's array position. Further identifying each button is the class attribute, which categorizes a button as either an up or down (by one line) action button. Scrolling the content upward requires subtracting the height of one line from the current vertical position of the element. One immediate call to the scrollBy( ) function comes within the function to let the buttons react instantaneously to a quick click. After that, the scrollBy( ) function is invoked every 100 milliseconds until other conditions (releasing the mouse button) turn off scrolling.

Adjusting the position of the inner content wrapper is the job of the scrollBy( ) function. It receives as parameters both the index number of the scroller object and the number of pixels to increment the vertical position. If the content is not scrolled completely to the top or bottom, the DHTML API moveBy( ) function moves the element along the vertical axis the number of pixels instructed by the calling function. But if the scrolling has reached an end point, the interval timer is turned off, and further holding of the mouse button over the image scrolls no more in the current direction.

The user interface possibilities for this kind of scrolling view port are endless. The code in this recipe can be adapted to a multitude of scroll controller buttons, whether they are images, hyperlinks, image maps, or widgets constructed out of div elements and text. It's just a question of assigning the desired event handlers to the hot spots and making sure that those spots have index properties associated with scrollBar objects (as shown in the scrollBar( ) constructor function).

At the same time, however, some designer choices can be disastrous. Using mouse rollover events to trigger the scroll may not be a good idea, despite its practice in some sites. Autoscrolling can also be frustrating if the content is important because good autoscrolling needs to be smoother (a scroll size of only one or two pixels), yet the time it takes to scroll through the content and start over can be frustratingly long for impatient visitors.

Choosing an object-oriented approach to the application is not as arbitrary as it might seem. The core, frequently repeated routines (especially the scrollBy( ) function invoked at short time intervals), rely on several properties of the content container and its outer wrapper. Some of those properties must be accessed (ultimately) through the DHTMLAPI.getComputedStyle( ) method, which must perform a fair amount of processing to do the job right. It is inefficient to invoke that function over and over while the interval is firing away. The values that don't change once the wrapper elements exist (such as dimensions) should be obtained only once. Preserving those values in an object representing the scroller simply makes good programming sense. As a by-product, the `scrollBar` object lets us preserve additional one-time calculated values throughout the entire session. Moreover, we can limit the button event handlers so that they are not active until the page is loaded. Premature clicking of the buttons causes no errors because the events aren't yet bound to the elements.

More about this application could be generalized, rather than governed by fixed-style sheet values for positioning. You can see an example of this (and the additional complexity it brings to the code) in Recipe 13.13, which produces a more fully loaded vertical scrollbar that controls the same kind of content.

See Also

Recipe 13.13 for a more complex scrollbar; Recipe 3.8 for creating a custom object; Recipe 11.12 for reading default style sheet property values as they apply to a rendered element.

13.13 Creating a Custom Scrollbar

Problem

You want to let users scroll through a separate block of content within the page via a scrollbar containing line and page regions, as well as a draggable scrollbar thumb.

Solution

This solution requires numerous HTML elements that are used as both scrollable content containers and a simulated scrollbar. You can see the HTML portion in Example 13-7 of the Discussion. You then use the *scrollBars.js* library, shown in Example 13-8 of the Discussion, as the script basis for both generating and controlling customized scrollbars on your page.

Your HTML page needs to link in three JavaScript libraries: *eventsManager.js* from Recipe 9.3, *DHTML3API.js* from Recipe 13.3, and *scrollBars.js*. The libraries are self-initializing.

Insert page-specific details by two calls to the *scrollBars.js* library at load time. For example, the following `initScrollbars()` function both creates a JavaScript object that governs the scrollbar associated with a fixed set of HTML elements, and creates the HTML pieces for the visible scrollbar:

```
function initScrollbars() {
    scrollBars[0] = new scrollBar("pseudoWindow", "outerWrapper", "innerWrapper");
    scrollBars[0].appendScroll();
}
addOnLoadEvent(function() {setTimeout("initScrollbars()", 0)});
```

The `initScrollbars()` function needs to operate in its own thread to avoid a "race" condition with the libraries.

Discussion

This solution is an extension of Recipe 13.12, but with far more complex issues involving the dragging of the scrollbar thumb and synchronizing the scroll of the document with the thumb location. It also employs dynamic creation of the scrollbar components (consisting of images and styled `div` elements) so that precise positioning isn't necessary: the positioning of elements depends on the specified dimensions of the content container and its various style sheet settings (borders, padding, and the like). Figure 13-4 shows the effect created by this solution.

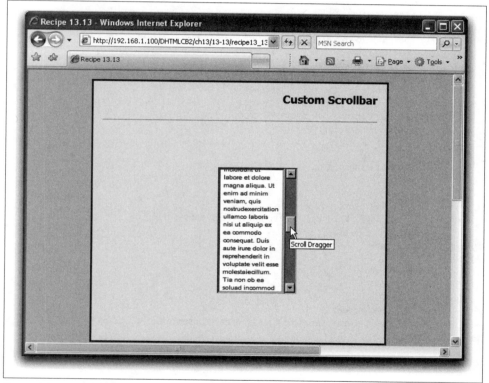

Figure 13-4. Scripted scrollbars for a div element

Two previous recipes play important roles in this solution. First is the DHTML API of Recipe 13.3. Second is the element dragging code from Recipe 13.12. One of the functions, `dragIt()`, is tailored to this scrollbar application, so all of the dragging functions are embedded within the *scrollBars.js* file.

The solution begins with the HTML for the pseudowindow container and its scrollable content, shown in Example 13-7. Missing is the HTML for the scrollbars themselves because they are generated by code later.

Example 13-7. HTML scrollbar region awaiting scripted scrollbars

```
<style type="text/css">
body {height: 400px}
#pseudoWindow {
            position: absolute;
            top: 160px;
            left: 45%
            }
#outerWrapper {
            position: absolute;
            top: 0px;
            left: 0px;
            height: 200px;
            width: 100px;
            overflow: hidden;
            border-top: 4px solid #666666;
            border-left: 4px solid #666666;
            border-right: 4px solid #cccccc;
            border-bottom: 4px solid #cccccc;
            background-color: #ffffff;
            }
#innerWrapper {
            position:absolute;
            top: 0px;
            left: 0px;
            padding: 5px;
            font: 10px Verdana, Ariel, Helvetica, sans-serif
            }
#myp {margin-top: 0em}
</style>
...
<div id="pseudoWindow" >
    <div id="outerWrapper">
        <div id="innerWrapper">
            <p id="myp">Lorem ipsum dolor sit amet, consectetaur ....</p>
        </div>
    </div>
</div>
```

Example 13-8 shows the extensive *scrollBars.js* library. It is divided into four sections: Scrollbar Creation, Event Handler Functions, Scrollbar Tracking, and Element Dragging (for the scrollbar thumb).

Example 13-8. The scrollBars.js library

```
/**********************
    SCROLLBAR CREATION
**********************/
// Global variables
var scrollEngaged = false;
var scrollInterval;
var scrollBars = new Array();

// Scrollbar constructor function
function scrollBar(rootID, ownerID, ownerContentID) {
    this.rootID = rootID;
    this.ownerID = ownerID;
    this.ownerContentID = ownerContentID;
    this.index = scrollBars.length;

    // one-time evaluations for use by other scroll bar manipulations
    this.rootElem = document.getElementById(rootID);
    this.ownerElem = document.getElementById(ownerID);
    this.contentElem = document.getElementById(ownerContentID);
    this.ownerHeight = parseInt(DHTMLAPI.getComputedStyle(ownerID, "height"));
    this.ownerWidth = parseInt(DHTMLAPI.getComputedStyle(ownerID, "width"));
    this.ownerBorder = parseInt(DHTMLAPI.getComputedStyle(ownerID, "border-top-width")) * 2;
    this.contentHeight = Math.abs(parseInt(this.contentElem.style.top));
    this.contentWidth = this.contentElem.offsetWidth;
    this.contentFontSize = parseInt(DHTMLAPI.getComputedStyle(this.ownerContentID,
        "font-size"));
    this.contentScrollHeight = this.contentElem.scrollHeight;
    // Boolean flag for overflow requiring scroll thumb
    this.overflow = this.contentScrollHeight >= this.ownerHeight;

    // create quirks object whose default (CSS-compatible) values
    // are zero; pertinent values for quirks mode filled in later
    this.quirks = {on:false, ownerBorder:0, scrollBorder:0, contentPadding:0};
    if (navigator.appName == "Microsoft Internet Explorer" &&
        navigator.userAgent.indexOf("Win") != -1 &&
        (typeof document.compatMode == "undefined" ||
        document.compatMode == "BackCompat")) {
        this.quirks.on = true;
        this.quirks.ownerBorder = this.ownerBorder;
        this.quirks.contentPadding = parseInt(DHTMLAPI.getComputedStyle(ownerContentID,
        "padding"));
    }

    // determined at scrollbar initialization time
    this.scrollWrapper = null;
    this.upButton = null;
    this.dnButton = null;
    this.thumb = null;
    this.buttonLength = 0;
    this.thumbLength = 0;
    this.scrollWrapperLength = 0
    this.dragZone = {left:0, top:0, right:0, bottom:0}
```

Example 13-8. The scrollBars.js library (continued)

```
    // build a physical scrollbar for the root div
    this.appendScroll = appendScrollBar;
}

// Create scrollbar elements and append to the "pseudo-window"
function appendScrollBar( ) {
    // button and thumb image sizes (programmer customizable)
    var imgH = 16;
    var imgW = 16;
    var thumbH = 27;

    // "up" arrow, needed first to help size scrollWrapper
    var lineup = document.createElement("img");
    lineup.id = "lineup" + (scrollBars.length - 1);
    lineup.className = "lineup";
    lineup.index = this.index;
    lineup.src = "scrollUp.gif";
    lineup.height = imgH;
    lineup.width = imgW;
    lineup.alt = "Scroll Up";
    lineup.style.position = "absolute";
    lineup.style.top = "0px";
    lineup.style.left = "0px";

    // scrollWrapper defines "page" region color and 3-D borders
    var wrapper = document.createElement("div");
    wrapper.id = "scrollWrapper" + (scrollBars.length - 1);
    wrapper.className = "scrollWrapper";
    wrapper.index = this.index;
    wrapper.style.position = "absolute";
    wrapper.style.visibility = "hidden";
    wrapper.style.top = "0px";
    wrapper.style.left = this.ownerWidth + this.ownerBorder -
        this.quirks.ownerBorder + "px";
    wrapper.style.borderTop = "2px solid #666666";
    wrapper.style.borderLeft = "2px solid #666666";
    wrapper.style.borderRight= "2px solid #cccccc";
    wrapper.style.borderBottom= "2px solid #cccccc";
    wrapper.style.backgroundColor = "#999999";
    if (this.quirks.on) {
        this.quirks.scrollBorder = 2;
    }
    wrapper.style.width = lineup.width + (this.quirks.scrollBorder * 2) + "px";
    wrapper.style.height = this.ownerHeight + (this.ownerBorder - 4) -
        (this.quirks.scrollBorder * 2) + "px";

    // "down" arrow
    var linedn = document.createElement("img");
    linedn.id = "linedown" + (scrollBars.length - 1);
    linedn.className = "linedown";
    linedn.index = this.index;
```

Example 13-8. The scrollBars.js library (continued)

```
linedn.src = "scrollDn.gif";
linedn.height = imgH;
linedn.width = imgW;
linedn.alt = "Scroll Down";
linedn.style.position = "absolute";
linedn.style.top = parseInt(this.ownerHeight) + (this.ownerBorder - 4) -
    (this.quirks.ownerBorder) - linedn.height + "px";
linedn.style.left = "0px";

// fixed-size draggable thumb
var thumb = document.createElement("img");
thumb.id = "thumb" + (scrollBars.length - 1);
thumb.className = "draggable";
thumb.index = this.index;
thumb.src = "thumb.gif";
thumb.height = thumbH;
thumb.width = imgW;
thumb.alt = "Scroll Dragger";
thumb.style.position = "absolute";
thumb.style.top = lineup.height + "px";
thumb.style.width = imgW + "px";
thumb.style.height = thumbH + "px";
thumb.style.left = "0px";
// set visibility per overflow
thumb.style.visibility = (this.overflow) ? "visible" : "hidden";

// fill in scrollBar object properties from rendered elements
this.upButton = wrapper.appendChild(lineup);
this.thumb = wrapper.appendChild(thumb);
this.dnButton = wrapper.appendChild(linedn);
this.scrollWrapper = this.rootElem.appendChild(wrapper);
this.buttonLength = imgH;
this.thumbLength = thumbH;
this.scrollWrapperLength =
    parseInt(DHTMLAPI.getComputedStyle(this.scrollWrapper.id, "height"));
this.dragZone.left = 0;
this.dragZone.top = this.buttonLength;
this.dragZone.right = this.buttonLength;
this.dragZone.bottom = this.scrollWrapperLength - this.buttonLength -
    (this.quirks.scrollBorder * 2)

// all events processed by scrollWrapper element
// if overflow is true
if (this.overflow) {
    this.scrollWrapper.onmousedown = handleScrollClick;
    this.scrollWrapper.onmouseup = handleScrollStop;
    this.scrollWrapper.oncontextmenu = blockEvent;
    this.scrollWrapper.ondrag = blockEvent;
}

// OK to show
this.scrollWrapper.style.visibility = "visible";
```

Example 13-8. The scrollBars.js library (continued)

```
        // handle Opera delay in reporting newly appended element height
        if (navigator.userAgent.indexOf("Opera") != -1) {
            var me = this;
            setTimeout(function( ) {
                me.scrollWrapperLength =
                    parseInt(DHTMLAPI.getComputedStyle(me.scrollWrapper.id, "height"));
                me.dragZone.bottom = me.scrollWrapperLength - me.buttonLength;
            }, 0);
        }

        // bind mousedown event to thumb
        dragObject.init( );

}


/***************************
    EVENT HANDLER FUNCTIONS
***************************/
// onmouse up handler
function handleScrollStop( ) {
    scrollEngaged = false;
}

// Prevent Mac context menu while holding down mouse button
function blockEvent(evt) {
    evt = (evt) ? evt : event;
    evt.cancelBubble = true;
    return false;
}

// click event handler
function handleScrollClick(evt) {
    var fontSize, contentHeight;
    evt = (evt) ? evt : event;
    var target = (evt.target) ? evt.target : evt.srcElement;
    target = (target.nodeType == 3) ? target.parentNode : target;
    var index = target.index;
    fontSize = scrollBars[index].contentFontSize;
    switch (target.className) {
        case "lineup" :
            scrollEngaged = true;
            scrollBy(index, parseInt(fontSize));
            scrollInterval = setInterval("scrollBy(" + index + ", " +
                parseInt(fontSize) + ")", 100);
            evt.cancelBubble = true;
            return false;
            break;
        case "linedown" :
            scrollEngaged = true;
            scrollBy(index, -(parseInt(fontSize)));
            scrollInterval = setInterval("scrollBy(" + index + ", -" +
                parseInt(fontSize) + ")", 100);
```

Example 13-8. The scrollBars.js library (continued)

```
                evt.cancelBubble = true;
                return false;
                break;
        case "scrollWrapper" :
                scrollEngaged = true;
                var evtY = (evt.offsetY) ? evt.offsetY : ((evt.layerY) ? evt.layerY : -1);
                if (evtY >= 0) {
                    var pageSize = scrollBars[index].ownerHeight - fontSize;
                    var thumbElemStyle = scrollBars[index].thumb.style;
                    // set value negative to push document upward
                    if (evtY > (parseInt(thumbElemStyle.top) +
                        scrollBars[index].thumbLength)) {
                        pageSize = -pageSize;
                    }
                    scrollBy(index, pageSize);
                    scrollInterval = setInterval("scrollBy(" + index + ", " +
                        pageSize + ")", 100);
                    evt.cancelBubble = true;
                    return false;
                }
        }
    }
    return false;
}

// Activate scroll of inner content
function scrollBy(index, px) {
    var scroller = scrollBars[index];
    var elem = document.getElementById(scroller.ownerContentID);
    var top = parseInt(elem.style.top);
    var scrollHeight = parseInt(elem.scrollHeight);
    var height = scroller.ownerHeight;
    if (scrollEngaged && top + px >= -scrollHeight + height && top + px <= 0) {
        DHTMLAPI.moveBy(elem, 0, px);
        updateThumb(index);
    } else if (top + px < -scrollHeight + height) {
        DHTMLAPI.moveTo(elem, 0, -scrollHeight + height - scroller.quirks.contentPadding);
        updateThumb(index);
        clearInterval(scrollInterval);
    } else if (top + px > 0) {
        DHTMLAPI.moveTo(elem, 0, 0);
        updateThumb(index);
        clearInterval(scrollInterval);
    } else {
        clearInterval(scrollInterval);
    }
}

/**********************
    SCROLLBAR TRACKING
**********************/
// Position thumb after scrolling by arrow/page region
function updateThumb(index) {
```

Example 13-8. The scrollBars.js library (continued)

```
    var scroll = scrollBars[index];
    var barLength = scroll.scrollWrapperLength - (scroll.quirks.scrollBorder * 2);
    var buttonLength = scroll.buttonLength;
    barLength -= buttonLength * 2;
    var docElem = scroll.contentElem;
    var docTop = Math.abs(parseInt(docElem.style.top));
    var scrollFactor = docTop/(scroll.contentScrollHeight - scroll.ownerHeight);
    DHTMLAPI.moveTo(scroll.thumb, 0, Math.round((barLength - scroll.thumbLength) *
        scrollFactor) + buttonLength);
}

// Position content per thumb location
function updateScroll( ) {
    var index = dragObject.index;
    var scroller = scrollBars[index];

    var barLength = scroller.scrollWrapperLength - (scroller.quirks.scrollBorder * 2);
    var buttonLength = scroller.buttonLength;
    var thumbLength = scroller.thumbLength;
    var wellTop = buttonLength;
    var wellBottom = barLength - buttonLength - thumbLength;
    var wellSize = wellBottom - wellTop;
    var thumbTop = parseInt(DHTMLAPI.getComputedStyle(scroller.thumb.id, "top"));
    var scrollFactor = (thumbTop - buttonLength)/wellSize;
    var docElem = scroller.contentElem;
    var docTop = Math.abs(parseInt(docElem.style.top));
    var scrollHeight = scroller.contentScrollHeight;
    var height = scroller.ownerHeight;
    DHTMLAPI.moveTo(scroller.ownerContentID, 0, -(Math.round((scrollHeight - height) *
        scrollFactor)));
}
/*******************
   ELEMENT DRAGGING
********************/
// dragObject contains data for currently dragged element
var dragObject = {
    selectedObject : null,
    offsetX : 0,
    offsetY : 0,
    index: 0,
    // invoked onmousedown
    engageDrag : function(evt) {
        evt = (evt) ? evt : window.event;
        var target = (evt.target) ? evt.target : evt.srcElement;
        if (target.id.indexOf("thumb") == 0) {
            var dragContainer = target;
            if (dragContainer) {
                dragObject.selectedObject = dragContainer;
                dragObject.index = dragContainer.index;
                DHTMLAPI.setZIndex(dragContainer, 100);
                dragObject.setOffsets(evt, dragContainer);
                dragObject.setDragEvents( );
```

Example 13-8. The scrollBars.js library (continued)

```
                    evt.cancelBubble = true;
                    evt.returnValue = false;
                    if (evt.stopPropagation) {
                        evt.stopPropagation( );
                        evt.preventDefault( );
                    }
                }
            }
        return false;
    },
    // calculate offset of mousedown within draggable element
    setOffsets : function (evt, dragContainer) {
        if (evt.pageX) {
            dragObject.offsetX = evt.pageX -
                ((typeof dragContainer.offsetLeft == "number") ?
                    dragContainer.offsetLeft : dragContainer.left);
            dragObject.offsetY = evt.pageY -
                ((typeof dragContainer.offsetTop == "number") ?
                    dragContainer.offsetTop : dragContainer.top);
        } else if (evt.offsetX || evt.offsetY) {
            dragObject.offsetX = evt.clientX -
                ((typeof dragContainer.offsetLeft == "number") ?
                    dragContainer.offsetLeft : 0);
            dragObject.offsetY = evt.clientY -
                ((typeof dragContainer.offsetTop == "number") ?
                    dragContainer.offsetTop : 0);
        }
    },
    // invoked onmousemove
    dragIt : function (evt) {
        evt = (evt) ? evt : window.event;
        var x, y, width, height;
        var obj = dragObject;
        if (evt.pageX) {
            x = evt.pageX - obj.offsetX;
            y = evt.pageY - obj.offsetY;
        } else if (evt.clientX || evt.clientY) {
            x = evt.clientX - obj.offsetX;
            y = evt.clientY - obj.offsetY;
        }
        var index = dragObject.index;
        var scroller = scrollBars[index];
        // set dynamically at scrollbar creation
        var zone = scroller.dragZone;
        width = scroller.thumb.width;
        height = scroller.thumb.height;
        x = (x < zone.left) ? zone.left :
            ((x + width > zone.right) ? zone.right - width : x);
        y = (y < zone.top) ? zone.top :
            ((y + height > zone.bottom) ? zone.bottom - height : y);
        DHTMLAPI.moveTo(obj.selectedObject, x, y);
        updateScroll( );
```

Example 13-8. The scrollBars.js library (continued)

```
            evt.cancelBubble = true;
            evt.returnValue = false;
        },
        // invoked onmouseup
        releaseDrag : function (evt) {
            DHTMLAPI.setZIndex(dragObject.selectedObject, 0);
            dragObject.clearDragEvents();
            dragObject.selectedObject = null;
        },
        // set temporary events
        setDragEvents : function () {
            addEvent(document, "mousemove", dragObject.dragIt, false);
            addEvent(document, "mouseup", dragObject.releaseDrag, false);
        },
        // remove temporary events
        clearDragEvents : function () {
            removeEvent(document, "mousemove", dragObject.dragIt, false);
            removeEvent(document, "mouseup", dragObject.releaseDrag, false);
        },
        // initialize, assigning mousedown events to all
        // elements with class="draggable" attributes
        init : function () {
            var elems = [];
            if (document.all) {
                // IE 5 & 5.5 don't know wildcard for getElementsByTagName
                // so use document.body.all, which lets IE 4 work OK
                elems = document.body.all;
            } else if (document.body && document.body.getElementsByTagName) {
                elems = document.body.getElementsByTagName("*");
            }
            for (var i = 0; i < elems.length; i++) {
                if (elems[i].className.match(/draggable/)) {
                    addEvent(elems[i], "mousedown", dragObject.engageDrag, false);
                }
            }
        }
    }
};
```

The code begins by defining some scrollbar and scroll action global variables. The scrollBars array manages more than one scrollbar per page.

The scrollBar() constructor function for the scrollbar objects receives three string parameters: the IDs for the div that holds the content and scrollbar (informally referred to here as the root container), the content's outer wrapper div (the content div's owner), and the content's inner wrapper (the owner content). The purpose of this constructor is to perform some one-time calculations and initializations per scrollbar (multiple scrollbars per page are allowed), facilitating several possible scrollbar actions later on. To help the buttons' event handlers know which set of scrollers is operating, an index value, corresponding to the position within the scrollBars array, is assigned to the index properties of the two button elements. The scrollBars.length value represents the numeric index of the scrollBars item being generated because the scrollBars array has not yet been assigned the finished object, meaning that the array length is one less than it will be after the object finishes its construction.

Numerous properties of each scrollBar object don't receive their active values until the function that creates the physical scrollbar executes. There is also a section in the constructor that concerns itself with browsers operating in quirks (i.e., non-CSS-compliant) mode, such as IE 5 and 5.5. When element dimensions affect element positioning, factors such as borders and padding are treated very differently in quirks and CSS-compatibility modes. Another property of this object, dragZone, is eventually used to guide the dragging of the thumb image to keep it restricted to the space within the scrollbar.

The next function, appendScrollBar( ), is a monster. It could be easily broken into multiple pieces, but the structure is simple enough to follow whole, as it assembles the DOM objects for the physical scrollbar. As relevant values become available, they are assigned to the abstract scrollBar object's properties created in the constructor function. The physical scrollbar consists of one scroll wrapper (which also serves as the background gray region for the scrollbar) and three img elements: clickable line-up and line-down buttons and the draggable thumb. Mouse-related event handlers are assigned to the scrollbar wrapper to process events from any of the components within the scrollbar. The scrollbar is initially created invisibly, and then shown at the end to overcome a rendering bug in IE that otherwise positions the scrollbar errantly.

The next section of the library contains the event handler functions. All that handleScrollStop( ) does is turn off the flag that other functions use to permit repeated scrolling, while blockEvent( ) stops the contextmenu event from carrying out its default action on the Macintosh. Event processing for clicks on the arrow images or in the page-up and page-down regions of the scrollbar is managed by the handleScrollClick( ) function. The function provides three branches for calculating the distance that scrolling is to jump in response to the click. Negative values move the content document upward. The trickiest part of this function is calculating whether the click on the scroll wrapper is above or below the thumb to reach the appropriate scroll direction (in the "scrollWrapper" case).

Compared to the simple scroll buttons of Recipe 13.12, this recipe's version of the scrollBy( ) function has more to worry about. When the user clicks an arrow or page area of the scrollbar, not only must the document scroll, but the thumb image must also move into a position that corresponds to the scrolled percentage of the document. Thus, after each invocation of the DHTML API's moveBy( ) or moveTo( ) function, the updateThumb( ) function gets a call. Notice that there are two extra branches of the scrollBy( ) function. They take care of the cases when the user clicks on the page regions and there is less than a full page to go. The result of the two extra branches forces the scroll (and thumb) to the top or bottom of the range, depending on direction.

The third section of the library is devoted to keeping the scrolled content and thumb position synchronized with each other. To keep the thumb image in sync with the scrolled position of the document, the updateThumb( ) function calculates the proportion of the document scrolled upward and applies that proportion to the position of the thumb element within the scroll wrapper element (offset by the up button image). Conversely, the updateScroll( ) function adjusts the scrolled position of the content to represent the same proportion as the location of the thumb along the scrollbar while the user drags the thumb. The known value (after some calculations involving the current size of the scrollbar and related images) is the proportion of the thumb along the area between the scroll buttons (the well). That factor is applied to the scroll characteristics of the content document. As the user slides the thumb up or down, the document scrolls in real time.

The last library code section contains functions needed for dragging the thumb. The basics of element dragging in Recipe 13.11 carry over to the scrollbar thumb-dragging operation here. Although we use the same event handler assignments and three primary dragObject methods (engageDrag( ), dragIt( ), and releaseDrag( )), a couple of items are modified to work specifically within this specialized scrollbar environment.

The biggest modifications apply to the dragIt( ) function. These changes deal primarily with restricting the drag of the thumb image within the vertical travel of the scrollbar, and preventing the thumb from exceeding the area between the scroll buttons. Values controlling the boundaries are set in the scrollbar object's dragZone property. If you use different scrollbar designs and sizes, you'll need to modify these object properties to fit your elements. The revised dragIt( ) function also invokes the updateScroll( ) function, which synchronizes the scroll of the content with the position of the thumb.

To create the scrollbar and prepare it for user interaction, initialize the process by calling the two key functions: the scrollBar( ) constructor function (passing IDs of the three hardwired HTML components shown at the beginning of this Solution), and the appendScroll( ) function. Activate these functions from the load event handler after initializing the DHTML API.

The design of the scrollbar shown in Figure 13-4 is very traditional. You're not limited to that style by any means. You might, for example, elect to eliminate the buttons, and include only a highly stylized slider to control scrolling. Or you could get more platform-specific, and include art that more closely resembles the user's operating system. Native scrollbars look very different in the Windows 9x, Windows XP, Windows Vista, and Mac OS X environments.

There is another factor to consider: Mac OS X displays scrollbar buttons together at the bottom of the scrollbar, rather than split to the top and bottom. Not that Mac users wouldn't know how to operate the split button kind of scrollbar, but the split design may not feel natural to users who are accustomed to the newer scrollbar interface. The code in the Solution could be modified to produce a scrollbar with the buttons together. This change impacts a lot of things, particularly the positioning of the thumb, but it is possible to branch your code (or perhaps load the scrollbar as separate external *.js* libraries) for the main operating systems.

Horizontal scrolling is not addressed in this recipe. If you need to scroll horizontally, you need to make several modifications to the code. Look first to all invocations of the scrollBy( ), moveBy( ), and moveTo( ) methods, which need to swap their parameters so that the y axis values are zero, and the x axis values are the ones that change. Dimensions of key elements, such as the scroll wrapper and content holders, need to focus on their widths, rather than heights. Fortunately, all of the technicalities of working in quirks mode apply directly to horizontal measures as well as to vertical measures, so you won't have to delve deeply in those parts of the code.

This scrollbar recipe is among the most code-intensive applications in this book. Yet it builds upon foundations from other recipes without reinventing infrastructure wheels (especially the DHTML- and element-dragging APIs). It also demonstrates that, at least for modern browsers, you can accomplish quite a lot from the user interface realm, even in the otherwise ordinary published document model.

See Also

Recipe 13.3 for the vital DHTML API library; Recipe 13.11 for the element-dragging routines; Recipe 13.12 for scrolling only with buttons rather than a complete scrollbar.

13.14 Creating a Slider Control

Problem

You want to provide users with a draggable slider control to interact with dynamic content on the page.

Solution

Use a combination of the *eventsManager.js* library (Recipe 9.3), the *DHTML3API.js* library (Recipe 13.3), and the *slideControl.js* library, shown in Example 13-9 in the Discussion. Although the new library is self-initializing, you need to pass some information to the library at load time for each slide control on the page. Your script in the HTML page would look like the following:

```
function initSlide( ) {
    if (slideObject) {
        slideObject.addSlide({zone:{left:-35, top:-11, right:227, bottom:-11},
            updateFunction:updateDisplay});
    }
}
addOnLoadEvent(initSlide);
```

As discussed more fully in the Discussion section, the `zone` object contains coordinates for the region in which the slide may travel while being dragged; the `updateFunction` is a reference to the page-specific function that modifies dynamic content on the page.

You must also include HTML for elements that comprise the slide control, usually consisting of an overall container (to provide a positioning context), an absolute-positioned background image, and an absolute-positioned slider. The CSS and HTML for one example follows:

```
<style type="text/css">
#sliderControl {position: absolute; top: 100px; left: 200px}
#sliderScale {position: absolute; top: 0; left: 0; z-index: 0; border: 3px ridge
black}
#slide {position: absolute; top: -11px; left: 97px; z-index: 1}
</style>
...
<div id="sliderControl">
<img id="sliderScale" src="slider_bg.png" width="300" height="141" alt="Slide Scale"
/>
<img id="slide" class="draggable" src="slider_slide.png" width="116" height="168"
alt="Slide" />
</div>
```

The class attribute value of `draggable` causes the slide controller initialization routine to assign the necessary `mousedown` event to enable dragging.

Discussion

This solution is a minor extension (with minor renaming) of the *dragManager.js* library from Recipe 13.11. As described in that recipe, it doesn't take much to limit the movement of a draggable item—something necessary for a slider that works horizontally or vertically.

As an example of the slider in action, this solution employs a background image of a scale and a movable foreground transparent image of a slide. While both examples are based on photographs of a real slider control, you can substitute artwork of your own creation. Figure 13-5 shows the slider, along with a color box below the slider. As the user slides the control, the color of the box changes dynamically from green to red (appearing yellow at the midpoint). Example 13-9 contains the complete *slideControl.js* library.

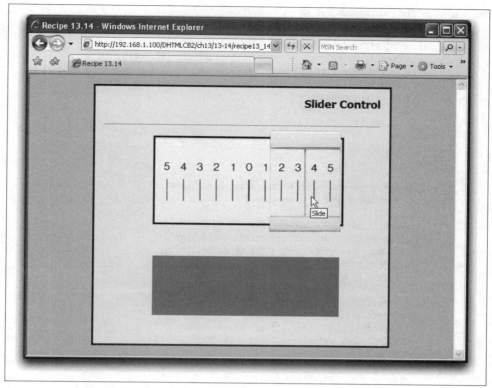

Figure 13-5. An example of a slider control operated by this solution

Example 13-9. The slideControl.js library

```
// slideObject contains data for currently dragged element
var slideObject = {
    selectedObject : null,
    offsetX : 0,
    offsetY : 0,
    sliders : new Array( ),
    zone: null,
    updateFunction: null,
    // invoked onmousedown
    engageDrag : function(evt, i) {
        evt = (evt) ? evt : window.event;
        slideObject.selectedObject = (evt.target) ? evt.target : evt.srcElement;
        var target = (evt.target) ? evt.target : evt.srcElement;
        var dragContainer = target;
        // in case event target is nested in draggable container
        while (target.className != "draggable" && target.parentNode) {
            target = dragContainer = target.parentNode;
        }
        if (dragContainer) {
            slideObject.selectedObject = dragContainer;
            slideObject.setOffsets(evt, dragContainer);
```

Example 13-9. The slideControl.js library (continued)

```
            slideObject.setDragEvents( );
            slideObject.zone = slideObject.sliders[i].zone;
            slideObject.updateFunction = slideObject.sliders[i].updateFunction;
            evt.cancelBubble = true;
            evt.returnValue = false;
            if (evt.stopPropagation) {
                evt.stopPropagation( );
                evt.preventDefault( );
            }
        }
    }
    return false;
},
// calculate offset of mousedown within draggable element
setOffsets : function (evt, dragContainer) {
    if (evt.pageX) {
        slideObject.offsetX = evt.pageX -
            ((typeof dragContainer.offsetLeft == "number") ?
            dragContainer.offsetLeft : dragContainer.left);
        slideObject.offsetY = evt.pageY -
            ((typeof dragContainer.offsetTop == "number") ?
            dragContainer.offsetTop : dragContainer.top);
    } else if (evt.offsetX || evt.offsetY) {
        slideObject.offsetX = evt.clientX -
            ((typeof dragContainer.offsetLeft == "number") ?
            dragContainer.offsetLeft : 0);
        slideObject.offsetY = evt.clientY -
            ((typeof dragContainer.offsetTop == "number") ?
            dragContainer.offsetTop : 0);
    }
},
// invoked onmousemove
dragIt : function (evt) {
    evt = (evt) ? evt : window.event;
    var x, y, width, height;
    var obj = slideObject;
    if (evt.pageX) {
        x = evt.pageX - obj.offsetX;
        y = evt.pageY - obj.offsetY;
    } else if (evt.clientX || evt.clientY) {
        x = evt.clientX - obj.offsetX;
        y = evt.clientY - obj.offsetY;
    }
    width = DHTMLAPI.getElementWidth(obj.selectedObj);
    height = DHTMLAPI.getElementHeight(obj.selectedObj);
    x = (x < obj.zone.left) ? obj.zone.left :
        ((x + width > obj.zone.right) ? obj.zone.right - width : x);
    y = (y < obj.zone.top) ? obj.zone.top :
        ((y + height > obj.zone.bottom) ? obj.zone.bottom - height : y);
    DHTMLAPI.moveTo(obj.selectedObject, x, y);
    // optimized for horizontal slider
    if (obj.updateFunction) obj.updateFunction((x - obj.zone.left)/
```

Example 13-9. The slideControl.js library (continued)

```
                    (obj.zone.right - obj.zone.left));
            evt.cancelBubble = true;
            evt.returnValue = false;
        },
        // invoked onmouseup
        releaseDrag : function (evt) {
            DHTMLAPI.setZIndex(slideObject.selectedObject, 0);
            slideObject.clearDragEvents();
            slideObject.selectedObject = null;
        },
        // set temporary events
        setDragEvents : function () {
            addEvent(document, "mousemove", slideObject.dragIt, false);
            addEvent(document, "mouseup", slideObject.releaseDrag, false);
        },
        // remove temporary events
        clearDragEvents : function () {
            removeEvent(document, "mousemove", slideObject.dragIt, false);
            removeEvent(document, "mouseup", slideObject.releaseDrag, false);
        },
        // add slider data to sliders array
        // data in object form {zone obj, updateFuncRef}
        addSlide : function(data) {
            this.sliders[this.sliders.length] = data;
        },
        // initialize, assigning mousedown events to all
        // elements with class="draggable" attributes
        init : function () {
            var elems = [];
            if (document.all) {
                // IE 5 & 5.5 don't know wildcard for getElementsByTagName
                // so use document.body.all, which lets IE 4 work OK
                elems = document.body.all;
            } else if (document.body && document.body.getElementsByTagName) {
                elems = document.body.getElementsByTagName("*");
            }
            var hitCount = 0
            for (var i = 0; i < elems.length; i++) {
                if (elems[i].className.match(/draggable/)) {
                    addEvent(elems[i], "mousedown", function(evt) {slideObject.engageDrag(evt,
                        hitCount++)}, false);
                }
            }
        }
    }
};
// set onload event via eventsManager.js
addOnLoadEvent(slideObject.init);
```

The library is implemented as a single object, named slideObject. Even though it is a single object, it can accommodate multiple sliders on the same page because the key details about each slider (the coordinate zone in which it travels and the function to be invoked at every movement) are stored in an array (called sliders) within the object. An index to that array is passed to the engageDrag( ) method, which then assigns the specific slider's details to the zone and updateFunction properties of sliderObject for the duration of the dragging process. For each slide control, invoke the slideObject.addSlide( ) method, passing an object consisting of two properties, as shown in the Solution section.

Determining the values to pass as the zone coordinates for a particular slider may take some trial and error. It's rare for the slide component to start and stop its travel at the exact edges of the positioning context. In the example shown in Figure 13-5, for instance, the left edge of the slide extends beyond the left edge of the positioning context, requiring the zone.left property to be a negative value. For a horizontal slider, the zone.top and zone.bottom values will be the same (to keep the slider on a fixed horizontal line); for a vertical slider, the zone.left and zone.right values will be the same.

Each time the sliderObject.dragIt( ) method runs (at each mousemove event while the slide is being dragged), the function passed as the second parameter to addSlide( ) is invoked. This function is one you write to respond to the new position of the slide control. The call to your function passes a single parameter, a value between 0 and 1 (inclusive) representing the percentage (0 to 100) at which the slide is positioned relative to the total travel distance for the slider. It is up to your function to convert that knowledge to something dynamic on the page. In the example shown in Figure 13-5, the update function changes the background color of a box on the page. The colors range from green (RGB value of 255, 0, 0) to red (RGB value of 0, 255, 0). Statements in the update function recalculate the necessary red and green values based on the passed value. Note that the passed value is a floating-point number. If your function needs integer values, perform the necessary conversions in your function, as shown in the following example:

```
function updateDisplay(pct) {
    var max = 255;
    var min = 0
    var red, green;
    if (pct < .5) {
        green = max;
        red = Math.round(max * (pct * 2));
    } else {
        red = max;
        green = Math.round(max * ((1-pct) * 2));
    }
    document.getElementById("colorbox").style.backgroundColor =
        "rgb(" + red + ", " + green + ", 0)";
}
```

As an aside, the reason the pct values above are multiplied by two is that in this application, the ranges of applied color values max out at the midpoint, where both red and green values are 255.

A slider control is fun and interactive for visitors. The downside, of course, is that without scripting enabled, the visitor derives no benefit from the design; similarly, special browsers for vision- or motor-skill-impaired visitors likely won't be able to use the sliders effectively. As with most DHTML implementations, apply techniques such as these to add value to otherwise accessible content.

See Also

Recipe 13.11 for other draggable element ideas; Recipe 13.3 for scripting DHTML features with the help of a JavaScript library.

CHAPTER 14
Creating Dynamic Content

14.0 Introduction

JavaScript-enabled browsers have always provided a level of control over page content so that scripts can influence what the visitor sees on the page. But it took sophisticated document object models and the automatically reflowing page features of browsers such as Internet Explorer 4 and Mozilla to give scripters carte blanche over the page content, both during page loading and after (within security boundaries, of course). This chapter focuses on how to generate content that goes into the page and manipulate the existing content of a page. The next chapter picks up where this one leaves off, showing several specific applications of these powers.

Web programmers who spend most of their time coding for server processing frequently overlook the power that a scripted client can provide to an otherwise dead and dull web page. Their (quite logical) train of thought is to have the server work its magic to assemble content that shoots its way to the browser, where users read it and perhaps enter various things into forms. The browser then sends the form back to the server, where more programming processes the user input. It's powerful stuff on the server, and applications involving transactions and database access need that power running right where it is.

Users, however, are accustomed to direct manipulation of data and instant feedback from their experience with standalone applications running on their computers. When you change the font characteristics of a selection in a word processing document, the change is instantaneous; when you sort the columns of a spreadsheet, the sorting occurs in the blink of an eye. Waiting for a submission to the server, remote processing, and delivery of the reconstituted page is not fun, even when you have a broadband connection to the Internet.

The broadband connection, combined with the now nearly ubiquitous XMLHttpRequest object in browsers, has unleashed an entirely new generation of web-based applications—applications that offer interactive communications with server processes and dynamically modified web pages. Incremental updates to page content mean that the user experience of a web-based application is as good as a standalone program—if not better, thanks to access to instant updates from a server.

This chapter and the next are all about pages that may look entirely different from the way they were delivered by the server because the user is able to sort tables, experiment with the body text content, retrieve incremental data, and even filter content based on user preferences. The focus here is on client-side solutions, all of which may be enhanced with server-side processes.

14.1 Writing Dynamic Content During Page Loading

Problem

You want to customize the content of the body based on client settings or cookie data, particularly in a backward-compatible way.

Solution

All scriptable browsers let you embed scripted document.write( ) statements anywhere in the body where you want customized content to appear. The following code displays a message tailored to the visitor's operating system:

```
<html>
<head>
<script type="text/javascript">
function yourOS( ) {
    var ua = navigator.userAgent.toLowerCase( );
    if (ua.indexOf("win") != -1) {
        return "Windows";
    } else if (ua.indexOf("mac") != -1) {
        return "Macintosh";
    } else if (ua.indexOf("linux") != -1) {
        return "Linux";
    } else if (ua.indexOf("x11") != -1) {
        return "Unix";
    } else {
        return "Computers";
    }
}
</script>
...
<body>
<h1>Welcome to GiantCo Computers</h1>
<h2>We love
<script type="text/javascript">document.write(yourOS( ))</script>
<noscript>Computer</noscript>
Users!</h2>
...
</body>
</html>
```

Discussion

The preceding Solution works on all scriptable browsers. Exercise care, however, when experimenting with document.write( ). When you embed this method in the page flow, as shown in the Solution, you do not use the document.open( ) or document.close( ) methods commonly associated with document.write( ). This is because the page-rendering stream is already open by virtue of the page loading from the server; the browser automatically closes the stream when the content ends.

A common beginner's mistake is to try to invoke document.write( ) after the page has loaded in an effort to modify or add to the content on the page. But if you invoke document.write( ) at that point, the current page automatically goes away, taking with it all scripts and data embedded in the page. Invoking document.write( ) by itself equates to three methods in sequence: document.clear( ), document.open( ), and document.write( ). In other words, after the current page has loaded, use document.write( ) only to replace the current page with other content that your scripts assemble (as shown in Recipe 14.2). To modify the existing page (to the extent that your target browsers support this feature), use the more direct element object manipulation shown throughout Chapter 15.

See Also

Recipe 15.1 for using document.write( ) to display a random slogan on the page; Recipe 15.7 for greeting users with the time of day in their local time zones.

14.2   Creating New Page Content Dynamically

Problem

You want to use scripts to assemble the content of a page that replaces the current page.

Solution

The following code gathers user-supplied text from a form on one page to provide some of the content for an entirely new page that replaces the first page:

```
<html>
<head>
<title>Welcome Page</title>
<script type="text/javascript">
// create custom page and replace current document with it
function rewritePage(form) {
    // accumulate HTML content for new page
    var newPage = "<html><head><title>Page for ";
    newPage += form.entry.value;
    newPage += "</title></head><body bgcolor='#ffffcc'>";
    newPage += "<h1>Hello, " + form.entry.value + "!</h1>";
```

```
        newPage += "</body></html>";
        // write it in one blast
        document.write(newPage);
        // close writing stream
        document.close();
    }
    </script>
    <body>
    <h1>Welcome!</h1>
    <hr />
    <form onsubmit="return false;">
    <p>Enter your name here: <input type="text" name="entry" id="entry"></p>
    <input type="button" value="New Custom Page" onclick="rewritePage(this.form);">
    </form>
    </body>
    </html>
```

Discussion

Because one swipe of the document.write( ) method invoked on a loaded page erases the current page, the technique is to assemble the replacement HTML as a single string value and then invoke document.write( ) just once, passing the string as the parameter. Bear in mind that you are supplying text for the entire page, so any content that you might typically put into a page's head section (such as the document title) goes into the string. If you fail to provide tags for the html, head, and body elements, the browser treats the written string as the body content of the new page, automatically inserting the html, head, and body elements around your content. But it is better practice to supply those parts of the page yourself.

You can put any well-formed HTML and script content into the string that gets written to the new page. Thus, you can pass along script variables and their numeric or string values within written script tags. For example, if you wanted to pass the value of string variable myName from the current document to the next, the following HTML string accumulation statement puts the correct value in place. Notice how explicit quote marks are placed around the evaluated value, just as you'd do in a regular script statement involving a string:

```
htmlString += "var myName = '" + myName + "';";
```

Using document.write( ) for script tags, however, can be tricky in earlier browsers because the </script> tag that you assemble into the string may be interpreted as an end to the script that is assembling the text. To avoid this problem, break up the end-script tag and escape the forward slash, as follows:

```
htmlString += '<script type="text/javascript">script statement here<\/scr' + 'ipt>';
```

It is vital that you follow the document.write( ) statement with a call to document. close( ). Even though the original page's script is blown away by document.write( ), the document.close( ) method call still executes. If you don't include document.close( ), not all of the content of the string written to the next page may render. This is especially true if the content contains images or other external content.

See Also

Recipe 1.1 for combining string segments into one string.

14.3   Including External HTML Content

Problem

You want to combine (include) content from another HTML document into a single document on the page.

Solution

Put the external content into an iframe element, and disguise the iframe so that it looks to be part of the regular document flow. Here is an example of an iframe element that blends seamlessly into a plain HTML page:

```
<iframe id="myFrame" frameborder="0" vspace="0" hspace="0" marginwidth="0"
marginheight="0" width="100%" src="external.html" scrolling="no"
style="overflow:visible"></iframe>
```

To size the iframe element correctly, you must wait for the content to load, and then use scripts to find out the content height. The following function is invoked by the load event handler of the main page, which passes the ID of the iframe to be adjusted:

```
function adjustIFrameSize(id) {
    var myIframe = document.getElementById(id);
    if (myIframe) {
        if (myIframe.contentDocument && myIframe.contentDocument.body.scrollHeight) {
            // W3C DOM iframe document syntax
            myIframe.height = myIframe.contentDocument.body.scrollHeight;
        } else if (myIframe.Document && myIframe.Document.body.scrollHeight) {
            // IE DOM syntax
            myIframe.height = myIframe.Document.body.scrollHeight;
        }
    }
}
```

To adjust the example iframe element, the load event binding can be by attribute in the main page's <body> tag:

```
onload = "adjustIFrameSize('myFrame');"
```

The user will see the page rearrange itself when the iframe resizes.

Discussion

For the resizing script to work, both the host and the external pages must be served from the same domain and server, to allow the script to dive into the otherwise protected realm of the iframe's content. Notice that the reference to the content of the iframe element is not as direct as you might be accustomed to from working with framesets. If you begin with a reference to the iframe element, you then need the DOM-compatible syntax to reach the document object within that frame: Document for IE and contentDocument for W3C DOM-based browsers. References to those documents point to the root document containing the content visible in the frame. From there, you can reach the body or other elements within the document. In the case of the embedded iframe, the total height of the rendered content (unknown until it loads) governs the ultimate height of the iframe.

Be aware that hyperlinks in the iframe's content will load their destination documents into the iframe, unless the targets of those links are set to _top. Also, any new content loaded into the iframe that is not the same height as the original either leaves a gap (too short) or is clipped (too long). The only fix is to resize the iframe for the new content.

To prepare the iframe for automatic resizing when a new document loads there, you must bind a load event handler to the iframe element. While a hardwired onload event handler or event property assignments may not work for the iframe element in Mozilla, more modern event binding does. Use the addEvent( ) function from Recipe 9.1 to revise the function shown in the Solution to bind the events as follows:

```
function adjustIFrameSize(id) {
    var myIframe = document.getElementById(id);
    if (myIframe) {
        if (myIframe.contentDocument && myIframe.contentDocument.body.scrollHeight) {
            // W3C DOM iframe document syntax
            myIframe.height = myIframe.contentDocument.body.scrollHeight;
        } else if (myIframe.Document && myIframe.Document.body.scrollHeight) {
            // IE DOM syntax
            myIframe.height = myIframe.Document.body.scrollHeight;
        }
        // bind load events to iframe
        addEvent(myIframe, "load", resizeIframe, false);
    }
}
```

The events invoke a function that processes the event to pass the desired information (the ID of the iframe) back to the adjustIFrameSize( ) function:

```
function resizeIframe(evt) {
    evt = (evt) ? evt : event;
    var target = (evt.target) ? evt.target : evt.srcElement;
    // take care of W3C event processing from iframe's root document
    if (target.nodeType == 9) {
        if (evt.currentTarget &&
            evt.currentTarget.tagName.toLowerCase( ) == "iframe") {
            target = evt.currentTarget;
        }
    }
    if (target) {
        adjustIFrameSize(target.id);
    }
}
```

The tricky part is that the `load` event fires for the content document of the `iframe` in W3C DOM browsers rather than for the `iframe` element directly. Fortunately, the event bubbles up to the containing `iframe`, and the W3C DOM event object's `currentTarget` property gives us a reference to the element that is actually processing the event, regardless of original target. The event bindings are invoked again in the `adjustIFrameSize( )` function, but there is no harm in doing so. If you have some other initializations on the page that occur in response to the main page's `load` event handler, you can shift these assignments to that initialization function so that they execute only one time.

See Also

Recipe 9.1 for handling conflicting event models together; Recipe 9.2 for details about the `load` event handler.

14.4   Embedding XML Data

Problem

You want to reference XML document data to support script activities in the main page.

Solution

IE 5 or later for Windows, Mozilla, Safari 1.2 or later, and Opera 8 or later allow you to create an invisible virtual document that holds raw XML data, which your scripts may then traverse using standard DOM node referencing methods and properties. For now, loading the XML data requires browser-specific handling, but once that occurs, you can reference the content and its node tree uniformly.

The following `XMLDoc( )` constructor function creates an object that stands ready to use the `XMLHttpRequest` object to load external XML data and then invoke a function of your own creation to handle the data:

```
// constructor function for an XML request object;
function XMLDoc( ) {
    var me = this;
    var req = null;
    // branch for native XMLHttpRequest object
    if (window.XMLHttpRequest) {
        try {
            req = new XMLHttpRequest( );
        } catch(e) {
            req = null;
        }
    // branch for IE/Windows ActiveX versions
    } else if (window.ActiveXObject) {
        try {
```

```
            req = new ActiveXObject("Msxml2.XMLHTTP");
    } catch(e) {
        try {
            req = new ActiveXObject("Microsoft.XMLHTTP");
        } catch(e) {
            req = null;
        }
    }
    } else {
        alert("This example requires a browser with XML support, such as IE5+/
Windows, Mozilla, Safari 1.2, or Opera 8.")
    }
    // preserve reference to request object for later
    this.request = req;
    // "public" method to be invoked whenever
    this.loadXMLDoc = function(url, loadHandler) {
        if (this.request) {
            this.request.open("GET", url, true);
            this.request.onreadystatechange = function () {loadHandler(me)};
            this.request.setRequestHeader("Content-Type", "text/xml");
            this.request.send("");
        }
    };
}
```

Create an instance of the XMLDoc object either at load time or whenever you need it.
Then instruct it to retrieve XML data from a known URL, firing your function upon
retrieval:

```
function initXML( ) {
    var outlineRequest = new XMLDoc( );
    outlineRequest.loadXMLDoc("myData.xml", handleDataFunction);
}
```

Discussion

The XMLHttpRequest object was first implemented in Internet Explorer as an ActiveX
control. There have been two generations of the ActiveX object. When the other
browsers began implementing this object, they did so as a native object—primarily
because the browsers needed to run on operating systems that didn't support ActiveX.
With IE 7, Microsoft has also implemented the native XMLHttpRequest object. But with
IE 6 still so prevalent, it's important that this solution continue to offer both ways,
depending on the capabilities of the browser. Priority is given to the native object, but
the operational result is inconsequential. Once the object is created, all styles have the
same basic properties, methods, and operating characteristics.

This solution builds an object (XMLDoc) that encapsulates the XMLHttpRequest object.
After your script creates an instance of the XMLDoc object, it needs to invoke only one
method of the object: loadXMLDoc( ). This method needs two parameters. The first is
the URL which responds to an HTTP GET to return an XML document (as well as
other types). The other parameter is a reference to a function that will be called by

the `XMLHttpRequest` object each time the `readystatechange` event fires. This event fires several times while data is coming from the server. Your script function will then have access to the XML document object, which has a DOM node tree you can read with the same W3C DOM node methods and properties that you use to manipulate an HTML document. You can see examples of this in Recipes 10.11, 14.6, and 14.8.

The reason that you need to load XML into these separate virtual documents is that loading them into a browser frame (hidden or visible) causes most browsers to HTML-ize the document. This type of conversion performs all kinds of formatting on the content so that it renders in the browser window with a variety of colors, indenting, and hierarchy symbols. The node tree of the raw document is buried and commingled with the browser-created window dressing.

See Also

Recipe 14.6 for generating an HTML table from XML data; Recipe 14.8 for creating JavaScript custom objects from XML data; Recipe 14.20 for walking a document node tree for XML or HTML documents; Recipe 14.17 for using the `XMLHttpRequest` object for a REST request; Recipe 14.18 for using the `XMLHttpRequest` object to make a SOAP call.

14.5 Embedding Data As JavaScript Objects

Problem

You want to include data retrieved by server processes in the JavaScript code of the page so that client scripts can manipulate the data and/or provide rendering options for the user.

Solution

Your server processing code can insert blocks of dynamically assembled data into portions of the HTML page about to be served to the client. While string data is typically sent to the client as values of hidden input elements, JavaScript data structures offer significantly more power and flexibility once the code loads into the client.

For simple collections of related values, JavaScript arrays are ideal mechanisms, especially with the shortcut syntax that simplifies code assembly on the server:

```
var dataArray = ["value0", "value1", "value2", ... "valueN"];
```

For repetitive database-record-like data, shortcut JavaScript object creation syntax makes it a snap to define properties and their values:

```
var dataObject = {prop0:"value0", prop1:"value1", prop2:"value2", ...    propN:
"valueN"};
```

To create an array of objects, take advantage of the length of a newly created array to get started. By using a calculated array index value, you can modify the sequence of array entries without having to renumber the indexes manually:

```
var dataArray = new Array();
dataArray[dataArray.length] = {prop0_0:"value0_0", prop0_1:"value0_1",
    prop0_2:"value0_2", ... prop0_N:"value0_N"};
dataArray[dataArray.length] = {prop1_0:"value1_0", prop1_1:"value1_1",
    prop1_2:"value1_2", ... prop1_N:"value1_N"};
...
```

Values assignable as array items or object values can be quoted strings (shown here), numbers, Booleans, and other arrays and objects. In fact, there is no practical limit to the amount of nesting you can do to create complex objects whose properties are, themselves, complex objects.

Discussion

If you define the JavaScript data objects in a script within the <head> tag, those objects are defined and ready to go when the body starts rendering. Therefore, you have the choice of utilizing those objects to generate dynamic HTML while the page loads, or of using the load event handler to trigger a function that modifies the body delivered with the page.

You don't have to embed the data formally within the HTML page. Instead, a separate server process (invokeable via URL) can serve as the source for the equivalent of a *.js* script library. Specify the URL of the process as the value of the <script> tag's src attribute. Make sure that the string content returned from the process is in the same script-only form as any valid *.js* file and that the content type for the output is text/javascript. Because of potential synchronization problems with a secondary server request, access the data delivered this way via the page's load event handler only.

One of the most convenient JavaScript data formats is an object utilizing string index values. These aren't arrays per se, since the object does not gain a length property, and iterating through its members requires the for-in style of object introspection. A little known fact is that JavaScript lets you build this pseudohash table on top of an array object, and the two sets of data do not collide (as shown in Recipe 3.9). For example, consider the following JavaScript data variation of the World Cup final match records, delivered initially as an array of objects:

```
var matchData = new Array();
matchData[0] = {loser:"Argentina", losscore:"2", location:"Uruguay",
winner:"Uruguay", winscore:"4", year:"1930"};
matchData[1] = {loser:"Czechoslovakia", losscore:"1", location:"Italy",
winner:"Italy", winscore:"2", year:"1934"};
...
```

Now imagine a page that has a select element containing a list of the years of all the matches, allowing a user to select a year to display the details of the final match. The slow way to reach the data is to use a for loop through the matchData array, looking at each year property value in search of a match of the chosen option value. For a sizable array, this could take a few seconds. But a one-time preprocessing of the array can create the pseudohash table with the years as string index values. Immediately after the matchData array is completely populated, the following statements generate the hash table:

```
for (var i = 0; i < matchData.length; i++) {
    matchData["_" + matchData[i].year] = matchData[i];
}
```

Notice an interesting twist that the sample data required: because the year property values being used as hash table indexes automatically cast to numeric values when placed in that context, a nonnumeric value (an underscore) is concatenated onto each value to force the index to be a string value. Otherwise, the numeric value increases the length of the array, without generating the string-indexed hash table. For nonnumeric property values, you can eliminate the concatenation trick and supply just the property reference.

Once the hash table is created, you can now reference the array object through the unique string index of the hash table, as in this oversimplified example:

```
<select onchange="alert('Winner was: ' + matchData[this.value].winner)">
<option value="_1930">1930</option>
<option value="_1934">1934</option>
...
</select>
```

A related technique, sometimes referred to as JavaScript Object Notation (JSON), can take advantage of the XMLHttpRequest object to retrieve data preformatted as JavaScript arrays and objects. The concept behind JSON is simple: deliver the data to the client as a string, and then use the JavaScript global eval( ) method to convert that string into live arrays and objects (the inverse of converting to strings shown in Recipe 3.13). In response to a request to a server URL, the XMLHttpRequest object receives data in two forms: an XML document (if applicable) and a string. That string can be changed into JavaScript objects and data that your scripts manipulate as if the data had arrived with the page. See Recipe 14.7 for more on handling data returned to an XMLHttpRequest object.

See Also

Recipe 3.1 for creating arrays; Recipe 3.8 for creating custom objects; Recipe 3.9 for generating hash tables from arrays or arrays of objects; Recipe 3.11 for sorting arrays of objects; Recipe 14.17 for working with XMLHttpRequest data.

14.6 Transforming XML Data into HTML Tables

Problem

You want to render embedded XML data as a traditional HTML table.

Solution

For a table of known column headings and XML data structure, you can set up the initial table element container, prepped for the addition of the data rows:

```
<table id="cupFinals">
<thead>
<tr><th>Year</th>
    <th>Host Country</th>
    <th>Winner</th>
    <th>Loser</th>
    <th>Score (Win - Lose)</th>
</tr>
</thead>
<tbody id="matchData"></tbody>
</table>
```

Use the XML-loading scenario described in Recipe 14.4. A load event handler function obtains an instance of the XMLDoc object and then loads a specific URL, while also indicating that drawTable( ) (shown in Example 14-1 of the Discussion) is to be invoked when the XML data is loaded:

```
function initXML( ) {
    var outlineRequest = new XMLDoc( );
    outlineRequest.loadXMLDoc("worldCupFinals.xml", drawTable);
}
addOnLoadEvent(initXML);
```

Discussion

Example 14-1 shows the drawTable( ) function, which assembles table rows and cells from the XML document's node tree.

Example 14-1. The drawTable( ) function dynamically generating a table's contents

```
// Draw table from XML document tree data
function drawTable(req) {
    req = req.request;
    if (req.readyState == 4 && req.status == 200) {
        // XML node tree
        var data = req.responseXML.getElementsByTagName("worldcup")[0];
        var tbody = document.getElementById("matchData");
        var tr, td, i, j, oneRecord;
        // for td class attributes
        var classes = ["ctr","","","","ctr"];
        for (i = 0; i < data.childNodes.length; i++) {
            // use only 1st level element nodes to skip 1st level text nodes in NN
```

```
            if (data.childNodes[i].nodeType == 1) {
                // one final match record
                oneRecord = data.childNodes[i];
                tr = tbody.insertRow(tbody.rows.length);
                td = tr.insertCell(tr.cells.length);
                td.setAttribute("class",classes[tr.cells.length-1]);
                td.innerHTML =
                  oneRecord.getElementsByTagName("year")[0].firstChild.nodeValue;
                td = tr.insertCell(tr.cells.length);
                td.setAttribute("class",classes[tr.cells.length-1]);
                td.innerHTML =
                    oneRecord.getElementsByTagName("location")[0].firstChild.nodeValue;
                td = tr.insertCell(tr.cells.length);
                td.setAttribute("class",classes[tr.cells.length-1]);
                td.innerHTML =
                    oneRecord.getElementsByTagName("winner")[0].firstChild.nodeValue;
                td = tr.insertCell(tr.cells.length);
                td.setAttribute("class",classes[tr.cells.length-1]);
                td.innerHTML =
                    oneRecord.getElementsByTagName("loser")[0].firstChild.nodeValue;
                td = tr.insertCell(tr.cells.length);
                td.setAttribute("class",classes[tr.cells.length-1]);
                td.innerHTML =
                    oneRecord.getElementsByTagName("winscore")[0].firstChild.nodeValue +
                    " - " +
                    oneRecord.getElementsByTagName("losscore")[0].firstChild.nodeValue;
            }
        }
    }
}
```

Once the drawTable( ) function runs, the table shown in Figure 14-1 appears on the page.

Because the XMLHttpRequest object's readystate event fires several times during the loading of the XML document, the first job of the drawTable( ) function is to filter out calls that occur before the entire document has loaded. Internal processing of this function occurs only if the request object's readyState property is 4 ("complete") and the status property is 200 ("success"). At that point, it is safe to fetch the XML data, which is stored in the responseXML property. XML data retrieved in this fashion is in the form of a W3C DOM document object. For this example, the structure of the XML document is as follows:

```
<?xml version="1.0"?>
<worldcup>
    <final>
        <location>Uruguay</location>
        <year>1930</year>
        <winner>Uruguay</winner>
        <winscore>4</winscore>
```

```
            <loser>Argentina</loser>
            <losscore>2</losscore>
        </final>
        <final>
            <location>Italy</location>
            <year>1934</year>
            <winner>Italy</winner>
            <winscore>2</winscore>
            <loser>Czechoslovakia</loser>
            <losscore>1</losscore>
        </final>
        ...
    </worldcup>
```

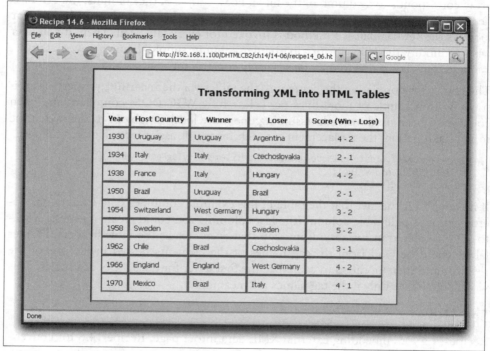

Figure 14-1. Sample table from embedded XML data

"Records" for this data are contained in the first (and only) element in the document whose tag name is worldcup. It is this XML structure that drawTable( ) maps to an HTML table. The regularity of the DOM node tree of record-based XML data provides an excellent analog to the row and cell formatting of an HTML table. Starting with the container of all record elements (the worldcup element in our example), it's a comparatively simple looping routine through the next level elements, each of which represents a record.

In order to generate the HTML for the table, Example 14-1 uses W3C DOM table-modification methods for inserting rows and cells. A style sheet, located in the head of the document, defines some rules for table components as well as a class called ctr:

```
<style type="text/css">
table {table-collapse:collapse; border-spacing:0}
td {border:2px groove black; padding:7px; background-color:#ccffcc}
th {border:2px groove black; padding:7px; background-color:#ffffcc}
.ctr {text-align:center}
</style>
```

An array called classes is near the top of the drawTable( ) function. Each entry of the array corresponds to a column of the table. For a couple of the columns, the ctr class needs to be assigned to the class attribute of the cell. This takes place within the for loop, as the setAttribute( ) method is invoked for every table cell. Then, if you later wish to modify the behavior of a particular column, simply define a new class rule, and add that class name to the classes array constructor.

The choice for populating the content of the tables via the innerHTML property is arbitrary. With a couple of more lines per cell, a fully W3C DOM-compliant approach could have been used instead. Assuming one more local variable, txt, defined at the top of the function, the replacement for each innerHTML assignment looks as follows:

```
txt = document.createTextNode(oneRecord.getElementsByTagName("year")[0].
    firstChild.nodeValue);
td.appendChild(txt);
```

If it weren't for the fact that the table in this example combines data from two properties into a single table column (the last column), you could create a generic XML-to-HTML table transformation function that even creates the table headers. Header labels could be read from the tag names of the elements nested inside one of the records, and then modified to capitalize the first letter for the sake of aesthetics. This works, of course, only if the tag names are meaningful.

See Also

Recipe 14.4 for embedding external XML data into a page; Recipe 14.8 for converting XML data into JavaScript objects; Recipe 14.20 for details on walking a document node tree.

14.7   Transforming JavaScript Objects into HTML Tables

Problem

You want to render embedded JavaScript data as an HTML table.

Solution

When JavaScript data is formatted as an array of objects, it is a relatively simple job to use the data to drive the creation of rows and cells of an HTML table. Here is an example of some repetitive data assembled on the server as a JavaScript array (perhaps from a database query):

```
// Table data -- an array of objects
var jsData = new Array( );
jsData[0] = {location:"Uruguay", year:1930, winner:"Uruguay", winScore:4,
             loser:"Argentina", losScore:2};
jsData[1] = {location:"Italy", year:1934, winner:"Italy", winScore:2,
             loser:"Czechoslovakia", losScore:1};
jsData[2] = {location:"France", year:1938, winner:"Italy", winScore:4,
             loser:"Hungary", losScore:2};
jsData[3] = {location:"Brazil", year:1950, winner:"Uruguay", winScore:2,
             loser:"Brazil", losScore:1};
jsData[4] = {location:"Switzerland", year:1954, winner:"West Germany", winScore:3,
             loser:"Hungary", losScore:2};
```

A skeleton of the table is delivered with the HTML, so that the column headings are already in place, and a table body section is set to receive the dynamically created table content:

```
<table id="cupFinals">
<thead>
<tr><th>Year</th>
    <th>Host Country</th>
    <th>Winner</th>
    <th>Loser</th>
    <th>Score (Win - Lose)</th>
</tr>
</thead>
<tbody id="matchData"></tbody>
</table>
```

The function that creates the table content utilizes W3C DOM table-modification methods:

```
// Draw table from 'jsData' array of objects
function drawTable(tbody) {
    var tr, td;
    tbody = document.getElementById(tbody);
    // loop through data source
    for (var i = 0; i < jsData.length; i++) {
        tr = tbody.insertRow(tbody.rows.length);
        td = tr.insertCell(tr.cells.length);
        td.setAttribute("align", "center");
        td.innerHTML = jsData[i].year;
        td = tr.insertCell(tr.cells.length);
        td.innerHTML = jsData[i].location;
        td = tr.insertCell(tr.cells.length);
        td.innerHTML = jsData[i].winner;
        td = tr.insertCell(tr.cells.length);
```

```
          td.innerHTML = jsData[i].loser;
          td = tr.insertCell(tr.cells.length);
          td.setAttribute("align", "center");
          td.innerHTML = jsData[i].winScore + " - " + jsData[i].losScore;
       }
   }
```

The `drawTable( )` function can be invoked via the load event handler of the page, or, if you prefer, by a script embedded in the body anywhere below the skeleton table elements:

```
   drawTable("matchData");
```

Discussion

The W3C DOM provides the key methods for making a table on the fly. The first is the `insertRow( )` method of the table element object; the second is the `insertCell( )` method of the table row element object. It's not enough just to insert a row or cell, however. You must also populate the inserted object with content.

When you invoke the `insertRow( )` method, the code returns a reference to the newly generated row object. That reference becomes the object you use to invoke `insertCell( )` for each cell in the row. The parameter for both methods is an integer indicating the position of the new row within the table or cell within the row. The example uses a simple programmatic technique of applying the `length` property of the collection of associated elements, which always points to the next one at the end of the series.

The choice to populate the content of the table cells via the `innerHTML` property is arbitrary. With a couple more lines per cell, a fully W3C DOM-compliant approach could have been used instead. Assuming one more local variable, `txt`, defined at the top of the function, the replacement for each `innerHTML` assignment looks as follows:

```
   txt = document.createTextNode(jsData[i].year);
   td.appendChild(txt);
```

Naturally, you are not limited to creating tables out of JavaScript data. JavaScript data objects can consist of the equivalent of lookup tables that interact with user input in forms. See Recipe 14.5 for an example of a select element being used as part of a user interface for embedded data lookup. Offloading these simple kinds of lookup tasks to the client frees the server for more important chores.

Note that IE 5 for the Macintosh does not support table modification methods. Other document tree modification techniques that involve tables and table components almost always crash the browser.

See Also

Recipe 14.5 for embedding JavaScript data into a page; Recipe 14.19 for sorting tables.

14.8 Converting an XML Node Tree to JavaScript Objects

Problem

You want to convert XML data (either loaded from an external file or embedded as an IE/Windows data island) into JavaScript objects for further manipulation by scripts.

Solution

The following XML2JS( ) function assumes a regular, record-like structure to the XML data (or portion of data that is significant to the page). Two parameters are required: a reference to the XML virtual document object (see Recipe 14.4) and the tag name of the XML document's element that is the parent node of the repeated records:

```
// convert XML data into JavaScript array of JavaScript objects
function XML2JS(xmlDoc, containerTag) {
    var output = new Array( );
    var rawData = xmlDoc.getElementsByTagName(containerTag)[0];
    var i, j, oneRecord, oneObject;
    for (i = 0; i < rawData.childNodes.length; i++) {
        if (rawData.childNodes[i].nodeType == 1) {
            oneRecord = rawData.childNodes[i];
            oneObject = output[output.length] = new Object( );
            for (j = 0; j < oneRecord.childNodes.length; j++) {
                if (oneRecord.childNodes[j].nodeType == 1) {
                    oneObject[oneRecord.childNodes[j].tagName] =
                        oneRecord.childNodes[j].firstChild.nodeValue;
                }
            }
        }
    }
    return output;
}
```

This function returns an array of JavaScript objects whose property names are the XML tag names, and whose property values are the text nodes of the XML tags.

Discussion

For an example of invoking the function shown in the Solution, consider the World Cup final match XML data file shown in the Discussion in Recipe 14.4. The element acting as the parent to the repeated record-like data is called worldcup. This is the tag name passed as the second parameter to the XML2JS( ) function. Capture the results in a global variable for use any time while the page remains loaded:

```
var matchData = XML2JS(req.responseXML, "worldcup");
```

The results are in the form of a JavaScript array of JavaScript objects. The object for the first record is the same object as if it were defined in JavaScript syntax:

```
matchData[0] = {loser:"Argentina", losscore:"2", location:"Uruguay",
                winner:"Uruguay", winscore:"4", year:"1930"};
```

With the data in JavaScript format, you have substantial flexibility in how you wish to mine the data for rendering in HTML. JavaScript's built-in array sorting capabilities substantially speed and simplify sorting the data according (over and above XSL transforms) to any one of the object properties, and then re-rendering the sorted data. If you are showing the data in tabular form, Recipe 14.19 demonstrates how to sort the data and redraw the table in an instant, rather than sending the request back to the server for reconstitution of the page.

You might wonder why you'd bother with the conversion process, since you can transform XML data into HTML directly (as in Recipe 14.6). The benefit, as you can see in Recipe 14.19, is that data in a JavaScript array of objects is much easier to access through scripts. Moreover, you can take advantage of powerful array-sorting routines that would be incredibly clumsy to reproduce using a DOM node tree as the data repository. Making tables that are sortable by a variety of columns is a comparative snap.

See Also

Recipe 14.4 for loading XML data into a page; Recipe 14.6 for converting XML data directly to an HTML table; Recipe 14.19 for sorting dynamically generated tables; Recipe 3.11 for sorting an array of objects.

14.9 Creating a New HTML Element

Problem

You want to generate a brand new HTML element and insert it into the body of the current page.

Solution

For IE 5 or later, Mozilla, Safari, and Opera 7 or later, use the W3C DOM element-creation method of the document object. The sole parameter is a string of the tag name for the element:

```
var elem = document.createElement("p");
```

You can now populate the element with properties and other content, and then insert it into the document.

Discussion

The tag name you supply as a parameter to the createElement( ) method can be upper- or lowercase, but in keeping with current trends in XHTML practice, lower-case is the preferred style. Your case choice does not influence the value returned by the element's tagName property, which uniformly returns values in all uppercase.

Invoking the createElement( ) method generates the element in the browser's memory, but the element is not yet part of the document node tree. To accomplish this task, use one of the node tree modification methods on the element that you want to be the parent node of the newly installed element:

appendChild(*newChild*)
> Adds the *newChild* node as the last child of the element invoking the method. Returns a reference to the newly appended child node.

insertBefore(*newChild,refNode*)
> Inserts the *newChild* in front of the existing child node referenced by *refNode*. Returns a reference to the newly inserted child node.

replaceChild(*newChild,oldChild*)
> Inserts the *newChild* in place of the *oldChild*. Returns a reference to the removed child node.

Here is a typical sequence that creates a new self-contained element, sets various attributes, and puts it at the end of the page's body:

```
var elem = document.createElement("img");
elem.setAttribute("src", "images/logo.jpg");
elem.setAttribute("height", "40");
elem.setAttribute("width", "120");
elem.setAttribute("alt", "GiantCo Logo");
document.body.appendChild(elem);
```

The previous sequence uses the setAttribute( ) method to assign values to what are normally attribute values of the tag. You can also assign values to the analogous properties of the element object, but the W3C DOM recommendation prefers the setAttribute( ) method for this purpose. Your choice is strictly based on programming style, in that browsers recognize both syntaxes equally (and the property assignment approach is less verbose).

You may, however, occasionally encounter problems with setAttribute( ). It's not unusual for IE to fail to act on attribute value changes when the attribute points to external content and other situations. This primarily affects elements that are already part of the document tree, but even setting a class attribute of an element under construction can fail. The workaround is to set the value by property rather than by the setAttribute( ) method. All browsers comply with this workaround, so it is safe.

You also are not required to set the attributes of the element prior to inserting the element into the document tree. Again, this is a programming style decision, but it is quite typical to load an object with all its values before presenting it to the environment. In rare instances, however, an element must become part of the document tree for a scripted property to be accessible because it needs a layout context for the property assignment to take effect (see Recipe 14.12).

Internet Explorer (dating back to version 4) has a supplementary vocabulary (and mind-set) for creating elements and inserting them into a document. The system is not node-oriented in the way the W3C DOM is. Instead, it works with HTML as strings. Rather than generating a new element object, simply assemble the HTML for the new element as a string, and then insert the string in the desired place within the document structure. The IE-only equivalent of the img element creation sequence shown earlier is:

```
var elem = "<img src='images/logo.jpg' height='40' width='120' alt='GiantCo Logo'>";
document.body.insertAdjacentHTML("BeforeEnd", elem);
```

The first parameter of the insertAdjacentHTML( ) method instructs the browser to insert the new string just inside the </body> tag of the document, while the method forces the browser to treat the string as HTML so that the tags are treated as markup, rather than as completely literal strings (displaying the angle brackets, attributes, and so on).

It's quite clear that the HTML-string approach is simpler in many respects. But the W3C DOM through Level 2 does not (and likely will not) provide a convenient way to deal with tagged content in string form. See Recipe 14.10 for one IE convenience that has made its way to the Mozilla browser for element text.

Although this recipe addresses creating an HTML element, the same concepts apply to creating an element that is to be appended or inserted in an XML document (as you might construct for submission to the server via Ajax). The only difference is that you should invoke the createElement( ) method from the XML document, not the current HTML document. For example, if the variable xDox contains an XML document (perhaps initially retrieved via XMLHttpRequest), you can add an element to the document via the following sequence:

```
var newElem = xDoc.createElement("product");
var catalogElem = xDoc.getElementsByTagName("catalog")[0];
catalogElem.appendChild(newElem);
```

See Also

Recipe 14.10 for generating text content of an element; Recipe 14.11 for creating a combination of element and text nodes for insertion into a document; Recipe 14.12 for inserting an iframe into a document.

14.10 Creating Text Content for a New Element

Problem

You want to use scripts to generate a portion of body content after the page loads.

Solution

Use the W3C DOM text node-creation method of the document object. The sole parameter is the string of text content destined for an element container:

```
var txt = document.createTextNode("My dog has fleas.");
```

You can now append or insert this text node as a new child node of any element node, including an element node that has been created but not yet inserted into the document tree.

Discussion

A typical sequence for creating both a new element and its text content is as follows:

```
var elem = document.createElement("p");
var txt = document.createTextNode("My dog has fleas.");
elem.appendChild(txt);
document.body.appendChild(elem);
```

The amount of nesting required for some combinations of elements and text can get somewhat complicated, but the principles are the same throughout. For example, the following sequence creates a p element with a sentence containing an em element:

```
var myEm, myP, txt1, txt2;
myEm = document.createElement("em");
txt1 = document.createTextNode("very");
myEm.appendChild(txt1);
myP = document.createElement("p");
txt1 = document.createTextNode("I am ");
txt2 = document.createTextNode(" happy to see you.");
myP.appendChild(txt1);
myP.appendChild(myEm);
myP.appendChild(txt2);
document.body.appendChild(myP);
```

The result of the previous sequence is an element whose HTML looks like the following:

```
<p>I am <em>very</em> happy to see you.</p>
```

You may create any combination of elements and text nodes, provided the result is well-formed HTML, a prospect that is nearly irrevocably enforced by the way node insertion methods work in the W3C DOM. In fact, you could conceivably append two text nodes next to each other. To the user, they would be rendered as one continuous string of text; to the document tree, they are siblings of the same node type (3). If you prefer to combine sibling text nodes into a single node, invoke the normalize( ) method on their parent containing element.

Internet Explorer 4 introduced two text-based properties of element objects that have gained wide usage in web development for that browser family: innerText and innerHTML. These two read/write properties let you assign a string of unmarked up text or text with HTML tags to the interior of an element container, respectively. If the text contains tags, assignment to the innerHTML property forces the browser to interpret the tags as if they were in the delivered page source code; assignment to the innerText property treats the contents as literal text, meaning that the angle brackets, tag name, and attributes are also rendered for users. This string-based approach to document modification is used by the IE-only document object model (in contrast to the W3C DOM node-based model).

Web content authors have found these properties so practical over the years that non-IE web browser makers relented in their predominantly strict adherence to W3C DOM precepts just enough to implement the innerHTML property. This convenience property saves coding because you don't have to go through the text node creation process. For example, the W3C DOM sequence:

```
var txt = document.createTextNode("My dog has fleas.");
document.getElementById("myP").appendChild(txt);
```

can be reduced to:

```
document.getElementById("myP").innerHTML = "My dog has fleas.";
```

The innerText property, however, is not supported by Mozilla.

See Also

Recipe 14.9 for creating a new (empty) element of any tag type; Recipe 14.11 for using the DocumentFragment object as a temporary container of element and text nodes during assembly.

14.11 Creating Mixed Element and Text Nodes

Problem

You want to generate content that consists of elements as well as text inside those elements.

Solution

Use the W3C DOM DocumentFragment object as an arbitrary container while assembling the content:

```
var frag, myEm, txt1, txt2;
frag = document.createDocumentFragment( );
```

```
myEm = document.createElement("em");
txt1 = document.createTextNode("very");
myEm.appendChild(txt1);
txt1 = document.createTextNode("I am ");
txt2 = document.createTextNode(" happy to see you.");
frag.appendChild(txt1);
frag.appendChild(myEm);
frag.appendChild(txt2);
```

At this point, the fragment (which starts and ends with text nodes) is ready for insertion or replacement at any existing element node in the document tree.

Discussion

Treat the DocumentFragment object like a scratch pad capable of containing any well-formed sequence of node types. The fragment exists solely in memory and is not a part of the document tree.

Internet Explorer implements the DocumentFragment object in version 5 for the Macintosh and Version 6 or later for Windows. For earlier versions of Internet Explorer, there is no node-related equivalent. You can simulate the document fragment in memory by assembling element and text nodes in any generic container (such as a div or span). When it's time to place the content into the document tree, you can remove each child node of the temporary container, and append the removed node into the document's destination element. This is ugly, but possible.

Assembling mixed content, not as nodes but as strings, plays nicely in the innerHTML property of all elements (available in IE, Mozilla, Safari, and Opera). The equivalent of the node approach just shown looks like the following:

```
var newContent = "I am <em>very</em> happy to see you.";
```

Then assign the new content to the innerHTML property of the desired element, which replaces the existing content with the new content.

The IE-only DOM equips elements with another method that assists insertion of strings containing text with or without HTML markup that is to be treated as renderable HTML. The insertAdjacentHTML( ) method (compatible back to IE 4 and in Opera 7 or later) lets you determine where the insertion goes in relation to the element. The method takes two parameters. The first is a case-insensitive string signifying the relative location of the insertion point for the new content. Here are the four possible values for the first parameter:

BeforeBegin
In front of the start tag of the current element

AfterBegin
After the start tag, but immediately before any existing content of the current element

BeforeEnd

At the very end of the content of the element, just in front of the end tag

AfterEnd

After the end tag of the current element, but before any subsequent element

The new content is the second parameter. For example, to append the HTML string created earlier to an existing element whose ID is myP, the backward-compatible IE-only syntax is:

```
document.all("myP").insertAdjacentHTML("BeforeEnd", newContent);
```

Internet Explorer offers a large set of proprietary content manipulation methods, shown in Table 14-1.

Table 14-1. IE element content manipulation methods

Method	Compatibility	Description
contains(elemRef)	IE 4, Opera 7	Returns Boolean true if current element contains elemRef
getAdjacentText(where)	IE 5 (Win)	Returns text sequence from position where
insertAdjacentElement(where, elemRef)	IE 5 (Win), Opera 7	Inserts new element object at position where
insertAdjacentHTML(where, HTMLText)	IE 4, Opera 7	Inserts text (at position where), which gets rendered as HTML
insertAdjacentText(where, text)	IE 4, Opera 7	Inserts text (at position where) as literal text
removeNode(deep)	IE 4, Opera 7	Deletes element or text node (and its child nodes if deep is true)
replaceAdjacentText(where, text)	IE 5 (Win)	Replaces current text at position where with text
replaceNode(newNodeRef)	IE 5 (Win)	Replaces current node with new node
swapNode(otherNodeRef)	IE 5 (Win)	Exchanges current node with otherNodeRef, and return reference to removed node

See Also

Recipe 14.9 for creating a new element; Recipe 14.10 for creating a new text node.

14.12 Inserting and Populating an iframe Element

Problem

You want to create an iframe element, insert it into the current document, and place content into the iframe.

Solution

This task requires a little more than just creating elements and appending them to the document. This is a case in which one of the elements you create—an iframe— requires a document tree context before you can stuff it with data. The following code takes place in the global space. If you bury it inside a function, predeclare the newIframe variable as a global.

First, we are going to append an iframe to the end of the body element, and then we will put a dynamically generated form into the iframe. Begin the expected way, by creating the iframe element in memory, and inserting the empty iframe into the document:

```
// create a frame element node
var newIframe = document.createElement("iframe");
newIframe.setAttribute("id","newIframe");
// insert it into the document to give it context;
// set a tiny size, or display:none if you don't want to see it
document.body.appendChild(newIframe);
```

Next, obtain a reference to the document context that is needed for creating elements that are to go inside the iframe. For IE, that context is the document object inside the iframe's window object; for others, the main document is the appropriate context:

```
// get the browser-appropriate document context for content creation
if (navigator.appName == "Microsoft Internet Explorer") {
    var doc = newIframe.contentWindow.document;
} else {
    doc = document;
}
```

Now create the form and elements inside the form using the browser-specific document context. Unfortunately, IE tends to race ahead with its processing of script statements, sometimes causing statements to execute before the components under construction arrive on the scene. Therefore, it is necessary to put the brakes on processing with a setTimeout( ) method (set to zero delay) so that the final action can take place in a stable environment:

```
// create a form node within suitable document context
var newForm = doc.createElement("form")
newForm.setAttribute("id","sendform");
// create an input element node in the same context
var newField = doc.createElement("input");
newField.setAttribute("id","alldata");
newField.setAttribute("type","text");
// insert the field into the form
newForm.appendChild(newField);
// create and insert more form controls here
...
// insert the form into the iframe via delay
setTimeout("finishIframe( )", 0);
}
```

Finally, the form can be inserted into the body of the iframe's document:

```
// complete content insertion
function finishIframe( ) {
    newIframe.contentWindow.document.body.appendChild(newform);
}
```

Discussion

If you code the HTML for the iframe and its content in a regular HTML page, the elements for the form simply exist between the start and end tags of the iframe. This leads you logically to imagine that creating and inserting a form into a new iframe would use the same kind of document tree insertion that you see in Recipe 14.9 and Recipe 14.10. The difference is that an iframe element is a type of window object, just as if it were a different frame in a frameset. Therefore, to work with the iframe's content in a script, you must be able to access the document that lives inside the iframe. When your scripting context is that of the main document and all you have is a reference to the iframe, the avenue to the iframe's document is via the iframe's contentWindow—a reference to the window in the frame. That window doesn't exist in the object model until the new iframe is inserted into the document.

This roundabout way of reaching the content of an element is limited to those elements that contain window and document objects: frame elements and iframe elements. An object element also has a level of indirection, but no window is involved. Instead, an object element (in the W3C DOM, but not supported in IE as of version 7) has a contentDocument property. You won't have to worry about this situation for any other HTML elements.

See Also

Recipe 14.3 for using an iframe to blend separate HTML documents together; Recipe 14.9 for creating a new element; Recipe 14.10 for creating element text content.

14.13 Getting a Reference to an HTML Element Object

Problem

You want to derive a valid element object reference starting with the string ID or tag name of an existing element.

Solution

Use the W3C DOM method that has scope over every element in the document:

```
var elem = document.getElementById("elementID");
```

If the element doesn't have an `id` attribute assigned to it, you can reach the element by tag name. The following example retrieves an array of elements with the same tag name:

```
var elems = document.getElementsByTagName("tagName");
```

Assuming you know the position of the desired element among all elements with the same tag name, use standard array syntax to obtain a reference to the single element:

```
var elem = document.getElementsByTagName("tagName")[2];
```

Discussion

The `getElementById( )` method belongs to the `document` object, so the scope of the method is always the entire document, including the head and body sections of an HTML document. In contrast, the `getElementsByTagName( )` method can be invoked on any container. This allows you to narrow the scope of the collection. You can also supply an asterisk wildcard character (in IE only, starting with IE 6) to retrieve an array of all element objects:

```
var allElems = document.getElementsByTagName("*");
```

How you assign identifiers to repetitive elements can assist for loop scripts that need to work with a series of similar elements. For example, if you use scripts to generate a table dynamically so that script processing is accessing the content of cells in one of the columns, you can assign IDs in sequence, such as `subTotal0`, `subTotal1`, and so on. In the function that later loops through the cells in the column, you can use string concatenation in the argument to `getElementById( )` to avoid use of the horribly inefficient `eval( )` function:

```
for (var i = 0; i < array.length; i++) {
    ...
    subTotCell = document.getElementById("subTotal" + i);
    ...
}
```

If you need a reference to an element in earlier browsers, you can use a pair of methods from Recipe 13.3's DHTML API that does the job across browsers and generations:

```
// Seek nested NN4 layer from string name
seekLayer : function (doc, name) {
    var elem;
    for (var i = 0; i < doc.layers.length; i++) {
        if (doc.layers[i].name == name) {
            elem = doc.layers[i];
            break;
        }
        // dive into nested layers if necessary
        if (doc.layers[i].document.layers.length > 0) {
            elem = this.seekLayer(doc.layers[i].document, name);
            if (elem) {break;}
        }
    }
```

```
            return elem;
        },

        // Convert element name string or object reference
        // into a valid element object reference
        getRawObject : function (elemRef) {
            var elem;
            if (typeof elemRef == "string") {
                if (this.browserClass.isW3C) {
                    elem = document.getElementById(elemRef);
                } else if (this.browserClass.isIE4) {
                    elem = document.all(elemRef);
                } else if (this.browserClass.isNN4) {
                    elem = this.seekLayer(document, elemRef);
                }
            } else {
                // pass through object reference
                elem = elemRef;
            }
            return elem;
        },
```

To use this pair of methods, invoke DHTMLAPI.getRawObject( ), passing a string of the desired element's ID. For IE 4, the function uses the document.all collection, which contains all elements in the document. For NN 4, however, only positioned elements (layers) are accessible in this manner (not all elements are exposed to the object model in NN 4). In case the NN 4 layer is nested inside another, the getRawObject( ) method invokes the seekLayer( ) method to iterate through all layers and nested layers in search of the one whose id attribute matches the parameter passed to getRawObject( ).

See Also

Recipe 13.3 for complete details about how the DHTML API library uses flexible object references in its dynamic positioning functions; Recipe 14.14 for obtaining a reference to an element by class attribute value.

14.14 Referencing All Elements of the Same Class

Problem

You want to reference an element based on the value assigned to its class attribute, rather than its id attribute.

Solution

Use the following function, which returns an array of elements whose class attribute is (or contains) the string passed as a parameter:

```
function getElementsByClassName(className) {
    var allElements = (document.all) ? document.all : document.
getElementsByTagName("*");
    var results = new Array();
    var re = new RegExp("\\b" + className + "\\b");
    for (var i = 0; i < allElements.length; i++) {
        if (re.test(allElements[i].className)) {
            results.push(allElements[i]);
        }
    }
    return results;
}
```

This function accommodates those cases in which you have assigned more than one value to the class attribute.

Discussion

The W3C DOM provides no built-in facility for retrieving all elements that share a class name. Because a class is another way to provide a semblance of context for elements—differentiating among all the divs in a document, for instance—your scripts may need to reach these elements, even when their IDs are not known. As long as you know the class name, you can use the function in the Solution to retrieve an array of all elements matching that class.

A bug in IE prior to version 6 causes the wildcard character to be ignored by the getElementsByTagName() method. Therefore, the function gives priority to the document.all version, if supported by the browser.

The HTML 4 spec allows multiple, space-delimited values to be assigned to the class attribute. The function uses a regular expression to inspect the className property value in search of the desired class value (including word boundaries around the name to prevent a mistaken match on a longer name that includes a shorter one).

Once your script receives the returned array, it can iterate through the smaller collection of elements and perform whatever manipulations are needed. You can even assign a new value to the property if, for example, you wish to assign a different style rule to all elements meeting the criteria.

See Also

Recipe 11.2 for more about CSS class selectors; Recipe 11.8 for changing style rule assignments by script.

14.15 Replacing Portions of Body Content

Problem

You want to replace content in the document with dynamically generated content.

Solution

There are different tactics, depending on whether the content to be replaced is simply the text content of an element or a series of HTML elements. To replace all text content inside an element, create a text node and replace the container's current child node with the new one:

```
var txt = document.createTextNode("Every good boy does fine.");
var elem = document.getElementById("someElement");
var oldTxt = elem.replaceChild(txt, elem.firstChild);
```

When the element's current content contains both text and interlaced elements (such as a paragraph element containing a portion of text marked up as an em element), delete each nested node prior to inserting the new content:

```
var txt = document.createTextNode("Every good boy does fine.");
var elem = document.getElementById("someElement");
while (elem.childNodes.length > 0) {
    elem.removeChild(elem.firstChild);
}
elem.appendChild(txt);
```

To replace one child element with a newly created element, use the replaceChild( ) method:

```
var newElem = document.createElement("span");
newElem.setAttribute("id", "newSpan");
var elem = document.getElementById("someElement");
elem.replaceChild(newElem, elem.firstChild);
```

For more complex content, especially content beginning or ending with a text node, use the DocumentFragment object as a temporary container of the created document, and then insert or replace in the destination element as needed (see Recipe 14.11).

Discussion

If you intend to replace just a portion of an existing text node, you have a couple of options—sthe more sophisticated of which entails text range objects, illustrated in Recipe 15.3. But for simpler cases, you can use unsophisticated string parsing on the old and new text. The basic sequence is to extract a copy of the element's text node, whose nodeValue property consists of the actual string. Then use the JavaScript string replace( ) method to put the new substring in place of the old. Next, reassign the text to the nodeValue property of the text node in the document tree. Here is a brief example, with some hardwired values, that replaces the string "coming" with "going":

```
var elem = document.getElementById("myP");
var srchText = /coming/g;
var replacement = "going";
var elemText = elem.firstChild.nodeValue.replace(srchText, replacement);
elem.firstChild.nodeValue = elemText;
```

If your design dictates knowing ahead of time that a particular portion of an element's text will be replaced on a regular basis, it is easier to surround that text in a span element and use that container as a localizer for the text to be swapped out. Similarly, if you design a page that arrives with a portion of the page empty, in anticipation of scripts filling in content upon loading or after user interaction, insert empty elements in position. You can see examples of this in Recipes 14.6 and 14.7, where an empty tbody element is pre-installed in a table element to act as a receptor for table rows and cells created by functions triggered after the page has loaded.

See Also

Recipe 14.9 for creating elements; Recipe 14.10 for creating text content; Recipe 14.11 for more about the DocumentFragment object; Recipe 1.8 for string search and replace with regular expressions; Recipe 15.3 for using text ranges for body text search-and-replace operations.

14.16 Removing Body Content

Problem

You want to eliminate an element or portion of text from the current document.

Solution

If you have a reference to the element you wish to delete, you can use the W3C DOM removeChild( ) method to remove the element. The method works only on child nodes, so you must step outward to the element's parent to invoke the method:

```
var elem = document.getElementById("spanToGo");
elem.parentNode.removeChild(elem);
```

To eliminate text from a text node, set its node value to an empty string:

```
var container = document.getElementById("someSpan");
// verify that the child node is a text node before emptying it
if (container.firstChild.nodeType == 3) {
    container.firstChild.nodeValue = "";
}
```

To remove the text node entirely, use the removeChild( ) method as shown above for the element node removal.

Discussion

When you remove repetitive elements, such as rows of a table, you may need to iterate through a collection when appropriate. For example, a table or tbody element object has a rows property that returns a collection of all tr element objects nested within. If you intend to remove all the rows, it is efficient to remove them via a tight while loop, acting on the first child until there are no more children:

```
var tbody = document.getElementById("myTableBody");
while (tbody.rows.length > 0) {
    tbody.removeChild(tbody.firstChild);
}
```

But if removal among a collection is meant to be selective, you also have to account for a changing collection of numeric indexes for the collection's array while the array gets smaller. To work around this potential problem, use a for loop that starts at the end and decrements the index counter so that the counter doesn't get off track with a changing collection.

For an example of selective deletion in action, consider the following table, in which each row contains a checkbox and some text. A button at the bottom of the table deletes any and all rows in which the checkbox is checked. The HTML for the table is as follows:

```
<form>
<table>
<tbody id="myTBody">
<tr>
    <td><input type="checkbox"></td><td>Item 1</td>
</tr>
<tr>
    <td><input type="checkbox"></td><td>Item 2</td>
</tr>
<tr>
    <td><input type="checkbox"></td><td>Item 3</td>
</tr>
<tr>
    <td><input type="checkbox"></td><td>Item 4</td>
</tr>
<tr>
    <td><input type="checkbox"></td><td>Item 5</td>
</tr>
<tr>
    <td colspan="2">
    <input type="button" value="Remove Checked" onclick="remove( )"></td>
    </td>
</tr>
</tbody>
</table>
</form>
```

The remove( ) function is as follows:

```
function remove( ) {
    var elem = document.getElementById("myTBody");
    for (var i = elem.rows.length-1; i >= 0 ; i--) {
        if (elem.rows[i].cells[0].firstChild.checked) {
            elem.removeChild(elem.rows[i]);
        }
    }
}
```

You could also use the deleteRow( ) method of the tbody object in the function.

See Also

Recipe 14.13 for ways to reference elements in the document.

14.17 Using XMLHttpRequest for a REST Request

Problem

You want to invoke a process on a server via a URL and process the results without disturbing the current HTML page in the browser.

Solution

Use the XMLDoc( ) object constructor (from Recipe 14.4) to create a cross-browser object for working with the XMLHttpRequest object:

```
// constructor function for an XML request object;
function XMLDoc( ) {
    var me = this;
    var req = null;
    // branch for native XMLHttpRequest object
    if (window.XMLHttpRequest) {
        try {
            req = new XMLHttpRequest( );
        } catch(e) {
            req = null;
        }
    // branch for IE/Windows ActiveX versions
    } else if (window.ActiveXObject) {
        try {
            req = new ActiveXObject("Msxml2.XMLHTTP");
        } catch(e) {
            try {
                req = new ActiveXObject("Microsoft.XMLHTTP");
            } catch(e) {
                req = null;
            }
        }
    } else {
```

```
            alert("This example requires a browser with XML support, such as IE5+/
    Windows, Mozilla, Safari 1.2, or Opera 8.")
        }
        // preserve reference to request object for later
        this.request = req;
        // "public" method to be invoked whenever
        this.loadXMLDoc = function(url, loadHandler) {
            if (this.request) {
                this.request.open("GET", url, true);
                this.request.onreadystatechange = function () {loadHandler(me)};
                this.request.setRequestHeader("Content-Type", "text/xml");
                this.request.send("");
            }
        };
    }
```

Create an instance of the object, and then invoke its loadXMLDoc( ) method, passing
the full request URL and a reference to a function to process the results:

```
function initXML( ) {
    var salesRequest = new XMLDoc( );
    salesRequest.loadXMLDoc("webservices.jsp?Operation=ItemRankLookup&ItemId=1234567",
        showSalesRanking);
}
```

Set up your post-query processing function to receive the request object and perform
work on the XML data once it is completely received, as in the following:

```
function showSalesRanking(req) {
    req = req.request;
    if (req.readyState == 4 && req.status == 200) {
        var xDoc = req.responseXML;
        // further processing of document here
    }
}
```

Discussion

REST is an acronym for Representational State Transfer, one of two popular and
standard ways of communicating with a server process via the HTTP protocol. The
choice between REST and SOAP is made by the designer of the server software at the
other end of an HTTP request. Your requests will have to conform to the format
imposed by the server software designer.

Typically, a REST request is formatted in a way similar to a web form submission (by
either the GET or POST method). The URL points to a server destination, appended
with one or more name/value pairs that provide details of the request. A question
mark delimits the appendage from the destination; name/value pairs have an equals
sign between each name and value, and an ampersand delimits each pair.

Most of the "heavy lifting" of an Ajax-style communication is handled by the
XMLHttpRequest object. Once an instance of the object is created (whether it come as

an IE 6 or earlier ActiveX object or native object in other browsers), a number of methods set the stage for transmission of the request. Table 14-2 lists the methods that all versions of the XMLHttpRequest object have in common.

Table 14-2. Methods of a request object

Method	Description
abort( )	Stops current request transaction
getAllResponseHeaders( )	Returns a list of headers arriving with the response
getResponseHeader( )	Returns a value of a specific header name
open( )	Assigns method, URL, and other attributes to a request waiting to be sent
send( )	Sends the previously specified request over the network
setRequestHeader( )	Sets a header name/value pair for a request waiting to be sent

You can see the key methods being invoked within the code shown in the Solution. Several methods must be called in a strict order. In particular, the sequence of open( ), setRequestHeader( ), and send( ) cannot be altered, although other statements can occur between these method calls.

In the example above, the open( ) method passes three parameters. The first is a string declaring the request type (GET or POST). The second is the URL of the process on the server. And the third is a Boolean value that indicates whether the request should be made asynchronously (true) or synchronously (false). All REST calls should be made asynchronously so that the browser won't hang while waiting for a slow or non-responsive server (the first "A" in Ajax stands for "Asynchronous").

The "data" portion of the request is contained by the search portion of the URL passed as the second parameter of open( ). Therefore, the send( ) method's parameter for a REST request is an empty string.

Other activities with the object involve getting or setting properties. Properties shared by all types of XMLHttpRequest objects are shown in Table 14-3.

Table 14-3. Lowest common denominator properties of a request object

Property	Description
onreadystatechange	Event property to bind to a function handler that acts during or after the request transaction
readyState	Request object status (0 = uninitialized; 1 = loading; 2 = loaded; 3 = interactive; 4 = complete)
responseText	String version of all data retrieved in last request
responseXML	XML document node (nodeType of 9) if data is an XML data type
status	Numeric status code returned by server (e.g., 200 for success)
statusText	Message string (if any) returned with status integer

Only one property, onreadystatechange, is adjusted prior to the request being sent. Its value is a reference to the function to be invoked each time the readystate event fires on the object. Each time the referenced function is invoked, a reference to the request object is automatically passed as the sole parameter to the function.

The state changes several times during reception of the data returned from the server. It is the job of your function to inspect the readyState and status properties of the request object to validate that the request was successful (a status value of 200) and the transmission is complete (a readyState value of 4). For cross-browser debugging purposes, you can insert alert( ) dialogs to view the readyState and status properties to make sure your request URL is formatted the way desired by the server process. If you receive status values other than 200, something is amiss.

At this point, your script may obtain a copy of the XML document object (responseXML) or a string representation of the data (responseText). If you intend to parse the document node tree, use the responseXML value. But a server process may also return a non-XML string that is written in the form of a JavaScript array and/or object notation. This so-called JavaScript Object Notation (JSON) can be retrieved from the responseText property and duly converted into real arrays and objects via the eval( ) function.

As its name implies, an XMLHttpRequest transaction is strictly a request-style communication. No open communication line exists between the browser and server once the returned data has been sent back to the browser. Therefore, this is not a server-push type of technology.

See Also

Recipe 14.4 for more about embedding XML data into a web page; Recipe 14.18 for making a SOAP call in the background; Recipe 14.8 for converting XML data into JavaScript objects.

14.18 Using XMLHttpRequest for a SOAP Call

Problem

You want to invoke a remote procedure by way of the SOAP protocol.

Solution

Use a SOAP-specific variation of the routine shown in Recipes 14.4 and 14.17. The new variation utilizes the same XMLHttpRequest object as its basis, but sends its data to the server separately from the URL:

```
// constructor function for an XML request object;
function SOAPCall() {
    var me = this;
```

```
        var req = null;
        // branch for native XMLHttpRequest object
        if (window.XMLHttpRequest) {
            try {
                req = new XMLHttpRequest();
            } catch(e) {
                req = null;
            }
        // branch for IE/Windows ActiveX versions
        } else if (window.ActiveXObject) {
            try {
                req = new ActiveXObject("Msxml2.XMLHTTP");
            } catch(e) {
                try {
                    req = new ActiveXObject("Microsoft.XMLHTTP");
                } catch(e) {
                    req = null;
                }
            }
        } else {
            alert("This example requires a browser with XML support, such as IE5+/
Windows, Mozilla, Safari 1.2, or Opera 8.")
        }
        // preserve reference to request object for later
        this.request = req;
        // "public" method to be invoked whenever
        this.loadSOAP = function(url, data, loadHandler) {
            if (this.request) {
                this.request.open("POST", url);
                this.request.onreadystatechange = function () {loadHandler(me)};
                soapReq.setRequestHeader("Content-Type","text/xml; charset=utf-8");
                soapReq.setRequestHeader("SOAPAction","");
                this.request.send(data);
            }
        };
    }
```

Processing data returned by the server is handled the same way as with a REST request, shown in Recipe 14.17.

Discussion

SOAP is an acronym for Simple Object Access Protocol or Service Oriented Architecture Protocol. It is a way for a client to invoke a process on the server, usually with the server responding with some type of result.

The big difference between SOAP and REST (Recipe 14.17) is that the "command" sent to the server is in the form of an XML document. The structure for this document is determined by the author of the server process. You will be provided with the structure of such an XML request by any service offering this capability.

Some of the structure is imposed by the SOAP standard, but there is plenty of room for variable pieces that are specific to the task running on the server. The following example is for a command requesting current conversion rates between two countries' currencies:

```
<SOAP-ENV:Envelope
    xmlns:SOAP-ENV="http://schemas.xmlsoap.org/soap/envelope/"
    xmlns:xsi="http://www.w3.org/1999/XMLSchema-instance"
    xmlns:xsd="http://www.w3.org/1999/XMLSchema">
    <SOAP-ENV:Body>
        <ns1:getCurrencyRate
            xmlns:ns1="urn:xmethods-CurrencyRate"
            SOAP-ENV:encodingStyle="http://schemas.xmlsoap.org/soap/encoding/">
            <countryfrom xsi:type="xsd:string">canada</countryfrom>
            <countryto xsi:type="xsd:string">india</countryto>
        </ns1:getCurrencyRate>
    </SOAP-ENV:Body>
</SOAP-ENV:Envelope>
```

Despite so much XML code, only two pieces—the country names in the countryfrom and countryto elements—change from one SOAP call to the next. Everything else remains the same (and would be provided to you by a SOAP service provider).

Your script needs to assemble this data, which it can do either as an XML document or as a string. As an example of performing this operation with string data, the following script segments create an instance of the SOAPCall object (from the Solution), assemble the SOAP data (the variable data shown in bold), and then send the data via the SOAPCall object:

```
function recalc(req) {
    // handles results of XMLHttpRequest retrieval
}
// assembles parameters for loadSOAP method and invokes
function fetchConversionRate(fromCountry, toCountry) {
    var url = 'soap.jsp';
    var data = '<?xml version="1.0" encoding="UTF-8"?><SOAP-ENV:Envelope xmlns:SOAP-
ENV="http://schemas.xmlsoap.org/soap/envelope/" xmlns:xsi="http://www.w3.org/1999/
XMLSchema-instance" xmlns:xsd="http://www.w3.org/1999/XMLSchema"><SOAP-ENV:Body><ns1:
getCurrencyRate xmlns:ns1="urn:xmethods-CurrencyExchange" SOAP-ENV:
encodingStyle="http://schemas.xmlsoap.org/soap/encoding/"><countryfrom xsi:type="xsd:
string">' + fromCountry + '</countryfrom><countryto xsi:type="xsd:string">' +
toCountry + '</countryto></ns1:getCurrencyRate ></SOAP-ENV:Body></SOAP-ENV:Envelope>
';
    var soapMachine = new SOAPCall();
    soapMachine.loadSOAP(url, data, recalc);
}
// trigger the SOAP call
fetchConversionRate("canada", "india");
```

The XMLHttpRequest object sends the data to the server as a text string. Unlike the example here, if you supply an XML document as a parameter to the send( ) method, the object automatically converts (serializes) the XML document to a string for transmission.

See Also

Recipe 14.17 for a REST-type of request via XMLHttpRequest.

14.19 Sorting Dynamic Tables

Problem

You want users to be able to view a table sorted according to different column values.

Solution

Sorting a table works best when the data for the table is delivered as JavaScript or XML data, using the kinds of table transformations shown in Recipes 14.6 and 14.7. The table data does not need to be any different from what was demonstrated in those recipes. The difference is in the fixed table column headings and the functions invoked from links surrounding the heading text.

Design your HTML structure such that clickable user interface elements let users control the table's sorting order. Table header text formatted as hyperlinks is most common. Next, define JavaScript array sorting functions for each of your sorting criteria. See the Discussion for an example. Finally, use a script routine to generate the body of the table based on the current sort order of the JavaScript data array (see the Discussion). Each time the user requests a sorting of the data array, the table body is refreshed with the data in the desired order.

Discussion

For an example of what a sortable table framework looks like, the hardwired HTML portion of the table from Recipe 14.7 is shown here, modified with th cell content fixed with clickable links.

```
<table id="cupFinals">
<thead>
<tr>
    <th><a href="#" title="Sort by Year"
        onclick="return sortTable(this)">Year</a></th>
    <th><a href="#" title="Sort by Country"
        onclick="return sortTable(this)">Host Country</a></th>
    <th><a href="#" title="Sort by Winning Team"
        onclick="return sortTable(this)">Winner</a></th>
    <th><a href="#" title="Sort by Losing Team"
        onclick="return sortTable(this)">Loser</a></th>
    <th>Score <a href="#" title="Sort by Winning Score"
            onclick="return sortTable(this)">Win</a> - <a href="#"
            title="Sort by Losing Score"
            onclick="return sortTable(this)">Lose</a></th>
</tr>
</thead>
```

```
<tbody id="matchData"></tbody>
</table>
```

All links invoke the same sortTable( ) function, which acts as a central switchboard
to individual array sorting routines. A switch statement branches execution based on
the text of the link's th element:

```
// Sorting function dispatcher (invoked by table column links)
function sortTable(link) {
    switch (link.firstChild.nodeValue) {
        case "Year" :
            jsData.sort(sortByYear);
            break;
        case "Host Country" :
            jsData.sort(sortByHost);
            break;
        case "Winner" :
            jsData.sort(sortByWinner);
            break;
        case "Loser" :
            jsData.sort(sortByLoser);
            break;
        case "Win" :
            jsData.sort(sortByWinScore);
            break;
        case "Lose" :
            jsData.sort(sortByLosScore);
            break;
    }
    drawTable("matchData")
    return false
}
```

Each of the sorting routines sorts the jsData array based on criteria that examine a
specific property of each jsData item's object:

```
// Sorting functions (invoked by sortTable( ))
function sortByYear(a, b) {
    return a.year - b.year;
}
function sortByHost(a, b) {
    a = a.location.toLowerCase( );
    b = b.location.toLowerCase( );
    return ((a < b) ? -1 : ((a > b) ? 1 : 0));
}
function sortByWinScore(a, b) {
    return b.winScore - a.winScore;
}
function sortByLosScore(a, b) {
    return b.losScore - a.losScore;
}
function sortByWinner(a, b) {
    a = a.winner.toLowerCase( );
    b = b.winner.toLowerCase( );
    return ((a < b) ? -1 : ((a > b) ? 1 : 0));
```

```
    }
    function sortByLoser(a, b) {
        a = a.loser.toLowerCase( );
        b = b.loser.toLowerCase( );
        return ((a < b) ? -1 : ((a > b) ? 1 : 0));
    }
```

Back in the sortTable( ) function, once the jsData table is sorted by the desired property, the drawTable( ) function executes. This is slightly modified over Recipe 14.7 to
include a call to another function that clears all rows from the tbody element reserved
for the dynamic cells. The modified drawTable( ) method is as follows:

```
// Draw table from 'jsData' array of objects
function drawTable(tbody) {
    var tr, td;
    tbody = document.getElementById(tbody);
    // remove existing rows, if any
    clearTable(tbody);
    // loop through data source
    for (var i = 0; i < jsData.length; i++) {
        tr = tbody.insertRow(tbody.rows.length);
        td = tr.insertCell(tr.cells.length);
        td.setAttribute("align", "center");
        td.innerHTML = jsData[i].year;
        td = tr.insertCell(tr.cells.length);
        td.innerHTML = jsData[i].location;
        td = tr.insertCell(tr.cells.length);
        td.innerHTML = jsData[i].winner;
        td = tr.insertCell(tr.cells.length);
        td.innerHTML = jsData[i].loser;
        td = tr.insertCell(tr.cells.length);
        td.setAttribute("align", "center");
        td.innerHTML = jsData[i].winScore + " - " + jsData[i].losScore;
    }
}
```

The clearTable( ) function is a simple loop that removes any rows in the table body
section:

```
// Remove existing table rows
function clearTable(tbody) {
    while (tbody.rows.length > 0) {
        tbody.deleteRow(0);
    }
}
```

Most of the sorting comparison functions in this recipe inspect properties of objects
that occupy each array entry. Because each jsData array entry is an object (see the
object definition in Recipe 14.7), the comparison functions repeatedly compare specific properties of the object, such as names of teams and score numbers. To ensure
accurate string comparisons regardless of case, they are converted to a uniform case
(lowercase in the example) so that the differing upper- and lowercase ASCII values
do not play a role in the comparisons.

Although the code above contributes a lot of functions to the global naming space, it is a simple matter to encapsulate many of them as nested functions. All of the individual sorting functions are perfect candidates for being nested inside the sortTable( ) function, for example.

See Also

Recipe 14.7 for embedding data as JavaScript objects and arrays (which enhance table sorting possibilities); Recipe 3.5 for simple array sorting; Recipe 3.10 for sorting an array of objects.

14.20 Walking the Document Node Tree

Problem

You want to iterate through the entire document node tree in search of nodes meeting desired criteria.

Solution

The following getLikeElements( ) function returns a collection of elements that share the same tag name, attribute name, and attribute value (specified as arguments):

```
function getLikeElements(tagName, attrName, attrValue) {
    var startSet;
    var endSet = new Array( );
    if (tagName) {
        startSet = document.getElementsByTagName(tagName);
    } else {
        startSet = (document.all) ? document.all :
            document.getElementsByTagName("*");
    }
    if (attrName) {
        for (var i = 0; i < startSet.length; i++) {
            if (startSet[i].getAttribute(attrName)) {
                if (attrValue) {
                    if (startSet[i].getAttribute(attrName) == attrValue) {
                        endSet[endSet.length] = startSet[i];
                    }
                } else {
                    endSet[endSet.length] = startSet[i];
                }
            }
        }
    } else {
        endSet = startSet;
    }
    return endSet;
}
```

Discussion

You can omit one or more arguments of the getLikeElements( ) function in specific combinations. For example, if you omit all three arguments, you receive a collection of all elements in the document. Specify only the first argument (the tag name) to retrieve all elements with the same tag name. If you supply the tag name and attribute name only, the returned collection contains elements that have the same tag name and have the same attribute specified, regardless of attribute value. If you specify an attribute value, you must also pass an attribute name. For empty arguments, pass either an empty string or null when they precede nonempty arguments. The following invocations of getLikeElements( ) are all valid:

```
var collection = getLikeElements();
var collection = getLikeElements("td");
var collection = getLikeElements("", "class");
var collection = getLikeElements("", "class", "highlight");
var collection = getLikeElements("td", "align", "center");
```

Use caution, however, when retrieving input elements that have value attributes. Mozilla returns only those elements with explicitly set value attributes, while IE returns all input elements because the browser automatically assigns a value attribute to input elements such as radio and checkbox buttons.

Another variation on the notion of walking a document tree is to use a script to diagram the document to reveal its nested node structure. Object model facilities for retrieving all elements in a document completely flatten the node hierarchy. To preserve the hierarchy and track it, you can use a routine like the following walkChildNodes( ) function, which accumulates a string that reveals the node structure of any object passed as the first parameter of the function. The function invokes itself recursively as it dives into nested hierarchies, and internally passes the second argument to help the function keep track of which nested level it is currently processing.

```
function walkChildNodes(objRef, n) {
    var obj;
    if (objRef) {
        if (typeof objRef == "string") {
            obj = document.getElementById(objRef);
        } else {
            obj = objRef;
        }
    } else {
        obj = (document.body.parentElement) ?
            document.body.parentElement : document.body.parentNode;
    }
    var output = "";
    var indent = "";
    var i, group, txt;
    if (n) {
        for (i = 0; i < n; i++) {
```

```
                indent += "+---";
        }
    } else {
        n = 0;
        output += "Child Nodes of <" + obj.tagName .toLowerCase( );
        output += ">\n=== == == == == == == == ==\n";
    }
    group = obj.childNodes;
    for (i = 0; i < group.length; i++) {
        output += indent;
        switch (group[i].nodeType) {
            case 1:
                output += "<" + group[i].tagName.toLowerCase( );
                output += (group[i].id) ? " ID=" + group[i].id : "";
                output += (group[i].name) ? " NAME=" + group[i].name : "";
                output += ">\n";
                break;
            case 3:
                txt = group[i].nodeValue.substr(0,15);
                output += "[Text:\"" + txt.replace(/[\r\n]/g,"<cr>");
                if (group[i].nodeValue.length > 15) {
                    output += "...";
                }
                output += "\"]\n";
                break;
            case 8:
                output += "[!COMMENT!]\n";
                break;
            default:
                output += "[Node Type = " + group[i].nodeType + "]\n";
        }
        if (group[i].childNodes.length > 0) {
            output += walkChildNodes(group[i], n+1);
        }
    }
    return output;
}
```

To invoke the walkChildNodes( ) function to capture the node structure of a document's body element, the call looks like the following:

```
walkChildNodes(document.body);
```

Output from walkChildNodes( ) displays the tags of each element node (with their IDs, if assigned), and samples of text nodes to help you identify them. The following trace shows the body of a document containing the Recipe 14.1 script plus a portion of the table from the discussion of Recipe 14.16:

```
Child Nodes of <body>
=== == == == == == == == == ==
<h1>
+---[Text:"Welcome to Gian..."]
<h2>
+---[Text:"We Love"]
```

```
+---<script>
+---[Text:" Windows "]
+---<noscript>
+---[Text:"Users!"]
<hr>
<form>
+---<table>
+---+---<tbody ID=myTBody>
+---+---+---<tr>
+---+---+---+---<td>
+---+---+---+---+---<input>
+---+---+---+---<td>
+---+---+---+---+---[Text:"Item 1"]
+---+---+---<tr>
+---+---+---+---<td>
+---+---+---+---+---<input>
+---+---+---+---<td>
+---+---+---+---+---[Text:"Item 2"]
+---+---+---<tr>
+---+---+---+---<td>
+---+---+---+---+---<input>
+---+---+---+---</td>
```

You can use the walkChildNodes() function as a diagnostic tool, particularly for dynamically created HTML content. If you embed the function into the document as well as into a temporary textarea element, your content creation function can end with a call to walkChildNodes() to output the results to the textarea for closer inspection, and comparison against what you think the node hierarchy should be.

One last technique to be aware of is the W3C DOM TreeWalker object, which is available in Mozilla, Safari 2 or later, and Opera 8 or later (but not in IE as of version 7). The TreeWalker object is a live, hierarchical list of nodes that meet criteria defined by the document.createTreeWalker() method. The list assumes the same parent-descendant hierarchy for its items as the nodes to which its items point. The createTreeWalker() method describes the node where the list begins and which nodes (or classes of nodes) are exempt from the list by way of filtering.

The TreeWalker object maintains a kind of pointer inside the list (so that your scripts don't have to). Methods of this object let scripts access the next or previous node (or sibling, child, or parent node) in the list, while moving the pointer in the direction indicated by the method you chose. If scripts modify the document tree after the TreeWalker is created, changes to the document tree are automatically reflected in the sequence of nodes in the TreeWalker.

While fully usable in an HTML document, the TreeWalker can be even more valuable when working with an XML data document. For example, the W3C DOM does not provide a quick way to access all elements that have a particular attribute name (something that the XPath standard can do easily on the server). But you can define a TreeWalker to point only to nodes that have the desired attribute and quickly access those nodes sequentially (i.e., without having to script more laborious looping through all nodes in search of the desired elements). For example, the following filter function allows only those nodes that contain the author attribute to be a member of a TreeWalker object:

```
function authorAttrFilter(node) {
    if (node.hasAttribute("author")) {
        return NodeFilter.FILTER_ACCEPT;
    }
    return NodeFilter.FILTER_SKIP;
}
```

A reference to this function becomes one of the parameters to a createTreeWalker( ) method that also limits the list to element nodes:

```
var authorsOnly = document.createTreeWalker(document, NodeFilter.SHOW_ELEMENT,
                    authorAttrFilter, false);
```

You can then invoke TreeWalker object methods to obtain a reference to one of the nodes in the list. When you invoke the method, the TreeWalker object applies the filter to candidates relative to the current position of the internal pointer in the direction indicated by the method. The next document tree node to meet the method and filter criteria is returned. Once you have that node reference, you can access any DOM node property or method to work with the node, independent of the items in the TreeWalker list.

See Also

Recipe 1.1 for concatenating string segments to build long strings.

14.21 Capturing Document Content

Problem

You want to grab a copy of the current HTML node tree, including any dynamic changes made to it by scripts.

Solution

The need for this feature most commonly occurs when you haven't prepared for it—for example, as an ad hoc debugging tool. Therefore, to get an emergency copy of the page's HTML, enter the following URL as one unbroken line into the Address/Location box of your browser:

```
javascript: void window.open("","","").document.write("<textarea cols=80
rows=20>" + document.body.parentNode.innerHTML + "</textarea>")
```

This code produces a new window containing a single textarea element displaying all HTML inside the <html> and </html> tags of the page at that instant.

Discussion

When you use dynamic element creation, it frequently becomes difficult to know if a rendering problem is due to a browser problem or a problem in the document tree caused by your element modification scripts. Viewing the source in the browser isn't much help here, because that view tends to mimic only the page as delivered to the browser, without any of the dynamic modifications your scripts make to the page after it loads.

An ideal way to diagnose these kinds of problems is to isolate a copy of the HTML as the browser sees it, paste it into a test document, and then load that test document into the browsers for which you develop. Sometimes, simply viewing the HTML quickly reveals problems such as improperly closed container tags (more common if you use the IE HTML string modification methods than the W3C DOM node-modification methods), unbalanced elements in tables, or a missing attribute. But even if the problem is more elusive, it is far easier to work in a scriptless and stable HTML environment, experimenting with tags and attributes to find the combination that works as desired in all target browsers. Then you can go back to your content modification scripts to plug the holes in content creation routines.

The javascript: pseudo-URL shown in the Solution can be modified to provide a larger or smaller textarea element. Once you find a combination that works best for you, create a bookmark for this URL. This kind of active JavaScript bookmark is commonly called a bookmarklet. It works on pages retrieved from any server.

You can even use it in a frameset. Simply reference the frame in which you're interested:

```
javascript: void window.open("","","").document.write("<textarea cols=80
rows=20>" + top.frames[1].document.body.parentNode.innerHTML + "</textarea>")
```

Be aware that IE for Windows may not produce all of the markup, particularly the head element contents, when the page is defined as a strictly XHTML file. You can experiment with the reference in the bookmarklet to point to the desired segment of the page you're looking at.

See Also

Recipe 14.20 for another way to examine a document's structure by walking the document node tree.

CHAPTER 15
Dynamic Content Applications

15.0 Introduction

This chapter's recipes attempt to provide solutions for real-world challenges that you may encounter in your DHTML development. The difficulty in arriving at such a roster of solutions is that DHTML is flexible enough to inspire the imaginations of every developer in different directions. While most of the recipes here can be used as-is, they are also meant to serve as basic foundations upon which you can build your specific application. If these recipes give you ideas for ways to add value to your site, all the better.

Several of the recipes in this chapter rely on scriptable objects whose powers are not always easy to grasp: the JavaScript core language Date object (covered in depth in Chapter 2), and an object representing text ranges (known as the TextRange object in IE for Windows and the Range object in the W3C DOM). The abstract nature of these objects and the technical details of their operation can cause numerous conceptual problems along the way.

Although the details of text range implementations in the IE for Windows and W3C DOMs are quite different, their fundamental operations are the same. At its core, a *text range* is a sequence of body text separate from the HTML elements that surround or are nested within the sequence. You don't see a text range, per se, although it is possible to highlight its text for the user to see, if it's important to your application.

A text range has a starting point and an ending point. When you create a text range, it has a default set of boundaries (again, the details vary with DOM type). Relocating those two boundaries may entail a reference to an HTML element, but the text range itself is devoid of any node hierarchy like that of the HTML document. The typical sequence of working with a text range is to create the abstract text range, position its boundary points, and then perform some operation on the text (such as removing the contents or grabbing a copy of the text). For example, you can convert a user selection of a portion of body text to a span element that is then under the control of a style sheet rule (see Recipe 15.2).

Between the two implementations, the IE TextRange object is the more flexible and better equipped for practical duty. It is the only one that offers facilities for searching within the body text for string matches (and positioning the boundary points around the found instance). Importantly, the IE TextRange object can also be applied to content in a textarea element. Therefore, while it may appear cool to be able to script a global search-and-replace operation in the body text (Recipe 15.3), it's more practical in a textarea containing a bunch of text supplied by the user.

Because many of the recipes in this chapter deal with positioning elements on the page, many rely on the importation of the DHTML API library shown in Recipe 13.3. Scripts with dependencies on the functions of that library are clearly marked. Although the library is not large, you are free to create a version of the library that includes only the functions needed for a specific application. Or you can copy and paste those functions into your in-document code or other .js library code. Also, be on the lookout for recipes that employ cookies to preserve settings across sessions— they use the *cookies.js* library from Recipe 1.10.

Several of the following recipes rely on the *eventsManager.js* library (Recipe 9.3) because they do their work after the page loads. In some cases, the scripts modify the page for scriptable browser visitors. The idea is to let the page convey its primary information for all visitors, and enhance the page for script-enabled visitors. This technique is sometimes referred to as *progressive JavaScript* or *unobtrusive JavaScript*. As stated throughout this book, for public sites in particular, JavaScript should add value by offering shortcuts or other enhanced experience features.

15.1 Displaying a Random Aphorism

Problem

You want a random choice from a library of famous quotes to appear in a location on your home page.

Solution

The backward-compatible (to version 4 browsers) solution is to use the document. write( ) method to insert your quotation element while the page loads. A more modern implementation uses the W3C DOM to insert an element containing the aphorism into an otherwise invisible placeholder element.

Start by creating an array of sayings in the head section. Each array entry is a custom object containing the saying and author's name:

```
var quotes = new Array( );
quotes[quotes.length] = {quote:"One should eat to live, and not live to eat.",
                         author:"Moliere"};
quotes[quotes.length] = {quote:"For man is man and master of his fate.",
                         author:"Tennyson"};
quotes[quotes.length] = {quote:"History is more or less bunk.",
                         author:"Henry Ford"};
quotes[quotes.length] = {quote:"You should never have your best trousers on when you
                                turn out to fight for freedom and truth.",
                         author:"Ibsen"};
quotes[quotes.length] = {quote:"It is vain and foolish to talk of knowing Greek.",
                         author:"Woolf"};
...
```

The following insertSaying( ) function uses a random number calculation to obtain
an index for the array to select a saying. The function then assembles the DOM element that is to appear in the page:

```
function insertSaying(targetElemID) {
    var currIndex = Math.floor(Math.random( ) * (quotes.length));
    var pElem = document.createElement("p");
    pElem.className= "quote";
    pElem.appendChild(document.createTextNode(quotes[currIndex].quote));
    var sElem = document.createElement("span");
    sElem.className = "author";
    sElem.appendChild(document.createTextNode(" -- " + quotes[currIndex].author));
    pElem.appendChild(sElem);
    document.getElementById(targetElemID).appendChild(pElem);
}
```

Then, in the place where you wish the saying to appear, include a script that invokes
the insertSaying( ) function, passing the ID of the placeholder element into which
the say is to go:

```
addOnLoadEvent(function( ) {insertSaying("placeholder")});
```

Discussion

The operative part of the Solution is the interaction between the array of objects and
the way the objects are retrieved when needed. The array creation code uses the
length of the array to determine the index values of the entries. This simplifies any
editing of the list, as you don't have to rearrange index numbers as you add or
remove objects from the array.

Computation of the (pseudo) random number is simplified here because we're looking
for a number between zero and the number of items in the array (inclusive). Once the
array index is available, it is used to access two properties of the array entry's object.

HTML formatting is strictly up to your page design. In the Solution, class names are
assigned to the two segments of the saying. A simple style sheet that supplies distinct
font characteristics for the saying and author's name might be like the following:

```
<style type="text/css">
  .quote {font:bold 12px serif}
  .author {font:italic 12px serif}
</style>
```

Your design is likely to be more detailed.

Note that the class names are assigned to the elements under construction by property name, rather than the typically more desirable setAttribute( ) method. This is a case where IE ignores setAttribute( ), failing to assign the class value correctly. Using property assignments does work in IE, as well as all other browsers.

The Solution displays a potentially different saying each time the user loads the page. If you'd like to preserve the same saying for all visits to the page on a given day, you need to add some cookie support to store the date and index number associated with that date. You can build this support into the insertSaying( ) function so that it first checks for a named cookie holding date information. If the date is different from the current date, the current date is preserved in the cookie and a new random index number is calculated. But if the cookie date matches the current date, the cookie's index number is assigned to the currIndex variable inside the function.

Numerous variations on the daily saying application abound on the Internet. Some like to peg a particular phrase or content to one of the seven days of the week or a date in the month. For example, each day of the week has a zero-based index number associated with it in the JavaScript Date object (values 0 through 6, with Sunday being 0). It's easy to create a new Date object and get the day number to use as an index for the array of sayings:

```
var today = new Date( );
var currIndex = today.getDay( );
```

Just be sure to have as many items in the array as the possible numbers that are assignable to the currIndex variable.

Another application is to display random pictures, such as one from a list of image URLs from a product catalog—a featured product. You can simply replace the image of an otherwise static product image on the page and the href attribute of the surrounding hyperlink (a) element. In this case, the array of custom objects contains image, URL, and alt attribute information:

```
var imgLinks = new Array( );
imgLinks[imgLinks.length] = {src:"images/prods/x25.jpg", url="products/x25.html",
    alt="X25 Super Widget"};
...
function getRandomImage(imgElemID) {
    var currIndex = Math.floor(Math.random( ) * (quotes.length));
    var imgElem = document.getElementById(imgElemID);
    var aElem = imgElem.parentNode;
    imgElem.src = imgLinks[currIndex].src;
    imgElem.alt = imgLinks[currindex].alt;
    aElem.href = imgLinks[currIndex].url;
}
```

At each visit, the user should see a different featured product, with a link directly to the product page.

See Also

Recipe 3.1 for creating an array; Recipe 3.8 for creating a custom object; Recipe 14.9 for creating a new HTML element; Recipe 14.10 for generating text content for an element node under construction.

15.2 Converting a User Selection into an Arbitrary Element

Problem

You want to wrap a user's body text selection in an element to assign a style that highlights the selection.

Solution

The following solution works with IE 4 or later, Mozilla 1.4 or later, Safari 2 or later, and Opera 9 or later. Begin by defining a CSS class rule that distinguishes the new arbitrary element from the rest of its surrounding text:

```
<style type="text/css">
.newSpan {font: bold 16px serif; background-color: yellow}
</style>
```

Assign a unique ID to a container that contains some HTML:

```
<p id="selectableParagraph">Lorem ipsum dolor sit amet, consectetaur
adipisicing elit, sed do eiusmod tempor incididunt ut labore et dolore magna aliqua.
</p>
```

Bind to that element two event handlers, one each for mouseup and the IE selectstart event (shown here with calls to *eventsManager.js* functions from Recipe 9.1 and Recipe 9.3):

```
function setEvents() {
    addEvent(document.getElementById("selectableParagraph"), "mouseup",
        function() {selectionManager.selection2Element("span", "newSpan");}, false);
    addEvent(document.getElementById("selectableParagraph"), "selectstart",
        function() {selectionManager.saveStart();}, false);
}
addOnLoadEvent(setEvents);
```

These events invoke methods of the custom selectionManager object, whose code is shown in Example 15-1 in the Discussion. The method contains code branches that work with both the W3C DOM Range object and the IE TextRange object.

Discussion

Example 15-1 shows the code for the selectionManager object, which acts as the interface between your scripts and the often complex worlds of the Range and TexRange objects.

Example 15-1. The selectionManager object

```
var selectionManager = {
    selectionStart : null,
    // invoked by selectstart event for IE
    saveStart : function() {this.selectionStart = event.srcElement;},
    // invoked by mouseup
    selection2Element : function(tagName, className) {
        if (document.selection && document.selection.createRange) {
            if (event.srcElement == this.selectionStart ||
                event.srcElement.parentNode == this.selectionStart ||
                event.srcElement == this.selectionStart.parentNode) {
                var rng = document.selection.createRange();
                var newHTML = "<" + tagName + " class='" + className + "'>" + rng.text +
                    "</" + tagName + ">";
                rng.pasteHTML(newHTML);
                this.selectionStart = null;
            } else {
                alert("Please restrict selections to within a single paragraph.");
            }
        } else if (document.createRange) {
            var sel = window.getSelection();
            // Safari 2.0.4 doesn't know sel.getRangeAt(), so do it the long way
            var range = document.createRange();
            range.setStart(sel.anchorNode, sel.anchorOffset);
            range.setEnd(sel.focusNode, sel.focusOffset);
            if (range.startContainer == range.endContainer ||
                range.commonAncestorContainer == range.startContainer.parentNode ||
                range.commonAncestorContainer == range.endContainer.parentNode) {
                var origContent = range.extractContents();
                var newElem = document.createElement(tagName);
                newElem.setAttribute("class", className);
                newElem.appendChild(origContent);
                range.insertNode(newElem);
            } else {
                alert("Please restrict selections to within a single paragraph.");
            }
        }
    }
}
```

IE's TextRange object and the W3C DOM's Range object are syntactically incompatible objects that both attempt to provide similar functionality—manipulating sequences of rendered text content in the browser window. Both object models also deal with user text selections in different manners, requiring additional DOM-specific coding.

The core of the `selectionManager` object is the `selection2Element( )` method. It requires two parameters: the name of the tag to use to surround the selected text and the class name to assign to the new container. Like most of IE's proprietary DOM, its Range object is also string-oriented (rather than DOM object-oriented). Therefore, the basis of converting the selection to a new element involves obtaining the text of the range, surrounding it with HTML tags, and pasting that new HTML string into the range.

Deploy this solution guardedly, as you can get yourself into substantial trouble without realizing it. If a user drags a selection across existing HTML container boundaries, the new HTML that the IE branch uses to replace the selection will, at best, be ill-formed HTML that has containers overlapping each other. At worst, the action will destroy the document structure in the vicinity of the replacement. The `selectstart` event invokes the `selectionManager.saveStart( )` method to record the node in which the selection began. If the beginning and end of the selection are not in the same node, the user receives an alert.

On the W3C DOM side, everything is handled within its branch of the `selection2Element( )` method. After obtaining a `selection` object (from `window. getSelection( )`), its properties are used to set parameters of a new TextRange object. After verifying that the range start and end are within acceptable related containers, the selection is initially removed from the DOM tree, inserted into a newly created element, and then reinserted into the DOM tree.

See Also

Recipe 15.3 for a more advanced application of the IE `TextRange` and W3C DOM `Range` objects.

15.3 Automating the Search-and-Replace of Body Content

Problem

You want to offer a search-and-replace function (with undo) for body content.

Solution

This recipe works only in Internet Explorer 4 or later for Windows and Mozilla-based browsers. On the IE side is a heavy dependence upon the Microsoft proprietary `TextRange` object (which also works with `textarea` element content); on the Mozilla side is a heavy dependence on the W3C DOM `Range` object, which isn't sufficiently implemented in Safari 2.0.4 or Opera 9 to be usable for this application. Observing how the W3C DOM `Range` object works in this recipe will help prepare you for the day when its deployment is more universal.

Use the *rangeReplace.js* library (Example 15-2 in the Discussion) to automate search-and-replace operations. You have your choice of two functions, depending on the type of search-and-replace user experience you prefer. Invoke the srBatch( ) function for unprompted batch replacement:

```
srBatch(document.body, "Law", "legislation", false);
```

The four parameters specify:

- A reference to the element to become the text range
- A string to search for
- A string to replace found strings
- A Boolean for case-sensitive search

The companion srQuery( ) function takes the same set of arguments, but highlights each match, and prompts the user to confirm each replacement:

```
srQuery(document.body, "Law", "legislation", false);
```

To undo the replacements performed by the last invocation of either function, invoke the undoReplace( ) function with no arguments.

Discussion

Example 15-2 shows the *rangeReplace.js* library. Link it into any document that requires this functionality.

Example 15-2. The rangeReplace.js library

```
// Return TextRange.findText( ) third parameter arguments
function getSearchArgs(caseSensitive) {
    return (caseSensitive) ? 4 : 0;
}

// Unprompted search and replace
function srBatch(container, search, replace, caseSensitive) {
    var rng;
    if (document.body.createTextRange) {
        // IE branch
        var args = getSearchArgs(caseSensitive);
        var found = "";
        rng = document.body.createTextRange( );
        rng.moveToElementText(container);
        clearUndoBuffer( );
        for (var i = 0; rng.findText(search, 1000000, args); i++) {
            found = rng.text;
            rng.text = replace;
            pushUndoNew(rng, search, replace, found);
            rng.collapse(false)  ;
        }
        alert("Search completed.");
    } else if (document.createRange && window.find) {
```

Example 15-2. The rangeReplace.js library (continued)

```
        // Mozilla (W3C) branch
        var sel;
        var args = caseSensitive || false;
        while (window.find(search, args)) {
            sel = window.getSelection( );
            if (sel.anchorNode) {
                rng = sel.getRangeAt(0);
                if (rng.intersectsNode(container)) {
                    pushUndoNew(rng, search, replace, rng.toString( ));
                    rng.deleteContents( );
                    rng.insertNode(document.createTextNode(replace));
                    rng.startContainer.parentNode.normalize( );
                }
            }
        }
        alert("Search completed.");
    }
}

// Prompted search and replace
function srQuery(container, search, replace, caseSensitive) {
    var rng;
    if (document.body.createTextRange) {
        // IE branch
        var args = getSearchArgs(caseSensitive);
        var found = "";
        rng = document.body.createTextRange( );
        rng.moveToElementText(container);
        clearUndoBuffer( );
        while (rng.findText(search, 10000, args)) {
            rng.select( );
            found = rng.text;
            rng.scrollIntoView( );
            if (confirm("Replace?")) {
                rng.text = replace;
                pushUndoNew(rng, search, replace, found);
            }
            rng.collapse(false)  ;
        }
        alert("Search completed.");
    } else if (document.createRange && window.find) {
        // Mozilla (W3C) branch
        var sel;
        var args = caseSensitive || false;
        while (window.find(search, args)) {
            sel = window.getSelection( );
            if (sel.anchorNode) {
                rng = sel.getRangeAt(0);
                if (rng.intersectsNode(container)) {
                    if (confirm("Replace?")) {
                        pushUndoNew(rng, search, replace, rng.toString( ));
                        rng.deleteContents( );
```

Example 15-2. The rangeReplace.js library (continued)

```
                            rng.insertNode(document.createTextNode(replace));
                            rng.startContainer.parentNode.normalize();
                        } else {
                            // move selection beyond current item for next find()
                            rng.collapse(false);
                            sel.addRange(rng);
                        }
                    }
                }
            }
            alert("Search completed.");
        }
    }


/***************
    UNDO BUFFER
***************/
// Temporary storage of undo information
var undoObject = {origSearchString:"",newRanges :[]};

// Store original search string and "bookmarks" of each replaced range
function pushUndoNew(rng, srchString, replString, foundString) {
    undoObject.origSearchString = srchString;
    if (rng.moveStart) {
        // IE branch
        rng.moveStart("character", -replString.length);
        var rngSpecs = {bookmark: rng.getBookmark(), found: foundString}
        undoObject.newRanges[undoObject.newRanges.length] = rngSpecs;
    } else if (rng.setStart) {
        // Mozilla (W3C) branch
        var rngSpecs = {node: rng.startContainer, start: rng.startOffset, end: rng.
startOffset + replString.length, found: foundString};
        undoObject.newRanges[undoObject.newRanges.length] = rngSpecs;
    }
}

// Empty array and search string global
function clearUndoBuffer() {
    undoObject.origSearchString = "";
    undoObject.newRanges.length = 0;
}

// Perform the undo
function undoReplace() {
    if (undoObject.newRanges.length && undoObject.origSearchString) {
        if (document.body.createTextRange) {
            // IE branch
            rng = document.body.createTextRange();
            for (var i = 0; i < undoObject.newRanges.length; i++) {
                rng.moveToBookmark(undoObject.newRanges[i].bookmark);
                rng.text = undoObject.newRanges[i].found;
            }
```

Example 15-2. The rangeReplace.js library (continued)

```
                clearUndoBuffer( );
        } else if (document.createRange) {
            // Mozilla (W3C) branch
            for (var i = undoObject.newRanges.length - 1; i >= 0 ; i--) {
                rng = document.createRange( );
                rng.setStart(undoObject.newRanges[i].node, undoObject.newRanges[i].start);
                rng.setEnd(undoObject.newRanges[i].node, undoObject.newRanges[i].end);
                rng.deleteContents( );
                rng.insertNode(document.createTextNode(undoObject.newRanges[i].found));
                rng.startContainer.parentNode.normalize( );
            }
            clearUndoBuffer( );
        }
    }
}
```

The library begins with a helper function, getArgs( ), invoked by both of the main search-and-replace functions. The IE TextRange object's findText( ) method, used in both of the main functions, takes three parameters. The first is the string to look for, followed by an integer of how many characters of the range to search through, and an integer corresponding to search detail codes. The four possible codes are: 0 (match partial words); 1 (match backwards); 2 (match whole words); or 4 (match case). Using binary arithmetic, these codes can be combined into a single value denoting two or more of these switches being on. The getArgs( ) converts the two Boolean argument values to the appropriate binary code for findText( ). Because this version of the recipe supports Mozilla, whose search facility does not offer a "whole word" option, the getArgs( ) function now works only with the "match case" value.

I'll first cover the IE branches of all functions. The object detection feature for most functions is IE's document.body.createTextRange( ) method.

Both of the search-and-replace functions, srBatch( ) and srQuery( ), operate the same way to create the IE text range, set the boundaries to the referenced element, clear the undo buffer (described next), and perform the search-and-replace operation via the TextRange's findText( ) method. The difference between the two functions is that srQuery( ) selects each found match to highlight the text, and then asks the user whether the highlighted text should be replaced.

Both search-and-replace functions are supplemented by the same undo capabilities. A global object (undoObject) keeps track of the changes made during a search-and-replace execution, using the IE TextRange bookmark feature (which preserves a range definition for reuse later). At each replacement operation, the pushUndoNew( ) function preserves information about the operation in the undoObject object's properties. Before the function stores the range, however, it adjusts the range to encompass the newly inserted text so that it can be selected and removed later. In case the search is not case-sensitive, the found text is also stored so that each instance may be restored correctly.

Prior to each search-and-replace traversal, the values of undoObject are cleared via the clearUndoBuffer() function so as not to interfere with previous operations. When the user wishes to undo the operation, the undoReplace() function iterates through the ranges stored in undoObject, and replaces those ranges with the original search string.

The first argument of either of the search-and-replace functions is a reference to the HTML container that bounds the text you wish to search. While you can supply a reference to the entire body if you like, doing so means that the operations will occur on things like form control labels and other elements you may not wish to have included. Therefore, structure your HTML document so that the target content is separate from any fixed content you don't want changed. You can always wrap a collection of paragraphs and their headings in an arbitrary span element to provide the necessary container.

Don't confuse IE's TextRange bookmark with the kinds of URL bookmarks you save in your browser. A bookmark value, derived from the *rangeObject*.getBookmark() method, is a string containing data that is gibberish to the human eye but is interpreted by the browser as a complete range specification. Supplying a bookmark value to the *rangeObject*.moveToBookmark() method sets the range to whatever specification had been preserved before. You can store as many range bookmarks as you like.

For the Mozilla (W3C DOM) branches, many of the basic operations are the same as the IE version, but the W3C DOM Range object is both conceptually and syntactically a different animal. The Range object offers no search facility. While one could build such an animal out of regular expressions, Mozilla does offer a window.find() method, which selects text that matches the search string. The selection object's getRangeAt() method generates an instance of a Range object whose specifications match those of the selection. The script then makes sure that the found range is within the context of the container passed as the first parameter to the search function. Details of the pre-replacement state are passed to pushUndoNew() where they are stored for use later, if needed. The found text is removed, new text is inserted, and all text nodes in the current container are normalized (because inserting a text node breaks up the original text node).

Because the W3C DOM Range object does not have an analogue to IE's bookmark mechanism, the undo buffer stores specifications piecemeal. In the undoReplace() function, the list of buffered ranges is traversed in reverse order because if there are two replacements in the same container, the range offsets will be out of whack for a later item when an earlier item is restored.

See Also

The introduction to this chapter for information about text ranges.

15.4 Designing a User-Editable Content Page

Problem

You want to offer a place for users to enter styled text for submission to the server.

Solution

This recipe for IE, Mozilla, and Opera 9 or later provides an `iframe` element that allows users to type new text into it, while customizing numerous style specifications, which appear within the element's content. Demonstrated here are only a few of the style editing choices available to page authors.

The *editor.js* library shown in Example 15-3 in the Discussion creates a single global object, `editableDoc`, which provides the interface to the editing commands. The HTML portion of the example offers a single `iframe` element and several controls for adjusting font characteristics (event assignments handled by functions in *eventsManager.js* from Recipes 9.1 and 9.3):

```
<script type="text/javascript">
function setEvents( ) {
    addEvent(document.getElementById("fontColorChooser"), "change",
        editableDoc.setFontColor, false);
    addEvent(document.getElementById("fontStyleChooser"), "change",
        editableDoc.setFontStyle, false);
    addEvent(document.getElementById("fontFamilyChooser"), "change",
        editableDoc.setFontFamily, false);
}
addOnLoadEvent(function( ) {editableDoc.init("editableIframe")});
addOnLoadEvent(setEvents);
</script>
...
<div>
<form>
Font Color: <select id="fontColorChooser">
    <option value="black" selected="selected">Black</option>
    <option value="red">Red</option>
    <option value="green">Green</option>
    <option value="blue">Blue</option>
</select>
Font Style: <select id="fontStyleChooser">
    <option value="removeformat" selected="selected">Normal</option>
    <option value="bold">Bold</option>
    <option value="italic">Italic</option>
    <option value="underline">Underline</option>
    <option value="strikethrough">Strikethrough</option>
</select>
Font Family: <select id="fontFamilyChooser">
    <option value="serif" selected="selected">Serif</option>
    <option value="sans-serif">Sans-serif</option>
    <option value="monospace">Mono</option>
    <option value="comic sans ms">Comic Sans</option>
```

```
    </select>
    </form>
    </div>
    <iframe id="editableIframe" src="sample.html" width="400" height="300"></iframe>
```

Discussion

One of the principles of Web 2.0 is the encouragement for site visitors to create input for others to see. In the past, this has meant using textarea elements for entering plain text, or using HTML tags the textarea to designate style changes and such—provided the author knew HTML.

These days, however, users are less likely to know HTML, but are familiar with styled text editing from their word processing programs. Microsoft developed a set of commands for IE that allow an element setup to be editable to display styled text and other HTML features through script control. Mozilla and Opera have implemented the same command structure (although not necessarily all of the same commands).

Example 15-3 is the code for a simple library that performs a limited number of stylistic changes to an editable element. It also includes the necessary initialization method to set the element to be editable.

Example 15-3. The editor.js library

```
var editableDoc = {
    doc : null,
    setFontColor : function(evt) {
        if (editableDoc.doc) {
            editableDoc.doc.execCommand("forecolor", false, editableDoc.getElem(evt).value);
        }
    },
    setFontStyle : function(evt) {
        if (editableDoc.doc) {
            editableDoc.doc.execCommand(editableDoc.getElem(evt).value, false, null);
        }
    },
    setFontFamily : function(evt) {
        if (editableDoc.doc) {
            editableDoc.doc.execCommand("fontname", false, editableDoc.getElem(evt).value);
        }
    },
    getElem : function(evt) {
        evt = evt || window.event;
        var elem = evt.target || evt.srcElement;
        return elem;
    },
    init : function(elemID) {
        var iframe = document.getElementById(elemID);
        if (iframe.contentWindow) {
            editableDoc.doc = iframe.contentWindow.document;
        } else if (iframe.contentDocument) {
            editableDoc.doc = iframe.contentDocument;
        }
```

Example 15-3. The editor.js library (continued)

```
    if (editableDoc.doc && editableDoc.doc.designMode) {
        editableDoc.doc.designMode = "on";
    }
  }
}
```

In the case of an `iframe` element, IE and the W3C DOM refer to its content document with different references, which are equalized in the `init()` method. Setting the `designMode` property of the document within the `iframe` to on makes it user-editable. The first three methods invoke the `execCommand()` method, passing appropriate parameters for each command. The `getElem()` method is used internally to help the first three methods obtain a reference to the select element that invoked the styling method. Command or parameter values are derived from the value of the currently selected option.

Table 15-1 provides an abbreviated list of commands that would be appropriate for a simple editing application. You can find more details in *Dynamic HTML: The Definitive Reference* (O'Reilly).

Table 15-1. Selected execCommand( ) method commands and browser support

Command	IE	Moz	Opera	Description	Value parameter
BackColor	●	●	●	Sets background color of current selection	Color value (name or hex triplet)
Bold	●	●	●	Makes the current selection bold weight	None
CreateLink	●	●	●	Wraps an `<a href=...>` tag around the current selection	A string of a complete or relative URL
FontName	●	●	●	Sets the font family of the current selection	A string of the font family name
FontSize	●	●	●	Sets the HTML font size of the current selection	A string of the font size (1–7)
ForeColor	●	●	●	Sets the foreground (text) color of the current selection	Color value (name or hex triplet)
FormatBlock	●	●	●	Wraps a block tag around the current object	HTML tag (e.g., `<p>`) as string
InsertOrderedList	●	●	●	Inserts an `<ol>` tag at the current insertion point	A string for the element ID
InsertUnorderedList	●	●	●	Inserts a `<ul>` tag at the current insertion point	A string for the element ID
Italic	●	●	●	Wraps an `<i>` tag around the range	None
JustifyCenter	●	●	●	Center justifies the current selection	None

Command	IE	Moz	Opera	Description	Value parameter
JustifyLeft	•	•	•	Left justifies the current selection	None
JustifyRight	•	•	•	Right justifies the current selection	None
Print	•	—	—	Displays Print dialog box (IE 5.5 or later)	None
RemoveFormat	•	•	•	Removes formatting from the current selection	None
SaveAs	•	—	—	Saves the page as a local file (optional file dialog)	A string of a URL for the path
Strikethrough	•	•	•	Formats the selection as strikethrough text	None
Subscript	•	•	•	Formats the selection as subscript text	None
Superscript	•	•	•	Formats the selection as superscript text	None
Underline	•	•	•	Wraps a `<u>` tag around the range	None

The quality of the HTML markup that results from these commanded edits varies with the browser. If the browser uses CSS to achieve the styles, the rules are embedded within span elements surrounding the affected text. But the fact that an `iframe`'s document is a genuine HTML document means that you can submit its content through facilities such as the `XMLHttpRequest` object's `send( )` method (with a POST type of transmission).

You can see a more fully fleshed-out editor at *http://developer.mozilla.org/en/docs/ Rich-Text_Editing_in_Mozilla*.

15.5 Creating a Slide Show

Problem

You want to deliver the equivalent of a PowerPoint presentation in a web browser.

Solution

There are dozens of ways to simulate a slide show, but this recipe is a simple, easy-to-implement solution for recent browsers. All of the content, style sheets, and scripts are contained in a single HTML page, whose code is shown in Example 15-4 in the Discussion.

To customize this slide show, place the content of each slide in its own div element with a class attribute set to slide. All of your slide div elements should be nested inside one master div element named slides. Keep the individual slide div elements in the same source code order as the presentation slide order.

You can also customize the style sheets that define the look of the slides. The format shown in Example 15-4 simulates a typical presentation software package's simple slide style.

Discussion

Example 15-4 shows the HTML page used for a slide show (with only one slide to save space). With the entire slide show arriving in a single document, there is no delay in navigating between slides. Additional support is provided by *eventsManager.js* (Recipe 9.1) and the DHTML API library (Recipe 13.3).

Example 15-4. A slide show HTML page and scripts

```
<!DOCTYPE html PUBLIC "-//W3C//DTD XHTML 1.0 Transitional//EN"
        "http://www.w3.org/TR/xhtml1/DTD/xhtml1-transitional.dtd">
<html>
<head>
<title>DHTML Slide Show</title>
<style type="text/css">
#slides {
        font-family: Verdana, Arial, sans-serif;
        position: absolute;
        top: 40px;
        width: 90%
        }
.slide {
        position: absolute;
        top: 0px;
        left: 0px;
        display: none;
        width: 80%;
        height: 500px;
        overflow: hidden;
        background-color: #ccffcc;
        font-size: 18px;
        padding: 20px;
        border: 5px solid #ff9900;
        margin: 10%;
        margin-top: 70px
        }
h1 {
    text-align: right;
    padding-right: 10%
    }
h2 {
    font-size: 36px;
    text-align: center
```

Example 15-4. A slide show HTML page and scripts (continued)

```
    }
li {
    list-style-image: url(end.gif);
    list-style-position: outside
    }
hr {
    width: 60%;
    height: 5px;
    background-color: #ff9900
    }
#titleBar {
            width: 100%;
            height: 10px
            }
body {background-color: #339966}
#controller {
              position: absolute;
              top: 30px;
              left: 10%
              }
</style>
<script src="../js/eventsManager.js"></script>
<script src="../js/DHTML3API.js"></script>
<script type="text/javascript">
// Array of all slides
var allSlides;
// Slide counter
var currSlide = -1;

// Set global with array of slide elements
function getAllSlides() {
    var allChildren = document.getElementById("slides").childNodes;
    var slideElems = new Array();
    for (var i = 0; i < allChildren.length; i++) {
        if (allChildren[i].nodeType == 1) {
            slideElems[slideElems.length] = allChildren[i];
        }
    }
    allSlides = slideElems;
}

// Set pixel heights of slide elements to fit window
function setHeights() {
    for (var i = 0; i < allSlides.length; i++) {
        allSlides[i].style.height = getInsideWindowHeight() - 200 + "px";
    }
}

// Advance to next slide
function next() {
    if (currSlide < 0) {
        allSlides[++currSlide].style.display = "block";
```

Example 15-4. A slide show HTML page and scripts (continued)

```
    } else if (currSlide < allSlides.length - 1) {
        allSlides[currSlide].style.display = "none";
        allSlides[++currSlide].style.display = "block";
    } else if (currSlide == allSlides.length - 1) {
        allSlides[currSlide++].style.display = "none";
    }
}

// Go to previous slide
function prev() {
    if (currSlide > allSlides.length - 1) {
        allSlides[--currSlide].style.display = "block";
    } else if (currSlide > 0) {
        allSlides[currSlide].style.display = "none";
        allSlides[--currSlide].style.display = "block";
    } else if (currSlide == 0) {
        allSlides[currSlide--].style.display = "none";
    }
}

// Initialize slide show
function initSlides() {
    getAllSlides();
    setHeights();
}
</script>
</head>
<body onload="initDHTMLAPI(); initSlides()" onresize="setHeights()">
<h1>U.S. Bill of Rights</h1>
<hr id="titleBar" />
<div id="controller">
<form>
<input type="button" value="Prev" onclick="prev()" />
<input type="button" value="Next" onclick="next()" />
</form>
</div>

<div id="slides">

<div id="slide1" class="slide">
<h2>ARTICLE I</h2>
<hr />
<p>
Congress shall make no law respecting an establishment of religion, or prohibiting
the free exercise thereof; or abridging the freedom of speech, or of the press; or
the right of the people peaceably to assemble, and to petition the government for
a redress of grievances.
</p>
<ul>
<li>Note 1</li>
<li>Note 2</li>
<li>Note 3</li>
```

Example 15-4. A slide show HTML page and scripts (continued)

```
</ul>
</div>
...

</div>
</body>
</html>
```

While the script code works in IE 5 or later, the CSS specifications in this example require IE 5.5 or later on Windows to achieve the consistent look shown in Figure 15-1.

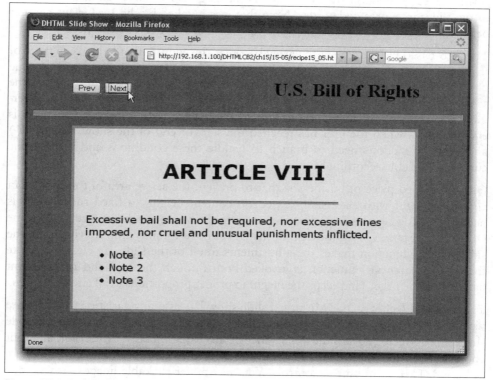

Figure 15-1. A slide show window

A lot of what a slide show looks like depends upon the CSS rules applied to a series of positioned div elements (of the slide class) nested inside one outer-positioned div element (with ID slides). Additional style rules control the look of elements within slides, such as headings, bullet lists, and horizontal rule dividers.

The HTML for the slide title area, controller buttons, and content has a straightforward structure. Controller buttons simply activate the prev( ) and next( ) functions to bring an adjacent slide into view. A style sheet rule positions the controller buttons where it is convenient within the rest of the design of the slides. The load event handler invokes initializations for both the DHTML API (Recipe 13.3) and the slide show scripts.

This slide show works under script control by hiding and showing individual div elements representing the slides. The script, therefore, simply needs to keep track of which slide is showing and display either the next or the previous slide in sequence. Rather than hardcoding IDs of the individual slides to establish the sequence, the scripts take advantage of the DOM node tree established for this document. Each slide is a child element node of an outer wrapper (whose ID is slides). The getAllSlides( ) function stores (in the allSlides global variable) an array reference to the slides in source code order. Note that it is invoked by the load event handler because the div elements must load and render before they can be counted.

The zero-based index value of the array becomes the counter that helps keep track of the currently displayed slide. A global variable, currSlide, is initialized with a value of -1, to signify that no slide is showing and the first slide (index of 0) is next in the sequence. Both the next( ) and prev( ) functions rely on the currSlide value to determine the next or previous slide to show in sequence until a border condition is encountered—when the user has reached the start or end of the show. The next( ) and prev( ) functions need to branch to handle these conditions and manage the currSlide variable accordingly.

One unfinished piece of business is that to prevent the active area of the slide from changing height with each slide (based on content height), a fixed slide height is needed. But to keep the height in proportion to the browser window size needs some DHTML assistance. With the help of the DHTML API library from Recipe 13.3, the setHeights( ) function makes the adjustments to all of the slide div elements. Note that the setHeights( ) function is invoked both through the load and resize event handlers of the page. This keeps the height in proper proportions in all circumstances.

The look and feel of a DHTML-based slide show has as many variations as there are web designers implementing the application. Most of the details shown for the style sheets in this recipe govern the appearance of this variation only. Size, color, and font choices are entirely up to you. The same goes for the controllers, implemented here as basic HTML form button controls. You may prefer clickable images, or you may not want any buttons at all, so that the slides advance by a click anywhere in the window. Adding the following code to the scripts just shown provides that functionality (except in IE on the Mac), along with a way to go backward by holding down the Shift key while clicking in the window:

```
function changeSlide(evt) {
    evt = (evt) ? evt : window.event;
    if (evt.shiftKey) {
        prev( );
    } else {
```

```
        next();
    }
}
document.onclick=changeSlide;
```

One aspect of typical slide shows not covered in the previous code is the transition effect. While it is possible to script numerous cross-browser effects, such as a discarded slide moving off to the left while the new one floats in from the right, the use of this kind of animation is of variable smoothness and speed, depending on browser and operating environment. But Internet Explorer for Windows makes good use of its integration with the operating system to provide a large set of transition filters that are specified as part of the style sheet rules.

The catalog of transition effects is long, as is the range of details you can specify for most transitions (see Recipe 12.12). But as a preview, the following style sheet rule can be added to the .slide class definition in the previously shown CSS rules:

```
filter:progid:DXImageTransform.Microsoft.Iris(irisStyle="circle")
```

Next, modify the next( ) and prev( ) functions to apply and play the transitions when needed. For example, the next( ) function becomes:

```
function next( ) {
    var allSlides = getAllSlides( );
    if (currSlide < 0) {
        allSlides[++currSlide].filters[0].apply( );
        allSlides[currSlide].style.visibility = "visible";
        allSlides[currSlide].filters[0].play( );
    } else if (currSlide < allSlides.length - 1) {
        allSlides[currSlide].style.visibility = "hidden";
        allSlides[++currSlide].filters[0].apply( );
        allSlides[currSlide].style.visibility = "visible";
        allSlides[currSlide].filters[0].play( );
    } else if (currSlide == allSlides.length - 1) {
        allSlides[currSlide++].style.visibility = "hidden";
    }
}
```

To allow these transitions to work in IE for Windows without causing script errors in IE for the Mac or Netscape browsers, you'll need to lengthen the code a little more to accommodate all supporting browsers:

```
function next( ) {
    var allSlides = getAllSlides( );
    var nextSlide;
    if (currSlide < 0) {
        nextSlide = allSlides[++currSlide];
        if (nextSlide.filters) {
            nextSlide.filters[0].apply( );
        }
        nextSlide.style.visibility = "visible";
        if (nextSlide.filters) {
            nextSlide.filters[0].play( );
        }
```

```
        } else if (currSlide < allSlides.length - 1) {
            allSlides[currSlide].style.visibility = "hidden";
            nextSlide = allSlides[++currSlide];
            if (nextSlide.filters) {
                nextSlide.filters[0].apply();
            }
            nextSlide.style.visibility = "visible";
            if (nextSlide.filters) {
                nextSlide.filters[0].play();
            }
        } else if (currSlide == allSlides.length - 1) {
            allSlides[currSlide++].style.visibility = "hidden";
        }
    }
```

Lastly, you can set up a slide show so that it automatically cycles through the slides, giving users a fixed amount of time to read each slide. Modify the next( ) function (you don't need prev( ) for this) to circle around when it reaches the end:

```
function next() {
    var allSlides = getAllSlides();
    if (currSlide < 0) {
        allSlides[++currSlide].style.visibility = "visible";
    } else if (currSlide < allSlides.length - 1) {
        allSlides[currSlide].style.visibility = "hidden";
        allSlides[++currSlide].style.visibility = "visible";
    } else if (currSlide == allSlides.length - 1) {
        allSlides[currSlide++].style.visibility = "hidden";
        currSlide = -1;
        next();
    }
}
```

Then use a load event handler of the page to initiate a setInterval( ) call to next( ) every several seconds. Because the load event handler shown earlier already performs an initialization in setHeights( ), you can enter the setInterval( ) call at the end of that function. But since that function is also invoked if the page is resized, you need to cancel the previous interval timer if the user resizes the window. Failure to do so starts another interval time, which gives the impression of speeding up the slide pacing. Therefore, preserve the interval identifier in a global variable:

```
var slideInterval;

function setHeights() {
    clearInterval(slideInterval);
    var allSlides = getAllSlides();
    for (var i = 0; i < allSlides.length; i++) {
        allSlides[i].style.height = getInsideWindowHeight() -200 + "px";
    }
    slideInterval = setInterval("next()", 5000);
}
```

See Also

Recipe 13.1 for how to make an element positionable on the page; Recipe 13.3 for details on the DHTML API library; Recipe 12.2 for an introduction to transition effects in IE for Windows.

15.6 Auto-Scrolling the Page

Problem

You want the entire browser page to automatically scroll vertically for the user.

Solution

All current mainstream scriptable browsers empower their window objects with a scrollBy( ) method. By invoking it repeatedly through a setInterval( ) call, you can scroll the browser window with no user interaction. The following function and setInterval( ) call do the trick:

```
function scrollWindow( ) {
    window.scrollBy(0, 1);
}
function initScroll( ) {
    setInterval("scrollWindow( )", 100);
}
```

The initScroll( ) function should be invoked by a load event of the window object.

Discussion

Determining the optimum scroll speed is not easy, and may even dissuade you from employing this application except perhaps in a kiosk environment. Scrolling speed is governed by two variables: the number of pixels of the increment (the second parameter of scrollBy( )) and how often the scrollWindow( ) function is invoked (the interval time specified in the setInterval( ) method call). If the pixel increment is too large, the page jumps in big steps that are difficult for the eye to track for any length of time. The smaller the increment, the better, as shown by the one-pixel jumps in the solution.

Frequency is specified by the nominal number of milliseconds between calls to the scrollWindow( ) function. Too large a number makes the page scroll painfully slowly for moderate reading speeds. Too small a number may lead to more comfortable reading in an ideal environment, but it points out a potential problem beyond your control: repetitive execution of the setInterval( ) method's function does not fire in absolutely uniform intervals. The smaller the interval, the more you see the results in bursts of smooth scrolling followed by brief stuttering.

To check on the progress of the autoscroll through the page, you can read the instantaneous scroll amount (in pixels); however, the syntax varies not only among browsers, but also between standards-compatible mode and quirks mode in IE 6 and 7. For Mozilla and Safari, get the read-only properties `window.scrollX` and `window.scrollY`. For older IE versions and IE 6/7 running in backward-compatible mode, use `document.body.scrollLeft` and `document.body.scrollTop`. In the CSS-compatibility mode of IE 6/7, use `document.body.parentElement.scrollLeft` and `document.body.parentElement.scrollTop`. The latter pair reads the scroll values for the entire `html` element filling the window.

See Also

Recipe 13.12 for an alternative way to scroll content (in a positioned `div` element) without scrolling the window.

15.7 Greeting Users with Their Time of Day

Problem

You want your page to include a greeting pertinent to the user's part of the day, such as "Good morning" or "Good afternoon."

Solution

First, create a function that returns strings associated with each day part, as calculated by a fresh `Date` object:

```
function dayPart( ) {
    var oneDate = new Date( );
    var theHour = oneDate.getHours( );
    if (theHour < 12) {
        return "morning";
    } else if (theHour < 18) {
        return "afternoon";
    } else {
        return "evening";
    }
}
```

To accommodate both scriptable and unscriptable browsers, be sure to encase the script statement inside HTML comment tags, and include the `noscript` element with the text to display for unscriptable browsers:

```
<script language="JavaScript" type="text/javascript">
document.write("Good " + dayPart( ) + " and welcome")
</script>
<noscript>Welcome</noscript>
  to GiantCo.
```

Discussion

As the page loads, it creates an instance of a Date object. By omitting the parameter for the Date object constructor function, the current time and date are used to generate the object. A Date object instance is not a ticking clock, but rather a snapshot of the clock when the object was created. The accuracy of the time is strictly dependent upon the computer's internal clock setting.

A Date object has numerous functions for getting and setting components of the date, ranging from the millisecond to the year. The getHours( ) method used in the Solution returns a number between 0 and 23, corresponding to the 24-hour clock set to the user's local time. The dayPart( ) function simply divides the day into three portions, breaking at noon and 6 P.M. to supply day parts ranging through morning, afternoon, and evening.

The example provides a <noscript> tag, which will cause browsers with scripting turned off to display a generic greeting. You could also use a load event to script the replacement of the generic greeting (assuming you encase the generic content within an identifiable container, such as a span element). The downside of using that approach is the chance that the display will flash between the default and scripted versions as the page loads. The document.write( ) version—though it may seem antique to some—avoids the visual disruption.

See Also

Recipes 2.9 through 2.11 for information about working with the Date object.

15.8   Displaying the Number of Days Before Christmas

Problem

You want to display the amount of time before a known date and/or time in the user's local time zone.

Solution

The following function returns the number of days prior to the next Christmas in the user's local time zone:

```
function getDaysBeforeNextXmas( ) {
    var oneMinute = 60 * 1000;
    var oneHour = oneMinute * 60;
    var oneDay = oneHour * 24;
    var today = new Date( );
    var nextXmas = new Date( );
    nextXmas.setMonth(11);
    nextXmas.setDate(25);
    if (today.getMonth( ) == 11 && today.getDate( ) > 25) {
```

```
        nextXmas.setFullYear(nextXmas.getFullYear() + 1);
    }
    var diff = nextXmas.getTime() - today.getTime();
    diff = Math.floor(diff/oneDay);
    return diff;
}
```

The value returned is an integer representing days, which you can insert into body text either while the page is loading or afterward, as in the following:

```
<p>Only
<script type="text/javascript">document.write(getDaysBeforeNextXmas())</script>
shopping days until Christmas.</p>
```

Discussion

Approaching the "How many days before?" problem has some side implications that you need to address before deploying a solution. In the case of the Solution in this recipe, the function operates year after year without maintenance because the target date is not pegged to any particular year. The extra if condition handles the case when the current date is sometime after Christmas but before January 1 of the following year. To make the calculation arrive at the correct count, the target comparative date is pushed out to the following year.

You could also rework the function to be more generic, whereby it accepts parameters for a target date in the future, complete with the year. Such a function looks like the following:

```
function getDaysBefore(year, month, date) {
    var oneMinute = 60 * 1000;
    var oneHour = oneMinute * 60;
    var oneDay = oneHour * 24;
    var today = new Date();
    var targetDate = new Date();
    targetDate.setYear(year);
    targetDate.setMonth(month);
    targetDate.setDate(date);
    alert(targetDate);
    var diff = targetDate.getTime() - today.getTime();
    diff = Math.floor(diff/oneDay);
    return diff;
}
```

If you are familiar with the Date object, you may wonder why the call to the constructor function for the target date object doesn't pass the getDaysBefore() arguments directly to the constructor. It is because the value for today includes the hours and minutes into the current day. To compare the current date against a future date, it's important to compare the same times in the two dates: if the target date only was handed to the constructor, the time would be 00:00:00 on that date.

Although this example shows calculations for the number of days, you can derive other time units by modifying the next-to-last statement's divisor from oneDay (for the number of days) to oneHour (for the number of hours) or oneMinute. The date calculations are performed at the millisecond level, so you can get even more granular if you like.

You aren't limited to displaying the results as text in the body content. If you have graphical images of each number from 0 through 9, you can convert the number returned into a graphical display comprising those images. For example, if you have your images named *0.jpg*, *1.jpg*, and so on, the following function assembles the HTML for a sequence of img elements:

```
function getDaysArt() {
    var output = "";
    var dayCount = getDaysBeforeNextXmas() + "";
    for (var i = 0; i < dayCount.length; i++) {
        output += "<img src='digits/" + dayCount.charAt(i) + ".jpg'";
        output += "height='120' width='60' alt='" + dayCount.charAt(i) + "' />";
    }
    return output;
}
```

As the page loads, use document.write( ) to insert this HTML where needed:

```
<p>Only
<script type="text/javascript">document.write(getDaysArt())</script>
shopping days until Christmas.</p>
```

See Also

Recipe 15.9 for a countdown timer pegged to a particular time zone in the world; Recipe 15.10 for a calendar-based date picker.

15.9 Displaying a Countdown Timer

Problem

You want to have a running countdown timer showing on the page.

Solution

Countdown timers can take many forms. Look to the combination of HTML and scripts in Example 15-5 of the Discussion for inspiration for your particular timer implementation. The example application sets the turn of the new year in the user's time zone as the "zero hour" for the timer, and displays a constantly updated display of the days, hours, minutes, and seconds until that time.

An onload event handler in the page invokes the countDown( ) function by way of the setInterval( ) method:

```
window.onload = function() {setInterval("countDown()", 1000)};
```

The display is updated approximately every second because the setInterval( ) method repeatedly invokes the countDown( ) function until a script cancels the timer.

Discussion

The display of the timer can be in a text input field (all scriptable browsers), swappable images, or body text. This example uses swappable images because it lends itself to the most flexible page designs of the choices. Figure 15-2 shows the output.

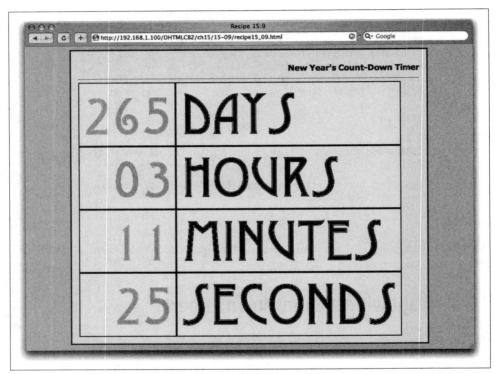

Figure 15-2. Countdown timer with swappable image

Example 15-5 shows the complete HTML document for this application, including the HTML and scripts.

Example 15-5. A countdown timer application

```
<html>
<head>
<title>Recipe 15.9</title>
<style type="text/css">
table {border-spacing: 0}
td {border: 2px groove black; padding: 7px; background-color: #ccffcc}
th {border: 2px groove black; padding: 7px; background-color: #ffffcc}
.ctr {text-align:center}
</style>
```

Example 15-5. A countdown timer application (continued)

```javascript
<script type="text/javascript">
if (document.images) {
    var imgArray = new Array( );
    imgArray[0] = new Image(60,120);
    imgArray[0].src = "digits/0.gif";
    imgArray[1] = new Image(60,120);
    imgArray[1].src = "digits/1.gif";
    imgArray[2] = new Image(60,120);
    imgArray[2].src = "digits/2.gif";
    imgArray[3] = new Image(60,120);
    imgArray[3].src = "digits/3.gif";
    imgArray[4] = new Image(60,120);
    imgArray[4].src = "digits/4.gif";
    imgArray[5] = new Image(60,120);
    imgArray[5].src = "digits/5.gif";
    imgArray[6] = new Image(60,120);
    imgArray[6].src = "digits/6.gif";
    imgArray[7] = new Image(60,120);
    imgArray[7].src = "digits/7.gif";
    imgArray[8] = new Image(60,120);
    imgArray[8].src = "digits/8.gif";
    imgArray[9] = new Image(60,120);
    imgArray[9].src = "digits/9.gif";
}

var nextYear = new Date().getYear( ) + 1;
nextYear += (nextYear < 1900) ? 1900 : 0;
var targetDate = new Date(nextYear,0,1);
var targetInMS = targetDate.getTime( );
var oneSec = 1000;
var oneMin = 60 * oneSec;
var oneHr = 60 * oneMin;
var oneDay = 24 * oneHr;

function countDown( ) {
    var nowInMS = new Date().getTime( );
    var diff = targetInMS - nowInMS;
    var scratchPad = diff / oneDay;
    var daysLeft = Math.floor(scratchPad);
    // hours left
    diff -= (daysLeft * oneDay);
    scratchPad = diff / oneHr;
    var hrsLeft = Math.floor(scratchPad);
    // minutes left
    diff -= (hrsLeft * oneHr);
    scratchPad = diff / oneMin;
    var minsLeft = Math.floor(scratchPad);
    // seconds left
    diff -= (minsLeft * oneMin);
    scratchPad = diff / oneSec;
    var secsLeft = Math.floor(scratchPad);
```

Example 15-5. A countdown timer application (continued)

```
        // now adjust images
        setImages(daysLeft, hrsLeft, minsLeft, secsLeft);
}

function setImages(days, hrs, mins, secs) {
    var i;
    days = formatNum(days, 3);
    for (i = 0; i < days.length; i++) {
        document.images["days" + i].src = imgArray[parseInt(days.charAt(i))].src;
    }
    hrs = formatNum(hrs, 2);
    for (i = 0; i < hrs.length; i++) {
        document.images["hours" + i].src = imgArray[parseInt(hrs.charAt(i))].src;
    }
    mins = formatNum(mins, 2);
    for (i = 0; i < mins.length; i++) {
        document.images["minutes" + i].src = imgArray[parseInt(mins.charAt(i))].src;
    }
    secs = formatNum(secs, 2);
    for (i = 0; i < secs.length; i++) {
        document.images["seconds" + i].src = imgArray[parseInt(secs.charAt(i))].src;
    }
}

function formatNum(num, len) {
    var numStr = "" + num;
    while (numStr.length < len) {
        numStr = "0" + numStr;
    }
    return numStr
}

window.onload = function() {setInterval("countDown( )", 1000)};
</script>
</head>
<body style="margin-left: 10%; margin-right: 10%">
<h1>New Year's Countdown Timer</h1>
<hr />

<table cellspacing="5" cellpadding="5">
<tr>
    <td align="right">
        <img name="days0" src="digits/0.gif" height="120" width="60" alt="days">
        <img name="days1" src="digits/0.gif" height="120" width="60" alt="days">
        <img name="days2" src="digits/0.gif" height="120" width="60" alt="days">
    </td>
    <td align="left">
        <img src="digits/days.gif" height="120" width="260" alt="days">
    </td>
</tr>
<tr>
    <td align="right">
```

Example 15-5. A countdown timer application (continued)

```
            <img name="hours0" src="digits/0.gif" height="120" width="60" alt="hours">
            <img name="hours1" src="digits/0.gif" height="120" width="60" alt="hours">
        </td>
        <td align="left">
            <img src="digits/hours.gif" height="120" width="360" alt="hours">
        </td>
    </tr>
    <tr>
        <td align="right">
            <img name="minutes0" src="digits/0.gif" height="120" width="60" alt="minutes">
            <img name="minutes1" src="digits/0.gif" height="120" width="60" alt="minutes">
        </td>
        <td align="left">
            <img src="digits/minutes.gif" height="120" width="450" alt="minutes">
        </td>
    </tr>
    <tr>
        <td align="right">
            <img name="seconds0" src="digits/0.gif" height="120" width="60" alt="seconds">
            <img name="seconds1" src="digits/0.gif" height="120" width="60" alt="seconds">
        </td>
        <td align="left">
            <img src="digits/seconds.gif" height="120" width="460" alt="seconds">
        </td>
    </tr>
    </table>

</body>
</html>
```

For this example, the target date of the countdown timer is the start of the next year in the user's local time zone. The HTML output display is a rudimentary table with place holders for the digit images. Because this application works with browsers that may experience CSS formatting problems, we use the old-fashioned, but still supported, align attribute in table cells and name attribute in img elements. The table is delivered to the browser with all of the swappable images set to the zero digit representation.

The script portion of the page begins by precaching the images that represent the numbers to prevent any delay the first time they are needed. Ten images, each the same height and width, are loaded into the browser's image cache while the page loads.

Several functions will execute repeatedly, and they benefit from the one-time predefinition of constants as global variables.

The function that executes repeatedly, countDown( ), performs the date math by comparing the current clock setting (read approximately every second) against the target date. Invoked by way of the window.setInterval( ) method, the countDown( ) function executes repeatedly once every second (plus or minus system latency).

Next is the setImages( ) function, which adjusts the swappable img element src properties. This function must convert the numeric values passed from countDown( ) into the URLs for the images. Calling formatNum( ) for each countdown component returns a string version of the number, including a leading zero where necessary.

This application is a good demonstration of a situation where it makes sense to use setInterval( ) to drive the repeated action. While setTimeout( ) is intended for a single invocation of a function after some delay, setInterval( ) automatically invokes a function repeatedly.

As with the timed autoscrolling of the page in Recipe 15.6, the repeated calls to the countdown timer can also exhibit less than smooth running. If you watch this code run for several seconds, you will notice an occasional and random unevenness to the flipping of the seconds. You can improve the smoothness by shortening the interval delay (to 100, for example), but this means that the function is being invoked 10 times per second, which could impact other script processing in your page. You can experiment with different settings to achieve the balance that feels best for your application.

So far, we have focused on the user's local time zone, but there may be other cases in which you want to peg the target date and time to a unique event occurring someplace on the planet, such as a corporate press conference announcing a new product release. To keep the timing accurate, you need to perform some additional calculations to get the time zone issues under control so that users from Australia to Greenland will see the exact same countdown times leading up to the singular event.

The coding for this is simple, but the timekeeping may not be. To peg the target time and date to a universal point in the future, change the global variable declarations shown in Example 15-5 from this:

```
var targetDate = new Date(nextYear,0,1);
var targetInMS = targetDate.getTime( );
```

to this:

```
var targetInMS = Date.UTC(nextYear, 0, 1, 0, 0, 0);
```

This is for the stroke of midnight on New Year's Eve at Greenwich Mean Time (GMT). If you have another date and time, simply plug the values into the six parameters in the order of four-digit year, month (zero-based), date, hour, minute, and second, but at Greenwich Mean Time. For example, if you plan to offer a web cast of a recital at 8 P.M. in Los Angeles on January 10, 2008, you need to determine what that time is in GMT so that you can provide a countdown timer on the announcement page. Los Angeles is in the Pacific Time Zone, and in that part of the year, the zone is Pacific Standard Time. The PST zone is eight hours earlier than GMT. When it's 8 P.M. in Los Angeles, it's 4 A.M. the next day at GMT. Thus, you'd set the target time for 4 A.M. on the 11th of January (month index is 2) like this:

```
var targetInMS = Date.UTC(2008, 0, 11, 4, 0, 0);
```

There is an even easier way to figure out this GMT stuff. Set your system clock and time zone to the local time of where the event is to occur (you may already be there). Then run this little calculator page to determine the GMT date and time:

```html
<html>
<head>
<script type="text/javascript">
function calcGMT(form) {
    var date = new Date(form.year.value, form.month.value, form.day.value,
                        form.hour.value, form.minute.value, form.second.value);
    form.output.value = date.toUTCString();
}
</script>
</head>
<body>
<form>
Year:<input type="text" name="year" value="0000" /><br />
Month (0-11):<input type="text" name="month" value="0" /><br />
Day (1-31):<input type="text" name="day" value="0" /><br />
Hour (0-23):<input type="text" name="hour" value="0" /><br />
Minute (0-59):<input type="text" name="minute" value="0" /><br />
Second (0-59):<input type="text" name="second" value="0" /><br />
<input type="button" value="Get GMT" onclick="calcGMT(this.form)" /><br />
<input type="text" name="output" size="60" />
</body>
</html>
```

If you change your system clock settings to use this calculator, be sure to change them back to your local time and time zone.

Another kind of counter is a short-term counter for applications like student quizzes or other controlled environments in which you need something to time out or navigate to another page. It's not uncommon in such cases to display, say, a 60-second counter.

The following code is a modified version of the script in Example 15-5 that displays a countdown timer for the number of seconds passed as a parameter to the primary function:

```javascript
// global variables
var targetInMS, timerInterval;
var oneSec = 1000;

// pass the number of seconds to count down
function startTimer(secs) {
    var targetTime = new Date();
    targetTime.setSeconds(targetTime.getSeconds() + secs);
    targetInMS = targetTime.getTime();
    // display starting image
    setImages(secs);
    timerInterval = setInterval("countDown()", 100);
}

function countDown() {
    var nowInMS = (new Date()).getTime();
```

```
        var diff = targetInMS - nowInMS;
        if (diff <= 0) {
            clearInterval(timerInterval);
            alert("Time is up!");
            // more processing here
        } else {
            var scratchPad = diff / oneSec;
            var secsLeft = Math.floor(scratchPad);
            setImages(secsLeft);
        }
    }

    function setImages(secs) {
        var i;
        secs = formatNum(secs, 2);
        for (i = 0; i < secs.length; i++) {
            document.images["seconds" + i].src = imgArray[parseInt(secs.charAt(i))].src;
        }
    }

    function formatNum(num, len) {
        var numStr = "" + num;
        while (numStr.length < len) {
            numStr = "0" + numStr;
        }
        return numStr
    }
```

This code is easily modifiable to extend the timer to minutes and seconds if you like.

See Also

Recipe 15.8 for displaying the number of days until Christmas; Recipes 2.9 and 2.10 for the Date object and its methods.

15.10 Creating a Calendar Date Picker

Problem

You want to provide a pop-up calendar to assist users in locating and entering a date into a form.

Solution

You can make the user interface part of a popup calendar date picker by using a dynamic table inside an absolute-positioned div container. Scripting behind the picker must accomplish two primary tasks:

- Populating the calendar with views of a selected month within a selected year
- Allowing the click of a date in the calendar to be delivered back to the main document form to fill in the date field(s)

See the Discussion for an example of an HTML-based date picker, along with style sheets and the scripts that power the calendar. One script function, shown in Example 15-6 in the Discussion, is called showCalendar( ). This function is invoked by a user interface element inside the displayed form.

To get everything initialized, a load event invokes all necessary routines in the current page:

```
addOnLoadEvent(function( ) {datePicker.init(document.getElementById("calendar"),
    document.getElementById("dateChooser"),
    document.getElementById("mainForm"))});
```

Discussion

This solution has a lot of code, including HTML, CSS, and scripts. But there is a lot going on here: dynamically creating table content for the calendar, setting the position and visibility of the calendar, supplying data from the calendar back to the main page, and more. Figure 15-3 shows the calendar being used with a very simple date form.

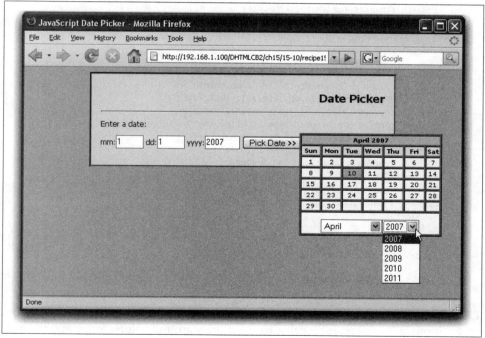

Figure 15-3. Pop-up calendar picker

We'll start with two segments of HTML. One is for the date form that ultimately receives the data from the date picker. A click of the button-type input element invokes a function that displays the calendar:

```
<form name="mainForm" id="mainForm" method="POST" action="...">
<p>Enter a date:</p>
```

```
<p>mm:<input type="text" name="month" id="month" size="3" maxlength="2" value="1" />
dd:<input type="text" name="day" id="day" size="3" maxlength="2" value="1" />
yyyy:<input type="text" name="year" id="year" size="5" maxlength="4" value="2003" />
<input type="button" id="showit" value="Pick Date  >>"
onclick="datePicker.showCalendar(event)" />
</p>
</form>
```

The other important HTML part is the positioned div element that holds the calendar table. It is delivered with the page in sparse form (and hidden from view) because scripts fill out the rest during initialization. Only the days-of-the-week headers and select list of months are preset in the code. Month names in the select list get used later on to supply the name for the current month of the calendar:

```
<div id="calendar">
<table id="calendarTable" border=1>
<tr>
    <th id="tableHeader" colspan="7"></th>
</tr>
<tr><th>Sun</th><th>Mon</th><th>Tue</th><th>Wed</th>
<th>Thu</th><th>Fri</th><th>Sat</th></tr>
<tbody id="tableBody"></tbody>
<tr>
    <td colspan="7">
    <p>
    <form id="dateChooser" name="dateChooser">
        <select name="chooseMonth" id="chooseMonth"
        onchange="datePicker.populateTable(this.form)">
            <option selected>January<option>February
            <option>March<option>April<option>May
            <option>June<option>July<option>August
            <option>September<option>October
            <option>November<option>December
    </select>
    <select name="chooseYear" id="chooseYear"
    onchange="datePicker.populateTable(this.form)">
    </select>
    </form>
    </p>
    </td>
</tr>
</table>
</div>
```

The table and its components are governed by a fairly extensive style sheet that covers positioning, visibility, table cell alignment, background colors, fonts, and the like. Mouse rollover effects for the date numbers in the calendar are controlled strictly by CSS pseudoclasses of a elements:

```
<style type="text/css">
#calendar {
        position: absolute;
        left: 0px;
```

```
                top: 0px;
                visibility: hidden;
                }
    table {
            font-family: Verdana, Arial, Helvetica, sans-serif;
            background-color: #999999
            }
    th {
        background-color: #ccffcc;
        text-align: center;
        font-size: 10px;
        width: 26px
        }
    #tableHeader {
                    background-color: #ffcccc;
                    width: 100%
                    }
    td {
        background-color: #ffffcc;
        text-align: center;
        font-size: 10px;
        width: 28px
        }
    #tableBody tr td {width: 26px}
    #today {background-color: #ffcc33}
    a:link {color: #000000; text-decoration: none}
    a:active {color: #000000; text-decoration: none}
    a:visited {color: #000000; text-decoration: none}
    a:hover {color: #990033; text-decoration: underline}
    </style>
```

Example 15-6 shows the script portion of this recipe, including the linked-in *eventsManager.js* library from Recipe 9.3 and the DHTML API library from Recipe 13.3. The calendar script is divided into five sections.

Example 15-6. Scripts for the pop-up date picker

```
<script src="../js/eventsManager.js"></script>
<script src="../js/DHTML3API.js"></script>
<script type="text/javascript">
var datePicker = {
    /*******************
      REFERENCE PROPERTIES
    *******************/
    calendarDiv : null,
    calendarForm : null,
    destinationForm : null,
    /*******************
      UTILITY METHODS
    *******************/
    // day of week of month's first day
    getFirstDay : function (theYear, theMonth){
        var firstDate = new Date(theYear,theMonth,1);
        return firstDate.getDay();
```

Example 15-6. Scripts for the pop-up date picker (continued)

```
        },
        // number of days in the month
        getMonthLen : function(theYear, theMonth) {
            var nextMonth = new Date(theYear, theMonth + 1, 1);
            nextMonth.setHours(nextMonth.getHours( ) - 3);
            return nextMonth.getDate( );
        },
        getElementPosition : function(elemID) {
            var offsetTrail = document.getElementById(elemID);
            var offsetLeft = 0;
            var offsetTop = 0;
            while (offsetTrail) {
                offsetLeft += offsetTrail.offsetLeft;
                offsetTop += offsetTrail.offsetTop;
                offsetTrail = offsetTrail.offsetParent;
            }
            return {left:offsetLeft, top:offsetTop};
        },
        // position and show calendar
        showCalendar : function(evt) {
            evt = (evt) ? evt : event;
            if (evt) {
                if (this.calendarDiv.style.visibility != "visible") {
                    var elem = (evt.target) ? evt.target : evt.srcElement;
                    var position = this.getElementPosition(elem.id);
                    DHTMLAPI.moveTo(this.calendarDiv.id, position.left + elem.offsetWidth,
                        position.top);
                    DHTMLAPI.show(this.calendarDiv.id);
                } else {
                    DHTMLAPI.hide(this.calendarDiv.id);
                }
            }
        },
        /***********************
          DRAW CALENDAR CONTENTS
        ************************/
        // clear and re-populate table based on form's selections
        populateTable : function(form) {
            // pick up date form choices
            var theMonth = form.chooseMonth.selectedIndex;
            var theYear = parseInt(form.chooseYear.options[form.chooseYear.selectedIndex].text);
            // initialize date-dependent variables
            var firstDay = this.getFirstDay(theYear, theMonth);
            var howMany = this.getMonthLen(theYear, theMonth);
            var today = new Date( );

            // fill in month/year in table header
            document.getElementById("tableHeader").innerHTML =
                form.chooseMonth.options[theMonth].text + " " + theYear;

            // initialize vars for table creation
            var dayCounter = 1;
```

Example 15-6. Scripts for the pop-up date picker (continued)

```
        var TBody = document.getElementById("tableBody");
        // clear any existing rows
        while (TBody.rows.length > 0) {
            TBody.deleteRow(0);
        }
        var newR, newC, dateNum;
        var done=false;
        while (!done) {
            // create new row at end
            newR = TBody.insertRow(TBody.rows.length);
            if (newR) {
                for (var i = 0; i < 7; i++) {
                    // create new cell at end of row
                    newC = newR.insertCell(newR.cells.length);
                    if (TBody.rows.length == 1 && i < firstDay) {
                        // empty boxes before first day
                        newC.innerHTML = " ";
                        continue;
                    }
                    if (dayCounter == howMany) {
                        // no more rows after this one
                        done = true;
                    }
                    // plug in link/date (or empty for boxes after last day)
                    if (dayCounter <= howMany) {
                        if (today.getFullYear() == theYear &&
                            today.getMonth() == form.chooseMonth.selectedIndex &&
                            today.getDate() == dayCounter) {
                            newC.id = "today";
                        }
                        newC.innerHTML = "<a href='#'onclick='datePicker.chooseDate(" +
                            dayCounter + "," + theMonth + "," + theYear +
                            "); return false;'>" + dayCounter + "</a>";
                        dayCounter++;
                    } else {
                        newC.innerHTML = " ";
                    }
                }
            } else {
                done = true;
            }
        }
    },
    /*******************
      INITIALIZATIONS
    *******************/
    // init dispatcher
    init: function(calendarDiv, calendarForm, destinationForm) {
        this.calendarDiv = calendarDiv;
        this.calendarForm = calendarForm;
        this.destinationForm = destinationForm;
        this.fillYears();
        this.populateTable(calendarForm);
```

Example 15-6. Scripts for the pop-up date picker (continued)

```
    },
    // create dynamic list of year choices
    fillYears : function( ) {
        var today = new Date( );
        var thisYear = today.getFullYear( );
        var yearChooser = document.getElementById("chooseYear");
        for (i = thisYear; i < thisYear + 5; i++) {
            yearChooser.options[yearChooser.options.length] = new Option(i, i);
        }
        this.setCurrMonth(today);
    },
    // set month choice to current month
    setCurrMonth : function(today) {
        document.getElementById("chooseMonth").selectedIndex = today.getMonth( );
    },
    /*******************
        PROCESS CHOICE
    *******************/
    chooseDate : function(date, month, year) {
        this.destinationForm.date.value = date;
        this.destinationForm.month.value = month + 1;
        this.destinationForm.year.value = year;
        DHTMLAPI.hide("calendar");
    }
}

addOnLoadEvent(function( ) {datePicker.init(document.getElementById("calendar"),
    document.getElementById("dateChooser"),
    document.getElementById("mainForm"))});
</script>
```

The first script section defines three properties whose values are initialized in the init( ) method (below) and are referred to several times throughout other method executions. Next comes a section that contains several utility functions that support others to come. First is a pair of functions, getFirstDay( ) and getMonthLen( ), that the calendar-creation routines use to find which day of the week the first day of a month falls on, and then the length of the month. The three-hour correction in getMonthLen( ) takes care of date calculation anomalies that can occur when the month includes a transition from summer to winter. The goal is to obtain a valid date of the day before the first of the next month.

When it's time to display the calendar, the next pair of functions come into play. The getElementPosition( ) function (Recipe 13.8) determines the position of a body element (the "Pick Date" button in our example), which the following showCalendar( ) function uses to position the calendar just to the right of the button before showing the calendar (positioning and visibility are controlled from DHTML API functions).

The core routine of this application, populateTable( ), calculates the date data and assembles the HTML for the table body portion of the calendar pop-up window. It begins by gathering important bearings for the calculations from select lists at the bottom of the calendar. Then it places the month and year text in the table's headers. After some DOM-oriented preparations, the script removes any previous table body content. At the heart of the script is a while loop that keeps adding rows to the table as needed. For each row, a for loop generates cells for each of the seven columns, filling cells with date numbers surrounded by links that pass the values back to the main form. A little extra touch is labeling the ID of the current day's cell so that it picks up one of the style sheet rules to make it stand out from the rest of the cells.

The primary initialization routine, init( ), takes three parameters, each being a reference to an HTML component of this system. The first parameter is a reference to the positioned div element that contains the entire calendar display. Within the calendar div is a form, which houses the month and year select elements. Because the populateTable( ) method uses those select element values to know which calendar to build, the form reference is an essential piece of information. Lastly, the third parameter is a reference to the form that is to receive the chosen date data. It is assumed that such a form has fields set for the month, day, and year (although the chooseDate( ) method's details can be easily modified to accommodate other date formats).

After storing the parameters as object properties, init( ) further calls fillYears( ) and setCurrMonth( ). These two methods prepare the select elements in the calendar so that the years in the list constantly move forward as time marches on. Also, the lists are set to the current month and year as a starting point for the user the first time the calendar appears.

When the user clicks on one of the dates in the calendar, the links for each date invoke the chooseDate( ) function, passing parameters for the date, month, and year. The parameters are assigned to the event handlers of the calendar date links while the calendar month's HTML is assembled back in populateTable( ). The chooseDate( ) function in this example distributes the values to the three date fields in the original form.

This pop-up calendar works in Internet Explorer 5 or later for Windows, Mozilla, Safari, and Opera 7 or later. Unfortunately, table modification bugs in IE 5 for the Mac prevent it from working in that environment.

Most of the visible, fun part of this application is governed by style sheets for the calendar table. You have wide flexibility in designing your calendar by using the HTML tags and IDs of the skeletal calendar table as a guide. If you adhere to those naming conventions, the calendar-generating and modifying code will work without any problems.

Another potential modification that might appeal to you is to make the calendar draggable by its titlebar. You can adapt the element-dragging code from Recipe 13.11 to add that functionality here, as well.

See Also

Recipe 2.9 and Recipe 2.10 for details about using date objects; Recipe 12.10 for hiding and showing elements; Recipe 13.3 for details on the DHTML API library; Recipe 13.8 for obtaining the position of a body element.

15.11 Displaying an Animated Progress Bar

Problem

You want to show a progress bar while a long, repetitive script operation takes place.

Solution

Components of this solution consist of a minimum of HTML, a style sheet to give the HTML its look and feel, and scripts to control the display and animation of the progress bar. The HTML included in the page consists of a group of nested div elements, each of which makes up a separate visible portion of the user interface: the wrapper around the entire progress bar, the label text, the empty bar, and the colored bar that expands to the right during the animation:

```
<div id="progressBar">
    <div id="progressBarMsg">Calculating...</div>
    <div id="sliderWrapper">0%
        <div id="slider">0%</div>
    </div>
</div>
```

The progress bar is hidden when the page loads, and the rest of its look and feel is controlled by an extensive style sheet described in the Discussion. You can customize the appearance by modifying the style sheet.

Apply the script shown in Example 15-7 to the progress bar. The sequence used to control the progress bar consists of calls to the showProgressBar( ), calcProgress( ), and hideProgressBar( ) functions. See the Discussion about how to repeatedly invoke calcProgress( ) to convey motion to the bar. The page must also include a load event call to the initProgressBar( ) function:

```
addOnLoadEvent(function() {initProgressBar()});
```

Discussion

Despite the simplicity of the HTML for the progress bar, it can convey a significant amount of information. Figure 15-4 shows what the progress bar looks like in the middle of its animation.

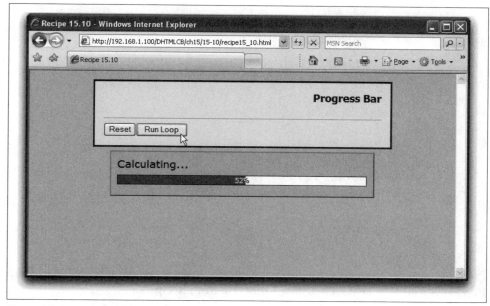

Figure 15-4. An animated progress bar in action

Other than the progress message and initial 0 percent indicators, the look and feel of the entire bar is controlled by the following style sheet rules:

```
<style type="text/css">
#progressBar {
            position: absolute;
            width: 400px;
            height: 35px;
            visibility: hidden;
            background-color: #99ccff;
            padding: 20px;
            border-width: 2px;
            border-left-color: #9999ff;
            border-top-color: #9999ff;
            border-right-color: #666666;
            border-bottom-color: #666666;
            border-style: solid;
            }
#progressBarMsg {
              position: absolute;
              left: 10px;
              top: 10px;
              font: 18px Verdana, Helvetica, sans-serif bold
              }
#sliderWrapper {
            position: absolute;
            left: 10px;
            top: 40px;
```

```
                    width: 417px;
                    height: 15px;
                    background-color: #ffffff;
                    border: 1px solid #000000;
                    text-align: center;
                    font-size: 12px
                }
    #slider{
            position: absolute;
            left: 0px;
            top: 0px;
            width: 420px;
            height: 15px;
            clip: rect(0px 0px 15px 0px);
            background-color: #666699;
            text-align: center;
            color: #ffffff;
            font-size: 12px
            }
    </style>
```

Progress bar scripting, as shown in Example 15-7, relies on the DHTML API from Recipe 13.3 and the centerOnWindow( ) function from Recipe 13.7.

Example 15-7. Scripts for the progress bar

```
<script src="../js/eventsManager.js"></script>
<script src="../js/DHTML3API.js"></script>
<script type="text/javascript">
// Center a positionable element whose name is passed as
// a parameter in the current window/frame, and show it
function centerOnWindow(elemID) {
    // 'obj' is the positionable object
    var obj = DHTMLAPI.getRawObject(elemID);
    // window scroll factors
    var scrollX = 0, scrollY = 0;
    if (document.body && typeof document.body.scrollTop != "undefined") {
        scrollX += document.body.scrollLeft;
        scrollY += document.body.scrollTop;
        if (document.body.parentNode &&
            typeof document.body.parentNode.scrollTop != "undefined") {
            scrollX += document.body.parentNode.scrollLeft;
            scrollY += document.body.parentNode.scrollTop
        }
    } else if (typeof window.pageXOffset != "undefined") {
        scrollX += window.pageXOffset;
        scrollY += window.pageYOffset;
    }
    var x = Math.round((DHTMLAPI.getInsideWindowWidth( )/2) -
        (DHTMLAPI.getElementWidth(obj)/2)) + scrollX;
    var y = Math.round((DHTMLAPI.getInsideWindowHeight( )/2) -
        (DHTMLAPI.getElementHeight(obj)/2)) + scrollY;
    DHTMLAPI.moveTo(obj, x, y);
    DHTMLAPI.show(obj);
```

Example 15-7. Scripts for the progress bar (continued)

```
}

function initProgressBar( ) {
    // create quirks object whose default (CSS-compatible) values
    // are zero; pertinent values for quirks mode filled in later
    if (navigator.appName == "Microsoft Internet Explorer" &&
        navigator.userAgent.indexOf("Win") != -1 &&
        (typeof document.compatMode == "undefined" ||
        document.compatMode == "BackCompat")) {
        document.getElementById("progressBar").style.height = "81px";
        document.getElementById("progressBar").style.width = "444px";
        document.getElementById("sliderWrapper").style.fontSize = "xx-small";
        document.getElementById("slider").style.fontSize = "xx-small";
        document.getElementById("slider").style.height = "13px";
        document.getElementById("slider").style.width = "415px";
    }
}

function showProgressBar( ) {
    centerOnWindow("progressBar");
}

function calcProgress(current, total) {
    if (current <= total) {
        var factor = current/total;
        var pct = Math.ceil(factor * 100);
        document.getElementById("sliderWrapper").firstChild.nodeValue = pct + "%";
        document.getElementById("slider").firstChild.nodeValue = pct + "%";
        document.getElementById("slider").style.clip = "rect(0px " + parseInt(factor *
417) + "px 16px 0px)";
    }
}

function hideProgressBar( ) {
    DHTMLAPI.hide("progressBar");
    calcProgress(0, 0);
}

// Test bench to see progress bar in action at random intervals
var loopObject = {start:0, end:10, current:0, interval:null};

function runit( ) {
    if (loopObject.current <= loopObject.end) {
        calcProgress(loopObject.current, loopObject.end);
        loopObject.current += Math.random( );
        loopObject.interval = setTimeout("runit( )", 700);
    } else {
        calcProgress(loopObject.end, loopObject.end);
        loopObject.current = 0;
        loopObject.interval = null;
        setTimeout("hideProgressBar( )", 500);
    }
```

Example 15-7. Scripts for the progress bar (continued)

```
}

function test( ) {
    showProgressBar( );
    runit( );
}
addOnLoadEvent(function() {initProgressBar( )});
</script>
```

The centerOnWindow( ) function is called each time the progress bar is shown (in the showProgressBar( ) function). Thus, if the user resizes the browser window between displays of the progress bar, the bar is still centered on the current window.

Due to the heavy use of borders and padding to define the look and feel of the progress bar, a bit of extra coding is needed to assist with the sizing of the nested div elements. The discrepancies in IE between backward- and CSS-compatible modes have a significant bearing on the various measures. The default specification from the style sheets is tailored for the CSS-compatible world and runs as-is in Mozilla, Safari, and Opera. For IE 5, 5.5, and the quirks mode of IE 6/7, the initProgressBar( ) function (invoked via the load event handler) makes critical adjustments to several dimensions.

Three functions control the visibility and animation of the progress bar. Two simply show and hide the bar, but the calcProgress( ) function is the key to the animation. The bar works by adjusting the clipping rectangle of the darker-colored, most deeply nested div element. It is initially set up to be clipped to zero pixel width. Calculations are based on some current value compared against a maximum value—notions that can be applied to any quantifiable operation. The factor (converted to a percentage for display within the bar space) is applied to the right edge of the clipping rectangle.

To experiment with the progress bar, I've created some test functions that simply repeat through a sequence of calculations with a little bit of irregularity thrown in to make the display interesting. A global object named loopObject contains properties to assist with the experimentation. The runProgressBar( ) function represents the kind of function you might be using that would benefit from the progress bar display. The key to successful deployment is a repeating script triggered by setTimeout( ) or setInterval( ) so that the page updates between iterations. Once the target value is achieved, the calcProgress( ) function is invoked with the same values as parameters to allow the bar to display the 100% value briefly, before the progress bar is hidden.

Identifying the kinds of operations to which the progress bar can be applied may not be easy. Prerequisites include an operation that takes sufficient time to warrant the display of the progress bar in the first place. But more important, the operations must be something that occurs after the page has loaded so that the progress bar div elements are already loaded and modified as needed for quirks-mode versions of IE for Windows.

The operation must also be something for which you have a known target quantity, so that the current progress can be measured against that target. One possibility is monitoring the precaching of images, provided the operation takes place triggered by the load event handler of the page (and after the progress bar is initialized). Your equivalent of the runProgressBar( ) function should loop through the array of image objects, checking whether the value of each object's complete property is true. If it is, the progress bar is incremented by one fraction of the image array's length, and your function should loop again via the setTimeout( ) method to test the next image in the array. If the value is false, the same index value is passed to the function again (via the setTimeout( )) to try once more. Of course, images don't always arrive from the server in source code order, so the progress bar is likely to be inconsistent in its progress. Also, if the images are already in the browser cache, the loop through the array may actually slow down the user's access to the finished page.

A progress bar is the right solution when the user might get impatient with something that is truly going on behind the scenes. Tolerance for delays is greatly extended when you entertain in the interim.

See Also

Recipe 12.10 for hiding and showing an element; Recipe 13.10 for how to make an element positionable; Recipe 13.3 for details on the DHTML API library; Recipe 13.7 for centering a positioned element in the browser window.

Keyboard Event Character Values

Keyboard events in recent browsers provide information about the keys and, where applicable, about the characters corresponding to the keys. Character values may be read from the keypress event. The following table reveals the codes for characters in the lower ASCII character set. Some of these codes are for action keys (such as Backspace and Tab), whose character values are also in this range.

Character	Value	Character	Value	
Backspace	8	0	48	
Tab	9	1	49	
Enter (Return on Mac)	13	2	50	
Space	32	3	51	
!	33	4	52	
"	34	5	53	
#	35	6	54	
$	36	7	55	
%	37	8	56	
&	38	9	57	
'	39	:	58	
(	40	;	59	
)	41	<	60	
*	42	=	61	
+	43	>	62	
,	44	?	63	
-	45	@	64	
.	46	A	65	
/	47	B	66	
C	67	b	98	

Character	Value	Character	Value
D	68	c	99
E	69	d	100
F	70	e	101
G	71	f	102
H	72	g	103
I	73	h	104
J	74	i	105
K	75	j	106
L	76	k	107
M	77	l	108
N	78	m	109
O	79	n	110
P	80	o	111
Q	81	p	112
R	82	q	113
S	83	r	114
T	84	s	115
U	85	t	116
V	86	u	117
W	87	v	118
X	88	w	119
Y	89	x	120
Z	90	y	121
[	91	z	122
\	92	{	123
]	93	|	124
^	94	}	125
_	95	~	126
`	96	Delete	127
a	97		

APPENDIX B
Keyboard Key Code Values

Key codes are numeric values that correspond to physical keys on the keyboard but do not necessarily correspond to a particular character. For example, the A key on the keyboard produces the same key code when pressed, even though its character code might be 65 (uppercase A) or 97 (lowercase a), depending on whether the Shift key is down at the same time. Key codes are not influenced by modifier keys. Character values (see Appendix A) may be read from the keypress event, while the key values, including navigation and function keys, are available from keydown and keyup events. The following table lists all keys on a typical U.S. English keyboard and their corresponding key codes.

Key	Key value	Key	Key value
Alt	18	F5	116
Arrow Down	40	F6	117
Arrow Left	37	F7	118
Arrow Right	39	F8	119
Arrow Up	38	F9	120
Backspace	8	F10	121
Caps Lock	20	F11	122
Ctrl	17	F12	123
Delete	46	Home	36
End	35	Insert	45
Enter	13	Num Lock	144
Esc	27	(NumPad) -	109
F1	112	(NumPad) *	106
F2	113	(NumPad) .	110
F3	114	(NumPad) /	111
F4	115	(NumPad) +	107

Key	Key value	Key	Key value
(NumPad) 0	96	P	80
(NumPad) 1	97	Q	81
(NumPad) 2	98	R	82
(NumPad) 3	99	S	83
(NumPad) 4	100	T	84
(NumPad) 5	101	U	85
(NumPad) 6	102	V	86
(NumPad) 7	103	W	87
(NumPad) 8	104	X	88
(NumPad) 9	105	Y	89
Page Down	34	Z	90
Page Up	33	1	49
Pause	19	2	50
Print Scrn	44	3	51
Scroll Lock	145	4	52
Shift	16	5	53
Spacebar	32	6	54
Tab	9	7	55
A	65	8	56
B	66	9	57
C	67	0	48
D	68	`	222
E	69	-	189
F	70	,	188
G	71	.	190
H	72	/	191
I	73	;	186
J	74	[	219
K	75	\	220
L	76	]	221
M	77	`	192
N	78	=	187
O	79		

ECMAScript Reserved Keywords

All of the words in the following table are reserved for use by the ECMAScript interpreter built into scriptable browsers. You may not use these words as identifiers for variables, functions, or objects. A majority of these words are already used by current implementations of JavaScript, while others may become part of the vocabulary in future versions.

abstract	double	in	super
boolean	else	instanceof	switch
break	enum	int	synchronized
byte	export	interface	this
case	extends	long	throw
catch	final	native	throws
char	finally	new	transient
class	float	package	try
const	for	private	typeof
continue	function	protected	var
debugger	goto	public	void
default	if	return	volatile
delete	implements	short	while
do	import	static	with

The following case-sensitive words may not be used as identifier names in scripts using ECMA for XML (E4X) scripts (currently supported only in Mozilla):

each	namespace	xml

Index

Symbols

< > (angle brackets)
    < (less-than) operator, using with for loop
      in array iteration, 59
    <= (less-than or equals) operator, array
      iteration and, 59
    >= (greater-than or equals) operator
      browser version detection, 114
      Internet Explorer version
        comparisons, 115
    tag names in CSS style rules, 333
@ (at sign), @import rule, 337
\ (backslash)
    \\ (double backslashes), escaping escape
      character, 15
    escape character, 15
: (colon), separating style property name
    from its value, 332
, (commas)
    delimiting style property values, 332
    in displayed numbers, 38
{ } (curly braces)
    containing statements belonging to a
      function, 90
    creating objects, 66
    placement of, 92
    style properties within, 332
. (dot), dots rule for custom objects, 52
" (double quotes) in strings, 1
= (equal sign)
    = = (equality) operator, 10, 34
      browser version detection, 114
      IE version comparisons, 115

= = = (strict equality) operator, 10
    testing numbers for equality, 35
    assignment operator, 52
! (exclamation mark)
    != (inequality) operator, 10
      testing for inequality of two
        numbers, 35
    != = (strict inequality) operator, 10
      testing for inequality of two
        numbers, 35
(hash mark)
    delimiter between page URL and anchor
      name in location.hash, 272
    preceding ID selectors, 336
( ) (parentheses), invoking functions, 90
+ (plus sign)
    += (add-by-value) operator, 4
      adding a number or appending a string
        to an array, 52
      performance problems with, 6
    addition operator, 4
      casting between string and number
        data types, 31
      priority to string concatenation over
        numeric addition, 32
? (question mark), search string
    delimiter, 272, 281
; (semicolon), separating style property/value
    pairs, 332
' (single quotes) in strings, 1
[ ] (square brackets)
    creating a multidimensional array, 56
    symbolizing array constructor, 55

We'd like to hear your suggestions for improving our indexes. Send email to *index@oreilly.com*.

hash table simulation for fast
lookups, 69–71
of items, element object references, 351
iterating through, 59
of objects, 68
form content converted to string, 228
simulated hash tables for lookups, 106
sorting, 72–74
objects vs., 52
sorting a simple array, 61
using as temporary storage device for
text, 6
using separately or with objects, 53
arrow keys, moving absolute-positioned
element, 258
ASCII character codes, 257, 548
assignLabelEvents( ) function, 300
assignment operator (=)
Asynchronous JavaScript and XML (see Ajax)
"at-rules", @import, 337
atob( ) method, 26
attachEvent( ) function, 238
functions bound via, order of
invocation, 243
authorAttrFilter( ) function, 498
autofocus( ) function, 223
availWidth and availHeight properties
(screen), 139

B

\b (backspace), 16
background color of an element,
alternating, 369
backgroundImage property, 377
base element
offset measures, 411
relative URLs and, 271
Base64 strings, encoding and
decoding, 23–26
character set for Base64-encoded
strings, 26
web site information on Base64
encoding, 26
base64.js library, 23
base64Encode( ) function, 26
BasicEvents module (DOM), 127
batch validation
forms, 196
master function calling individual
validation functions as needed, 204
preventing form submission upon
validation failure, 204

binary attachments to email, 26
binding events, 231
addEventListener( ) method (W3C
DOM), 237
attachEvent( ) method (IE), 238
to elements, pre-W3C DOM ways, 238
keyboard event to document node, 259
load event handler triggering scripted
bindings, 240
via property assignments, 241
to select element, 275
blankFrame( ) function, 178
blendTrans( ) filter, 382
block value (style.display property), 408
blockEvent( ) function, 431, 444
blockEvents( ) function, 152, 250
blocking double clicks, 251
blockIt( ) function, 251
block-level elements in HTML, default
behavior, 407
body content
automating search and replace, 506–511
removing, 483
replacing dynamically, 482
body element
attributes, 374
background-related style properties,
changing, 375
connecting a positioned element to, 398
OPML documents, 329
positioning HTML elements in IE, 395
bookmark values (TextRange), 511
bookmarking
framesets and, 178
just one frame, 183
bookmarklets, 320
border of the currently selected control
button set to red color, 373
borders (positioned elements), 246
bottlenecks in your code, eliminating, 103

 tag compared to newline character, 5
branching execution, 97–100
assigning browser global variables, 112
break statement, 98
Browser Archive, 131
browsers
browser detection, 110
canvas element, 385
carriage return codings in textarea
elements, 16
collapsible XML navigation menus, 321
color values, 370
cookies, 19

select element
    changing options, 224
    using for navigation, 275
    W3C DOM Level 2 specification, xiii
btoa( ) method, 26
button property (event), 254
    possible values of, 255
buttons for scrolling, 428
button-type input element
    invoking function displaying a
        calendar, 535
    invoking validation routines and form
        submission, 196
    Submit button, 217
    using for client-side form validation, 207

C

caching
    HTTP headers preventing caching in
        browsers, 355
    a page for navigation to anchor on same
        page, 272
    precaching images, 354
        monitoring, 547
calcBlockState( ) function, 317, 328
calcProgress( ) function, 542, 546
calendar date picker, 203
    creating, 534–542
        scripts for, 537–540
cancelAll( ) function, 300
cancelBubble property (event object), 246,
    250
cancelHide( ) function, 304
canvas element, drawing charts in, 385–391
    properties and methods of canvas context
        object, 385
capturing document content, 498
carriage returns
    codings in textarea element contents, 16
    in JavaScript source code, 5
Cascading Style Sheets (see CSS)
case
    character comparisons, 222
    converting in strings, 8
    language codes, 127
    sorting and, 73
case branch, 98
case-insensitive (i) regular expression
    modifier, 3
case-sensitivity, variable names, 88

casting between number and string data
    types, 31
ceil( ) method (Math), 35
center cell event handlers, HTML for, 263
centered window, opening, 142
centering an element, 345
    in a window or a frame, 412–414
        recentering after user actions, 414
    on top of another element, 410–412
centerOnElement( ) function, 410
    offset properties used, 412
centerOnWindow( ) function, 412, 546
change event handlers
    binding to select element, 275
    in input element, real-time validation of
        text box entries, 199
changeSizeStyle( ) function, 370, 372
character codes
    allowing only numbers or letters in a text
        box, 221
    analysis to allow Shift-Tab to move focus
        in reverse direction, 224
    ASCII, 548
    key codes vs., 258
    Unicode, converting between string values
        and, 20
character key presses, reading, 256
character values, keyboard events, 548
characters, case comparison, 222
charCodeAt( ) method, 20
charts, drawing in the canvas
    element, 385–391
checkDate( ) function, 47
    basic version, 48
    enhanced version, 49
checkModal( ) function, 157
childNodes property (olData), 319
chooseDate( ) function, 541
circular element paths, animating, 419–421
class attribute, 480
    set to draggable, 422
class names, 335
class selectors and class attributes
    assigning style sheet rules to a subgroup of
        elements, 334
    toggling style for an element, 342
className property (elements), 342
clearDragEvents( ) method, 166
clearTable( ) function, 493
clearTimeout( ) method, 95
clearUndoBuffer( ) function, 511

H

handleArrowKeys( ) function, 258
handleCancel( ) and handleOK( ) methods
    (parent), 153
handleCancel( ) function, 152
handleClick( ) function, 232
handleOK( ) function, 152
handleScrollClick( ) function, 431, 444
handleScrollStop( ) function, 431, 444
hasFeature( ) method, 125
hash property (location)
    # delimiter character and, 272
    assigning anchor name string to, 271
    navigating to any element on a page, 273
hash tables
    indexes, numeric and non-numeric
        values, 462
    simulated, using for array lookups, 106
    simulated. in drop-down navigation
        menu, 299
    simulating for fast array lookups, 69–71
height, width, and top style sheet properties
    (iframe), 172
hexadecimal numbers, converting between
    decimal numbers, 39
hidden frame, using as temporary data
    store, 280
hide( ) function, 405
hideMenus( ) function, 300
    menu component state, restoring to
        initial, 304
hideProgressBar( ) function, 542
hiding subsidiary groups of form controls
    until needed, 219
history, keeping pages out of, 273
horizontal scrolling, 445
hover (CSS pseudo-class), 343
href property (location)
    assigning new page URL string to, 271
    changing frame content from another
        frame, 179
href property (styleSheet), 340
HTML
    binding event handler functions to
        elements, 203
    blocks rendering for specific IE
        versions, 339
    comment tags, masking scripts from
        nonscriptable browsers, 110
    countdown timer application, 528–531
    creating new elements, 470
    element objects, getting references to, 478

grabbing copy of current HTML node
    tree, 498
JavaScript objects, transforming into
    HTML tables, 466–468
positioning elements, 392–451
scrollbar region awaiting scripted
    scrollbars, 434
scrolling region and controller, 427
slide control elements, 446
slide show page and scripts, 516–519
transforming XML data into HTML
    tables, 463–466
html element, 395
HTML module (DOM), 126
HTMLDocument object, URL property, 272
HTMLEvents module (DOM), 126
HTTP USERAGENT string, 110
hyperlink element (<a>), 268
hyperlinks (see links)

I

i (case-insensitive) regular expression
    modifier, 3
id attribute
    <map> tags, 359
    of an element, assigning ID selector name
        to, 336
    <img> tags, 358
    toggling style for a single element, 343
ID attributes, 195
ID names, 336
ID selectors
    assigning style sheet rules to an
        element, 336
    defining for a style rule and assigning to
        element id attribute, 336
    toggling style for a single element, 343
identifiers (class names), 335
IE (Internet Explorer)
    (see also browsers)
    a:active pseudoclass, 374
    carriage returns, 16
    conditional comments, 339
    cookie storage, 19
    creating different versions on a
        computer, 131
    creating elements and inserting them into
        a document, 472
    currentStyle object, 346
    detecting early versions, 113
    DHTML event, 233
    disabling form controls, 217

About the Author

Danny Goodman has been writing about personal computers and consumer electronics since the late 1970s. In 2006, he celebrated 25 years as a freelance writer and programmer, having published hundreds of magazine articles, several commercial software products, and, with the release of this volume, 45 computer-related books. Through the years, his most popular book titles—on HyperCard, AppleScript, Java-Script, and Dynamic HTML—have covered programming environments that are accessible to nonprofessionals, yet powerful enough to engage experts. His *Dynamic HTML: The Definitive Reference*, now in its third edition, is an O'Reilly bestseller.

Colophon

The animal on the cover of *JavaScript & DHTML Cookbook* is a howler monkey. Howler monkeys are so named because of the very loud sounds they make, which can be heard up to two miles away. They are considered the loudest landliving animals. They have two hollow hyoid bones that allow them to make the powerful sounds for which they are known.

Male howler monkeys are black, and females range from a brown to a light tan color. They have a large neck and a large lower jaw (containing the large hyoid bones), short legs, and a long, prehensile tail. All baby howler monkeys are born with brown fur, but the fur on the males eventually changes to black. These monkeys can grow up to 2 feet in height and can weight up to 16 pounds. The males are usually significantly larger than the females.

Howlers travel and live in packs of one to three males and two to seven females. There is one dominant male in each group. They spend the majority of their time in trees. Their howling vocalizations are used to mark their territories as well as to communicate with other packs of monkeys. Their diet consists mostly of leaves, but they also eat fruit and bugs. They are becoming an endangered species due to the shrinking size of the forests in which they live.

The cover image is from *Cuvier's Animals*. The cover font is Adobe ITC Garamond. The text font is Linotype Birka; the heading font is Adobe Myriad Condensed; and the code font is LucasFont's TheSans Mono Condensed.

70502

Related Titles from O'Reilly

Web Authoring and Design

ActionScript 3.0 Cookbook

Ajax Hacks

Ambient Findability

Creating Web Sites: The Missing Manual

CSS Cookbook, *2nd Edition*

CSS Pocket Reference, *2nd Edition*

CSS: The Definitive Guide, *3rd Edition*

CSS: The Missing Manual

Dreamweaver 8: Design and Construction

Dreamweaver 8: The Missing Manual

Dynamic HTML: The Definitive Reference, *3rd Edition*

Essential ActionScript 2.0

Flash 8: Projects for Learning Animation and Interactivity

Flash 8: The Missing Manual

Flash Hacks

Head First HTML with CSS & XHTML

Head Rush Ajax

HTML & XHTML: The Definitive Guide, *6th Edition*

HTML & XHTML Pocket Reference, *3rd Edition*

Information Architecture for the World Wide Web, *3rd Edition*

Information Dashboard Design

JavaScript: The Definitive Guide, *5th Edition*

Learning JavaScript

Learning Web Design, *2nd Edition*

PHP Hacks

Programming Flash Communication Server

Web Design in a Nutshell, *3rd Edition*

Web Site Measurement Hacks

Our books are available at most retail and online bookstores.

To order direct: 1-800-998-9938 • *order@oreilly.com* • *www.oreilly.com*

Online editions of most O'Reilly titles are available by subscription at *safari.oreilly.com*